AF765263

INSOLVENCY LAW IN EAST ASIA

Insolvency Law in East Asia

Edited by
ROMAN TOMASIC

Routledge
Taylor & Francis Group
LONDON AND NEW YORK

First published 2006 by Ashgate Publishing

2 Park Square, Milton Park, Abingdon, Oxfordshire OX14 4RN
52 Vanderbilt Avenue, New York, NY 10017

Routledge is an imprint of the Taylor & Francis Group, an informa business

First issued in paperback 2020

British Library Cataloguing in Publication Data
Insolvency law in East Asia
1. Bankruptcy - East Asia
I. Tomasic, Roman
346.5'078

Library of Congress Cataloging-in-Publication Data
Tomasic, Roman.
Insolvency law in East Asia / by Roman Tomasic.
p. cm.
Includes index.
ISBN 0-7546-2125-1 (alk. paper)
1. Bankruptcy--East Asia. I. Title.

KNC362.T663 2005
346.507'8--dc22

2005015921

ISBN 978-0-7546-2125-6 (hbk)
ISBN 978-0-367-60396-0 (pbk)

Contents

List of Tables

List of Abbreviations

ADB	Asian Development Bank
ADR	Alternative Dispute Resolution (Hong Kong)
AMC	Asset Management Company (China)
AMLT	Asset Management and Liquidation Team (Vietnam)
APEC	Asia-Pacific Economic Cooperation group
A$	Australian dollar
ASEAN	Association of South East Asian Nations
ASIC	Australian Securities and Investments Commission
BA	Bankruptcy Act (Korea)
BBC	Bangkok Bank of Commerce (Thailand)
BHP	Balai Harta Peninggalan (Indonesian insolvency courts)
BI	Bank Indonesia
BIS	Bank for International Settlement (Korea)
BOT	Bank of Thailand
BRO	Business Registration Ordinance (Hong Kong)
BSP	Bangko Sentral ng Pilipinas (Central Bank of the Philippines)
CA	Composition Act (Korea)
CA	Court of Appeals (Philippines)
CC	Commercial Code (Korea)
CCC	Civil and Commercial Code (Thailand)
CCFI	Council of Creditor Financial Institutions (Korea)
CDRAC	Corporate Debt Restructuring Advisory Committee (Thailand)
CDRC	Corporate Debt Restructuring Committee (Malaysia)
CLERP	Company Law Economic Reform Programme (Australia)
CLRFC	Company Legislation and Regulatory Framework Committee (Singapore)
CRA	Corporate Reorganization Act (Korea)
EAEC	East Asian Economic Caucus
FAIR	Forum for Asian Insolvency Reform
FIDF	Financial Institutions Development Fund (Thailand)
FSC	Financial Supervisory Commission (Korea)
GATT	General Agreement on Tariffs and Trade
GFI	Government Financial Institutions (Philippines)
GITIC	Guangdong International Trust and Investment Company (China)
GOCC	government-owned and controlled corporation (Philippines)
GPCL	General Principles of Civil Law (China)
GSP	Generalized System of Preferences
HKAB	Hong Kong Association of Banks

HKMA	Hong Kong Monetary Authority
HKSAR	Hong Kong Special Administrative Region (of the People's Republic of China)
IBRA	Indonesian Bank Restructuring Agency
IBRD	International Bank for Reconstruction and Development (World Bank)
IFC	International Finance Corporation
IMF	International Monetary Fund
INSOL	International Association of Restructuring, Insolvency and Bankruptcy Professionals
IPAA	Insolvency Practitioners Association of Australia
IRM	Insolvency Risk Management
ISDA	International Swaps and Derivatives Association
ITSA	Insolvency Trustee Service, Australia
IVA	Individual Voluntary Arrangements (Hong Kong)
KAMCO	Korea Asset Management Company (Korea)
KMT	Kuomintang (Taiwan)
LCHR	Lawyers Committee for Human Rights
LRC	Law Reform Commission (Hong Kong)
MOF	Ministry of Finance (China)
MOU	Memorandum of Understanding
NEM	New Economic Mechanism
NPC	National People's Congress (of China)
NPL	non-performing loan
OECD	Organization for Economic Cooperation and Development
ORO	Official Receiver's Office (Hong Kong)
PBOC	People's Bank of China
PHILJA	Philippine Judicial Academy
PMLT	Property Management and Liquidation Team (Vietnam)
PSR	Purchase-Sale Restructuring (China)
PWOIO	Protection of Wages on Insolvency Ordinance (Hong Kong)
RHC	Rules of the High Court (Hong Kong)
RMB	Renminbi (currency of China)
SAFE	State Administration of Foreign Exchange (China)
SAR	Special Administrative Region (Singapore)
SC	Supreme Court (Philippines)
SEC	Securities and Exchange Commission (Philippines)
SIDA	Swedish International Development Authority
SOCB	state-owned commercial bank (China)
SOE	state-owned enterprise (China)
TAMC	Thai Asset Management Corporation
UNCITRAL	United Nations Commission on International Trade Law
UNDP	United Nations Development Program
USAID	United States Agency for International Development
WTO	World Trade Organization

Chapter 1

Diversity and Convergence in Insolvency Laws in East Asia

ROMAN TOMASIC
Victoria University, Melbourne

This volume seeks to provide an overview of insolvency laws and related rules and procedures in the countries of East Asia. This introductory chapter seeks to provide a brief introduction to the field of insolvency law reform as it has occurred in East Asia over the last decade and especially since the 1987 Asian financial crisis. There are fourteen chapters which each look at the principal jurisdictions in this region,[1] as well as two other general chapters dealing respectively with issues such as legal culture and cross-border insolvency. This book is a successor volume to *Company Law in East Asia* that was published in 1999 by Ashgate.[2] It also picks up themes raised in an earlier empirical study on insolvency law and practice in Asia which saw the value of systematic comparisons of different insolvency regimes.[3] The preparation of this volume has also benefited from the vigorous practitioner debate in regard to insolvency law reform that has in part been funded and organised by a range of multilateral bodies, such as the Asian Development Bank and the OECD, and most vividly articulated in the annual meetings of the Forum on Asian Insolvency Law Reform.

Insolvency law reform has become a subject of some public policy urgency in many countries over the last two decades, and this is especially so in many parts of Asia over the last decade. Many countries have been seeking to overhaul their existing laws with a view to bringing them more closely into line with international standards of best practice. Such standards have been developed by such multilateral bodies as the Asian Development Bank,[4] the World Bank,[5] the IMF,[6] the OECD[7] and

1 The East Asian jurisdictions examined are as follows: Japan; Korea; The People's Republic of China; Taiwan; Hong Kong; Vietnam; Laos; Thailand; Malaysia; Indonesia; Singapore; The Philippines; New Zealand and Australia. It was not possible to include chapters on Burma and Cambodia, nor on some smaller jurisdictions.

2 R. Tomasic (ed.), *Company Law in East Asia*, Aldershot, Dartmouth, 1999.

3 See further, R. Tomasic and P. Little, *Insolvency Law and Practice in Asia*, Hong Kong, FT Law & Tax, 1997.

4 See for example, ADB, *Report on RETA 5795: Insolvency Law Reforms in the Asian and Pacific Region*, at http://www.adb.org/Documents/Others/Law_ADB/1pr_2000_1.asp?p+lawdevt (accessed 19 April 2005). See further, W. Willms, 'The ADB's role in encouraging and facilitating Asset Reconstruction Companies', 6 November 2004, paper presented to the Forum on Asian Insolvency Reform, 2004, New Delhi.

UNCITRAL[8] as well as by practitioner communities such as INSOL International.[9] Ad hoc groupings such as the Forum for Asian Insolvency Reform (FAIR)[10] have also greatly contributed to the development of insolvency ideas in Asia; their proceedings have been disseminated widely through the OECD.

These efforts have sought to create a degree of convergence in basic insolvency procedures across different jurisdictions, as well as a greater recognition of orders made in insolvency proceedings taking place in other jurisdictions. Understandably, this has been a slow process but it has generally been moving forward. However, given the pace of globalisation and international trade, an insolvency system that accords with generally accepted principles is widely seen as a means of facilitating risk taking and investment by foreign companies.

All of the above kinds of bodies have worked to develop guidelines, broad standards and model laws relating to insolvency. This has been a great start, but the success of insolvency law reform initiatives in Asia has also depended greatly on the appropriateness of proposed insolvency law reforms to local conditions as well as the degree to which it has been possible to effectively implement these reforms; this suggests that the social, historical and cultural contexts in which insolvency law reforms occur are quite crucial.[11] This has led the World Bank and others to focus upon the problem of risk management in insolvency law reform efforts. Also, sociologists Halliday and Carruthers refer to what they describe as the problem of insolvency risk management (IRM).

These writers argue that the: '… establishment of an effective IRM system depends on the successful interplay of three processes: design, lawmaking, and

---

5 World Bank, *Principles and Guidelines for Effective Insolvency and Creditor Rights Systems*, April 2001. In January 2003 the World Bank organised a Global Forum on Insolvency Risk Management and is continuing to organise what it describes as the 'World Bank Insolvency Initiative' which seeks to identify principles and guidelines to assist in the establishment of sound insolvency systems and to strengthen debtor-creditor rights in emerging markets; see further: http://www4.worldbank.org/legal/insolvency_ini/overview.htm (accessed 19 April 2005).

6 See for example, the IMF report *Orderly and Effective Insolvency Procedures: Key Issues*, May 1999, and C.J. Lindgren *et al.*, *Financial Sector Crisis and Restructuring – Lessons from Asia*, IMF, London, 2000; see further at: http://www.imf.org/external/pubs/ft/op/opfinsec/.

7 The OECD's work in supporting insolvency-related conferences, such as the Forum on Asian Insolvency Reform, should be noted. The parallel work of the OECD in supporting the development of corporate governance principles (such as its *Principles of Corporate Governance*, revised 2004) has been important in standardising corporate practices. See also the OECD's *White Paper on Corporate Governance in Asia*, June 2003.

8 See for example UNCITRAL's *Legislative Guide on Insolvency Law* (final provisional version, 6 August 2004). This guide was approved by the UNCITRAL Commission in June 2004. See further at: http://www.uncitral.org/english/texts/insolven/insoguide.pdf. Also see *UNCITRAL Model Law on Cross-Border Insolvency with Guide to Enactment*, New York, United Nations, 1999.

9 See for example, INSOL International, *Statement of Principles For A Global Approach to Multi-Creditor Workouts*, London, INSOL International, 2000; also see: http://www.insol.org/crossBorder.htm.

10 The fourth Forum of FAIR was held in New Delhi in November 2004. Earlier meetings of FAIR took place in Bali (2001), Bangkok (2002) and Seoul (2003). A preliminary meeting took place in Sydney in 1999.

11 See generally, R. Tomasic and P. Little, *Insolvency Law and Practice in Asia*, Hong Kong, FT Law & Tax, 1997.

implementation. Without as much attention to the processes by which laws are made and the impediments to implementation, no matter how sophisticated the design it will not succeed.' Halliday and Carruthers also argue that there is a considerable degree of interdependence of different variables in the reform process and, as a consequence, '[n]o part of an insolvency system can be successfully implemented without adequate understanding of how it relies upon and contributes to the functioning of other elements in the system.'[12] This makes it very difficult to simply seek to uncritically transplant an insolvency regime from a developed country in one part of the world to a developing country in Asia. Having said this, it is useful to look at some of the broad insolvency law reform efforts that are currently taking place.[13]

The Asian Development Bank has played a leading role in supporting the development of insolvency law reform in Asia. It has funded law reform initiatives in China over the years as well as supporting various international conferences aimed at spreading advanced insolvency ideas. Speaking in November 2004 at the fourth meeting of the Forum on Asian Insolvency Reform (co-sponsored by the Asian Development Bank, the World Bank and the OECD), Louis de Jonghe, the ADB's country director of India, observed that:

> ADB is committed to join its member countries, development partners, and other stakeholders, to undertake the journey to reform insolvency laws and systems. Indeed, ADB has long been associated with such reforms ... ADB has contributed to insolvency law reform, primarily through the provision of country-specific technical assistance, as well as through our loan projects with insolvency components, since the 1970s. In addition to country-specific assistance, ADB's work concerning insolvency and secured transactions has helped to articulate some of the core principles that underlie all well-functioning financial systems ... [B]etter substantive laws on insolvency are a necessary condition for the development of a market-based economy, but alone, cannot achieve this in the absence of a proper enforcement machinery ...[14]

In 2000 the ADB published an influential report by Ronald Harmer on 'Insolvency Law Reforms in the Asian and Pacific Region'. Harmer had been responsible for drafting the Australian corporate insolvency law reforms that were introduced in the early 1990s and had been involved in a number of multilateral insolvency law reform

---

12 T.C. Halliday and B.G. Carruthers, 'Insolvency Systems and Risk Management in Asia: How (Not) to Implement Effective Insolvency Risk Management Systems: Lessons for Asia – and Elsewhere', paper presented to the Forum on Asian Insolvency Reform 2004, New Delhi, 3–5 November 2004, p. 3.

13 See further some earlier works in this area by T.C. Halliday and B.G. Carruthers such as 'Sociological Reflections on Insolvency Reform in East Asia', pp. 19–36 in *Maximizing Value of Non-Performing Assets in Asia: proceedings from the Third Forum for Asian Insolvency Reform*, November 2003, Paris, OECD; T.C. Halliday and B.G. Carruthers, 'Foiling the Hegemons: Limits to the Globalization of Corporate Insolvency Regimes in Indonesia, Korea and China', Chicago, American Bar Foundation Working Paper, 2212 (2003); and B.G. Carruthers and T.C. Halliday, 'The Global Production of Law: The Diffusion of Corporate Bankruptcy Law 1973–1998', Chicago, American Bar Foundation Working Paper 2213 (2003), and B.G. Carruthers and T.C. Halliday, *Rescuing Business: Making Corporate Bankruptcy Law in the United States and England*, Oxford, Oxford University Press, 1998.

14 L. de Jonghe, '4th Forum on Asian Insolvency Reform (FAIR): Special Address', at http://www.adb.org/documents/speeches/20045/sp2004037.asp (accessed 19 April 2005).

initiatives.[15] The 2000 ADB report sought to advance a number of 'good practice standards' which were applicable to corporate insolvency; this report also assessed whether these standards had been accepted into the laws of eleven Asian legal jurisdictions.[16] The legal jurisdictions covered in this report did not include the People's Republic of China, but included Hong Kong, India, Indonesia, Korea, Malaysia, Pakistan, the Philippines, Japan, Singapore, Taiwan and Thailand.

Whilst acknowledging that standards may not always fit neatly with a particular country's systems and traditions, Harmer has noted that there are still some 'common basic policies and principles of approach in the insolvency law regimes of countries with different legal traditions.'[17] He added that because there are some basic common features related to the operation of companies, this suggests that there should be some similar laws or principles regarding the financial viability and stability of such companies. Harmonisation of insolvency standards may also arise from the similarity in needs and expectations found within the commercial community. Harmer has labelled these as: (1) the need for certainty and predictability in commercial affairs; (2) the need for sensible commercial stability and order; (3) a need for commercial efficiency; (4) a need for fair commercial or equitable treatment; and (5) a need for transparency. These parallel some of the principles that underlie many national bodies of insolvency law.[18]

The ADB's 'Good Practice Standards', as developed by Harmer, are worth paraphrasing and setting out; these include the following general propositions:

1. There should be a clear distinction in any legal system between corporate insolvency and personal or individual bankruptcy.[19]
2. The same insolvency regime should apply to all types of corporations, whether they be state owned or privately owned.[20]
3. Ideally, any insolvency regime should provide for both corporate rescue and winding up within the same law; this suggests the existence of two systems within any one insolvency law regime, allowing for a movement to liquidation where the rescue or reorganisation efforts have failed.[21]

---

15 See further: R.W. Harmer, *General Insolvency Inquiry, Report No 45*, Australian Law Reform Commission, Canberra, AGPS, 1988. Also see generally R. Tomasic and K. Whitford, *Australian Insolvency and Bankruptcy Law*, 2nd Edition, Sydney, Butterworths, 1997, Ch. 1, 'Principles of Corporate Insolvency Law'.

16 R.W. Harmer, 'Insolvency Law Reforms in the Asian and Pacific Region' (2000) Vol. 1 *Law and Policy Reform at the Asian Development Bank* pp. 8–86 (hereinafter referred to as R.W. Harmer, 'Insolvency Law Reforms'.

17 Ibid. at p. 25.

18 See generally, R.M. Goode, *Principles of Corporate Insolvency Law*, London, Sweet & Maxwell, 1990; and P.R. Wood, *Principles of International Insolvency*, London, Sweet & Maxwell, 1995.

19 R.W. Harmer, 'Insolvency Law Reforms' at p. 28. The ADB report notes that six of the 11 Asian jurisdictions surveyed had such a dual system in place; Harmer op. cit. at p. 28.

20 Ibid. at p. 29.

21 Ibid. at p. 30. The ADB report notes (at p. 30) that only five of the 11 jurisdictions surveyed had such a dual system in place.

4. Easy access to the use of legal mechanisms should be available to a debtor, such as a simple trigger of presumed insolvency (for example, an inability to pay a matured debt as and when it is due).[22]
5. In the event of a liquidation, if it is decided that a company should be liquidated due to inability to pay its debts, an independent manager should be appointed to run the company and conduct the liquidation, and the powers of existing management should be terminated.[23] In regard to a reorganisation, an independent administrator should be able to take over control of the company and the powers of the existing management should be limited to the extent that the administrator sees fit.
6. A most important feature of the commencement of insolvency proceedings is the immediate 'stay or suspension of actions and proceedings against the property of the debtor corporation … '[24] Such a stay should also arise in regard to reorganisation proceedings.
7. Regarding the initial process for the handling of insolvent corporations, it is desirable that strict and swift time limits be put into place and that relevant courts be properly resourced for the handling of this process. Sensible time limits should also be applied in regard to the administration of any reorganisation procedure.[25]
8. An insolvency law should provide for a commercially safe system and for priority to be given to fund the urgent and necessary business needs of the debtor during the rescue process.[26]
9. The administration of the liquidation process should be part of the overall regulation of companies and should be seen as a public responsibility best placed into the hands of a specialist government agency.[27]
10. The ADB has suggested that the legal system should specify the types of information about the debtor that should be available and that this information be subject to independent analysis.[28]
11. In regard to creditors, the insolvency law should ensure that they are involved as part of the liquidation or rescue process and that the law should clearly define the voting rights of creditors and set out procedures for the approval of a rescue plan.[29] Most Asian insolvency systems make provision for such procedures.
12. The ADB urges that the 'law should not proscribe the nature of a [reorganisation] plan, except in regard to fundamental requirements and to prevent commercial abuse.' This plan should be able to be subjected to objective

22 Ibid. at p. 32.

23 Ibid. at p. 34. The ADB report notes at p. 34 that all 11 Asian jurisdictions surveyed had applied such a moratorium procedure in their laws.

24 Ibid. at p. 35. The ADB report notes at p. 35 that six out of 11 of the countries surveyed had such a stay or suspension procedure.

25 Ibid. at p. 38.

26 Ibid. at p. 37. This mechanism was not widely available across Asia, with only three of 11 jurisdictions having such a mechanism in place.

27 Ibid. at p. 39.

28 Ibid. at p. 41.

29 Ibid. at p. 43.

analysis by an independent adviser.[30] Such requirements have only partially been adopted in Asian insolvency law regimes.

13. Courts should have a general supervisory role in regard to the rescue process and should be empowered to set a reorganisation or rescue plan if it is considered to be in the best interests of the creditors as a whole.[31]
14. During the administration of a rescue plan, it is desirable that an independent person should control or supervise this process and the plan should be capable of being changed. In the event of the debtor failing to perform in accordance with the plan, the law should provide for the liquidation of the debtor company.[32]
15. A fundamental principle that needs to be preserved in any insolvency law is the equal treatment of creditors and as such the number of priorities should be kept to a minimum.[33]
16. Because there is a danger that creditors may be damaged or that the equal treatment of creditors may be undermined, an insolvency law should contain rules for dealing with efforts to avoid such transactions.[34]
17. Insolvency laws should also seek to deal with possible damage or loss to creditors by putting in place civil sanctions for fraudulent or similar conduct in the management or operation of a company.[35]
18. Finally, in relation to cross-border insolvency, insolvency systems should provide for the recognition of foreign judgements and cooperation with foreign insolvency administrators, preferably by adopting the UNCITRAL model rules on cross-border insolvency.[36]

It might be added that it is also desirable to impose some sanctions upon corporate officers to ensure that the financial position of a company does not deteriorate to such an extent that rescue or reorganisation is impossible. Some jurisdictions have sought to deal with this problem by imposing personal liabilities upon directors for engaging in insolvent trading.

Asian insolvency laws have increasingly been reworked to provide for alternatives to liquidation, such as rescue-based models like reorganisation and restructure. The growth of interest in rescue-based ideas parallels similar reforms that have been introduced in developed countries such as the US, the UK and Australia. This has to some degree been easier to accept in some Asian countries due to the difficulty that many have had in accepting liquidation as an option, especially where it is likely to lead to considerable social upheaval, such as the displacement of employees.

In addition to the kinds of insolvency law provisions that have been suggested above by the ADB, it has also been widely argued that it is essential that an integrated system for dealing with secured transactions be set up to support the corresponding

---

30 Ibid. at p. 45.
31 Ibid. at p. 47.
32 Ibid. at p. 48.
33 Ibid. at p. 49.
34 Ibid. at p. 50.
35 Ibid. at p. 51.
36 Ibid. at p. 53.

insolvency and rescue systems.[37] As Harmer has observed, in regard to the 'creation, registration and enforcement of secured property interests there is a high degree of compatibility between secured transactions and insolvency.'[38]

Both the World Bank and the IMF have developed similar principles which also have sought to reflect good practice in insolvency. In May 1999 the IMF issued a report dealing with *Orderly and Effective Insolvency Procedures: Key Issues* whilst in February 2000 the World Bank issued a background paper on *Building Effective Insolvency Systems: Toward Principles and Guidelines*.

UNCITRAL's *Legislative Guide on Insolvency Law* has sought to provide a comprehensive statement of the key objectives of any insolvency and debtor-creditor regime and to set out a series of flexible approaches to the implementation of such objectives.[39] This guide was adopted by UNCITRAL in New York in June 2004. In keeping with many earlier similar statements, the *Guide* sets out the following key objectives of any insolvency regime:

1. the insolvency regime should provide certainty in the market to promote economic stability and growth;
2. the insolvency regime should maximise the value of assets to reduce the burden of the insolvency;
3. the insolvency regime should strike a balance between liquidation and reorganisation (balancing near-term debt collection through liquidation against preserving value through a reorganisation);
4. the insolvency regime should ensure the equitable treatment of similarly situated creditors (not that all creditors need to be treated identically);
5. the insolvency regime should provide timely, efficient and impartial resolution of the insolvency (this enhances the maximisation of asset value and equitable treatment of creditors);
6. the insolvency regime should preserve the insolvent estate so as to facilitate the equitable treatment of creditors;
7. the insolvency regime should ensure a transparent and predictable insolvency law that contains incentives for gathering and dispensing information;
8. the insolvency regime should recognise existing creditor rights and establish clear rules for the ranking of priority claims;
9. the insolvency regime should establish a framework for cross-border insolvency.[40]

The UNCITRAL *Legislative Guide* goes on to provide a detailed analysis of each of these objectives. It is clear from the work of bodies such as UNCITRAL and the Asian Development Bank that a great deal of progress has been achieved over the last decade in developing broad principles or guidelines to be followed by reformers

37 ADB, 'The Need for an Integrated Approach to Secured Transactions and Insolvency Law Reforms, written by R.W. Harmer' (2000) Vol. 1 *Law and Policy Reform at the Asian Development Bank* pp. 87–100. The nature of secured transaction systems in operation in Asia is also discussed in R. Tomasic and P. Little, *Insolvency Law and Practice in Asia*, Hong Kong, FT Law & Tax, 1997.

38 Ibid. at p. 99.

39 See further at: http://www.uncitral.org/english/texts/insolven/insoguide.pdf.

40 Ibid. at pp. 12–18.

whose task it is to fashion the insolvency law regimes of their own jurisdictions. Whilst it is clearly inappropriate to seek to simply impose an insolvency law regime from a developed country upon a developing country in Asia, broad principles provide a degree of flexibility to give law makers greater freedom in adjusting their reform proposals to local legal and political conditions and pathways.

As research work commissioned by the Asian Development Bank has shown, there is clearly considerable diversity in the nature of corporate insolvency systems in different parts of East Asia.[41] The extent to which there will be greater convergence in Asian insolvency regimes clearly depends upon a number of factors, but probably the most important of these has been the degree to which there has been an increasingly open and vigorous debate about the importance of insolvency laws to economic development and market development.

When this book was first conceived an effort was made to try to achieve some degree of integration by asking authors to consider some key themes that run through different insolvency regimes. Many of the chapters in this collection have been able to systematically address these themes. However, in some cases, the poor development of insolvency and bankruptcy laws has made this difficult. In any event, the Appendix at the end of this chapter sets out some of these key themes that run through many of the chapters that follow. The insolvency regimes of some countries were not sufficiently well developed to be able to allow them to be neatly discussed under these headings, but in the interests of comparability, some effort has been made to advance this goal of comparison. It is left to the user of this book to determine the degree to which such comparisons will be useful or meaningful.

---

41 See generally: R.W. Harmer, 'Insolvency Law Reforms' pp. 8–86 and Tomasic and Little, supra.

Appendix: Some Key Insolvency Law Themes covered by Chapters dealing with Individual Legal Jurisdictions

1 INTRODUCTION

1.1 Introduction to the legal system and local legal culture, attitudes to debt and debt enforcement.

1.2 Discussion of the history, sources and philosophy of insolvency laws in the jurisdiction.

1.3 Identification of key insolvency law principles in the jurisdiction.

1.4 General introduction to the statutory, regulatory and judicial approach to corporate insolvency and personal bankruptcy laws in the jurisdiction.

2 PERSONAL INSOLVENCY LAWS (if any)

2.1 Introduction to the personal insolvency/bankruptcy laws in the jurisdiction, sources of laws, their constitutional basis and the extent of their usage.

2.2 The regulatory structures for the control of bankruptcy proceedings.

2.3 The principal institutions for the application of these laws (e.g. courts, bankruptcy practitioners, trustees in bankruptcy).

2.4 Powers of courts in handling bankruptcy petitions.

2.5 Duties of bankruptcy practitioners in the jurisdiction.

2.6 Rules regarding creditors' petitions for bankruptcy; timing for a creditor to initiate bankruptcy proceedings (e.g. acts of bankruptcy).

2.7 Rules regarding debtors' petitions for bankruptcy.

2.8 Powers of secured creditors.

2.9 Nature of bankruptcy petitions by creditors and debtors.

2.10 Creditors' meetings.

3 PERSONAL BANKRUPTCY LAW PROCEDURES

3.1 Controls placed on debtors once a bankruptcy petition has been lodged (e.g. overseas travel, use of property, books, etc.).

3.2 Collection of information about debtors; examination of debtors.

3.3 Offshore collection of information.

3.4 Rules regarding the proof of debts; illicit transfers of property, etc. by the bankrupt.

3.5 What orders may be made in regard to the property of the debtor.

3.6 Rules for the distribution of the assets of the bankrupt.

3.7 Creditors of the debtor and debt agreements.

3.8 Creditors' meetings and debt agreements/their termination.

4 CORPORATE INSOLVENCY RULES

4.1 An introduction to the different corporate insolvency rules in the jurisdiction (e.g. voluntary administration, schemes of arrangements, compositions, court-ordered winding up, voluntary winding up, receivership, judicial management, etc.).

4.2 Corporate rescue and the use of informal (non-legal) mechanisms of dealing with corporate debtors (e.g. workouts, etc.); advantages and disadvantages of these mechanisms.

4.3 The nature of legally prescribed mechanisms of voluntary administration.
4.4 Methods of initiating voluntary administration schemes (court-based or otherwise).
4.5 Effect of the appointment of an administrator (or such like person) on the assets and management structures of the company.
4.6 Powers, liabilities and qualifications of the administrator and duration of administration.
4.7 Protection of corporate assets during administration.
4.8 Role of creditors during administration, creditors' meetings, etc.
4.9 Powers of the courts in relation to administration and the administrator.
4.10 Termination of the administration.
4.11 Other related matters.

5 COURT-BASED SCHEMES OF ARRANGEMENT, RECONSTRUCTION OR ARRANGEMENT
5.1 Discussion of other legal mechanisms, apart from winding up, which may impact on the company (e.g. court-based schemes of arrangement, the provision of safe harbours/moratoriums, etc.).
5.2 Reconstructions and arrangements.
5.3 Judicial or official management.
5.4 Other schemes.

6 WINDING UP PROCEDURES
6.1 An introduction to the range of winding up procedures available in the jurisdiction.
6.2 Initiation of winding up proceedings; powers of the court and powers of creditors.
6.3 Grounds for winding up; when winding up proceedings may be commenced (e.g. inability to pay debts when due; rules which facilitate the finding that there is an inability to pay debts when due); the test of insolvency.
6.4 Effect of the commencement of winding up upon the company's management (i.e. the powers of the board and of directors), other creditors' claims and members' rights.
6.5 Creditors' meetings.
6.6 The role of the court in the winding up process.
6.7 Proof and ranking of claims by creditors against the company.
6.8 Set off of debts.
6.9 Voidable transactions.
6.10 Procedures for the dissolution (and restitution) of the company.

7 LIQUIDATORS: Appointment, powers and duties
7.1 Appointment of liquidators, qualifications, registration, etc.
7.2 Powers of liquidators, powers of investigation, inspection of books examination of witnesses, etc.
7.3 Duties of liquidators (e.g. fiduciary and statutory duties).
7.4 Status, independence, etc., of liquidators.
7.5 Powers of the court in relation to liquidators.

7.6 Suspension or revocation of registration, powers of liquidators.
7.7 Reports by liquidators.
7.8 Remuneration and fees of liquidators.

8 ENFORCEMENT OF SECURITIES OVER A DEBTOR'S ASSETS IN THE JURISDICTION
8.1 The position of secured creditors; rules regarding the protection of property interests, such as receivership and mortgages or charges over assets and secured title.
8.2 The appointment of receivers and managers of property of a debtor (i.e. who may appoint them).
8.3 Powers and duties of an external controller, such as a receiver and manager.
8.4 Effect of the appointment of an external controller of corporate assets (such as a receiver and manager).

9 OFFENCES
9.1 Insolvent trading rules.
9.2 Other insolvency-related offences by corporate controllers.
9.3 Other relevant corporate law offences.

10 RULES REGARDING CROSS-BORDER INSOLVENCY AND JUDICIAL ASSISTANCE TO FOREIGN INSOLVENCY OFFICIALS
10.1 Broad policy of the jurisdiction in regard to the recognition of foreign judgements and court orders.
10.2 Procedures for the assistance of courts in foreign jurisdictions.
10.3 Such other rules as may apply to foreign-based assets.

Chapter 2

Insolvency Law in Japan*

STACEY STEELE**
University of Melbourne

1 Introduction

1.1 Introduction to the Legal System and Local Legal Culture, Attitudes to Debt and Debt Enforcement

Japan's corporate law reforms for the past century have followed the pattern of other industrialised countries, that is, most have been induced by economic or financial crises. It is not surprising, then, that insolvency law reform in Japan accelerated dramatically during the late 1990s and early years of the 21st century, just as the effects of a prolonged recession were becoming increasingly obvious.

During Japan's high growth period from the 1960s to the late 1980s Japanese bank lending was often characterised as a relationship-driven, 'main-bank system' of preferential lending to members of large *keiretsu* or corporate groupings. Large Japanese corporations were predominantly financed by bank borrowing and banks monitored client corporations relationally or through direct intervention in the management of the borrower.[1] Small and medium-sized corporations depended on a range of sources for credit: regional banks; *shinkin* banks (akin to building societies); housing loan corporations (*jûsen*); credit cooperatives and other non-bank financial institutions. For small and medium-sized corporations, payment of creditors on time was regarded as a core business ethic and was reinforced indirectly through banks' willingness to suspend accounts of commercial clients who repeatedly dishonoured promissory notes or bills (*tegata*). When a corporation dishonoured a bill

---

* In this chapter, I have generally followed the template suggested by the editor with a view to making comparisons of different aspects of each jurisdiction dealt with in this book easier for readers. In a few sections in this chapter, this has led to repetition or required cross-references to other sections. I hope that the benefits of the book's comparative approach outweigh the inconvenience this might cause to readers. Japanese names have been referenced following English conventions: for example, in the Bibliography 'Hatano, Takeshi and Noriaki Takizawa' = Takeshi (first name) and Hatano (surname) and Noriaki (first name) and Takizawa (surname).

** Associate Director (Japan), Asian Law Centre, Melbourne Law School, University of Melbourne and Solicitor, Financial Services Group, Blake Dawson Waldron, Melbourne, Australia. I thank Professor Taylor, Professor of Law and Director, Asian Law Centre, University of Washington (Seattle, USA) and Professor Tagashira, Sophia University (Tokyo, Japan) for their comments and assistance.

1 In line with American legal usage, the Japanese for company (*kaisha*) is usually rendered as 'corporation' in English. For consistency, we follow this American/Japanese usage in this chapter.

it was generally interpreted as a prelude to insolvency, partly because small and medium-sized Japanese corporations were under-capitalised and relied heavily on their line of credit in trade.[2] When a bill is dishonoured, the Japanese Financial Clearing House (*Tegata kôkan sho*) notifies all its member banks who are then on notice that something is amiss. If a bill from a debtor is dishonoured a second time within six months, suspension of trade measures (*ginko torihiki teishi shobun*) are taken and the issuer's bank accounts are frozen. Ancillary legal doctrines permit, for example, the cancellation of long-term contracts on the basis of industry intelligence about a corporation's inability to pay debts. This reliance on bills in Japanese trade, and lack of registration of movable assets, contributed to an environment where inside information was critical[3] and gave some creditors an effective early warning system, but arguably did not provide for a transparent and orderly workout process.

During the high-growth period corporate insolvency and personal bankruptcy were concepts that attracted social stigma and evoked traumatic memories of the 1920s worldwide economic collapse and the immediate post-World War II period in Japan. The 'bubble economy' of the late 1980s, fuelled by speculative investments and borrowings against highly inflated real estate values, contributed to a widespread sense of Japan's financial invulnerability. When the 'bubble' burst in 1990, however, a very different landscape of Japanese credit emerged. Small financial institutions and non-bank institutions collapsed or merged and depositors fled to more creditworthy banks. Consumers and small businesses were exposed to an under-regulated market in loan-sharking. The *jûsen* loan crisis of 1995 onward directly affected larger banks, which had supplied much of the capital on which small financial institutions relied. Since much of the large bank lending had been secured by real estate that was now dramatically overvalued, available credit contracted and the banks' existing loan portfolios became skewed with bad, or at least highly suspect, loans.[4] One consequence of the credit squeeze was that debt issue as a primary means of corporate financing became more commonplace in the late 1990s. From 1997 onward a series of major financial institutions collapsed, beginning with Yamaichi Securities and Hokkaido Takushoku Bank, followed by the Long-Term Credit Bank of Japan (now Shinsei Bank) and Nippon Credit Bank (now Aozora Bank). By 2001, every major bank in Japan had merged or been reconstructed. During the same period, the Japanese economy continued to contract and corporate and individual bankruptcies became increasingly visible.

What changed between the mid-1990s and the commencement of the 21st century is the spread of bankruptcies across a wide range of industries and the tacit acceptance that large corporations are not immune from business failure. Newsworthy corporate failures included large department store retailer Sogô, medium-sized life insurance companies Kyôei Life and Chiyoda Life and major supermarket operator Mycal Corporation. Recent bankruptcies include a growing number of long-established

2 Grondine (1996: 140–1). Takagi (1997: 98) suggests that the use of bills and under-capitalisation in Japan may be on the decline.

3 Bennett (1994: 219).

4 One of the indirect results of deflation and this type of lending was the introduction of the Security Interest Extinguishing Scheme provisions. See Steele (2003).

firms, defined as those in business for longer than 30 years. Of the 14,174 corporate failures for January–October 2001, most were attributed less to speculation during the 1980s than to the policy changes and tightened lending practices of banks; price-cutting competition and sluggish consumer spending; and a social and legal environment that has inhibited rapid corporate restructuring during the prolonged recession.[5]

The historically high levels of corporate failure in Japan have led to complex international insolvency cases and in the consumer sector are paralleled by record numbers of individual voluntary bankruptcies and greater public awareness of bankruptcy as a social and legal policy issue.[6] The number of bankruptcy petitions increased dramatically by 33 per cent from 168,811 in 2001 to 224,467 in 2002. Of these petitions, 160,741 petitions in 2001 and 214,996 petitions in 2002 were for personal bankruptcy proceedings, an increase of approximately 35 per cent. The corresponding figures for corporate insolvency filings reveal an increase of approximately 15 per cent.[7] Tagashira suggests that recently in Japan the community is beginning to see insolvency as just another aspect of the economic cycle.[8] Another interpretation of the increased use of formal insolvency procedures by corporations in Japan may be that banks no longer perceive great benefits from participating in informal workouts.[9]

Against this economic and social background, the Japanese government officially began restructuring its insolvency laws in 1996. The reform process commenced with the setting up of a Committee on Insolvency Law Reform (*Tôsan hô bukai*) (the 'Committee') within the Legislative Deliberative Council (*Hôsei shingikai*) in October 1996.[10] As this chapter was being finalised, the Committee was completing a draft new Bankruptcy Law that was due to be presented to the Diet as a bill in the later part of 2003 and was expected to become effective on 1 April 2004. The new Bankruptcy Law provisions will impact on the substantive provisions of other insolvency-related laws discussed in this chapter because they are to be amended to bring them into line with the new Bankruptcy Law. This chapter states the law as available to me at 1 April 2003. Where possible, however, I anticipate further changes to the law.

---

5 'Big firms going under in alarming numbers', *Nikkei Net Interactive*, 5 November 2001, www.nni.nikkei.co.jp. This figure represents the number of corporate failures involving liabilities of more than 10,000,000 yen.

6 On attitudes to individual or so-called 'consumer' bankruptcies, see Anderson and Itô (2003).

7 Hatano and Takizawa (2003: 32–33).

8 Tagashira (2003: 34). Hatano and Takizawa (2003: 32) also note the increased community interest in the insolvency law system and cases.

9 Cf. Corbett (1998: 113). Corbett suggests that, despite anecdotal evidence to the contrary, banks are not dramatically changing their practices in relation to assisting financially troubled clients. Corbett's research is based mainly on data collected in 1996. In any event, as Anderson and Steele (2003: [19-601]) note, the use of informal workouts to resolve financial difficulties is not limited to Japan. See also their comments on systems facilitating informal insolvency resolution at [19-601].

10 On the reform process see Steele (2000: 54–55) and Anderson and Steele (2003) at [19-20].

1.2 Discussion of the History, Sources and Philosophy of Insolvency Laws in Japan

The Japanese insolvency law regime has developed haphazardly according to historical circumstance. The current legislation was established for the most part in the 1920s and 1930s,[11] with additions in 1952 during the Occupation period and reforms in the mid-1960s. However, as early as the middle of the Tokugawa era (1600–1867), creditors used customary law (called *Osadamegaki hyakkajô*) and formal collection proceedings to enforce repayment of debts.[12] Japanese insolvency law has been influenced by German, Austrian, English and American statutes. The influence of the insolvency law from each of these countries has grown out of the tendency for Japanese reformers to take whatever law was perceived to be the best in the world at the time and closely follow debate on the disadvantages and advantages of that law. Consequently, trends in Japan have followed a timeline of worldwide changes in attitudes towards debt and debt enforcement which have generally created a movement away from bankruptcy or liquidation per se, to giving options to debtors and creditors that include procedures which conflate liquidation and reorganisation aims.[13]

The Japanese insolvency law regime comprises five different court procedures established in four different pieces of legislation (see Table 2.1). Two of the procedures are traditionally described as liquidation-type procedures: Bankruptcy and Special Liquidation. Three are said to be reconstruction-type procedures: Civil Rehabilitation, Corporate Arrangement and Corporate Reorganisation. In addition to these main procedures, there is also a special procedure for dealing with insolvent financial institutions, and securities and insurance companies (see 5.4) and a separate statute dealing with cross-border insolvencies called the Law on Recognition and Assistance for Foreign Insolvency Proceedings (*Gaikoku tôsan shori tetsuzuki no shônin enjo ni kan suru hôritsu* Law No. 129, 2000). Further, special procedures are available for the mediation of financial difficulties between debtors and creditors under the Civil Conciliation Law (*Minji chôtei hô* Law No. 222, 1951), as supplemented by the Special Mediation Law (*Tokutei saimui tô no chôsei no sokushin no tame no tokutei chôtei ni kan suru hôritsu* Law No. 158, 1999). Finally, as in other countries, many insolvencies in Japan are dealt with informally without reference to the courts.[14] The different procedures have diverse objectives, different commencement requirements and apply to different entities.

---

11 From the turn of the century to around this time the whole of the Japanese legal system was being redrafted in line with the Westernisation policy of the Meiji government. Drafters sought ideas from all around the world, but generally used civil law jurisdictions as their models.

12 Itô (2000:45) and Anderson and Steele (2003: [19-111]).

13 Anderson and Steele (2003: [19-113]) note the desire for a functional and pragmatic regime in Japan which has softened in modern times.

14 According to Miki (1997: 67 and n. 10), most insolvencies in Japan are resolved by informal workout; however there are no official statistics regarding the number of workouts which occur outside of the umbrella of the courts. See also Anderson and Steele (2003: [19-601] to [19-644]) on informal insolvencies in Japan.

Table 2.1 Formal insolvency procedures in Japan

Procedure	Legislation	Coverage
Bankruptcy	Bankruptcy Law (*Hasan hô* Law No. 71, 1922)	Corporate and personal
Special Liquidation	Special Liquidation Commercial Code (*Shô hô* Law No. 48, 1899, amended 1938)	Joint-stock corporations
Civil Rehabilitation	Civil Rehabilitation Law (*Minji saisei hô* Law No. 225, 1999) as amended[15]	Corporate and personal
Corporate Arrangement	Corporate Arrangement Commercial Code (*Shô hô* Law No. 48, 1899, amended 1938)	Joint-stock corporations
Corporate Reorganisation	New Corporate Reorganisation Law (*Kaisha kôsei hô* Law No. 154, 2002)	Joint-stock corporations and non-incorporated entities via the Financial Institutions' Rehabilitation Law
Private Agreement	Civil Conciliation Law (*Minji chôtei hô* Law No. 222, 1951) and Special Mediation Law (*Tokutei saimu tô no chôsei no sokushin no tame no tokutei chôtei ni kan suru hôritsu* Law No. 158, 1999)	Corporate and personal
Financial Institutions Rehabilitation	Special Procedures for Reorganisation of Financial Institutions Law (*Kinyû kikan no kôsei tetsuzuki no tokurei tô ni kan suru hôritsu* Law No. 95, 1996)	Financial and insurance institutions
Recognition and Assistance for Foreign Insolvency	Law on Recognition and Assistance for Foreign Insolvency Proceedings (*Gaikoku tôsan shori tetsuzuki no shônin enjo ni kan suru hôritsu* Law No. 129, 2000)	Insolvency proceedings commenced in foreign jurisdictions

15 The Civil Rehabilitation Law was subsequently amended by the Law to Amend the Civil Rehabilitation Law (*Minji saisei hô tô no ichibu o kaisei suru hôritsu* Law No. 128, 2000) and the Law Relating to Recognition and Assistance for Foreign Insolvency Proceedings (*Gaikoku tôsan shori tetsuzuki no shônin enjo ni kan suru hôritsu* Law No. 129, 2000). For a translation of the Civil Rehabilitation Law prior to the amendments, see Steele (trans) (2000).

1.3 Key Insolvency Law Principles in Japan

The haphazard development and mix of historical sources of Japanese insolvency law has resulted in a regulatory scheme that does not reflect a single set of insolvency law principles. Underlying French-influenced statues passed in the Meiji period (1868–1912) were suspension of payments principles based on mercantilist practice, with a trustee being appointed to realise assets under the close supervision of a judge.[16] Later laws reflect reliance on German bankruptcy law concepts such as the right of separation for secured creditors, the English focus on court-driven winding up of corporations and American-influenced reorganisation (see 1.2 and 1.4).

Broadly stated, a leading Japanese insolvency law textbook describes the principles on which Japanese insolvency law is based as being 'equity, equality and fairness' and guaranteeing the integrity of insolvency workout processes.[17] However, each of the laws that make up the Japanese insolvency law regime has a separate aim. The aim of the Bankruptcy procedure in the Bankruptcy Law is the orderly liquidation of assets of a debtor in financial difficulty and the fair and equitable distribution of liquidated assets to creditors.[18] The other liquidation-type procedure, Special Liquidation under the Commercial Code, is an extension of Ordinary Liquidation where the parties want more court supervision of the process. Parties must consent to an agreement aimed at liquidating the debtor's assets.

There are also subtle differences between the aims of the different reorganisation-type procedures. The ostensible purpose of the Civil Rehabilitation Law is to gain consensus amongst creditors for a rehabilitation plan that will lead to the rehabilitation of a financially distressed debtor's business or economic well-being (Civ RL Art. 1). The purpose of the Corporate Arrangement procedure in the Commercial Code is to support private negotiations between debtors and creditors, but the autonomy of the parties is emphasised. The aims of these two laws are very similar because the Civil Rehabilitation Law is based in part on concepts found in the Corporate Arrangement procedure. However, the aim of the third reorganisation-type procedure, the Corporate Reorganisation Law, is to preserve the going concern value of large corporations under the supervision of a trustee with the assistance of a post-commencement prohibition on the payment of creditors, including secured creditors.

During the early stages of the current reform process in Japan, debate focused on whether to introduce a one-stop insolvency regime or maintain the current collection of laws distinguished by their purpose and the type and size of the debtor. The system of separate legislation is said to be confusing for petitioners and the transfer rules between each procedure do not work well. The introduction of a consolidated

---

16 Itô (2000: 47).

17 Itô (2000: 11 and 14).

18 The Bankruptcy Law also includes a procedure for Compulsory Composition that can only be commenced after a Bankruptcy proceeding has begun. Previously this procedure interacted with the Composition procedure under the Composition Law and was aimed at preventing bankruptcy. The Composition Law was repealed and replaced by the Civil Rehabilitation Law in 2000 and it is likely that the Compulsory Composition procedure will be repealed by the new Bankruptcy Law expected to come into effect in 2004.

insolvency regime arguably requires consensus amongst reformers on a single purpose for the law and a single set of conditions that debtors must meet in order to use a particular procedure. The issue has not been resolved and it is doubtful that a consolidated system will now emerge, but there may be movement towards collecting the various procedures left over from the reform process in one law.

1.4 General Introduction to the Statutory, Regulatory and Judicial Approach to Corporate Insolvency and Personal Bankruptcy Laws in Japan

In Japan, district courts have jurisdiction over insolvency cases. Specialist insolvency divisions exist in the district courts in Osaka and Tokyo, Japan's two major commercial centres. Although Japan is traditionally categorised as a civil law country where statutes, rather than case law, take precedence, there is a large body of judicial precedent interpreting insolvency statutes.[19] The courts in Osaka and Tokyo are well known for the divergence in their approach to insolvency law.[20] Lawyers hoped that the new legislation will be interpreted and implemented in a consistent manner, but it seems that the courts continue to apply the legislation differently depending on the commercial realities current in the jurisdiction in which they operate.[21] Some lawyers also called for a 'hands off' approach from the courts, which will allow parties to progress insolvency proceedings without a high level of judicial supervision. Certainly the courts have improved the speed with which cases are being processed, despite the dramatic increase in the number of cases. However, it is not clear whether this is mostly as a result of court procedures, flexible juridical interpretation, changes in judicial attitudes or government and community pressure.[22]

2 Personal Insolvency Laws

2.1 Introduction to the Personal Insolvency/Bankruptcy Laws in Japan, Sources of Laws, their Constitutional Basis and the Extent of their Usage

Personal bankruptcy was a major problem in Japan even before the collapse of the so-called 'bubble' economy (1987–90), reflecting the rapid expansion of the consumer credit industry in the 1980s. Until recently, Japan has never had procedures designed specifically to deal with personal insolvency (see 3.7), although court rules were often modified to reflect the special needs of individuals as opposed to corporations.[23] Natural persons and corporations are both dealt with under the Bankruptcy Law and the Civil Rehabilitation Law. Thus, the rules with respect to corporations under these laws also apply to personal insolvencies. As the statistics in

---

19 See, for example, the collection of cases in Shindô *et al.* (1990).

20 See Anderson and Steele (2003: [19-300]).

21 Tahara (1998: 8).

22 See Anderson and Steele (2003: [19-120]) citing Tsutsumi and Kosuga (2002: 11). Hatano and Takizawa (2003: 32) suggest that it is a result of improved processing of matters and the establishment of policies and procedures within the courts.

23 On this point see Anderson and Itô (2003) under the heading 'Administering Consumer Insolvencies'.

Table 2.2 reveal, the Bankruptcy proceeding is by far the most popular method of court-based insolvency workout and personal bankruptcies make up the majority of filings.[24]

Many personal bankruptcy cases in Japan involve individuals who have no assets that can be distributed to creditors. They file for voluntary bankruptcy in order to receive a discharge from their debts and the cases usually end without a trustee ever being appointed.[25] This is because a court must discontinue a bankruptcy case at the same time that it declares a person bankrupt where it believes that the bankrupt's estate will not be sufficient to pay the expenses of the bankruptcy court. This is known as the 'Simultaneous Bankruptcy Abolition' rule (*dôji hasan haishi*) (BL Art. 145). In 2002, the court granted Simultaneous Bankruptcy Abolition rulings in 89.5 per cent of Personal Bankruptcies.[26] Even after a Bankruptcy proceeding is commenced, if the court believes that the estate is not sufficient to pay the expenses of the bankruptcy, it may discontinue the Bankruptcy proceeding on the petition of the trustee after obtaining the opinion of a meeting of creditors (BL Art. 353). The court may also discontinue a Bankruptcy proceeding where all the creditors who filed a proof of claim within the designated period approve the termination (BL Art. 347).

The concept of a discharge was introduced into the Bankruptcy Law in 1952 under the influence of the American Occupation authorities. A bankrupt may apply for a discharge order at any time (BL Art. 366-2). The discharge will be granted by the court after a hearing (BL Art. 366-4) unless the bankrupt has performed certain disqualifying acts, such as fraud or failing to cooperate with the trustee (BL Art. 366-9).

Individuals are encouraged to apply for bankruptcy as a means of dealing with their debts because they can receive a discharge. A debtor may also be able to file for a discharge in some jurisdictions at the same time as they file for bankruptcy.[27] However, after obtaining a discharge, a bankrupt is still liable for some bankruptcy claims, including for:

- taxes;
- damages for torts committed by the bankrupt with malicious intent;
- priority employee wages;
- employee deposits;
- claims knowingly not included on the list of creditors by the bankrupt; and
- certain penalties and fines (BL Art. 366-12).

24 Each year the Supreme Court publishes statistical data in respect of the judicial system (*Shihô tôkei nenpô*). These figures are based on a preview of the Supreme Court publication published in a leading Japanese legal journal (see Hatano and Takizawa (2003)).

25 On these points generally, see Anderson and Itô (2003).

26 Hatano and Takizawa (2003: 34).

27 Anderson and Itô (2003).

Table 2.2 New filings of insolvency proceedings in Japan in 2002

	Bankruptcy	Civil Rehabilitation			Corporate Reorganisation	Corporate Arrangement	Special Liquidation
		Ordinary	Small debtor	Wage earner			
Nationally[28]	224,467	1,093	6,054	7,444	88	4	336
Tokyo	24,795	400	589	521	50	0	147
Yokohama	10,966	42	296	305	0	0	18
Saitama	8,982	27	344	317	0	0	4
Chiba	8,693	25	233	237	0	0	7
Shizuoka	6,047	22	164	142	0	0	7
Osaka	20,924	117	845	835	23	0	53
Kyoto	5,143	13	125	296	4	0	7
Kobe	9,806	27	362	376	3	0	5
Nagoya	9,148	41	400	293	4	1	12
Hiroshima	5,932	24	53	115	0	0	4
Fukuoka	13,810	59	479	429	2	0	9
Sapporo	9,003	19	122	354	0	0	4

28 Only those district courts that received 5,000 or more petitions for Bankruptcy have been included in this list. The Supreme Court statistics include all district courts.

3 Personal Bankruptcy Law Procedures

As the Civil Rehabilitation Law, the Bankruptcy Law and the Civil Conciliation Law apply to both personal and corporate insolvencies, this part 3 should be read in conjunction with parts 2.1, 4 and 6. Where relevant, the appropriate part is referenced below.

3.1 Controls Placed on Debtors once a Bankruptcy Petition has been Lodged

A Bankruptcy proceeding may be initiated by a debtor or a creditor filing a petition in the debtor's local district court (BL Art. 105) (see also 6.2 below). Because filing a petition does not automatically cause a Bankruptcy proceeding to commence, once a bankruptcy petition has been lodged the court may order measures to preserve the bankruptcy estate and protect it from dissipation ('Preservation Measures') (BL Art. 155). Preservation Measures are usually ordered on the application of an interested person, but the court may also order Preservation Measures on its own motion. A Preservation Measure, for example, might consist of an order requiring the debtor to provide a court officer with his/her financial accounts. If Preservation Measures are ordered, an interested party may make an immediate *kôkoku* appeal; however, this does not have the effect of suspending the Preservation Measures (BL Art. 155(4)).[29]

When a Bankruptcy proceeding is commenced, the bankrupt's assets vest in the trustee (BL Art. 7) and the court may also order that a bankrupt:

- cannot leave his/her dwelling place without court permission (BL Art. 147);
- be brought before the court (BL Art. 148);
- be put under surveillance if there is a likelihood that s/he will abscond, conceal or destroy property (BL Art. 149); and
- (who has been put under surveillance) may not communicate with outsiders without the permission of the court (BL Art. 150).

These provisions also apply to persons such as the bankrupt's legal representative (BL Art. 152).

Other controls and restrictions relating to a bankrupt include:

- any juridical acts performed after the declaration of bankruptcy by the bankrupt cannot be claimed against bankruptcy creditors (BL Art. 53(1));
- the delivery of all of the bankrupt's mail to the trustee, who may open it and examine its contents (BL Art. 190);
- the prohibition against a bankrupt becoming a guardian (Civil Code Art. 847(3)) executor of a will (Civil Code Art. 1009), trustee (Trusts Act, *Shintaku hô* Law No. 62, 1922, Art. 5), or director of a joint-stock corporation (*Japan* v. *Mizutani*, Supreme Court, 21 Minshû 274, 9 March 1967 and Commercial Code Art. 254-2(2));

29 A *kôkoku* appeal, or protest, is a summary procedure to object to a judicial determination other than a judgement.

- the duty of the bankrupt, his/her agent or other analogous persons to provide information about the bankruptcy if requested by the trustee, investigator or creditors' meeting (BL Art. 153); and
- the prohibition against professionals such as lawyers, notaries, patent agents and certified public accountants participating in their respective occupations.[30]

3.2 Collection of Information about Debtors; Examination of Debtors

The court is not bound to hear oral arguments before making a declaration of bankruptcy (BL Art. 110). However, it will dismiss a petition to commence a Bankruptcy proceeding if the following requirements are not met:

- proof of a ground for bankruptcy;
- in the case of a debtor's petition, provision of information as to the debtor's assets and liabilities; and
- the payment of costs into court[31] (see also 6.3 below).

3.3 Offshore Collection of Information

The rules relating to cross-border insolvency are discussed in part 10.

3.4 Rules regarding the Proof of Debts, Illicit Transfers of Property, etc., by the Bankrupt

These are the same as for corporations (see part 6.7 below).

3.5 Orders in regard to the Property of the Debtor

As discussed at 3.1 above, the court may order Preservation Measures, including moratoriums, prohibiting execution in respect of a debtor's property.

3.6 Rules for the Distribution of the Assets of the Bankrupt

The provisions relating to the distribution of assets are discussed at 6.10, but note the comments in respect of discharge at 2.1.

3.7 Creditors of the Debtor and Debt Agreements

As noted above, the Civil Rehabilitation Law applies to corporations and individuals (see also part 4 below). The procedure is particularly popular in respect of personal insolvencies, with 6,210 individuals filing for Civil Rehabilitation in 2001 and

---

30 *Bengoshi hô* (Lawyer Law) Art. 6(5), *Kôshônin hô* (Public Notary Law) Art. 14(2), *Benrishi hô* (Patent Attorney Law) Art. 5(6) and *Kô'nin Kaikei shi hô* (Certified Public Accountant Law) Art. 4(3).

31 See Anderson and Steele (2003 at [19-213] in relation to costs and at [19-214] in relation to the grounds for bankruptcy.

approximately 13,498 in 2002.[32] The Law to amend the Civil Rehabilitation Law (*Minji saisei hô tô no ichibu o kaisei suru hôritsu* Law No. 128, 2000) amended the Civil Rehabilitation procedure to add new provisions dealing specifically with the rehabilitation of debtors who are natural persons. Those provisions enable debtors to propose a plan, not unlike a debt agreement in the Australian context. In particular, they deal with:

- rehabilitation for small individual debtors ('Individual Rehabilitation') (Chapter 13, Arts 221–238);
- rehabilitation for wage earners ('Wage Earner Rehabilitation') (Chapter 13, Arts 239–245); and
- special rules in relation to claims in respect of the debtor's home loan ('Home Loan rules') (Chapter 10, Arts 196–206).[33]

These provisions simplify the Civil Rehabilitation procedure in order to provide a simple and effective method of:

- assisting individual debtors to avoid bankruptcy;
- increasing returns for creditors; and
- enabling individual debtors who are in financial difficulties to keep their home.

Given the large number of Individual Rehabilitation and Wage Earner Rehabilitation cases, it is likely that many of the cases and thus precedents developed in respect of the Civil Rehabilitation Law will deal with personal bankruptcies.[34]

3.7.1 Individual Rehabilitation The Individual Rehabilitation procedure accounts for 41.5 per cent of cases under the Civil Rehabilitation Law (see Table 2.2). The procedure is aimed at what the legislation calls 'small-scale individual debtors' who are those debtors that have future earning capacity and whose unsecured debts do not total more than 30,000,000 yen (Civ RL Law Art. 221).[35] The provisions provide the court with discretion to appoint one or more supervisors to oversee the Individual Rehabilitation ('Individual Rehabilitation Officers') and ensure the plan proposed by the debtor conforms to the legislative requirements.

Statistics from the Tokyo, Osaka and Nagoya District Courts suggest a divergence in approach to the appointment of Individual Rehabilitation Officers. In Tokyo, the court always appoints an Officer (based on data up to July 2002). However, in Osaka

---

32 Hatano and Takizawa (2003: 34).

33 On the Individual Rehabilitation process generally, see Iwanami (2002).

34 Anderson and Steele (2003: [19-375]).

35 This amount excludes any amount in respect of home loans, any amount which remains owing after enforcement of a secured claim and any amount for arising before the commencement of the Civil Rehabilitation proceedings (Civ RL Art. 221(1)). There is a proposal to increase this amount to 50,000,000 yen which may be included in draft legislation in late 2003. See 'Individual debtors may get a break', *The Japan Times* (Tokyo), 13 July 2003. According to this newspaper report, Ministry of Justice officials are in favour of increasing the limit because the scheme has been able to help many individuals avoid bankruptcy.

and Nagoya the court generally will not appoint an Officer if the debtor's petition is filed by a lawyer as opposed to the debtor himself/herself. This is presumably because the court feels it can rely on the lawyer to have fulfilled the functions of the Officer.[36]

If a debtor is eligible for Individual Rehabilitation, she/he may propose a rehabilitation plan that provides for the repayment of debts within three years with at least one payment to be made every three months (Civ RL Art. 229(2) 1 and 2).[37] With the court's permission and subject to the performance of the plan, the remainder of the individual's unsecured debts will be discharged. The court must not confirm a plan even if it is approved by creditors if, amongst other things, it does not provide for repayment of at least one fifth (up to 3,000,000 yen) or 1,000,000 yen (whichever is the greater) of unsecured claims (Civ RL Art. 231-2(3)).

3.7.2 Wage Earner Rehabilitation The Wage Earner Rehabilitation procedure is aimed at individuals who fall within the scope of the Individual Rehabilitation procedure referred to above, who have an expectation of earning a wage or equivalent type of income that is unlikely to vary greatly in amount in the future (Art. 239(1)). In such cases, the provisions relating to the Individual Rehabilitation procedure are simplified. Filings under the Wage Earner Rehabilitation procedure accounted for 51 per cent of cases under the Civil Rehabilitation Law in 2002 (see Table 2.2).

3.7.3 Home Loan rules Special provisions in the Civil Rehabilitation procedure deal with individual debtors who have a home loan (Civ RL Ch 10, Arts 196–206). If there is a likelihood that the debtor's home loan will be rescheduled as part of the rehabilitation plan, the court may order a stay against a secured creditor enforcing its security in respect of the home or home site. The court may specify the period of the stay at the time that the debtor files a petition to commence a proceeding. Only a debtor may file a plan that includes a proposal for rescheduling home loan repayments (Civ RL Art. 200-1). When deciding whether to approve a plan, the court must listen to the opinions of those secured creditors whose rights will be affected by the provisions in the plan relating to the home loan; however, those creditors do not have a right to vote on the plan (Civ RL 201-1 and 201-2).

3.8 Creditors' Meetings and Debt Agreements and their Termination

In respect of the Civil Rehabilitation Law, see 4.8 and 4.10 below. In respect of the Bankruptcy Law, see 6.5 on meetings and 2.1 on discharge.

---

36 Anderson and Steele (2003: [19-374]), based on statistics provided by the courts themselves.

37 This three-year period for the payment of debts may be extended in special circumstances, but only up to five years (Civ RL 229(2)-2).

4 Corporate Insolvency Rules

4.1 Legislative Procedures for Corporate Insolvencies

All five of the insolvency procedures in Japan can be used in respect of corporate debtors (see 1.2). Special Liquidation and Corporate Arrangement under the Commercial Code and Corporate Reorganisation under the Corporate Reorganisation Law were designed specifically for joint-stock corporations (*kabushiki kaisha*) and do not apply to individuals. The Civil Rehabilitation Law was initially designed with small and medium-sized enterprises in mind; however, since its introduction it has also been used by large corporations such as the MyCal supermarket chain[38] and has been amended to include special provisions for personal insolvencies (see 3.7).

4.2 Corporate Rescue and the Use of Informal (Non-legal) Mechanisms of dealing with Corporate Debtors

4.2.1 Overview Similarly to most other countries, in Japan many insolvency workouts occur outside the legal procedures mentioned above; that is, the solvency problems of the debtor are worked out privately without court participation.[39] Informal workouts have the advantage of being flexible because they are based on private agreements between the parties and to some extent avoid the stigma of court proceedings, which in the case of a rehabilitation may be particularly damaging to business confidence.

Private informal workouts (*shiteki seiri*) may focus on either winding up or continuation of a debtor-corporation's business. An informal workout in Japan is sometimes also described as a discretionary workout (*nin'i seiri*) or an internal workout (*nai seiri*). In general, once a corporation is insolvent, the creditors will come together for a meeting to decide a plan of action.[40] Often one or more creditors will be chosen to form an informal creditors' committee, which will be responsible for overseeing the workout process.[41] The committee will then choose a chairperson who will virtually take over the management of the business, with responsibility for preserving the accounting books and corporate seal. Equipment, raw materials, bank accounts and the like will be transferred into the chairperson's name.

Next, the creditors' committee considers the events leading up to the corporation's insolvency: for example, were there any voidable antecedent acts and was the debtor solely responsible for the insolvency? Based on this investigation and the opinions of

38 MyCal was eventually forced into Corporate Reorganisation by its bank. See Anderson and Steele (2003: [19-380]).

39 This phenomenon is not unique to Japan. Much has been made, for example, of successful bank-driven informal workouts under the London Approach in England.

40 Aoyama *et al.* (1992: 20). The following summary of informal workouts is based on Aoyama *et al.* (1992: esp. 20–1). As Itô (1991: 29) notes, informal procedures are flexible and may vary from case to case, although there are rules which are followed as a matter of custom.

41 Itô (1991: 29) documents some other possibilities: the chairperson may appoint a lawyer to oversee the workout; the creditors' committee may choose not to elect a chairperson and appoint a lawyer directly; or the creditors' meeting may not elect a committee and simply choose a chairperson.

the debtor and secured and preferential creditors, the committee will decide whether or not to liquidate the corporation and/or conclude an agreement with the debtor. Where it is decided to wind up the corporation, the agreement will often involve transferring all of the debtor's assets in trust to the committee; in the case of continuation of a business, an agreement usually provides for future investment in the corporation, forgiveness of some debts and extension of payment periods for others.

Even if there are some creditors who do not agree with the contents of an agreement, where the majority agrees, the workout process will usually proceed, but the majority will continue to try to obtain the approval of the dissenting minority. When creditors consent to the agreement, they notify the other creditors of the amount and basis of their claim. The committee then checks this notification against the books and records already in its possession. Where the claim cannot be confirmed in this way, the committee may ask the creditor to provide more information to support its claim.

In the case of an informal workout aimed at winding up a corporation, the committee tries to realise the debtor's assets as quickly as possible at the best possible price and distribute the proceeds amongst the creditors. Where the creditors have decided to try to rehabilitate the debtor, non-essential assets and private assets of the debtor will be disposed of and new capital will be raised if there are assets that might be used as collateral or persons willing to go guarantor for the debtor. The creditors will then receive payments over a long period from the future profits of the debtor.

4.2.2 Disadvantages of informal insolvency workouts in Japan A common problem with informal workouts everywhere is that they rely on agreement amongst the creditors: if even one creditor does not agree, it is difficult to proceed with a collective workout procedure outside of a court. There is no mechanism for binding creditors to a workout agreement and no moratorium to prevent them from exercising their rights individually.[42] Furthermore, informal workouts are essentially dealt with on a private contractual basis, so the procedure is not transparent and there is no supervision by a public body such as a court or an administrator. Thus, there is potential for committee chairpersons to abuse their position to obtain preferential payment for themselves.[43]

4.2.3 Guidelines for Out-of-Court Workouts In an effort to make informal workouts more transparent, guidelines for private or informal workouts were drafted by a panel composed of representatives from the Japanese Bankers' Association (*Zenginkyô*), Japan Federation of Economic Organisations (*Keidanren*), academics, lawyers and government agencies including the Financial Services Agency and the

---

42 The Tokyo District Court has found that decisions made at informal creditors' meetings are only binding on those creditors who attend the meeting and agree to the proposal. See Aoyama *et al.* (1992: 21) citing Tokyo District Court, 31 May 1974 ruling on Case No. 290, 1970 (*wa*), dealing with a demand for compensatory damages, reported in (1974) 312 *Hanrei taimuzu* 233.

43 Itô (1991: 30–1) argues that there is support in academic literature in Japan for interpreting the chairperson's relationship with other creditors and the debtor according to fiduciary principles and that recent cases have been influenced by this way of thinking.

Ministry for Finance. The Guidelines for Out-of-Court Workouts (*shiteki seiri ni kan suru gaido rain*) were released on 19 September 2001.[44]

The Guidelines are designed to be a uniform reference point for banks to use when deciding whether to forgive loans made to a corporation that is in financial difficulty. Trade creditors generally do not participate in the workout and would continue to be paid as usual.[45] The Guidelines provide for the waiver of bank loans to corporate debtors and the resolution of the workout within three years. Although there are no formal sanctions against the debtor, the Guidelines suggest that top executives be dismissed and shareholders of the firm must incur a reduction of capital. The debtor must hold a creditors' meeting within two weeks of making the request and provide a reconstruction plan and obtain the agreement of all participating creditors (*taishô saikensha*) within three months of that meeting. The reconstruction plan is to contain profit forecasts for the next ten years and a debt repayment schedule. The Guidelines do not clarify how the burden of the rescheduling of the debt should be shared amongst the debtors' banks. In practice, the main burden in the rescheduling is likely to fall to the debtor's main bank or banks, particularly if the bank is heavily involved in the management of the debtor.

4.2.4 Civil Conciliation Many insolvency workouts (both corporate and personal) are dealt with under the Civil Conciliation Law (*Minji chôtei hô* Law No. 222, 1951).[46] In these cases, court-sanctioned lay and professional mediators assist corporate and individual debtors to come to an agreement with creditors, usually by providing creditors with some sort of attachment rights to a debtor's future earnings. However, because a mediation plan cannot be created without the consent of all parties (Civil Conciliation Law Art. 16), mediation was perceived to be ineffective for debtors with many large debts.[47] Supplementary provisions were introduced in 1999 that make agreements binding on all creditors without unanimous consent but only in certain circumstances, including requirements such as the parties having jointly applied for conciliation and the debtor being a corporation.[48]

4.2.5 Industrial Revitalisation Corporation A further development in private insolvency workouts in Japan is the establishment of the Industrial Revitalisation Corporation on 8 May 2003 by the Japanese Government. The Corporation's brief is to provide government assistance to help reconstruct the financial and corporate sectors. At the time this chapter was being finalised, the Corporation had received

---

44 For a translation, see the Japanese Bankers' Association's web site: http://www.zenginkyo.or.jp/news/pdf/GL010919.pdf. The nine points are: objects of private workout; working rules; enterprises which may become [private workout] debtors; commencement of private workouts; first meeting of creditors and creditors' committee; temporary moratorium; contents of a reconstruction plan; formation of a reconstruction plan; and miscellaneous [issues].

45 Sudo (2003: 4).

46 Anderson and Steele (2003: 19-632]).

47 Aoyama *et al.* (1992: 23).

48 Law Concerning Special Conciliation for the Promotion of Conciliation of Certain Debts (*Tokutei saimu tô no chôsei no sokushin no tame no tokutei chôtei ni kan suru hôritsu* Law No. 158, 1999). See Anderson and Steele (2003: [19-632]).

few cases and its officials expressed frustration at the lack of interest in its activities by the banks.[49]

4.3 The Nature of Legally Prescribed Mechanisms of Voluntary Administration: Civil Rehabilitation

The Civil Rehabilitation Law was designed to be the primary reorganisation or reconstruction statute in Japan.[50] Because of its popularity in comparison to other reorganisation-type proceedings, and thus its importance for insolvency proceedings in Japan, the focus of this part 4 is the Civil Rehabilitation procedure. The other types of reorganisation-type proceedings are dealt with by way of overview in part 5 below.

4.4 Methods of Initiating a Civil Rehabilitation Proceeding

Filing a petition for a Civil Rehabilitation proceeding does not automatically commence the proceeding. The national average time between filing and commencement of a case that meets the requirements (discussed below) is less than one month and is even shorter in commercial centres like Tokyo (about two weeks).[51]

The grounds for commencement of a Civil Rehabilitation proceeding are different depending on whether the petition is brought by a debtor or a creditor. A debtor may petition for commencement of a Civil Rehabilitation proceeding where there are: (1) grounds to suspect that the liabilities of the corporation are in excess of its assets; or (2) an inability to pay debts without causing a serious obstacle to the continuation of a debtor's business (Civ RL Law Art. 21-1). A creditor, on the other hand, may only petition for commencement on the first ground (Civ RL Law Art. 21-2). In either case the grounds must be proven prima facie to exist at the time of filing (Civ RL Law Art. 23). In any event, petitions by creditors are rare.[52]

The petitioner must also meet certain other commencement requirements to initiate a proceeding, because the court must dismiss a petition where:

---

49 See 'Tanigaki: Sick firms passing up IRC's help', *The Asahi Shimbun* (Tokyo), 3 July 2003, www.asahi.com/english/business, accessed on 5 August 2003. See also the comments in 'Bus company wants IRC to get on board', *The Asahi Shimbun* (Tokyo), 25 July 2003, www.asahi.com/english/business, accessed on 5 August 2003.

50 Hatano and Takizawa (2003: 32) refer to the Civil Rehabilitation procedure as the fundamental law in respect of reconstruction-type procedures for dealing with insolvency. See Table 2.2 for the number of Civil Rehabilitation filings compared to Corporate Reorganisation filings. Although I note that the lower number of Corporate Reorganisation filings could be attributed to the fact that some debtors may have been discouraged from filing or delayed filing under the procedure because it was about to be amended, even before the reforms which introduced the Civil Rehabilitation Law and repealed the Composition Law, the Composition proceeding was far more popular than the Corporate Reorganisation proceeding. See Hatano and Takizawa (2003: 34). However, as Hatano and Takizawa note (2003: 33), filings under the old Corporate Reorganisation Law increased dramatically in 2002 (88 cases) compared to 2001 (47 cases), so it will be interesting to see if there is any change in the relevant popularity of the Civil Rehabilitation procedure in future given that the new Corporate Reorganisation procedure has been drafted to reflect the procedural provisions under the Civil Rehabilitation Law.

51 Anderson and Steele (2003: [19-312]).

52 Anderson and Steele (2003: [19-312])

1. the costs of the rehabilitation proceeding have not been paid into court;
2. there is a Bankruptcy, Corporate Arrangement or Special Liquidation proceeding pending and in light of the general interests of creditors it is appropriate to deal with the case as part of that proceeding;
3. it is clear that there is no possibility of a rehabilitation plan being created or consented to by creditors or that there is no possibility of the plan being confirmed by a court; or
4. a petition is found to have been made in bad faith (Civ RL Art. 25).

4.5 Effect of the Appointment of a Supervisory Officer on the Assets and Management Structures of the Corporation

In principle, the Civil Rehabilitation procedure allows debtors to retain the right to manage and dispose of assets after commencement (Civ RL Law Art. 38). However, where the court finds it necessary, it may appoint supervisory officers with varying powers of control over the debtor:

- Supervisor (*kantokui'in*) (Civ RL Arts 54–61);
- Investigator (*chôsai'in*) (Civ RL Arts 62–63);
- Trustee (*kanza'nin*) (Civ RL Arts 64–78);
- Provisional administrator (*hozen kanri'nin*) (Civ RL Arts 79–83); and
- Individual Rehabilitation Officer (*kojin saisei i'in*) (Civ RL Art. 223) (see 3.7.1 above).

Statistics from the first 2.5 years of the Civil Rehabilitation procedure's operation show that despite the prima facie 'debtor-in-possession' nature of the Civil Rehabilitation Law, supervisors are appointed in most cases once a petition is filed; that is, before a case is even commenced.[53]

4.5.1 Supervisors and investigators The office of supervisor and investigator are very similar. The court may appoint a supervisor and/or investigator at any time after a petition for a Civil Rehabilitation proceeding is filed on its own motion or a petition from an interested party (Civ RL Arts 54-1 and 62-1).

4.5.2 Provisional administrators and trustees The appointment of a trustee or a provisional administrator has a much greater effect on the management of the debtor. A provisional administrator may be appointed during the period beginning from when a petition for commencement is filed until a decision to commence a proceeding or reject the petition is made (Civ RL Art. 79-1). After a proceeding is commenced, a trustee may be appointed (Civ RL Law Art. 64-1). A provisional administrator/trustee will only be appointed where the court finds that it is especially necessary for the rehabilitation of the debtor's business (see also 4.6). They can be appointed on the court's own motion or a petition of an interested party but only where the debtor is a juridical person. The right to manage and dispose of the assets of the debtor vests in

---

53 Anderson and Steele (2003: [19-322]).

the provisional administrator/trustee automatically upon appointment (Civ RL Arts 66 and 81-1). However, in the case of a provisional administrator, she/he must obtain court permission in respect of any acts that are not within the everyday scope of the debtor's business (Civ RL Art. 81-1). This is logical given the timing distinction between the office of provisional administrator and trustee, with provisional administrators being appointed after filing but prior to commencement.

4.6 Powers, Liabilities and Qualifications of Supervisory Officers and Duration of Administration

4.6.1 Supervisors and investigators Each supervisor, investigator, provisional administrator and trustee:

- has the power to request that auditors, directors and liquidators of the rehabilitation debtor provide reports on the state of the business and assets of the debtor, and to inspect any documents or accounts, and any objects described in them (Civ RL Arts 59, 63, 78 and 83-1);
- is under a duty of care to conduct their duties as good managers (Civ RL Arts 60-1, 63, 78 and 83-1); and
- will receive pre-payment of costs and have their remuneration decided by the court (Civ RL Arts 61-1, 63, 78 and 83-1).

Each supervisory officer acts under the supervision of the court (Civ RL Arts 57, 63, 78 and 83-1).

Where two or more supervisors or investigators are appointed, they must perform their duties in common (Civ RL Arts 58 main sentence and 63), but a supervisor may obtain court permission to act separately or to divide certain functions among the group of supervisors (Civ RL Arts 58 proviso). Both supervisors and investigators may be juridical persons (Civ RL Arts 54-3 and 63).

The main difference between the powers of a supervisor and those of an investigator is that only supervisors may be given authority by the court on its own motion or a petition of an interested party to exercise avoidance powers (*hi'nin ken*) with respect to certain acts once a Civil Rehabilitation proceeding is commenced (Civ RL Art. 56-1).[54] The supervisor may also be given authority to manage and dispose of the monetary earnings/expenses and other assets of the debtor to the extent that it is necessary to exercise its authority to exercise avoidance powers (Civ RL Art. 56-2). Investigators, on the other hand, are appointed by the court to compile reports that the court and creditors will rely on when deciding how to proceed with respect to the debtor. The court will set a deadline for the presentation of any reports at the time of the appointment (Civ RL Art. 62-2).

In practice, investigators have rarely been appointed by the courts, possibly because of the limited powers of that office when compared to supervisors.[55] In most

---

54 This may result in supervisors being appointed to exercise rights of avoidance. On this point and for a detailed explanation of the avoidance provisions in the Civil Rehabilitation Law, see Steele (2000).

55 Anderson and Steele (2003: [19-322]).

cases, the court will appoint a licensed lawyer (*bengoshi*) to act as supervisor, but the preference in the Nagoya District Court appears to be for a licensed accountant, because the court finds that the accountant's financial reports are useful to creditors.[56]

With respect to the duration of the proceeding, see 4.10 below.

4.6.2 Provisional administrators and trustees These have been appointed by the court in only a few Civil Rehabilitation cases. This is probably because the courts have not found it necessary given that they appoint a supervisor in most cases (see 4.6.1).[57] In respect of the power of provisional administrators and trustees, see the beginning of this 4.6 and 4.5.2 above. In addition to those powers, the court may also request that postal agencies redirect the debtor's mail to the trustee (Civ RL Art. 73-1) who may open and inspect it (Civ RL Art. 74-1). If the debtor wishes to view the contents of the mail or have mail that is not relevant to his/her assets returned, the debtor may make a request to the trustee (Civ RL Art. 74-2).

4.7 Protection of Assets in respect of a Civil Rehabilitation Proceeding

Assets are protected during two distinct periods under the Civil Rehabilitation Law: (1) after filing a petition, but before the court makes a ruling to commence a proceedings ('pre-commencement'); and (2) after the court makes a ruling to commence a proceeding ('post-commencement').

4.7.1 Pre-commencement protection Assets may be preserved for use during a Civil Rehabilitation proceeding by preventing creditors from enforcing their rights after a petition has been filed on the basis of a number of discretionary Preservation Measures and moratoriums or stays. The court may make the following orders on its own motion or a petition from an interested party in respect of unsecured creditors:

- prohibition against unsecured creditors commencing actions against a debtor's business or assets such as attachment or disposition ('Preservation Measures') (Civ RL Art. 30);
- a stay against a particular action which has already been commenced by an unsecured creditor. This stay also covers other insolvency proceedings and litigation involving an administrative agency ('Individual Stay') (Civ RL Art. 26); and
- a stay against all actions by unsecured creditors, whether or not they have been commenced ('Comprehensive Stay') (Civ RL Art. 27).

Before a court will order a Comprehensive Stay, it must find that there are special grounds that clearly make an Individual Stay ineffective to achieve the aims of the proceedings (Civ RL Art. 27-1). Further, given the serious consequences of granting a Comprehensive Stay for unsecured creditors, the court must also have already appointed or appoint at that time a supervisor or provisional administrator when it

---

56 Anderson and Steele (2003: [19-322]).

57 Anderson and Steele (2003: [19-323]).

orders a Comprehensive Stay (Civ RL Art. 27-1). Given the statistical evidence that the courts will appoint a supervisor in most cases anyway, it would appear that this second requirement is unlikely to deter debtors from applying for a Comprehensive Stay.[58]

In addition to these stays in respect of unsecured creditors, courts may also grant individual stays to prevent secured creditors from enforcing security by way of official auction before the commencement of a proceedings for a period of time specified by the court ('Secured Creditor Stay') (Civ RL Art. 31) (see 8.4 below in relation to official auctions).

A Secured Creditor Stay will only be granted by the court if it: (1) corresponds to the general interests of unsecured creditors; and (2) does not unfairly prejudice the secured creditor (Civ RL Art. 31-1). Further, before granting a Secured Creditor Stay, the court must take into account the opinion of the secured creditor (Civ RL Art. 31-2).

Although the Secured Creditor Stay upsets the traditional deference paid to secured creditors in Japan, few have been granted. This suggests that the requirements are difficult to meet.[59] Further, as the average length of a stay specified by the Tokyo District Court is only three months, a secured creditor may wait and enforce its security once the stay has lapsed (subject to any grant of an extension of the stay by the court).[60] At best, it provides the debtor with breathing space and a possible negotiating tool against the secured creditor. The Security Interests Extinguishing Scheme (*tanpo shômetsu seikyû seidô*) will also have an impact on the position of secured creditors (see 4.11).

4.7.2 Post-commencement protection Once a Civil Rehabilitation proceeding commences, the debtor is prohibited from making payments to unsecured creditors (Civ RL Art. 85-1). However, the court may grant exceptions for the payment of small to medium-sized enterprises where the continuation of their business would otherwise be seriously threatened (Civ RL Art. 85-2).

4.8 Role of Creditors during a Civil Rehabilitation Proceeding, Creditors' Meetings, etc.

The Civil Rehabilitation Law provides for limited participation by creditors through a voluntary Creditors' Committee system (Civ RL Art. 118). A Creditors' Committee must obtain court approval to participate in a proceeding. To receive court approval, creditors must take the initiative and form a committee that has:

1. at least three persons but not more than ten (Supreme Court Rules, rule 52);
2. consent from a simple majority of unsecured creditors to the Committee's participation; and

---

58 Anderson and Steele (2003: [19-335]).

59 Steele (2003) and Anderson and Steele (2003: [19-336]).

60 Anderson and Steele (2003: [19-336]). I do not know of any other District Court that has provided this type of detailed statistics. In any event, if the courts must specify a time period the same argument applies once that period comes to an end.

3. the ability to appropriately represent the interests of all creditors (Civ RL Art. 118-1).

The court may seek the Committee's opinion and the Committee may present opinions to the court, rehabilitation debtor and/or supervisor (Civ RL Art. 118-2 and 118-3). There is no provision for the Committee to present its opinion to a provisional administrator or trustee and the court may withdraw its approval for the Committee at any time on the petition of an interested party or its own motion (Civ RL Art. 118-5).

In addition to Creditors' Committees, creditors may choose to participate in the proceedings through a Creditors' Representative (*dairii'in*). With the court's permission, a creditor or creditors may appoint a representative, usually a lawyer, to manage their interests in a Civil Rehabilitation proceeding (Civ RL Art. 90-1 and 90-2). The representative has all the rights and authority of the creditor(s), but permission to act as a representative may be revoked by the court at any time if the representative exercises its authority in a seriously unfair manner (Civ RL Art. 90-4). Representatives may receive compensation from the assets of the debtor as determined by the court (Civ RL Art. 91-1). Creditor Representatives would prove useful in cases where there are many creditors of a particular type who require representation on a Creditor's Committee, for example, the members of a golf club under Civil Rehabilitation.[61]

4.9 Powers of the Courts in Relation to Administration and the Administrator

Supervisors, investigators, provisional administrators and trustees perform their duties under the supervision of the court (Civ RL Arts 57, 63, 78 and 83-1). The court may vary or cancel an appointment at any time (Civ RL Arts 54-5, 62-3, 64-4 and 79-4).

4.10 Termination of a Civil Rehabilitation Proceeding

A Civil Rehabilitation proceeding will usually terminate when the court confirms a plan (Civ RL Art. 188-1).[62] However, where a supervisor has been appointed the court may delay termination of the proceeding for three years when it confirms the plan (Civ RL Art. 188-2). Similarly, where a trustee has been appointed, the court may delay termination of the proceeding until it is convinced that the plan will be performed in its entirety (Civ RL Art. 188-3). This means that a proceeding may last as long as ten years, the time limit set down for any obligations to be repaid under a plan.

---

61 Anderson and Steele (2003: [19-235]).

62 For more details on drafting plans, performing, amending and revoking plans and completing plans, see Anderson and Steele (2003: [19-351] to [19-360]).

4.11 Other Related Matters

4.11.1 Security Interest Extinguishing Scheme ('Scheme') This is aimed at assisting debtors to deal with assets that are secured for more than they are worth as a result of the collapse of the Bubble economy, deflation and imprudent lending practices during the 1980s.[63] The Scheme is set out in the Civil Rehabilitation Law articles 148–153 and allows for a secured creditor's claim over assets that are indispensable to the Civil Rehabilitation to be cancelled in return for a reasonable current price being paid into court by the debtor. This will prevent secured creditors from selling assets necessary to a debtor's rehabilitation and it is intended that ordinary creditors will benefit from some of the proceeds from the price paid. However, under the Scheme a debtor may be able to avoid paying second or lower ranking secured creditors who will be forced to join the ranks of ordinary unsecured creditors. Even if the Scheme is not used in practice, the threat of a debtor being able to extinguish secured creditors' interests may provide debtors with leverage in their negotiations with secured creditors and provide potential new financiers or buyers of the debtor's business with an incentive to participate in a refinancing or sale under the umbrella of the Civil Rehabilitation proceedings (see 4.11.2 below).

4.11.2 Pre-packaged Rehabilitation The Scheme (see 4.11.1) will complement the business transfer provisions in the Civil Rehabilitation Law (Arts 42–43), by enabling debtors and their supporters to prepare a corporation for a sale with the aim of restructuring and reorganising its business.[64] The business transfer provisions allow a debtor to apply to the court to transfer the whole or part of its business where necessary for the debtor's rehabilitation as soon as a proceeding is commenced (Civ RL Art. 42-1). Further, an application for a transfer need not be made as part of a plan, so the transfer can occur very quickly. Given that the Tokyo District Court, for example, only takes about two weeks to process a Civil Rehabilitation petition before giving a ruling in respect of commencement, these provisions provide a great incentive for debtors and their advisers to use the Civil Rehabilitation for pre-packaged rehabilitations involving a merger and/or acquisition.[65] The provisions also provide protection for prospective buyers who suspect that the company may later be subject to scrutiny by the court or a trustee in respect of voidable transactions as the business transfer will have received the court's blessing.[66]

4.11.3 Simplified and Consensual Rehabilitation Two schemes in the Civil Rehabilitation Law simplify the ordinary procedure. They are helpful in the case of smaller debtors where there are only a few creditors involved and agreement between them is possible.

First, under the Simplified Rehabilitation Scheme (Civ RL Arts 211 to 216), the process of investigating and proving claims may be dispensed with if the petition

63 Steele (2003) discusses the origins and drafting of the Scheme provisions in detail.

64 Steele (2003).

65 Anderson and Steele (2003: [19-372]).

66 Anderson and Steele (2003: [19-372]).

for commencement certifies that three fifths of the registered creditors agree to: (1) dispensing with the investigation and certification of claims; and (2) the rehabilitation plan submitted by the debtor (Civ RL Art. 211-1).[67] Second, under the Consensual Rehabilitation Scheme (Civ RL Arts 217 to 220), if a debtor can obtain the consent of all creditors who have filed a proof of claim, the court may confirm a plan under the Consensual Rehabilitation Scheme and dispense with the need for a creditors' resolution (Civ RL Art. 217). These Schemes have yet to be used extensively, but would be useful, for example, in the context of a pre-packaged rehabilitation.[68]

5 Court-based Reorganisation, Arrangement, Reconstruction of Financial Institutions

5.1 Discussion of Other Legal Mechanisms which may Impact on the Corporation

As discussed at 1.2 and 4.3 above, in addition to the reorganisation-type procedure under the Civil Rehabilitation Law, there are two other formal reorganisation-type procedures in Japan: Corporate Reorganisation and Corporate Arrangement.

5.2 Corporate Reorganisation

The new Corporate Reorganisation Law (*Kaisha kôsei hô* Law No. 154, 2002) replaced the old Corporate Reorganisation Law (*Kaisha kôsei hô* Law No. 172, 1952) when the new law came into effect on 1 April 2003. Although the new law has been updated to make it procedurally consistent with the Civil Rehabilitation Law, it has retained a number of characteristics from the old law that are not contained in the Civil Rehabilitation Law because of their differing objectives.

The new Corporate Reorganisation Law is specifically aimed at rehabilitating the business of joint-stock corporations so that they can continue to maintain their business (CRL Art. 1). The court must reject a petition for Corporate Reorganisation if it finds that there is no possibility of a reorganisation plan that includes, as part of its terms, the continuation of the corporation's business being approved by creditors or confirmed by the court (CRL Art. 41). Similarly to Civil Rehabilitation, Corporate Reorganisation includes pre-commencement discretionary stays (CRL Chapter 2, Sections 1–2, Arts 24–29). However, it also includes a post-commencement prohibition on the payment of all creditors, including secured creditors (see CRL Arts 2-12 and 47). Further, there are provisions for pre-commencement supervisory officers to be appointed similarly to Civil Rehabilitation (Chapter 2, Sections 3–5, Arts 30–40). However, unlike Civil Rehabilitation, after the commencement of a Corporate Reorganisation proceeding, a trustee will automatically be appointed by the court (CRL Arts 67 and 72). Given that the procedure deals only with joint-stock

---

67 Where such a petition is made, the relevant labour union or employee representative must be notified (Civ RL Art. 200-2).

68 See Anderson and Steele (2003: [19-372]) and Fujiwara (1999: 72).

corporations, it also includes specific provisions dealing with shareholders (for example, Art. 45 and Chapter 6, Arts 165–166).

The Corporate Reorganisation procedure also applies to non-incorporated entities such as savings and loans companies and credit unions via the Financial Institutions' Rehabilitation Law (see 5.4).

5.3 Corporate Arrangement Procedure

In 1938 the Corporate Arrangement procedure was introduced into the Commercial Code (*Shô hô* Law No. 48, 1899). It was designed as a quick and cheap rehabilitation procedure to deal specifically with small-scale joint-stock corporations, by codifying informal workout practices.[69] The Corporate Arrangement procedure is similar to methods of informal workout, because it relies on negotiation between interested parties and lacks detailed formal requirements. It is likely that this procedure will be repealed shortly and it is mentioned here for completeness only.[70] In fact, the procedure is rarely used: in 2002 there were only four cases.[71]

Despite the Corporate Arrangement procedure's unpopularity for corporate workouts, many of the provisions from the Civil Rehabilitation Law have been adapted from it. Similarly to Civil Rehabilitation, for example:

- the Corporate Arrangement discretionary moratorium provisions enable a court to suspend enforcement of security interests by official auction after commencement of a proceeding (Commercial Code Art. 384);
- a Corporate Arrangement proceeding may be commenced where the corporation is in danger (*osore*) of bankruptcy (Commercial Code Art. 381-1); and
- although the incumbent management may retain the right to manage and dispose of a corporation's assets, their behaviour is checked by the threat of the court appointing a supervisory officer (Commercial Code Arts 386(1)-11 and 398).

It will be interesting to see if courts and practitioners look to previous decisions relating to Corporate Arrangements in order to interpret the Civil Rehabilitation provisions.

5.4 Financial Institutions and Insurance Companies

The financial failure of banks, securities companies and insurance companies in Japan led to the enactment of laws in 1996 and 2000.[72] The existing insolvency laws

69 Shinomiya (1997: 81) and Aoyama *et al.* (1992: 302).

70 Anderson and Steele (2003: [19-130]).

71 Hatano and Takizawa (2003: 33, table 1). The district courts in which the Corporate Arrangement proceedings were brought were Maebara (1), Nagoya (1) and Yamagata (2). In contrast, in those jurisdictions there were respectively 12, 41 and 7 ordinary Civil Rehabilitation cases.

72 The *Special Procedures for Reorganisation of Financial Institutions Law (Kinyû kikan no kôsei tetsuzuki no tokurei tô ni kan suru hôritsu* Law No. 95, 1996) ('RFIL'), as amended by the Law to amend part of the RFIL (*Kinyû kikan no kôsei tetsuzuki no tokurei tô ni kan suru hôritsu no ichibu wo kaisei suru hôritsu* Law Nos 92–93, 2000).

were considered inappropriate for financial, securities and insurance sectors, because of the special nature of these businesses.[73] The legislation gives special standing to government regulators to file for a modified Bankruptcy or Corporate Reorganisation proceeding.[74] The modifications take into account the special interests of financial institutions and depositors as debtors and creditors respectively.

6 Winding Up Procedures for Corporations

6.1 An Introduction to the Range of Winding Up Procedures Available in Japan

The main insolvency statute governing winding up of corporations in Japan is the Bankruptcy Law, which also applies to individuals as discussed above in part 3 (*Hasan hô* Law No. 71, 1922). A second procedure for winding up a joint-stock corporation is the Special Liquidation procedure under the Commercial Code (see part 7 below). As noted above, these laws were still being redrafted as this chapter was being finalised. Accordingly, this chapter is based on the pre-reform legislation, but where possible it highlights areas of the law which are expected to change.

6.2 Initiation of Bankruptcy Proceedings; Powers of the Court and Powers of Creditors

A debtor or its creditor(s) (in practice, the debtor or creditor's legal representative) may petition for the commencement of a Bankruptcy proceeding in the local district court of the debtor (BL Arts 105 and 132-1). The vast majority of petitions are by debtors.[75] Conditional and future creditors may petition for bankruptcy and it does not matter whether a creditor is secured or unsecured. There is also no requirement as to the amount of the creditor's claim. If the petitioner is a creditor, she/he or it must provide information relating to the specific debt owed and evidence as to grounds for bankruptcy (BL Art. 132-2). Further, the petitioning creditor must advance costs into court to cover the cost of the administration of the Bankruptcy proceedings.[76] If the court finds that the requirements for commencement are met, it will make a bankruptcy declaration (*hasan senkoku*) and this commences the proceeding. This means that there is a time lag between filing and commencement during which the court may order Preservation Measures or stays to preserve the assets of the debtor.

6.3 Grounds for Bankruptcy: When may Bankruptcy Proceedings be Commenced?

A petitioner for bankruptcy must show that there are grounds for bankruptcy (*hasan gen'in*) by proving that: (1) the debtor is unable to pay its debts (*shiharai funô*) (BL Art. 126-1); (2) in the case of a juristic entity such as a corporation, the entity's

73 See also Anderson and Steele (2003: [19-520]) on this point.

74 See Anderson and Steele (2003: [19-520]).

75 Anderson and Steele (2003: [19-212]).

76 See Anderson and Steele (2003: [19-213]) in relation to costs.

liabilities exceed its assets (*saimu chôka*) (BL Art. 127-1). The first requirement refers to a cash flow or equitable test of insolvency and the second to balance sheet insolvency. Grounds for bankruptcy require acts by the debtor that suggest to the outside world that they are unable to ordinarily or continuously pay debts that are due, for example, suspension of payments (*shiharai teishi*) (BL Art. 126-2).[77] The case law suggests that a temporary cash flow problem would not evidence the existence of grounds for bankruptcy; however, dishonouring two promissory notes (giving rise to a suspension of payments under the clearing house system) is generally accepted as evidence that grounds for bankruptcy exist.[78]

6.4 Effect of Commencement of Bankruptcy on Corporation Management and Creditors' Claims

The effect of the commencement of bankruptcy is that a trustee will be appointed to manage and dispose of the bankruptcy estate (BL Arts 7, 185). Assets that are excluded from the bankruptcy estate are exempt property, including those obtained by the bankrupt after the Bankruptcy proceeding was commenced, and (in the case of a personal bankruptcy) a minimum amount of money and assets such as household goods allowed for personal use by the debtor (BL Art. 6). It has been suggested that the amount in respect of personal use will increase from 210,000 yen per month under the new Bankruptcy Law.[79]

6.4.1 Lawsuits Lawsuits will be suspended when a Bankruptcy proceeding is commenced, but the trustee or the other party to the lawsuit may request that the trustee take over lawsuits which relate to assets falling within the bankruptcy estate. Lawsuits relating to claims against the bankruptcy estate will be suspended at least until the date set down for the investigation of claims.

6.4.2 Enforcement proceedings Proceedings initiated by unsecured creditors which cease to have effect when a Bankruptcy proceeding is commenced are: compulsory executor (*kyôsei shikkô*), provisional attachments (*kari sashiosae*) and provisional injunctions (*kari shobun*). Once a Bankruptcy proceeding is commenced, there is a general prohibition on enforcement by unsecured creditors outside the proceedings (BL Art. 16). Prior to commencement, the court may grant a temporary stay prohibiting specific unsecured creditors from enforcing rights (BL Art. 155). Enforcement proceedings for rarely-used floating charges (*kigyô tanpo*) will also cease to have effect, but enforcement proceedings by secured creditors with a right of separation are not affected (BL Art. 92) (see 8.1.1 below).

Drafts of the new Bankruptcy Law suggest that moratoriums similar to those discussed above in respect of the Civil Rehabilitation procedure may be introduced in future.[80]

---

77 Aoyama *et al.* (1992: 35).

78 See Anderson and Steele on the clearing house system at [19-631] and the comments at 1.1 of this chapter.

79 'Bankrupt people to lose less assets', *The Asahi Shimbun* (2003).

80 Anderson and Steele (2003: [19-231]).

6.5 Creditors' Meetings

Meetings of creditors may be convened by the court. At a creditors' meeting, creditors may, among other things, decide to:

1. resolve to request the court to remove a trustee (BL Art. 167);
2. resolve to appoint investigators (*chôsai'in*) and seek the court's approval for their appointment (BL Arts 170 and 172-1);
3. resolve to remove investigators (BL Art. 174);
4. suspend or continue the operation of the debtor's business (BL Art. 194);
5. raise objections and offer opinions about the discontinuance of the Bankruptcy proceeding for lack of funds (BL Arts 351 and 353(2)); and
6. discontinue a Bankruptcy proceeding in favour of commencing a compulsory composition proceeding (BL Arts 299, 306(1)).

Creditors may only vote if they have filed a proof of claim, but they may vote by proxy (BL Art. 181). Deferred claims do not give rise to voting rights (BL Art. 182(5)). A creditor's right to vote is determined by the amount of its proved claims (BL Art. 182-1). If a creditor has claims which are conditional, future or yet to be proved, the court has the power to determine whether such a creditor may vote and the extent of the creditor's voting rights (BL Art. 182-2).

Creditors' meetings in Japan are not well attended. Only about 10 per cent of those creditors who have filed a proof of claim attend even the first meeting and it is not unusual for there to be zero attendance at the last meeting where the trustee is required to give a final report to creditors.[81] The lack of attendance arises for a number of reasons, not just because creditors are disinterested. Itô suggests two reasons: (1) the trustee's report on the financial state of the debtor – due at the first meeting under Bankruptcy Law Art. 193 – is often postponed to the second creditors' meeting, leaving creditors wary of the trustee's ability to sort out the debtor's problems; and (2) trustees often do not provide creditors with enough information.[82] On the other hand, it seems that there is a general impression amongst trustees that because creditors in a Bankruptcy proceeding are only interested in a distribution, detailed explanations about the financial prospects of the debtor are unnecessary. Itô argues that trustees can help maintain creditors' confidence by explaining, for example, what assets are available and how they intend to realise them. In light of these problems, there are likely to be amendments to the provisions relating to creditors' meetings in the new Bankruptcy Law.[83]

---

81 Itô (2000: 131).

82 Itô (2000: 131).

83 For example, the *Questionnaire on Reforms* suggested making meetings other than the first meeting discretionary. See *The Questionnaire* [Dai 1 bu dai 1 shô dai 1-10(2) *a*]. *The Questionnaire* was published by the Committee in 1997 as a means of obtaining public comment on proposed insolvency law reforms. *Hômushô minjikyoku sanjikan shitsu* (Office of the counsellor of the Civil Affairs Bureau of the Ministry of Justice) (December 1997), *Tôsan hôsei ni kan suru kaisei kentô jikô* (Questionnaire on reforms relating to insolvency laws), reproduced in (1997), *Bessatsu NBL*, 46. See Steele (2000) on the reform process

6.6 *The role of the Court, Trustees and Investigators in the Bankruptcy Process*

As discussed at 6.4, when a Bankruptcy proceeding is commenced, the court will appoint a trustee (*kanzai'nin*) to control and manage the debtor's assets (BL Art. 185). The right to manage and dispose of those assets vests in the trustee (BL Art. 7). The court's role is to supervise the trustee (BL Art. 161).

There are no particular restrictions on who may be a trustee, but it must be a natural person. In principle, the court appoints one person as the trustee, usually a licensed lawyer (*bengoshi*), although it may appoint more than one in large or complex cases (BL Arts 158, 163). It is understood that in order to ensure the speedy progress of the proceeding, there can be no objection to the court's choice of trustee.[84] Once a lawyer expresses an interest in doing insolvency law cases, judges will start to give them insolvency cases.[85] The judges then keep notes on those lawyers and their previous insolvency experience with comments – like a school report card. Trustees are thus graded on how well they perform their responsibilities, which include: managing, collecting and disposing the assets of the bankruptcy estate, investigating creditors' claims, exercising avoidance powers and distributing the proceeds from the bankruptcy estate to creditors. The trustee is subject to a duty of care to perform these responsibilities as a good manager (BL Art. 164). The trustee will be discharged by the court once accounts have been presented to the Creditors' Committee and settled, all assets liquidated and all proceeds distributed to creditors (BL Arts 168, 169). In addition to appointing a trustee, the Creditors' Committee may also resolve to appoint one or more investigators (*kansai'in*) (BL Arts 170, 171-1). If the appointments are confirmed by the court (BL Art. 171-2), the role of the investigator is to investigate the condition of the assets that make up the bankruptcy estate and provide reports to the trustee (BL Art. 173). The Creditors' Committee may resolve to discharge the investigator at any time (BL Art. 174-1).

6.7 *Proof and Ranking of Claims by Creditors against the Corporation*

6.7.1 Types of claims by creditors In general, the concept of *pari passu* applies to the rules relating to the ranking of claims in a Bankruptcy proceeding. However, like most modern insolvency laws, there are exceptions which provide for priority in respect of certain types of claims (see 6.7.3). Of the claims which are general unsecured claims, the Bankruptcy Law provides for priority for the costs of administering the Bankruptcy ('estate claims', *zaidan saiken*) and claims prioritised for other public policy reasons ('priority claims', *yûsen saiken*). Secured claims that give rise to a right of separation (see part 8) rank higher than any other claim because they can be enforced without reference to a Bankruptcy proceeding. Thus, in order of

---

generally. Other reform proposals include allowing for a meeting to be called on the motion of the court, trustee or a certain number of creditors, and creating a scheme whereby creditors can vote and present opinions in writing (Ito, 2000: 132) not unlike the Simplified Rehabilitation Scheme discussed at 4.11.3 above.

84 Aoyama *et al.* (1992: 158–63).

85 See comments by Nagai in Takahashi (1998: Part 2, 35).

priority, the types of claims in Bankruptcy are: (1) secured claims; (2) priority estate claims; (3) general priority claims; (4) general unsecured claims; and (5) deferred claims.

6.7.2 Priority estate claims Priority estate claims must be paid in full before any other general priority or unsecured claims and may be paid at any time (BL Arts 40, 49, 50 and 51-1). Estate claims, in order of priority, include (BL Arts 47 and 48):

- costs of judicial proceedings incurred for the benefit of the creditors as a group;
- taxation claims which may be collected under the National Tax Collection Law (*Kokuzei chôshû hô* Law No. 147, 1959);[86]
- expenses arising out of the management, realisation or distribution of the Bankruptcy estate;
- claims arising due to acts done by the trustee with respect to the Bankruptcy estate;
- claims arising after the commencement of the Bankruptcy proceeding due to the management of the bankrupt's affairs without a mandate or unjust enrichment;
- claims arising after the commencement of the Bankruptcy proceeding due to acts done out of urgent necessity after the termination of a mandate or extinction of an agent's powers;
- claims under an executory contract where the trustee has performed the contract;
- claims arising prior to the termination of an executory contract where the trustee has made an offer to rescind the contract;[87]
- a living allowance payable to the bankrupt and his/her dependants; and
- costs to the Bankruptcy estate arising from the receipt of a testamentary gift.

6.7.3 General priority claims Once all priority estate claims have been paid, the ranking of general priority claims under the legislation which gives them priority applies (BL Art. 39). For example:

- claims encompassing a lien over the general assets of the bankrupt (including unpaid wages of the employees of a bankrupt joint-stock corporation (Commercial Code Art. 295) and unpaid wages for the last six months for other employees (Civil Code Arts 306 and 308)); and
- ordinary priority claims such as floating charges (Charge on an Enterprise Act, *Kigyô tanpo hô* Law No. 106 1958, Art. 2).

6.7.4 General unsecured claims Claims for payment or rights against property that are based on grounds arising before the commencement of the Bankruptcy proceeding are provable (*hasan saiken*) (BL Art. 15). They include conditional

---

86 The high priority placed on taxation claims has been criticised in Japan and has been a topic of debate in the reform process.

87 Where the trustee cancels an executory contract, the other party under the contract may demand the return of any consideration still existing in the Bankruptcy estate. If no consideration continues to exist, then the other party may demand any benefit existing in the Bankruptcy estate arising from the consideration. Such a claim will be an estate claim (BL Art. 78(1)).

claims, claims not yet due and unsettled claims such as disputed claims. These claims will be paid out of the assets of the bankrupt by way of equal distribution, but they are unlikely to receive anything, because the vast majority of distributions in Bankruptcy pay less than 25 per cent of the amount owed to unsecured creditors.[88]

Where possible, general unsecured claims are converted into monetary amounts when the Bankruptcy proceeding is commenced. The following special rules also apply:

- claims to become due in the future are deemed to have become due on the date the Bankruptcy proceeding was commenced;
- general unsecured claims with a fixed future due date include the principal and any interest accrued up until the original due date in addition to liquidated damages after the due date, but any interest that accrued after the commencement of the Bankruptcy proceeding and any liquidated damages will become subordinated claims (BL Arts 46(1), (5));
- non-monetary claims and claims in a foreign currency will be converted into a yen-monetary amount as of the date of the commencement of the Bankruptcy proceeding (BL Art. 22); and
- conditional claims will not be paid at distribution unless they have become unconditional.[89]

6.7.5 Deferred claims The following bankruptcy claims will be paid after all other claims have been met if there are any proceeds remaining (BL Art. 46):

- interest accrued after the commencement of the Bankruptcy proceeding;
- damages and penalties arising due to defaults by the bankrupt after the commencement of the Bankruptcy proceeding;
- expenses incurred due to participation in the Bankruptcy proceeding;
- criminal penalties and costs of the related criminal proceeding;
- an amount corresponding to the interest after the commencement of Bankruptcy with respect to any fixed amount claims falling due on a fixed date in the future;
- any difference between the evaluated amount and the face value of claims falling due on a date in the future which is yet to be fixed.

6.7.6 Filing of proof of claims General unsecured creditors must file a proof of claim with the court (BL Art. 228). Secured creditors may also file a proof of claim, but only for the amount that could not be recovered from enforcing a right in respect of the assets over which the secured creditor held security (BL Art. 96) (see further

---

88 See Anderson and Steele (2003: [19-244]) citing figures for 2001: '54% of bankruptcies paid from nothing to 5% of recognised claims, while 89% of debtors' estates were only able to pay between 0 and 25% of what they owed to their unsecured creditors'.

89 If there are any amounts to be paid to conditional claims once the conditions have been met, these amounts are held in trust after the final distribution for a period determined by the court (BL Art. 271(4)). If the period determined by the court elapses without the conditions being fulfilled, the conditional creditor loses its right to distribution and the money held in trust will be distributed to the other creditors (BL Art. 275).

8.1 with respect to the rights of secured creditors in Bankruptcy). A creditor with a non-monetary claim or a conditional claim must provide an estimate.

A proof of claim must be filed within the period determined by the court at the time the Bankruptcy proceeding was commenced. This period must be no less than two weeks and no more than four months after commencement (BL Arts 142(1) and 228). Creditors who do not file a proof of claim within this period may still file a proof of claim but they will be liable for any extra costs incurred due to the lateness of the claim (BL Art. 234). However, the claim may not be considered after the date determined by the court for final distribution which will be no less than two weeks and no more than one month after public notice of the amount to be distributed is given. There may be no appeal against the date determined by the court (BL Art. 273).

The clerk of the court will prepare a list of claims consisting of the claims for which a proof of claim has been filed. The list must include:

- the name and address of each creditor;
- the amount claimed by each creditor;
- the transaction which gave rise to each claim;
- whether the claim should have priority or be deferred and why; and
- the amount which could not be recouped by a secured creditor as a result of enforcing its right under its security.

6.7.7 Investigation and filing of proof of claims As discussed above, the court will determine the date for investigation of claims at the commencement of the Bankruptcy proceeding (BL Art. 142). On that date, the bankrupt (or the bankrupt's agent) and creditors may attend the court and review the claims (BL Art. 232). The trustee must be present before the investigation may commence (BL Art. 233). The trustee, creditors or the bankrupt may give an opinion about the claims or make an objection. Objections are noted on the list of claims and may be challenged by the creditor in court (BL Arts 241, 244).[90]

If there are no objections to a claim or a challenge to an objection is successful, the claim is deemed to have been proved (BL Arts 240, 244). Any estimated amounts with respect to secured claims will also be deemed to have been proved if there are no objections, but the amounts will be finalised and the list amended after any security has been enforced (BL 263(3)). The list of claims has the effect of a final judgement with respect to the claims that are proved (BL Art. 242).

Once claims against the bankrupt have been proved and there is a reasonable amount of money from the realisation of the bankrupt's assets, the trustee may begin to make interim distributions to creditors in accordance with a list approved by the court or the investigator (if any) (BL Arts 256, 257). A final distribution will only be made by the trustee with the permission of the court even if it already has the consent of the investigator (BL Art. 272).

---

90 If there are several persons who objected to the claim, the creditor must name them as co-defendants (BL Art. 244(2)).

6.8 *Set Off of Debts*

A creditor may set off debts owed to a bankrupt at commencement of the Bankruptcy proceeding (BL Art. 98). However, it is generally accepted that a creditor may exercise a right of set off at any time prior to the termination of the Bankruptcy proceedings.[91] Set off is prohibited where, with the knowledge that there has been a suspension of payments or a petition for bankruptcy against the debtor, a creditor has assumed an obligation or acquired another person's claim against a debtor (BL Art. 104). This provision is designed to prevent the exercise of rights of set off which contravene the notion of equality amongst creditors and to thus stop creditors from profiteering from bankruptcy.

The use of rights of set off to gain an advantage in a Bankruptcy proceeding and the relationship between set off and voidable transactions have been the subjects of debate in Japan.[92] The conflation of set off and voidable transactions can be seen, for example, where a creditor acquires an obligation against a debtor who is clearly going bankrupt, but before a suspension of payments is imposed on the debtor. However, the Supreme Court has held that set off by a creditor can only be challenged under article 104 and that article 72 (discussed below at 6.9) is limited in its application to voidable transactions.[93] Some commentators suggest that such a transaction should come within article 72, thus making it voidable.[94]

6.9 *Voidable Transactions: Avoidance Powers*

In Japan, voidable transactions are referred to as rights of avoidance or avoidance powers (*hi'nin ken*). Rights of avoidance may be divided into three general categories: (1) intentional or fraudulent transfers (*koi hi'nin*, 'intentional avoidances'), (2) transactions in time of financial distress (*kiki hi'nin*, 'crisis avoidances') and (3) gratuitous or under-valued transactions (*musho hi'nin*, 'gratuitous avoidances') (see Table 2.3).[95] In a Bankruptcy proceeding, rights of avoidance are exercised by the trustee (BL Art. 76). The exercise of a right of avoidance means that the transferred assets must be restored to the Bankruptcy estate (BL Art. 77(1)). Once restitution occurs, the claim against the Bankruptcy estate of the creditor who received the benefit is restored (BL Art. 79).

In practice, in addition to the statutory requirements for each category, there are two or three general requirements before a right of avoidance will arise. First, the transaction must affect the assets of the bankrupt for it to fall within the category of a crisis avoidance. Second, the transaction must be unfair to the creditors in Bankruptcy. When considering the second requirement, the court will inquire into, for example, the benefit lost by the bankruptcy creditors, the benefit being enjoyed by the beneficiary and the motivation for the transaction. The trustee must prove that

91 Itô (2000: 330).

92 Itô (2000: 327).

93 *Trustee for Kajiro Shôten K.K.* v. *Mitsui Ginkô K.K.*, Supreme Court, 410 Hanrei Jihô 23, 22 April 1965.

94 Itô (2000: 328).

95 Itô (2000: 338) and Anderson and Steele (2003: [19-232]).

the transaction was prejudicial and intentional for it to give rise to an intentional avoidance, but it is also open for the beneficiary to show that the act was not unfair. In the case of a crisis avoidance, the beneficiary must show that there was no unfairness.

Lastly, the transaction must generally be done by the bankrupt. There is debate about whether this requirement applies to all three categories of rights of avoidance.[96] For a transaction to give rise to an 'intentional avoidance', it arguably must be done by the bankrupt, because intent on the part of the bankrupt is a necessary requirement. However, if an act by a third party has the same effect as an act by the bankrupt – for example, paying off a creditor – this may be enough to give rise to a right of avoidance based on the categories crisis avoidances and gratuitous avoidances (BL Arts 72(2)–(4)). This is because intent is not required for these categories.

Table 2.3 Rights of avoidance under Japanese bankruptcy law

Category of transaction	Specific requirements	Burden of proof	General requirements
Intentional avoidances	Bankrupt must have intent Beneficiary must have knowledge	Trustee: prejudice and intent Beneficiary: did not know	Affect estate Unfair Act by bankrupt
Crisis avoidances	Beneficiary must have knowledge	Trustee: did know (Art. 72(2)) Beneficiary: did not know (72(3)(4)) see 6.9.2 in text	Affect estate Unfair [Act by bankrupt]
Gratuitous avoidances	Intent/knowledge not necessary to prove	Trustee: Gratuitous acts or acts deemed to be gratuitous per circumstances	Affect estate Unfair [Act by bankrupt]

6.9.1 Intentional avoidances Intentional or fraudulent transfers will be voidable where: (1) the bankrupt does an act that is prejudicial to creditors; (2) the bankrupt intended it to be prejudicial; and (3) the beneficiary knew that the act would prejudice other creditors (BL Art. 72(1)). The trustee seeking to exercise a right of avoidance must prove (1) and (2), but the beneficiary must show (3) (that is, it did not know that the transfer would prejudice other creditors).

96 Itô (2000: 336–8).

6.9.2 Crisis avoidances The following transactions will give rise to a right of avoidance if the beneficiary knew that the debtor was experiencing financial distress, thus knowledge is determinative:

- any act prejudicial to creditors, or any act that would furnish security or extinguish an obligation, done after a suspension of payments, filing of a petition to commence a Bankruptcy, provided that the beneficiary knew of the suspension of payments or that it would be prejudicial (BL Art. 72(2));
- any act, as defined above, where the beneficiary was a relative or co-habitant of the bankrupt, provided that this does not apply where the beneficiary did not know of the suspension of payments or that it would be prejudicial (BL Art. 72(3)); or
- any act relating to the furnishing of security or extinguishing a debt done after or thirty days prior to a suspension of payments, which does not fall within the duties of the bankrupt or is not within the duties of the bankrupt because of the method or timing in which it was performed, provided that this does not apply where creditors did not know that it would be prejudicial to other creditors or that there had been a suspension of payments (BL Art. 72(4)).

6.9.3 Gratuitous avoidances: transfers for less than value A trustee must set aside any gratuitous transaction or any other transaction which must be deemed to be similar to a gratuitous transaction due to the circumstances involved if it occurred: (1) after a suspension of payments or petition for bankruptcy, or (2) within the six-month period before a suspension of payments or petition for bankruptcy (BL Art. 72(5)). Gratuitous transactions or transactions for less than value include gifts (but not customary gifts given in Japan, for example, *Oseibo* gifts traditionally given at the end of each calender year, see Civil Code Art. 549), discharge of an obligation (see Civil Code Art. 519) and giving up a right. Where a gratuitous transaction gave rise to the right of avoidance and the recipient of the benefit received it in good faith, the recipient need only restore the benefit that the recipient is actually enjoying (BL Art. 77(2)).

6.9.4 Avoidance of perfection of transfers In addition to these three categories of voidable transactions, perfection of an interest – that is, registration or recording an interest – may also give rise to a right of avoidance (BL Art. 74).[97] Article 74 of the Bankruptcy Law says:

1. acts performed after the suspension of payment or after the petition in bankruptcy, which are necessary to protect a transfer or alteration of rights against third parties, may be avoided if they are performed in bad faith, 15 days or more after the transfer or alteration itself. However, with respect to registrations and recordings, this will not apply to conversion of a provisional registration or a provisional recording to a final registration or recording (respectively); and
2. the preceding provision also applies to recordings giving rise to an interest.

97 For an analysis of the relationship between Arts 72 and 74 of the Bankruptcy Law, see Bennett (1994: 230).

6.9.5 Voidable transactions under the Civil Code A transfer may also be voidable under Civil Code Arts 424 and 425. Article 424 of the Civil Code dealing with avoidance of fraudulent transfers says:

1. a creditor may apply to the court to void a legal act performed by the debtor with knowledge that this would prejudice creditors. However, this will not apply where the recipient of such benefit, or a transferee, does not know facts at the time of the receipt or transfer sufficient to alert the recipient to such prejudice; and
2. the preceding paragraph does not apply to legal acts which do not affect rights in assets.

Because Art. 425 of the Civil Code says that exercising a right of avoidance under Art. 424 is effective for the benefit of all creditors, a plaintiff-creditor will not receive punitive damages from the debtor, only damages to compensate them for the amount owed by the debtor. Other creditors can only obtain a share of the proceeds from an action under article 424 by commencing a Bankruptcy proceeding. When a Bankruptcy proceeding is commenced, the bankruptcy trustee will take over any claims pending under article 424 for the benefit of all creditors (BL Art. 86).

6.9.6 Penalties relating to fraudulent transfers A debtor, officer of the debtor or a creditor, may be imprisoned for up to ten years for:

- concealment or destruction of assets;
- disposing of assets in a way that is disadvantageous to creditors; and
- fraudulently increasing the liabilities of the bankruptcy estate (BL Arts 374(1), (2)).

In the case of a personal bankruptcy, a debtor involved in a fraudulent transfer may also be refused a discharge from bankruptcy if convicted of misconduct (BL Art. 366-9) (see penalties below also). These penalties are not often enforced because of the difficulty of differentiating between these acts and ordinary business conduct.[98]

6.10 Procedures for the Dissolution (and Restitution) of the Corporation

The Bankruptcy proceeding will continue until the final distribution of the debtor's assets in accordance with the distribution list.[99] When the final distribution is made, the trustee asks the court to convene a final creditors' meeting where the trustee will submit a final report of accounts to the creditors (BL Art. 168). If the accounts are approved, the court will order the termination of the proceeding and give public notice of the text of the order and its reasons (BL Art. 282(1)). The date of the public

98 Bennett (1994: 226).

99 Aoyama *et al.* (1992: 215–16) note that even where notice has been given that there has been a final distribution, it is possible to distribute any further funds arising out of the Bankruptcy estate. This additional distribution will then become the final distribution.

notice is deemed to be the date of the conclusion of the Bankruptcy proceeding, as complaints against a ruling terminating a proceeding are prohibited (BL Art. 282(2)).

7 Special Liquidation in the Commercial Code

In addition to Bankruptcy, the other so-called liquidation-type insolvency procedure in Japan is Special Liquidation. The Special Liquidation procedure in the Commercial Code (*Shô hô* Law No. 48, 1899, amended 1938, Arts 431–456) is a simplified dissolution procedure for joint-stock corporations. Very few liquidations are brought about under this procedure and of these a majority are for restructuring and tax purposes.[100] This is probably because of the low profile of the procedure and the fact that it only applies to joint-stock corporations that are already in Ordinary Liquidation.

7.1 Appointment of Liquidators, Qualifications, Registration, etc.

An Ordinary Liquidation procedure may be commenced by a corporation's shareholders by deciding to dissolve the corporation by a resolution at a general meeting (Commercial Code Art. 404).[101] In Ordinary Liquidation, the general meeting of shareholders will usually appoint the directors of a corporation to act as its liquidators (Commercial Code Art. 417).

Once an Ordinary Liquidation has been commenced, a Special Liquidation procedure may be commenced by the court upon the application of any creditor, liquidator, auditor or shareholder or at the court's discretion, where there are circumstances which seriously impede the progress of the Ordinary Liquidation of the corporation (Commercial Code Art. 431-1). Where the corporation is in danger of its liabilities exceeding its assets, for example, a Special Liquidation procedure may be commenced in order to protect the interests of creditors and shareholders. The liquidator is also under a duty to apply for a Special Liquidation where the liquidator deems that there are grounds to suspect that the liabilities of the corporation are in excess of its assets (Commercial Code Art. 431-2).

Usually the liquidator appointed by the shareholders at a general meeting of the corporation to oversee the Ordinary Liquidation continues in his/her position. However, Commercial Code Art. 435 gives the court power to remove a liquidator where an important reason exists (Commercial Code Art. 435-1) and to appoint another liquidator (Commercial Code Art. 435-2).

7.2 Court Involvement and Termination

Compared to an Ordinary Liquidation proceeding, under a Special Liquidation proceeding, court supervision increases. The court may appoint an investigator to examine the business affairs and assets of the corporation and report back to the

100 Tahira (1997: 88).

101 The Ordinary Liquidation procedure may not be used where a company is being dissolved as a result of a merger or bankruptcy (Commercial Code Art. 417).

court (Commercial Code Art. 452 and 453). On the basis of that report, the court may order Preservation Measures to prevent the dissipation of the corporation's assets (Commercial Code Art. 454).

After commencement, a Special Liquidation may proceed as per an Ordinary Liquidation where creditors are paid in proportion to the amount of their claims (Commercial Code Art. 438). However, the main method of dissolution is the payment of creditors according to the terms of an agreement proposed by the liquidator and approved by creditors holding three quarters of the total amount of claims of creditors entitled to vote (Commercial Code Arts 447-50 and 450). The procedure comes to an end when the liquidation of the corporation according to the terms of the agreement is complete after the liquidator has settled the final accounts at a general meeting of shareholders (Commercial Code Arts 399, 456).

8 Enforcement of Securities over a Debtor's Assets

8.1 The Position of Secured Creditors; Rules regarding the Protection of Property Interests

The position of secured creditors in Japanese insolvency proceedings varies depending on the type of proceeding. In general, they will not be affected by the commencement of proceedings. In common with other civil law jurisdictions, the range of secured transactions used in Japan is fairly narrow. Until fairly recently, the primary form of security was a hypothec over immovable property (with or without a title transfer), or pledge of, or lien over, immovable or movable property. While the enterprise hypothec *(kigyô tanpo)* exists and is akin to a charge over the assets of the corporation, the fixed or floating charge has not been used in transactions in Japan to the extent that it has in the common law world; consequently the scenario in which chargees have the right to appoint a receiver does not frequently arise and so is not dealt with explicitly in Japanese insolvency law. However, official auctions (*kyôsei keibai*) have been a visible feature of Japanese commercial life for the last decade. Lists of property scheduled for court-supervised auction appear regularly in major financial newspapers. At law, the effect of the procedure is a sanctioned foreclosure sale.[102]

8.1.1 Bankruptcy Once a Bankruptcy proceeding is commenced, a person holding a security interest over a specific asset belonging to the Bankruptcy estate becomes a person holding a right of separation (generally referred to below as a 'secured creditor') (BL Art. 92). A person with a right of separation may enforce a security interest without reference to the Bankruptcy proceeding (BL Art. 95). This applies to security interests such as hypothecs (*teitôken*) and the base hypothecs (*ne-teitôken*), the most common form of securities over immovable assets in Japan. To enforce a hypothec, a creditor must petition the court for an official auction (see 8.4). Official auctions are time-consuming, open to interference from third parties and usually

102 Anderson (2001: 384).

bring a lower price than a sale on the open market. Other security interests which give rise to a right of separation in bankruptcy are special preferential rights, rights of pledge and Commercial Code rights of retention (BL Arts 92 and 93).

Another common form of security over a specific asset is the *jôto tanpo*, or title-security transfer. Under a *jôto tanpo*-type security arrangement, title to the asset which forms the collateral for the loan is transferred to the lender at the time the loan is made. The lender contracts to transfer title back to the borrower when the loan is repaid. This means that the lender need not resort to an official auction to enforce its security because the lender already has undisputed title and can sell the property if there is a default.

In contrast, a person with a security interest over a debtor's entire property, such as an ordinary preferential right (Civil Code Art. 306) or an enterprise hypothec (Enterprise Hypothecation Law (*Kigyô tanpo hô* Law No. 106 1958) Art. 1), does not have a right of separation upon declaration of bankruptcy. Thus, a person holding this type of security must file a proof of claim under a Bankruptcy proceeding and seek repayment as a creditor with a priority claim (see 6.7.2 above and BL Art. 39).

A person with a right of separation may claim against a Bankruptcy estate to the extent that the full amount of the debt/obligation owed to it is not satisfied from the proceeds of a sale of the collateral property (BL Art. 96). If a secured creditor registers the amount still owed to it (the remainder, *zangaku saiken*), it may receive a distribution from the Bankruptcy estate. To do this, the secured creditor must provide the trustee with prima facie proof of claim within the prescribed period[103] that it has commenced the disposal of the collateral property and an estimate of the remainder amount that is still owed by the debtor (BL Arts 96, 228, 261, 262, 277, 278) (see also 6.7).

If a secured creditor with a right of separation does not provide prima facie evidence that there will be a remainder after enforcement of the security within the time set down for a distribution from the Bankruptcy estate, then the creditor will be disqualified from that distribution even if the disposal has been commenced (BL Art. 262). Even if there is prima facie evidence that a remainder will arise, until the amount is confirmed the secured creditor cannot receive a distribution and any amount owing to it will be held in trust (BL Art. 271-3). If the person with a right of separation provides no evidence of the amount of the remainder by the time set down for notice of the final distribution, then they will be disqualified from receiving any distribution from the estate, including any money held in trust, and that amount will be distributed to other creditors (BL Arts 277 and 278).

The procedure relating to remainders causes problems for secured creditors in Japan, particularly in the current economic environment. Because there has been a fall in the value of immovable assets that form collateral for security, secured creditors require a reasonable amount of time to realise the collateral for a reasonable price; in fact, it may be impossible to realise the collateral at all. However, technically the secured creditor may not receive a distribution from the Bankruptcy estate until the

103 Bankruptcy Law Arts 261 and 262 give a creditor two weeks from the day public notice is given of a distribution to provide prima facie proof that it has commenced a proceeding to dispose of the collateral property.

amount of the remainder owed to them is confirmed. One proposal for reform of the remainder procedure is to adopt a self-evaluation system, like the scheme for proving debts by secured creditors under Australian insolvency law.[104] Under that scheme, a secured creditor can still prove a claim against a debtor even if the collateral has not been realised by estimating the value of the collateral and proving for the balance (remainder) after deducting the estimated value. Thus, they do not have to wait until the collateral is realised to receive a distribution from the Bankruptcy estate.

8.1.2 Special Liquidation The rules that apply in a Bankruptcy proceeding also apply with respect to rights of separation under the Special Liquidation procedure (Commercial Code Art. 440). However, unlike bankruptcy, the court may order a moratorium on the enforcement of debts for a specified period (Commercial Code Arts 384, 433).

8.1.3 Other procedures Moratoriums and the treatment of secured creditors in Civil Rehabilitation, Corporate Reorganisation and Corporate Arrangement proceedings are dealt with in parts 4 and 5 above.

8.2 Additional Powers and Duties of Trustees and Special Liquidators

In principle, a person with a right of separation may enforce its security by realising the assets which form the collateral for its security (see 8.1). However, a trustee or special liquidator also has power to dispose of assets under the Civil Execution Law (*Minji shikkô hô* Law No. 4, 1979) (BL Arts 203(1) and 204; Commercial Code Art. 456, applying Arts 203(1) and 204 of the Bankruptcy Law *mutatis mutandis*). A trustee or special liquidator may petition the court to determine a period for realisation by the secured creditor and if the secured creditor fails to commence disposal of the collateral property within that time the secured creditor forfeits its right to realise the collateral (BL Art. 204).

However, even if a trustee intervenes in the realisation process, secured creditors still have a priority right to the proceeds of the realisation. Proposals in the current reform process suggest that part of the proceeds should be contributed to the Bankruptcy estate to cover the administrative costs of the realisation. Suggestions include figures from three to ten per cent of the price obtained for the asset. The current practice of trustees is to reserve a certain percentage of the price obtained for the bankruptcy estate, but this is not based on any legislative requirement.

9 Offences

9.1 Offences in Bankruptcy

9.1.1 Offence of fraudulent bankruptcy It is an offence of fraudulent bankruptcy if the debtor does any of the following acts before or after a declaration of bankruptcy

---

104 See Ikeda (1999: 24) referring to the Corporations Law (as it was then) of Australia, sec 554E(1).

(see 6.2) for the purpose of benefiting themselves or a third party, or prejudicing creditors:

- concealing or destroying property relating to the Bankruptcy estate (BL Art. 374(1));
- fraudulently increasing the obligations owed by the Bankruptcy estate (BL Art. 374(2));
- failing to prepare commercial records required by law[105] or failing to make entries that do not sufficiently describe the present state of the assets contained in the commercial records, or making fraudulent entries or concealing or destroying the commercial records (BL Art. 374(3)); and
- modifying, concealing or destroying commercial records closed by the clerk of the court under Art. 187 of the Bankruptcy Law (the commercial records of the bankrupt are closed immediately after the adjudication of bankruptcy under Art. 187) (BL Art. 374(4)).

The offence of fraudulent bankruptcy applies to debtors who are natural persons and their legal representatives, but not to juridical persons per se. In the case of a juridical person such as a corporation, the offence can apply to persons such as directors (*riji*) or analogous persons, the debtor's legal representatives and corporate controllers (BL Art. 376). A third party who does any of the acts set out in Art. 374 of the Bankruptcy Law will also be guilty of an offence of fraudulent bankruptcy, as will a person who fraudulently exercises a right as a bankruptcy creditor for the purpose of benefiting themselves or another person (BL Art. 378).

To be guilty of an offence of fraudulent bankruptcy, a person must have intended to benefit themselves or a third party or prejudice a creditor. In the case of transactions aimed at prejudicing creditors, the purpose must be to prejudice all creditors and not just a particular creditor. In the case of transactions aimed at benefiting themselves or a third party, a person must have known that the transaction would prejudice creditors in addition to having the purpose of receiving a benefit.[106] Intention would be established where the debtor/bankrupt has dealt fraudulently with commercial records and/or they knew that there were grounds to suspect that the debtor was bankrupt.

Although an offence of fraudulent bankruptcy may arise from a transaction which occurred before or after a declaration of bankruptcy, in reality, article 374(3) of the Bankruptcy Law is limited to transactions occurring before a declaration and Art. 374(4) of the Bankruptcy Law is limited to transactions occurring after a declaration, because the commercial records of the debtor/bankrupt are closed at the time a declaration of bankruptcy is made (BL Art. 187).[107]

105 The term 'commercial records' (*shôgyô chôbô*) refers to accounting records and lists of debtors and creditors (Commercial Code Art. 32(1)). There is debate whether the term includes other types of profit/loss accounts, etc (Itô, 2000: 492, n. 9).

106 Itô (2000: 487).

107 Itô (2000: 487).

The other requirement which makes up the offence of fraudulent bankruptcy is confirmation of a declaration of bankruptcy (BL Arts 374, 376 and 378). This requirement has been criticised for restricting the scope of the offence because only a small number of insolvency cases lead to a declaration of bankruptcy.[108] A better approach may be to require that there be grounds for bankruptcy such as an inability to pay debts when due.[109] The reforms to the insolvency-related offences under the Civil Rehabilitation Law make those provisions broader in scope when compared to the offences under the current Bankruptcy Law and it is likely future reforms will follow this trend (see 9.3).

The penalty for fraudulent bankruptcy is up to ten years' imprisonment (BL Art. 374).

9.1.2 Offence of negligent bankruptcy A person will be guilty of an offence of negligent bankruptcy if he/she does any of the following acts before or after a declaration of bankruptcy:

- drastically reduces assets or assumes excessive debts through extravagance, gambling or other speculative undertakings (BL Art. 375(1));
- assumes obligations under seriously disadvantageous terms with the purpose of delaying a declaration of bankruptcy or purchases goods on credit and disposes of them on seriously disadvantageous terms (BL Art. 375(2));
- gives security or forgives obligations with the purpose of bestowing special benefits on some creditors, even though s/he knew that there were grounds for bankruptcy, and the transaction did not come within the responsibilities of the debtor, or the manner or timing of the transaction was such that it did not come within the responsibilities of the debtor (BL Art. 375(3));
- fails to prepare commercial records required by law, fails to make entries that sufficiently describe the present state of the properties contained in the commercial records, or conceals or destroys commercial records (BL Art. 375(4)); and
- modifies, conceals or destroys commercial records closed by the clerk of the court as a result of a declaration of bankruptcy under article 187 of the Bankruptcy Law (BL Art. 375(5)).

The offence of negligent bankruptcy differs from that of fraudulent bankruptcy in that it does not require an intent to benefit or prejudice (BL Art. 375). Thus, the penalty for the offence is not as harsh as the penalty for fraudulent bankruptcy. The penalty for negligent bankruptcy is up to five years' imprisonment or a fine of up to 300,000 yen.

The offence of negligent bankruptcy applies to debtors and persons analogous to the debtor such as a director (*riji*) or corporate controller (BL Arts 375 and 376). However, unlike fraudulent bankruptcy, there is no offence of negligent bankruptcy with respect to third persons (Art. 378 of the Bankruptcy Law only applies to Art. 374).

---

108 Itô (2000: 489).

109 Itô (2000: 489).

9.2 Other Insolvency-related Offences by Corporate Controllers

9.2.1 Breach of a surveillance order and breach of the duty to explain The offences of breach of surveillance (BL Art. 377) and breach of duty to explain (BL Art. 382) are both aimed at obtaining the bankrupt's cooperation in the Bankruptcy proceeding. A bankrupt, the bankrupt's legal representative, a director (*riji*) or analogous person or a manager who has been put under surveillance under Arts 149, 150, 152 or 154 of the Bankruptcy Law, will be guilty of an offence if s/he breaches the surveillance order by absconding, talking to people other than those living with them (BL Art. 377-1) or leaving his/her dwelling place without obtaining the permission of the court (BL Art. 377-2). Where a bankrupt, his/her agent, a director or analogous person fails to respond or responds falsely to a demand to explain made by a trustee, investigator or Creditors' Committee under Art. 153 of the Bankruptcy Law without good cause, s/he will be guilty of the offence of breach of duty to explain (BL Art. 382-1).

The penalty for breach of surveillance and breach of duty to explain is up to one year's imprisonment or a fine of up to 50,000 yen. However, in the case of a breach of the duty to explain under Art. 382-1 of the Bankruptcy Law, the penalty may be reduced or remitted if the person who has committed the offence reports the fact of the breach to the court (BL Art. 382-2).

9.2.2 Taking and offering bribes A bankruptcy trustee or investigator (*kansai'in*) who takes, demands or promises a bribe in connection with his/her duties will be guilty of an offence (BL Art. 380-1, first sentence). Similarly, a bankruptcy creditor, his/her representative, a director (*riji*) or analogous person who takes, demands or promises a bribe in connection with a resolution to be adopted at a creditors' meeting will be guilty of an offence (BL Art. 380-1, second sentence). Any person offering a bribe to a trustee, investigator, a bankruptcy creditor, his/her representative, a director (*riji*) or analogous person will also be guilty of an offence (BL Art. 381-1).

In all cases involving bribes, the penalty is up to three years' imprisonment or a fine of up to 200,000 yen (BL Arts 380-1 and 381-1). However, if a person who has offered a bribe turns him/herself in to the authorities, the penalty may be reduced or remitted (BL Art. 381-2). Any bribes that have been paid will be confiscated, or if it is impossible to confiscate them, the value of the bribes will be collected (BL Art. 380-2).

9.3 Other Relevant Corporate Law Offences

9.3.1 Offences under the Civil Rehabilitation Law Compared to its predecessor, the Composition Law, the scope of the offences under the new Civil Rehabilitation Law have been broadened. Previously under the Composition Law, there were no offences equating to the offence of fraudulent bankruptcy or negligent bankruptcy as discussed above. The offences only dealt with taking and offering bribes and breach of duty to explain, report or investigate.

Under the Civil Rehabilitation Law, it is an offence to do the following acts before or after the commencement of a Civil Rehabilitation proceeding with the intent of creating a benefit for oneself or another person or prejudicing creditors:

- conceal, destroy or dispose (to the detriment of creditors) assets of the debtor (Civ RL Law Art. 246-1(1));
- drastically increase the obligations of the debtor (Civ RL Art. 246-1(2)); or
- fail to create commercial records required by law, or make untrue entries in, conceal or destroy commercial records (Civ RL Art. 246-1(3)).

These provisions also apply to the legal representative of a debtor, its board and its directors or any person supporting the debtor (Civ RL Art. 246-2) and third parties (Civ RL Art. 247). The penalty for these offences is up to ten years' imprisonment or a fine of up to 2,000,000 yen (Civ RL Arts 246, 247).

Other offences under the Civil Rehabilitation Law include doing an act which impedes the making of a report or an investigation in respect of the Civil Rehabilitation proceeding (Civ RL Art. 250). This applies to debtors, a debtor's legal representatives, directors (*riji*), secretary, auditor and liquidator, and any person holding an analogous position. The penalty is up to one year's imprisonment or 500,000 yen. Similarly to the Bankruptcy Law (see 9.2.2), it is also an offence for a supervisory officer such as a trustee to take, demand or promise a bribe (Civ RL Art. 248-1) and the penalty for this offence is up to three years' imprisonment or 1,000,000 yen. The same applies for third parties (Civ RL Art. 249) and any person committing the offence outside Japan (Civ RL Art. 251-1).

Finally, under provisions akin to the Australian provisions relating to insolvent trading, officers of a corporation in a Civil Rehabilitation proceeding may also be held liable by the court to pay for debts incurred by the company before commencement of the proceeding (Civ RL Art. 143). An action against an officer may be brought by the corporation, a provisional administrator, a trustee, a creditor or the court on its own motion. Further, if the court finds it necessary, for example because the officer may attempt to dispose of or conceal assets, it may issue Preservation Measures in respect of the officer's assets after commencement of the proceeding (Civ RL Art. 142-1) and, in emergency cases, even before commencement (Civ RL Art. 142-2).

According to available statistics up to 31 July 2002 for the Tokyo District Court, there have only been ten cases involving claims for compensatory damages from directors.[110] Of these cases, an officer availed him/herself of appeal/objection rights (Civ RL Art. 142-146) in only one case and two other cases settled. Although ten cases are too few to suggest a trend, a preliminary assessment of these statistics suggests that officers are accepting of at least some responsibility for the corporation's insolvency with or without proceedings being successfully brought against them.

110 Anderson and Steele (2003: [19-321]) citing Sonoo (2002: 12).

10 Rules regarding Cross-border Insolvency, Judicial Assistance to Foreign Insolvency Officials

10.1 Broad Policy of Japan in regard to the Recognition of Foreign Judgements and Court Orders

Japan was involved in the discussions which produced the UNCITRAL Model Law on Cross-border Insolvency ('UNCITRAL Model Law').[111] The reforms introduced on 1 April 2001 by the Law Relating to Recognition and Assistance for Foreign Insolvency Proceedings (*Gaikoku tôsan shori tetsuzuki no shônin enjo ni kan suru hôritsu*, Law No. 129, 2000, 'Recognition and Assistance Law')[112] reflect the principles set out in the Model Law, but do not replicate it. The reforms mean an end to the strict territorial principle (previously based on Bankruptcy Law Art. 3) and the introduction of a modified universalism.[113] The strict territorial principle meant that, on its face, the Japanese insolvency law regime provided that a proceeding commenced in Japan was not effective with respect to the assets of a debtor situated overseas and, conversely, that a foreign proceeding had no effect on a debtor's assets situated in Japan. However, in practice, the principle was not strictly applied by judges, leading to a discrepancy between the legislation and case law and considerable legal debate about how to process international insolvency proceedings in Japan and those involving Japanese companies overseas.[114]

The aim of the Recognition and Assistance Law is to provide for the international coordination of the liquidation of assets or the economic rehabilitation of debtors involved in international business activities, by stipulating a procedure for recognition and assistance in relation to foreign insolvency proceedings which have been commenced in respect of such debtors (RAL Art. 1). Although the law does not achieve the harmonisation synergies that might have resulted from adopting a system closer to the UNCITRAL Model Law, it is certainly an improvement on the previous ambiguous situation brought about by the conflict between the statutory position and the more pragmatic case law.

10.2 Procedures for the Assistance of Courts in Foreign Jurisdictions

10.2.1 Recognition proceedings Under the Recognition and Assistance Law, foreign entities are to be treated in the same way as Japanese entities (RAL Art. 3). Jurisdiction in relation to the Recognition proceedings lies with the Tokyo District Court (RAL Art. 4); however, the court may order that the proceedings be moved to a more appropriate district court based on factors such as the location of the debtor and the business or the assets being dealt with (RAL Art. 5).

---

111 UNCITRAL Model Law on Cross-Border Insolvency, Report of UNCITRAL on the Work of Its Thirtieth Session, UNGAOR (52d Sess) Annex I, 68–78, UN Doc A/52/17(1997).

112 For a translation see http://www.moj.go.jp/ENGLISH/CIAB/1r+r01-1.html (Matsushita and Steele trans.)

113 Article 3 of the Bankruptcy Law was repealed by the Law relating to Recognition and Assistance for Foreign Insolvency Proceedings (Supplementary provisions, Art. 2)

114 Matsushita (1998: 76–9).

As the name of the new proceeding suggests, a foreign trustee may apply to a Japanese court for a decision recognising the foreign insolvency proceeding where there are assets in Japan (RAL Chapter 2). When the foreign trustee files the petition it must also pay into court an amount to be decided by the court for the costs of the Recognition procedure (RAL Art. 20).

After a petition for Recognition, the court may grant Preservation Measures in order to preserve the assets existing in Japan (RAL Arts 25(2), 26(2) and 27(2)). This includes an order suspending domestic proceedings and prohibiting unsecured and secured creditors from enforcing their claims. The court may decide to appoint a provisional administrator to manage the business and assets of the debtor which are located in Japan during the period from the filing of a petition for a decision recognising a foreign insolvency proceeding until it hands down its decision (RAL Art. 51). The provisional administrator will be responsible for the continuation of the debtor's business and management and disposal of the debtor's assets in Japan, but must obtain the court's permission for any acts which do not fall within the scope of the debtor's ordinary business (RAL Art. 53).

At the same time as making a ruling recognising the foreign proceeding, the court has the power to make similar orders if it finds that it is necessary for achieving the purpose of the Recognition proceeding (RAL Arts 25(1), 26(1), 27(1) and 28(1)). The court also has the power to appoint a recognition trustee to manage and dispose of the business and assets of the debtor that are located in Japan (RAL Art. 32(1)). The recognition trustee:

- must obtain the court's permission before it disposes or repatriates any of the debtor's assets located in Japan or does an act ordered by another court (RAL Art. 35(1));
- is under the supervision of the court and may be dismissed by the court on the petition of an interested party or on its own motion (RAL Art. 38);
- may demand a report in relation to the condition of the business and assets of the debtor in Japan from the debtor (if it is a natural person) or the debtor's officers (if it is a juridical person) (RAL Art. 41);
- inspect the accounts, documents and other items of the debtor (RAL Art. 41);
- is under a duty of care to conduct his/her duties as good managers (*zenryô na kanrisha no chûi*) (RAL Art. 45); and
- must report to the court within the time stipulated by the court (RAL Art. 46).

10.2.2 Concurrent insolvency cases The Recognition and Assistance Law also deals with situations where an insolvency proceeding has been commenced in Japan before the filing of a petition for Recognition (see Chapter 5). In such cases, the court must reject the petition unless all of the following criteria are met:

- the foreign insolvency proceeding is the main proceeding;
- it is found that the assistance measures provided for in the law would be compatible with the interests of ordinary creditors; and
- there are no grounds to suspect that it would unfairly prejudice the interests of creditors in Japan, by using the assistance measures provided for in the law (RAL Art. 57(1)).

If all of these criteria are met, the court must order a stay of any insolvency proceedings in Japan when it makes a decision recognising the foreign insolvency proceeding (RAL Art. 57(2)).

Where there is already a Recognition and Assistance proceeding afoot in Japan in relation to the same debtor, the court must reject a petition for Recognition where one of the following criteria are met:

- the earlier foreign insolvency proceeding is the main insolvency proceeding; or
- if the earlier foreign insolvency proceeding is not the main proceeding, the application of the assistance measures provided for in the law to the subsequent non-main insolvency proceeding would not be compatible with the interests of ordinary creditors (RAL Art. 62(1)).

References

Anderson, Kent and Makoto Itô (2002), 'Insolvency Law of a New Century: Japan's Revised Framework for Economic Failures', in Foote, Daniel (ed.), *Law in Japan: A Turning Point*, Tokyo/Seattle: Asian Law Center/University of Washington School of Law.

Anderson, Kent and Stacey Steele (2003), 'Insolvency Law', *Japan Business Law Guide*, CCH [loose-leaf].

Anderson, Kent (2002), 'The Cross-Border Insolvency Paradigm: A Defense of the Modified Universal Approach Considering the Japanese Experience', *University of Pennsylvania Journal of International Economic Law*, 21.

Anderson, Kent (2001), 'Small Business Reorganisations: An Examination of Japan's Civil Rehabilitation Act Considering U.S. Policy Implications and Foreign Creditors' Practical Interests', *American Bankruptcy Law Journal*, 75.

Aoyama, Yoshimitsu, Makoto Itô, Harunori Inoue and Aritoshi Fukunaga (1992), *Hasan hô gaisetsu* (Outline of Bankruptcy Law), 2nd edition, Tokyo: Yûhikaku.

Bennett, Frank (1999), 'Civil Execution in Japan: the legal economics of perfect honesty', *Nagoya University Law Review*, 177.

Bennett, Frank (1994), 'Preference Rules in Japanese Bankruptcy Law', in Oda, Hiroshi (ed.), *Japanese Commercial Law in an Era of Internationalisation*, London: Graham and Trotman.

Corbett, Jenny (1998), 'Changing Corporate Governance in Japan', in Balling, Morten, Elizabeth Hennessy and Richard O'Brien (eds), *Corporate Governance, Financial Markets and Global Convergence*, London: Kluwer Academic Publishers.

Fujiwara, Sôichirô (1999), *Minji saisei tetsuzuki no kaisetsu* (Interpretation of the Civil Rehabilitation Procedure), Tokyo: Shôji hômu kenkyûkai.

Grondine, Robert F. (1996), 'Financing Direct Investments and Operations in Japan', in McAlinn, Gerald Paul (ed.), *The Business Guide to Japan*, Singapore: Butterworth-Heinemann Asia.

Hatano, Takeshi and Noriaki Takizawa (2003), 'Kinnen no tôsan jiken môshitate no gaijyô – Heisei 14 nen no shinjuken sû wo chûshin toshite' (Outline of recent

insolvency cases petitions – Focusing on statistics of matters newly received in 2002), *NBL*, 760.
Hômushô minjikyoku sanjikan shitsu (Office of the Counsellor of the Civil Affairs Bureau of the Ministry of Justice) (December 1997), *Tôsan hôsei ni kan suru kaisei kentô jikô* (Questionnaire on reforms relating to insolvency laws), reproduced in (1997) *Bessatsu NBL*, 46.
Horiuchi, Akiyoshi (1998), 'Nihon no furyô saiken mondai no ichibunseki' (A brief analysis of Japan's bad debt problem), *Kinyû*.
Ikeda, Tetsuo (1999), 'Tôsan tanpo hô no shinjidai' (A new era for insolvency security law), *Hanrei taimuzu*, 991.
Itô, Makoto (2000), *Hasan hô* (BL), Tokyo: Yûhikaku.
Itô, Makoto (1999), 'Minji saisei tetsuzuki (kashô) hôan no seiritsu wo kitai suru' (Expecting the establishment of the civil rehabilitation procedure (tentative title) bill), *Saiken kanri*, 86.
Itô, Makoto, Morio Takeshita, Munehide Nishizawa *et al.* (1993), 'Proposed Reforms in Japanese Law and Practice in International Bankruptcy – Preliminary Draft of the international bankruptcy related provisions in Japanese insolvency proceedings', *International Insolvency Review*, 2(1).
Itô, Makoto (1991), *Hasan hô* (BL), 2nd edition, Tokyo: Yûhikaku.
Iwanami, Hideaki (2002), 'Kojin saisei jiken no gaikô – Hôshikô go ichinenkan no jyôkyô wo fumaete' (Individual rehabilitation cases: based on the general situation one year since enactment), *NBL*, 741.
Matsushita, Jun'ichi (1998), 'Present and Future Status of Japanese International Insolvency Law', *Texas International Law Journal*, 33.
Miki, Kôichi (1997), 'Hasan hô ni okeru rippôteki kadai' (Legislative problems with the Bankruptcy Law), *Juristo*, 1111.
Shindô, Kôji, Kôji Shimojiama and Yoshimitsu Aoyama (eds) (1990), 'Shintôsan hanrei hyakusen' (New selection of 100 insolvency law cases), *Juristo Bessatsu*, 106.
Shinomiya, Akio (1997), 'Kaisha seiri ni okeru rippôteki kadai' (Legislative problems with corporate arrangement), *Juristo*, 1111.
Sômu chô tôkei kyoku (Statistics Bureau, Management and Coordination Agency, Government of Japan) (November 1990, October 1997 and May 1999), *Nihon tôkei geppô* (Japan Statistical Monthly).
Steele, Stacey (2003), '"Too Hot to Handle": Extinguishing Secured Creditors' Interests in Insolvency under Japan's Civil Rehabilitation Law', 8(16) *Journal of Japanese Law*, 223.
Steele, Stacey (2000), 'Evaluating the new Japanese Civil Rehabilitation Law', *Asian Law*, 2(1).
Steele, Stacey (trans) (2000), 'Civil Rehabilitation Law (Law No. 225, 1999) (Japan)', *Asian Law*, 2(2).
Sudo, Hideaki (2003), 'Shiteki seiri no ukezara toshite no kaisha kôsei tetsuzuki' (Private workouts as the saucer for the Corporate Reorganisation procedure), *Ginkô hômu 21*, 620.
Tagashira, Shôichi (2003), 'Kyôsô shakai no naka de no tôsan shori tetsuzuki no yakuwari' (The role of insolvency law procedures in a competitive society), *Hôgaku seminâ*, 580.

Tahira, Makoto (1997), 'Tokubetsu seisan no rippôteki kadai' (Legislative problems of special liquidation), *Juristo*, 1111.
Takagi, Shinjirô (1997), 'Kaisha kôsei hô no rippôteki kadai' (Legislative problems of the Corporate Reorganisation Law), *Juristo*, 1111.
Takahashi, Hiroshi (Moderator), 'Tôsan Tetsuzuki ni okeru saibankan, shokikan, bengoshi no kyôryoku to kanyo' (Co-operation and participation of judges, clerks and lawyers in insolvency proceedings) (Published as a series, Parts 1–5) (1998) *NBL*, 645; (1998) *NBL*, 646; (1998) *NBL*, 647; (1998) *NBL*, 648; (1998) *NBL*, 649.
Tsutsumi, Chieko and Kazuhiro Kosuga (2002), 'Minji saisei jiken-hô shikô 90 2 nenkan no gaikyô wo furikaette' (Looking back on the general situation of Civil Rehabilitation cases two years after enactment of the law), *NBL*, 741.

Newspaper Articles

'Big firms going under in alarming numbers', *Nikkei Net Interactive*, 5 November 2001, www.nni.nikkei.co.jp.
'Bankrupt people to lose less assets', *The Asahi Shimbun* (Tokyo), 16 June 2003, www.asahi.com/english/business, accessed on 5 August 2003.
'Bus company wants IRC to get on board', *The Asahi Shimbun* (Tokyo), 25 July 2003, www.asahi.com/english/business, accessed on 5 August 2003.
'Corporate rehabilitation drive set to take off', *The Asahi Shimbun* (Tokyo), 2 May 2003, www.asahi.com/english/business, accessed on 19 May 2003.
'Individual debtors may get a break', *The Japan Times* (Tokyo), 13 July 2003, www.japantimes.co.jp accessed on 5 August 2003.
'Tanigaki: Sick firms passing up IRC's help', *The Asahi Shimbun* (Tokyo), 3 July 2003, www.asahi.com/english/business, accessed on 5 August 2003.

Websites

Japanese Bankers' Association (2001), *Shiteki seiri ni kan suru gaido rain* (Guidelines for Out-of-Court Workouts), http://www.zenginkyo.or.jp/news/pdf/GL010919.pdf (copy on file with author).

Japanese Legislation

Auditing Special Exceptions Law (Kabushiki kaisha no kansa tô ni kan suru Shô hô no tokurei ni kan suru hôritsu Law No. 22, 1997)
Bankruptcy Law (Hasan hô Law No. 71, 1922)
Enterprise Hypothecation Law (Kigyô tanpo hô Law No. 106, 1958)
Civil Code (Minpô Law No. 89, 1899)
Civil Execution Law (Minji shikkô hô Law No. 4, 1979)
Civil Conciliation Law (Minji chôtei hô Law No. 222, 1951)
Civil Rehabilitation Law (Minji saisei hô Law No. 225, 1999)
Code of Civil Procedure (Minji soshô hô Law No. 109, 1996)
Commercial Code (Shô hô Law No. 48, 1899)
Composition Law (Wagi hô Law No. 72, 1922)
Corporate Reorganisation Law (Kaisha kôsei hô Law No. 172, 1952)

Corporate Reorganisation Law (Kaisha kôsei hô Law No. 154, 2002)
Insurance Sector Law (Hoken gyô hô Law No. 105, 1995)
Law Relating to Exceptions etc for Financial Institutions Rehabilitation Proceedings (Kinyû kikan no saisei tetsuzuki no tokurei tô ni kan suru hôritsu Law No. 95, 1996)
Law Relating to Recognition and Assistance for Foreign Insolvency Proceedings (Gaikoku tôsan shori tetsuzuki no shônin enjo ni kan suru hôritsu Law No. 129, 2000)
Law to Amend the Civil Rehabilitation Law (Minji saisei hô tô no ichibu o kaisei suru hôritsu Law No. 128, 2000)
Limited Companies Law (Yûgen gaisha hô Law No. 74, 1938)
National Tax Collection Law (Kokuzei chôshû hô Law No. 147, 1959)
Non-litigious Case Procedure Law (Hishô jiken tetsuzuki hô Law No. 14, 1956)
Special Mediation Law (Tokutei saimu tô no chôsei no sokushin no tame no tokutei chôtei ni kan suru hôritsu Law No. 158, 1999)
Special Procedures for Reorganisation of Financial Institutions Law (Kinyû kikan no kôsei tetsuzuki no tokurei tô ni kan suru hôritsu Law No. 95, 1996) ('RFIL'), as amended by the Law to amend part of the RFIL (Kinyû kikan no kôsei tetsuzuki no tokurei tô ni kan suru hôritsu no ichibu wo kaisei suru hôritsu Law Nos 92–93, 2000)
Trusts Act (Shintaku hô Law No. 62, 1922)

Chapter 3

Insolvency Law in Korea[1]

SOOGEUN OH
Ewha Womans University, Seoul

1 Introduction

1.1 General Introduction to the Legal System and Local Culture

The rule of the king had been the principle of government and society for several centuries before the Western legal system based on the philosophy of the rule of law was introduced to Korea. The king was expected to have enough integrity to exercise his power with dignity. The king and upper-class people were not subject to the law but to moral standards. Although necessary statutes for governing the nation were enacted in an organized way in the early 15th century, they served for the systematic governance, not for the restriction of power. Law was an inferior norm to morality.

Western law and legal thoughts were first introduced to Korea in the late 1800s. It was a challenge to analyze a legal relationship based on right and duty rather than moral and comity. The judiciary was separated from administration in 1895 for the first time in Korea. The colonial Japanese regime implanted the Western legal system from the early 1900s, which it had accepted mainly from Germany a few decades previously. The new legal system replaced the traditional one, but people did not think the new law functioned for their welfare because it was implemented for the benefit of the oppressive colonial government.

After the liberation in 1945, new governments were established separately in the south and the north of the Korean peninsula. South Korea is a capitalistic country whereas the North is a communistic one. South Korea has maintained the same legal system since colonial days. Statutes are the main source of law and the judiciary is separated.

People's attitudes toward law were not positive even under independent governments. Traditional perceptions of law still remained in the minds of people. They did not feel much need to use the law as a social norm because the basic structure of the nation was still in the form of an agricultural society.

As the industrialization and urbanization of the country progressed, the law was frequently referred to in daily life. Most surveys showed that people changed to view it positively. Among many reasons, the changes in political power after the early

---

1 This chapter deals with insolvency law and practice which was in place before the new consolidated insolvency law of Korea (Debtor Rehabilitation and Bankruptcy Law) came into effect on April 1, 2006. Please consult the author's forthcoming book *Korean Insolvency Law: an Introduction and the Text* for the new Korean Insolvency Law (soh@ewha.ac.kr).

1990s were the most critical in the enhancement of the rule of law in Korean society. The law cannot be a tool of domination as in the days of military governments. Arbitrary applications of law are frequently criticized judicially as well as politically. The activities of non-governmental organizations (NGOs) have been remarkable since the 1990s in that regard. The expansion of the application of the rule of law is seemingly in the stage of ripeness.

1.2 Introduction to Insolvency Laws

Korea did not have a tradition of a trustee who handled the property of the deceased or the bankrupt for the beneficiary. The concept of a third party managing the entire property collectively for heirs or creditors was quite alien to Koreans. Without such a tradition, people did not bring insolvency cases for collective collection. Individual enforcement of claims was common. In the case of the value of debtor's property being less than the amount of debts, debtors often got together and distributed debtor's property. It was called *bitjanchi*, which is literally translated into 'debts festival'.

Table 3.1 Treatment of the insolvent in Korea

Major Role Players	Business Entity		
	Dissolution	Maintenance	Transformation
Debtor	Liquidation		Sales of Business
			Merger
			Private Arrangement
Creditors	Foreclosure		Bank Management
Court	Bankruptcy		Corporate Reorganization
			Composition
Government		Rationalization Measures	Big Deals Workout

Insolvent debtors are treated in various ways, as shown in Table 3.1. Insolvency, where a debtor cannot repay debts as they fall due, could be settled by a private arrangement between a debtor and creditors. In the case of business corporations, shareholders can liquidate business entities according to the Commercial Code. The negotiations between them might be performed in a pre-structured procedure as in a 'workout on bank management'. Creditors bring many cases to court to enforce their claims individually according to the Civil Enforcement Act. The formal bankruptcy procedure is possible for the collective enforcement of claims.

The government intervenes directly in some important insolvency cases under the industrial policy of Rationalization Measures, Big Deal and Workout. In addition to the dissolution of business entities, business activities might continue after restructuring, sale of business and mergers. Some of these modes are implemented in the judicial procedure including composition or corporate reorganization.

As far as a business enterprise is concerned, insolvency procedures usually start with '*budoe*', literally meaning a non-payment of checks or promissory notes. Checks and promissory notes are the major mediums of payment for commercial transactions in Korea. They are usually endorsed and transferred several times from debtors to creditors before they are due for payment. Default on payment results in the issuer of dishonored checks or promissory notes being severely restricted in financial transactions. For example, banks will refuse to deal with the issuer and the issuers' properties will be subject to public auction for payment of debt to check or promisory note holders through a judicial enforcement process. However, most *budoe* cases are settled through private arrangements between the debtor and creditors. Only a handful of *budoe* cases go as far as involving court intervention as shown in Table 3.2.

Private arrangements according to general contract law and individual enforcement procedure under the Civil Enforcement Act are out of the scope of this article.

Table 3.2 Number of insolvency cases in Korean courts

Year	*Budoe**	Bankruptcy	Composition	Corporate Reorganization
1983	**	**	**	65
1984	**	**	**	52
1985	**	11	2	40
1986	**	26	**	26
1987	**	20	**	30
1988	**	21	–	26
1989	**	37	2	27
1990	4,108	27	–	15
1991	6,159	16	–	64
1992	10,769	14	–	87
1993	9,502	26	–	45
1994	11,255	18	–	68
1995	13,992	12	13	79
1996	11,589	18	9	52
1997	17,169	38	322	132
1998	22,828	467	728	148
1999	**	733	140	37

* *Budoe*: The number of companies that could not pay checks or notes
** 6,718

Source: Court Administration Agency (2002), Bank of Korea (2002)

1.3 History, Sources and Philosophy of Insolvency Laws

In Korean traditional society, insolvent debtors were punished as criminals. The punishment usually entailed strokes of cudgels. There was no collective collection measure from a debtor. Indemnity did not exist either. Under the colonial regime from 1910 through 1945 when the Bankruptcy Act existed, Korea had very little experience in insolvency cases. The bankrupt was treated in a customary manner instead of being put into judicial procedure. The economy of Korea was not capitalistic enough for a corporate reorganization procedure to be required. This situation remained unchanged until the 1960s when President Park Jung Hee launched the economic development plan.

Three statutes on insolvency, the Bankruptcy Act, the Composition Act, and the Corporate Reorganization Act, were enacted in 1962. The Bankruptcy Act deals with the liquidation of individuals and companies. The Composition Act provides composition (arrangement) proceedings for individuals and companies. The Corporate Reorganization Act covers the reorganization process of stock corporations.

At that time, Korea still followed pre-existing Japanese statutes without enacting its own acts. President Park's military government hurried to draft many laws and had them passed in the Supreme Council for National Reconstruction that had legislative power during the *coup d'etat* regime. For unclear reasons, insolvency laws were among those laws passed by it.

Insolvency laws are the offspring of a free market economy because competition in a free market inevitably produces winners and losers. Korea, however, made insolvency laws in 1962 when industrialization was just beginning. These insolvency laws had problems from the outset. One problem was that there was no socio-economic basis for the enactment. People did not understand the necessity for insolvency laws. Moreover, these Acts were an entire translation of Japanese acts (Bankruptcy Act, Composition Act, Corporate Rehabilitation Act). Without the need or understanding of business society and experts in the professional field, insolvency laws were quickly forgotten.

Before the foreign currency crisis in 1997, there was little application of insolvency laws and the concept itself was unfamiliar even to lawyers, not to mention the public. It was said that judges handled just one insolvency case on average during their tenure.

One technical impediment to a wider use of judicial insolvency procedures was Article 7-3 of the Act on Special Measures for Unpaid Loans of Financial Institutions. It gave the Korea Asset Management Corporation (KAMCO) exclusive authority to auction a defaulting company's assets even in the midst of the corporate reorganization process. This provision virtually paralyzed the Corporate Reorganization Act since KAMCO could halt the process at any time.

In 1990, the Korean Constitutional Court declared this provision unconstitutional on the grounds that it was unfair and unreasonable. With this ruling, financial institutions, usually represented by KAMCO, were forced to undergo judicial process.

Another factor for the infrequency of insolvency cases was the high liability-asset ratio in Korea. Simply put, business corporations and individual debtors do not have enough assets for creditors. In most cases, cooperative collection measures are not necessary because most assets of a debtor are already utilized for security. Secured creditors get their portion according to the Civil Enforcement Act on an individual basis. Thus, almost nothing is left for unsecured creditors.

Moreover, the word 'bankruptcy' contains the connotation that the bankrupt has been broken morally or mentally, not to mention financially. Many creditors in Korea have hesitated turning to the court for insolvency because their reputations seemed to be severely damaged.

Though the number of court cases increased in the 1990s, there was a negative assessment of the corporate reorganization process. Critics pointed out such problems as: outside political influence; abuse of criminal proceedings for evasion of dishonored checks; ambiguous rules; delays in processing; insufficient recovery of claims by creditors; and the low success rate of reorganization.

The Supreme Court could not ignore some criticisms against court practices, so it tightened the process by enacting the Rule on Corporate Reorganization Procedure in 1992 (hereinafter 'the 1992 Rule'), which provided detailed requirements for the reorganization process and for approval of a reorganization plan. The 1992 Rule established three requirements for the commencement of the procedure: high social value, financial distress, and the possibility of rehabilitation. It also enumerated detailed factors to be considered for each requirement. The 1992 Rule, however, went beyond its limits of interpretation, which totally diverged from pre-existing legislation.

Again, the Corporate Reorganization Act came under fire when a corporation went bankrupt again during the reorganization process. The CEO of Non-No Corp. fled abroad after issuing a series of bounced checks. As a result, in 1996, the Supreme Court amended the 1992 Rule to reinforce the monitoring function of the court over corporations under reorganization. The 1996 Rule mandated that the court wipe out shares owned by controlling shareholders responsible for mismanagement of the company. It also excluded the incumbent management from the reorganization process.

The 1996 Rule, however, bore unexpected results. It essentially removed any incentive for insolvent companies to apply for the corporate reorganization procedure. Incumbent controlling shareholders and management looked for other avenues to maintain insiders' shares and control of the company. In 1997, clever lawyers in major insolvency cases such as Kia Motors Corp. found loopholes in the composition procedure and filed for the procedure, even though the composition procedure was originally intended for independent businesspersons and small companies. Although Kia Motors was eventually put into corporate reorganization, a flood of companies followed the suit as evident in Table 3.2.

Most countries show development of insolvency laws during periods of economic turmoil and Korea is no exception. However, a study to amend insolvency statutes began in 1996, before the crisis hit the Korean economy, by the Ministry of Finance to enhance the efficiency of the exit mechanism in the economy. The financial crisis and the agreements with the International Monetary Fund (IMF) and the International Bank for Reconstruction and Development (IBRD or World Bank) only hastened the effort.

Since the first enactment of insolvency statues in 1962, there was no significant amendment until 1998. The 1998 Amendments introduced several new concepts and mechanisms: an economic value test, management committees, time limitations, amortization of shares, mandatory assessment, and the creditors' conference.

Soon after the institution of the 1998 Amendments, the IMF and the IBRD suggested that the Korean government add other schemes including automatic stay, pre-packaged plans, and a bankruptcy court. The Ministry of Justice prepared the 1999 amendment draft and the National Assembly passed the bill on the last day of 1999 in spite of criticisms on the frequent revision of acts. There were two significant changes under the 1999 Amendments: increased accessibility of the corporate reorganization procedure and the composition procedure and, in the event of failure of these procedures, mandatory transfer of the failed cases to the bankruptcy procedure. The new provisions mandate the courts to decide the commencement of these procedures after reviewing the formal requirements within one month after the petition. However, the court shall adjudge the applying corporation bankrupt if it disapproves of the reorganization plan (or the composition condition) or discontinues the procedures.

2 Bankruptcy Procedure

2.1 Source and Structure of Bankruptcy Procedure

Bankruptcy proceedings, governed by the Bankruptcy Act (BA), are intended to collect the debtor's assets and distribute them collectively to creditors in the event of a debtor's insolvency. Generally, bankruptcy occurs when the debtor is unable to make the payments demanded by a creditor or creditors after mobilizing all of its available assets and funds. Suspension by the debtor of overdue payments is presumed to signal the inability to pay (BA Art. 116). The Bankruptcy Act also provides that a corporation may be declared bankrupt when its liabilities exceed its assets (BA Art. 117). The debtor may be any form of legal entity, including individuals and legal persons.

2.2 Bankruptcy Petition

The debtor, creditors, or a third party may petition for bankruptcy. In the case of a corporation, a corporate director may also file the petition. In the case that a petition for bankruptcy is not filed by a debtor or by all directors of an incorporated body, the applicant shall establish prima facie evidence of valid grounds for bankruptcy (BA Art. 122 through 128).

When such a petition is filed, the court may issue an order temporarily suspending the disposition of the debtor's assets except as permitted by law or by the court. Upon review of a petition for bankruptcy, the court declares the debtor bankrupt if it determines that the grounds for bankruptcy exist based on the information included in the petition and examination by the court. Otherwise, the court dismisses the petition.

The court must also notify the appropriate government offices or agencies as well as the public prosecutor of the adjudication of bankruptcy. Anyone having a legal interest may appeal the court's decision adjudicating bankruptcy within 14 days of the date of public notice of bankruptcy.

2.3 *Receiver*

At the time of adjudication of bankruptcy, the court appoints a receiver with the consultation of the administration committee (BA Art. 147). It also sets the period for the filing of claims, the date of the first meeting of creditors, and the date of the examination of claims (BA Art. 132). All such information regarding an adjudication of bankruptcy shall be made public, and the creditors, debtors and other concerned parties notified (BA Art. 133).

The receiver has exclusive rights to manage and dispose of the bankruptcy estate. The Bankruptcy Act also provides for the right of the receiver to set aside transactions in the bankruptcy procedure. The substance of these provisions is largely analogous to that of the Corporate Reorganization Act. The receiver's authority to terminate executory contracts is the same as the trustee's power under the corporate reorganization procedure.

The receiver has the discretionary right to liquidate the bankruptcy estate and determine when and how such liquidation should be done. However, this right is subject to certain limitations. For example, the receiver cannot liquidate the estate before the conclusion of a general investigation of the debtor's obligations. If a request for mandatory composition has been submitted prior to the conclusion of the general investigation, the court's ruling on the request is compulsory before the receiver can dispose of the estate.

2.4 *Bankruptcy Estate*

Upon the court's adjudication of bankruptcy, the bankrupt estate is established with all properties of the debtor (BA Art. 6). The right to manage and dispose of the bankruptcy estate is vested exclusively with the receiver, subject to court supervision (BA Art. 7). The receiver takes possession of and manages the bankruptcy estate (BA Art. 175). The receiver shall have all properties in the bankruptcy estate appraised in the presence of the court clerk, bailiff or notary public, make the inventory and a balance sheet, and submit them to the court. Interested parties have the right to inspect such documents (BA Art. 178, 179).

2.5 *Claims of Creditors*

All creditors are required to file their claims with the court within the period fixed by the court, which should be not less than two weeks and not more than four months. The Bankruptcy Act, in effect, provides a hierarchy of five separate categories of claims, as described below:

1. Secured claims: Secured creditors can proceed against their collateral on the same terms as would be available if the debtor were not bankrupt.
2. Estate claims: Estate claims are senior to all unsecured obligations and can be paid by the receiver at any time. They are not subject to the limitations of distribution imposed on other liabilities. Examples of estate claims include: costs of judicial proceedings incurred for the common benefit of creditors; expenses incurred in the management, liquidation, or distribution of the bankruptcy estate;

claims resulting from the acts of the receiver in managing the bankruptcy estate; and reimbursement claims resulting from the termination of bilateral contracts.
3. Claims with statutory preference: The most significant is the claim for unpaid wages to employees, which are superior to general claims.
4. Bankruptcy claims: Although general creditors do not hold as much authority as those mentioned above, they are nevertheless entitled to set off any amount they owe to the bankrupt against their claims.
5. Less preferred claims: Examples of such claims include interest accrued after the adjudication of bankruptcy, damages and penalties resulting from a failure of performance after adjudication of bankruptcy, and costs of participating in the bankruptcy proceedings.

The creditor's right to set off his debt to the insolvent company under the Bankruptcy Act is substantially the same as that under the Corporate Reorganization Act. There is, however, one procedural difference between them. This is that the creditor's right to set off under the corporate reorganization procedure must be exercised on or before the last day of the period specified for filing the claims of all creditors, whereas there is no such time limit in the case of the creditor's right to set off under the bankruptcy procedure.

2.6 Distribution

At the first creditors' meeting, the receiver reports on the circumstances that led to the adjudication of bankruptcy, interim developments, and the present status of the bankrupt and the bankrupt estate (BA Art. 183). The validity of claims filed by creditors can be examined at the first creditors' meeting. If the receiver or any creditor does not object to filed claims, it will become conclusive (BA Art. 217). If the receiver or any creditor opposes a filed claim, the holder of the claim may bring action to obtain a court judgment.

A resolution at the creditors' meeting requires that the majority of the creditors present vote for it, and the claims of the creditors voting for the resolution must exceed 50 per cent of the amount of the claims of all creditors present at the meeting (BA Art. 163). If the resolution adopted at the creditors' meeting goes contrary to the general interests of the creditors, the court may prohibit implementation of the resolution (BA Art. 168).

Immediately after the general examination of claims, the receiver shall perform the distribution whenever he or she recognizes any money appropriate for the distribution (BA Art. 228). The receiver distributes the proceeds from the bankruptcy estate to the creditors in proportion to their claims according to the distribution schedule prepared by him or her, and inspected by creditors (BA Arts 229–231). Permission from the court is required for the final distribution.

A bankruptcy proceeding is concluded with a court decision after the receiver has made the final distribution and presented a report at the creditors' meeting. The court may also discontinue a bankruptcy proceeding in the following cases: (1) when the bankrupt applies for the discontinuance under the agreement of creditors, and (2) when the court acknowledges that the value of the bankrupt estate is smaller than the amount of the expenses for the bankruptcy proceeding.

2.7 Constraint and Indemnity of Debtors

As mentioned earlier, the Bankruptcy Act was seldom used in the past because it did not offer incentives to creditors or debtors. The procedure was not an effective way for creditors to collect claims. There were several statutory discriminations against the bankrupt in addition to social degradation. A person adjudged bankrupt had to resign his position as a public servant. In the case of medical doctors or lawyers, their license to practice was revoked. The number of such revoked jobs surpasses 300.

Until the mid 1990s, credit card usage was not as high in Korea as in some countries that also experienced a plethora of consumer bankruptcy cases. As credit cards become more popular, however, the number of defaults on credit card debts and personal bankruptcy increased.

It is noteworthy that a unique Korean custom has also aided in causing personal bankruptcy. Local financial institutions commonly demand a personal guarantee on a loan as a condition for loan approval. Family members, friends, relatives, and colleagues often act as co-signers purely as a personal favor and at no charge to the debtor. Although these personal guarantees are based on social relationships, a potential outcome is economic ruin for the guarantors. Even before the financial crisis, this practice of personal guarantee was frequently criticized. The Supreme Court tried to mitigate the situation by limiting the liability of a guarantor in some cases, but this did not fundamentally solve the problem. The burden of reform is on legislators and banks. The first case in which the court ordered the exemption of debts was for a debtor who was a guarantor for her brother.

3 Corporate Reorganization

3.1 Scope of Application

Korea has four types of business corporations which have independent legal personality from their equity holders: *habmyunghoesa*, *habjahoesa*, *joosikhoesa*, and *youhanhoesa*. *Habmyunghoesa* consists of partners with unlimited liability. *Habjahoesa* has both partners with limited liability and partners with unlimited liability. *Habmyunghoesa* and *habjahoesa* are similar to partnerships with separate legal personalities. *Joosikhoesa* are joint-stock corporations whose shareholders assume limited liability up to their contribution to acquire outstanding stocks. *Youhanhoesa* can be defined as a small *joosikhoesa* because the Code applies simpler requirements and procedures to the former.

Corporate reorganization procedure is applied only to *joosikhoesa*. Other types of business corporations, partnerships and sole proprietorships have to apply for the composition procedure instead of the corporate reorganization procedure when they aim at being rehabilitated. The Corporate Reorganization Act (CRA) governs the procedure.

3.2 Filing of the Corporate Reorganization Procedure

Corporate reorganization proceedings are initiated by a petition for commencement presented to the proper court by the insolvent corporation. This process is for joint-stock corporations only. The petition may also be filed by at least one of the creditors whose claims against the company are no less than 10 per cent of the company's equity capital, or by shareholders who hold no less than 10 per cent of the issued shares of the company (CRA Art. 30). The court that has venue on the main office of a corporation has exclusive venue on a corporate reorganization case (CRA Art. 6).

As the Corporate Reorganization Act does not allow an automatic stay, the applicant files a petition of temporary protection order that appoints an interim trustee, prohibits disposal of assets and repayment of debt by the insolvent company, and/or halts other enforcement procedures (CRA Arts 37, 39). Without this temporary protection order, the reorganization proceedings cannot continue due to the creditors' eagerness to collect their claims individually. The court issues a temporary protection order after reviewing petition documents and interviewing applicants. The court hears the opinion of the management committee before issuing the order.

The interim trustee acts as the legal representative of the insolvent company and performs the daily duties of the company (CRA Arts 39-3, 53). Thus, incumbent members of the board of directors lose their authority. As its authority is almost the same as that of a trustee, most provisions on trustees are applied to interim trustees. Commercial banks, merchant banks and trust companies, and individuals may be appointed as interim trustees. The interim trustee must obtain the approval of the court to perform certain actions specified by the court, such as disposing of the company's assets.

Before the 1999 Amendments, the court deliberated whether to render the order of the commencement of the reorganization process during the interim trustee's term. The court rejected any petition for the commencement of proceedings if it carried even one of the stipulated factors. The most frequently debated factor was the comparison between liquidation value and going concern value. The court-appointed examiner performed due diligence and appreciation of liquidation value and going concern value. It took several months for the court to decide the commencement upon the opinion of the examiner.

The 1999 Amendment, however, changed the requirements as well as the process. The court dismisses the petition in cases where it is clear that the liquidation value is greater than the going concern value. The court does not appoint the examiner before it decides on the commencement of the procedure. Moreover, the Act mandates that the court shall decide the order of commencement within one month from the petition (CRA Art. 45-2). The intention is to base the decision of the commencement on procedural review instead of deliberation on merit.

3.3 Commencement Order and Appointment of Trustee (Powers, Liabilities and Qualifications)

When ordering the commencement of the reorganization procedure, the court also appoints one or more trustees and fixes the period for the filing of claims, the date of the first meeting of interested parties, and the date for examining the claims. The trustee has full authority to manage the corporation like an interim trustee. He or she has to report to the court and the management committee regarding such information as the comparison between liquidation value and going concern value.

The court may appoint the examiner to hear opinions on the evaluation of corporate assets, financial statements, and suitability of the requirements of the proceedings. The court usually appoints accountants as examiners and the opinion of the examiner is critical with regard to the comparison of the liquidation value and going concern value. The Act does not prescribe any specific method for calculating those values. The 1998 Supreme Court Rule on Corporate Reorganization, however, suggests one possible method – to figure out liquidation value, sum up the discounted price of individual assets on a balance sheet; and for going concern value, evaluate the present value of future cash flow in addition to the value of not-for-business assets. Other reasonable methods are permissible, but the practice generally follows the suggested method.

Upon the commencement of the corporate reorganization procedure, all creditors are required to file their claims with the court within the period fixed by the court, which should not be less than two weeks and not more than four months. This period can be extended up to one month for creditors who could not file claims without their faults. Shareholders can also file their stock with the court at this time. The court will then examine each of the filed claims together with the chairman of the board of directors and the trustee.

The trustee has the authority to set aside the transactions that are enumerated in CRA Art. 78. The trustee also has the authority to decide whether or not to perform or terminate any executory contract under which there remain obligations to be performed by the company and the counter party. This signifies that the trustee has the power to either terminate or seek action on an executory contract. He or she may exercise this power in such a manner as to allow contracts that are advantageous to the insolvent company and terminate those unfavorable to the company, also generally known as 'cherry picking'.

3.4 Reorganization Plan

Creditors under the reorganization procedure are classified into three categories: (1) creditors with common benefit claims; (2) creditors with secured claims; and (3) creditors with general claims. Common benefit claims are to be repaid irrespective of the reorganization plan and in advance of secured claims and general claims. Art. 208 stipulates that common benefit claims, including administrative fees for the procedure, employees' salaries, and retirement allowances and claims are to occur after the commencement under the approval of the court. General claims and secured claims, however, are subject to the corporate reorganization plan unless the court approves separate payments.

Based upon the fixed claims and the result of due diligence, the trustee makes a draft of the reorganization plan (the Plan), which must be presented to the court within the period prescribed by the court. The period shall not exceed four months from the last day of the period for filing claims. The prescribed period may be extended within two months. For small and medium-sized companies, the extension shall not exceed one month. The Act entitles the corporation's creditors and shareholders to submit the Plan. However, only one case has been reported in which the Plan was drafted by any one other than the trustee.

The most important aspect of the Plan is how to change the liabilities of debtors and rights of shareholders. The change of liabilities is usually done by reducing the amount of debts or postponing the due date. Before the 1998 Amendments, the repayment of debts could be extended up to 20 years. It meant that some firms were under the reorganization procedure for that length of time. Reflecting the criticism against the prolonged process, Art. 213 limits the duration of the Plan to ten years.

Shareholders' rights are usually restricted during the corporate reorganization procedure, with their voting rights frozen. Art. 221 authorizes the court to amortize over one-half of the outstanding shares in cases where the total amount of debt exceeds that of the assets. The court is authorized to amortize over two-thirds of the stocks in cases where the owners are responsible for mismanagement.

In the past, creditors, usually banks and other financial institutions, were not prone to cut off their claims even in the reorganization procedure. The officers of banks did not have the authority or ability, in certain situations, to decide the cut-off on a commercial basis under the government-led corporate structure in banking institutions. They did not have ample knowledge and skill to handle non-performing loans and hesitated to decide on anything that might incur suspicion.

Debt-for-equity swaps were seen and treated in a similar manner as debt cut-offs. Moreover, banks did not want to be major shareholders because they did not want to take any responsibility for the management of troubled corporations. As financial markets were underdeveloped in the past, the bad debts or equities of reorganized corporations had no place in which to be traded. For these reasons, the only methods used in the Plan were to postpone the due dates and/or reduce the interest rates. Banks preferred to maintain the amounts of loans in the accounting statements even though they were non-performing.

The financial crisis of late 1997 changed this practice. Non-performing loans had grown so big that creditor banks were almost destroyed under their pressure. Banks have slowly begun to prefer cash to unreduced amounts in accounting statements. Banks have agreed to cut down or cut off their claims in return for collecting some parts of their claims in cash. Debt-for-equity swaps have also been adopted as a method of restructuring. Banks now hope to collect their claims by selling their shares of their newly restructured company in the near future.

In the normal debt collection process, the claimants with junior priority are not entitled to get anything at all before those with senior priority are fully paid. In the corporate reorganization process, the highest priority is given to wage claims, the second to secured claims, the third is to unsecured claims, and the last is to shareholders. So in the normal judicial enforcement process, the shareholders take nothing before the unsecured creditors are fully paid. Priority among creditors and shareholders is strictly observed in the normal judicial enforcement process. The Plan, however, usually allows junior claimants to be partly paid even if senior claimants have not acquired full payment. The common means for discrimination between secured creditors and unsecured creditors are interest rates and duration of payment.

It is useful to note that under the same category of creditors there are several sub-categories: (1) primary financial institution creditors, such as commercial banks versus the secondary financial institution creditors, including investment banks; (2) principle creditors versus surety creditors; and (3) trading creditors versus financial creditors. The payment schedule might be slightly different from one sub-category to another. The Plan is usually drafted reflecting inflation, so it normally adds expected inflation rates to the estimated growth rate of sales.

The Plan is deliberated on and admitted to by creditors and shareholders at interested parties meetings. There is usually a series of three meetings. The first meeting is for the presentation of the trustee's report on the company's financial condition and examination of the filed claims. The second meeting is for the deliberation of a draft reorganization plan. The third meeting is for the resolution of the draft reorganization plan. Usually the second and third meetings are held at the same time. Admission of the Plan requires consent of over two-thirds of general creditors, three-quarters of secured creditors, and a majority of shareholders.

Once a draft reorganization plan has been consented to at the interested parties meeting, the court determines whether or not to approve it. The consent of the employees is not required for the approval of the Plan by the court. Public interests are not a factor to be considered either. Instead, the court shall examine whether the draft reorganization plan satisfies all the statutory requirements (Art. 233).

The most frequently visited requirements are fairness and equality. In recent rulings, the Supreme Court found these requirements lacking in the reorganization plan, and thus reversed an appellate court's decision with respect to the Plan's different payment schedule for damage claimants (in *re Korea Takoma*, 92Kue10, June 15, 1992). The Supreme Court made a similar reversal with respect to unfair and inequitable early payments and higher interest rates as applied to a state-owned bank (in *re Samik*, 98Kue11, August 28, 1998).

The Corporate Reorganization Act has a provision authorizing the court to approve the Plan even though any one class of claimants fails to reach an agreement on the proposed reorganization plan, but only under the condition that the court determines the necessary clauses to protect the rights of interested parties. Though 'cram-down' has not been much utilized in insolvency practice, it has prevented selfish creditors from halting the process.

Absolute priority rule is not stated in the Act nor accepted in practice. The normal reorganization plan allows junior claimants to be paid even if some of the senior claimants have not been fully paid. Conjectures can be made as to why senior creditors agree to such a plan. In most cases, secured creditors have unsecured claims too. Their concern is to maximize the total amount of collection regardless of a claim's priority. There should be some compromise between interested parties to prevent a holdout. No case has been filed yet in which the plaintiff complains that the reorganization plan violates the absolute priority rule.

The best interest test is used in the US as a tool to protect the dissenting creditors, within a consenting class of creditors. This means that the dissenting claimants are guaranteed to receive the amount that they might get in liquidation. The Corporate Reorganization Act does not provide this rule explicitly. However, the liquidation value will be preserved in practice because the total value distributed in the reorganization process will be bigger than the liquidation value if the distribution is fair.

The feasibility test can be applied throughout the whole process from the filing of the petition to the successful conclusion of the Plan. If the court discovers that there is no possibility of rehabilitation before issuing the provisional protection order or commencement order, it must dismiss the petition. Even before a reorganization plan is adopted at the interested parties meeting, the court shall discontinue the process if the court recognizes that there is no possibility of rehabilitation (CRA Art. 272). Feasibility is one requirement for the approval of the Plan by the court (CRA Art. 233). Even after the implementation of the Plan, the court shall discontinue the procedure unless the Plan is feasible (CRA Arts 273, 276).

3.5 Protection of Corporate Assets during the Corporate Reorganization Procedure

Once a corporate reorganization proceeding begins, the authority to manage the operation and assets of the company is vested exclusively with the trustee, subject to court supervision. Although formally the Act did not exclude the incumbent management or major shareholders as a trustee in the reorganization process, the 1992 Supreme Court Rule clearly stated that any attempts should be blocked for the former owner to regain control of the firm. The Rule reflected public sentiment that someone should be held responsible for the failure of the corporation. Retired officers of financial institutions are often appointed trustees because the creditors' opinion was receptive to the court. The problem is that such officers do not know the business and the firm undergoing the reorganization process.

The 1998 Supreme Court Rule repealed the provisions and recommended that the court appoint the trustee, with due consideration given to the opinions of the corporation, the management committee and creditors' conference. Though it does not exclude the former manager from being a candidate for a trustee, it is still so cautious as to suggest that a co-trustee recommended by the creditors' conference be appointed in cases where the incumbent manager is named as the trustee.

The Corporate Reorganization Act does not fix the term of the trustee, but the court usually nominates a trustee with a two-year term. The court supervises the trustee in a general sense. The trustee must manage the firm with the care of a good manager. He is liable for any damage that he causes by neglecting his duty of care (CRA Art. 101, 43). The court is entitled to dismiss the trustee in cases of serious cause (CRA Art. 101, 44). It is generally understood that serious cause means bribery or false reporting.

In addition to the regular salary, the court may allow the trustee a special bonus or stock option for the compensation of his or her achievements. According to the Seoul District Court's internal guidelines, the total of the special bonus can amount to one hundred million Korean won.

3.6 Role of Creditors

Creditors are entitled to set off debt owed to the company against claims to the company except under certain circumstances as prescribed in Art. 163. The creditor's right to set off under reorganization proceedings, however, must be exercised on or before the last day of the period specified for filing the claims of creditors.

The 1998 Amendments introduced the creditors' committee as a communication channel between creditors and the corporation. As the trustee is responsible to the court, not to the creditors, the creditors did not have an appropriate way to communicate with the court and the trustee. The creditors' committee, composed of major creditors up to the number of ten, disseminates information among creditors and submits the opinion of the creditors to the court. In addition to the presentation of their opinion to the court, creditors can file a formal petition in some instances, including discontinuance of the procedure and the exercise of avoidance of power. As to the application of these two petitions, actual practice to date has not been as successful as expected.

The management committee was established by the 1998 Amendments and serves two purposes. One is to provide expertise to the court and the other is to aid the court with routine managerial work.

3.7 Termination of the Corporate Reorganization Procedure

Once the court approves the Plan, a trustee implements the Plan under court supervision. If the Plan has been implemented completely or if it is deemed certain that it will be successfully implemented, the court may conclude the reorganization proceeding. As the Plan is usually organized for up to ten years, it takes several years to fully implement it. One common reason for an early conclusion of the Plan is merger and acquisition (M&A). Upon the conclusion of the procedure, the authority for managing the company reverts to the company's directors.

If it becomes apparent that the company cannot be rehabilitated either before or after the approval of the Plan, the court may decide to discontinue the reorganization proceedings. In this case, the court shall declare the corporation bankrupt as in the case of disapproval of the Plan (CRA Art. 23). Even with the discontinuance of the procedure, the change of claims or discharge according to the Plan is still effective. The cessation of the procedure does not have a retroactive effect.

4 Composition

4.1 Scope of Application

There are no restrictions on the applicants for the composition procedure, which is governed by the Composition Act (CA). Individuals as well as corporations can apply for it in principle. Individuals, however, do not usually use the composition procedure. Private arrangements are more convenient than the composition procedure if creditors cooperate with a debtor. The bankruptcy procedure can indemnify a debtor from unpaid debts, which is impossible in the composition procedure. In recent years, however, sole proprietorships or professionals increasingly apply for the composition.

As far as business corporations are concerned, the composition procedure has strong merits for managers and controlling shareholders. Contrary to the corporate reorganization procedure, which has the same goal of rehabilitation, the composition procedure does not expel the incumbent managers from the management of a debtor company. Moreover, controlling shareholders can possess their shares, which would be amortized in most cases of corporate reorganization.

For these reasons, there was a flood of applications for the composition procedure right after the foreign currency crisis in 1997. The Supreme Court has put a restriction on this trend by forbidding big companies to apply for the composition procedure through its ruling as mentioned before.

4.2 Filing of the Procedure

Only a debtor is eligible to petition for the composition procedure. An individual as well as a corporation can be a petitioner. However, the composition case for non-business entities is difficult to find. If the debtor is a legal entity, a unanimous resolution by all of the board members is required. A petition for commencement of composition should state the condition of composition (the Condition), such as the method of payment and the nature and extent of collateral (CA Art. 13). The Condition can be modified under the approval of the court. The petitioner should also provide the court with a detailed statement of its assets and a list of creditors and debtors.

Automatic stay is not allowed in the composition procedure either. Before deciding on a petition for commencement of composition, the court may issue a temporary protection order appointing an interim administrator and/or prohibiting the disposal of assets and repayment of debt by the debtor (CA Art. 20). An order to stop other enforcement procedures is not allowed in the composition procedure by interpretation. This interim administrator has virtually the same powers as those granted to the administrator who is appointed following commencement and who is entitled to monitor the activities of the debtor.

4.3 Commencement Order and Appointment of Administrator

With the commencement of the composition procedure, which shall be rendered within one month from the petition (CA Art. 26-2), the court appoints an administrator and an inspector. It also sets the period for filing claims and the date for the creditors' meeting (CA Art. 27). All information regarding the commencement of composition should be conveyed through public notice to known creditors and other concerned parties.

The Composition Act stipulates negative requirements with which the court shall dismiss the petition (CA Arts 18, 19 and 19-2). The court may order the debtor company to provide personal or material security, including the shares of major shareholders, as collateral to the creditors as a precondition to the commencement of the composition procedure.

The filing of claims in the composition process has a different meaning from that in the corporate reorganization process. Creditors file their claims in order to exercise their voting right at the creditors' meeting. If a creditor does not file its claims by the fixed date and its claims are not included in the list of debts, the creditor does not lose its claims. The filing is just for participation in the creditors' meeting and for exercising voting rights. There is no process for the confirmation of claims. The list of claims is not deemed to the title of debts. Priority claims that are superior to general claims are not subject to composition proceedings. Thus, secured claims are out of the scope of the composition procedure.

4.4 Composition Condition

The creditors meet on a date fixed by the court and review the reports and opinions of the administrator and the inspector concerning the debtor's situation. The creditors then vote on the proposed Condition. The consent to the Condition requires affirmative votes by a majority of the creditors present, representing three-quarters or more of the total amount of claims filed (CA Art. 53, BA Art. 278).

The Condition of composition consented to at the creditors' meeting will be examined by the court to see if it satisfies all the legal requirements. Art. 55 lists occasions where the court may oppose the composition. Those negative requirements include where the composition procedure or consent does not conform with the provisions of the Act, where the consent was done in an illegitimate manner, and where the consent goes against the general interests of the composition creditors. If the Condition is found satisfactory, the court will approve the plan.

4.5 Protection of Corporate Assets during Administration

An administrator in the composition procedure does not have full authority like the trustee in the corporate reorganization procedure. The appointment of an administrator in the composition procedure does not affect the power of the debtor to manage and dispose of assets. The administrator has authority to monitor the activities of a debtor. Transactions outside the scope of the ordinary course of business are subject to the consent of the administrator, and even transactions falling within the scope of the ordinary course of business may not be undertaken if the administrator raises an objection (CA Art. 31, 32).

4.6 Role of Creditors during Administration, Creditors' Meetings, etc.

Creditors with priority claims are not subject to the approved Condition. A creditor with secured claims, for example, may foreclose its collateral at any time. For this reason, a debtor usually persuades priority creditors to be involved in the Condition voluntarily.

Under the Composition Act, the creditor has the right to set aside any acts of the insolvent party that occurred after filing the petition and that are not part of the ordinary course of business. The creditor may also set aside any acts taken by the insolvent party after the commencement of the proceeding without the required consent of an administrator. The Composition Act has almost similar provisions on the management committee and creditors' meeting as those of the Corporate Reorganization Act (CA Arts 11-2, 49-2, 49-3, 49-4, 50).

4.7 Powers of the Courts in relation to Administration and the Administrator

Practically speaking, the company is no longer under the court's control once the court approves the Condition of composition. The directors of the company do not have any direct duty to the court. The administrator of the composition procedure is not directly involved in the management.

There are two kinds of intervention of the court after the Condition is approved. The first is the discontinuance of the composition procedure and the other is the revocation of the composition procedure. The court shall render the decision of discontinuance when a debtor is unable to implement the condition of the composition. It may also discontinue the procedure upon the illegal activities of a debtor (CA Arts 63, 64). The court shall revoke the composition procedure when a debtor is in the fault of non-performance (CA Arts 67, 68). In both cases, the court shall declare the debtor bankrupt.

4.8 Termination of the Administration

The court may decide to discontinue a composition procedure if the debtor wishes to do so before the creditors' vote on the Condition or if a majority agreement cannot be reached within two months of the first creditors' meeting.

The debtor runs the business without any interference by the court after the approval of the composition. The implementation of the Condition is laid in the hands of the debtor. Following the approval of the composition, the debtor company must report to the court every six months with respect to its payment under the Plan. The court has discretion to discontinue the composition proceedings if it finds that the debtor has not met, or may not be able to meet in the future, repayment obligations according to the condition. In case of discontinuance, disapproval or cancellation of the composition, the court shall, *ex officio*, adjudicate the bankruptcy of a debtor (CA Art. 9).

5 Non-judicial Procedure on Insolvent Corporations

5.1 Rationalization Measures

The economic development policy of the Park government (1962–1979) adopted quite a unique capitalist system. To solve the problems caused by the lack of funds necessary for investment, President Park took over the financial market as well as state-owned banks and virtually ran them as government businesses. When those corporations that were supported by government-led financial institutions became insolvent, the government tackled the situation by adopting an industrial policy perspective. Instead of resorting to formal insolvency procedures, the government used measures under the title of 'Industrial Rationalization Policy'.

The first rationalization measures were implemented during the period of 1969 through 1971 by employing debt reduction, tax benefits, mergers and takeover by creditor banks. Over 100 companies were liquidated under this policy and only a few were put into the corporate reorganization procedure. However, there were no statutory grounds for these measures. They were executed by the unchecked power of the government over the financial sector and in the name of economic development policy. Under such circumstances, even lawyers developed the notion that the government, not the court, decided the future of big insolvent companies.

Another rationalization measure, the so-called 8-3 Measure, was proclaimed as a presidential emergency decree on 3 August 1972 to save over-indebted companies suffering from the oil crisis. The decree nullified existing loan contracts and changed them in favor of debtor companies. The decree was recorded as a rare example of the government unilaterally infringing creditors' rights. The rationalization measures continued without statutory foundation until the Industrial Development Act was enacted in 1986. Under this Act, the ownership of 57 large insolvent companies was transferred to third parties, for which the government granted special financial and tax favors. In turn, the Bank of Korea provided commercial banks with a special loan to compensate for their losses stemming from these rescue loans.

These ad hoc measures may have served the purpose of preventing the systemic collapse of the economy when each of the measures was implemented. But on the whole, they led to an institutional environment under which both debtor companies and their creditors had little incentive to use the formal insolvency procedures with the expectation that the government would solve their problems for them. As a consequence, the judicial system and resources for the formal procedures were left underdeveloped. The government-directed measures also negatively affected the formal insolvency mechanism by impeding the development of financial institutions and markets, which are essential to an efficient insolvency mechanism in the court.

During the 1990s, the rationalization measures were not frequently used because industrial policy ceased to focus on target industries. However, as a result of the expansion policy based on the government-controlled financial system, big corporations, including *chaebols* – massive Korean corporate groups controlled by families – have been so deeply indebted that the possibility of insolvency was always there. Until 1997, the government sometimes saved some *chaebols* by providing rescue loans.

5.2 Bank Management

There are two types of bank management: court management and private management. Court management means that a bank is nominated as a trustee of the corporate reorganization procedure. Private management is a contract between a debtor and creditor.

When a creditor bank finds out that a debtor company is in danger of insolvency, it may sign a contract for management. The contract usually uses very broad terms so the scope of management differs from one case to another. There are two core elements: the creditor bank dispatches bank staff to the debtor company in order to check the cash flow and the bank supplies rescue loans. In some cases, bank staff take positions in the line of management and directly manage the company. In other cases, they just monitor the cash flow of the company.

Bank management, in its pure form, may work as a type of monitoring on a debtor company. Instead of collecting information from a debtor, a bank can directly watch a debtor inside the company and effectively monitor the financial status of the debtor. In reality, however, bank management was not an efficient procedure in preventing bankruptcy and restructuring a debtor in a timely manner. In many cases, there was moral hazard on both sides. The debtor company did not do its best, with the expectation that it would not be bankrupt. The creditor bank preferred the status quo, with the fear that its loss might be revealed upon bankruptcy. In the 1990s, the number of bank management cases decreased drastically. Banks became reluctant to be involved in the management of debtors.

5.3 Workout and Big Deals

A year before the 1997 crisis, Korea faced an enormous insolvency case. Hanbo Steel Corp. requested rescue loans from banks and eventually from the government. Its total debts to financial institutions amounted to 1.3 trillion Korean won (exchange rates were about 1,000 Korean won for 1 US$ at that time). The Kim Young Sam government's (1992–1997) approach to the Hanbo case was vastly different from prior cases under previous governments. The Kim administration stated negatively: 'It is creditor banks who decide whether to provide additional loans.' Major creditor banks, usually accustomed to following the guidelines set by the government, were not brave enough to make a decision without government endorsement. Eventually Hanbo Steel collapsed and creditor banks were put in danger.

There was another shock with Kia Motors' insolvency. Kia Motors, among the top ten largest groups, was unique because it was neither a *chaebol*, nor state-owned. The government handled this situation in the same manner as it did in the Hanbo case, even though there was much public sympathy. Kia Motors filed a petition for the composition procedure just before becoming insolvent.

The downfall of these two big corporations awakened the country to the notion that nothing is too big to be destroyed. The size of a company is no longer a safeguard. Koreans became aware of the fragility that exists in business enterprises.

The Hanbo and Kia cases set off a domino effect. Many large companies and corporate groups were soon on the edge of bankruptcy. In the face of such overall instability, the government was not prepared to adequately address the insolvency issue.

The government did not want to be directly involved in issues between creditor banks and debtor companies. Instead, the government forced banks to stop declaring *budoe* (non-payment of promissory notes or checks) in some cases. All banks signed the Anti-Budoe Agreement in April 1997. The Agreement, however, failed to mitigate the situation because the non-bank financial institutions, which were not parties to the agreement, abused the payment by signatory banks for the collection of their claims.

When the Anti-Budoe Agreement was not as effective as the government had hoped, a series of big corporate groups with relatively strong reputations were pushed to insolvency. In October 1997, the Minister of Finance and Economy urged the presidents of merchant banks as well as commercial banks to stop grab-first competition against those companies and to provide loans necessary for survival.

Due to government pressure, the Co-operative Loan Agreement was drafted and every financial institution, including the second and the third tiers of financial institutions, signed it. According to the Agreement, the main creditor bank could choose which companies deserved cooperative loans. Pursuant to the selection, every creditor bank of the company must stop collecting loans and provide additional loans.

Many controversies arose regarding the program. There was a conflict of interest among creditors and corruption was inevitable since creditor banks were not free from the influence of politicians and high officials. The firms that received cooperative loans were benefited in ways such as low interest rates and non-security. Around 2.1 trillion won in cooperative loans were fed through to 11 big corporate groups by April 1998.

In December 1997, the foreign currency crisis hit Korea, which had yet to resolve the insolvency issues. The crisis almost doubled the foreign exchange rate as the value of one US dollar went from 902 won in August 1997 to 1,642 won in February 1998. Interest rates also increased two-fold from 12.39 per cent in August 1997 to 25.34 per cent in January 1998. Many companies, including *chaebols*, heavily dependent on debt financing for their investments, teetered on the edge of bankruptcy. As the companies within each *chaebol* were closely connected through cross-loan guarantees and other intra-group transactions, one company's bankruptcy could produce a domino effect, thus seriously crippling the entire economy.

Many small and medium-sized companies went bankrupt due to a lack of effective policy measures. At first, the government focused its effort on preventing a systematic collapse of *chaebols*, and only later turned its attention to the general state of the economy.

The government addressed the bankruptcy of the top 64 *chaebols* and several large independent companies in three ways. Firstly, there was an exit order given to companies that were deemed unable to be rehabilitated. The exit order, implemented through consultation with creditor financial institutions, was initiated by the largest creditor. The chairperson designated the most troubled firms among the top 64 *chaebols*. The Financial Supervisory Commission (FSC) finally selected 55 companies and ordered financial institutions to stop extending new loans and to call in existing loans when they were due. However, the purpose of this measure and its ultimate effect remain unclear, since most of the companies designated to exit were merged into their affiliated companies or filed for formal insolvency procedures. Only a handful of them were actually in the process of liquidation.

Secondly, the government created an informal rehabilitation procedure, the so-called 'Workout'. It was an attempt to prevent a systemic corporate bankruptcy amid mounting non-performing loans in the aftermath of the economic crisis. It was also conceived partly out of concern that the existing formal insolvency procedures were not well-developed nor efficient enough to simultaneously handle such a large number of firms in financial distress. The Workout will be discussed in more detail later in this section.

The last measure was an exchange of companies between the top five *chaebols*, the so-called 'big deals', which were first mentioned by some politicians as a method to reform *chaebol* structure. The basic idea was to exchange or merge some business sectors among *chaebols* in order to reduce their debts and increase their strength in the market. Some business sectors, such as the aeromechanics, train, and petrochemical sectors, were successfully restructured with mutual understanding among *chaebols*. The semiconductor sector was traded between the Hyundai and LG group at the strong urging of the government. In spite of government pressure, the 'big deals' in automobile and electronics between Samsung and Daewoo groups were not realized because of disagreements on the debt appreciation of Samsung Motors.

The Workout is based on the Financial Institutions Agreement for Promotion of Corporate Restructuring ('Corporate Restructuring Agreement') signed on 25 June

1998 by all domestic creditor financial institutions, including commercial banks, investment trust corporations, and merchant banks. It was supposedly modeled after the London Approach, in which the central bank plays an arbitrator's role in the voluntary negotiations between debtor companies and their banks. But the Korean Workout differs in a number of ways in its implementation. First, every financial institution was urged to participate in this agreement, including insurance companies and security brokerage companies, unlike the case of the failed Anti-Bankruptcy Agreement of 1997, which was signed only by commercial banks. Second, the FSC has in effect assumed a central role in the process since it is in charge of both corporate and financial sector restructuring, even though the Corporate Restructuring Committee is the official arbitrator according to the Agreement. Third, the government retains another way to directly influence the process, as it is the majority shareholder of many of the large commercial banks. The government became the absolute majority shareholder of many commercial banks as a result of the restructuring.

The Workout is initiated when the main bank of a debtor company, or financial institution having loans amounting to more than 25 per cent of the company's total credit, selects a targeted firm and calls for a Council of Creditor Financial Institutions (CCFI). The targeted firms mainly consist of firms that are economically viable but are temporarily suffering from financial distress. The Workout should provide a more reasonable loan call rate than what a legal procedure such as composition and reorganization would entail. But selection of the targeted firms is largely dependent on the main bank's discretion.

When the main bank selects the targeted firm and notifies the credit financial institutions, the CCFI convenes and decides on the Workout procedure. At this time, debt collection by the financial institutions on loans is immediately suspended for a maximum of six months. In addition, the CCFI also selects the institution that will examine the situation of the target firm during the standstill.

The purpose of due diligence on the firm is mainly to verify its real liquidation value from a conservative perspective. The investigation looks into the company's assets, liquidation value, future value, liabilities and liabilities not necessarily listed in books or contingent liabilities. Based on the results of the investigation, each creditor knows the minimum value it can collect, and compares the various alternatives provided by the main bank with that basic information. During the investigation, the main bank prepares a Workout plan with the assistance of an external advisory group.

A Workout plan prepared by the main bank is negotiated by the CCFI. The plan can include a wide range of restructuring measures: debt rescheduling, interest reductions, additional financing, dissolution of cross-loan guarantees in the case of conglomerates, debt-equity swaps and amortization of issuing stock, asset and business sales, injection of fresh capital from foreign investors, and the appointment of a manager. After the Workout plan is established, the CCFI approves the Workout plan with the approval of 75 per cent or more of the total of those holding the company's debts. The CCFI then decides whether or not the Workout procedure will begin. The approval of the proposed Workout plan requires at minimum a 75 per cent majority vote by the creditors, otherwise the firm is excluded from the Workout procedure. In the event where neither a 75 per cent agreement nor objection is reached, the agenda is rolled over to the second or third convention of the council.

If the second and third convention cannot decide on the Workout procedure, the main bank may request arbitration by the Committee of Corporate Restructuring

Once the plan is approved, the main bank concludes a Memorandum of Understanding (MOU) on corporate restructuring with the targeted firm. The Workout procedure principally requires the shareholder, manager and other employees to be equally responsible for the losses suffered by the creditors. Thus, the MOU must include and specify elements of self-rescue, reduction of capital and adjustment of personnel. In concluding the MOU, the main bank must specify the management target measurable with quantitative and qualitative measures and the time schedule to carry out the target to protect the credit financial institutions and fulfill the Workout procedure correctly.

After the conclusion of the MOU, the main bank establishes and dispatches a management team to the targeted firm for monitoring. In addition, the main bank may construct a regular reporting system, appoint and dispatch an independent director, and construct a committee to assess the management and monitor the process of executing the MOU.

As of 30 July 2000, 106 companies were under the Workout procedure, 68 of which had an approved Workout plan. The total amount of credits of those 68 companies subject to the Workout program was 104.9 trillion won. Three trillion won were converted into equity while 62.4 trillion won were treated to extension of due dates. In addition, the debtor companies pledged to improve their financial condition by asset sales, new capital injection, and divestment of affiliated firms, by the amount of 8.3 trillion won.

But the actual restructuring performance of debtor companies was disappointing. Asset sales, foreign investment and management improvement made 2.7 trillion won available. Creditor banks and debtor companies were criticized at the same time. The former were more interested in securing their claims than in rehabilitation, and the latter were reluctant to debt-equity swap for fear of losing management control.

The most frequent criticism of the Workout stems from the fact that the government is the actual director of the program, not the creditor financial institutions. There is much doubt as to whether the government is capable of making sound decisions concerning business. The Corporate Restructuring Agreement does not provide any transparent or persuasive criteria for decisions in the Workout process. Though the FSC plays a vital role in the Workout, it hides itself behind a curtain. Rationalization measures in the 1970s and 1980s seem to survive in the 1990s under a different name and pretense.

5.4 Bank Insolvency

Financial institutions, including commercial banks, merchant banks, securities companies, and insurance companies, require more focus during restructuring or liquidation because their businesses have a prevailing impact on general economic activities. Hence, many states have separate laws on the restructuring or liquidation of financial institutions.

A relevant law is the Act on Structural Improvement of the Financial Industry, which was originally known as the Act on Merger and Transfer of Financial Institutions of 1991. This law underwent comprehensive revision in 1996 and was given a new name in order to encourage healthy financial institutions to merge and weak institutions to exit. Until the financial crisis, this act was never employed to restructure or liquidate financial institutions, even though there were serious concerns regarding poor business practices as Korea's banking industry grew. Most of the problems were not exposed publicly or legally. Some financial institutions were merged or acquired by other institutions under the guidance of the Ministry of Finance.

The financial crisis provided the proper circumstances to apply this act openly. The act gives the FSC the authority to order management improvement measures, including the amortization of stocks, mergers, suspension of directors, appointment of trustees, transfer of business, and third party acquisitions. The FSC can also suspend a bank's business for a stipulated period and ask the Minister of Finance to cancel its license.

On 22 December 1997, the FSC issued a management improvement order to the Seoul Bank and the Korea First Bank, two of the five largest banks. Two months later, the FSC issued management improvement orders to 12 banks that did not meet the BIS (Bank for International Settlement) ratio. After reviewing management normalization plans and performing on-the-spot examination of assets, the FSC announced the exit of five banks and their counterpart banks that would acquire their assets. Seven other banks have been restructured through mergers, new investment of foreign capital, and trimmed business operations.

The implementation of the act raised controversy over the legitimacy of some provisions. The act provides that, through the decision of contract transfer by the FSC and newspaper notices, all assets and debts of a target bank are transferred collectively to the acquiring bank. This provision is criticized for lacking creditor protection measures that are generally provided under the Civil Code and the Commercial Code. Another point of contention is over transfers which take place without a special resolution at the general meeting of shareholders, which is required by the Commercial Code. The issue of constitutionality has also been raised regarding the provision that the FSC solely determines the take-over bank. These criticisms, however, have not deterred the implementation of this act.

6 Winding Up Procedures

6.1 An Introduction to the Range of Winding Up Procedures

The Commercial Code, which regulates matters of business corporations, distinguishes dissolution of corporate entities from winding up. Dissolution means that the business corporation as a legal entity is dissolved and no longer exists. Winding up or liquidation, however, is the process that allocates corporate property to interested parties including creditors and stakeholders before dissolution. As most business corporations are stock corporations in Korea, the following description is on the winding up procedure of stock corporations. The winding up of other business corporations is dealt with in a separate section of this chapter.

Art. 517 of the Code enumerates the causes of dissolution: satisfaction of the causes stipulated in the articles of incorporation including the completion of duration of incorporation, merger, split-off (spin-off), bankruptcy, court order of dissolution, court decision of dissolution, resolution of dissolution by the general meeting of shareholders. Wind up is mandatory in dissolution except in the case of a merger, split or bankruptcy. In addition, corporations are dissolved in the practical sense by the court decision to revoke or nullify the establishment of corporation. Upon those decisions of revocation or nullification, winding up procedures are to follow the court order or decision of dissolution.

In case of partnership and sole proprietorship, the law does not require winding up. As they do not have the status of an independent legal entity they are taken as an individual as far as legal matters are concerned. General contract law decides their liability with creditors similar to a consumer liability case. A debtor in partnership and sole proprietorship may sell out all his/her property and pay his/her debts, whether completely or not. Though we can name the process individual winding up, no special rules are applied to it except those under general contract law.

6.2 Who may Initiate the Winding Up Procedure and When?

The winding up procedure of stock corporations starts upon the dissolution except in the case of a merger, split or bankruptcy. In case of merger and split of stock corporations, the winding up procedure is not necessary because all the liabilities are handed over to a successive corporation. The bankruptcy procedure has an independent process for liquidation.

Contrary to the bankruptcy procedure, neither creditors nor courts can initiate winding up directly. Winding up is the successive procedure following dissolution. Creditors shall apply for the bankruptcy procedure in case of the insolvency of a debtor.

The Commercial Code (CC) allows stock corporations and limited liability corporations a statutory winding up because the protection of creditors is urgent under the limited liability of shareholders in stock corporations.

The statutory winding up requires the liquidators to do some tasks in addition to basic functions, including closing of current business, collection of claims, conversion into money, payment, and allocation of remaining properties. Liquidators shall give notice publicly that all the claims are to be filed within two months (CC Art. 535). This should include all claims that a debtor already has knowledge of, even though they are not filed. A debtor may not pay its debts during the period of filing claims. Only small claims and secured claims can be repaid with the permission of the court (CC Art. 536). After the completion of the period of filing claims, a debtor may repay its debts, but it must file a petition for bankruptcy immediately after it finds the assets are insufficient for the repayment of debts (CC Art. 542). Upon the completion of repayment, remaining properties are to be distributed to shareholders in proportion to their shares.

Liquidators must submit the report on closing accounts immediately after they finish the business of liquidation. When the report is approved at the shareholders' meeting, the liability of liquidators is exempted except in case of wrongdoings (CC Art. 540).

6.3 Effect of the Commencement of Winding Up upon the Company's Management

Upon the winding up, the governance structure of stock corporations changes. The directors, board of directors and chairman of the board are replaced by liquidators, a board of liquidators and a chairman of the board of liquidators. Directors become liquidators in principle. The articles of incorporation or shareholders' meeting can nominate liquidators (CC Art. 531). The court may select liquidators when it renders an order or a decision of dissolution upon the petitions of interested parties including shareholders or *ex officio* parties. The board of liquidators has power to decide the business of liquidation. The chairman of the board of liquidators is entitled to execute the business of liquidation according to the decision of the board of liquidators. Most provisions on directors in the Commercial Code are also applied to liquidators.

Shareholders' meetings and auditor(s) have the same authority as before the dissolution as far as the corporation under the winding up procedure exists for the purpose of liquidation.

6.4 Creditors' Meetings

Creditors are not treated collectively in the winding up procedure. The Commercial Code does not provide for any assembly of creditors, which is the main difference from the bankruptcy procedure. The reason for the absence of any assembly of creditors can be found in the fact that the winding up under the Commercial Code is a repayment procedure when full payment is possible. There is no need to require the collective opinion of creditors, whose claims are fully paid. If the debtor's property is not enough for the full repayment of debts, the winding up procedure cannot be continued. The liquidator must apply for the bankruptcy procedure instead.

6.5 The Role of the Court in the Winding Up Process

The court does not play as major a role in the winding up procedure as in the bankruptcy procedure. It selects liquidators when they are not nominated by shareholders' meetings or by the articles of incorporation or when the nomination is inappropriate or impossible. Liquidators lead the winding up procedure and the court assumes a limited task as a neutral third party, a place to which liquidators file financial statements for liquidation.

6.6 Claims

If a debtor denies any claim of a creditor, the dispute is settled in a separate suit according to the general contract law. Priority among claims are decided by the Civil Code and other related statutes including the Act for the Protection of Housing Rent, the Labor Standard Act and the Basic Act for Taxation. A debtor as well as creditors can set off their claims with liabilities in the winding up procedure without any restriction. Relevant law on winding up does not have different provisions on these issues.

Voidable transactions are not discussed in the winding up procedure. There is no need for any creditors to argue the legitimacy of repayment or transaction because there are enough properties for full payment.

6.7 Winding Up of Other Corporations

Every ground for the dissolution of stock corporations is the same as the ground for dissolution of other kinds of corporations. In addition, other corporations are to be dissolved when the number of constituents become one, whereas stock corporations are not to be dissolved for that reason.

In stock corporations, the Commercial Code provides the procedures of winding up and the corporation cannot decide or follow different procedures. However, the disposal of corporate properties can be decided by the articles of incorporation or the consent of total constituents in the process of private winding up of *habmyunghoesa* and *habjahoesa* because their constituents assume unlimited liabilities for the debts of corporations. The Commercial Code calls this private winding up (CC Art. 247). In private winding up, the Commercial Code requires two things to protect creditors. The first is the appeal against the private winding up. The corporation shall give notice that any creditors may file an appeal for at least one month. The other is the consent of creditors with securities on shares to the private winding up. If the corporation disposes its properties out of the due process, the transaction is to be revoked.

6.8 Procedures for the Restitution of the Corporation

Even if business corporations are dissolved, the restitution of the dissolved corporation to the former legal entity is desirable instead of establishing a new corporation. The Commercial Code provides the requirements and procedures of restitutions in each corporation respectively (CC Arts 229, 285, 519, 610).

*6.8.1 Corporation with unlimited liability partners (*habmyunghoesa*)* When the corporation is dissolved for reasons satisfying the articles of corporation and every constituent agrees with the dissolution, the restitution of the dissolved corporation is possible with the consent of more than two constituents. Constituents who do not agree with the restitution are required to quit from the corporation (CC Art. 229). The restitution is possible by admitting a new constituent in the case that the corporation is dissolved due to a single constituent (CC Art. 229). If a new member has limited liability, the corporation is transformed into *habjahoesa*.

If the court revokes or nullifies the establishment of corporation because of any reasons peculiar to some constituents, other constituents can agree with the restitution excluding those with problems (CC Art. 194). In the process of bankruptcy, the restitution is possible by the resolution of compulsory composition or court decision of discontinuance of bankruptcy procedure (BA Arts 283, 320).

*6.8.2 Corporation with unlimited and limited liability partners (*habjahoesa*)* The rules on restitution of *habmyunghoesa* can be applied to *habjahoesa* except the one on the change of constituents. If one kind of constituent quits the corporation altogether, the remaining constituents restitute the corporation by admitting new constituents or changing their liability (CC Art. 285).

*6.8.3 Stock corporation (*joosikhoesa*)* The restitution of *joosikhoesa* can be done by a special resolution at the general meeting of shareholders when the corporation is dissolved because of the satisfaction of requirements provided by the articles of incorporation or the resolution by the shareholders' meeting (CC Art. 519). The resolution of compulsory composition or court decision of discontinuance of bankruptcy procedure is also the ground for the restitution of *joosikhoesa*.

*6.8.4 Limited liability corporation (*youhanhoesa*)* The rules on restitution of *joosikhoesa* are applied to *youhanhoesa*. In addition, the restitution is possible by admitting new constituents when the corporation is dissolved because of a single constituent (CC Art. 610).

7 Offences

7.1 Insolvent Trading Rules

The insolvency laws do not penalize a late filing. This means a debtor company does not have a legal obligation to file a corporate reorganization petition. Members of the board of directors, however, have a duty of care or fiduciary duty to their companies in a general sense under the Commercial Code. Thus they have to compensate for any damages that come about if a filing is late as a result of negligence of duties.

The act of insolvency is not criminal behavior and the managers of insolvent companies are not considered criminals. Neither the Corporate Reorganization Act nor the Criminal Code orders any criminal investigation upon the commencement of the corporate reorganization procedure. Criminal charges against corporate directors are unusual in Korea even in a bankruptcy situation. But the conflicts between creditors and the management of a debtor company sometimes reveal evidence of embezzlement or breach of trust, so that the prosecutor may bring an indictment against the managers. The situation in insolvency proceedings is almost the same as in the normal business process as far as criminal matters are concerned.

7.2 Other Insolvency-related Offences by Corporate Controllers

Directors can be sued by their own company if they act against their duty or law and cause damages to the company (CC Art. 399). Derivative suits may be brought by the shareholder(s) with 3 per cent or more of issued shares (0.01 per cent for listed corporations) if the company does not exercise its claim. The Corporate Reorganization Act stipulates a summary procedure, named 'assessment', against the director who is liable for the damages of the corporation (CRA Art. 72). When the court discovers any damage caused by the director to the corporation, the court orders the director to pay the damages to the corporation, bypassing much of the time and expense involved in a regular damage recovery suit.

Civil and criminal charges against directors have not often been exercised. This has been particularly so in the case of large companies, including listed companies. But the crisis in 1997 has changed the situation to some extent. The rights of minority shareholders have become an important agenda item in citizen activism. An activist group brought a derivative action against the former president and directors of Korea First Bank. The court ordered them to pay compensation of US$33 million for the damages incurred by them to the Bank. The case was reported as the first derivative suit against a listed company in Korea's economic history. It is doubtful whether the accused directors can pay the damages because they do not have liability insurance or sufficient property to use as recompense. However, legal actions with respect to the responsibilities of directors are expected to increase, as shareholder activism has grown more prevalent after the crisis.

7.3 Other Relevant Corporate Law Offences

The Korean law confines the liability of each legal entity to itself and does not extend to other legal entities without any statutory provisions. The liabilities of a business corporation do not extend to its shareholders and/or directors. Shareholders and directors are not liable for the debts of the corporation. The only possibility whereby shareholders may be liable for the debts of the corporation is when the principle of piercing the corporate veil is applied. The Korean courts have applied the principle only in a few cases and, in these, extended the liability of the corporation to the shareholders.

8 Rules regarding Cross-border Insolvency and Coordination with Foreign Insolvency Proceedings

Insolvency laws in Korea do not reflect the current situation of increasing cross-border insolvency cases. These statutes were enacted when multinational corporations were rather uncommon. The basic approach of insolvency laws on international matters is territorialism. The corporate reorganization procedure and the bankruptcy procedure are effective on property in Korea (BA Art. 3, CRA Art. 3). Any foreign judgment on bankruptcy and any corporate reorganization procedure commenced by a foreign court cannot be applied to properties placed in Korea (BA Art. 3, CRA Art. 3).

Foreigners are not discriminated against in the area of insolvency law. In the bankruptcy procedure and corporate reorganization procedure, they have the same legal status as Koreans and Korean corporations (BA Art. 2, CRA Art. 3). The Bankruptcy Act, in addition, requires reciprocal treatment to Koreans and Korean corporations by the foreign national law in question.

Chapter 4

The Long March Towards China's New Bankruptcy Law

ROMAN TOMASIC and MARGARET WANG
Victoria University, Melbourne

China's insolvency regime has been in a state of transition for a relatively long period of time, although a new Bankruptcy Law is likely to be passed in the very near future. The draft of the Bankruptcy Law of the People's Republic of China (hereinafter referred to as the 'Draft Bankruptcy Law'), went to the 10th session of the Standing Committee of the National People's Congress (NPC), China's top legislative body, for deliberation on 21 June 2004.[1] The Draft Bankruptcy Law has also been submitted to the meeting of the National People's Congress in March 2005. Due to heated debates about priorities to be accorded to insolvency claims by employees, it is now expected that the new PRC Bankruptcy Law will not be enacted before the end of 2006.

Until the new Bankruptcy Law comes into effect, bankruptcy will be governed by a variety of legal instruments and procedures that will be discussed in this chapter. It is also likely that the pre-existing approaches to dealing with insolvency in China will also have some effect. In a recent study of insolvency law in China and a number of other East Asian countries the fragmented and under-developed state of China's bankruptcy laws was evident; as one participant in the Chinese market observed:

> China doesn't have much of a legal system. And it will be a rule of men rather than a rule of law for some time yet, as the legal system in China will take years to develop. In the meantime, the implementation of bankruptcy laws will rely upon the Chinese way of doing things ...[2]

It should be said that this situation is now rapidly improving.

Traditionally, the concept of 'bankruptcy' was not recognized in Chinese law until the first bankruptcy law was introduced during the late Qing Dynasty.[3] Before that

---

1 Lan, X., 'Outdated Bankruptcy Law Upgraded' – http://www.bjreview.com.cn/200430/Business-200430(B).htm (accessed on 14 December 2004) and Li, J., 'NPC Weighs Momentous New Bankruptcy Law', *China Daily*, 22 June 2004 – http://www.chinadaily.com.cn/english/doc/2004-06/22/content_341275.htm (accessed on 14 December 2004).

2 Tomasic, R. and Little, P., *Insolvency Law and Practice in Asia*, Hong Kong, FT Law and Tax Asia Pacific, 1997, at 21.

3 Li, S., 'Bankruptcy Law in China: Lessons of the Past Twelve Years', at http://www.fas.harvard.edu/~asiactr/haq/200101/0101a006.htm.

time, the role of bankruptcy law was filled by the legal and ethical tradition that 'the son pays for the debts of his father'.[4] In feudal society, this notion was extended so that even a grandson could be responsible for his grandfather's debt. It has been said that 'a grandson may even have a debt or obligation before he is born …'[5] In 1906, the Qing government followed the civil law system, especially the laws of Japan, China's more developed neighbour, and enacted a bankruptcy law. Due to difficulties in its implementation, this law was annulled by China's Emperor Guang Xu in 1908. In 1915, during the era of the Republic of China, the then Northern Warlords Government also drafted a bankruptcy law. In 1935, the Nationalist Government published and implemented a bankruptcy law in China, one that is still in force in Taiwan today.[6]

In 1949, with the founding of the People's Republic of China, the new government abolished all laws enacted by the former Nationalist Government. As a result, China ceased to have an insolvency law for the next 30 years or so until the enactment in 1986 of the broadly based Law on Enterprise Bankruptcy (For Trial Implementation) (hereinafter referred to as the 'Enterprise Bankruptcy Law'). During this intervening period, the Chinese government practised a uniform policy of centralized assumption of profits and losses of state-owned enterprises (SOEs) under the planned economic system. Enterprises with chronic and serious deficits suffered one of two fates; firstly, they were closed, suspended, consolidated or had their production changed by administrative orders, or secondly, they went 'bankrupt' automatically without going through any legal procedure.[7]

In the early 1980s, Chinese economists, legal experts and government officials started to realize the drawbacks of the way in which the planned economic system dealt with insolvent enterprises, and advocated the need for a law dealing with enterprise bankruptcy. After the strong push by experts and scholars and fierce debates in the Standing Committee of the National People's Congress (NPC), the Law of the People's Republic of China on Enterprise Bankruptcy (For Trial Implementation) was finally promulgated by the 18th Session of the Standing Committee of the 6th NPC on 2 December 1986.[8]

Despite the enactment of the Enterprise Bankruptcy Law, China is still a country that is oriented to a 'rule by man' approach rather than the 'rule of law'. This is reflected in the way that many provisions of the Enterprise Bankruptcy Law were drafted and how the procedures for bankruptcy are implemented in China, as it has a unitary system (rather than one in which there is a separation of powers) under which the government appoints judges and allocates budgets for China's courts,[9] and under which the courts look to the legislature and other political bodies for guidance as to the meaning of a particular law. Inevitably, this will mean that governments at the central and local levels will exert influence over decisions regarding bankruptcy cases made by the courts. This chapter outlines the complex insolvency law regime

---

4 Ibid.

5 Tomasic and Little, supra at 51.

6 Li, supra at 1.

7 Ibid., at 1 and 2.

8 Ibid., at 2.

9 Ibid., at 6.

which exists in China today, discusses the bankruptcy laws which apply to different types of enterprises, the government's involvement in this area, key issues in Chinese bankruptcies, obstacles to the implementation of bankruptcy law and, finally, alternatives to bankruptcy which exist for enterprises in China.

The Insolvency Regime in China: 1986–2004

Like many other areas of law in China, China's insolvency regime has been seen by some to be 'like an onion', with many layers of different laws applicable to different types of companies and situations. Understandably, in many of these situations, there will be uncertainty as to which law or laws apply in a particular situation, and there may also be conflict between different laws. Nevertheless, it is possible to categorize the insolvency regime in China into various categories, as follows: national legislation, opinions of the Supreme People's Court, specific national legislation dealing with particular types of insolvency (such as the insolvency of a bank or a foreign investment vehicle) and regional insolvency regimes. The absence of a comprehensive national insolvency or bankruptcy statute has provided room for these other insolvency law pronouncements and statements to operate.

National Legislation

There are a number of bodies of national legislation dealing with enterprise bankruptcy in China; these include the 1986 Enterprise Bankruptcy Law, the 1986 General Principles of Civil Law of the People's Republic of China, the 1991 Civil Procedure Law and the 2006 Company Law.

Enterprise Bankruptcy Law The Law of the People's Republic of China on Enterprise Bankruptcy (For Trial Implementation) 1986 (effective from 1 November 1988) applies exclusively to 'enterprises owned by the whole people',[10] or state-owned enterprises.[11] It does not apply to the bankruptcy of individuals.

Company Law Chapter X of the 2006 Company Law of the People's Republic of China (effective from 1 July 1999: as amended in October 2005) deals with bankruptcy of a company.[12] Article 2 of the Company Law defines 'company' to be a limited liability company or a joint stock company limited. Both types of companies are regarded as enterprise legal persons.[13]

Civil Procedure Law and General Principles of the Civil Law Chapter XIX of the 1991 Civil Procedure Law of the People's Republic of China (effective from 9 April 1991) deals with the bankruptcy of enterprises as legal persons. The term 'legal

---

10 Article 2, Enterprise Bankruptcy Law.

11 Tomasic and Little, supra at 24.

12 Article 184, Company Law.

13 Ibid., Article 3.

person' has been defined by General Principles of the Civil Law[14] to mean 'an organization that has capacity for civil rights and capacity for civil conduct and independently enjoys civil rights and assumes civil obligations in accordance with the law.'[15] Further, Article 37 of the General Principles stipulates that a legal person shall have the following qualifications:

1. establishment in accordance with the law
2. possession of the necessary property or funds
3. possession of its own name, organization and premises
4. ability to independently bear civil liability.

Article 41 of the General Principles of Civil Law (hereinafter referred to as the 'GPCL') also states that:

> An enterprise under ownership by the whole people or under collective ownership shall be qualified as a legal person when it has sufficient funds as stipulated by the state; has articles of association; an organization and premises; has the ability to independently bear civil liability; and has been approved and registered by the competent authority …

Regarding Chinese-foreign joint ventures (whether equity or contractual) and foreign capital enterprises established within the PRC, Article 41 of the GPCL states that they must also be qualified as legal persons in China and have been approved and registered by the administrative agency for industry and commerce in accordance with the law. Whilst a foreign company is a legal person of the foreign country, its branch in China is not recognized as a legal person in China and therefore does not enjoy such a legal status.[16]

Opinions of the Supreme People's Court

In addition to the national legislation outlined above, the Supreme People's Court of China has issued supplementary opinions regarding the implementation of the Enterprise Bankruptcy Law, the Civil Procedure Law and the Civil Law. These opinions include:

- Supreme People's Court, Law of the People's Republic of China On Enterprise Bankruptcy (For Trial Implementation) 1986 Opinion (7 November 1991) ('Enterprise Bankruptcy Law Opinion')
- Supreme People's Court, Code of the Civil Procedure Law of the People's Republic of China Opinion (14 July 1992) ('Civil Procedure Law Opinion')
- Supreme People's Court, Civil Law General Principles Opinion (26 January 1988) ('Civil Law Opinion')

14 General Principles of Civil Law of the People's Republic of China (effective from 12 April 1986).

15 Article 36, General Principles of Civil Law.

16 Article 196, Company Law.

- Supreme People's Court, 'Provisions on Some Issues concerning the Trial of Enterprise Bankruptcy Cases' (Promulgated 30 June 2002; Effective from 1 September 2002).

National Legislation Dealing with Foreign Investment Vehicles

There is also specific national legislation and various other rules dealing with different types of foreign investment vehicles in China, such as equity joint ventures, cooperative joint ventures and wholly foreign-owned joint ventures. This legislation includes:

- Law of the People's Republic of China on Sino-Foreign Joint Equity Enterprises (effective from 1 July 1979 and amended 4 April 1990)
- Chapter 14 of the Regulations for the Implementation of the Law of the People's Republic of China on Sino-Foreign Joint Equity Enterprises (effective from 20 September 1983 and Article 100 of Chapter 14 amended 15 January 1986)
- Law of the People's Republic of China on Sino-Foreign Cooperative Enterprises (effective from 13 April 1988)
- Detailed Rules for the Implementation of the Law of the People's Republic of China on Sino-Foreign Co-operative Enterprises (effective from 4 September 1995)
- Law of the People's Republic of China Concerning Enterprises with Sole Foreign Investment (effective from 12 April 1986)
- Detailed Rules for the Implementation of the Law of the People's Republic of China on Sole Foreign Investment Enterprises (effective from 12 December 1990).[17]

Furthermore, Chapter VII of the Commercial Banking Law deals with the liquidation and receivership of foreign commercial banks, branches of foreign commercial banks and Sino-foreign equity joint venture commercial banks.[18]

Regional Insolvency Regimes

In addition to general and specific pieces of national legislation and Supreme People's Court opinions, there are also a number of regional insolvency regimes. However, where these local regulations conflict with national laws, the latter will prevail. The most important pieces of regional legislation include:

- Guangdong Province Company Insolvency Regulations (effective from 1 August 1993)
- Shenzhen Special Economic Zone, Enterprise Insolvency Regulations (effective from 1 March 1994)
- Shenzhen Special Economic Zone, Enterprise Liquidation Regulations (effective from 1 October 1995)

---

17 Tomasic and Little, supra at 24.

18 Ibid.

- Shanghai Municipality, Foreign Investment Enterprise Liquidation Procedures (effective from 1 October 1991)
- Beijing Municipality, Foreign Investment Enterprise Liquidation Procedures (effective from 1 June 1992)
- Beijing Municipality, Foreign Investment Enterprise Dissolution Regulations (effective from 15 July 1995)
- Tianjin Municipality, Foreign Investment Enterprises Liquidation Rules (effective from 1 June 1995).

It is also of interest to note that China has had experience with regional bankruptcy courts; for example, in the case of Shenzhen Special Economic Zone, the Third Section of the Economic Division of the Shenzhen Intermediate People's Court, dealing specifically with bankruptcy, was established on 1 December 1993.[19]

Bankruptcy Law in China

As noted above, different national legislation and opinions of the Supreme People's Court apply to different types of enterprises; these will be discussed below.

State-owned Enterprises (SOEs)

The 1986 Enterprise Bankruptcy Law applies exclusively to SOEs; as Article 2 states, 'this Law applies to enterprises owned by the whole people'.[20] Article 3 of this Law stipulates that 'enterprises which, owing to poor operations and management that result in serious losses, are unable to repay debts that are due shall be declared bankrupt in accordance with the provisions of this Law.' Whilst the law provides for bankruptcy of SOEs, in practice, this has been difficult to achieve; as Article 3 further provides that:

> Enterprises for which creditors file for bankruptcy shall *not* be declared bankrupt under any of the following circumstances:
>
> 1. Public utility enterprises and enterprises that have an important relationship to the national economy and the people's livelihood, for which the relevant government departments grant subsidies or adopt other measures to assist the repayment of debts;
> 2. Enterprises that have obtained guarantees for the repayment of debts within six months from the date of the application for bankruptcy.[21]

---

19 Ibid., at 25.

20 In contrast to the current situation prescribed by the Enterprise Bankruptcy Law, the November 2004 version of the Draft Bankruptcy Law currently being considered by the Standing Committee of the 10th National People's Congress would seem to apply to all forms of ownership, whether state-owned or non-state-owned, as there is no express provision contained in the draft indicating its applicability or non-applicability to any type of enterprise/s.

21 Article 3, Enterprise Bankruptcy Law.

The language of Article 3 effectively makes bankruptcy subject to government discretion, in the sense that the government will be the party making a determination on the meaning of phrases such as: 'important relationship', 'national economy', 'the people's livelihood', and on whether or not to grant assistance to repay debts.[22]

Further, Article 3 also blocks bankruptcy where 'enterprises have obtained guarantees for repayment of debts within six months'. According to Chang of the law firm, Paul, Weiss, Rifkind, Wharton and Garrison, in Beijing, whilst this provision is less offensive to creditors, it still lacks details.[23]

Another barrier to mobilizing this 1986 Law is found in Article 17, which states that 'with respect to enterprises for which creditors file for bankruptcy, bankruptcy proceedings shall be suspended if the enterprise's superior departments in charge have applied for reorganization and if the enterprise and its creditors have reached a settlement agreement through consultation.'[24] This effectively gives the bankrupt's department-in-charge two years to 'fashion a reorganization (and, thereby, delay bankruptcy proceedings).'[25]

It seems that much effort has been taken to prevent the SOEs from being declared bankrupt. Another such example is to be found in Article 5, which stipulates that 'bankruptcy cases shall be under the jurisdiction of the people's courts[26] in the location of the debtor.'[27] Article 1 of the Enterprise Bankruptcy Law Opinion supplements the meaning of 'location of the debtor' to mean 'the place of the debtor's domicile'.[28] Debtor's domicile is referred to as 'the place where the debtor has its principal office. If the debtor does not have a principal office, such a case shall be under the jurisdiction of the people's court of the place where the debtor is registered.'[29] Therefore, this makes it inconvenient for the creditor located at a different place to bring bankruptcy proceedings against the debtor.

---

22 The November 2004 Draft of the Bankruptcy Law prescribed a much lower threshold regarding when an enterprise can be liquidated, as Article 2 states 'where enterprise legal persons are unable to pay off the debts due, and their assets are unable to pay off all of their debts or they obviously lack the ability to pay off the debts, they shall be liquidated in accordance with the provisions of this Law.' Therefore, it appears to no longer require government approvals for an enterprise to be declared bankrupt under the Draft Bankruptcy Law.

23 Chang, G., 'Bankruptcy Law in China: Too Much or Too Little?', *China Law and Practice*, June/July 1999, at 23.

24 Article 3, Enterprise Bankruptcy Law.

25 Chang, supra at 23.

26 Article 2 of Bankruptcy Law Opinion stipulates that the basic-level people's courts shall generally have the jurisdiction over bankruptcy cases of enterprises approved by and registered in the administrative organs for industry and commerce of counties, county-level cities or districts. The intermediate people's courts shall generally have the jurisdiction over bankruptcy cases of enterprises approved by and registered in the administrative organs for industry and commerce of prefectures, cities at the prefecture level or above. Enterprise bankruptcy cases under state plans shall be subject to the jurisdiction of the intermediate people's courts.

27 Article 5, Enterprise Bankruptcy Law.

28 This jurisdictional requirement is broadly similar under the Draft Bankruptcy Law, as Article 3 of the Draft Bankruptcy Law also states: 'Bankruptcy cases shall be under the jurisdiction of the people's court or in the place of debtor's domicile'.

29 Article 1, Supreme People's Court, Law of the People's Republic of China On Enterprise Bankruptcy (For Trial Implementation) 1986 Opinion (7 November 1991) ('Enterprise Bankruptcy Law Opinion').

Such obstacles as these are not surprising, given the social implications of bankruptcy and the impact on China's financial system that would result from bankruptcy of unprofitable SOEs; a high percentage of SOEs are in such parlous financial circumstance. According to the World Bank and International Finance Corporation:

> Because of their heavy reliance on bank financing since the mid-1980s, most SOEs are over-indebted and many are insolvent. An assets evaluation organized by the government in the mid-1990s found that nearly 40 per cent of the 302,000 non-financial SOEs were empty shells, in the sense that their debt obligations exceeded their assets. The percentage would certainly be much higher if assets were recorded at their market value and off-balance-sheet liabilities were taken into account.[30]

Further, Article 4 specifically places the burden on the state to take care of employees of bankrupt SOEs, as it provides that 'the state through various means shall arrange for the appropriate reemployment of the staff and workers of bankrupt enterprises and shall guarantee their basic living needs prior to reemployment; specific measures shall be separately stipulated by the State Council.'[31] If all of the SOEs which are suffering 'serious losses and unable to repay debts that are due'[32] are permitted to be declared bankrupt, this would place an extraordinary burden on the State to take care of the employees of those SOEs. Therefore, it is not surprising that many obstacles are in place in China's bankruptcy regime when dealing with SOEs. Such obstacles are evident throughout the provisions in the Enterprise Bankruptcy Law, and they are also reflected in practice.

Having said that, it should be noted that 'since 1994, the central government has changed its approach to reforming SOEs from attempting to revitalize every single SOE to saving only the viable ones and preserving the overall sector.'[33] This is a major step forward.

Submission and acceptance of bankruptcy applications Under the Enterprise Bankruptcy Law in China, both the creditor and the debtor have the right to file bankruptcy applications.[34]

A creditor has the right to file an application to declare the debtor bankrupt pursuant to Article 7 where the debtor is unable to repay debts that are due.[35] When the creditor is submitting a bankruptcy application, it must provide relevant evidence

---

30 Tenev, S. and Zhang, C., 'Corporate Governance and Enterprise Reform in China: Building the Institutions of Modern Markets', *The World Bank and International Financial Corporation*, 2000, at 29–30 (http://www2.ifc.org/publications/pubs/corp_gov/China-Corp-Cov.pdf – website accessed on 24 October 2003).

31 Such provision is absent in the Draft Bankruptcy Law.

32 Article 3, Enterprise Bankruptcy Law.

33 Li, S., 'Bankruptcy Law in China: Lessons of the Past Twelve Years' (http://www.fas.harvard.edu/~asiactr/haq/200101/0101a006.htm – website accessed on 31 January 2003).

34 The situation appears similar under the Draft Bankruptcy Law, as both debtor and creditor also have the right to file such application – Article 9, Draft Bankruptcy Law.

35 The equivalent provision in Draft Bankruptcy Law is Article 9.

relating to the amount of the claim, whether or not it is secured with property, and in regard to the inability of the debtor to repay debts that are due.[36] A detailed list of material to be submitted by the creditor to the People's Court is set out in Article 7 of the Enterprise Bankruptcy Law Opinion.

Debtors, on the other hand, also have the right to file a bankruptcy application.[37] Article 8 provides that:

> The debtor, upon the agreement of the superior departments in charge, may apply for the declaration of bankruptcy. When the debtor is submitting the bankruptcy application, it shall explain the circumstances of the enterprise's losses and deliver relevant accounting statements, a detailed list of debts and a detailed list of claims.[38]

The detailed list of information to be submitted by the debtor to the people's court is stipulated by Article 6 of the Enterprise Bankruptcy Law Opinion.

After the People's Court has accepted a bankruptcy case, it must notify the debtor within ten days and make a public announcement.[39] Within ten days of receiving the detailed list of debts provided by the debtor, the people's court must notify all known creditors. A public announcement and notice must stipulate the date of the first convening of the creditors' meeting.[40]

After the public announcement is made by the court, creditors have the burden of reporting their claims to the court, as Article 9 states that:

> Creditors who have been notified shall, within one month after receiving the notice, and creditors who have not been notified shall, within three months after the date of the public announcement, report their claims to the people's court and explain the amount of the claims, as well as whether or not they are secured with property, and also deliver relevant materials of proof.[41]

Most importantly, 'creditors who do not report their claims during these periods shall be deemed to have automatically abandoned their claims.'[42]

Settlement and reorganization China's reluctance to bankrupt SOEs is also reflected in the fact that Chapter IV of the Bankruptcy Law provides for the making of

---

36 Article 7, Enterprise Bankruptcy Law.

37 The Draft Bankruptcy Law also provides an equivalent provision, Article 9.

38 Article 8, Enterprise Bankruptcy Law.

39 The procedures for acceptance appear to be different under the Draft Bankruptcy Law, as it has provided a timeline for the courts to comply; for example, Article 12 provides 'the people's court shall decide whether or not to accept the application within fifteen days ... Where it need be prolonged in special cases, it may prolong fifteen days subject to approval of the superior people's court.' This appears to be designed to make the courts more accountable and to avoid delays in dealing with bankruptcy cases, as would be possible under the current regime.

40 Article 9, Enterprise Bankruptcy Law. (This timeline would be shortened to five days by Article 12 of the Draft Bankruptcy Law.)

41 Ibid.

42 Ibid.

a settlement between the creditor and debtor and the reorganization of the debtor enterprise.

Article 17 stipulates that where the creditor has applied for the bankruptcy of a particular debtor enterprise, the superior departments in charge of the debtor's enterprise may, within three months of the people's court accepting the case, apply to carry out the reorganization of the enterprise;[43] and the period of reorganization must not exceed two years.[44]

After the enterprise and the creditors' meeting have reached a settlement agreement which has been recognized by the people's court, the court must make a public announcement and suspend the bankruptcy proceedings.[45]

Creditors do not have a great deal of involvement in the reorganization process, as 'the reorganization of the enterprise shall be supervised by its superior departments in charge.'[46] Further, 'the reorganization plan of the enterprise shall be discussed by a congress of the staff and workers of the enterprise.'[47] It is only the circumstances of the reorganization which are required to be reported periodically to the creditors' meetings.[48]

Where an enterprise has undergone reorganization and is able to repay debts in accordance with the settlement agreement, the people's court will terminate the bankruptcy proceedings for such an enterprise, and also make a public announcement to this effect.[49]

Whilst the provisions dealing with the settlement agreement and reorganization appear to suggest China's desire to protect SOEs and hence a reluctance to bankrupt them, the Enterprise Bankruptcy Law also provides for the declaration of bankruptcy of these enterprises where the following circumstances arise during the period of reorganization:

1. The enterprise is not implementing the settlement agreement
2. The enterprise has continued to worsen its financial condition, for which reason the creditors' meeting has applied for the termination of reorganization

---

43 Article 17, Enterprise Bankruptcy Law. (The Draft Bankruptcy Law allows for different applicants to apply for reorganization. Instead of the 'superior department in charge of the enterprise' as stipulated by Article 17 of current law, the Draft law permits the 'debtor or the investor who holds more than one-tenth of the debtor's registered capital' to apply for reorganization – Article 65, Draft Bankruptcy Law. This shows China's effort to move from a planned economy towards a market economy.)

44 Article 17, Enterprise Bankruptcy Law.

45 Ibid., Article 19.

46 Ibid., Article 20. (This is in contrast with the Draft Bankruptcy Law which prescribes that such supervision be carried out by the administrator subject to the approval of the people's court (Article 69). In accordance with Article 19 of the Draft Bankruptcy Law, an administrator shall be designated by the people's court. Therefore, it demonstrates China's desire and effort to move away from rule by man (evidenced by the current regime of reorganization supervised by its superior department in charge) to rule of law (shown by the court's involvement in appointing an administrator to supervise reorganization).)

47 Ibid.

48 Ibid.

49 Ibid., Article 22.

3. The enterprise has committed any of the acts listed in Article 35[50] and has caused serious harm to the interests of creditors.[51]

Further, Article 22 provides that 'with respect to an enterprise that, on the expiration of the period of reorganization, is unable to repay debts in accordance with the settlement agreement, the people's court shall declare the enterprise bankrupt, and shall re-register the claims in accordance with Article 9.'[52] The Enterprise Bankruptcy Law Opinion also deals with the situation where the debtor does not repay all debts in accordance with the contents of the settlement agreement, and permits creditors to apply to the people's court for compulsory execution.[53] Further, the Opinion also states that 'where the debtor does not or is unable to implement the [settlement] agreement, the people's court shall, upon application by creditors, order the resumption of the bankruptcy proceedings.'[54]

Bankruptcy declarations and bankruptcy liquidations Chapter V of the Enterprise Bankruptcy Law provides for bankruptcy declarations and the liquidation of enterprises. Thus, Article 23 stipulates that:

---

50 Article 35 stipulates:

> During the period from six months before the people's court accepts the bankruptcy case until the date that bankruptcy is declared, the following actions of bankrupt enterprise are null and void:
>
> 1. Concealment, secret distributions or transfer of property without compensation;
> 2. Sale of property at abnormally depressed prices;
> 3. Securing with property claims that originally were not secured with property;
> 4. Early repayment of claims that are not yet due; and,
> 5. Abandonment of the enterprise's own claims.

51 Article 21, Enterprise Bankruptcy Law. This is in contrast to the Draft Bankruptcy Law which, whilst also providing for the grounds to declare a debtor bankrupt, the grounds for such are different and include the following:

1. the situation of management and finance of the debtor continue deteriorating and the possibility or save it lacks;
2. the debtor conducts fraud, decreasing the enterprise's property maliciously, delaying without reasons, or other behaviors that apparently are disadvantageous to creditors;
3. the behaviors of the debtor lead to the administrator being unable to perform his duties. (Article 76, Draft Bankruptcy Law.)

It is also important to note that the Draft Bankruptcy Law also seems to further demonstrate China's desire to move towards 'rule of law', as the court is only permitted to terminate the reorganization procedure and declare debtor bankruptcy after 'confirmation by trial' (Article 76). This is in contrast to the existing regime where such actions may be exercised 'upon judgment of the people's court' (Article 21, Enterprise Bankruptcy Law).

52 Article 22, Enterprise Bankruptcy Law.

53 Article 26, Enterprise Bankruptcy Law Opinion.

54 Ibid., Article 27.

> In any of the following circumstances, after the judgment of the people's court, an enterprise shall be declared bankrupt:
>
> 1. If, in accordance with the provisions of Article 3 of this Law, it should be declared bankrupt;
> 2. If reorganization has been terminated in accordance with the provisions of Article 21 of this Law; and,
> 3. If, upon the expiration of the period of reorganization, it is unable to repay debts in accordance with the settlement agreement.[55]

Article 3 of the Enterprise Bankruptcy Law states that 'enterprises which, owing to poor operations and management that result in serious losses, are unable to repay the debts that are due shall be declared bankrupt in accordance with the provisions of this Law.' Article 31 of the Enterprise Bankruptcy Law Opinion defines the term 'unable to repay the debts that are due' to mean that 'the period for the implementation of the debts has expired and the debtor obviously lacks the capacity to repay the debts.'[56] Further, where the debtor ceases repaying the debts that are due and this situation continues, it may be presumed that the debtor is 'unable to repay the debts that are due', provided that there is no contrary evidence.[57] However, the terms of 'poor operations and management' and 'serious losses' are not defined.

Liquidation team When an enterprise is declared bankrupt, the people's court must establish a liquidation team to take over the bankrupt enterprise within 15 days after such a declaration is made.[58] The liquidation team shall be 'responsible for the keeping, putting into order, appraisal, disposition and distribution of the bankruptcy property. The liquidation team may carry out necessary civil actions in accordance with the law.'[59]

Article 50 of the Enterprise Bankruptcy Law Opinion supplements the duty of the liquidation team to include the following:

1. Take over the bankrupt enterprise
2. Clean up the bankrupt enterprise's properties, work out the supporting schedule of properties, the balance sheet and the detailed list of the claims and debts, and organize and appraise, auction and dispose of the bankruptcy properties
3. Recover the bankrupt enterprise's properties, and exercise the rights to properties against the bankrupt enterprise's debtor or property holders in accordance with the law
4. Manage and dispose of the bankruptcy properties, and decide on whether to implement contracts or carry out their operation within the scope of the liquidation; and confirm the rights to exemption, offset and recapture

55 Article 23, Enterprise Bankruptcy Law.
56 Article 31, Enterprise Bankruptcy Law Opinion.
57 Ibid.
58 Article 2, Enterprise Bankruptcy Law and Article 47, Enterprise Bankruptcy Law Opinion.
59 Article 2, Enterprise Bankruptcy Law.

5. Carry out the entrusted appraisal, auction of the bankruptcy properties and other related work
6. Propose and execute the proposals on disposition and distribution of the bankruptcy properties in accordance with the law
7. Submit the liquidation report
8. Represent the bankrupt enterprise to participate in litigation and arbitrations
9. Carry out the cancellation of registration of the enterprise and other bankruptcy termination matters
10. Complete other matters designated by the people's court in accordance with the law.[60]

Article 24 of the Enterprise Bankruptcy Law stipulates the composition of the liquidation team and states that:

> The members of the liquidation team shall be designated by the people's court from among the superior departments in charge, government finance departments, and other relevant departments and professional personnel. The liquidation team may hire necessary work personnel and is responsible to, and shall report its work to, the people's court.[61]

Article 48 of the Enterprise Bankruptcy Law Opinion supplements this by stating that:

> The members of the liquidation team may be selected from the higher-level department in charge of the bankrupt enterprise, the liquidation intermediation institutions, the accountants and lawyers, or be selected upon designation from the governmental departments of finance, industrial and commercial administration, planning, economy, auditing, taxation, price, labor, social insurance, land administration, state asset administration and personnel, etc. The branches (sub-branches) of the people's bank may send persons to participate in the liquidation team in accordance with the relevant provisions.[62]

Further:

> The liquidation team may, upon consent of the people's court, retain such intermediation institutions as bankruptcy liquidation institution, law firm, accounting firm, etc. to undertake certain bankruptcy liquidation work. The intermediation institutions shall be responsible to the liquidation team with respect to the liquidation work.[63]

Bankruptcy property Article 28 of the Enterprise Bankruptcy Law provides that the bankruptcy property[64] comprises the following:

---

60 Article 50, Enterprise Bankruptcy Law Opinion.

61 Article 24, Enterprise Bankruptcy Law. (The provision regarding the establishment of a liquidation team is absent in the Draft Bankruptcy Law.)

62 Article 48, Enterprise Bankruptcy Law Opinion.

63 Ibid., Article 49.

64 Article 28 of the Draft Bankruptcy Law provides that 'all the property that belongs to the debtor at the time when the bankruptcy case is accepted and the property the debtor obtains after the acceptance of the bankruptcy case but before the termination of bankruptcy procedures, shall be the debtor's property.'

- all property that the bankrupt enterprise operated and managed at the time that the bankruptcy was declared
- property obtained by the bankrupt enterprise during the period from the declaration of bankruptcy until the conclusion of the bankruptcy proceedings
- other property rights that the bankrupt enterprise should exercise.[65]

Property that already constitutes security collateral is not regarded as bankruptcy property.[66] However, the portion of the value of the security collateral exceeding the amount of the debt that it secures is regarded as bankrupt property.[67]

Article 71 of the Enterprise Bankruptcy Law Opinion also supplements this by stating that the following properties shall not belong to bankruptcy properties:

- the properties of others which are occupied or used by the debtor on the basis of any of such legal relationships as warehouse keeping, storage, contract for processing, entrusted transaction, sale by proxy, loan for use, deposit, lease, etc.
- mortgaged, retained and pledged properties, with the exception of the part remaining from the obligee's waiving the right to receive repayment in priority or from payment of guaranteed claims in priority
- such subrogated things as insurance, compensation, indemnity, etc. that have occurred after the guaranteed properties are lost
- the properties with priority in accordance with the legal provisions, with the exception of the part that has remained from the obligee's waiving their right to receive repayment in priority or from payment of particular claims in priority
- the properties which have been sold and the titles of those have not been transferred, however, the purchasers have already paid the full consideration
- the properties which have been delivered to the other party but whose property right certificate has not been obtained or the formalities on transfer of the name of the property right have not been completed
- the properties over which the debtor has not obtained ownership from the sale or preservation of ownership
- the properties over which the state has the exclusive ownership and cannot be transferred
- the properties owned by the work unit of the bankrupt enterprise.[68]

If the properties or property rights (such as things, claims, intellectual properties) are jointly owned by the debtor and others, then such property must be partitioned in the bankruptcy liquidation, and the part owned by the debtor will belong to bankruptcy properties.[69] If such properties cannot be partitioned, then the debtor must transfer

---

Further, 'after the people's court accepts the bankruptcy case, the secondary debtor shall pay off its debts and deliver the property to the administrator.'

65 Article 28, Enterprise Bankruptcy Law and Article 64, Enterprise Bankruptcy Law Opinion.

66 Article 28, Enterprise Bankruptcy Law.

67 Ibid.

68 Article 71, Enterprise Bankruptcy Law Opinion.

69 Ibid., Article 65.

the part which it owns, and the proceeds from the transfer will belong to the pool of bankruptcy properties.[70]

Whilst China's bankruptcy laws seem to be well-drafted for the purpose of determining whether something is bankrupt property, there are serious practical problems in making such determinations. According to Chen,[71] there are two types of property which have caused most difficulty – land and other state-affiliated facilities, such as schools, hospitals and nurseries. With respect to land, in 1949, the Communist government seized ownership of all land in China. As land belongs exclusively to the state, no real market existed for real property in China at the time. However, in the 1990s, the national government realized that real estate plays an important economic role. 'Land use' rights started to be capable of being conveyed. In light of the fact that most enterprises received land from the state for free, the law provides that, under these circumstances, the land should revert back to the state upon termination or expiration of the 'use'. When this reversion occurs, the state should pay proper compensation for any buildings on the land and any fixtures.[72] However, according to Chen, the term 'proper compensation' has an elastic meaning and he concluded that 'a more likely scenario is that the government will simply take the land back and the creditor will receive nothing.'[73] In relation to other state-affiliated facilities, Chen also observes that:

> Unlike Western society, every state-run factory constitutes an independent society. Schools, hospitals, nurseries, and other facilities all belong to the enterprise. Should these assets be included in the bankruptcy estate? The majority view asserts that because these facilities exist for the employee's welfare, they cannot be treated as part of the bankruptcy estate. Again, the law is ambiguous.[74]

Bankruptcy claims These are defined as 'claims not secured with property and claims secured with property for which the priority right to receive repayment has been abandoned, which were established before bankruptcy was declared.'[75] Further, the expenses of creditors incurred while participating in the bankruptcy proceedings may not constitute bankruptcy claims.[76]

The Enterprise Bankruptcy Law Opinion also supplements this definition, as Article 55 of the Opinion provides that the following claims will be treated as being covered by bankruptcy claims:

- claims occurring prior to the bankruptcy declaration but not guaranteed with property

---

70 Ibid.

71 Feng Chen is a Professor of Law at Sichuan Union University, Chengdu, Sichuan.

72 Chen, F., 'Chinese Bankruptcy Law: Milestones and Challenges', 31 *St. Mary's Law Journal* 49, 1999.

73 Ibid.

74 Ibid.

75 Article 30, Enterprise Bankruptcy Law.

76 Ibid.

- claims occurring prior to the bankruptcy declaration and which are guaranteed with property, but in regard to which the creditors waive the right to receive repayment in priority
- the excessive amount of a claim occurring prior to the bankruptcy declaration, which are guaranteed with property, but the amount of the claim exceeds the value of the guaranteed properties
- claims occurring in the circumstance where the drawer of a negotiable instrument is declared bankrupt, but the drawee or the acceptor makes the payment or acceptance to the holder without knowledge of these facts
- claims occurring upon rescission of the contract by the liquidation team, which are to be enjoyed by the other party in accordance with the law or as stipulated in the contract, and which may be calculated by currency of the debtor
- claims occurring from the debtor's handling of trust matters made for the debtor's benefit after the bankruptcy of the debtor
- claims formed from the debtor's issuance of bonds
- claims which the debtor's surety may recover from the debtor after repaying the debts for the debtor
- claims which the debtor's surety reports for a pre-existing right of recourse in accordance with Article 32 of the Guaranty Law of the PRC
- if the debtor is a surety, the suretyship liability which has been determined by an effective legal document prior to the bankruptcy declaration
- the indemnity liability occurring under the circumstance that the debtor causes property losses to others prior to the bankruptcy declaration due to an act of tort or breach
- other claims ratified by the people's court.[77]

The Supreme People's Court's Enterprise Bankruptcy Law Opinion also supplements the Enterprise Bankruptcy Law by stating that the following claims shall not belong to bankruptcy claims:

- fines and other relevant expenses imposed by administrative or judicial organs upon the bankrupt enterprise
- the fee for the debtor's late payment of a payable amount after the people's court's acceptance of a bankruptcy case, including the fee for the debtor's late payment of the interest for delay or labour insurance which should be doubled due to its failure to execute an effective legal document
- interest on the debts after the bankruptcy declaration
- the expenses paid by creditors for participating in the bankruptcy proceedings
- the share rights of the bankrupt enterprise, and the rights of the stockholders on their share rights and stocks
- the claims reported to the liquidation team after the distribution of the bankruptcy property began
- the claims having exceeded the limitation of action

77 Article 55, Enterprise Bankruptcy Law Opinion.

- the management fee and contract fee that the manager of the debtor has not collected from the debtor.[78]

Furthermore, funds gratuitously allocated by the government to the debtor do not belong to bankruptcy claims.[79] However, the money granted by administrative departments of finance, poverty reduction, scientific management and technological management, etc., through the conclusion of contracts and pursuant to the principles of paid use and regular return, may be regarded as bankruptcy claims.[80]

Priority in bankruptcy property distribution Article 34 of the Enterprise Bankruptcy Law provides that priority will be given to the following bankruptcy expenses:

- the expenses needed for the management, sale and distribution of the bankruptcy property, including the expenses of hiring work personnel
- the litigation expenses of the bankruptcy case
- other expenses paid in the course of bankruptcy proceedings for the common interest of creditors.[81]

With respect to enterprises whose bankruptcy property is insufficient to cover bankruptcy expenses, the people's court will terminate bankruptcy proceedings.[82] Article 37 provides that the distribution plan for the bankruptcy property must be proposed by the liquidation team, adopted by the creditors' meeting and submitted to the people's court for judgment before implementation. Further, after the prior deduction of bankruptcy expenses from the bankruptcy property, repayment must be made in the following order:

1. wages of staff and workers and labour insurance expenses that are owed by the bankruptcy enterprise
2. taxes that are owed by the bankrupt enterprise
3. bankruptcy claims.[83]

---

78 Ibid., Article 61.

79 Ibid., Article 62.

80 Ibid.

81 Article 34, Enterprise Bankruptcy Law.

82 Ibid.

83 Ibid., Article 37. (Article 127 of the Draft Bankruptcy Law provides for a slightly more comprehensive list of the order of priority in the distribution of bankruptcy property by stating:

> After bankruptcy expenses and common benefits are paid preferentially, the repayment order shall be as follows:
>
> 1. salaries of staff and employees and basic social insurance fees owed by the bankrupt as well as compensation that should be paid to staff and employees provided by law and regulation;
> 2. taxes owed by the bankrupt; and
> 3. common bankruptcy credits.

Where the bankruptcy property is insufficient to meet all the repayment needs within a single order of priority, it must be distributed on a pro-rata basis.[84]

In practice, 'secured creditors have a long way to go before they realize the true value of their security.'[85] Since the enactment of the Enterprise Bankruptcy Law, the State Council has issued (on 2 March 1997) the Supplementary Notice on Issues Concerning the Trial Implementation in Several Cities of State-owned Enterprises Bankruptcy and Merger and Re-employment of Staff and Workers (the '1997 Notice'). According to Chang,[86] the 1997 Notice is at odds with the scheme for the distribution of assets contained in the Enterprise Bankruptcy Law and is also inconsistent with some of the NPC's other enactments, namely the PRC, Security Law and the Civil Procedure Law. The 1997 Notice, in general outline, provides that resettlement expenses of workers of a bankrupt enterprise located in any of 111 cities, including Guangzhou and Shenzhen, are to be provided for first. This is done by taking revenues from the disposition of land use rights, even if such rights are encumbered for the benefit of creditors (Article 5). If such revenues are insufficient, revenues can be taken from unencumbered property and then from other encumbered property.[87]

If this were not enough, Article 5 of the 1997 Notice also deems workers' living expenses to be administrative expenses of a bankruptcy: this enjoys a high priority according to Article 34 of the Enterprise Bankruptcy Law.[88] Therefore, it seems that, in practice, secured creditors do have a long way to go before being able to recover the value of their security.

Companies

Bankruptcy of companies (whether a limited liability company or a joint-stock company incorporated within the territory of the People's Republic of China in accordance with this Law)[89] is dealt with by Chapter X of the Company Law of the People's Republic of China (as amended in October 2005, with effect from 1 January 2006).[90] As with the relevant provisions in the Enterprise Bankruptcy Law (dealing with bankruptcy of SOEs), Article 184 of the Company Law provides that 'where a company is to be dissolved in accordance with the provisions of item (1), (2), (4) or (5) of Article 181, a liquidation committee shall be formed within 15 days after the reason for the dissolution occurs and commences the liquidation.'[91] The roles of the

84 Ibid.

85 Chang, G., 'Examination of Technical Bankruptcy Issues Crucial for GITIC Creditors', *China Law and Practice*, February 1999, at 68.

86 Ibid.

87 Chang, supra.

88 Ibid.

89 Article 2, Company Law.

90 As discussed above, the Draft Bankruptcy Law would apply to all kinds of companies, whether state-owned or non-state-owned. Therefore, it would appear that if the Draft Bankruptcy Law is enacted, there would no longer be different laws which would apply to different kinds of companies, as is the case under the current regime.

91 Article 184, Company Law.

liquidation committee are stipulated by Article 185, and these are comparable to the roles that the liquidation team is expected to play in the case of the bankruptcy of SOEs, as stipulated by the Enterprise Bankruptcy Law. However, unlike the Bankruptcy Law, the Company Law not only provides for the bankruptcy of companies, it also provides for the dissolution of such entities.[92]

Enterprises as Legal Persons

Procedures for the bankruptcy of enterprises as legal persons are governed by Chapter XIX of the PRC Civil Procedure Law (effective 9 April 1991). As outlined above, a 'legal person' has been defined by Article 36 of the General Principles of Civil Law[93] to mean 'an organization that has capacity for civil rights and capacity for civil conduct and independently enjoys civil rights and assumes civil obligations in accordance with the law.'[94] Further, Article 37 states that:

> A legal person must be qualified by reference to the following criteria:
>
> 1. It must be established in accordance with the law
> 2. It must possess the necessary property or funds
> 3. It must possess its own name, organization and premises
> 4. It must have the ability to independently bear civil liability.[95]

Article 41 of the General Principles of Civil Law also stipulates that:

> An enterprise under ownership by the whole people or under collective ownership shall be qualified as a legal person when it has sufficient funds as stipulated by the state; has articles of association; and organization and premises; has the ability to independently bear civil liability; and has been approved and registered by the competent authority.[96]

A Chinese-foreign joint venture (equity or contractual) or foreign capital enterprise established within the People's Republic of China will also be qualified as a legal person in China, if it has the qualifications of a legal person and has been approved and registered by the administrative agency for industry and commerce in accordance with the law.[97] It is important to note that, in relation to the branch of a foreign company in China, Article 196 of the Company Law expressly stipulates that 'A branch established by a foreign company within the territory of the People's Republic of China shall not have the status of a Chinese legal person. A foreign company shall bear civil liability for the operational activities engaged in by its branch within the territory of the People's Republic of China.'[98]

---

92 Ibid., Article 181.

93 General Principles of Civil Law of the PRC (effective 12 April 1986) ('Civil Law').

94 Article 36, Civil Law

95 Ibid., Article 37.

96 Ibid., Article 41.

97 Ibid.

98 Article 196, Company Law.

Bankruptcy procedures Article 199 of the Civil Procedure Law provides that 'if an enterprise as legal person is in serious losses and unable to repay the debts that are due, the creditors may apply to a people's court to declare the debtor's bankruptcy repayment, the debtor may also file at a people's court to declare bankruptcy repayment.'[99] The procedures for declaring and ordering bankruptcy, formation and composition of a liquidation team, settlement and reorganization, priority in repayment and jurisdiction for bankruptcy cases[100] under the Civil Procedure Law are similar, if not identical, to those under the Enterprise Bankruptcy Law, except that the Civil Procedure Law is more brief and contains fewer provisions.

One difference though, arises in relation to enterprises as legal persons:

> With respect to property that already constitutes security for such obligatory rights as loan from a bank and for other surety, the bank and other creditors shall have priority in receiving repayment with respect to such security or other surety. If the value of the security and other surety exceeds the amount of debts that they secure, the exceeding portion shall be the bankruptcy repayment property.[101]

This may be contrasted with Article 28 of the Enterprise Bankruptcy Law, where it is prescribed that 'property that already constitutes security collateral is not bankruptcy property; the portion of the value of the security collateral exceeding the amount of the debt that it secures is bankruptcy property.'[102]

Enterprises as Legal Persons Owned by the Whole People

Confusion often occurs where some enterprises are within the definition of 'legal persons' under the General Principles of Civil Law and the Civil Procedures Law, but are also 'owned by the whole people' (i.e., SOEs that are also legal persons). Article 206 of the Civil Procedure Law resolves this puzzle by stating that 'with respect to the procedure for bankruptcy repayment of enterprises owned by the whole people, the provisions of the Law of the People's Republic of China on Enterprise Bankruptcy (Bankruptcy Law) shall apply.'[103]

Article 206 also states that 'with respect to enterprises without legal personality, individual businesses, leasehold farm households and individual partnerships, the provisions of this Chapter shall not apply.'[104] However, it fails to specify which laws will apply with respect to the bankruptcy of these types of enterprises.

With respect to the bankruptcy of state-owned companies (whether a limited liability company or a joint-stock company owned by the whole people), it is less clear which laws would apply.

Where creditors have a choice between the application of the Enterprise Bankruptcy Law and the Civil Procedure Law, one very important consideration

---

99 Article 199, Civil Procedure Law.

100 Articles 200 to 202 and Articles 204 and 205, Civil Procedure Law.

101 Article 203, Civil Procedure Law.

102 Article 28, Enterprise Bankruptcy Law.

103 Article 206, Civil Procedure Law.

104 Ibid.

in choosing a law is the right to appeal.[105] According to Chang, the Enterprise Bankruptcy Law Opinion takes the position that creditors do not have appeal rights in bankruptcy proceedings (except where a people's court rejects a bankruptcy petition).[106] Chang further argues that 'the theoretical underpinning for this position is dubious with regard to proceedings under the Bankruptcy Law.'[107] This is illustrated by the recent insolvency of GITIC (Guangdong International Trust and Investment Company).[108]

The Civil Procedure Law Opinion, in Article 252, also adopts this 'no appeal' rule. According to Chang, 'that position, unlike the position of the Bankruptcy Law Opinion, is defensible in this regard.'[109] Chang drew his conclusion by reviewing the table of contents of that law, which is as follows: a litigant's appeal rights (found in Chapter XIV), a litigant's retrial rights (Chapter XVI), and the bankruptcy provisions (Chapter XIX) are all found in Part II (Trial Procedure). Chang then commented that, 'If the National People's Congress, China's legislature, intended appeal and retrial rights to apply to bankruptcy proceedings, it should have put the bankruptcy chapter in a different portion of the law (or included appropriate cross references).'[110] He further stated that 'as now organized, the appeal and retrial rights appear to apply to all civil litigation except those special proceedings (such as bankruptcy proceedings that are authorized by Part II).'[111] He then concluded that 'although this analysis assumes that the drafters of the Civil Procedure Law intended that the organization of that statute have substantive significance, it nonetheless gives a basis for Civil Procedure Law Opinion.'[112]

Key Issues in Chinese Bankruptcies

Professor Li Shuguang has previously served as an expert advisor on bankruptcy and reorganization in China's State Economic and Trade Committee, and as an expert advisor on enterprise merger and bankruptcy for the World Bank and the Asian Development Bank, and has participated in the drafting of the new Bankruptcy Law. He has reviewed the lessons arising from experience during a dozen years since the passing of the 1986 law and identified thirteen key issues from these in Chinese bankruptcies.[113] Professor Li's key issues are as follows:

105 Chang, supra at 24.
106 Ibid.
107 Ibid.
108 See further in note 85.
109 Chang, supra at 24.
110 Ibid.
111 Ibid.
112 Ibid.
113 Li, S., supra note 33, http://www.fas.harvard.edu/~asiactr/haq/200101/0101a006.htm – website accessed on 31 January 2003.

1 In Regards to the Government's Excessive Role in Bankruptcies

It had been stated that the Chinese government plays a 'special role' in enterprise bankruptcies in China. Li notes that the government's role is both

> … dominant and multi-faceted in SOE bankruptcies. It initiates these bankruptcies, yet at the same time, is the policymaker, the leader, and the direct operator in them. The government not only controls their number, scale, and speed, but also decides what industries and trades are covered under the bankruptcy law. It also covers the costs of SOE bankruptcies.[114]

2 The Court's Role in Bankruptcies

Professor Li also observed that as the government grants the power to the court with respect to bankruptcy matters, particularly as the government appoints judges and allocates budget for courts, the courts are not independent from the government. Without approval by the government, courts are often hesitant to accept and hear bankruptcy cases. Further, the majority of Chinese judges are not experienced in dealing with bankruptcy cases because Chinese courts had never dealt with a single bankruptcy case prior to the implementation of the Enterprise Bankruptcy Law in 1988.[115]

3 Who is the Real Debtor?

It has also been commented by Li that as the ownership structure of SOEs is not clear, it is difficult to identify the real debtor. Whilst SOEs are technically 'owned by the state', it is unclear as to who represents the state in exercising its ownership. Further, SOEs are often owned by multiple governmental entities that frequently evade their responsibilities when an SOE is faced with bankruptcy. Parent-subsidiary relationships add additional complexity. In practice, many SOEs are not independent legal persons even though they are powerful enterprises. It is often the case that an SOE and its subsidiaries have business relationships without ever establishing any clear legal relationships.[116]

4 The Anti-bankruptcy Stance of Creditors

On this point, Li notes that creditors often have difficulty recovering debts from bankrupt SOEs. Current policy requires that money recovered from a bankrupt SOE be used to settle employees first. As there is often little money left after employee settlement, the state-owned banks, which are often hardest hit by bankruptcy, therefore often oppose SOEs' efforts to file for bankruptcy.[117]

---

114 Ibid., at 6.
115 Ibid.
116 Ibid., at 6–7.
117 Ibid., at 7.

5 Difficulties in Settling Employees

An issue central to bankruptcy is employee settlement. Li Shuguang notes that 'Employee settlement is the most difficult and thorny issue in SOE bankruptcies.'[118] The problem is manifold. First, SOE employees are reluctant to accept bankruptcy because bankruptcy means that they lose their identity as state employees, and thus lose their 'right' of having an 'Iron Rice Bowl', or lifetime employment. Second, when an enterprise is bankrupt, laid-off employees become a serious potential source of social instability, particularly as China does not seem to have an adequate social welfare system. Third, questions remain concerning the logistics and terms of settlement, such as, how should employees be settled? Where does the money for employee settlement come from? Should the government be responsible for the settlement or should the employees find their own way out? Fourth, the legal rights and interests of employees of the bankrupt enterprises are not protected due to the lack of contract enforcement mechanisms.[119]

6 Scarcity of Professional Intermediary Service Organizations Involved in Bankruptcy Cases

Whilst Article 48 of the Enterprise Bankruptcy Law Opinion permits the professionals to be involved in dealing with bankruptcy, Professor Li has commented that the use of such professional services are uncommon and rudimentary in China. The majority of Chinese liquidation professionals lack experience in handling complicated bankruptcies, resulting in low efficiency and high cost for their work. Only a few law firms and accounting firms have been involved in bankruptcy cases. Moreover, there is no trustee system for handling bankruptcies.[120]

7 Inadequacy of the Bankruptcy Law and Policies

Professor Li also observed that the existing Bankruptcy Law is difficult to implement, as much of its content does not adequately address the complex economic realities of China. On this point, he noted that the SOE bankruptcy procedures are vague and those governing non-SOE bankruptcies are deficient. Further, there is no legal basis for filing bankruptcy for a natural person, partnership, or corporation. In addition, there are conflicts and inconsistencies between the Bankruptcy Law and existing government policies.[121]

8 Fake Bankruptcy Cases

It has been commented by Professor Li that some enterprises dodge their liabilities by declaring bankruptcy after dividing their businesses and changing licences. Li

118 Ibid., at 8.
119 Ibid., at 8.
120 Li, supra at 8.
121 Ibid., at 8.

observed that a large number of enterprises practise ill-will bankruptcy – a 'disappearance act from an entangled situation' – they shift their assets and repudiate their debts by taking advantage of the bankruptcy procedure.[122]

Such a view has been echoed by Chang in which he commented that 'in some parts of China, local authorities encourage debtors to declare bankruptcy to avoid paying banks and creditors from other provinces.'[123]

9 Confusing Guarantee Relations

Furthermore,

> In China, enterprises often give unsubstantiated guarantees to each other, resulting in duplicate pledges of the same asset. Guarantees are often given without careful documentation, creating hidden liabilities that lead to chain reaction bankruptcies. One reason for such confusing guarantee relations is that governmental administrative agencies designate guarantees.[124]

10 Difficulty of Evaluating Creditors' Rights and Liabilities

Professor Li noted another difficulty, which arises from the unsound accounting system for SOEs, thereby making it difficult to accurately ascertain creditors' rights and liabilities. Further, it appears that enterprises in China often keep two books – their own accounting books and their 'official' book, thereby making it extremely burdensome for creditors to produce concrete evidence from accounting records to substantiate their claims. In addition, a two-year statute of limitation exists for allowing creditors to assert their rights in courts. To complicate things further, government funding to SOEs could be converted into debt upon the occurrence of certain triggering events, making the nature of liabilities unclear.[125]

In a book titled *Corporate Governance and Enterprise Reform in China: Building the Institutions of Modern Markets*, published by the World Bank and International Finance Corporation,[126] the authors commented that:

> The incomplete and vague legal framework for bankruptcy remains a severe constraint to the influence that creditor banks might otherwise have over insolvent debtors. As one banker put it, the only hope for substantial recovery of unsecured credit is to 'react immediately to early distress signals and obtain immediate payment or additional collateral by using all kinds of threats against the firm and its managers and owners as long as they are legal.'[127]

---

122 Ibid., at 9.

123 Chang, supra at 24.

124 Li, supra at 9.

125 Ibid.

126 Tenev, S. and Zhang, C., *Corporate Governance and Enterprise Reform in China: Building the Institutions of Modern Markets*, World Bank and International Finance Corporation, 2002.

127 Ibid., at 61.

11 The Difficulty of Converting Bankruptcy Assets into Cash

Li further observed that 'there is often a discrepancy between the appraisal value of bankruptcy property and its market value.'[128] According to Li's observations, property values are currently determined by governmental assessment agencies, which are often at levels substantially higher than market values. It is thus difficult to sell bankruptcy property to settle employee and creditor claims.[129]

12 Bankruptcy Concerning Enterprises with Foreign Participation

It has also been said that 'myriad problems arise in the bankruptcy of Sino-foreign joint ventures.'[130] The main issue with respect to bankruptcy of Sino-foreign joint ventures is that it is unclear who bears the responsibility after the bankruptcy. This is because there is no adequate bankruptcy procedure for enterprises with foreign investment or participation, as the current bankruptcy law does not provide sufficient protections for foreign investors. The 1999 bankruptcy case of GITIC (Guangdong International Trust and Investment Company) may provide an illustration of this problem.[131]

The GITIC case In early January 1999, GITIC, an investment arm of the Guangdong government, informed its creditors that the organization did not have sufficient assets to cover all liabilities and accordingly GITIC filed for bankruptcy in the Guangdong Higher People's Court in Guangzhou.[132]

The PRC foreign exchange regulations require that all international borrowing by domestic entities (with very few exceptions) be approved by State Administration of Foreign Exchange ('SAFE') and all foreign debts be registered with SAFE in accordance with *Administration of Borrowing of International Commercial Loans by Domestic Organizations Procedures* (promulgated by SAFE on 24 September 1997 and effective as of 1 January 1998).[133] It appears that many of GITIC's foreign debts were not registered with SAFE because such borrowings were not approved by SAFE in the first instance.[134]

The failure to register a debt that should be registered will lead to the debt being unenforceable. The application of this principle to foreign parties can be found in Article 7 of the PRC, Foreign Economic Contract Law (the 'Foreign Contract Law').[135] The article also provides that contracts requiring approval must be considered to be formed only when such official approval has been obtained.

---

128 Li, supra at 9.

129 Ibid.

130 Ibid., at 10.

131 Ibid.

132 Hickman, M. and Chen, M., 'Cross-Border Financing', *China Law and Practice*, February 1999, at 78.

133 Ibid. and Chang, G., 'Examination of Technical Bankruptcy Issues Crucial for CITIC Creditors', *China Law and Practice*, February 1999, at 69.

134 Hickman and Chen, supra at 78.

135 The Foreign Economic Contract Law was adopted on 21 March 1985 and became effective as of 1 July 1985.

The GITIC Notice announced that 'legal principal and interest of deposits of natural persons inside China' have priority.[136] Chang notes that 'GITIC, at the time of its closure, had taken about US$94 million in deposits from approximately 25,000 individuals.'[137] Article 11 of the PRC Commercial Banking Law[138] provides that approval by the People's Bank of China (PBOC) is required for an enterprise to engage in a 'commercial banking business such as taking deposits from the public'. GITIC did not have a commercial banking licence.[139] As illegal contracts in China are unenforceable,[140] depositors therefore did not have a valid claim against GITIC.

Although the GITIC depositors' claims were, as a technical legal matter, void, depositors will be paid back.[141] According to the GITIC Liquidation Group, Guangdong Province will transfer to the Bank of China, in its capacity as administrator of GITIC, funds meant to equal the principal amount of all deposits.[142] The funds will then be distributed to the 25,000 depositors outside the bankruptcy proceedings, and the only thing that depositors will lose will be the interest that they would have earned had there been no closure.[143]

According to Chang:

> By not paying depositors interest, China has put GITIC and its depositors back in the same position that they would have been had there been no illegal deposits. The same rationale, of course, applies to unregistered debt. Working under this theory, holders of this debt should get back their principal but no interest.[144]

Coincidentally, this is a result that can be justified by Article 11 of the Foreign Contract Law, which states that: 'When one party is responsible for the invalidity of a contract, it shall bear responsibility for compensation to the other party for losses suffered as a result of the contract's invalidity.'[145]

Whilst it may be correct to suggest that by failing to register the debts with SAFE, GITIC harmed its lenders, which arguably now have no claim in the bankruptcy proceedings,[146] the Enterprise Bankruptcy Law, as the current bankruptcy regime in China, nonetheless provided little guidance on the rights, if any, of the foreign lenders, or what they can possibly do to try to recover.

---

136 Ibid.
137 Ibid.
138 The Commercial Banking Law was adopted on 10 May 1995 and became effective as of 1 July 1995.
139 Ibid.
140 Ibid.
141 Ibid.
142 Ibid.
143 Ibid.
144 Ibid.
145 Ibid., at 69–70 and Article 11, Foreign Contract Law.
146 Ibid.

13 Unfair Preferential Policies on Bankruptcy

Finally, Professor Li has noted that only SOEs in the 111 pilot cities (out of 665 cities nationwide) that are part of the government's experimental programme may be benefiting from preferential bankruptcy policies, which include the ability to write off bad debts. In contrast, all enterprises in non-pilot cities and non-SOEs in pilot cities do not seem to enjoy such preferential treatment.[147]

Alternatives to Bankruptcy

It is clear that government policy in China has sought to discourage the bankruptcy of SOEs. This is partly due to the possibility of having the problems associated with massive unemployment (such as social unrest) if all non-performing SOEs were to be declared bankrupt. Also, if all SOEs were liquidated, many banks would also fail.[148] This has been referred to as the problem of triangular debt. Given that the government either still owns or has a majority shareholding in a high percentage of enterprises in China,[149] the government has sought to devise other methods of dealing with the problems with non-performing enterprises. Two of the most commonly used methods are, firstly, the use of Asset Management Companies (AMCs) to take over and seek to dispose of bad debts and, secondly, the use of reorganizations which rely on methods such as debt for equity swaps (as occurred in Changchun-style restructuring); these are discussed below.

Asset Management Companies (AMCs)

Origins of China's Bank AMCs From the late 1980s through the 1990s, as the Chinese economy underwent major structural reform, most of the country's SOEs came to be increasingly reliant on financial support from the state-owned commercial banks (SOCBs). Many SOCB loans made to SOEs during this period were on a non-commercial basis. Bank lending was made in order to prop up uncompetitive SOEs as China moved from being a centrally planned economy to a market economy. Much of the bank credit so extended was used to finance enterprise losses, to pay workers' wages and to fund pension obligations. The magnitude of this 'policy lending' is difficult to assess, but even based on officially reported statistics, the growth of bank credit to SOEs in the recent past was reported to be very high.[150]

Given the nature of these credits and the difficult condition of China's state-owned sector, it is not surprising that large numbers of SOEs defaulted on loans from the

147 Li, supra at 10.

148 'International Insolvency: Corporate/Debt Restructuring: Japan, the Hong Kong SAR and the People's Republic of China: A Roundtable Discussion', 10 *American Bankruptcy Institute Law Review*, Spring 2002.

149 Tenev and Zhang, supra at 78.

150 Pierce, D. and Yee, L., 'China's Bank Asset Management Companies: Gold in Them Thar Hills?', *Topics in Chinese Law – O'Melveny & Myers LLP*, July 2001, at 2.

SOCBs.[151] Furthermore, in the vast majority of cases, the SOEs have not been held accountable for these defaults.[152] According to Pierce and Yee, 'as a result, by the late 1990s China's four major SOCBs were reportedly each holding huge portfolios of "bad" or "distressed" debts, in some cases reportedly amounting to more than half of total assets, mainly comprising non-performing loans ("NPLs") made to SOEs.'[153]

In 1999, the Chinese government recognized the seriousness of this situation and the potential problems that may result from such a fragile financial system, and this led to the State Council approval being given to the establishment of the four AMCs to take over bad debts from the four major Chinese banks.[154] These AMCs then proceeded to rapidly acquire a significant proportion of the big four SOCBs' NPLs and other troubled assets.[155]

It should be noted that these Bank AMCs are wholly state-owned, non-bank financial institutions. Each of them has registered capital of RMB (renminbi) 10 billion (approximately US$1.2 billion), and all of them are directly funded by China's Ministry of Finance (MOF).[156] In 2000, the Bank AMCs each issued ten-year bonds, guaranteed by the MOF, to their respective 'partner' SOCBs in order to finance the purchase of the SOCB assets transferred to them.[157]

It is important to note that 'a crucial feature of the purchase of assets by the Bank AMCs is that they were transferred at current book value.'[158] According to Pierce and Yee, as a result of this, assets have been transferred at valuations not set by reference to any market.[159] Such valuations, which may be inevitably unrealistic, mean that in most if not all cases, when the Bank AMCs eventually divest the assets, large losses will be incurred. The willingness of Bank AMC managers to accept steep losses has been questioned by many commentators, some of whom have argued that bureaucratic fear of recognizing losses has and will continue to seriously hamper the divestment process.[160]

Disposition of assets by the Bank AMCs Pierce and Yee also observed that 'initially, at least, the Bank AMCs appeared to make good progress toward their stated goal of asset disposition for value.'[161] They further commented that 'In 2000, they each reported active use of three methods to dispose of assets: collection, sale or lease of real property, and restructuring of debts.'[162] By using these methods, it has been reported that:

---

151 Ibid.
152 Ibid.
153 Ibid.
154 Ibid., at 2–3.
155 Ibid., at 3.
156 Ibid.
157 Ibid.
158 Ibid., at 5.
159 Ibid.
160 Ibid.
161 Ibid.
162 Ibid.

> Huarong AMC [had] a 45% recovery rate of assets with a book value of RMB 7,858 billion in 2000, of which around 26% was recovered in case and around 15% was recovered as real property. Great Wall AMC reported that it disposed of assets worth RMB 73.2 billion; Cinda AMC reported the divestment of assets to the value of RMB 38 billion, including the recovery of RMB 5.2 billion in cash; and China Orient AMC reported the disposition of RMB 18.8 billion worth of assets.[163]

On the high recovery rates, it has been commented that 'these recovery rates appear to be high but almost certainly do not reflect the overall quality of the Bank AMCs' assets.'[164] Further, Pierce and Yee also stated that:

> Naturally, the best assets have been disposed of first and the more troubled remain in the Bank AMCs' portfolios. Some bankers have predicted that the most optimistic overall recovery rate is likely to be in the region of 25% of book value, while other analysts believe that recovery in the range of 5% to 15% of book is more likely.[165]

Why have Bank AMCs been successful in disposing of debts which SOCBs had difficulties getting rid of? Gesteland provided an explanation for this when he noted that 'banks in China are not allowed to discount debt. Borrowers are given the choice of paying what is owed in full or going bankrupt.'[166] AMCs, on the other hand, 'are allowed to discount debt and negotiate with borrowers, and, as a result, they are reporting a high success rate in recovering non-performing loans.'[167] Gesteland illustrated his view by using Huarong as an example, which had 'claimed it has been able to recover more than 70 percent of its bad loans through negotiated settlement.'[168]

It may be appropriate to ask why anyone would wish to buy these bad loans. According to *Asiaweek*:

> The loans are being sold by Huarong at 15% of their original value. They were collateralized with assets like machinery, factories and the land they are standing on. The feeling is that if you can match Huarong's collection rate of 35%, you can make money off a cheaply priced asset.[169]

In regard to the Chinese government being creative in the method of disposing of non-performing loans, it has been noted that 'a large pool of non-performing assets valued at about 21 million yuan (US$2.53 million) was sold through online auctions … [Furthermore], the Tianjin-based Jinqiao Hotel was purchased by a local investment company via online auctions.'[170]

---

163 Ibid., at 5–6.
164 Ibid., at 6.
165 Ibid.
166 Gesteland, L., 'China – Jack Rodman thinks bad debt can be golden opportunity', *ChinaOnline*, 22 April 2002.
167 Ibid.
168 Ibid.
169 'The Sell-off', *Asiaweek*, 30 November 2001.
170 'Online sale of NPAs goes well', *CBNet*, 21 September 2001.

Changchun-style Debt Restructuring

Background of Changchun approach Changchun City, situated in Northeast China, is an old industrial city with a majority of SOEs and assets. In the past two decades, the local SOEs endured hard times due to heavy debt burdens, redundant workers, low quality assets, inflexible management systems and obsolete technology and equipment. The SOEs were insolvent, their trademarks and names were forgotten and market resources were lost.[171]

In 1995, Changchun City began to look for ways to rescue the profitable assets of its insolvent SOEs. Initially, Changchun used administrative power to hive the profitable assets off from the old enterprises, and registered new companies. However, they soon found that this practice was illegal and that there was no way in which they were able to sever the joint liability between the new enterprises and the old ones. Thus, since 1996, a new approach, named 'Purchase-Sale Restructuring' ('PSR') was devised. By about July 2001, 40 or so of Changchun's SOEs had adopted this approach to restructuring and some were proven to be successful. From that time, this approach, known locally as PSR and nationally as the 'Changchun Approach', attracted the attention of many people and other cities in China began to adopt this approach to the restructure of their SOEs.[172]

According to Professor Weiguo Wang,[173] under the Changchun approach, an enterprise adopting the PSR approach would remain an insolvent entity holding profitable assets that can contribute to future profits. Before applying the PSR theory, the government used liquid assets and leased land to set up a new company. After undergoing the cycles of asset transaction, this company gradually converts itself into a multi-shareholder entity. This new company acquires the profitable assets of the old company. The three entities involved in this transaction are the new company, the old company and the primary creditors, usually the bank holding the debts of the old company. These three entities enter into an agreement and develop a package of measures. This package relates to the profitable assets of the old company; the valuation of these assets, the sale of these assets and future debt payment, form the key elements of the transaction. This transaction can be further broken down into four stages: the bank will first approve a loan to the new company to allow it to purchase the profitable assets of the old company. The amount that is lent will be close to the valuation of the profitable assets. This then enables the old company to transfer its profitable assets to the new company at the contractual amount. The old company then uses the capital generated by the sale of the profitable assets to pay off the debt amount.

While this transaction may appear to be a simple movement of funds across the balance sheets of two different entities, there are certain considerations that govern the dynamics of the process. An important aspect of the transaction is assessing, or rather differentiating, between profitable and non-profitable assets. A valuation has to

---

171 Wang, W., 'Changchun Approach: A New Scheme for Debt Restructuring in China', Paper presented at *The Second Forum for Asian Insolvency Reform* held in Bangkok, Thailand on 16–17 December 2002.

172 Ibid., at 1–2.

173 Ibid., at 2–3.

be performed by an authorized entity and the results of the valuation have to be approved by the Administration of State-owned Assets and the creditor (usually the primary creditor). A plan for restructuring has then to be developed and presented by the old company. Approval of this plan is also required from the workers' congress. Further, the transaction has to be undertaken in the Center of Title Transaction. Based on the asset valuation, both entities will exchange cash and assets, once the agreement becomes binding.

Some other secondary (but centrally important) measures that need to be resolved deal with questions raised by workers; the redress of grievances is undertaken by the Communist Party of China. Usually, the majority of the jobs are transferred from the old company to the new company and the workers then sign a labour contract with the new company. The floating assets of the old company are acquired by the new enterprise and then used to produce marketable goods. Shortly thereafter, the property rights are reformed and the new company assumes the dimension of a multi-shareholder enterprise. This may assume various forms, such as: a share-issuing enterprise, a shareholding cooperative enterprise, an enterprise group, a cooperative enterprise and a Sino-foreign joint venture. Finally, the disposition of the old company's residual assets has to be undertaken. For those assets that cannot be readily disposed of, bankruptcy will ensue, but those assets that are still effective remain in operation. The decision to support an old enterprise in business or to apply a restructuring to its operations is the prerogative of the new enterprise.[174]

Conclusion

China has come a long way in the development of its bankruptcy laws and related systems, starting from the traditional concept (requiring a son to repay his father's debts) to a complex bankruptcy regime with different sets of laws and regulations, as well as Supreme People's Courts' opinions applying to the insolvency of different types of enterprises.

Whilst numerous bankruptcy laws exist, China is still effectively a country 'ruled by men', as the government has wide discretion in determining which enterprises will be declared bankrupt. Further, the government also exercises control through its courts, as judges are appointed by the government and court budgets are also allocated by the government.

Therefore, it is not surprising to see that the government, in preventing the potential serious problems associated with declaring enterprises bankrupt (particularly with the vast number of non-performing SOEs and the potential social unrest that may result), puts forth all types of obstacles in deterring the declaration of bankruptcy against enterprises. Further, as employees must be treated as a first priority in the distribution of bankruptcy property, creditors are often left with few assets to be distributed to them. In order to minimize the number of enterprises being declared bankrupt, the Chinese government has put forth alternative strategies in an attempt to

174 Ibid.

resolve the issue, including the use of asset management companies and the use of Changchun-style restructuring.

In the wake of China's accession to the World Trade Organization and the pressure placed on China to transform from a centrally planned economy to a market economy, it is clear that a new bankruptcy system is needed. In an attempt to resolve some of the problems that exist in China's existing bankruptcy regime and to foster China's transformation to a market economy, a number of new drafts of the bankruptcy law have been developed in China, the latest one being the November 2004 draft. It is anticipated that a new bankruptcy law for China will come into force soon, given that a draft has already been submitted to the Standing Committee of the 10th National People's Congress for deliberation. If the draft bankruptcy law does become effective, China will no doubt move into a new phase of economic and legal development. However, in the meantime, the 1986 bankruptcy law and subsequent regulations and opinions remain operative in China.

Chapter 5

Insolvency Law in Taiwan: The Interplay between Official and Unofficial Law

ANGUS FRANCIS
Griffith University, Brisbane
and
NEIL ANDREWS*
Victoria University, Melbourne

1 Introduction

1.1 Introduction to the Taiwanese Legal System and Legal Culture

Taiwan's legal system displays the distinction between official and unofficial law, between the 'law in the books' and the 'law in practice', that has been highlighted in studies of other Asian and non-Asian legal systems.[1] There is also evidence of the interaction between official and unofficial law produced by the presence, or absence of, shared values: where they are present, the unofficial (or informal) law may both justify and orientate the application of the official (or formal) law; where they are absent, the unofficial law may directly affect the implementation of the official law by supplementing, opposing, modifying or undermining it.[2] The complexity of Taiwanese history and the influence of its different communities have heightened the distinction between formal and informal law in the jurisdiction. This chapter begins with a brief outline of the historical factors influencing the interplay between official and unofficial law in Taiwan before considering this relationship in more detail in the context of Taiwan's insolvency laws.

Taiwan before 1895 The existence of distinct ethnic societies in Taiwan has arguably produced a narrower overlap of shared values between official and

---

* Professor of Law and Deputy Director, Centre for International Corporate Governance Research, Victoria University, Melbourne, Australia.

1 For example see: Macaulay, S. (1963), 'Non-contractual Relations in Business: A Preliminary Study', 28 *American Sociological Review* 55; Macaulay, S. (1966), *Law and the Balance of Power: The Automobile Manufacturers and Their Dealers*, New York: Russell Sage Foundation; Yasuda, N. (1991), 'Law and Development in ASEAN Countries', in Radhie, T., and N. Yasuda, *Law and Development in ASEAN Countries*, Tokyo: Institute of Developing Economies.

2 Chiba, M. (1986), 'Introduction', in Chiba, M. (ed.), *Asian Indigenous Law in Interaction with Received Law*, London: KPI, 1, 5–9.

unofficial law. The original inhabitants are Malayo-Polynesian peoples, who form one to two per cent of the present population.[3] It is difficult to identify the laws and customs of Taiwan's indigenous population prior to and during the Han Chinese migration that commenced from the 1590s.[4] Early Chinese studies of the laws and customs of the original inhabitants of Taiwan tend to adopt a simplistic and sinocentric view of indigenous culture to the extent that they characterize the 'savages' as either 'backward and culturally inferior' or 'as the preserver of an ancient [Chinese] righteousness lost among the moderns'.[5]

For example, it was with the aim of recovering lost Chinese antiquity on Taiwan that Deng Chuan'an (fl. 1830), who served in Taiwan as a Subprefect for Savage Affairs (*Lifan tongzhi*) around 1822, wrote *Fansu jin' gu shuo* (A Discourse on the Resemblance of Savage Customs to those of Antiquity). Deng writes in his Discourse:

> They cannot communicate in their language with those outside their borders; how could they understand writing? If one side has a credit in trading, they use knotted strings in place of promissory notes. When the amount is paid back as arranged, then the knot is untied. This is an example of how their customs resemble those of high antiquity.[6]

The reference to 'knotted strings', also found in earlier studies of Taiwan's indigenes (such as Chen Di's *Dongfan ji* (Record of the Eastern Savages)), arguably alludes to the Daoist *Dao de jing* and the *Zhuangzhi*, which 'called for a return to a way of life that antedated the invention of writing, when people used knotted strings for calculations and record keeping'.[7] The sinocentricity of these early studies found its way into official gazettes and policy documents, rendering it difficult to discern whether the laws and customs of Taiwan's indigenous inhabitants had any lasting impact on Taiwan's legal system.

The early Han migrants were few in number until the Dutch East Indies Company claimed Taiwan in 1624.[8] The Dutch encouraged further migration of Han Chinese to Taiwan with the aim of producing cultivated crops, such as sugar, on the island.[9] The migrants who arrived in Taiwan during the 39 years of Dutch control came from

---

3 Shepherd, J. (1993), *Statecraft and Political Economy on the Taiwan Frontier, 1600–1800*, Stanford, California: Stanford University Press, 7. However, there has been significant controversy over the ethnic identity of the original inhabitants of Taiwan: see Stainton, M. (1999), 'The Politics of Taiwan Aboriginal Origins', in Rubenstein, M. (ed.), *Taiwan: A New History*, Armonk, New York: M.E. Sharpe.

4 Hsu, Wen-hsiung (1980), 'From Aboriginal Island to Chinese Frontier: The Development of Taiwan Before 1683', in Knapp, R. (ed.), *China's Island Frontier: Studies in the Historical Geography of Taiwan*, Honolulu: The University Press of Hawaii and The Research Corporation of the University of Hawaii, 3–29, 10. Hsu notes (at 6) that Chinese had inhabited the Penghu (Pescadores) islands in the Taiwan Straits from at least the 11th century.

5 Teng, E. (1999), 'Taiwan as a Living Museum: Tropes of Anachronism in Late-Imperial Chinese Travel-Writing', 59 *Harvard Journal of Asiatic Studies* 2, 445–484, 448.

6 As note 5, above, 471.

7 As note 5, above, 452.

8 Allee, M. (1994), *Law and Local Society in Late Imperial China: Northern Taiwan in the Nineteenth Century*, Stanford, California: Stanford University Press, 23.

9 As note 8, above, 24.

the southern Chinese province of Fujian.[10] The Han Chinese population may have increased to between 40,000 and 50,000 during Dutch rule.[11] Migration was mainly limited to a small area around modern Tainan in southwestern Taiwan and into the northern sector of modern Gaoxiong county.[12]

Zheng Chenggong, a Chinese loyalist of the fallen Ming dynasty, drove the Dutch from Taiwan in 1662.[13] Given that the Dutch had control over the island for only 39 years, their continuing influence on the legal system was limited.[14] Han Chinese continued to migrate to Taiwan during the Zheng period, the population doubling to 100,000.[15] The new Qing dynasty seized the island in 1683. Han Chinese migration to Taiwan persisted under Qing rule. In the 18th and 19th centuries, Hokkienese-speaking natives of Fujian's Quanzhou and Zhangzhou prefectures, and Hakkas,[16] a distinct minority Han group in China, comprised the bulk of Han Chinese migration to Taiwan.[17]

The following migration and demography patterns emerged during the early Han Chinese migration to Taiwan in the Dutch, Zheng and Qing periods:

- Han Chinese spread and became dominant with indigenous tribes either being pacified and assimilated (referred to by Chinese as *shu fan* or 'cooked' aborigines) or remaining hostile and outside Chinese control (referred to by Chinese as *sheng fan* or 'raw' aborigines);[18]
- Qing government policies attempting to control migration to Taiwan and to establish a boundary confining Chinese expansion on the island to prevent conflict between Chinese migrants and indigenous tribes were gradually overcome with an activist Qing policy to pacify aboriginal tribes remaining outside Chinese jurisdiction, particularly when Japan was seen to threaten Qing sovereignty over the island following an incident in 1874; and
- there were widespread intra-ethnic disputes, both economic and violent, between Hokkienese (the majority Han population) and Hakka (about 10 to 15 per cent of

10 As note 4, above, 17.

11 As note 8, above, 24.

12 As note 8, above, 24.

13 As note 8, above, 24.

14 See further: Hung, Chienchao (1981), *Taiwan under the Cheng Family 1662–1683: Sinicization after Dutch rule*, PhD dissertation, Georgetown University, 68, cited in Wang, Taysheng (1997), 'Taiwan', in Tan, Pohling, *Asian Legal Systems*, Sydney: Butterworths, 124.

15 As note 8, above, 24.

16 Hakkas migrated to Taiwan from, amongst other areas, Huizhou and Chaozhou prefectures in Guangdong and Tingzhou prefecture in Fujian (Chen, Yundong (1978), *Kejia ren* (Hakkas), Taibei: Lianjing, 97 cited in Allee, as note 8, above, ff 7, 282.

17 As note 8, above, 25–27.

18 Teng notes (as note 5, above, ff 34, 460–61) that the terms *sheng* and *shu* – 'raw' and 'cooked', or 'unfamiliar' and 'familiar' – meant different things for different writers. The terms could be used in a cultural and linguistic sense to distinguish those 'savages' that lived in Han settlements and 'who speak our language' and those that did not (Lu Zhiyu, *Taiwan shimo ouji*, in *Taiwan yudi huichao*, 9). They could also refer to the submission of 'savages' to the state, such as whether they paid taxes or wore the queue, or to the geographical location of the indigenes.

the Han population by the end of this period), primarily caused by issues like competition over land and resources, land use and boundaries, rent payment, and debt repayment, but exacerbated by differences in language, social arrangements, and customary practices.[19]

The predominant continuing influences during this period of Han migration was the customary or unofficial law of the Han Chinese migrants and the administrative and legislative intervention of the Qing state.

The Qing state inherited the imperial form of centralized, bureaucratic government that had first been implemented in the Qin dynasty as early as 221 B.C. Under the Qin nobles and officials of the former states were removed and replaced with a centrally appointed, non-hereditary, salaried bureaucracy.[20] This was the model for all dynastic governments until the founding of the Republic in 1912. The Qing also inherited the traditional Chinese concept of law that arose from an eclectic mix of Confucianism, Legalism and Chinese cosmology.[21]

Official state law in Imperial China was employed as a means of state administration.[22] The state existed to ensure the maintenance of social and political stability.[23] As a result, central official law was chiefly penal and administrative in character.[24] Following Qing conquest, Taiwan fell under the Qing Code (which assumed definitive form in 1740). Taiwan was administered by the Qing state as part of the adjacent Fujian province until achieving full provincial status in 1886.[25]

The Code had little relevance to commercial life in Taiwan. Firstly, the Code almost totally neglected commercial affairs, aside from general penal provisions relating to usury and debt (Article 149), bailment (Article 150), lost property (Article 151), licensing commercial agents (Article 152), valuation of merchandise (Article 153), monopolizers and unfair traders (Article 154), false weights, measures and scales, and substandard manufacture (Article 156).[26]

The Code was mainly applied by county or district magistrates as a part of the myriad demands to be dealt with at this lowest administrative level. The administration of justice was a part of the general administration of the state; the role of the local county or district magistrate embraced judge, tax collector and general

---

19 As note 8, above, 33–35. Allee (at 34) notes that there was also conflict between Hokkienese-speaking Zhangzhou and Quanzhou natives of Fujian.

20 Bodde, D. and C. Morris (1967), *Law in Imperial China: Exemplified by 190 Ch'ing Dynasty Cases*, Cambridge, Mass.: Harvard University Press, 27.

21 As note 20, above, 27–29 and 43–48.

22 Chen, J. (1999), *Chinese Law: Towards an Understanding of Chinese Law, Its Nature and Development*, The Hague: Kluwer Law International, 16.

23 As note 20, above, 184.

24 Chiu, Hungdah and Fa, Jyh-pin (1994), 'Taiwan's Legal System and Legal Profession', in Silk, M. (ed.), *Taiwan Trade and Investment Law*, Hong Kong: Oxford University Press, 21–42, 22.

25 Brockman, R. (1980), 'Commercial Contract Law in Late Nineteenth-Century Taiwan', in Cohen, J., R. Edwards and Fu-mei Chang Chen, *Essays on China's Legal Tradition*, Princeton, NJ: Princeton University Press, 76–137, 78.

26 As note 25, above, 76–137.

administrator.[27] Magistrates turned to local custom rather than statutory law as a source of rules in any given case.[28] If a case did go to court in Taiwan involving debt, Article 149 was used as a last resort should the debtor not pay.[29]

There is disagreement between scholars whether the imperial Chinese state considered unofficial customary law to be trivial – and therefore not a part of official state law – or whether the regulation of civil matters by local custom was an instance of controlled delegation.[30] Regardless of how customary law is characterized, what is of importance is that customary law played an essential role in regulating commercial relationships in Imperial China.[31]

Commercial cases in Taiwan rarely ended up in court and those that did were resolved by recourse to local commercial custom.[32] Commercial cases were either mediated outside the formal judicial structure through the intervention of merchant guilds or lineage ties acting in accordance with local custom[33] or, where no guild or clan or common custom bound the parties (as was often the case in the export-driven market of Taiwan), by recourse to a developed system of standard contracts.[34] The primacy of unofficial customary law on Taiwan was a mirror of the mainland.[35]

---

27 Chü, T'ung-tsu (1962), *Local Government in China under the Ch'ing*, Cambridge, Mass.: Harvard University Press, cited in Jones, W. (1994), 'Introduction', in Jones, W. (trans.) *The Great Qing Code*, Oxford: Clarendon Press, 10.

28 As note 25, above, 91.

29 As note 25, above, 95. Article 149 read:

> Interest on a loan may not exceed 3 percent of principal per month. On repayment, the total interest may not exceed the amount of the principal. Punishment for violation shall be 40–100 blows in proportion to the amount of illegitimate interest charged. A debtor who fails to pay a valid debt when due shall be punished with 10–60 blows depending on the amount due and the period the debt has remained unpaid. The debt shall remain lawfully due.
>
> A creditor who himself violently seizes the property of a defaulting debtor in satisfaction of the debt shall be punished with 80 blows. A creditor who accepts the wives or children of his debtor as security shall be punished with 100 blows.

30 As note 22, above, ff 106, 17 citing Alford, W. (1995), *To Steal a Book Is an Elegant Offence: Intellectual Property Law in Chinese Civilization*, Stanford, California: Stanford University Press, 11, and Liang, Zhiping (1997), *The Pursuit of Harmony in Natural Orders: A Study of Traditional Legal Culture (Xunqiu Ziran Zhixu Zhong De Hexie: Zhongguo Chuantong Falü Wenhua Yanjiu)*, Beijing: China University of Science and Law Press, 249. Allee (as note 8, above, ff 9, 313) also suggests that state law may appear more interested in commercial matters if attention is shifted from centrally sanctioned legislation to provincial government regulations, e.g. *Fujian shengli* (Fujian provincial regulations).

31 Zhang, Jinfan (1988), *A Collection of Papers on Legal History (Fashi Jianlüe)*, Beijing: Press of the Masses, 6; As note 20, above, 5–6; MacCormack, G. (1996), *The Spirit of Traditional Chinese Law*, Athens and London: The University of Georgia Press, 1.

32 As note 25, above, 91. Although Allee (as note 8, above, 259) suggests that the courts did provide one of the only means for peacefully resolving disputes crossing ethnic lines.

33 As note 8, above, 259.

34 As note 25, above, 76–137.

35 Jamieson, G. (1970), *Chinese Family and Commercial Law*, Hong Kong: Vetch and Lee Limited, i. Jamieson writes (at i):

The local magistrate courts in Taiwan, in an attempt to lessen inter-ethnic and intra-ethnic conflict and to encourage 'standard, traditional societal structures of China', tried to foster lineage ties instead of native place links by forcing mediation by lineage relatives when possible.[36] Courts in Taiwan also recognized collective or corporate legal personae in litigation, such as corporate lineages, retail businesses, partnerships, tenant groups, multiplex village organizations, and corporate commercial bodies.[37]

By the late Qing period there were numerous joint-stock companies and de facto recognition of them as legal persons in Taiwan.[38] However, fear of liability limited their size.[39] Under Chinese unofficial customary law, managing partners were liable for debts of the company, irrespective of shares.[40] Silent partners (those only contributing capital) could only be made liable for remaining debt with difficulty, although negotiation often secured contribution.[41] On the mainland, these entities were described as 'merchant practices under official supervision'.[42] The model was designed to further state economic policies.[43] The use of this model was subsequently rejuvenated by the Kuomintang (KMT).[44]

Taiwan after 1895 Taiwan's political history after 1895 has also fractured the values which might be shared by official and unofficial law and produced an unusually complex relationship between them. The Qing dynasty ceded Taiwan to

---

> It was therefore hopeless to attempt to construct a system of mercantile law from the books. Inquiries among those who might be expected to know as to what were the principles which guided Chinese Courts in cases, for instance of partnership, bankruptcy and so forth, elicited the reply that every case was decided on its merits, and there was no general rule; or that it was a matter of custom in particular places or of the particular guild to which the trader belonged.

36 As note 8, above, 259. On the issue of the delegated authority of clan and guild, see van der Sprenkel, S. (1966), *Legal Institutions in Manchu China: A Sociological Analysis*, New York: The Athlone Press, 96:

> The tsu [clan] and guild tribunals may perhaps be thought of as subsidiaries of the official courts, exercising delegated powers, the one as a community, the other as an association, in connection with matters which came within their range of operation. On this view, they were part of the hierarchy of courts, from which the magistrate's court constituted the first court of appeal.

37 As note 8, above, 166–168.

38 Andrews, N. and A. Francis (1999), 'Company Law in Taiwan', in Tomasic, R. (ed.), *Company Law in East Asia*, Aldershot: Dartmouth/Ashgate, 219–295, 226–227.

39 As note 38, above, 226–227.

40 As note 35, above, 121.

41 As note 35, above, 121.

42 Feuerwerker, A. (1995), 'China's Nineteenth Century Industrialization: The Case of the Hanyeping Coal & Iron Company Ltd.' in Feuerwerker, A. (ed.), *Studies in the Economic History of Late Imperial China: Handicraft, Modern Industry and the State*, Michigan: Center for Chinese Studies, University of Michigan, 181–182.

43 As note 38, above, 226.

44 Kirby, W.C. (1995), 'China Unincorporated: Company Law and Enterprise in Twentieth-Century China', *Journal of Asian Studies*, 54, 43, 54.

Japan in 1895 under the Treaty of Shimonoseki. The Japanese colonization of Taiwan between 1895 and 1945 saw the introduction of Japan's Western-styled civil and commercial codes in Taiwan, including the introduction of Japan's Western-style bankruptcy law in 1923.[45] Japan's bureaucracy and court system on Taiwan were well managed, efficient, and complied with written law and administrative directions.[46] As part of a system of colonial social control the official Japanese legal system and its courts were more prone to intervene in the lives of families and individuals, although matters of family law and succession continued to be largely unaffected by it.[47]

There is evidence that the Japanese did attempt to accommodate elements of Taiwan's unofficial customary law.[48] For example, a traditional Taiwanese practice that had evolved during the Qing period was the concept of *daohao* ('closed business'). If a debtor's assets were insufficient to meet creditor demands a meeting of creditors could be called by the debtor or creditors. The meeting would consider any proposal put forward by the debtor. If the proposal was rejected or the debtor failed to subsequently comply with creditor demands, the debtor's assets would be sold off and distributed. All outstanding claims were extinguished after the disposal of the assets. The Japanese bankruptcy code offered a similar court process. However, due to the perceived expense of court-controlled insolvency proceedings, and because debtors enjoyed automatic discharge on completion of the *daohao* process, 'few Taiwanese resorted to modern bankruptcy proceedings during the Japanese period'.[49]

There were also instances of the hybridization of official and unofficial legal forms under Japanese rule. The idea of the borrower transferring title to land to the lender where there was no personal relationship was brought to Taiwan by migrants from China as their custom and also in the Qing Code as official law. This agreement prevented the borrower from disposing of land. In 1905 a Japanese law gave the lender upon default of the borrower the power to apply to the court for the land to be auctioned. Thus the agreement was transformed into a mortgage. The agreement continued under the same name but it was recognized as having a different legal status. After the end of Japanese rule in 1945 the agreement as modified was no longer recognized in the official law but continued to be used by the business community in Taiwan. Now, as Taiwanese custom, it is enforced by the official law administered in the courts.[50]

---

45 Tomasic, R. and A. Francis (1997), 'Taiwan', in Tomasic, R. and P. Little (eds), *Insolvency Law and Practice in Asia*, Hong Kong: Pearson Professional (Hong Kong) Limited, 68.

46 Wachman, A. (1989), *National Identity and Democratization*, Armonk, NY: East Gate, 93–5.

47 Wang, Taysheng (1997), 'Taiwan', in Tan, Pohling, *Asian Legal Systems*, Sydney: Butterworths, 124, 131–132.

48 The Temporary Commission for the Survey of Traditional Customs in Taiwan was established in 1901 by the Japanese colonial government-general. The resulting publication considering Taiwan's customary law, *Taiwan Shiho* [The Private Law of Taiwan] 1910, was a six-volume study of land law, family law, personal property and commercial law. See further Brockman, R. (1980), 'Commercial Contract Law in Late Nineteenth-Century Taiwan', in Cohen, J., R. Edwards and Fu-mei Chang Chen, *Essays on China's Legal Tradition*, Princeton, NJ: Princeton University Press, at pp. 76–137.

49 Wang, Tay-sheng (1992), *Legal reform in Taiwan under Japanese colonial rule (1895–1945): the reception of Western law*, Ann Arbor, Mich.: U.M.I., 368–9.

50 As note 47, above, 151–152.

In the 50 years of Japanese rule the identity of the Hokkienese, who now form approximately 63 per cent of the population, and the Hakka, who form about 20 per cent, emerged as distinctively Taiwanese.[51] The arrival of the KMT signalled a further Han Chinese migration of two million people from the mainland in 1948–1950 following the Chinese civil war. Those associated with the KMT assumed a monopoly over Taiwanese government, law, education and culture until the late 1980s. For the greater part of the period since 1945 the earlier Han Chinese communities, identifying themselves as Taiwanese, have been the victims of systematic discrimination.[52] The underlying social and political tension between the Han Chinese communities is now in decline. Many Taiwanese speak Mandarin and there are marriages and many other ties between the Han Chinese.[53]

The discussion so far has briefly indicated the impact of Taiwan's complex history on the jurisdiction's official and unofficial law. The influence of various communities historically produced a narrower overlap of values between official and unofficial law than would be presumed. However, there are also examples of the hybridization of official and unofficial law following the arrival in the jurisdiction of external legal values. The interplay between Taiwan's official and unofficial law becomes more apparent when consideration is given to the history of Taiwan's insolvency regime.

1.2 History, Sources and Philosophy of Insolvency Laws in Taiwan

The impact of the arrival of the KMT Following the arrival of the KMT, insolvency in Taiwan has been governed by the Bankruptcy Law (*Pochan Fa*) 1935 ("Bankruptcy Law") and the Company Law 1929 ("Company Law"). The Bankruptcy Law and the Company Law formed part of an array of Western-styled commercial and civil laws enacted in the early 20th century in China. China's first bankruptcy code was promulgated by the Qing dynasty in 1905 only to be revoked in 1907.[54] The Qing dynasty had attempted to accommodate both traditional Chinese attitudes to the resolution of disputes over debt and bankruptcy principles found in the provisions of contemporary European bankruptcy regimes.[55]

The Civil Codification Commission of the Legislative Yuan was given the task of drafting a new law on bankruptcy under the Nationalist Government. The drafting committee had at its disposal the Qing dynasty's law on bankruptcy, the draft of the Beijing Codification Commission of 1915, the draft of the Ministry of Justice, and the Provisional Rules for the Liquidation of Indebtedness of Merchants (repealed by Article 5 of the Law Governing the Application of the Bankruptcy Law, 1935).

---

51 Chiou, C. (1994), 'Emerging Taiwanese Identity in the 1990s: Crisis and Transformation', in Klintworth, G. (ed.), *Taiwan in the Asia Pacific in the 1990s*, Sydney: Allen and Unwin, 21, 26.

52 As note 47, above, 125–6.

53 As note 51, above, 21.

54 'The bankruptcy code initiated by the Board of Commerce and sanctioned by the throne in 1905 was expressly revoked in 1907. This law has not been revived and is consequently no longer applicable': Decision of the Chinese Supreme Court, A.C. No. 16 3rd Yr. C.R. Tr., cited in Allman, N. (1925), 'Bankruptcy Laws in China', *The China Law Review* 2, 218–225, 220.

55 Mitrano, T. (1978), 'The Chinese bankruptcy law of 1906–1907: a legislative case history', *Studies in East Asian Law*, Boston, Mass.: Harvard Law School.

The Bankruptcy Law and the Company Law have remained largely in the same form since enactment. In response to growing American influence, the Company Law was amended in 1966 to include a court-ordered company reorganization regime. Taiwan has four official insolvency procedures: bankruptcy, composition (*hejie*), reorganization and special liquidation.[56]

The Taiwanese, who staged 20 revolts against Japanese rule, were alienated from the new government and its legal institutions.[57] The incident of 28 February 1947 led to an authoritarian and corporatist state.[58] The Taiwanese came to accept economic opportunities in exchange for the mainland elite amongst the civil war migrants dominating the government and the military.[59] This division still marks the Taiwanese economy and society,[60] particularly commercial activities where the KMT exchanged entry rights to a lucrative oligopoly for cooperation and loyalty.[61] It is reflected in a large, but decreasing, informal economy as it is steadily formalized. In 1990 it still accounted for 57 per cent of the total Taiwanese economy, compared with 3 to 21 per cent in other developed economies.[62] The KMT amassed great wealth during its period in power and the distinction between the property of the KMT and of the government remains unclear.[63]

The close connection between the KMT and business has had a perceived effect on the application of official insolvency laws in the jurisdiction:

> Over the past 40 years the KMT has had every level of business beholden to them. The KMT is often the principal shareholder and controller. This brings in connections and the old boy network. The KMT are worth an estimated NT$40 billion. This has deferred any application of the Bankruptcy Law as companies have not been under any pressure as they have had recourse to other arrangements.[64]

---

56 As note 45, above, 67.

57 As note 46, above, 93–5.

58 Wade, R. (1990), *Governing the Market: Economic Theory and the Role of Government in East Asian Industrialization*, Princeton, NJ: Princeton University Press, 27.

59 Gold, T. (1986), *State And Society In The Taiwan Miracle*, Armonk, New York: M.E. Sharpe, 51–2; Clough, R. (1981), 'The Political System of Taiwan', in Hsiang, J. (ed.), *Contemporary Republic of China: The Taiwan Experience, 1950–1980*, New York: Praeger, 351, 355; Kaufman Winn, J. (1993), 'Relational practices and marginalization of law: informal financial practices of small businesses in Taiwan', 28 *Law & Society Review* 2, 193–232; Kaufman Winn, J. (1991), 'Banking and Finance in Taiwan: The Prospects for Internationalisation in the 1990s', *International Lawyer*, 907, 944.

60 Wen-hui Tsai (1994), *Towards Greater Democracy: An Analysis of the Republic of China on Taiwan's Major Elections in the 1990s*, Baltimore: School of Law, University of Maryland, 33 and ff 31.

61 Yun-han Chu, 'The Realignment of Business-Government Relations and Regime Transition in Taiwan', in McIntyre, A. (ed.) (1994), *Business and Government in Industrialising Asia*, St Leonards, Allen & Unwin, 1994, 113, 116–17, 136.

62 As note 59, above, Kaufman Winn (1993), 211.

63 As note 58, above, 175–182.

64 An unidentified partner with a Taiwan accounting firm quoted in: Tomasic and Francis, as note 45, above, 84. For example, see the proposal to float on the Taipei Stock Exchange the China Ship Building Corporation as a way of saving it from insolvency: 'Taiwan to abolish support of shipyard', *South China Morning Post*, 1 April 1998, Freight and Shipping Post, 6.

As the KMT also owns and controls banks, there has been, until now, a perceived ready source of further loans for troubled companies.[65] Insolvency practitioners also complain of the excessive reliance of courts on the views of government agencies in corporate reorganizations.[66] However, in an International Monetary Fund study of six Asian economies following the Asian Financial Crisis, it was concluded that one of the reasons Taiwan more successfully weathered the crisis was that credit is now allocated primarily on commercial grounds based on adequate risk assessment by banks.[67]

The official legal system and the unofficial legal culture The development of official and unofficial legal institutions on Taiwan has blurred the boundaries between official and unofficial insolvency law. Firstly, Chinese law has influenced both the official law represented in the Bankruptcy Law and the unofficial law of the Chinese ethnic groups who migrated to Taiwan before and after 1945. Both the official and unofficial systems of law before 1895 and after 1945 shared a number of legal values.[68]

Secondly, Japanese law, which was official law in Taiwan from 1895 to 1945, also affected the unofficial law of the Taiwanese. Yet Japanese law had assimilated, over 1,000 years before, a number of values from Chinese law and these values had also been used in modifying the provisions of Western law it had adopted in its legal codes, promulgated in the Meiji period, which were applied in Taiwan. It had little effect on the practices of the Taiwanese who continued with their customary processes rather than the remedies which the official law provided.[69]

The official law applied in Taiwan after 1945 was that of the Republic of China, which was modelled partly on Japanese codes. Japanese lawyers, as well as Chinese lawyers educated in Japan, had drafted them. Again, this gives rise to shared values between the official systems before and after 1945.[70] An example of a common value in both Chinese and Japanese official law and Taiwanese unofficial law which blurs the boundary between these two forms of law is the shared preference for mediation. In the official and unofficial law of Taiwan there has been a strong preference for the resolution of disputes by compromise rather than enforcement of the official law.[71]

---

65 In 1991, the government or the KMT held majority shares in and were board members of the 24 banks: 'Econews', *Agence France Presse*, 25 June 1991 (Lexis Nexis, All News database, 22 February 2000); As note 45, above, 84–87; Glosseman, B., 'Asia's Banks: Flat and Broke', *Japan Times*, 16 June 1999 (Lexis Nexis, All News database, 22 February 2000).

66 As note 45, above, 82–83.

67 Hussain, Q. and C. Wihlborg (1999), 'Corporate Insolvency Procedures and Bank Behaviour: A Study of Selected Asian Economies', a *Working Paper of the International Monetary Fund* (WP/99/135), 34.

68 Chiba refers to the assimilation of Islamic law in Egypt and Iran, Indian law in Thailand and Dutch-Roman law in Sri Lanka as examples of assimilation of official law to unofficial law: Chiba, M. (1986), 'Conclusion', in Chiba, M. (ed.), *Asian Indigenous Law in Interaction with Received Law*, London: KPI, 378, 389.

69 As note 49, above, 367–369.

70 As note 68, above, 389–90.

71 See generally: Chiba, M. (1986), 'Three level structure of contemporary law in Japan – the Shinto society', in Chiba, M. (ed.), *Asian Indigenous Law in Interaction with Received Law*, London: KPI, 301, 335–336.

This is significant as the way in which communities settle disputes is a central part of their social structure and value systems.[72] In mid-19th century Taiwan, going to court was considered bad form and plaintiffs went to some lengths to explain why they were litigating: for instance, their business would otherwise be in trouble; they too were troubled by creditors; winter was coming and they would have trouble getting enough food; or that the person owing the money was a soldier and, given soldiers' reputations, there was no way in which the plaintiff could recover the money or the property.[73]

The Taiwanese began to litigate in increasing numbers under Japanese official law, which was, as a colonial form of social control, intrusive. Paradoxically, as distrust of the courts by the Taiwanese grew after 1945 the amount of litigation also increased. This appears to have reflected a separation between the values of the official legal system, which continues to prefer compromise in civil matters, and the values of the unofficial law. These latter values changed as a result of the breakdown in traditional relationships which had both required mediation and provided the mediators. The breakdown was caused by the influx of civil war migrants from China and by the industrialization of a previously rural Taiwanese society. A similar phenomenon existed on Taiwan's early frontier as different ethnic groups struggled to live together. Many potential Taiwanese litigants now make decisions based on the calculation of benefits and costs in deciding to go to court. The assessment in bankruptcy matters includes whether the costs of litigation would exceed the benefits.[74]

Also official and unofficial law relating to debts and their payment, deriving from the Japanese period, came to continue as unofficial law recognized by official law after 1945. Three types of unofficial forms of debt which are favoured transactions in the informal finance sector show this pattern. Counter-intuitively, until it is remembered that at least one form was once part of the official law, and all are recognized by official law as Taiwanese custom, and that they are mainly used in transactions where there are no personal relationships, they often involve legalistic arrangements and documents.[75]

Tai*: official, unofficial and then official ... unofficial* The idea of the borrower transferring the title to land to the lender where there was no personal relationship was brought to Taiwan both by migrants from China as their custom and also in the Qing Code as official law. This agreement, *tai*, prevented the borrower from disposing of the land.[76] As already noted, in 1905 a law made by the Japanese administration gave the lender, when the borrower had defaulted, the power to apply to the court for the land to be auctioned. The *tai* was transformed into a mortgage or hypothec. In 1923 rights based in Taiwanese custom were deemed to be analogous rights under

72 See generally: Baxi, U. (1986), 'People's law in India – The Hindu society', in Chiba, M. (ed.), *Asian Indigenous Law in Interaction with Received Law*, London: KPI, 216, 240.

73 As note 25, above, 99–100.

74 As note 47, above, 153–154.

75 This is because they often involve the lending of money outside a relationship structure: As note 59, Kaufman Winn, 1993, 222–225.

76 As note 47, above, 151.

the Japanese Civil Code, and the *tai* became a true mortgage in official law. Both after 1905 and 1923 Taiwanese continued to call the arrangement *tai* but also recognized that its legal nature had changed. After 1945 the *tai*, as modified, was no longer recognized in the official law but was widely used by the extensive informal banking system conducted by money lenders where there was no relationship with the borrower. Now, as a Taiwanese custom, it is enforced by the official law administered in the courts.[77]

Nei-teto: non-existent, then unofficial continues to be unofficial *Nei-teto* – fixed collateral – was a widespread Japanese credit practice. Under *nei-teto*, land was offered as a security for an unlimited number of debts within a limited amount. It was not provided for in the Japanese Civil Code but it was recognized by the Japanese Supreme Court in 1901.[78] By 1907 it had become a common form of credit in Taiwan. After 1945 the official law of Taiwan also made no provision for it but it continued to be widespread. It was also subsequently endorsed by the Taiwanese Supreme Court as a Taiwanese custom and is recognized by the official legal system in two approved precedents.[79]

Rotation credit association: always unofficial The rotation credit association is another form of credit indigenous to the Chinese and Taiwanese jurisdictions, but not recognized by the official law in the civil codes of either Japan or those of China introduced in 1945. Members each contribute an agreed amount to a common pool which is given to the highest bidder. The right to bid is reserved to those who have not yet received the pool until each has received it once. This was also recognized by both the Japanese courts and the present Taiwanese courts as a Taiwanese custom.[80]

As with Japan and other non-Western states, the adoption of Western legal processes and codes created a major discontinuity between official and unofficial law in China and, after 1945, in Taiwan. The Qing imperial edict on bankruptcy in 1905 was repealed in 1907 as the concepts used were inconsistent with business practice and also the courts were not equipped to administer it. Many did not have a copy of the law.[81] Even after the promulgation of the Bankruptcy Law custom and tradition remained significant.[82] The Drafting Commission itself anticipated this,

---

77 As note 47, above, 151–152.

78 As note 71, above, 331. The Japanese Civil Code in 1971 was amended to include 21 articles to deal with this form of security.

79 As note 47, above, 156–157 and ff 151, citing judgment No T'ai-shang 776 of 1973 and No T'ai-shang 1097 of 1977.

80 As note 47, above, 151. See further, as note 59, above, Kaufman Winn, 1993, 203. Gray, John, William Gow Gregor (eds) (1878), *China: a history of the laws, manners and customs of the people*, London: Macmillan, 84–86.

81 Teesdale, J. (1907), 'Editorial', in Cahng Nieh-Yün (trans.), *Translation of the Chinese Bankruptcy Code of 1905*, Shanghai: American Presbyterian Mission Press, 1, 1; Foo, Ping Sheung (1936), 'Introduction', in *The Bankruptcy Law of the Republic of China*, Shanghai: Kelly & Walsh, vii, viii.

82 The plethora of legal reforms made by the KMT in the period after the reunification of China in 1928 made little impact. Stephens observes:

acknowledging that the law had to be simple and concise and deal only with essentials as 'customs vary from place to place in this vast country, a law too detailed and too rigid in all its provisions would be quite unsuitable'.[83]

The official law's attitude to insolvency The continuing presumption in the official law of Taiwan is that the law is based on the official law made by the Republic of China. That Republic has its antecedents in the Revolution of 1911 which ended the Qing dynasty and a tradition of imperial law which was over 2,000 years old.

No bankruptcy system providing for the compulsory liquidation of the bankrupt's property existed in the imperial codes. Debtors, whether they were in trade or not, would seek to settle their debts in full. When that failed debtors would engage third parties to negotiate an amicable arrangement with the creditors. When debtors were unwilling to negotiate or had shown bad faith, the creditors would exert pressure on the debtors and their families which could lead to imprisonment to try to obtain reasonable terms for the payment of the debts. The courts, and law, were rarely invoked.[84]

The imperial law was regarded as based heavily on Confucianism represented more by the use of *li* – compliance with the spirit of proper behaviour – than *fa* – the text of the law. The Legalists, who had insisted on the element of *fa* rather than *li* in the Qin dynasty, are often contrasted with the Confucians. This ignores that Confucianism is 'a highly eclectic thought system – one that borrowed extensively from its philosophical rivals'.[85] It is now generally acknowledged that the origin of the Chinese legal system was more pluralist than once thought. The codification of the law which was based on the supreme power of the Emperor and which was a creation of the discredited Legalists in the Qin, for example, endured until the end of the last dynasty over 2,000 years later.[86]

Insolvency law as social harmony Underlying the successive imperial codes was the idea of reinforcing harmony between the human and the natural world through the theory of *yin* and *yang* and the five elements. Legal codes, as statements of law, were *yin* – the dark side – of social control as opposed to the *yang* of ritual, morality

---

> The Nationalist government ... built up in China an impressive array of modern courts administering Western style codes of rules in the adjudicative mode ... But the whole structure was an elaborate façade without any real substance behind it. The Western system never won acceptance by the Chinese people, the great bulk of whom simply ignored it and continued in their traditional ways and practices unaffected. So slight was the penetration of the Western system that the communists, when they achieved power, had no difficulty at all in cancelling it out completely with a few strokes of the brush.

Stephens, T. (1987), 'The Shanghai mixed court and the Ming Sung Umbrella Case 1926', 33 *Australian Journal of Politics and History*, 77, 85.

83 As note 81, above, Foo, xi.

84 As note 81, above, Foo, vii. Foo was the Chairman of the Civil Codification Commission, Legislative Yuan.

85 Liu, Yongping (1998), *Origins of Chinese Law: Penal and Administrative Law in its Early Development*, Hong Kong: Oxford University Press, 325.

86 As note 85, above, 325.

and education.[87] This concern with harmony is seen in Tang law. The Miscellaneous Statute of 737 set limits to parties' freedom to contract, including interest rates, the jurisdictions of the courts and the problem of enslavement of family members to repay debt.[88] The Ming and Qing codes were also concerned with creditors who interfered with the proper relationships within families.[89] These provisions can be seen as symbolic. Discouraging too much debt was a proper function for the Emperor as part of his concern with the welfare of the people. There is a balance in recognizing the necessity of repaying what was borrowed.[90] These lofty principles survived the fall of the Qing. In 1916, the Supreme Court at Beijing considered them in deciding that during a father's lifetime a son has no authority over the family's property and that that property cannot be executed upon because of the son's debts.[91]

Insolvency law as a by-product of administrative law The Qing code gave magistrates jurisdiction to punish defaulting debtors but it would be wrong to argue that in cases of debt, punishment was the unavoidable consequence of legal action. In late-19th century Taiwan punishments were almost never imposed for a failure to pay a debt. A debtor who failed to obey a magistrate's order to pay might be punished for disobeying the court's order. Matters which went to court were frequently resolved expeditiously as purely civil matters.[92]

The imperial codes in this context can be seen as more analogous to administrative law whereby the state was concerned to advance its own interests; but that goal also sometimes protected the interests of individuals.[93] The codes also did not seek to

---

87 Johnson, W. (1997), 'Introduction', in Johnson, W. (trans.), *The Tang Code*, Princeton, NJ: Princeton University Press, Vol. 1, 14; As note 20, above, 43–48.

88 The Tang writer and statesman, Han Yü (768–824), referred to the problem in his essays. As a prefect he memorialized the Emperor on discovering 731 free men and women pledged to creditors in breach of the law and who were treated like slaves. He assessed the value of the labour which they had performed for the creditors and released them: MacCormack, G. (1990), *Traditional Chinese Law*, Edinburgh: Edinburgh University Press, 247–248.

89 A creditor who took a debtor's wife, concubine or child in repayment of a debt faced 100 blows with the heavy stick and, when force was used, the punishment was increased by two degrees to penal servitude for 18 months and 70 blows with the heavy stick. The relatives were to be released and no further action was to be taken. The commentary to the codes makes it clear that the creditor is to be punished and not the debtor, as a wealthy and powerful creditor may have forced a poor debtor to surrender their family members. Article 9.1 of the Ming Code and Article 134 of the Qing Code: As note 88, above, 249.

90 As note 31, above, MacCormack, 50–51.

91 Van der Valk, M. (trans.) (1949), *Interpretations of the Supreme Court at Peking: Years 1915 and 1916*, Batavia: Sinological Institute, Faculty of Arts, University of Indonesia, 286–287.

92 Some simple matters, which still required investigation by the magistrate, took less than 15 days from the issuing of the originating process to the judgment: As note 25, above, 99. In a case reported by the governor-general of Chilhi province in 1825 a plaintiff and his son, seeking to recover a debt, were beaten with heavy bamboos after they became unruly on being urged to forget it, possibly because the debtor was unable to pay. The plaintiff committed suicide and the military officer, who was acting outside his power, was punished for pressing another into committing suicide: As note 20, above, 458–460.

93 Van der Sprenkel (as note 36, above, 64) noted this in the context of the punishment of debtors and creditors; See also: As note 91, above, 1, 28–31; As note 85, above.

order property rights for the purpose of facilitating economic efficiency.[94] So the commercial law provisions of the Qing Code focused on taxation, also covering interests rates, breaches of loan agreements and the recovery of the debt from other property of the debtor.

More detailed regulation was left to the guilds. Guilds were societies for mutual support formed by all merchants in the same trade or all merchants from another district trading in a particular town. Their powers represented a compromise reached in the Song when greater government intervention in commercial matters was successfully resisted.[95] In addition families also had their own power to regulate the affairs of family members, within the wider law. British observers in the 19th century saw families as being like an English company with the power to frame by-laws but also liable where its powers were exceeded.[96]

The Qing Code also prohibited mortgages of land which refused to allow redemption.[97] While it punished creditors who pressed debtors so hard that they committed suicide, debtors needed to be careful that they did not provoke the creditors into hanging themselves at the debtor's door as they would be strangled under the same provision.[98]

Insolvency law as social mediation Mediation was widely used in commercial disputes in the late Qing on Taiwan, but guilds and families found that when disputes involved members of other guilds or families, there were significant limits to their powers and courts were resorted to, although courts too favoured arbitration which was unlikely to give a party all their demands.[99] Guilds sought to appoint secretaries of sufficient social standing to be able to deal directly with mandarins and avoid the lower level of the bureaucracy. When matters did go to court the secretary generally represented the guild and its members.[100]

Going to court meant that a plaintiff ran the risk of losing control of the Case. It might become an adversarial process between the magistrate and the parties. When in 1893 at Heng-ch'un in Taiwan the butcher Ch'en Liang sued Yü Yüan for 39 yuan owing on credit purchases from the butcher shop, Yü claimed that he had kept it as

---

94 As note 20, above, 11.

95 As note 36, above, 89–90.

96 As note 36, above, 96.

97 George Thomas Staunton (trans.) (1810), *Ta Tsing Leu Lee: Being the Fundamental Laws and A Selection from the Supplementary Statutes of the Penal Code of China*, London: T. Cadell and W. Davies, Section XCV, 101–102, Appendix XV, 529; As note 27, above, Jones, Article 95 (3), 119. Land was often inalienable: As note 87, above, Vol. 11, Specific Articles, Article 163, 137–138; As note 35, above, 99–102.

98 As note 20, above, 459. In addition the Qing punished households which had not paid all of the tax due: As note 97, above, Staunton, Section CXLVIII, 158–160; As note 27, above, Jones, Article 148, 159–160. For its antecedants in earlier codes see: As note 87, above, Vol. 11; Articles, Article 217, 205. Debts due to the government continued to take precedence during the period of the early Republic, of the war lords and in the period after reunification. The property of the family of the person in default could also be seized in such cases: As note 35, above, 122.

99 As note 25, above, 81–83.

100 As note 36, above, 95.

interest on a loan. The magistrate's inquiries revealed that Yü had lent 700 yuan to Ch'en and his stepson, Wang Neng. It was, however, related to another loan and dispute between Yü and a relation, Yü Chiang. The magistrate ordered that both disputes be mediated by the village headman. The dispute between the Yüs was resolved but not between Yü and Ch'en. The magistrate ordered that Ch'en repay the 700 yuan immediately.[101]

Parties could only regain control by agreeing to settle the matter under a process called *hexi*, agreement and settlement, from the characters the magistrate drew on the pleadings.[102] The Qing Code forbade private settlements of cases before magistrates but little regard was had to the provision. In Taiwan most matters were referred by the magistrates to mediation by guilds or village headmen.[103]

The President of the Supreme Court in Beijing, Yao Tseng, observed in 1919 the absence of the application of official law in the imperial period:

> In the days of the old regime civil cases were decided by a method more like arbitration than a judicial process; for except the law of succession and marriage there was hardly any law to go by; while in criminal cases decisions could be based on analogy and the judge was even allowed to make punishable an act which in his opinion should not have been done, though it had not been expressly made an offence by law.[104]

The unofficial law's attitude to insolvency There is a cultural norm toward repayment of debt in Taiwan. The Chinese custom was for debts to be paid in full by New Year. When creditors were unable to shame debtors or their families into paying they might force themselves onto the debtors' family, refusing to leave the house until the debt was paid.[105]

There were alternatives to this self-help. Families and magistrates could seek the assistance of local guilds to have debts paid. The guilds bound their members by rules, including the primacy of honesty and fair dealing as well as the periods of credit to be given. The heads of the guild were often arbitrators in disputes between members. Merchant guilds in particular required their members not to go to court but to submit to arbitration by a meeting of the guild. Rules might stipulate procedures:

> It is agreed that members having disputes about money matters with each other shall submit their cases to arbitration at a meeting of the guild where the utmost will be done to arrive at a satisfactory settlement of the dispute. If it be impossible to arrive at an understanding, appeal may be made to the authorities; but if the complainant have recourse to the official

---

101 As note 25, above, 94.

102 As note 25, above, 94.

103 As note 25, above, 101; As note 31, above, MacCormack, 48. But see: Huang, P. (1994), 'Codified Law and Magisterial Adjudication in the Qing', in Bernhardt, K. and H. Philip (eds), *Civil Law in the Qing and Republican China*, Stanford, California: Stanford University Press, 142–186.

104 As note 91, above, 1, 21 quoting Yao Tseng (1923), 'Foreword', in Cheng, F. (trans.) (1923), *The Chinese Supreme Court Decisions*, Peking: Commission on Extra-Territoriality. Van der Sprenkel (as note 36, above, Appendix 4, 133–134) provides examples of deeds of sale, mortgage and loan from the Qing period.

105 As note 35, above, 114. An example of the practice appears in the Case of Chu Pai-Mu in Appendix I, as note 35, above, 140–141.

> direct, without referring to the guild, he shall be subjected to a public reprimand and any future case he may present for the opinion of the guild will be dismissed without a hearing.[106]

If members of other guilds were involved, the heads of the respective guilds could give their support to the members involved and assist them in litigation or negotiate with the heads of the other guilds concerned.[107] By the late 19th century merchants who failed placed their affairs in the hands of their creditors who selected responsible people to settle their debts.[108] In Taiwan similar practices, known as *daohao* ('closed business'), were followed.[109] This continued after the introduction of the Japanese Bankruptcy Law in 1923. As *daohao*, like the official Japanese law, also constituted a discharge for debts on completion there was little incentive to use the formal law.[110]

The practice of the courts using official law has also affected the unofficial law. In the early 1990s business failures were significant in Taiwan as so much small business was undercapitalized. The approach favoured in unofficial law was for creditors to accept 30 per cent of what was owed as this was the penalty imposed by courts for passing a bad cheque. Consequently, as post-dated cheques were frequently used as a way of borrowing, debtors offered this amount to their creditors who then had little reason to take the matter further.[111] Again in the context of small business and individuals the inability of the official banks to provide them with debt capital led them to rely upon many informal financial institutions including unofficial money lenders, rotating credit lotteries *(biaohui)*, post-dated cheques, and real estate loans from scriveners *(daishu)*. Gangsters have been particularly associated with the recovery of debts of the informal money lenders.[112]

Even in larger commercial insolvencies the official law is used reluctantly because of the tradition of having primary recourse to compromise and mediation, the embarrassment of insolvency, the lack of interest of practitioners to become involved, the inadequacies of the Bankruptcy Law and the Company Law, and the questionable outcome of court-administered insolvencies.[113] In corporate reorganizations directors

106 As note 36, above, 94.

107 As note 35, above, 114. In *Tate & Hawkes* v. *Chun Kee*, 26 April 1873, Shanghai Taotai's Court, the Taotai, in spite of the vigorous dissent of the British judge, adopted the report of the Guild involved although it did not reflect the law: As note 35, above, Appendix II, 168–169. Van der Sprenkel (as note 36, above, 90–96) describes the power and the functions of the guilds in the Qing period. Brockman (as note 25, above, 102) gives an example from Taiwan of the magistrate accepting the village headman's decision completely.

108 The financial crisis in Shanghai in 1883–1884 was produced by a stagnant silk market and speculative demand for shares in joint-stock companies. Their failure also led to a fall in the value of commodities and real estate, which had commonly been used as security for loans. McEldery, A. (1976), *Shanghai Old Style Banks (Chien-Chunag) 1800–1935: A Traditional Institution in a Changing Society*, Ann Arbor: Center for Chinese Studies, University of Michigan, 88–89.

109 As note 45, above, 90–91.

110 As note 49, above, 367–369.

111 As note 59, above, Kaufman Winn, 1993, 207–208.

112 As note 59, above, Kaufman Winn, 1993, 213.

113 Tomasic, R. (1997), 'Insolvency Law and Practice in Asia', in Tomasic, R. and P. Little (eds), *Insolvency Law and Practice in Asia*, Hong Kong: FT Law and Tax Asia, 3, 11; As note 45, above, 87–95.

of the company in difficulty may be appointed as managers and this has occurred even when they are facing criminal charges.[114]

Judges are also regarded as unable to administer the law effectively. Many are regarded as young and inexperienced and without the status which common law jurisdictions in particular give to judges:

> Judges don't have enough business sense or expertise or knowledge of the law itself or sufficient experience to handle bankruptcy cases. Once you call the creditor's meeting the process becomes very complicated and judges and professionals don't have enough expertise to handle it.[115]

The scarcity of cases means that they have difficulty in acquiring the necessary skills.[116]

As Taiwan is caught up in the latest period of economic globalization, international investors have brought to Taiwan a different attitude which at the present produces conflict and resistance but which, in the future, may produce a change in local, unofficial law.[117]

The last imperial code, that of the Qing, nominally punished the failure to pay debts in giving magistrates power to deal with them, but it also prevented creditors from relying on their own powers to seize assets of the debtor instead of applying to a magistrate.[118] Where a debtor absconded creditors generally used self-help and raided the debtor's premises and seized whatever assets remained on a first-come first-served principle. If the magistrates were informed of the flight before others the premises were sealed, until the debtor was arrested, with strips of official paper over the windows and doors.[119] On the debtor's arrest it was still usual to negotiate a settlement with the creditors. Again, there was considerable pragmatism. A person from a wealthier family would be expected to offer more than a person from a poorer family. When a compromise was reached the magistrate would approve it and release the debtor.[120]

The penal provisions of the Qing Code were mainly invoked in establishing what the assets of a debtor were and enforcing judgments. Failure to pay a debt did not lead to punishment. The purpose was to force the debtor to restore the property due. If it was clear that debtors were insolvent and not concealing property they could be

---

114 As note 45, above, 79–80.

115 An unidentified partner in a Taiwanese law firm quoted in Tomasic and Francis (as note 45, above, 81).

116 As note 45, above, 81–82.

117 As note 45, above, 91–92, 95.

118 They were subject to punishment by 80 blows, provided that if the value of the property seized did not exceed the amount owed, a fine could be paid: As note 97, above, Staunton, Section CXLIX, 158–160; As note 27, above, Jones, Article 149, 161–162. For its antecedants in earlier codes see: As note 87, above, Vol. 11, Specific Articles, Articles 398–399, 464–465.

119 An illustration of the shop of a bankrupt appears in Gray, as note 80, above, 84.

120 As note 35, above, 122. Alabaster describes the arrest for debt procedure in the case of Chin Shéng-chang by petitioning a magistrate who issued an arrest warrant to the bailiff: Alabaster, E. (1968) (originally published London, 1899), *Notes and Commentaries on Chinese Criminal Law*, Taipei: Ch'ang-Wen, 551.

released.[121] There were exceptions. When Hu Kuang-yung, a particularly wealthy silk merchant and customs banker, went bankrupt in Shanghai through a failure to corner the market in export silk in 1883 the imperial government directly intervened. Hu's banks held customs revenue and private investments of members of the imperial family. It ordered that he be stripped of his title, his affairs investigated and, if his financial obligations were not met, he was to be punished.[122]

Once a party obtained a judgment, or sought to have a settlement given the force of a court order, courts had limited powers to enforce payment. They interpreted the Code as not permitting them to order the seizure of the assets of the debtor. Where parties had no resources, or a poor reputation, they could be required to provide a guaranty bond from a third party promising to pay if the judgment debtor did not. Courts could also order that recalcitrant judgment debtors be flogged or imprisoned. While these may appear to be criminal sanctions, they are criminal in the same way as in most common law jurisdictions, where parties who breach injunctions granted in civil matters or refuse to comply with an order for specific performance may be fined or imprisoned.[123]

The growing impact of Western capitalism and colonialism on China after the mid-19th century resulted in the development within China of commercial and manufacturing firms, the expansion of trade within China and foreign trade between China and other states, the presence of foreign companies and traders, and the use of non-Chinese trading practices which had had no previous existence.[124]

Pragmatic practices overlaid the application of the Qing Code. For example, the Qing Code was silent on the liability of partners in a partnership but rules were developed if the partnership became bankrupt:

- If all partners participated in the business and were known to the public they were each liable to pay a share of the debts in proportion to their share in the total capital.[125]
- If only some partners conducted the business and silent partners (who had contributed capital) took no part in it, the partners managing the business were primarily liable for the whole of the debts, particularly where there was reckless trading or other misconduct. Silent partners lost their capital and could not appear

121 A Ming and Qing sub-statute permitted claims for the restitution of specific property. In its final form, following a revision in 1835, where the property sought to be reclaimed was worth more than 30 ounces of silver, a person could be imprisoned for six months. If it was of less value the period of imprisonment was reduced to three months. At the end of that period the Emperor was petitioned about the case and advised on exercising clemency or exiling the debtor having regard to the circumstances of the case. Both the imprisonment and the possible exposure to a sentence of exile were intended to bring pressure on the debtor and the family to make restitution: As note 88, above, 251.

122 As note 108, above, 88–89.

123 As note 25, above, 94–95.

124 Jamieson (note 35, above, 116–120) provides an example in the conflicting consequences for the guarantors of guarantee bonds or 'security chops' leading to the appeal to the Supreme Court in Beijing of the decision in *Sassoons* v. *Fan Teh-sheng*, Shanghai Mixed Court, 15 May 1885, Appendix II, 169–170.

125 As note 35, above, 128–130. This principle appears to have been followed in *Guerrier* v. *Wang Tso-Ming*, 31 March 1904, Shanghai Mixed Court, Appendix II, as note 35, above, 163.

as creditors competing with the ordinary competitors, but were treated differently; yet, as no rule was rigid, if they had substantial means there was an expectation that they would contribute to the amount to be paid to creditors on the winding up.[126]
- There was to be an equal division of the assets of the partnership amongst the creditors.[127]

These pressures led in 1905 to the promulgation of the first bankruptcy law as an imperial edict. As noted, it was repealed in 1907 as the impact of Western business practices was far from uniform and many parts of China remained unaffected by them.[128]

The Bankruptcy Code of 1905 This was made in the period of increasing globalization and internationalization of national economies that preceded World War I. It was drafted by staff of the Ministry of Commerce who had been educated in Japanese law schools. The draft was revised before promulgation by Wu Ting-fan, who had been admitted to the English Bar, and who was in charge of the Imperial Law Reform Commission.[129]

The Code consisted of 69 Articles, and applied both to merchants and to individuals.[130] It required the involvement of the local chamber of commerce as well as the courts if the merchant was the petitioner or the subject of a petition by creditors.[131] The chamber of commerce selected a trustee in bankruptcy from the reputable merchants with sufficient assets in the debtor's trade.[132] Creditors notified outstanding debts to the chamber of commerce. The chamber forwarded them to the trustee who was required to organize the creditors' meetings.[133] Resolutions at these meetings required a simple majority of creditors present but the votes of creditors whose claims constituted 75 per cent of the indebtedness were binding.[134] The trustee was entitled to take possession of the debtor's property subject to mortgages and to sell it where the amount realized would exceed the amount secured.[135] Those owing money to the bankrupt, once notified by the court, were required to pay outstanding amounts to the chamber of commerce within one month.[136] Where debts were owed to government it participated *pari passu* with other creditors but the bankrupt was

126 As note 35, above, 128–130.

127 In *Re Chen Dah and Sin Dah*, Shanghai Mixed Court, 26 August 1904: as note 35, above, 163–164. These customs were recognized in a Hong Kong ordinance as a result of complaints by Chinese merchants about the severity of English partnership law which held all partners responsible for all the debts: An Act to provide for the registration of Chinese partnerships and to enable partners therein to register and thereby to limit their liability, Ordinance No 53 of 1911, as note 35, above, 128–130.

128 As note 81, above, Foo, viii.

129 As note 81, above, Teesdale, 2.

130 Articles 1 and 8.

131 Articles 1 and 5.

132 Article 9.

133 Articles 17 and 20.

134 Article 22.

135 Article 34.

136 Article 39.

to be investigated for embezzlement and punished if found guilty.[137] Property of others, including family members, held by the bankrupt was not to be used to pay the debts.[138] If the bankrupt was without any assets the trustee, with the permission of the creditors, could show compassion and pay to the bankrupt enough money to support the bankrupt and his family for two years.[139] Where there were extenuating circumstances and more than 50 per cent of the money owed was paid, or where all the money owed was paid, the bankrupt could be discharged.[140] Where fraud was involved special procedures were to be followed to ensure that the bankrupt was punished and to ensure that any sureties paid any amounts outstanding.[141]

In addition to these procedures merchants in financial difficulties could apply to the chamber of commerce to negotiate a compromise with creditors in order to be able to trade out of those difficulties.[142] A creditor was entitled to insist on payment and to petition to bankrupt the debtor.[143]

Although revoked in 1907 the Qing Bankruptcy Law gained a unique status. Until the Bankruptcy Law of 1935 was promulgated it continued to be used as a persuasive guide by the courts when it was not contrary to other laws or local customs. It became the primary source of bankruptcy law principles for courts in the Republican period after 1911 and was applied to individuals, partnerships and companies.[144] Its significant principles, particularly those parts which represented Chinese tradition and custom, survived to reappear in the Bankruptcy Law of 1935. Both gave a significant role to chambers of commerce. These had grown out of the old guilds as Chinese merchants in different trades came to engage in greater cooperation to regulate the new ways of doing business. They enabled merchants to compete effectively with foreign enterprises but also excluded non-establishment businesses which were too competitive.[145]

---

137 Article 40. Allman (as note 54, above, 225) citing a Supreme Court decision: '"In the purview of private law, a Government is in the same position as an individual. Consequently public funds deposited with mercantile concerns for interest bearing purposes are subject to bankruptcy rules when such firm becomes insolvent and no preferential right is acquired by reason of being public funds." (Legal Rules and Explanations of the Chinese Supreme Court, Vol. 3, p. 5 Bankruptcy).'

138 Articles 43 and 45. Allman (as note 54, above, 222) citing Supreme Court decision AC No 2416, 4th Yr CR Tr and AC 253 3rd Yr CR reported in Cheng, F. (trans.) (1923), *The Chinese Supreme Court Decisions*, Peking: Commission on Extra-Territoriality, 26.

139 Article 48.

140 Articles 66–68.

141 Articles 49–62.

142 Articles 63–65.

143 As note 54, above, 221.

144 Allman (as note 54, above, 220–222) citing the following decisions of the Supreme Court: AC No 16 3rd Yr CR Tr and AC No 1028 3rd Yr CR Tr and AC No 718 3rd CR Tr. Subsequently the Supreme Court stated: 'In the case of the bankruptcy of a merchant or trader, should there be a special local custom relating to the bankruptcy of commercial firms, such custom should be observed in preference to any legal principles governing bankruptcies', cited in Tomasic and Francis (as note 45, above, 69).

145 In Shanghai the imperial governor and the Imperial Bank of China as well as the exclusive guilds, including those in banking which ran a clearing association, cooperated to form a Western-style chamber of commerce: As note 108, above, 92–93.

The Bankruptcy Law drafted in Beijing in 1915, the fourth year of the Republic, by the Codification Commission was not promulgated for the same reason that the edict of 1905 had been repealed: the absence of uniform adoption of non-traditional business practices and the countervailing strength of custom.[146]

In 1920 the Ministry of Justice promulgated detailed rules for the enforcement of judgments in which Articles 46–51 and 79 permitted the property of the debtor to be distributed among the creditors, apart from the judgment creditors, if it could be proved that the debtor was also indebted to them. These were an inadequate basis on which courts could supervise the liquidation of assets and the payment of creditors. In 1934 the same ministry promulgated tentative rules for the bankruptcy of merchants and also produced a revised version of the draft Bankruptcy Law of 1915. By that time the need for a bankruptcy law was acute. Manufacturers and commercial firms were failing at an unprecedented rate as China was caught in the global depression.[147]

The history of Taiwan's legal system reflects the commercial and cultural interaction between communities on Taiwan, as they brought with them their own legal values, and between Taiwan's official and unofficial laws and other external influences. The interaction between Taiwan's official and unofficial laws shows the hallmarks of this process, such as the promulgation of legislation to cater for changes in commercial custom. The remaining sections of this chapter look at this interplay between official and unofficial law in the context of Taiwan's insolvency laws and practice.

1.3 Key Insolvency Law Principles in Taiwan

*Bankruptcy Law (*Pochan Fa*) 1935* The Civil Codification Commission of the Legislative Yuan was instructed to draft a Bankruptcy Law in 1933 and a seven-member Commission commenced the task in 1934. The drafting Commission drew on a wide range of sources:

- existing Chinese custom and practice in the settlement of debt;
- the draft bankruptcy laws of 1915 and 1934 and the tentative rules for the bankruptcy of merchants of 1934; and
- 'the most modern, most scientific and most characteristic foreign bankruptcy law, where the Commission could find the latest accomplishments of Western juridical science.'[148]

---

146 As note 81, above, Foo, viii.

147 As note 81, above, Foo, viii.

148 These included: (a) the English bankruptcy legislation of 1914 which had been amended in 1926 and the adaptations reflected in the bankruptcy ordinances of Hong Kong and the Straits Settlements 'as adaptations of English law to Far Eastern countries'; (b) the Morocco Bankruptcy Law of 1913, revised in 1922 which was accepted to represent current French law; (c) the German and Japanese Bankruptcy Law on which the 1915 and 1934 draft laws were largely based; (d) the Swiss Law on Execution for Debts and Bankruptcy (1889) and the Turkish Bankruptcy Law of 1932 which was based on it; (e) the related laws of Yugoslavia (1929), Persia (1932), Peru (1932) and Argentina (1933); and, (f) the Italian draft revised Commercial Code of 1925: As note 81, above, Foo, ix–x.

A draft law of 160 articles was produced and subject to review by the Legislative Yuan and its advisers, the Judicial Yuan, the Ministry of Judicial Administration, the courts, chambers of commerce, bar associations and law schools. In addition it was advertised in newspapers within China and circulated to a number of foreign legal bodies for comment. A number of amendments were made to the final draft before its introduction into the Legislative Yuan and a number of amendments were made in the course of its discussion in the legislature.[149]

*The principles of the Bankruptcy Law (*Pochan Fa*) 1935* As drafted and enacted, the law was intended to embody five important principles. It:

- reflected the spirit of new Chinese legislation provided for in the Constitution;
- met the needs of the general public;
- preserved what was good of traditional practices and customs;
- embodied those features of foreign laws which were progressive and adapted to the requirements of Chinese business; and
- was clear and concise.[150]

In addition to the law itself there are the interpretations of the Judicial Yuan, which has inherited the power of the Supreme Court at Beijing created in the early years of the Republic, to make binding interpretations and to establish precedents. In its introduction to the summary of its decisions the Supreme Court observed in 1919:

> Since the establishment of the Republic … the Supreme Court strictly abides by the law. When, at times, the law is found to be defective or inconsistent with the spirit of the age, a remedy, if possible, is affected through interpretation, and where there is no law to go by at all, a precedent is created, having first considered the special condition of the country as well as legal principles.[151]

The Drafting Commission identified the key features of the Bankruptcy Law as it was enacted in 1935:

- The amicable settlement provisions which draw on Chinese legal concepts and ethics which permit any debtor up to the last moment to submit a scheme of composition to the creditors' meeting.
- The extension of amicable bankruptcy procedures to both merchants and non-merchants, which was inconsistent with a number of other jurisdictions which sought to separate commercial law from civil law, as it would have been contrary to the principles of the KMT's policy of 'the social unification of the nation' to permit merchants to have a special juridical statement.
- The discharge of debtors, where there is no fraud, free of any further liability once the creditors are paid according to a composition or the assets are liquidated and

149 As note 81, above, Foo, x.

150 As note 81, above, Foo, x–xi.

151 As note 91, above, 21 quoting Yao Tseng (1923), 'Foreword', in Cheng, F. (trans.) (1923), *The Chinese Supreme Court Decisions*, Peking: Commission on Extra-Territoriality.

distributed according to the Bankruptcy Law (Article 149). This gives bona fide bankrupts the chance of a new start free from new civil actions, which is both humane and consistent with Chinese ethics.

- The right of a creditor with a secured right over that asset to exercise rights outside any bankruptcy proceedings, subject to a bankruptcy administrator being entitled to recover the property and dispose of it where the property may yield more than the secured debt so that the balance is available to other creditors (Article 108).
- Bankruptcy could be pronounced by a court in any civil proceedings where the debtor is found to be unable to discharge the debts owing: this protects other creditors who may be unaware of the debtor's real situation (Article 60).
- Bankruptcy proceedings can apply to inheritances at the request of the creditors or the heir managing the deceased's property (Article 59).
- Penalties for fraudulent bankruptcy and other frauds related to bankruptcy, including collusion between bankrupt creditors and administrators, fixed to deter such actions being taken, particularly to prevent debtors from harming the interests of the creditors.[152]

1.4 General introduction to the Statutory, Regulatory and Judicial Approach in Taiwan

Corporate insolvency laws in Taiwan are found in the Bankruptcy Law and Company Law. The Bankruptcy Law also governs personal bankruptcy. There are other pieces of legislation impacting on corporate insolvency and personal bankruptcy in the jurisdiction, including the Civil Code, the Chattel Secured Transactions Law, and the Statute of Conflict of Laws.

Regulatory authorities have significant supervisory roles in the reorganization process found in the Company Law. For instance, the court is required to seek opinions on the reorganization plan from the following regulatory authorities:

- the central authority (the Ministry of Economic Affairs);
- the central authority in charge of special purpose enterprises (usually the Industrial Development Board); and
- the authority in charge of securities exchanges (the Taiwan Securities Exchange Commission).[153]

However, there is some doubt about the extent to which government agencies take an active role in the supervision of financially distressed companies within their jurisdiction. There is a perception among practitioners in Taiwan that regulatory bodies are reluctant to get involved in the supervision of financially distressed companies unless influenced by government policy considerations.[154] In a study of Taiwan's insolvency laws and practice in 1995 and 1996, a local accountant stated that 'once a company's liabilities exceed its assets then it is considered bankrupt

---

152 As note 81, above, Foo, xiii–xv.

153 Company Law, Article 283.

154 As note 45, above, 82–87.

(according to the Bankruptcy Law). But as long as the piece of paper is not sent into the Ministry of Economic Affairs, then it doesn't matter and no-one is concerned about bankruptcy.'[155] Practitioners also questioned the ability of the regulatory bodies in Taiwan to deal with a large corporate bankruptcy.[156]

There is also the view that the court system in Taiwan has difficulties in dealing with complex insolvencies.[157] Local magistrates, as noted, during the Qing period dealt with insolvencies as a part of their administrative duties. Taiwan has since been subject to considerable influence from the Japanese legal system, which in turn has been influenced by European civil law models. These influences are reflected in the nature of courts and the judiciary in contemporary Taiwan. In particular, the courts in Taiwan have a greater investigative and interrogative role in the insolvency process than their counterparts in Western common law jurisdictions. Another major difference is that the judiciary is an early vocational appointment for law graduates in Taiwan, as opposed to a final step in the career of experienced commercial practitioners called from the bar. There are moves to reform the judiciary to ensure that judges have the expertise to deal with the demands of the insolvency procedures under the Bankruptcy Law and Company Law.[158]

2 Personal Insolvency Laws

2.1 Introduction: Sources of Laws, Basis and Extent

The Bankruptcy Law, which applies to both personal and business insolvencies, was promulgated in 1935, under a previous Constitution of the Republic of China.[159]

Article 111 of the present Constitution allocates legislative and executive powers between the Central, Provincial and County governments by providing that matters not specifically dealt with in other provisions:

> … shall fall within the jurisdiction of the Central Government if it is national in nature, within that of the Province if it is provincial in nature, and within that of the County if it is county in nature. In case of dispute, the matter shall be settled by the Legislative Yuan.

The Central Government has a number of powers under Article 107(2) to make and administer laws on bankruptcy. It has power over foreign affairs, national law and criminal, civil, and commercial laws, the judiciary, state-operated economic enterprises and financial and economic matters affecting aliens or foreign countries, any of which might relate to bankruptcy. Under Article 108(1) it also has the specific, but delegable, legislative and administrative powers over the demarcation of administrative areas, commerce, banks and stock exchanges. The provincial

155 As note 45, above, 83–84.
156 As note 45, above, 86.
157 As note 45, above, 82.
158 As note 45, above, 82.
159 The Provisional Constitution of the Political Tutelage Period promulgated in 1931.

government of Taiwan may legislate separate rules and regulations provided they do not contravene any national law.

Chapter XIII of the Constitution established fundamental national policies to be followed by government. Now of reduced significance they reflect the historic socialist platform of the KMT in 1947 which was also consistent with older Chinese traditions on harmony in the distribution of wealth and which underpin the considerable scale of state-owned enterprise in Taiwan. Article 142 states that:

> The national economy shall be based on the Principle of People's Livelihood and shall seek to effect the equalization of land rights and regulation of private capital in order to assure an equitable distribution of national wealth and sufficiency for the people's livelihood.

Article 145 complements this principle:

> With respect to private wealth and privately operated enterprises, the State shall restrict them by law if they are deemed detrimental to the balanced development of national wealth and people's livelihood. Cooperative enterprises shall receive encouragement and assistance from the State.

Article 149 puts beyond doubt that in implementing such policies: 'financial institutions shall, in accordance with law, be subject to State control'.

More contemporary statements of the role of the state in business and commerce appear in the Additional Article 9, promulgated in 1994, which declares that:

> The State shall encourage the development of and investment in science and technology, facilitate the upgrade of industry, promote the modernization of agriculture and fishery, emphasize the exploitation and utilization of water resources, and intensify international economic cooperation.

The Bankruptcy Law came towards the end of the period of the substantial reform of the law of China which had commenced under the last emperors of the Qing dynasty at the beginning of the 20th century. The reform accelerated after the reunification of China in 1928 and was ended by Japan's attack on Manchuria. Like many of the other laws enacted in that period it was influenced by Japanese and German civil law models.[160] Like the other codified laws of this period, the Bankruptcy Law was to make little impact on the embedded Confucian respect for traditional moral and social behaviour.[161] Long periods of economic growth have also led to less insolvency. The use of the legal process has been unusual.[162]

---

160 As note 113, above, 11.

161 As note 83, above, 193.

162 Kamarul, B. and R. Tomasic (1999) 'The rule of law and corporate insolvency in six Asian legal systems', in Jayasurya, K. (ed.) *Law, Capitalism and Power in Asia: the rule of law and legal institutions*, Routledge: London, 151, 170-1.

2.2 *The Regulatory Structures for the Control of Bankruptcy Proceedings*

Regulatory bodies do not have as great a role in the administration of bankruptcy procedures as they do in the reorganization process.[163] As a result, bankruptcy administration is largely left to the courts. When they become involved they do not handle it well. The borrowed civil law traditions of the judiciary also mean that judges tend not to have had experience as practising commercial lawyers. This becomes self-perpetuating, as few cases in bankruptcy do not give them any experience.[164] The courts also do not accord bankruptcy much priority. Bankruptcy cases are frequently transferred between judges.[165] A significant feature of corporate reorganizations is the role played by government agencies.[166] Courts, following the tradition of both civil law systems and the tradition of Chinese imperial administration, do not see themselves as separate from these other agencies and their views can be very influential.[167] Intervention by the Executive Yuan may be more indirect by assisting the insolvent company with access to finance from state-owned banks or through transactions with state-owned companies.[168]

The combination of these factors has made some business people with Anglo-American commercial backgrounds in Taiwan sceptical of the capabilities of the Taiwanese insolvency regime, particularly if it were faced with a large insolvency.[169]

2.3 *The Principal Institutions for the Application of these Laws*

Bankruptcy proceedings will involve a district court judge, the trustee in bankruptcy appointed by the court and the inspector, or supervisor, elected at the creditors' meeting. Where composition before the court is sought a district court judge will be involved as supervisor. The appointment of an inspector or assistant supervisor may involve chartered public accountants or people nominated by the local chamber of commerce. Where composition is sought at the local chamber of commerce it will handle the matter without the intervention of the court. Such a composition may involve public chartered accountants, other specialists or its own members as supervisors of the business, as well as representatives appointed by the creditors' meeting.[170]

---

163 As note 45, above, 83.

164 As note 45, above, 81.

165 As note 45, above, 81.

166 Company Law, Article 283.

167 As note 45, above, 82–3.

168 As note 45, above, 84–85.

169 As note 45, above, 86–7. At 86, a foreign banker in Taipei is cited as saying:

> It would be impossible for them [to handle a large insolvency]. There is a complete lack of skills to handle anything as big and complex as BCCI (Bank of Credit and Commerce International]. The SEC here is incompetent, not very diligent, and has no teeth. They never go in and say 'stop'. They don't enforce anything. In a case we are involved in at the moment, the company was still trading on the stock exchange until recently, despite its bankruptcy.

170 Bankruptcy Law, Chapter II – Composition: Section 1 – Composition before the Court, and Section 2 – Composition at the Chamber of Commerce, and Chapter III – Bankruptcy.

In a bankruptcy the trustee in bankruptcy must be appointed by the court, and:

- selected from certified public accountants or other persons qualified for the management of the corporate debtor's assets; or
- appointed from the creditors present at the creditors' meeting.[171]

The inspector, or supervisor, must be elected at the creditors' meeting to supervise the progress of the bankruptcy on behalf of the creditors.[172]

In compositions before the court a district court judge must be the supervisor.[173] The assistant supervisor must be:

- selected from certified public accountants;
- elected by the local chamber of commerce; or
- one or two other appropriate persons.[174]

There is limited expertise and experience in the accounting and legal professions in Taiwan in fulfilling the role of trustee or being involved in bankruptcy administration or corporate liquidation.[175] Possible practitioners refer to the negative publicity and poor status associated with insolvency work and the constant controversy and professional and physical harassment involved.[176] There are also other reasons in the lower levels of the economy. A Taipei lawyer, and member of the Judicial Review Committee, is reported as saying: 'Lawyers decline to become involved as administrators because often the underground is involved. If these sort of people lose their money they become crazy and mad. People who get involved risk their lives.'[177] Trustees in bankruptcy are seen to be under the greatest pressure and as getting the least support.[178]

2.4 Powers of Courts in Handling Bankruptcy Petitions

Bankruptcy and composition proceedings are within the jurisdiction of the district court where the debtor is domiciled. If the debtor has a business office the jurisdiction falls to the district court where that office is located. If the jurisdiction cannot be determined using these principles the district court of the principle place where the debtor's property is situated has jurisdiction.[179]

---

171 Bankruptcy Law, Articles 64, 83.

172 Bankruptcy Law, Article 120.

173 Bankruptcy Law, Article 11.

174 Bankruptcy Law, Article 11.

175 As note 162, above, 170–1.

176 As note 45, above, 88–9.

177 As note 162, above, 161.

178 As note 45, above, 89, 94.

179 Bankruptcy Law, Article 2.

2.5 *Duties of Bankruptcy Practitioners*

A trustee must exercise the functions with the care expected from a good administrator.[180] If the duty of care is breached the trustee is jointly liable together with the bankrupt for any damage which results to other people. Where the loss or damage is suffered by the bankrupt the trustee is liable to the bankrupt. If there is a breach of the fiduciary duty of the trustee a criminal offence will have been committed.[181]

Particular actions by the trustee will require the agreement of the inspector, or supervisor. They are:

- assigning rights over immovable property;
- assigning mining rights, fishing rights and intellectual property rights;
- assigning the stock of a business or the whole business;
- borrowing money;
- assigning of movable property worth more than NT$100 when this does not form part of the continuation of the bankrupt's business;
- assigning claims and valuable securities;
- recovery of currency, securities or valuable items in special custody;
- claiming the performance of a bilateral contract;
- mediating or arbitrating disputes in respect of the bankrupt's properties;
- waiving any rights held by the bankrupt;
- recognizing the right of others to recover or exclude property from the bankrupt's estate and the expenses incurred in the administration of the estate; and
- instituting legal proceedings to recover property for inclusion in the estate.[182]

Trustees in bankruptcy are supervised by the district court that may require them to post a bond.[183] The court may replace a trustee on its own motion or following a resolution of the creditors' meeting or a request from the inspector or supervisor.[184]

No legal proceeding has been taken against practitioners for any breach of their duties.[185]

Assistant supervisor in composition Assistant supervisors in a composition may be required by the court to post securities.[186] Their functions, under the direction of the supervisor, are to:

- supervise the management of the business by the debtor and prevent any action which would be prejudicial to the interests of the creditors;

---

180 Bankruptcy Law, Article 86.

181 Deng, Y. (1998), *Report on Taipei, China*, Asian Development Bank, Technical Assistance No. 5795-REG, Insolvency Law Reform, para. J4.

182 Bankruptcy Law, Article 92.

183 Bankruptcy Law, Article 83.

184 Bankruptcy Law, Article 85.

185 As note 181, above, para. J4.

186 Bankruptcy Law, Article 11.

- keep business receipts and assets of the debtor secure, except for those required to be disposed of in managing the business and maintaining the debtor and the debtor's family;
- complete the list of creditors; and
- investigate the business of the debtor, properties and their value.[187]

2.6 Rules regarding Creditors' Petitions for Bankruptcy and Initiation of Bankruptcy Proceedings

The creditor can apply for a debtor to be made bankrupt.[188] A failure by a debtor to continue to pay debts will raise a presumption that the debtor is unable to pay and provides the grounds for the application.[189] The petition must state the nature and amounts of outstanding claims and other factors relating to the inability to be able to pay off debts.[190] The court can also initiate a bankruptcy. If a court ascertains in the course of civil litigation or civil execution that a debtor cannot pay or is unable to pay off debts, it may of its own power order that the debtor is bankrupt.[191]

A creditor of a deceased debtor may also petition for the bankruptcy of the estate.[192]

A bankruptcy petition can be filed where a composition is under way but the court may dismiss the petition if it believes that it is possible to reach a composition.[193] The failure of any composition will lead to bankruptcy by operation of the Bankruptcy Law.[194] Only the debtor may apply for composition[195] but a creditor can prevent an application succeeding by applying for bankruptcy. Debtors may not apply for composition if there is already a bankruptcy application in existence.[196]

The court must rule on a bankruptcy petition within seven days from its receipt. If the investigations required cannot be completed in that time the court may extend the period for less than seven days. The court may make its own investigations and summons debtors and creditors and other interested people for questioning.[197]

If it decides to grant the petition the court must:

- appoint a trustee in bankruptcy; and
- fix a period for reporting claims of more than 15 days and less than three months from the date of its order.[198]

---

187 Bankruptcy Law, Article 11.
188 Bankruptcy Law, Articles 57, 58.
189 Bankruptcy Law, Article 1.
190 Bankruptcy Law, Article 61.
191 Bankruptcy Law, Article 60.
192 Bankruptcy Law, Article 59.
193 Bankruptcy Law, Article 58.
194 Bankruptcy Law, Articles 52–54.
195 Bankruptcy Law, Article 6.
196 Bankruptcy Law, Articles 6, 41.
197 Bankruptcy Law, Article 63.
198 Bankruptcy Law, Article 64.

The court must give a public notice, which is sent to each of the debtors, creditors and holders of the bankrupt's property of which it is aware, advertised on the court's bulletin board, and published in any public gazette and newspaper in the district. The notice must indicate:

- the court's decision to make the debtor bankrupt;
- the name and address of the trustee in bankruptcy;
- the period for submitting claims;
- that the debtors of the bankrupt and holders of the bankrupt's property must pay any debt owed or hand the property to the trustee in bankruptcy or notify the trustee of the debt or the property; and
- that creditors of the bankrupt must report their claims to the trustee in the period fixed for this.[199]

2.7 Rules regarding Debtors' Petitions for Bankruptcy

Bankruptcy A debtor may also file an application for bankruptcy. The debtor's petition for bankruptcy must list the status of any assets, and a list of creditors and debtors.[200]

The heir, manager of a deceased's property, or the executor of the will may apply for the bankruptcy of the deceased's estate.[201] If such an order is made the creditors of the heir may not exercise any rights over such property even though the heir has not given acceptance of succession.[202]

Composition The debtor may apply to the district court for composition where the debtor's assets are insufficient to satisfy debts. A failure by a debtor to pay will raise a presumption that the debtor is unable to pay.[203] Alternatively the debtor may apply to a local chamber of commerce for composition as discussed below in para. 3.7.

In applying to the district court for composition the debtor must submit a statement of assets and their status and a list of creditors and debtors as well as a composition plan and provide securities for the carrying out of the composition plan.[204] The court may summons the debtor to appear to make supplementary statements, to provide relevant documents or to make other necessary inquiries.[205] The court must rule on the application within seven days and there is no appeal against its decision.[206] The court must dismiss the application if the debtor has not provided the required information either on the initial application or as a result of being summonsed by the court.[207]

199 Bankruptcy Law, Article 65.
200 Bankruptcy Law, Article 62.
201 Bankruptcy Law, Article 59.
202 Bankruptcy Law, Article 115.
203 Bankruptcy Law, Article 6.
204 Bankruptcy Law, Article 7.
205 Bankruptcy Law, Article 8.
206 Bankruptcy Law, Article 9.
207 Bankruptcy Law, Article 10.

The court must, after approving a petition for composition, advertise the application, the names of the supervisor and assistant supervisor, the place where the composition will be conducted and the period in which claims are to be notified. It must also send this information and a copy of the proposed composition arrangements to the creditors and the applicant.[208]

2.8 Powers of Secured Creditors

Secured creditors and or preferred creditors have the right not to participate in a bankruptcy. A person with a pledge, mortgage or lien over a property of the bankrupt may exclude that property from the bankruptcy proceedings and need not comply with those proceedings.[209] They may choose to participate in the bankruptcy in respect of any unpaid amount of the debt still owing.[210]

Other creditors may also enjoy some protection under the Bankruptcy Law:

- a debtor who has paid the bankrupt a debt unaware of the bankruptcy order may set the payment up against the creditors. If the debtor had knowledge, only the benefits received by the assets divisible among creditors may be set up;[211]
- a seller, who has made an agreement with a buyer who has become bankrupt, but is yet to supply the goods and receive the payment for them, may rescind the agreement and recover the goods. The trustee in bankruptcy may insist on delivery but is then obliged to pay the whole price for the goods;[212] and
- a creditor who is also a debtor at the time of the bankruptcy may claim a set-off without complying with the bankruptcy procedure.[213]

Set-offs cannot be claimed where:

- a creditor in bankruptcy becomes indebted to the bankrupt's estate after the bankruptcy order;
- the debtor of a bankrupt acquires a claim against the bankrupt's estate after the bankruptcy order; and
- the debtor of a bankrupt acquires a claim against the bankrupt's estate after becoming aware that a petition for bankruptcy has been filed (except where the claim is acquired by operation of statute or an obligation which existed prior to the knowledge of the application).[214]

---

208 Bankruptcy Law, Article 12. The publication may be on the court's notice board, in newspapers and public gazettes, or at the chamber of commerce or other appropriate places: Bankruptcy Law, Article 13.
209 Bankruptcy Law, Article 108.
210 Bankruptcy Law, Article 109.
211 Bankruptcy Law, Article 76.
212 Bankruptcy Law, Article 111.
213 Bankruptcy Law, Article 113.
214 Bankruptcy Law, Article 114.

In compositions secured creditors and or preferred creditors have the power not to agree to a composition and moratorium.[215]

2.9 Nature of Bankruptcy Petitions by Creditors and Debtors

Except for a bankruptcy ordered by the court itself the bankruptcy proceeding can be commenced by a petition filed by a creditor or the debtor. Composition, as noted, is available only on the debtor's petition.[216]

A composition application or scheme may be terminated by the court and the debtor adjudicated bankrupt by the court:

- where the creditors disagree at the creditors' meeting over the conditions of the composition, or where a creditor failed to attend the meeting where the composition was adopted and the composition shows bias in favour of the interests of other creditors and is, therefore, prejudicial to some creditors;[217]
- within one year from the court's approval of the composition, and the creditors show that the debtor made a false report of the debts, concealed property or promised preferential treatment to some creditors;[218] or
- where the debtor is unable to fulfil the terms of the composition and a majority of the outstanding creditors holding more than two thirds of the total amount owed resolve to end the composition.[219]

2.10 Creditors' Meetings

Bankruptcy The court, on the application of the trustee in bankruptcy or supervisor, may order the convening of a creditors' meeting to participate in the bankruptcy.[220] A judge must preside at a creditors' meeting.[221]

The bankrupt must be present and must answer questions raised by the presiding judge, the trustee in bankruptcy, any inspectors or supervisors, or the creditors.[222]

Resolutions are to be passed by majority vote of the creditors present at the meeting who together represent more than one half of the aggregate amount claimed.[223] They can deal with:

- election of one or more supervisors, or inspectors, to supervise the progress of the bankruptcy procedures on behalf of the creditors;
- measures for the management of the bankrupt's estate;

---

215 Bankruptcy Law, Article 17.
216 Bankruptcy Law, Article 6.
217 Bankruptcy Law, Article 50.
218 Bankruptcy Law, Article 51.
219 Bankruptcy Law, Article 52.
220 Bankruptcy Law, Article 116.
221 Bankruptcy Law, Article 117.
222 Bankruptcy Law, Article 122.
223 Bankruptcy Law, Article 123.

- continuing or discontinuing the business of the debtor;[224]
- election, appointment and change of the trustee in bankruptcy;[225]
- approval or disapproval of the reconciliation plan – terminating the bankruptcy if it is approved by the court;[226]
- giving instructions for the auction or other disposal of the properties of the bankrupt;[227] and
- disputes over claims.[228]

Composition Compositions must have a creditors' meeting for them to take place. The creditors' meeting is required to negotiate with the debtor. The meeting must be held within seven days to one month following the close of the period for notifying claims. That period is from ten days to two months from the grant of the application by the court.[229]

The supervisor, a district court judge, is the chair. The assistant supervisor should also attend.[230] The debtor, or a representative, must be present at the meeting and answer issues raised by the supervisor, the assistant supervisor and any creditors.[231]

A resolution, agreeing to composition, must be passed by majority vote of the creditors present at the meeting who together represent more than two thirds of the aggregate unsecured amount claimed.[232]

3 Personal Bankruptcy Law Procedures

The Bankruptcy Law is infrequently applied to personal insolvencies. A family's connections, the related *guanxi*, and a reluctance to be seen as the person who pushed another into bankruptcy leads to unofficial and negotiated solutions.[233] A local partner in an international accounting firm in Taipei is reported as saying: 'The use of … non-legal means depends on the level of the economy you are at. At the lower levels there are loan sharks and more criminal activity. I have heard that some companies may hire a company to collect debts – "I'll break your knees if you don't pay shortly – like yesterday".'[234]

---

224 Bankruptcy Law, Article 121.
225 Bankruptcy Law, Article 85.
226 Bankruptcy Law, Article 132.
227 Bankruptcy Law, Article 138.
228 Bankruptcy Law, Article 125.
229 Bankruptcy Law, Article 12.
230 Bankruptcy Law, Article 22.
231 Bankruptcy Law, Article 24.
232 Bankruptcy Law, Article 27.
233 As note 162, above, 160–161.
234 As note 162, above, 161.

3.1 Controls Placed on Debtors once a Bankruptcy Petition has been Lodged

Bankrupts lose the ability to conduct their own financial and business affairs. Any property rights are transferred to the estate in bankruptcy. The trustee in bankruptcy takes the bankrupt's place in contractual arrangements to recover any debts or property.[235] The trustee, with the permission of the court and before the creditors' meeting, may continue to trade in the bankrupt's business to the extent required to facilitate its liquidation.[236]

In a composition the financial and business affairs are conducted by the debtor subject to the supervision of the supervisor. The supervisor has no right to take any action in the debtor's place.[237]

The court has considerable power over the place of living and freedom of movements of bankrupts. In certain cases the court of its own power, or on the application of the creditors, may arrest or detain the person the subject of a bankruptcy petition, or make other precautionary orders, on the receipt of a petition for bankruptcy.[238] The bankrupt should not leave a place of residence without the court's permission.[239] The court may arrest, or summons, the bankrupt when it deems it necessary and, in such cases, the court's powers are enlarged to those found in the Code of Criminal Procedure.[240] If it is feared that the bankrupt may abscond or hide, or destroy or abandon any property, the court may arrest the bankrupt and detain the bankrupt for a period up to one month. On the application of the trustee the period can be extended by periods of one month.[241] The detention of the bankrupt must cease when the reason for it no longer exists.[242] Since amendments to the Bankruptcy Law in 1993 the maximum period of detention is six months.[243]

A bankrupt must hand over to the trustee in bankruptcy all the books and documents relevant to any properties owned by the bankrupt and all properties in the bankrupt's control except for those protected against attachment.[244]

3.2 Collection of Information about Debtors and the Examination of Debtors

Bankruptcy The trustee in bankruptcy may:

- apply to the court to summon people interested in the bankrupt's affairs to investigate the bankrupt's assets;[245]

---

235 Bankruptcy Law, Articles 75, 82.
236 Bankruptcy Law, Article 91.
237 Bankruptcy Law, Article 14.
238 Bankruptcy Law, Article 72.
239 Bankruptcy Law, Article 69.
240 Bankruptcy Law, Article 70.
241 Bankruptcy Law, Article 71.
242 Bankruptcy Law, Article 73.
243 As note 45, above, 73.
244 Bankruptcy Law, Article 90.
245 Bankruptcy Law, Article 70.

- require the bankrupt to supply a list of assets and their status, nature and location and of creditors and debtors;[246]
- require the bankrupt to provide all documents relating to the bankrupt's property and to hand over all property in the bankrupt's control or possession;[247] and
- require the bankrupt to provide information about properties and businesses.[248]

The supervisor or inspector in bankruptcy may:

- require the bankrupt and other people to provide information about the bankrupt's properties and businesses;[249] and
- request a report on the status of the bankrupt's estate from the trustee and investigate any aspect of the status of the estate.[250]

At the creditors' meeting the trustee must present a statement of claims against the estate and a statement of the estate's assets which have been collected or which may be collected, as required under Article 94, as well as a report on the progress of the bankruptcy administration and any reconciliation plan proposed by the bankrupt.[251] The statement under Article 94 is required by the Article to be kept in the trustee's office for free perusal by interested parties.

The bankrupt is required to be present at the creditors' meeting and must answer questions asked by the judge presiding, the trustee, the inspector and the creditors.[252]

Composition The supervisor in composition must report on a number of matters relating to the debtor's assets and business affairs within 30 days of the appointment. The report must cover:

- the business, financial condition and value of the bankrupt's assets;
- whether any business is still viable, using the standard of reasonable financial and commercial practice;
- whether there was negligence or improper conduct on the part of the debtor; and
- whether there is any fraudulent or false statement in the petition.

Supervisors may make investigations to do such a report and may inspect the debtor's property and books and the financial condition of any businesses. The debtor must answer all inquiries made by the supervisor.[253]

The assistant supervisor has a similar power and may also, on the supervisor's

---

246 Bankruptcy Law, Articles 74, 87.
247 Bankruptcy Law, Article 88.
248 Bankruptcy Law, Articles 87–89.
249 Bankruptcy Law, Article 90.
250 Bankruptcy Law, Article 121.
251 Bankruptcy Law, Article 119.
252 Bankruptcy Law, Article 122.
253 Bankruptcy Law, Article 14.

instructions, keep safe the current assets and business receipts of the debtor. The debtor must answer all inquiries made by the assistant supervisor.[254]

3.3 Offshore Collection of Information

There are no specific provisions in the Bankruptcy Law permitting information to be obtained in foreign jurisdictions. Most states do not recognize the Republic of China as the government of all China. They recognize the People's Republic of China as the *de jure* government of China, including Taiwan. This creates significant problems with the execution of international agreements between these states and Taiwan to establish a legal framework for the exchange of information, particularly as such bilateral arrangements are based on an expectation by both governments, their agencies and courts of reciprocity.[255] Article 4 of the Bankruptcy Law at present precludes any substantive reciprocity in respect of any foreign bankruptcies or compositions. Such proceedings have no affect on the properties of the bankrupt or debtor within Taiwan. This may come to be a new area of conflict.[256]

3.4 Rules regarding the Proof of Debts and Illicit Transfers of Property

Bankruptcy: proof of debts Claims may only be proved in accordance with the Bankruptcy Law.[257] What is a claim is not defined but it appears to be any debt or obligation owed by the bankrupt which is not specifically avoided by the Bankruptcy Law. Claims against the bankrupt which have been made before the bankruptcy order are admissible, unless they are excluded by its other provisions. Those exclusions include property in the bankrupt's control which is not the bankrupt's and property which is subject to a pledge, mortgage or lien to another.[258] Where a debt is to be paid at the end of a fixed period which has not yet expired, it becomes payable on the making of the bankruptcy order.[259] Future debts that become payable 15 days after the bankruptcy order are not admitted.[260] Debts subject to a condition yet to be fulfilled may be admitted provided that if the condition's occurrence:

---

254 Bankruptcy Law, Article 14.

255 McGowan, H. (1994), 'Banking, credit, and finance: the transactional aspects', in Silk, M. (ed.) *Taiwan Trade and Investment Law*, Hong Kong: Oxford University Press, 377, 401–2.

256 *Haarhuis* v. *Kunnan Enterprises Ltd*, US Court of Appeals, No 98–7175 (DC Cir, 28 May 1999). See: Schmertz, John R. and Mark Meier, 'In action by professional tennis players against insolvent Taiwanese company for its failure to perform sponsorship contracts, DC Court affirms as case of first impression that US bankruptcy law Section 304 does not require presence of debtor's assets in US for bankruptcy court to exercise jurisdiction' (1999) 5 (6) *International Law Update* (June) (Lexis Nexis News Allwld 22 February 2000). Section 304 permits a US court to grant relief to a company undergoing reorganization or relief in another jurisdiction but in s 304(c) comity is a factor to be considered: Sharon L Babbin, 'US Court decision supports Taiwan reorganization proceeding: US firms subject to foreign bankruptcy laws and courts', 15 June 1997 19(6) *East Asian Executive Reports* 9.

257 Bankruptcy Law, Article 98.

258 Bankruptcy Law, Articles 98, 108, 110.

259 Bankruptcy Law, Article 100.

260 Bankruptcy Law, Article 142.

- cancels the claim, the party posts a bond with the court or the payment, when it occurs, is deposited with the court;[261] or
- cancels the claim, the payment is deposited with the court, and, if the claim cannot be made within 15 days after the distribution table is approved by the court, the claim is not admitted.[262]

The Bankruptcy Law does not admit as claims:

- interest accruing after the bankruptcy order;
- expenses incurred in participating in the bankruptcy process;
- compensation for damages for breach of contract for non-performance after the bankruptcy order;
- fines and retrospective payments;[263]
- secured claims and claims with priority.[264]

The amount of admitted claims is calculated on the final date for registering claims; that date is notified in the public notice that the debtor has been made bankrupt.[265]

Unexpired lease contracts made by the bankrupt may be renounced by the trustee with no specific remedy being available to the lessor.[266]

No particular form for the proof of a claim is required. It must be 'sufficient'. Sufficiency is a matter to be determined by the trustee.[267] If there is a dispute it may be raised and voted on at the creditors' meeting. If that does not resolve the matter the court may rule upon it. On its resolution a new statement of claims is to be presented to the creditors' meeting.[268]

Composition: proof of debts The Bankruptcy Law does not specify the claims admitted under a composition. The prevailing opinion is that as composition exists to avoid bankruptcy, the same claims as for bankruptcy would be admitted.[269]

The claims must be notified within the time specified in the notice of the application advertised and sent to creditors by the court: a time not less than ten days nor more than two months from the grant of the application.[270]

Bankruptcy: illicit transfers of property Gratuitous transfers of property is a serious issue. The head of a family may transfer property to other close relations in the family knowing that, after the title is transferred, he will be able to continue to control the

261 Bankruptcy Law, Article 140.
262 Bankruptcy Law, Articles 141, 142.
263 Bankruptcy Law, Article 103.
264 Bankruptcy Law, Articles 108, 109, 112.
265 Bankruptcy Law, Articles 65(5), 94.
266 Bankruptcy Law, Article 77.
267 Bankruptcy Law, Article 94.
268 Bankruptcy Law, Articles 125–126.
269 As note 181, above, para L1.
270 It may be extended if the debtor has a branch office at a distant place: Bankruptcy Law, Article 12.

property through his powers as the head of the family.[271] The Civil Code permits creditors to avoid gratuitous transfers if they have the effect of making the debtor insolvent. It also permits them to set aside transfers if a creditor can show that the debtor knew that the transfer would be prejudicial.[272] What is required for a transaction to be 'gratuitous' is uncertain. The prevailing view among Taiwan legal practitioners in the mid-1990s was that even if the guarantor received an indirect benefit through profits from the enterprise, it may still be gratuitous. The only guarantees which would not be cancelled on a guarantors' bankruptcy would be those involving the payment of a real guarantee fee to a commercial guarantor.[273]

The trustee may repudiate any guarantee made within six months prior to the court's bankruptcy order where:

- the bankrupt provided security for outstanding debts, unless the bankrupt had promised to provide such security more than six months before the bankruptcy order; or
- made payment of debts which were not yet due.[274]

The avoidance can extend to transferees who knew, when the right was acquired, that there was a cause for avoidance.[275]

The trustee in bankruptcy may apply to the court for an order enabling the trustee to repudiate any gratuitous or onerous acts done by the bankrupt prior to the bankruptcy order, if they are prejudicial to creditors' rights and may be repudiated under provisions of the Civil Code.[276]

Composition: illicit transfers of property Any gratuitous act done by the debtor subsequent to the application for composition has no effect. A gratuitous act is an onerous act with spouses, lineal relatives, or relatives of dependents or an act where the debtor disposes of property at more than 50 per cent below the market price.[277] In addition all onerous acts from the date of the application, other than those within the course of normal management or ordinary business, have no effect.[278]

271 Kaufman Winn, J. (1988), 'Security interests under the laws of the Republic of China on Taiwan: an introductory guide', 23 *Texas International Law Journal*, 395–416, 397, ff 7.

272 Civil Code, Article 244. Kaufman Winn cites Supreme Court Judgment, 45 [1956] Tai Shang Tze No 1316 to the effect that: '[I]f, due to the acts of the debtor, circumstances arise that result in the debtors' inability to carry out the obligation or cause the debtor to have difficulty in carrying out the obligation, then the acts of the creditor will be deemed prejudicial to the creditor.': As note 271, above, 398, ff 9.

273 Article 244 of the Civil Code makes such gratuitous guarantees liable to cancellation. See further: As note 255 above, 381–2.

274 Bankruptcy Law, Article 79.

275 Bankruptcy Law, Article 80.

276 Bankruptcy Law, Article 5.

277 Bankruptcy Law, Article 15.

278 Bankruptcy Law, Article 16.

3.5 Orders which May be Made in Regard to the Property of the Debtor

Bankruptcy Bankrupts lose the power to manage their affairs and assets. These powers vest in the trustee in bankruptcy.[279]

The court may authorize the trustee to renounce, on the petition of the trustee in bankruptcy, a contract representing any gratuitous or onerous acts made by the insolvent prior to the bankruptcy. The contract must be detrimental to the creditors' rights and voidable under the Civil Code.[280] The order can extend to transferees who knew, when the right was acquired, that there was a cause for avoidance.[281]

The court may order a moratorium on the payment of all unsecured debts. It can also approve a reconciliation plan, approved by the creditors' meeting, to settle the bankruptcy on terms other than those otherwise specified in the Bankruptcy Law.[282]

Composition The insolvent person may continue to conduct business but under the supervision of the supervisor and the assistant of the supervisor. Any transaction not supported by adequate consideration will be deemed to be null and void. No unsecured creditor may initiate compulsory execution proceedings and any on foot are terminated. Secured or preferred creditors may continue to exercise their rights.[283] Creditors with claims arising after the commencement of the moratorium may initiate compulsory acquisition proceedings.

3.6 Rules for the Distribution of the Assets of the Bankrupt

Bankruptcy All assets of the bankrupt, apart from (1) those held by secured creditors or preferred creditors, and (2) those exclusively belonging to the bankrupt or non-attachable property, are available to the creditors. Secured and preferred creditors are able to exercise their rights without regard to the bankruptcy proceedings.[284]

Priority in payment is given to expenses and debts relating to the bankruptcy in preference to any claim on the bankrupt's estate.[285] The expenses include:

- any expenses incurred in connection with the administration, disposal or distribution of the estate;
- any expenses and litigation costs incurred in pursuing the common interests of the creditors;
- the remuneration of the trustee; and
- the living expenses and funeral expenses of the bankrupt and any dependents.[286]

---

279 Bankruptcy Law, Article 75.
280 Bankruptcy Law, Article 78.
281 Bankruptcy Law, Article 80.
282 Bankruptcy Law, Article 136.
283 Bankruptcy Law, Article 17.
284 Bankruptcy Law, Article 108.
285 Bankruptcy Law, Article 97.
286 Bankruptcy Law, Article 95.

The trustee's remuneration is set by the court.[287]

The debts of the bankrupt's estate include:

- debts arising from acts done by the trustee in bankruptcy in connection with the bankrupt's estate;
- debts arising from a request from the trustee for performance of a bilateral contract on account of the bankrupt's estate or as a result of the performance of a bilateral contract after the bankruptcy order was made;
- debts representing managing without mandate pertaining to the bankrupt's estate; and
- debts representing undue enrichment pertaining to the bankrupt's estate.[288]

Some claims are entitled to be paid in advance of other claims. Where there is more than one preferred claim of the same priority they are to be repaid in proportion to the total amount of each.[289] The preferred status of these claims derives from legislation apart from the Bankruptcy Law. They include debts referred to in the Business Tax Law, the Workers Financial Welfare Law and the Labour Standards Law. The last law, for example, which applies to specified industries, states in Article 28: 'In the case of business closure, liquidation or bankruptcy of an employer, if the cumulative outstanding wages owed to workers based on the stipulations of the labour contract amount to less than 6 months pay, such outstanding wage payment shall have the top priority in settlement.'[290]

Method of distribution The bankrupt's property, where the creditors' meeting has not given contrary instructions, is to be disposed of, where necessary, by auction.[291] If the property may be distributed after the first creditors' meeting the trustee must proceed to do so after preparing a distribution list showing the method and proportion to be paid. Any objection to the proposal must be made to the court within 15 days from the list being published.[292] Where it appears that objections or litigation may delay distribution the trustee may lodge that amount with the court and distribute the remainder amongst the creditors.[293] If, after the final distribution, further property is found in the estate, the trustee may, with the approval of the court and within three years of the ruling that the bankruptcy be closed, distribute that property amongst the creditors.

Immediately after the final distribution the trustee in bankruptcy is to report to the court on the distribution.[294] The court is to immediately rule on the closing of the bankruptcy.[295]

287 Bankruptcy Law, Article 84.
288 Bankruptcy Law, Article 96.
289 Bankruptcy Law, Article 112.
290 Quoted in Tomasic and Francis (as note 45, above, 73).
291 Bankruptcy Law, Article 138.
292 Bankruptcy Law, Article 139.
293 Bankruptcy Law, Article 144.
294 Bankruptcy Law, Article 145.
295 Bankruptcy Law, Article 146.

Reconciliation in bankruptcy The bankrupt, prior to the distribution of the estate in bankruptcy, may submit a plan for reconciliation.[296] This follows a procedure similar to composition before the court.[297] It must specify (1) the percentage of debt being paid, (2) the time limits for payment, and (3) security, if any, available.[298] A reconciliation plan cannot be submitted if (1) the whereabouts of the bankrupt is unknown, (2) the bankrupt is being prosecuted for the offence of fraudulent bankruptcy contained in Article 154, or (3) has been prosecuted for that offence.[299] The plan must be submitted to the trustee in bankruptcy and to the creditors' meeting.[300] If it is approved by the creditors' meeting it is to be considered by the court and approved if the terms are considered equitable.[301] The trustee, the inspector or supervisor and the creditors, as well as the bankrupt, are to be heard and they may be summonsed for questioning by the court. The judge presiding at the creditors' meeting should also be present to express an opinion on the plan.[302] Once approved the plan will apply to all creditors.[303] If the bankrupt breaches the agreement or has concealed assets the plan may be terminated.[304]

Composition Where a composition scheme is approved by the court it binds all unsecured creditors. There are no assets available for distribution. Secured or preferred creditors who also agreed to it may participate in it but are able to continue to exercise their rights. Priority in payments will be according to the composition scheme made at the creditors' meeting, except for the remuneration, fixed by the court, of the assistant supervisors which must be paid ahead of other payments.[305]

3.7 Creditors of the Debtor and Debt Agreements

The Bankruptcy Law has a specific provision for out-of-court 'workout' agreements between creditors and the debtor. This is composition at a local chamber of commerce. The provision is not borrowed from recent developments in insolvency law in other jurisdictions. It represents older Chinese custom and law and the traditional role of guilds in the resolution of commercial disputes. These mediation practices, as discussed, were drawn on in the first Qing legislative reforms in dealing with insolvency. Many Taiwanese prefer to use these customs associated with the unofficial law without bringing themselves within the official law's recognition of them.[306]

---

296 Bankruptcy Law, Article 129.
297 Bankruptcy Law, Article 137.
298 Bankruptcy Law, Article 130.
299 Bankruptcy Law, Article 131.
300 Bankruptcy Law, Article 132.
301 Bankruptcy Law, Article 135.
302 Bankruptcy Law, Articles 133–135.
303 Bankruptcy Law, Article 136.
304 Bankruptcy Law, Articles 51–53, 56, 137.
305 Bankruptcy Law, Article 11.
306 Bankruptcy Law, Article 11.

Chapter II, Section 2 of the Bankruptcy Law deals with merchants who are unable to pay off their debts. They may make a request to the local chamber of commerce for a composition provided they have not filed such an application with the district court.[307] The chamber of commerce should ascertain the identity of the creditors and request that they take part in the composition and attend a creditors' meeting.[308] In exercising this function the chamber of commerce may appoint its own members, public chartered accountants or other specialists to inspect the properties and books of the debtor, supervise a debtor's business and prevent the debtor from doing acts prejudicial to the interests of the creditors.[309] If the creditors' meeting agrees, a written agreement is made between the debtor and the chamber of commerce.[310]

The creditors' meeting must be held within two months of the debtor's request.[311] It may elect up to three members both to inspect the debtor's properties and books and, after a composition agreement has been made, to supervise its execution.[312] The scheme is administered according to the scheme for compositions approved by the district court, discussed above in para. 3.4.[313]

The scheme is terminated if the debtor:

- conceals books, documents or properties or makes a false report of debts;
- refuses to answer inquiries or makes false statements; or
- commits acts in the conduct of the business which are detrimental to the interests of the creditors where the supervisors have sought to prevent such acts from occurring.[314]

The composition scheme, which can only be initiated by the debtor, and is presided over by a judge as a supervisor, provides the broad structure in which a formal workout agreement could be implemented. It is not likely that Taiwan, in the near future, will have provision for a more informal scheme.[315]

3.8 Creditors' Meetings and Debt Agreements and their Termination

Bankruptcy proceedings are terminated by either the division of the estate or a reconciliation plan adopted by creditors and approved by the court. Immediately after the final distribution the trustee in bankruptcy is to report to the court on the distribution.[316] The court is to immediately rule on the closing of the bankruptcy.[317]

---

307 Bankruptcy Law, Article 41.
308 Bankruptcy Law, Article 42.
309 Bankruptcy Law, Articles 19, 43.
310 Bankruptcy Law, Article 47.
311 Bankruptcy Law, Article 44.
312 Bankruptcy Law, Articles 45, 48.
313 Bankruptcy Law, Article 46.
314 Bankruptcy Law, Article 46.
315 As note 181, above, para R (a).
316 Bankruptcy Law, Article 145.
317 Bankruptcy Law, Article 146.

If a bankrupt discharges all of his debts through repayment, or by other means, the court, on the bankrupt's petition, may grant the restoration of rights. If the debts are not discharged, and if the bankrupt has not been convicted for fraudulent bankruptcy or fraudulent composition under Articles 154 or 155, rights may be restored by the court three years after the close of the bankruptcy or the execution of the composition in reconciliation.[318]

If a reconciliation plan proposed by the bankrupt is approved by the court it becomes binding on all creditors and the debtors.[319] Upon termination all restrictions imposed on the bankrupt cease and the bankrupt may resume the control and management of assets, subject to the restrictions of the reconciliation plan. If the bankrupt has concealed assets or fails to adhere to the plan the court can terminate it.[320]

Composition proceedings are terminated by their success, or failure. If it succeeds the debtor is restored to the control and management of assets as the creditors have been paid. It may also terminate if:

- the terms of composition are not acceptable to the creditors;
- the composition is based on a false representation of the debtor;
- the debtor is imprisoned for breach of the Bankruptcy Law;[321] or
- the corporate debtor fails to observe the terms of the composition.[322]

4 Corporate Insolvency Rules

4.1 Introduction to the Different Corporate Insolvency Rules in Taiwan

Taiwan's insolvency regime includes four official mechanisms: bankruptcy, special liquidation, composition, and reorganization. The bankruptcy and composition proceedings are governed by the Bankruptcy Law. The Company Law governs reorganization and special liquidation proceedings.

The bankruptcy procedure is designed to ensure the equitable distribution of the bankrupt's total assets between creditors. The bankruptcy process also includes a mechanism for a court-approved reconciliation plan between the corporate bankrupt and its creditors. The composition and reorganization mechanisms seek the rehabilitation of the corporate debtor. The special liquidation process attempts to reach a settlement between an insolvent company, which has entered the normal liquidation process, and its creditors. All the procedures are subject to court supervision, although an application for composition may alternatively be made to the local chamber of commerce.

---

318 Bankruptcy Law, Article 150.

319 Bankruptcy Law, Articles 135, 136.

320 Bankruptcy Law, Articles 51–53, 56, 137.

321 Bankruptcy Law, Article 10.

322 Bankruptcy Law, Article 10.

4.2 Corporate Rescue and the Use of Informal Mechanisms of Dealing with Corporate Debtors

A recent International Monetary Fund study of six Asian insolvency law regimes quantified responses to a questionnaire distributed by the Asian Development Bank to practitioners in the jurisdictions.[323] The findings indicate that informal workout is preferred to formal procedures due to the better outcomes perceived to flow from informal workouts.[324] This is despite the fact that responses indicated that the average time for an informal workout was 12 to 18 months whereas the average time for a formal reorganization was eight to 12 months.[325] The reason for the favourable view of informal workouts may be found in the responses to the question of the predictability of a positive outcome of judicial handling of bankruptcy/liquidation or rehabilitation: on a scale of one to five (one = very high and five = very low) responses rated both at five.[326]

These responses are consistent with the previous discussion of the importance traditionally placed on unofficial legal procedures, such 'closed business' workouts, in Taiwan. The responses are also consistent with the discussion of the role of the judiciary in the insolvency process and the apparent lack of qualification of judges in dealing with complex commercial insolvency cases. However, formal procedures do contribute to workouts to some degree in Taiwan. Comparing jurisdictions, the International Monetary Fund study concludes:

> In Malaysia the existence of formal procedures provides incentives for informal workouts, while in Korea the government encourages workouts. In addition to Malaysia, formal procedures in Taiwan Province of China contribute to workouts to some degree while in Indonesia, the Philippines, and Thailand, the formal rules do not have such an effect.[327]

Arguably, official insolvency law in Taiwan reinforces – through a number of mechanisms for the compromise of claims and rehabilitation of the corporate debtor prior to and after an adjudication of bankruptcy – the existing informal workout culture in Taiwan. The importance of official insolvency law processes in encouraging informal workouts in Taiwan becomes apparent when we consider the number of mechanisms in the official law that allow for compromise between the parties.

Mechanisms or procedures that allow for the efficient and informal administration or rehabilitation of financially distressed companies have gained favour in a number

---

323 As note 67, above. The authors note that there is a risk that each group of practitioners would employ a different scale when answering the questionnaires of the Asian Development Bank. However, the authors of the working paper suggest that the answers are consistent with the other major source for their study, namely Tomasic, R. and P. Little (eds) (1997), *Insolvency Law and Practice in Asia*, Hong Kong: Pearson Professional (Hong Kong) Limited.

324 As note 323, above, 13.

325 As note 323, above, 13.

326 As note 323, above, 13.

327 As note 323, above, 12.

of countries.[328] The closest mechanism under Taiwan's Bankruptcy Law is the composition procedure, which permits a corporate debtor to make a request to the courts or a local chamber of commerce for a composition. The Company Law also contains the somewhat more cumbersome reorganization process and the special liquidation process.

The next section will look at, amongst other issues, the method of initiating these processes, the appointment of supervisors, the effect of these procedures on the assets and management structures of the company, the powers, liabilities and qualifications of the supervisor, the duration of these processes, the role of creditors, creditors' meetings, and the termination of the process.

5 Court-based Schemes of Administration, Reconstruction or Arrangement

Composition and reorganization are the two court based schemes of administration, reconstruction or arrangement available to financially distressed companies in Taiwan. The underlying philosophy of the composition provisions in the Bankruptcy Law and the reorganization provisions of the Company Law is to seek the rehabilitation of the corporate debtor. There is also provision in the Company Law for a special liquidation process.

Composition

Taiwan's composition (*hejie*) process is intended to encourage reconciliation between the corporate debtor and creditors through a compromise of outstanding claims sanctioned by the courts or formalized by the corporate debtor's local chamber of commerce (*dangdi shanghui*).[329] The composition provisions in the Bankruptcy Law accord with the early unofficial law in Taiwan, which saw the involvement of the local guilds. In particular, section 2 of the Bankruptcy Law (Articles 41 to 49) permits a corporate debtor, who is unable to 'pay off' its debts, to make a request to the local chamber of commerce for a composition. The chamber of commerce process embodies an out-of-court negotiation scheme between corporate debtors and their

328 For UK provisions and a discussion of the voluntary administration regime incorporated into the Insolvency Act 1986 (UK) following recommendations of the 1982 Cork Report, see Fletcher, I. (1994), 'Administrative Orders under the Insolvency Act 1986 (UK): Results, Reflections and Prospects for Future Reform', 2 *Insolvency Law Journal* 110. For a discussion of the position in the United States, see Griggs, L. (1994), 'Voluntary administration and Chapter 11 of the Bankruptcy Code (US)', 2 *Insolvency Law Journal* 93.

329 If the court considers that the composition is equitable and the security provided by the debtor for carrying out the proposed repayment is adequate the court must approve the composition passed at the creditors' meeting: Bankruptcy Law, Article 32. This requirement does not apply to compositions entered under the supervision of the local chamber of commerce, which merely require that the composition be passed at the creditors' meeting and a written agreement, signed by the chairman of the chamber of commerce and affixed with the seal of the chamber of commerce, is executed: Bankruptcy Law, Article 47 and Article 48.

creditors. However, only the insolvent debtor may apply to the court or chamber of commerce to arrange a composition.[330]

The role of the local chamber of commerce in the composition process includes:

- calling a meeting of creditors and arranging for all creditors to attend the creditors' meeting;[331]
- appointing members of the chamber, public chartered accountants, or other specialists (*zhuanmen renyuan*) to inspect the creditor's properties and books, supervise the management of the business, and prevent any acts of the debtor prejudicial to the creditors;[332] and
- signing and affixing the chamber's seal to any composition, in the form of a written agreement, passed at the creditors' meeting.[333]

There is limited court involvement in a chamber of commerce composition, except where the composition fails and the debtor applies to the court for a composition or the creditor does not cooperate with the appointed supervisors.[334] The creditors' meeting may elect representatives to supervise the implementation of the composition.[335] The creditors' meeting also has the power to elect representatives to inspect the debtor's properties and accounts.[336] The official law seeks to preserve the cordiality, informality and efficiency that was perceived to exist in merchant custom or unofficial law. Accordingly, the chamber of commerce may withdraw the benefit of its composition process if the debtor does not act in good faith.[337]

The corporate debtor has the option of applying to the court for a composition prior to filing an application for bankruptcy.[338] The corporate debtor may also apply to the court for a composition if the chamber of commerce mechanism has failed.[339] A court-arranged composition, like bankruptcy, falls under the jurisdiction of the district court of the place of domicile of the debtor.[340] Both the court and chamber of commerce compositions are initiated by the debtor prior to filing an application for

330 Bankruptcy Law, Articles 6, 41.

331 Bankruptcy Law, Articles 42, 44. The meeting must be called within two months of the receipt of the request for a composition from the debtor: Bankruptcy Law, Article 44.

332 Bankruptcy Law, Article 43.

333 The agreement must then be executed: Bankruptcy Law, Article 47.

334 The supervisors appointed by the chamber of commerce or the creditors' meeting are arguably required under Article 19 of the Bankruptcy Law to report to the court if the creditor conceals accounts, documents or property, makes a false report of debts, refuses to answer the supervisor's (or assistant supervisor's) inquiries, or commits acts detrimental to the interests of the creditors.

335 This would replace the interim supervision approved by the chamber of commerce: Bankruptcy Law, Article 48.

336 The election is expressed to be in conjunction with the inspectors appointed by the chamber of commerce under Article 43: Bankruptcy Law, Article 45.

337 Bankruptcy Law, Article 46. The grounds for withdrawing the chamber's conduct of the composition are set out in Article 19. For example, concealing accounts, refusing to assist with inquiries or doing an act detrimental to the creditors: Bankruptcy Law, Article 19.

338 Bankruptcy Law, Article 6.

339 Bankruptcy Law, Article 6.

340 Bankruptcy Law, Article 2.

bankruptcy on the grounds that the corporate debtor is unable to 'pay off' its debts.[341] After the commencement of composition proceedings, all acts by the debtor corporation without consideration or with inadequate consideration will be deemed null and void.

Court or chamber of commerce approval of the application for composition places a moratorium on civil proceedings against the corporate debtor, except in the case of secured creditors and preferential claims.[342] The corporate debtor may also continue in business under the supervision of the supervisor (*jianduren*) in the case of a court-arranged composition. There is no equivalent express stipulation allowing the debtor to continue in business under the chamber of commerce provisions. Instead, the Bankruptcy Law merely provides that the chamber of commerce may appoint members of the chamber, public chartered accountants or other specialists, to supervise the management of the business of the corporate debtor.[343]

The supervisor has the following responsibilities:

- supervising the business of the corporate debtor;[344]
- instructing the assistant supervisor;[345]
- reporting to the court any improper act of the corporate debtor;[346]
- acting as the chairperson of the creditors' meeting;[347]
- reporting the absence of the debtor at the creditors' meeting to the court (provided the debtor was given adequate notice);[348]
- inspecting the accounts and property of the corporate debtor;[349]
- reporting on the status of the corporate debtor's assets and business;[350]
- providing an opinion on the composition plan;[351]
- seeking a reconciliation between the corporate debtor and its creditors;[352]
- ruling and resolving disputes between the creditors' claims;[353]
- declaring the composition closed;[354]
- reporting to the court if the composition plan is rejected at the creditors' meeting;[355]

---

341 Bankruptcy Law, Article 6.
342 Bankruptcy Law, Article 17.
343 Bankruptcy Law, Article 43.
344 Bankruptcy Law, Article 14.
345 Bankruptcy Law, Article 18.
346 Bankruptcy Law, Article 19.
347 Bankruptcy Law, Article 22.
348 Bankruptcy Law, Article 24.
349 The debtor has an obligation to answer all inquiries of the supervisor or assistant supervisor in connection with the business: Bankruptcy Law, Article 14.
350 Bankruptcy Law, Article 25.
351 Bankruptcy Law, Article 25.
352 Bankruptcy Law, Article 25.
353 Bankruptcy Law, Article 26.
354 Bankruptcy Law, Article 28.
355 Bankruptcy Law, Article 28.

- submitting the successfully passed composition to the court for approval or disapproval;[356] and
- providing the court with the reasons for a ruling on a dispute between creditors.[357]

The assistant supervisor has similar responsibilities.[358] Unlike the trustee in bankruptcy, the supervisor or assistant supervisor does not have any power to overturn past transactions, for example, unfair preferences or uncommercial transactions, or to initiate legal proceedings to recover assets of the corporate debtor.

Both composition proceedings are commenced by a debtor's petition that attaches a preliminary composition plan, including a statement of the debtor's assets and creditors.[359] Creditors have the limited protection of the court's or chamber of commerce's discretion, which is non-appellable, to accept or reject the application for a composition on the grounds set out in Article 10 of the Bankruptcy Law.[360] Court-arranged compositions arguably offer greater protection to creditors than the chamber of commerce provisions. For example, under a court-arranged composition the court may require the debtor to make a supplementary composition statement or produce relevant documents.[361] The court may interrogate the debtor upon receipt of the supervisor's report.[362] The court is also required to issue a public notice setting out the following:

- its reasons for approving the application;
- the name and address of the supervisor and assistant supervisors and the place where the composition is to be conducted;
- the period within which claims are to be reported; and
- the date of the first creditors' meeting.[363]

---

356 Bankruptcy Law, Article 29.

357 A creditor may appeal against a ruling of the supervisor or the composition plan to the court within ten days of the date of the decision or resolution: Bankruptcy Law, Article 30. The court may summons the creditor and debtor for interrogation prior to the ruling. The court may also order the supervisor or assistant supervisor to provide reasons for the decision: Bankruptcy Law, Article 31.

358 The duties of the assistant supervisor are set out in Article 18 of the Bankruptcy Law and include, amongst others, safekeeping the assets and receipts of the debtor.

359 Bankruptcy Law, Articles 7, 49.

360 Bankruptcy Law, Article 9. The grounds, as set out in Article 10 of the Bankruptcy Law, are:

- the applicant debtor has not provided an adequate composition plan;
- the debtor has previously been sentenced to imprisonment under the Bankruptcy Law;
- the debtor fails to comply with an agreed condition after the approval of the composition by the court; or
- the applicant fails to appear after summoned by the court without justifiable reason, or appears before the court but fails to make a genuine statement, or refuses to produce relevant documents.

361 The court also has the power to institute 'other necessary investigations': Bankruptcy Law, Article 8.

362 Bankruptcy Law, Article 20.

363 Bankruptcy Law, Article 12. Creditors must report claims not less than ten days and not more than two months from the date the application for composition is approved. The date of the creditors' meeting must be between seven days and one month after the expiration of the period for reporting claims. The publication requirements of the public notice are dealt with in Bankruptcy Law, Article 13.

The court must send the applicant and any known creditors a notice in the same form as the public notice.[364] There are no equivalent provisions under the chamber of commerce composition process.

Under a court-arranged composition a judge is appointed supervisor with the assistance of a chartered public accountant or other appropriate persons from the local chamber of commerce.[365] As already noted, local magistrates in Taiwan under the Qing dynasty also employed the services of the local guild to resolve disputes, including those involving outstanding debt and insolvency. Unlike the bankruptcy proceeding, there must be a creditors' meeting to approve or disapprove the composition proposal and negotiate with the corporate debtor.[366]

Creditors that agree to the composition proposal adopted at the creditors' meeting and approved by the court must abide by the proposal in the satisfaction of their claims. Secured creditors and preferred creditors will not be bound to the proposal unless they have given their consent to the proposal.[367] Secured creditors are exempt from composition proceedings (unless consenting to the proposal) and have the right to enforce their security at any time.[368] The Bankruptcy Law does not provide for the admissibility of claims under the composition procedure. However, given that the composition procedure is designed to pre-empt the bankruptcy process the claims admissible under the bankruptcy procedure should arguably be admissible under the composition procedure. Claims will be ranked in accordance with the proposal adopted at the creditors' meeting. The Bankruptcy Law does not prevent creditors or the corporate debtor from applying for adjudication of the corporate debtor's bankruptcy or for reorganization during the composition process.

The court will terminate the composition procedure where:

- the creditors reject the composition proposal;
- the composition proposal is accepted on the basis of false representations made by the corporate debtor; or
- the corporate debtor does not abide by the terms of the composition.

The court has the power to order the commencement of bankruptcy proceedings if the court-arranged composition proposal fails. The court may also order the commencement of bankruptcy proceedings where the agreement entered into under either composition process is subsequently revoked by the court because it was

364 Bankruptcy Law, Article 12.

365 Bankruptcy Law, Article 11.

366 A resolution for composition must be adopted by a majority vote of the creditors present at the meeting (proxies are provided for under Bankruptcy Law, Article 23). The majority must represent more than two thirds of the total amount of unsecured claims: Bankruptcy Law, Article 27. In the case of court-arranged compositions, if the composition is rejected the chairman of the creditors' meeting must declare the composition procedure closed and make a report to this effect to the court: Bankruptcy Law, Article 28.

367 Bankruptcy Law, Article 37.

368 Bankruptcy Law, Article 108.

unconscionable, or because it was made fraudulently, or where it was not duly performed by the debtor.[369]

Reorganization

Taiwan's Company Law was amended in 1966 to include a reorganization regime. The reorganization process provides for a court-supervised restructuring of a potentially viable but insolvent company. The process is available to public companies only.[370] In contrast to the composition process, a board of directors, shareholders, or creditors (whether secured, preferred or unsecured) of a corporate debtor need only establish that the corporate debtor has suspended business due to 'financial difficulty', or there is an apprehension of this, to apply to the court for reorganization.[371] The applicant must convince the court that the company would cease operations (temporarily or permanently) if there were no reorganization.[372] The company must be advised of both the application and ruling for reorganization by the court.[373]

The court must reject an application for reorganization where:

---

369 Bankruptcy Law, Article 35 and Section 3 (Revocation of Composition and Composition Concession). Revocation may also be ordered if a creditor, who expressed disagreement to the conditions of the composition at the creditors' meeting or did not attend personally or by proxy, can show that the composition shows bias and is prejudicial to their own interests: Bankruptcy Law, Article 50.

370 Company Law, Article 282. Article 156 of the Company Law states that 'when the capital of a company has reached or exceeded a specific amount fixed by the central authority, its share certificates shall be issued in public'. The Ministry of Economic Affairs is charged with setting the prescribed amount: Company Law, Article 5. Many companies limit their paid-in capital to one dollar less than the minimum required for being publicly held because of the more onerous disclosure requirements of public companies. See further Kaufman Winn, J. (1988), 'Creditors' Rights in Taiwan: a Comparison of Corporate Reorganization Law in the United States and the Republic of China', 13 *North Carolina Journal of International Law and Commercial Regulation* 3, 409–471, 441.

371 The chairman of the board of directors may apply to the court for reorganization upon a majority vote of two thirds of the directors present in a board meeting. Shareholders may also petition the court if holding more than 10 per cent of the total shares of the company over the prior six months. Creditors may also apply for a reorganization if they have a claim that is at least 10 per cent of the debtor's total issued shares: Company Law, Article 282.

372 The petition for reorganization must also include:

- the name and domicile or residence and a statement on the status of the petitioner;
- the name and location of the company and the names of the responsible persons;
- the grounds on which the petition is filed;
- the business undertaken by the company and the condition of the business;
- the assets, liabilities, profits and losses and other financial conditions of the company; and
- opinions on the reorganization of the company.

Company Law, Article 283.

373 Company Law, Articles 284, 291. Article 291 also requires that the court send the notice of ruling to the supervisor, reorganizers, the creditors and the shareholders.

- the company has been adjudged bankrupt under the Bankruptcy Law;
- a resolution for composition has been passed under the Bankruptcy Law;
- the company has been dissolved; or
- the company is 'not worthy of operation according to the standard of reasonable financial bearing of expenses'.[374]

Following the court's adjudication of the commencement of reorganization, the management and power of disposal of the property of the corporate debtor is delegated to the reorganizers.[375] The shareholders' meeting as well as the directors and ordinary supervisors cease to function upon transfer.[376] All creditors' claims that arose prior to the adjudication must be pursued through the reorganization plan.[377] Unlike the bankruptcy and composition process, the secured creditor is not exempt from the reorganization procedure.[378]

The adjudication of the commencement of reorganization suspends any other civil proceeding involving the debtor, including bankruptcy, composition, special liquidation and compulsory execution.[379] The court also has the power to make an interim ruling prior to deciding the reorganization application to suspend proceedings for bankruptcy, composition, or compulsory execution 'and others'.[380] In addition, the court may order an amendment of a reorganization plan to transfer the property held as security by secured creditors to the company in reorganization.[381] There are indications that practitioners and foreign bankers in Taiwan consider that many corporate debtors misuse the reorganization process to avoid liability.[382]

The court will appoint an examiner, a reorganizer, and a supervisor[383] to oversee the reorganization process. The examiner and supervisor in reorganization must be non-interested persons with special knowledge or experience in the operation of the company in reorganization.[384] The reorganizer is a suitable person appointed from among the directors, creditors or shareholders.[385] Each position is assigned the duties thought necessary to ensure the transfer of the company's operations to a court-supervised reorganization.

The role of the examiner in reorganization is primarily to examine the business and financial condition (including assets) of the company at the outset and to advise the court:

374 Company Law, Article 288.

375 Company Law, Article 293.

376 Company Law, Article 293.

377 Company Law, Article 296.

378 Company Law, Article 296.

379 Company Law, Article 294.

380 Company Law, Article 287.

381 Company Law, Article 306.

382 As note 45, above, 75.

383 The supervisor in reorganization is to be contrasted with the ordinary supervisor of a company limited by shares appointed under Article 216 of the Company Law.

384 Company Law, Article 285 and Article 289 respectively.

385 Company Law, Article 290.

- whether the company is still viable;
- whether there was any neglect or improper act on the part of the responsible persons of the company; and
- whether the petition for reorganization contains any fraudulent or false statements.[386]

The supervisor is responsible for overseeing the transfer of the operation of the company's business to the reorganizer and the performance of the reorganizer once the transfer is complete.[387] The supervisor may apply to the court for an order replacing the reorganizer if he or she acts improperly. The supervisor's other responsibilities include:

- preparing a list of preferred creditors, secured creditors, unsecured creditors and shareholders (noting their respective claims and voting rights);[388]
- reporting to the court if the interested parties' meeting does not pass the reorganization plan;[389]
- petitioning the court to instruct the interested parties to reconsider the reorganization plan given that new factors indicate the plan is unworkable or no longer necessary;[390]
- attending and answering any questions at court hearings concerning the rights of creditors;[391] and
- convening and acting as chairperson of the meeting of interested parties.[392]

The reorganizer prepares and executes the reorganization plan and performs the day-to-day business of the company under reorganization.[393] After the transfer of the business to the reorganizer, the shareholders' meeting, directors and ordinary supervisors cease to have power over the company.[394] The reorganizer must secure the prior consent of the supervisor prior to the following:

- disposing of the property of the company outside the scope of its business;
- changing the business or operations of the company;
- entering a loan contract;
- concluding or rescinding important long-term contracts;
- proceeding in litigation or arbitration;
- waiving or assigning the rights of the company;
- dealing with other parties who seek to rescind agreements or effect set-off; or

---

386 Company Law, Article 285.
387 Company Law, Article 293.
388 Company Law, Article 298.
389 Company Law, Article 306.
390 Company Law, Article 306.
391 Company Law, Article 299.
392 Company Law, Article 300.
393 The business of the company and the power of controlling and disposing of the property of the company is transferred to the reorganizers after delivery of the ruling for reorganization: Company Law, Article 293.
394 Company Law, Article 293.

- appointing or removing important officers of the company.[395]

Like the supervisor, the reorganizer attends court hearings that concern creditors' and shareholders' rights and petitions the court if the reorganization plan becomes unworkable or unnecessary.[396] The reorganizer has the additional responsibility of petitioning the court for the adjudication of completion of reorganization.[397] The reorganizer must also be available to answer any questions at the interested parties' meetings and must convene a meeting of shareholders after the adjudication of reorganization.[398]

The reorganizer, like the supervisor in composition and the liquidator, does not have the power to initiate legal proceedings to recover assets of the corporation that are available for distribution to creditors. The powers of the reorganizer do not extend to recovering assets of the corporation that may have been subject to an unfair preference, an invalid charge, or were the subject of an uncommercial transaction prior to the reorganization. The supervisor and reorganizer may be liable for losses or damages caused to the corporate debtor or other person due to his or her failure to exercise due care.[399]

All creditors and shareholders of the company are required to attend the interested parties' meetings during the reorganization process.[400] The functions of the interested parties' meeting include:

- reviewing reports on the condition of the company and the opinions of the reorganizer;
- approving or rejecting the reorganization plan; and
- resolving any other matters concerning the reorganization.[401]

The interested parties are divided into four groups: secured, unsecured, preferred, and shareholder.[402] Creditors or shareholders holding more than one half of the total claims or equity (as the case may be) in each group must approve any resolutions of the meeting. This is subject to the proviso that the decision on the reorganization plan must be made by a majority of over two thirds of the total votes.[403]

Claims established prior to the adjudication of reorganization will be admissible, except non-admissible claims of the kind applicable in the bankruptcy process of the Bankruptcy Law. The method of proving the claim is not set out in the Company Law. Article 297 states that all creditors must 'produce documents to sufficiently prove the existence of their rights for declaring their rights to the reorganizers …'. There

395 Company Law, Article 290.
396 Company Law, Articles 299, 306.
397 Company Law, Article 310.
398 Company Law, Article 300.
399 Company Law, Article 313.
400 Company Law, Article 300.
401 Company Law, Article 301.
402 Company Law, Article 298.
403 Company Law, Article 302.

is no issue of priority of claims in the composition, reorganization, or liquidation processes, as payments are made in accordance with the proposal adopted at the creditors' or interested parties' meeting. This is subject to Article 312, which provides for the priority of debts incurred during the reorganization to ensure the continued operation of the company or expenses of the reorganization. Any interested person may contest in court the right of a creditor or shareholder.[404] The reorganization plan must clearly state any change in the rights of creditors or shareholders.[405]

The court will terminate the reorganization plan if the interested parties reject the plan or the court does not approve the plan.[406] The court may also terminate the plan if the plan becomes unworkable or no longer necessary (as mentioned). Bankruptcy may be ordered upon termination of the reorganization if the 'circumstances are so serious as to fall into the provisions in connection with bankruptcy'.[407] Upon the successful completion of the reorganization plan, the directors and ordinary supervisors of the corporate debtor may apply for registration or a change of registration as well as a ruling from the court that the reorganization process is complete.[408]

Completion of the reorganization has the following effects:

- unpaid portions of claims already declared expire except where otherwise provided for in the reorganization plan;
- the changed, decreased or cancelled parts of the right of shareholders in consequence of the reorganization expire; and
- bankruptcy, composition, compulsory execution or other litigation or procedures involving the property of the company prior to the reorganization ruling become ineffective.[409]

Special Liquidation

Creditors, shareholders or the liquidator may apply to the court for an order that a company limited by shares enter special liquidation if circumstances exist which apparently impede the execution of the ordinary liquidation process.[410] However, only liquidators appointed under the ordinary liquidation provisions of the Company Law can bring an application to the court for the institution of a process of special liquidation if they suspect that the liabilities of a company limited by shares exceed its assets.[411] In the case of unlimited companies the liquidator must also file an application for a declaration of bankruptcy if the assets of the company are not sufficient to meet its liabilities: Company Law, Article 89. The functions of the

404 Company Law, Article 299.
405 Company Law, Article 304.
406 Company Law, Article 306.
407 Company Law, Article 307.
408 Company Law, Article 310.
409 Company Law, Article 311.
410 Company Law, Article 329.
411 Company Law, Article 335.

liquidator are then terminated and their duties transferred to a receiver in bankruptcy: Company Law, Article 89.[412]

After the court rules that the company institute a process of special liquidation all bankruptcy, composition, compulsory execution and other litigation involving the property of the debtor is suspended.[413] Prior to the ruling for special liquidation the liquidator, creditors or shareholders may apply to the court for any of the following interim orders:

- measures for the preservation of the property of the company;
- prohibitions on the transfer of shares;
- prohibitions on or annulments of the release of the responsibilities of any of the promoters, directors, supervisors, managerial officers or liquidators;
- prohibitions on the transfer of shares; and
- measures for the preservation on the property of any of the promoters, directors, managerial officers or liquidators for damages against them.[414]

The court has the power to instigate any of the above measures whenever it deems it necessary for the supervision of the liquidation.[415] In addition to the above, the court may also order prohibitions on or annulments of the release of the responsibilities of any of the promoters, directors, supervisors, managerial officers or liquidators following the report of a court-appointed inspector into the affairs of the company.[416]

The liquidator may convene a meeting of creditors at any time it is deemed necessary during the liquidation process.[417] Creditors having claims totalling not less than 10 per cent of the total amount of claims may file a written application requesting the liquidators to convene a creditors' meeting.[418] Resolutions at the creditors' meeting require a majority vote of creditors present at the meeting who represent more than two thirds of the total amount of claims.[419] The voting rights of creditors are determined in proportion to the monetary amount of their claim.[420] Subject to court approval, the creditors' meeting may resolve to appoint or remove a liquidation inspector at any time during the proceedings.[421]

After consulting the liquidation inspector, the liquidator may also make a proposal for a settlement agreement to the creditors' meeting.[422] The creditors' meeting may

---

412 The dissolution and liquidation provisions applicable to unlimited companies apply to the limited company as defined in Article 98 of the Company Law: Company Law, Article 113. In the case of an unlimited company with limited liability shareholders, liquidation is undertaken by all shareholders of unlimited liability: Company Law, Article 127.

413 Company Law, Articles 294, 335.

414 Company Law, Articles 336, 339, 354.

415 Company Law, Article 339.

416 Company Law, Article 354.

417 Company Law, Article 341.

418 Company Law, Article 341.

419 Company Law, Article 343 and Bankruptcy Law, Article 123.

420 Company Law, Articles 343, 298.

421 Company Law, Article 345.

422 Company Law, Article 347.

adopt the settlement agreement by a majority of unsecured creditors holding at least three quarters of the total amount of unsecured claims.[423] The resolution adopting the agreement is subject to court approval.[424] The settlement agreement then binds all creditors in liquidation.[425]

The liquidator also requires the creditors' meeting to approve (if the liquidator examiner does not) the following acts:

- disposal of any property of the company;
- borrowing of money;
- commencing legal proceedings;
- agreement to a composition or an arbitration; or
- waiver of any right.

If there is no prospect of an agreement of settlement or no prospect of an agreement of settlement being duly carried out, the court will make an adjudication of bankruptcy in accordance with the Bankruptcy Law.[426] If the agreement is successfully carried out the provisions governing the normal liquidation procedure will apply to the company.[427] The liquidation provisions of the Company Law, discussed in greater detail in Part 7 below, apply to special liquidation where applicable.

6 Winding Up Procedures

6.1 Introduction to the Winding Up Procedures

The winding up of a company on the grounds of insolvency is provided for in the bankruptcy procedures of the Bankruptcy Law. The provisions of the Bankruptcy Law apply to corporate, as well as individual, debtors (*zhaiwuren*). Corporate debtors who are unable to pay off their debts must liquidate their debts in accordance with the composition or bankruptcy procedures set out in the Bankruptcy Law.[428] In addition, a company will be subject to the bankruptcy procedures if there is no prospect of settlement or no prospect of a settlement being duly carried out following an order for special liquidation.[429]

Any measures that can be taken against a debtor or bankrupt under the Bankruptcy Law can also be taken against:

- the shareholders of an unlimited company or shareholders of an unlimited company with limited liability shareholders who conduct the business of the corporate debtor;

423 Company Law, Article 350.
424 Company Law, Article 350.
425 Company Law, Article 350 and Bankruptcy Law, Article 136.
426 Company Law, Article 355.
427 Company Law, Article 356.
428 Bankruptcy Law, Article 1.
429 Company Law, Article 355.

- the directors of a company limited by shares;
- the shareholders of a company limited by shares who conduct the business of the company; or
- the liquidator of the corporate debtor.[430]

There is a statutory presumption that a corporate debtor which has ceased to make repayments is unable to pay off its debts.[431] A trustee in bankruptcy is appointed to administer the corporate bankrupt's estate in bankruptcy under the supervision of the court.[432] The trustee in bankruptcy must submit a final report to the court upon completion of the distribution of the bankruptcy estate.[433] The court will then give a ruling on the close of the bankruptcy.[434] If the bankruptcy process runs its course, the corporate debtor may be dissolved under the provisions of the Company Law.

The Bankruptcy Law includes a reconciliation mechanism in which the corporate bankrupt may submit a plan for reconciliation to the creditors prior to accepting the distribution of the bankruptcy estate.[435] The trustee in bankruptcy, the inspector, the creditors and the corporate bankrupt may all submit their opinions to the court on whether the plan should be approved.[436] The court may interrogate (*xunwen*) the trustee, the inspector, the creditors and the corporate bankrupt, and the chairman of the creditors' meeting prior to making a ruling on the reconciliation plan.[437] The court may approve a reconciliation plan passed by the creditors' meeting if the court considers the plan is equitable.[438] The plan takes effect toward all creditors in bankruptcy if the court approves the plan.[439] The relevant provisions of the composition process then apply to the reconciliation.[440]

A bankruptcy petition may be filed during a composition. However, the court will reject the petition if it considers that there is a chance of reaching a composition.[441]

6.2 *Initiation of Winding Up Procedures*

Bankruptcy proceedings may be initiated by the corporate debtor (including the directors, shareholders or management) or creditors.[442] The petition must include the nature and amount of the claims, a statement on the status of the company's assets, a list of creditors and debtors, and the facts in connection with the corporate debtor's

430 Bankruptcy Law, Article 3.
431 Bankruptcy Law, Article 1.
432 Bankruptcy Law, Article 83. The trustee must be a chartered accountant or other person qualified to administer the corporate bankrupt's estate. The trustee may be appointed from among the creditors at the creditors' meeting.
433 Bankruptcy Law, Article 145.
434 Bankruptcy Law, Article 146.
435 Bankruptcy Law, Article 129.
436 Bankruptcy Law, Article 133.
437 Bankruptcy Law, Article 134.
438 Bankruptcy Law, Article 135.
439 Bankruptcy Law, Article 136.
440 Bankruptcy Law, Article 137.
441 Bankruptcy Law, Article 58.
442 Bankruptcy Law, Article 58.

inability to pay off its debts.[443] The court may institute investigations and interrogate creditors and other interested persons prior to making an adjudication.[444] The court may also adjudicate the corporate debtor bankrupt if it becomes apparent during the course of civil proceedings or civil execution proceedings that the corporate debtor is unable to pay off its debts.[445]

6.3 Grounds for Winding Up

The corporate debtor will be adjudicated bankrupt if it is unable to pay off debts.[446] There is no guidance in the Bankruptcy Law whether this test embodies a 'cash flow test' or 'balance sheet test'. As noted, the only statutory presumption of insolvency offered in the Bankruptcy Law applies to a debtor who stops payment of debts. The court may also adjudicate the corporate debtor bankrupt if it becomes apparent during the course of civil execution proceedings, presumably where a judgment debt is returned unsatisfied, that the corporate debtor is unable to pay off its debts.[447] There is no provision for a statutory demand nor is there a presumption of insolvency if a receiver or other controller is appointed over some or all of the company's assets.

6.4 Effect of the Commencement of Winding Up

The corporate bankrupt loses the right to manage and dispose of the properties forming the bankrupt's estate.[448] Members or shareholders of the corporate bankrupt will be required to pay up their subscribed capital on adjudication of bankruptcy.[449] The trustee in bankruptcy is obligated to take 'necessary precautions' in respect of the corporate bankrupt's rights forming a part of the bankruptcy estate.[450] The corporate bankrupt's estate includes all properties belonging to the corporate bankrupt at the time of adjudication, any future claims on property, and any properties acquired by the corporate bankrupt after adjudication but before the close of bankruptcy.[451]

The trustee in bankruptcy may request that the corporate bankrupt provide a statement on the status of the bankrupt's assets and a list of creditors and debtors.[452] Furthermore, the corporate bankrupt must hand over to the trustee all the books and documents relating to the properties in the bankruptcy estate.[453] The trustee in bankruptcy may continue the business of the corporate bankrupt, but only to the degree necessary to liquidate.[454]

---

443 Bankruptcy Law, Articles 61, 62.
444 Bankruptcy Law, Article 63.
445 Bankruptcy Law, Article 60.
446 Bankruptcy Law, Article 57.
447 Bankruptcy Law, Article 60.
448 Bankruptcy Law, Article 75.
449 Bankruptcy Law, Article 93.
450 Bankruptcy Law, Article 90.
451 Bankruptcy Law, Article 82.
452 Bankruptcy Law, Article 89.
453 Bankruptcy Law, Article 88.
454 Bankruptcy Law, Article 91.

There is a moratorium on the claims of unsecured creditors, who must follow the bankruptcy procedures to satisfy their claims. Unsecured creditors who fail to register their claims with the court will be deprived of their claims against the corporate debtor. However, secured creditors are not required to follow the bankruptcy procedures. All assets of the company are available for the satisfaction of the creditors' claims except assets held by secured creditors or those exclusively belonging to the bankrupt. If the creditors in bankruptcy have received payment in accordance with the reconciliation or bankruptcy procedure, their claims to any outstanding portion of the claim is deemed to be extinguished on the close of bankruptcy.[455]

6.5 Creditors' Meetings

Under the bankruptcy procedure in the Bankruptcy Law, the court will convene a creditors' meeting upon the application of the trustee in bankruptcy or the examiner.[456] The court appoints a judge to oversee the creditors' meeting.[457] Resolutions must be adopted with a majority vote of creditors present at the meeting who represent at least two thirds of the total amount of claims.[458]

The creditors' meeting may consider the following matters:

- the election of supervisors to monitor the bankruptcy process on behalf of creditors;[459]
- measures for the management of the bankrupt estate;[460]
- the future of the business of the corporate debtor;[461]
- the election, appointment, and substitution of the trustee in bankruptcy;[462]
- the approval or disapproval of a reconciliation plan; and
- instructions to dispose of the properties of the bankruptcy estate.

Resolutions passed at a creditors' meeting may be overturned on application to the court if not in the interests of the creditors in bankruptcy.[463] Any objections to claims must be raised at the first creditors' meeting and the dispute ruled upon by the court.[464] The trustee in bankruptcy may be appointed from among the creditors at the creditors' meeting.[465]

---

455 This is subject to instances of fraudulent bankruptcy: Bankruptcy Law, Article 149.
456 Bankruptcy Law, Article 116.
457 Bankruptcy Law, Article 117.
458 Bankruptcy Law, Article 123.
459 Bankruptcy Law, Article 120.
460 Bankruptcy Law, Article 120.
461 Bankruptcy Law, Article 120.
462 Bankruptcy Law, Articles 83, 85.
463 Bankruptcy Law, Article 124.
464 Bankruptcy Law, Article 125.
465 Bankruptcy Law, Article 83.

6.6 The Role of the Court in the Winding Up Process

The functions of the court in the winding up of a corporate debtor include:

- adjudicating the bankruptcy of the corporate debtor following a petition or independently in other proceedings;
- making any necessary investigations and interrogations prior to adjudication of bankruptcy;
- appointing the trustee in bankruptcy;[466]
- ruling on the period for the reporting of claims;[467]
- convening the first creditors' meeting on application by the trustee in bankruptcy or examiner;[468]
- setting the date and agenda for the first and subsequent creditors' meeting;[469]
- giving public notice of the adjudication;[470]
- giving written notification of the adjudication to the creditors and debtor;[471]
- effecting registration of the bankruptcy;[472]
- preparing an abridged version of the corporate debtor's accounts;[473]
- summoning or arresting the bankrupt;[474]
- ordering the detention of the bankrupt;[475]
- ordering interim measures prior to the adjudication;[476] and
- ruling on a plan of reconciliation submitted by the corporate bankrupt.[477]

6.7 Proof and Ranking of Claims by Creditors Against the Company

Claims provable in bankruptcy must be pursued through the bankruptcy procedure.[478] Creditors' claims established prior to adjudication of bankruptcy are admissible claims provable in bankruptcy unless excluded under the Bankruptcy Law.[479] Unmatured claims for a fixed period will be deemed to have matured upon adjudication of bankruptcy.[480] Future claims that cannot be exercised within 15 days of adjudication of bankruptcy are not admissible. The total amount of conditional claims are provable in bankruptcy.[481]

466 Bankruptcy Law, Article 64.
467 Bankruptcy Law, Article 64.
468 Bankruptcy Law, Article 116.
469 Bankruptcy Law, Articles 64, 118.
470 Bankruptcy Law, Article 65.
471 Bankruptcy Law, Article 65.
472 Bankruptcy Law, Article 66.
473 Bankruptcy Law, Article 67.
474 Bankruptcy Law, Article 70.
475 Bankruptcy Law, Article 71.
476 Bankruptcy Law, Article 74.
477 Bankruptcy Law, Article 135.
478 Bankruptcy Law, Article 99.
479 Bankruptcy Law, Article 98.
480 Bankruptcy Law, Article 100.
481 Bankruptcy Law, Article 102.

The Bankruptcy Law expressly excludes the following claims:

- interest accruing after the adjudication of bankruptcy;
- fines and retroactive payments;
- damages for breach of contract resulting from non-performance after adjudication of bankruptcy; and
- expenses incurred from participation in the bankruptcy process.[482]

Preferred claims (e.g. costs of the bankruptcy, tax claims, and employees' claims) have priority over other creditors' claims, which rank *pari passu* on a *pro rata* basis.[483] Secured creditors are not subject to the bankruptcy procedure and may enforce their rights against the subject property.[484] The expenses and debts arising from the bankruptcy process have preference over other claims provable in bankruptcy.[485] There is scope for retention of title clauses found in Article 110, which provides that property not belonging to the corporate bankrupt may be recovered from the trustee in bankruptcy without complying with the bankruptcy procedure.[486] A seller may also rescind a contract of sale and recover goods not yet delivered nor fully paid for, subject to the trustee in bankruptcy's discretion to pay off the whole price and request delivery of the goods.[487]

6.8 Set-off of Debts

Set-off may be effected where the creditors in bankruptcy are obligated to the corporate debtor at the time of adjudication.[488] Set-off may not be effected in the following circumstances:

- if the creditors in bankruptcy become indebted to the corporate bankrupt after adjudication;
- if the debtors of a corporate bankrupt acquire claims against the bankrupt from other persons after adjudication; or
- if the debtors of a corporate debtor acquire a claim with the knowledge that a petition for bankruptcy has been filed or the corporate debtor has stopped paying debts.[489]

A debtor of the corporate bankrupt who effects repayments without the knowledge of an adjudication of bankruptcy may set the repayments up against the creditors in bankruptcy.[490]

---

482 Bankruptcy Law, Article 103.
483 Bankruptcy Law, Article 112.
484 Bankruptcy Law, Articles 98, 108.
485 Bankruptcy Law, Article 97.
486 Bankruptcy Law, Article 109.
487 Bankruptcy Law, Article 111.
488 Bankruptcy Law, Article 113.
489 Bankruptcy Law, Article 114.
490 Bankruptcy Law, Article 76.

6.9 Voidable Transactions

The trustee in bankruptcy may apply to the court to avoid transactions involving the property of the corporate bankrupt where:

- the transaction occurred at any time prior to the adjudication of bankruptcy and was gratuitous or onerous and prejudicial to the creditors' rights and repudiatable under the Civil Code;[491] and
- the act occurred within six months after the adjudication of bankruptcy and provided securities for outstanding debts or repaid debts not yet due.[492]

The trustee in bankruptcy must exercise the right of avoidance within two years from the date of adjudication of bankruptcy.[493]

6.10 Procedures for the Dissolution (and Restitution) of the Company

Article 315 of the Company Law provides for dissolution of a company limited by shares upon the occurrence of bankruptcy.[494] Article 71 of the Company Law provides for dissolution of an unlimited company on the occurrence of bankruptcy.[495] In the case of a company limited by shares, there must be a resolution for dissolution adopted by a majority vote at the shareholders' meeting attended by shareholders representative of over three quarters of the total number of issued

---

491 Bankruptcy Law, Article 78.

492 Bankruptcy Law, Article 79.

493 Bankruptcy Law, Article 81.

494 A company limited by shares may be dissolved under Articles 315 to 319 of the Company Law on the occurrence of any of the following:

- the satisfaction of the conditions for dissolution set out in the company's Articles of Incorporation;
- the completion or impossibility of completion of the company's business;
- a resolution to dissolve the company adopted at a shareholders' meeting;
- the shareholders of registered share certificates numbering fewer than seven persons;
- consolidation or merger with another company;
- bankruptcy; or
- an order or judgment of the court dissolving the company.

Company Law, Article 315.

Generally, Article 11 of the Company Law provides that 'in the event of apparent difficulty in the operation of a company or serious damage thereto, the court may, upon the application of shareholders and after receiving the opinion of the central authority and the central authority having jurisdiction over such specific enterprise and demanding the company's reply thereto, rule for dissolution.'

495 The dissolution and liquidation provisions applicable to unlimited companies apply to the limited company as defined in Article 98 of the Company Law: Company Law, Article 113. In the case of the unlimited company with limited liability shareholders (as defined in the Company Law, Article 114), dissolution occurs upon the withdrawal of all shareholders of unlimited liability or of limited liability: Company Law, Article 126.

shares.[496] There are no provisions in the Company Law dealing with the reinstatement of dissolved or deregistered companies.

7 Liquidators: Appointment, Powers and Duties

The Company Law (as well as the Bankruptcy Law) has provisions relevant to the liquidation of companies. Article 10-1 permits the Ministry of Economic Affairs by itself, or on the application of a relevant local authority or another interested party, to dissolve a company which has not engaged in its approved business activities for more than six months. Article 10-2 gives the same Ministry the power to act where the company has failed to comply with the law or the Articles of Incorporation following a direction to do so. If the direction is not observed the Ministry may order that the company be dissolved. If the breach of the law is serious the Ministry may order that the company be dissolved immediately. Article 11 enables shareholders who have held more than 10 per cent of the issued shares for more than six months to apply to dissolve the company where it has an apparent difficulty in its operation or it has suffered serious damage.[497] Article 315(6) makes bankruptcy a ground for the dissolution and liquidation of a company. A liquidation bankruptcy of a company is a rare event in Taiwan. The extensive use of secured credit and the use of unofficial measures generally leaves insufficient assets to justify a formal liquidation.[498] Some larger companies avoid liquidation by using the reorganization provisions of the Company Law previously discussed.[499]

7.1 Appointment, Qualifications and Registration of Liquidators

There are no formal requirements for the accreditation or registration of liquidators apart from those recognizing professional qualifications in law or accountancy.[500] As with other forms of insolvency law and insolvent company reorganization there is a reluctance for practitioners to be involved.[501] Legal practitioners in particular may have neither the requisite skills nor interest. Until 1989, admission to legal practice affected lawyers' abilities to professionally perform skilled complex corporate matters. Admission was tightly controlled, privileging judges, procurators or retired military officers over the pre-1945 Taiwanese in admission to the profession. Judges,

---

496 Company Law, Article 316. Article 25 of the Company Law states that a dissolved company in the process of liquidation is deemed not yet dissolved. A dissolved company may temporarily transact its business during the liquidation process for the purposes of settling affairs and facilitating liquidation: Company Law, Article 26. Article 24 of the Company Law provides that 'a dissolved company shall be liquidated, unless such dissolution is caused by consolidation or merger or bankruptcy'.

497 Under the Company Law, Article 24, dissolved companies must be liquidated. Under Article 26 of the Company Law they have a limited power to transact business to facilitate in the liquidation.

498 As note 255, above, 397.

499 As note 45, above, 74.

500 Admission to these professions is controlled by the Examination Yuan which was retained by Sun Yat-sen from the imperial system of administration: As note 47, above, 138.

501 As note 45, above, 87.

including the Council of Grand Justices, and procurators are still not required to have professional legal training.[502] The regulatory environment of 'public restrictions, private disregard' and the connection of a number of lawyers with government and political parties make lawyers significant intermediaries between companies and the state in obtaining approvals and indications that regulatory agencies will not take action.[503]

There are two forms of liquidation, leading to the appointment of liquidators, for companies limited by shares. These are ordinary and special liquidation.

Ordinary liquidation An ordinary liquidation is a voluntary one in which the directors act as the liquidators. The Articles of Association may have a provision authorizing the appointment of some other person as liquidator, or, in the absence of any other person acting as a liquidator, an interested person may request the court to appoint one.[504] The dissolution resolution must be carried by a majority vote of shareholders at a general meeting where the shareholders present represent over 75 per cent of the issued shares. If the shares are publicly issued the resolution must be passed by 75 per cent of the shareholders present where they also represent a majority of the total issued shares. If there are stricter requirements in the Articles of Incorporation they will apply in place of these.[505] If assets are found after an ordinary liquidation has concluded the court may, on the application of an interested party, appoint a liquidator to distribute them.[506]

Special liquidation A special liquidation is one where circumstances exist which impede the liquidation of the company. Creditors, an existing liquidator, or a shareholder may apply for the court to appoint a liquidator. The court can also appoint one on its own motion. In circumstances where there is a suspicion that the liabilities of the company exceed its assets the liquidator in an ordinary liquidation may make such an application.[507] In special liquidations, if there is no prospect of reaching an agreement or settlement the court must of its own motion order the bankruptcy of the company in accordance with the Bankruptcy Law. It must also do so if there is no prospect of any agreement or settlement being successfully carried out.[508]

---

502 Hungdah Chiu (1991), 'Contract Management and Dispute Resolution', in McDermott, J. (ed.), *Legal Aspects of Investment and Trade with the Republic of China*, Baltimore: School of Law, University of Maryland, 44, 53.

503 As note 59, above, 952; Hawk, B. (1995), 'Book Review: UK Merger Control: Law and Practice', 18 *Fordham International Law Journal*, 1588, 1588.

504 Company Law, Article 322.

505 Company Law, Article 316.

506 Company Law, Article 333.

507 Company Law, Article 335.

508 Company Law, Article 355.

7.2 Powers of Liquidators, Powers of Investigation, Inspection of Books and Examination of Witnesses

Ordinary liquidation Liquidators in an ordinary liquidation have the rights of directors, unless there is a contrary requirement, including access to corporate information and property.[509] On appointment they must examine the financial condition of the company and prepare a balance sheet and inventory. These reports should be sent to any inspectors or supervisors and also presented to a meeting of shareholders as well as submitted to the court. Obstructing liquidators in this examination is a criminal offence punishable by fines of up to NT$60,000.[510]

Special liquidation Liquidators in special liquidations have similar powers to the liquidator in an ordinary liquidation.[511] In addition, on the application of the liquidator, the inspector or supervisor, shareholders holding more than 3 per cent of the issued shares, creditors who have applied for a special liquidation, or creditors representing 10 per cent of the amount claimed, the court may order the inspection of the company's business or property.[512] The inspector or supervisor, rather than the liquidator, is required to report to the court whether:

- there are any incidents for which any promoter, director, supervisor, executive officer or liquidator should be held responsible;
- measures to preserve the company's property are necessary; and
- measures to preserve the property of any promoter, director, supervisor, executive officer or liquidator are necessary to enable the company to claim for any damage it has suffered.[513]

7.3 Duties of Liquidators

Ordinary liquidation Liquidators have the duties of a director under the Company Law unless the contrary is indicated.[514] Directors are required to comply with the specific provisions in the Company Law and, where there is no specific provision, with Title 10 of the Book of Obligations in the Civil Code. Generally they must conduct the affairs of the company applying the standards which ordinary people use in their own affairs. If they receive some benefits they must observe the standard used by a good administrator.[515] If these standards are breached they are liable to compensate the company for any damages which it suffered.[516] If they cause damage

509 Company Law, Article 316.
510 Company Law, Article 326.
511 Company Law, Article 355.
512 Company Law, Article 352.
513 Company Law, Article 353.
514 Company Law, Article 316.
515 Civil Code, Article 535.
516 Civil Code, Article 544.

to another person by any breach of the law they, and the company, are jointly liable to compensate that person.[517]

Many of the directors' duties in the Company Law are subject to the contrary intention exclusion because of the functions of the liquidator. Directors must act in accordance with the Articles of Incorporation, the resolutions adopted at shareholders' meetings, and the general laws and regulations of Taiwan. Directors will be liable to compensate the company for any damage or loss caused by a resolution that was adopted in contravention of these. However, directors who disagree with the resolution, on the record or in writing, will not be liable.[518] The most significant of the obligations not inconsistent with the application of these provisions to liquidators is that they must act in accordance with the general laws and regulations or be liable for any resulting damage to the company. Liquidators who are remunerated would also attract the standard of the good administrator.

Liquidators, after taking up their position, must advertise at least three times for creditors to submit claims within three months or risk not having the debt included in the liquidation. Where a creditor is known to a liquidator the creditor must be directly notified.[519] Liquidators must not pay any creditor, except for secured creditors where the court has given its approval, until the end of the period fixed for the notification of debts. The company will be liable for any damage to the creditors caused by this delay. Where the company appears to have sufficient assets to pay all of its debts the liquidator may, with the approval of the court, pay those creditors who may hold the company liable for damages.[520] Creditors who failed to notify the liquidator of their debts may, while the liquidator holds the undivided residual assets of the company, require that their debts be paid out of that residue.[521] Once the debts have been paid the liquidator must distribute the assets between the shareholders in accordance with the proportion of shares held and their ranking in a winding up as specified in the Articles of Incorporation.[522]

Within 15 days of the final distribution of the residue liquidators must prepare a list of receipts and payments and a profit and loss statement. Together with all statements and accounts they must be sent to the supervisors or inspectors for them to submit to the shareholders. The shareholders may appoint another inspector to review them. Once the shareholders approve them the liquidator is released from any liability except for any unlawful acts. The statements must also be filed with the court. Failure by a liquidator to lodge these documents with the court is an offence punishable by a fine of NT$3,000 to NT$15,000.[523]

Special Liquidation The purpose of special liquidations and the functions of liquidators in them will lead to fewer duties of a director under the Company Law

517 Company Law, Article 23.
518 Company Law, Article 193.
519 Company Law, Article 327.
520 Company Law, Article 328.
521 Company Law, Article 329.
522 Company Law, Article 330.
523 Company Law, Article 331.

being applicable to liquidators as a contrary intention will be apparent.[524] Except for two additional provisions the liquidator in a special liquidation has similar specific duties and immunities as a liquidator in an ordinary liquidation. In a special liquidation the liquidator is specifically required to prepare a report on the investigations into the company's business and property as well as an inventory of assets. The report should state an opinion on how the liquidation should proceed.[525] This directs the attention of the liquidator to consider whether a settlement could be reached and whether any settlement would be viable. If neither are likely, an order for bankruptcy is provided for in Article 355 of the Company Law. The property must also be distributed in any settlement in proportion to the debt owed to a creditor with the rights of secured creditors and those with the rights of exclusion preserved.[526] The same equal distribution is required in respect of any settlement agreed between the liquidator and the creditors.[527]

7.4 Status and Independence of Liquidators

Ordinary liquidation In an ordinary liquidation liquidators are subject to provisions providing for supervision and direction by the court, the creditors' meeting, or any inspector or supervisor appointed by the creditors' meeting. They may be removed by the court and inspectors or supervisors may also apply for such an order.[528]

Special liquidation Liquidators may convene a meeting of creditors if it is necessary to do so. Creditors representing at least 10 per cent of the debt owed, excluding secured and excluded debts, may also make a written request for such a meeting to be held. The holders of secured and excluded debts may be invited to attend any creditors' meeting.[529] Resolutions must be passed in accordance with the requirement in the Bankruptcy Law that there be a majority of those present and who hold more than 66 per cent of claims in support.[530]

Liquidators may be supervised by an inspector or supervisor appointed by the creditors' meeting and approved by the court.[531] Liquidators must get the approval of inspectors or supervisors:

- to dispose of any property of the company;
- to borrow money to bring an action;
- to agree to a compromise or to seek the arbitration of a claim; or
- to relinquish any right.

---

524 Company Law, Article 316.
525 Company Law, Article 344.
526 Company Law, Article 340.
527 Company Law, Article 348.
528 Company Law, Article 341.
529 Company Law, Article 341.
530 Company Law, Article 343 and Bankruptcy Law, Article 123.
531 Company Law, Article 345.

No approval is required if the value of the item is worth less than 0.1 per cent of the total value of the assets. If the supervisor does not agree, the liquidator may seek to have the creditors' meeting approve the transaction.[532]

If a liquidator intends to put a proposal for a settlement to the creditors' meeting, the liquidator should also consult the inspector or supervisor.[533] The liquidator, where necessary, may request that creditors participate in negotiating such an agreement.[534] Any settlement must be approved by the court and creditors holding more than 75 per cent of the total amount claimed at a meeting attended by over half the creditors entitled to vote. The settlement binds all creditors.[535] Any settlement may be altered following a similar procedure.[536]

7.5 Powers of the Court in relation to Liquidators

Ordinary liquidation Generally liquidators may be removed by a resolution of the shareholders. Liquidators appointed by the court may only be removed by the court. The court can also remove liquidators appointed by shareholders on the application of the supervisor or inspector or by the shareholders who have held more than 3 per cent of the issued capital for more than one year.[537]

Special liquidation Liquidators in special liquidations are appointed by the court.[538] Additional liquidators may be appointed by the court whenever it is necessary to do so or a vacancy exists. The court may also remove liquidators for any significant reason.[539] It may require liquidators to report on the state of the liquidation at any time, including on the assets of the company and it may make any investigation required to properly supervise the liquidation.[540]

Before ordering a special liquidation the court may make interim orders for the preservation of the property of the company and prohibit the transfer of shares. It may also make orders to preserve the property of any promoters, directors, executive officers or liquidators where the company may have a claim for damages against them.[541] It may also make these orders in the course of a liquidation.[542]

In a special liquidation where there is a need to preserve the property of the company or of people involved in its management to ensure that the company can claim damages from them, the court can make a wide range of orders:

---

532 Company Law, Article 346.
533 Company Law, Article 347.
534 Company Law, Article 349.
535 Company Law, Article 350 and Bankruptcy Law, Article 136.
536 Company Law, Article 351.
537 Company Law, Article 323.
538 Company Law, Article 335.
539 Company Law, Article 337.
540 Company Law, Article 338.
541 Company Law, Articles 336, 339, 354.
542 Company Law, Article 339.

- preserving the company's property;
- prohibiting the transfer of shares;
- prohibiting the release of promoters, directors, supervisors, executive officers or liquidators from their responsibilities;
- annulling the release of promoters, directors, supervisors, executive officers or liquidators from their responsibilities;
- assessing the claim to damages from the breach of their responsibilities by promoters, directors, supervisors, executive officers or liquidators from their responsibilities; and
- preserving the property of promoters, directors, supervisors, executive officers or liquidators to compensate the company for any breach of responsibilities.[543]

7.6 Suspension or Revocation of Registration of Liquidators

As there is no formal process of accreditation or registration, apart from the requirement for professional qualifications in law or accountancy, the only means for revocation are through those bodies which discipline such professionals. Lawyers are disciplined by the Committee on the Discipline of Lawyers and the Committee of Appeal on the Discipline of Lawyers. These Committees are constituted by lawyers and judges and procurators in the higher courts.[544]

7.7 Reports by Liquidators

The circumstances in which liquidators are required to report are set out in the context of their duties. Many believe that liquidators do not have a sufficient understanding of industrial sectors in which companies operate to do complete and in-depth reports and that they fail to notice and report on clear instances of impropriety by managers.[545]

7.8 Remuneration and Fees of Liquidators

Ordinary liquidation The remuneration of a liquidator not appointed by the court is to be determined by the shareholders. Where the court made the appointment it is also to determine the remuneration. The liquidator's expenses and remuneration are to be paid immediately from the assets of the company.[546]

Special liquidation In a special liquidation the remuneration of the liquidator is to be fixed by the court and expenses and remuneration are to be paid in the same way as in ordinary liquidations.[547]

---

543 Company Law, Article 354.

544 As note 47, above, 150.

545 As note 255, above, 399–400.

546 Company Law, Article 325.

547 Company Law, Articles 325, 356.

8 Enforcement of Securities over a Debtor's Assets in Taiwan

8.1 The Position of Secured Creditors and the Protection of Property Interests

Taiwanese official law offers several forms of security over property including mortgages of immovables and chattel mortgages including trust receipts, conditional sales and pledges. These three last forms of securities are provided for by the Chattel Secured Transactions Law which was promulgated in 1963. It does not provide for a floating charge over stock of a fluctuating value. Non-residents of Taiwan may not hold mortgages over real estate or chattels, except for ships and aircraft, nor can they hold trust receipts.[548] Securities over personal property are problematical. The foreign banks which opened in Taiwan in the late 1970s and early 1980s found that all the movable property of a debtor had disappeared by the time they learnt of a default.[549]

Secured creditors are exempt from composition proceedings and may bring a civil action, which unsecured creditors cannot do, once a composition is on foot.[550] They have exclusive rights on a bankruptcy in property over which they hold their securities and remain entitled to exercise their rights outside the bankruptcy procedure.[551] The reorganization provisions in the Company Law, however, do not exempt secured creditors.[552] They may face delays of up to 15 years before the money is repaid to them. In the two years it takes for the reorganization plan to be approved, assets of the company may be dissipated at the same time as their rights are deferred for continuing periods of three months and indefinitely once the plan is approved.[553] Consequently secured creditors are reluctant to rely on the courts protecting their interests in the return of their capital in the framework of official insolvency law.[554]

Domestic financing in Taiwan has historically concentrated more on securing assets than cash flows. It is not unusual to find a lender holding at least four or five forms of the following securities:

- mortgages over immovables owned by the borrower and used in the business;
- chattel mortgages over equipment or machinery;
- trust receipts over the stock and inventory;
- pledges over the business's bank accounts;
- post-dated cheques from the business's customers endorsed by the business to the lender;
- personal guarantees from the proprietor of the business or the members of its board; and
- guarantees from a parent or related companies.

548 Land Law, Article 17; As note 255, above, 387.

549 As note 271, above, 398.

550 Bankruptcy Law, Articles 17, 108.

551 Bankruptcy Law, Article 108.

552 Bankruptcy Law, Article 108 and Company Law, Article 296.

553 Company Law, Article 294. Article 287 does allow interested parties to apply for an order that the business of, and obligations to be performed by, a company be restricted: As note 45, above, 80–81.

554 As note 45, above, 84–85; As note 255, above, 400–401.

The emphasis in disputes has been less on representations, warranties and covenants and more on securities and the legal provisions relating to their status. Some of these provisions rely to a greater extent on unofficial law than they do on official law.[555]

Mortgages of land and buildings A mortgage of immovable property is a lien over the land or things affixed to the land. It is defined in the Civil Code as the right to receive performance of an obligation from the proceeds of the sale of an immovable asset which has been given as security for the obligations of the debtor.[556] A mortgage does not lead to a transfer of title from the mortgagor to the mortgagee. The mortgagee has no title to the land nor is entitled to possession until the mortgagor has defaulted. The mortgagee has the right to have an obligation performed by the payment from the proceeds of sale of an immovable property.[557] The mortgage agreement is void if it provides for title to pass automatically on default.[558] This form of mortgage is the Roman law hypothec, a charge on the land, as opposed to the common law mortgage which requires the transfer of the title to the mortgagee, giving rise to an equity of redemption in the mortgagor.[559] Immovable property may be the land or the building on the land and it is not uncommon in Taiwan for them to be separately owned. The Civil Code seeks to address the conflict which may result from this division. The practice is to avoid mortgages in these circumstances.[560]

Two other interests in land are now recognized in official law. The *tai* of both official Chinese imperial law and of unofficial Chinese custom had features of the common law mortgage. It was changed, at least in official law, in the Japanese period into a hypothec based on the official law's recognition of Taiwanese custom and finally, in 1923, into a true hypothec. Not recognized in official law after 1945 it continued to be extensively used and was finally recognized by the Supreme Court again as a Taiwanese custom which would be recognized in the official law.[561] The right to move against the payment of a price for the possession of an immoveable belonging to another for the user and usufruct found in official Chinese imperial law has been taken up in the Civil Code in Articles 911 onward. It is like a sale of land with a right of pre-emption. It was used by people selling family land which they had inherited from ancestors as an attempt to minimize the effect of an outright sale.[562]

555 As note 255, above, 379.

556 Civil Code, Article 66.

557 Civil Code, Article 860.

558 Civil Code, Article 873.

559 In some translations of the Civil Code the term is translated as hypotheca: see 'Chapter VI: Hyoptheca' in Liu, Francis S. (trans.) (no date), *The Civil Code of the Republic of China: Book III: Law of Things*, (no place of publication): Boyer PH Chu and Li Chong Chen; Walker, D. (1980), *The Oxford Companion to Law*, Oxford: Clarendon Press, 597.

560 As note 255, above, 379; Loh, Jen-Kong, D. Allen, M. Hiscock, D. Roebuck (1973), *Credit and Security in the Republic of China: the Legal Problems of Development Finance*, St Lucia, Queensland: University Press, 137–8.

561 See above notes 76–77.

562 It is sometimes explained in terms of the French *antichrese*, the German *grundschuld*, the Welsh mortgage or the Japanese pledge of immovables but it is different from all of them: 'Translator's note on the right of dien', As note 559, above, 48–50.

The Civil Code generally treats rights associated with this right as if it were a mortgage of immovables.[563]

The Civil Code provides that a mortgage interest cannot be severed from the obligation it secures. The Supreme Court, apparently contrary to the Code, has approved maximum mortgages which permit revolving credits to be secured. These mortgages are not destroyed when all the debt is paid off and further advances are secure.[564] This also represents the recognition in the official law of the unofficial practice of *nei-teto* – fixed collateral. This is a Japanese credit practice adopted in Taiwanese custom before becoming part of the official Japanese law for Taiwan. Again, having lost its official status in 1945, it continued in general use and was resurrected into its pre-1945 status by decisions of the Supreme Court recognizing it as creating rights and liabilities enforceable in the official legal system.[565]

Taiwanese law also recognizes accommodation mortgages where the security is provided by a third party, the accommodation party, rather than the borrower.[566] In addition the Banking Law recognizes negative pledges. They can only be made by companies with authorization from the board. They prevent others from obtaining a mortgage over the property used as security. If it is breached, the directors are personally liable and are subject to criminal penalties.[567]

Mortgages must be in writing and registered. Registration confers priority on a mortgage.[568] Agreements to make a mortgage can be specifically enforced.[569] The mortgagee's rights in the mortgage are not subject to bankruptcy proceedings.[570]

Chattel securities The Chattel Secured Transactions Law imposes the same requirements for valid chattel mortgages, trust receipts, conditional sales and pledges. It is based on the US Uniform Commercial Code. The agreement must be written. It must be registered to be effective against third parties.[571]

Chattel mortgages A chattel mortgage is a lien over a chattel securing a debt or promised future action. It is a hypothec which does not transfer the title or the possession of the chattel.[572] It may be a maximum mortgage, i.e., it may stipulate the maximum amount which is to be advanced to permit revolving credit.[573]

To be valid a chattel mortgage must contain:

---

563 Civil Code, Article 914.

564 Civil Code, Articles 294, 870; Supreme Court Judgments, 62 [1973] Tai Sheng Tze No 776 and 66 [1977] Tai Sheng Tze No 1097, cited in: As note 271, above, 400 and ff 19 and 20.

565 See above notes 78–79.

566 Civil Code, Article 860.

567 Banking Law, Articles 30, 126.

568 Civil Code, Articles 758, 760, 865.

569 Civil Code, Articles 153, 760.

570 Bankruptcy Law, Article 108.

571 Chattel Secured Transactions Law, Article 5.

572 Chattel Secured Transactions Law, Article 15.

573 Chattel Secured Transactions Law, Article 16.

- the name and business or residential addresses of the parties;
- the amount secured and the interest rate;
- the name, quantity, price, description, serial number, identifying mark, if any, of the chattel;
- the manner in, and location at, which the debtor or a third party is to keep the chattel;
- the manner in which the secured obligation is to be performed;
- the method of foreclosing if there is a default by the debtor;
- where the chattel is insured against loss or damage, a statement that the mortgagee is the beneficiary under the policy;
- the name of the court with jurisdiction over the agreement;
- the statement of other terms and conditions, if any; and
- the date of the execution of the agreement.[574]

It must be registered to be valid. Similar particulars must be supplied together with additional information and copies where the agreement is registered.[575] The agency with which the chattel is registered varies depending on its nature. If the mortgaged property is in more than one administrative region or may be moved to another administrative region, it should also be registered in that region.[576] In addition a plaque indicating the existence of the mortgage should be placed on the chattel by the mortgagee.[577]

The chattel mortgagee's rights in the mortgage are not subject to bankruptcy proceedings.[578]

Trust receipts A trust receipt requires a *trustee*, the debtor, and a person who trusts – the *trustor*, the creditor. The secured interest is a possession in trust created by the trustor providing the credit to the trustee to buy a chattel with the title being held by the trustor. The trustee is entitled to the possession of the chattel and is able to sell or otherwise dispose of it.[579] Its appearance in the Chattel Secured Transactions Law represents the official law taking up a practice followed in unofficial law. In the *ya-hui* the lender retained receipts for goods bought and sold as security for payment under a letter of credit.[580]

The formalities required for trust receipts are similar to those required for chattel mortgages but with necessary variations including:

- a statement that the trustor retains title to the chattel and the manner in which the trustee may have possession and dispose of it;

574 Chattel Secured Transactions Law, Article 16.

575 Chattel Secured Transactions Law, Article 9.

576 These requirements are set out in the Enforcement Rules, Chattel Secured Transactions Law. See further: As note 271, above, 407–408, ff 80 and 81.

577 As note 255, above, 380.

578 Bankruptcy Law, Article 108.

579 Chattel Secured Transactions Law, Article 32.

580 As note 271, above, 410.

- the manner in which the credit advanced will be repaid including, where the trustee is to sell the chattel, a statement that the trustee will pay to the trustor the amount advanced;
- the manner in which the trustor will exercise any rights if the trustee defaults; and
- where the chattel is insured against loss or damage, a statement that the trustor is the beneficiary under the policy.[581]

Trust receipts must be registered in the same way as chattel mortgages.[582] The trustor's rights in the trust receipt are not subject to bankruptcy proceedings.[583]

Conditional sales These require buyers and sellers. The buyer takes possession of, but not title to, the goods on the condition that the title will pass from the seller on part, or full, payment of the price or performance another condition. The effect is that the seller extends credit to the buyer but takes a security over the goods. It cannot be used to secure further advances of money or credit.[584]

The formalities required for conditional sales are similar to those required for chattel mortgages but with necessary variations including:

- a statement that the seller retains title to the chattel and the manner in which the buyer may have possession of it and use it;
- the manner of payment of the amount outstanding;
- the conditions under which the buyer may acquire title;
- the manner in which the seller will exercise any rights if the buyer defaults; and
- where the chattel is insured against loss or damage, a statement that the seller is the beneficiary under the policy.[585]

Conditional sales must be registered in the same way as chattel mortgages.[586] The seller's rights in the conditional sale are not subject to bankruptcy proceedings.[587]

Pledges A pledge is a right to take possession of property as security for an obligation to be performed by a debtor or third party. It is a security interest in the proceeds of sale from the thing which is the subject of the pledge. Except where the agreement is to the contrary the pledge secures not only the principal, it also secures the interest, the cost of executing the pledge, and any injury which the pledgee suffers from a concealed defect in the property or the right.[588]

Where a movable is pledged, the movable must be delivered into the possession of the pledgee.[589] Where a right is pledged, the agreement must be in writing and any

---

581 Chattel Secured Transactions Law, Article 33.
582 Chattel Secured Transactions Law, Article 9.
583 Bankruptcy Law, Article 108.
584 Chattel Secured Transactions Law, Article 26.
585 Chattel Secured Transactions Law, Article 33.
586 Chattel Secured Transactions Law, Article 9.
587 Bankruptcy Law, Article 108.
588 Civil Code, Article 887.
589 Civil Code, Article 885.

document which is proof of the rights must be delivered to the pledgee.[590] Shares must be transferred into the name of the pledgee.[591]

If the pledge secures an obligation to repay a debt, the debtor can pay the amount to either the pledgor or the pledgee without the consent of both. Where agreement is not reached, the debtor may lodge the payment with the public lodgement office of the district court which has jurisdiction over the debt.[592]

Generally pledges are used where ownership of the thing pledged can be proved by a written instrument such as shares, bonds and bank accounts which, if transferred to the lender, do not significantly interfere with the benefits of ownership. But it is also possible for them to be used in respect of the stock or inventory of a business. The lender may have a warehouse in which the pledged items are kept, or may be the lessee of a shop and require the pledged inventory to be kept in the warehouse or the shop. In these ways the lender has taken the required 'possession' of them.[593]

A pledge agreement which seeks to automatically transfer title to the pledgee on default is invalid.[594] Movable property and transferable claims or other rights can be the subject of a pledge. Immovable property and rights which are not transferable cannot be pledged.[595] Nor can property which cannot be subject to judicial attachment.[596]

The pledgee's rights in the pledge are not subject to bankruptcy proceedings.[597]

Guarantees and negotiable instruments A large amount of financing in Taiwan uses promissory notes from third parties complying with the Law of Negotiable Instruments. Inevitably, given their prevalence, they have featured in litigation. They are frequently assigned or endorsed as a form of security.[598] Their interesting position between official and unofficial law is discussed in the context of criminal offences.[599]

In addition personal guarantees and corporate guarantees are common. They also straddle both legal systems. If they are given gratuitously, they may be cancelled by any creditor of the guarantor if the creditor can show that they jeopardized any rights of the creditor which pre-existed the guarantee. There is no agreement on what 'gratuitous' means in this context.[600]

Guarantees given by companies may also be found to be unenforceable as 'gratuitous' or for other reasons. Firstly, Article 16 of the Company Law requires that the company must be specifically authorized by its articles to give a guarantee in respect of the obligations of a third party. Most are not. Rather than amend their

590 Civil Code, Article 296, 904.
591 Company Law, Article 902; Civil Code, Article 161.
592 Civil Code, Article 907.
593 As note 255, above, 380; As note 45, above, 78.
594 Civil Code, Article 893.
595 Civil Code, Article 900.
596 Civil Code, Article 294.
597 Bankruptcy Law, Article 108.
598 As note 255, above, 378–9.
599 See below notes 653–654.
600 Article 244 of the Civil Code makes such gratuitous guarantees liable to cancellation. See further: As note 255, above, 381–2.

articles they seek to create a guarantee using other devices. Secondly, to avoid the lack of power in the Articles, the company may in substance guarantee loans to third parties by declaring that the company is jointly liable with another to repay the loan. Joint liability by declaration is possible under Article 272 of the Civil Code. This liability is argued not to be the contingent liability required to have a guarantee as the joint liability is a present liability. But such arrangements are vulnerable to being found to be a guarantee in substance. Thirdly, and alternatively to the second reason, the company may issue a promissory note to the borrower who endorses it in favour of the lender. This relies on the separate legal liability of a person who gives a promissory note which is present and not contingent, as with a guarantee. Nevertheless the courts may look at the real intention of the company, the borrower and the lender, and to the substance of the transaction in considering whether there has been a breach of Article 16 of the Company Law.[601]

Companies are further restricted in official law by a number of other prohibitions in the Company Law. They may not raise finance to increase fixed assets to be used as productive equipment by using short-term debt. The company officers who breach this provision have committed an offence punishable with a fine up to NT$20,000. They are also liable to the company for any damage caused to it.[602] Unless the commercial activities between companies in a group require it, the capital of the company cannot be lent to another person, including any shareholders.[603] A company cannot redeem or buy back shares in itself, or accept them as security unless the shareholder is a bankrupt. If the provision is breached, the officers involved have committed an offence punishable with imprisonment of up to one year and a fine up to NT$20,000.[604]

8.2 The Powers of the Court on Default

Mortgages of land If the mortgagor defaults on repayment the mortgagee can request the court to sell the property. If the obligation under the mortgage is fully mature the mortgagee can negotiate with the mortgagor to buy it without a judicial sale. If there is no agreement the mortgagor must petition the court to sell the property by auction and then petition for the execution of that order.[605] If unsecured creditors have attached the land it will be difficult for the mortgagor to agree to a private sale because of the right of the general creditors to force an auction.[606]

Chattel mortgages If the mortgagor defaults on performing the contract, or if the mortgaged property is removed, sold, pledged, transferred or otherwise disposed of to impede foreclosure, the mortgagee may take possession of the property without a

601 As note 255, above, 382–3.
602 Company Law, Article 14.
603 Company Law, Article 15.
604 Company Law, Article 167.
605 Civil Code, Article 873.
606 As note 255, above, 379.

court order.[607] Otherwise, without the agreement of the mortgagor, the mortgagee may only take possession by order of the court.[608]

Where a mortgagor refuses to surrender a chattel under the agreement, the mortgagee may apply to the court for the provisional seizure of the chattel. If the agreement specifies that there can be 'compulsory execution', the mortgagee can proceed directly to a judicially ordered sale.[609]

If the mortgagor sold the chattel to a third party who was acting in good faith and the chattel has been moved to an administrative region where the mortgage has not been registered, the mortgagee's interest ceases to exist and the chattel cannot be recovered.[610] The same applies if a third party acting in good faith has obtained a statutory chattel security over it.[611] The debtor may have committed criminal offences in doing any of these things as well as being liable to the mortgagee for any damage.[612]

The mortgagee must give the person in possession of the chattel three days' notice of the intention to repossess the chattel. The notice must specify the basis on which the repossession is taking place. It may also state the terms on which the mortgagor could make good any breach of the agreement. If the debtor continues to remain in default, the mortgagor may sell the property and any right to redeem held by the mortgagor is extinguished.[613] Where the required notice was not given, the person in possession who took the chattel from the mortgagor has ten days in which to cure any defect. If the defect is cured the chattel should be returned. The expenses of the mortgagor in repossessing the chattel must also be paid. If the chattel is perishable or likely to quickly lose value, the mortgagee may sell it immediately after taking possession, whether or not three days' notice was given.[614]

Trust receipts If the trustee defaults under the trust receipt agreement, the trustor, as the holder of the title in the chattel, is able to take possession without an order from a court. The trustor may also take possession where the trustee removes the chattel without the trustor's consent, pledges or mortgages the chattel or disposes of it in ways not provided for in the agreement.[615] A major problem for the trustor is that the trust receipt does not float and so if the thing which is secured by it is processed or manufactured into something else, the trust ownership ceases.[616]

The provisions relating to sale by the trustor, either privately by agreement or under a court order, match those of the mortgagee under a chattel mortgage.[617]

---

607 Chattel Secured Transactions Law, Articles 17, 18.
608 Chattel Secured Transactions Law, Article 17.
609 Chattel Secured Transactions Law, Article 17.
610 Chattel Secured Transactions Law, Articles 5, 6.
611 Chattel Secured Transactions Law, Article 25.
612 Chattel Secured Transactions Law, Articles 38, 40.
613 Chattel Secured Transactions Law, Article 18.
614 Chattel Secured Transactions Law, Article 18.
615 Chattel Secured Transactions Law, Article 34.
616 As note 255, above, 380; As note 45, above, 77.
617 Chattel Secured Transactions Law, Article 37.

Conditional sales If the purchaser defaults under a conditional sales agreement, the seller, as the holder of the title in the chattel, is able to take possession without a court order. The seller may also take possession where the purchaser fails to pay the purchase price as required in the agreement, fails to perform another obligation which the agreement requires, or sells, pledges, or otherwise disposes of the chattel. If the chattel has lost value, the seller can recover damages from the seller.[618]

Pledges Unless there is agreement to the contrary, pledgees are entitled to collect any benefits accruing to the thing pledged.[619] The pledgee must look after the thing pledged as a 'good administrator' would.[620] Where a pledgee believes the thing pledged may lose value and that the rights of the pledgee will be extinguished or endangered, the pledgee may sell it at auction and keep the proceeds in its place.[621]

If the thing pledged is lost or destroyed, the pledge is extinguished. The pledgee retains the right to subrogation.[622] Once the obligation represented by the pledge is performed the pledge is extinguished and the pledgee must return the thing to the person entitled to it.[623]

Guarantees and negotiable instruments The use of guarantees is intended to put the holder of the guarantee in the position where they can take action to enforce it. Generally if the money due is not paid the holder will have to sue in debt. Post-dated cheques and promissory notes endorsed in favour of the lender also leave the lender in this situation. The unofficial popularity of post-dated cheques in part relies on the Law of Negotiable Instruments as a speedy and efficient method for enforcing securities. Under Article 123 of the Negotiable Instruments Law the holder of a promissory note can apply for an order that the note be enforced by execution against the property of the note maker. The court need only be satisfied that:

- the note amount is certain;
- the issuance date is specified;
- there is language which identifies the document as a promissory note; and
- payment under the note is unconditional.[624]

Such judgments are rendered in one month and for nominal fees. If action were to be taken under the Civil Code, it would take many months and the maker of the note is permitted to raise substantive defences.[625] Tomasic and Francis quote a leading foreign lawyer in Taipei who observed that promissory notes are 'an effective debt

618 Chattel Secured Transactions Law, Article 28.

619 Civil Code, Article 889.

620 Civil Code, Article 888.

621 Civil Code, Article 892.

622 Civil Code, Articles 898, 899.

623 Civil Code, Article 897.

624 Negotiable Instruments Law, Article 123.

625 Kaufman Winn, J. (1986), 'Decriminalising bad checks should help to raionalize Taiwan's financial system', 15 August 1986, 8 (8) *East Asian Executive Reports* 9.

collection method because once there has been a default and a seal has been put in place on the assets, it is a criminal offence for the debtor to touch the assets'.[626] This effectiveness of the mere seal of the official legal system in unofficial law has echoes of the effectiveness of the paper seals of imperial magistrates on the windows and doors of the premises of a bankrupt.[627]

8.3 The Powers of the Court to Sell or Transfer Property used as Security

Mortgages of land If the court grants the creditor's petition for attachment, it will attach the property secured by the mortgage, have it valued, set a minimum price and announce the time of the auction.[628] Auctions are conducted by sealed bid. If the highest price is below the price set by the court, it may arrange for a second auction with the price reduced by up to 20 per cent. A third auction may be ordered in a similar way. If that does not succeed the court may offer the property to the mortgagee at the final reduced minimum price. If the mortgagee declines the process starts again after a six-month delay.[629]

Chattel mortgages The mortgagee in possession may arrange for the auction of the chattel. Except where the required three days' notice was not given, the notice of the auction must be given within 30 days of the mortgagee obtaining possession. It must also be given at least five days before the auction. The mortgagor or the person previously in possession must be given ten days' notice of the auction. The mortgagee and members of their family may bid at the auction. If the property can be divided, the auction is to stop once an amount sufficient to pay the mortgagee's claim and any costs and expenses has been obtained.[630]

The mortgagee must obtain a certificate from a court, notary, police, or chamber of commerce of a local authority that the sale was at market value.[631] A mortgagee who does not follow the requirements specified in the Chattel Secured Transactions Law is liable to the mortgagor for any damage suffered.[632] The priority in applying the proceeds of the sale are, firstly, the costs of the sale; secondly, any interest outstanding; and, thirdly, the principal. The mortgagee retains the right to sue the mortgagor for any outstanding debt.[633]

Trust receipts The provisions relating to sale by the trustor either privately, by agreement, or under a court order match those of the mortgagee under a chattel mortgage.[634]

---

626 As note 45, above, 78.

627 See above note 119. An illustration of the shop of a bankrupt appears in: As note 80, above, 84.

628 Compulsory Execution Law, Articles 4, 76, 80, 81.

629 Compulsory Execution Law, Articles 91–95. See further: As note 255, above, 380.

630 Chattel Secured Transactions Law, Article 19.

631 Chattel Secured Transactions Law, Article 21.

632 Chattel Secured Transactions Law, Article 22.

633 Compulsory Execution Law, Article 20.

634 Chattel Secured Transactions Law, Article 37.

Conditional sales The purchaser may request the seller in possession of the chattel to sell it. The seller may sell the chattel within 30 days of taking possession of it. The agreement ceases to have effect. Whether or not the seller sells the chattel, the seller is not required to refund any part of the purchase price paid by the purchaser.[635]

The provisions relating to sale by the seller, either privately, by agreement, or under a court order, match those of the mortgagee under a chattel mortgage.[636]

Pledges If the pledgor defaults on the maturity of the obligation, the pledgee may sell the thing at auction, without a court order, and pay to themselves any amount owing from the proceeds of the sale.[637] Notice must be given to the pledgor unless it is impracticable to do so.[638] The pledgor may agree with the pledgee to transfer title of the thing or to dispose of it otherwise than by auction.[639]

8.4 The Effect of the Appointment of a Liquidator or Reorganizers on Corporate Assets

The appointment of a liquidator in either an ordinary or special liquidation will have little effect on securities held by third parties over corporate property. Secured creditors with registered interests should be known to the liquidator who is required to notify them individually of the liquidation.[640] Secured creditors are exempt from the general prohibition that liquidators must not pay any creditors until the end of the period fixed for the notification of debts.[641] In special liquidations secured creditors are excluded from the process and voting in the creditors' meeting although they may still attend these meetings.[642] In such liquidations, if it becomes clear that the company is insolvent and no settlement is likely to be reached, the company will be bankrupted. The special liquidator is required to consider how the liquidation should proceed.[643] If it is unlikely that a settlement will be reached, the Company Law in Article 355 provides for a bankruptcy order to be made. The secured creditors' rights are reserved under that law in Article 108.

The major problems for secured creditors occur when company directors avoid the liquidation provisions and bring the company within the reorganization provisions of the Company Law.[644] They are assisted in this by the inability or unwillingness of interested parties to intervene in the process by raising issues which are detrimental to the shareholders or institutional creditors. Even when insolvency is imminent or has commenced, companies may engage in fraudulent preferences.[645]

---

635 Chattel Secured Transactions Law, Article 29.

636 Chattel Secured Transactions Law, Article 37.

637 Civil Code, Article 893.

638 Civil Code, Article 894.

639 Civil Code, Articles 878, 893, 895. See further: As note 255, above, 381.

640 Company Law, Article 327.

641 Company Law, Article 328.

642 Company Law, Article 341.

643 Company Law, Article 344.

644 As note 45, above, 74.

645 McGowan (as note 255, above, 398–399) has identified three examples: payments are disguised to

Courts frequently make interim orders, in the absence of creditors, to protect companies from bankruptcy proceedings but without restricting the powers of the company and its managers. As there is no requirement to advertise such petitions, the creditors generally learn of the orders after they have been made.[646] Only upon completion of the reorganization, which may be many months or years later, does their right to take action revive.[647] In most cases the court appoints a member of the existing management to conduct the affairs of the company while it operates under the reorganization provisions.[648] By the mid-1990s the courts exercising bankruptcy jurisdiction were showing some inclination to curb abuses and shortcomings in previous practices.[649] Still, creditors wishing to participate in any court proceedings are confronted by time-consuming and complicated processes. Even to apply to review the court files they must have the relevant file numbers. These are not matters of public record. There is no formal procedure to disclose them. Except for listed companies, company records held by government agencies are difficult to locate and access.[650]

The government continues to be an important stakeholder in any corporate insolvency and its interests in, and policies towards, industries which 'support Taiwan' distort the implementation of the official law.[651] In smaller companies, as mentioned, family control, its associated *guanxi*, and the reluctance to play the ugly role of pushing the company into bankruptcy, marginalizes the official law. Negotiation and compromise, based in unofficial law, take over.[652]

9 Offences

The relationship between the official criminal law and the unofficial law of the Taiwanese commercial community is also complex. In the 1980s business failures were significant in Taiwan as so much small business was undercapitalized. The approach favoured in unofficial law was for creditors to accept 30 per cent of what was owed as this was the penalty imposed by courts on charges of uttering a bad

---

aggressive private creditors by transfer pricing, and leasing and distributorship arrangements which are not at arm's length; the transfer of assets to management, particularly through dealings by affiliated companies in the group; and the creation of fictitious debts in the hands of family and friends to stack any creditors' pool and to skim payments in a reorganization into the hands of management.

646 They have to make orders, under Articles 287 and 295 of the Company Law: suspending proceedings relating to bankruptcy, composition or compulsory execution against the company's assets; preserving its property; limiting the claims which are made against the company; relieving it from performing obligations; prohibiting the transfer of its shares; and investigating and establishing liability for damage caused to the company and preserving management owned property. See further: As note 255, above, 399; As note 45, above, 84–85.

647 Company Law, Article 311(3).

648 As note 255, above, 400.

649 As note 255, above, 400–401.

650 As note 255, above, 400.

651 Kamarul and Tomasic (as note 162, above, 160–161) indicate that this is particularly so of companies in the financial and banking sectors. Another company was rescued as 'the brand value it has for Taiwan is tremendous'.

652 As note 162, above, 166–167.

cheque. There was no automatic criminal penalty for failing to honour a promissory note. Consequently, post-dated cheques were favoured by lenders to secure loans. Lenders could use the threat of a criminal penalty under the official law in any negotiations on default. Debtors came to offer, as a standard amount, 30 per cent to their creditors who then had little reason to take the matter further. The response in the official legal system was to de-criminalize the writing of cheques not met on presentation in order to remove official legal support for this unofficial practice.[653] This practice, once established, did not change with the change in the official law and post-dated cheques are still preferred over promissory notes as the negotiable instrument to secure a debt.[654]

The criminal courts of Taiwan have not enjoyed a reputation for the effective enforcement of the criminal law or the confidence of the Taiwanese legal profession or the people.[655] Some judges are believed to take bribes. Prosecutors describe the rigorous and uniform enforcement of the criminal law but only act on complaints. Notorious criminal conduct is not prosecuted.[656] As in other jurisdictions fraud is frequently revealed only in insolvency proceedings. In Taiwan it will be punished, but only if the evidence permits courts to convict. The complexity of the conduct may make that difficult.[657]

The Bankruptcy Law creates a number of specific offences relating to insolvencies. Under Article 154 the offence of fraudulent bankruptcy is committed if, within one year before the bankruptcy order or in the course of the bankruptcy procedure, for the purpose of injuring the interests of the creditors, the bankrupt:

- conceals, destroys or abandons properties or otherwise disposes of properties to the disadvantage of the creditors;
- forges evidence of debts or incurs debts which are not genuine; or
- destroys, abandons or forges the whole or a part of the account books or other accounting documents which result in the false or inaccurate presentation of the status of the bankrupt's assets.

The penalty is imprisonment for up to five years.

Article 156 makes it an offence for a bankrupt, in the year prior to the making of the bankruptcy order, to:

- engage in lavish acts, gambling or other speculative acts which result in evident decrease in properties or the undertaking of excessive obligations;
- undertake obligations or purchase or dispose of goods under disadvantageous conditions in order to delay the making of a bankruptcy order; or

---

653 As note 59, Kaufman Winn 1993, 207–208; As note 271, above, 398.

654 As note 255, above, 381.

655 As note 47, above, 153. Wang reports that in 1985 50–60 per cent of people surveyed in Taipei 'partly' or 'considerably' agreed that the courts were fair. Twenty to 25 per cent 'partly' or 'completely' disagreed. Thirty-one per cent of practising lawyers in Taiwan 'partly' disagreed and 8 per cent 'completely' disagreed.

656 As note 59, above, Kaufman Winn 1993, 204.

657 As note 181, above, para KK(b), (c) and (d)(iii).

- furnish security or extinguish debts to benefit select creditors while knowing that a ground for making a bankruptcy order exists.

The penalty is imprisonment for up to one year.

Article 155 makes any of the actions in Article 154 an offence of fraudulent composition, carrying up to five years' imprisonment, where they are committed by a debtor to cause injury to the creditors after a petition for composition has been approved.

Bankrupts who (1) fail to provide, at the request of the trustee in bankruptcy, a statement of assets – including their nature and location – and a list of creditors and debtors under Article 87; or (2) fail to hand over to the trustee in bankruptcy all the books and documents relevant to their properties or properties which are in their custody under Article 88; have committed an offence punishable with imprisonment for up to one year.[658]

Failure to answer questions or to provide an explanation is also an offence, carrying imprisonment of up to one year and a fine of up to NT$1,000, when the failure is by:

- the bankrupt's relations or other interested people who have been summonsed by the court under Article 74;
- the bankrupt when requested by the trustee in bankruptcy or inspector, or supervisor, under Article 89; and
- the bankrupt when requested by the presiding judge, trustee in bankruptcy, inspector, or supervisor, or creditors at the creditors' meeting under Article 122.[659]

Assistant supervisors in a composition, trustees in bankruptcy, inspectors or supervisors in bankruptcy who demand or agree to accept bribes or other improper benefits for any action they undertake have committed an offence punishable with imprisonment for up to three years and the imposition of a fine of up to NT$3,000.[660]

Creditors, or their agents, who demand, agree to accept or accept bribes or other improper benefits for the adoption of a resolution at the creditors' meeting have committed an offence punishable with imprisonment for up to three years and the imposition of a fine of up to NT$3,000.[661]

Mortgagors under chattel securities It is a criminal offence for a debtor who has given a statutory chattel security over a chattel to:

- remove, sell, pledge, transfer, mortgage or otherwise dispose of the chattel the subject of the security with the intention of obtaining an unlawful benefit which injures the creditor's rights;[662]

---

658 Bankruptcy Law, Article 152.

659 Bankruptcy Law, Article 153.

660 Bankruptcy Law, Article 157.

661 Bankruptcy Law, Article 158.

662 Chattel Secured Transactions Law, Articles 38.

- intentionally cause any reduction in the value of, or damage to, the chattel which injures the creditor's rights;[663] or
- intentionally cause another right of retention, including a statutory chattel security, to be created in right of a third party which injures the creditor's rights.[664]

9.1 Insolvent Trading Rules and Other Relevant Corporate Law Offences

Where assets are evidently insufficient to meet the company's liabilities, the board of directors must immediately file an application for bankruptcy unless an application for reorganization has been filed. Directors who fail to take either of these actions commit an offence punishable by a fine of up to NT$20,000.[665]

The Company Law has a number of disclosure and other requirements which will lead to disclosure of the solvency of a company limited by shares. The supervisors have access to company records including financial records.[666] Supervisors are required to check the financial records which the directors submit to the general meeting and to check the actual financial condition of the company, engaging a public accountant to assist them if necessary. It is an offence for them to make a false statement in their reports to the shareholders.[667] Supervisors must act as ordinary people would in managing their own affairs or, where they are remunerated, as good administrators would.[668] They are liable to compensate the company for any damage it suffers through their negligence.[669] Directors must report to them any possibility that the company may suffer substantial damage.[670] The supervisors must take action to prevent the directors breaching any law, including those relating to the company's solvency.[671]

The directors must prepare financial reports to shareholders within ten days of the close of the company's business year. They must be made available for inspection by shareholders at the company's office and also circulated to shareholders for consideration at the shareholders' meeting. It is an offence for directors not to prepare and circulate such reports. It is also an offence for them to make false reports.[672]

The Company Law requires directors of a company limited by shares to call a meeting of the shareholders where the company has lost more than one half of its capital.[673]

In addition a company limited by shares is required to maintain a surplus reserve of 10 per cent of surplus profits, after taxes and other expenses have been paid.

---

663 Chattel Secured Transactions Law, Article 39.
664 Chattel Secured Transactions Law, Article 40.
665 Company Law, Article 211.
666 Company Law, Article 218.
667 Company Law, Article 219.
668 Company Law, Article 216; Civil Code, Article 535.
669 Company Law, Article 224.
670 Company Law, Article 218(1).
671 Company Law, Article 218(2)
672 Company Law, Article 230.
673 Company Law, Article 211.

However, if this amounts to the same amount as the authorized capital, there is no need for the company to set it aside. It may maintain a special surplus reserve.[674] It must keep a capital reserve in which the premiums above par value paid for new shares are kept as well as other assets.[675] The surplus reserve and the capital reserve must not be used except to make up for a deficiency or loss by the company unless the surplus is sufficient to do so.[676] Companies are also not to distribute a surplus unless all losses have been covered.[677]

Shareholders who produce a certificate which states their interest in the company and the nature of their business may inspect the books and other financial records of a company. It is an offence by the director responsible not to make the records available or to falsify them.[678] Shareholders who have held 3 per cent of the issued shares for more than three months may apply to the court for an inspector to inspect the financial records of the company. It is an offence to hinder the inspector. Subsequently, if the court thinks it necessary to do so on the basis of the inspector's report, it may order that a supervisor call a shareholders' meeting. It is an offence for the supervisor not to do so. The Ministry of Economic Affairs' power to have its officers inspect the books of a company at any time could also be used where it is suspected that a company is insolvent.[679]

9.2 Other Insolvency-related Offences by Corporate Controllers

Where the Bankruptcy Law creates an offence which may be committed by the bankrupt or the debtor in composition proceedings, the following will also be taken to have committed the offence:

- shareholders of an unlimited company or an unlimited company with shareholders of limited liability who conduct the company's business;
- directors of a company limited by shares;
- shareholders of a company limited by shares with shareholders of unlimited liability who conduct the business;
- statutory representatives, managers or liquidators of the debtor or bankrupt; and
- the heir, administrator or executor of the estate which has been the subject of a bankruptcy order.[680]

---

674 Company Law, Article 237.

675 Company Law, Article 238. The company must also set aside in the capital reserve: the amount of appreciation of assets less the amount of depreciation as a result of asset valuation to be made in each business year; the proceeds in excess of the cost in the disposition of assets; the value of assets retained from a company which has been dissolved as a result of a merger less the amount required to meet its obligations; and earnings from gifts received.

676 Company Law, Articles 238, 239.

677 Company Law, Article 63.

678 Company Law, Article 210.

679 It is an offence to hinder these officers in their inspection: Company Law, Article 21.

680 Bankruptcy Law, Article 3.

Liquidators in ordinary liquidations who make false reports are subject to punishment under the Criminal Code and the Special Criminal Code.[681] Those who interfere with the final review of the accounts submitted by a liquidator in an ordinary liquidation may be liable to a fine of up to NT$60,000.[682]

10 Rules regarding Cross-border Insolvency and Judicial Assistance to Foreign Insolvency Officials

10.1 Broad Policy of Taiwan in regard to Recognition of Foreign Judgments and Court Orders

Foreign insolvency procedures will not be recognized over assets located in Taiwan.[683] Article 2 of the Bankruptcy Law provides that cases of composition or bankruptcy are under the sole jurisdiction of the district court where the corporate debtor is domiciled. If the head office of the corporate debtor is located outside Taiwan, then the district court of the place of the corporate debtor's head office in Taiwan has sole jurisdiction.[684] If there is no district court at these locations, then the district court at the place where the corporate debtor's principal assets are located will have jurisdiction.[685]

Taiwan is not a party to any convention or treaty governing cross-border insolvency. There are no indications that Taiwan is considering implementation of the UNCITRAL Model Law on Cross-border Insolvency approved by the United Nations in June 1997.

10.2 Procedures for the Assistance of Courts in Foreign Jurisdictions

Pursuant to the Statute of Conflict of Laws, the courts will recognize the authority of foreign insolvency administrators in accordance with the applicable foreign law.

10.3 Such Other Rules as may Apply to Foreign-based Assets

Under the law, there is no difference between the security held by foreign or local creditors over properties located in Taiwan. Government agencies, such as the Ministry of the Interior, tend to take the view that a foreign corporation must have a branch office in Taiwan to entitle registration as a chattel mortgagee or real estate mortgagee or pledgee. However, legislation in Taiwan does not require additional steps for foreign parties when creating a valid security interest.[686]

---

681 Company Law, Article 326.

682 Company Law, Article 331.

683 Bankruptcy Law, Article 4.

684 Bankruptcy Law, Article 2. The official translation reads 'if the head office is located abroad (*waiguo*)'.

685 Bankruptcy Law, Article 2.

686 As note 181, above, para. P.

11 Conclusion

In conclusion, Taiwan's contemporary insolvency regime must be understood as representing the continued interaction between official and unofficial law in the jurisdiction. In this respect, Taiwan's insolvency regime is evidence of the extent to which the assumption cannot be made that Taiwan's official law accurately reflects commercial or legal practice. Arguably, to understand Taiwan's insolvency regime – and legal system generally – it is necessary to grasp the distinction between formal and informal law in the jurisdiction and how the two interact with each other and outside influences.

Chapter 6

Insolvency Law in Hong Kong

E.L.G. TYLER
City University of Hong Kong

1 Introduction

1.1 Introduction to the Hong Kong Legal System and Legal Culture, Attitudes to Debt and Debt Enforcement

Until midnight on 30 June 1997 Hong Kong Island had been a British colony since 1843. In fact the British had occupied it since 1841. In 1843 the criminal and admiralty courts established by the British at Canton in 1833 were removed to Hong Kong and in 1844 a Supreme Court was established.[1] English law was formally introduced into Hong Kong in 1844. For legislation the cut-off date was 5 April 1843. There was no cut-off date for the common law. In 1966 under the Application of English Law Ordinance it was provided that English common law and the rules of equity applied in Hong Kong so far as they were applicable to the circumstances of Hong Kong. This was not so straightforward as it seemed, but we need not go into the problems it caused, as they are now purely of historical interest. As to legislation, some 70 English Acts specified in the schedule to the Application of English Law Ordinance were applicable in Hong Kong and English Acts and Orders in Council could be made applicable to Hong Kong.[2]

In 1861 Kowloon and Stonecutters Island were ceded to Great Britain and declared to be part of the colony of Hong Kong. In 1898 the New Territories were leased to Great Britain and absorbed into the colony. These later additions with their larger populations, and for the New Territories a different status, were and still are important for the application of Chinese law and custom, mainly in the context of New Territories land law and the law of succession.[3]

Though it is now generally accepted that Hong Kong Island was not the barren uninhabited rock it was once thought to be, it was certainly no thriving commercial centre and Kowloon and the New Territories were made up of a military garrison and rural communities. While it can be said that there was some customary Chinese

---

1 See generally for the historical background to the constitution of Hong Kong, Wesley-Smith, P., *Constitutional and Administrative Law in Hong Kong*, Longman Asia, 2nd ed. 1994.

2 See generally on the reception of English law, Wesley-Smith, P., *The Sources of Hong Kong Law*, Hong Kong University Press, 1994 (hereafter referred to as '*Sources*').

3 On Chinese law and custom as a source of law see *Sources*, Ch. 12.

commercial law, for example in the context of partnership,[4] it did not survive the change from Chinese to British control.

Over the nearly 150 years of British control most of the local legislation (known as ordinances) were copies of their English equivalents.[5] Until quite recent times British and other expatriates predominated in the Legislative Council and the majority of the judges, magistrates and law teachers were British or other expatriates. Hong Kong did not have a Law School until 1969. Until law teaching started at the University of Hong Kong would-be lawyers from Hong Kong had to go to England to study. Until quite recent times, English was the language of the courts. Over the past five years or so criminal trials in Cantonese have become common in the Magistrates' Courts and in the District Court (though less so in the High Court) but most civil work and all insolvency work is currently conducted in English, with translation if necessary. Even today Queen's Counsel from England appears in weighty trials in Hong Kong. It is not surprising therefore that the legal system and legal culture in Hong Kong was a British system and a British culture.

And that has not really changed with Hong Kong's reunification with the People's Republic of China at midnight on 30 June 1997. The 1984 Joint Declaration and the Basic Law of the Hong Kong Special Administrative Region of the People's Republic of China (HKSAR) guaranteed the continuity of the existing system.[6] The Basic Law confirms the concepts of 'one country, two systems' and 'a high degree of autonomy for Hong Kong'. In preparation for the reunification it was necessary to localize all the British Acts and Orders in Council applying in Hong Kong, for example, the Copyright Act 1956 extended to Hong Kong by Orders in Council applied in Hong Kong until replaced by the Copyright Ordinance (cap 528) in 1997, and to establish the Court of Final Appeal to replace the Privy Council as the final appeal court for Hong Kong.[7] The Hong Kong Supreme Court (taking its title by analogy to the Supreme Court of Judicature of England and Wales) had to be changed to the High Court of the HKSAR as the Supreme Court for China was the Supreme People's Court in Beijing.[8] It was also necessary to localize legal personnel, for under the Basic

---

[4] The best treatment of commercial law in Imperial China is Jamieson, G., *Chinese Family and Commercial Law*, Kelly & Walsh, Shanghai 1921, reprinted by Vetch & Lee Ltd in 1970. A form of limited liability partnership was recognized. And see Kirby, W.C., 'China Unincorporated: Company Law and Business Enterprise in Twentieth Century China' (1995) *Journal of Asian Studies*, 54.1, 43–63.

[5] Copycating or 'xeroxing' English legislation in colonies where the socio-economic and cultural situation was very different has been the subject of criticism in recent years; see, for example, in the context of company law Rungta, R.S., *The Rise of Business Corporations in India 1851–1900*, Cambridge University Press, 1970 and McQueen, R., 'Company Law as Imperialism' (1995) 5 *Australian Journal of Corporate Law* 187.

[6] There is now a large corpus of material on the Joint Declaration and the Basic Law. For an overview see Wesley-Smith, P., *Constitutional and Administrative Law in Hong Kong* (see note 1) and for a more detailed treatment Ghai, Y., *Hong Kong's New Constitutional Order: The Resumption of Chinese Sovereignty and the Basic Law*, Hong Kong University Press, 2nd ed. 1998.

[7] Court of Final Appeal Ordinance (cap 484).

[8] Interpretation and General Clauses Ordinance (cap 1) Schd. 8, para. 9, added by the Hong Kong Reunification Ordinance, No. 110 of 1997, s 8.

Law the highest legal offices can only be held by Chinese citizens who are permanent residents of Hong Kong with no right of abode in any foreign country.

Article 8 of the Basic Law provides that the laws previously in force in Hong Kong, that is the common law, rules of equity, ordinances, subordinate legislation and customary law, shall be maintained, except for any that contravene the Basic Law, and subject to any amendment by the legislature of the HKSAR.[9] So the bankruptcy law and the company liquidation law of Hong Kong, both based on their British background, continue to apply in Hong Kong.

Despite some blips and interferences by mainland authorities in the political system in Hong Kong and, arguably, some pressures in the criminal justice system,[10] it seems unlikely that the familiar civil and commercial aspects of Hong Kong's legal system, including insolvency, will be affected by the change of sovereignty. Indeed, there has already been a decision by the Court of Appeal in the bankruptcy area that gives hope for a robust judicial attitude to maintaining the existing system in commercial matters. In *Ting Lei Miao* v. *Chen Li Hung & others* [1999] 1 HKLRD 123 the majority of the Court of Appeal, Mortimer V-P and Godfrey JA, applying general private international law principles, recognized the right of a trustee in bankruptcy appointed by a Taiwanese court to sue for movables situate in Hong Kong. Only Rogers JA dissented, on the basis that if the Court were to give effect to the bankruptcy order it would become part of the judicial process of Taiwan, namely the process of administration of assets in what was in effect rebel territory under the control of a court of the rebel government.

The attitude of Hong Kong people to debt varies according to their age. Despite an appearance of being highly Westernized, Hong Kong is still very much a traditional Chinese society. Indeed research into Chinese culture and tradition is probably more fruitfully done in the New Territories than in most parts of the mainland, where ancient traditions and culture were sought to be rooted out in 1949 and later by the Cultural Revolution. China has a long tradition of money lending, pawnbroking and informal money lending and borrowing groups, all of which the Communist Government sought to stamp out in 1949, but which continued in Hong Kong.[11] We tend to forget how comparatively recent is the concept of credit, as we know it today, particularly consumer credit. Chapter 1 of the Cork Report (Insolvency Law and Practice – Report of the Review Committee) 1982, entitled 'The Credit World', gives a convenient overview of the topic. It was the Cork Report that led to the major reform

---

9 Article 8 does not impose a new cut-off date (on earlier cut-off dates see text above at note 2): Wesley-Smith, P., 'The Content of the Common Law in Hong Kong', Ch. 1 of Wacks, R. (ed.) *The New Legal Order in Hong Kong*, Hong Kong University Press, 1999.

10 Such as the decisions by the Secretary for Justice (successor to the Attorney-General) not to prosecute Xinhua News Agency for an offence under the Personal Data (Privacy) Ordinance and not to prosecute Sally Au, newspaper proprietor and member of the Chinese People's Political Consultative Conference (a state organ of the PRC), for conspiracy to defraud by inflating the sales figures of the Hong Kong Standard newspaper, despite senior executives being charged with conspiring with her.

11 See the Money Lenders Ordinance (cap 163) (consumer credit legislation has not yet become an issue in Hong Kong), Pawnbrokers Ordinance (cap 38) and Chit-Fund Businesses (Prohibition) Ordinance (cap 262) (which permits funds where there are not more than 30 participants and the fund does not exceed HK$20,000).

of insolvency law in the UK in 1985/86. Hong Kong has accepted credit and debt with open arms. The per capita ratio of banks is high – there are 211 authorized institutions, of which 186 are owned by interests from 31 countries, and 85 representative offices of foreign banks.[12] Many of the local banks are small, family controlled banks. There is a long tradition of bank lending, both in the commercial and domestic areas, and despite the development of the Stock Exchange of Hong Kong over the past 25 years, bank borrowing still remains a major source of finance for most companies.

The extended family has been a source of finance, but with that concept breaking down, is now less so. Small companies (and most commercial companies in Hong Kong are small[13]) have in the good times in the past been able to fund much expansion and development from internal funds.

The modern Hong Kong Chinese attitude to debt can be summed up in one comment: 'Why use my own money, when I can borrow money and get a better return on my own money!' As in the West, attitudes to debt often vary between generations, with the older generation being more wary of credit. For the young, one has only to see their purses and wallets stuffed with 'Hello Kitty' and 'Batman' and other credit cards to see what their attitude to credit is.

Debt enforcement became the subject of a reference to the Law Reform Commission of Hong Kong in 1998. In *Wong Wai Hing & anor* v. *Hui Wei Lee* (2000) HCt unreported Action No. 2901 of 1998 (judgment delivered 29 March 2000) Sakhrani J said at p. 31:

> There can be nothing wrong per se in engaging a debt collector to collect a debt. After all, it is common knowledge that reputable banks and credit card companies do from time to time engage debt collectors to collect debts from customers. What is wrong, however, is the unlawful manner in which some debt collectors have used to collect debts by threats of assaults to the person and damage to property and sometimes actually carrying out their threats. Such disgraceful and unlawful conduct deserves the strongest condemnation. Unfortunately, there are no regulations governing debt collectors in Hong Kong. There is as yet no requirement for debt collectors to be licensed in Hong Kong. It is, in my view, important to determine whether, on the facts of each case, the employer is liable for the unlawful acts of the agent that he has employed.

The *Sunday Morning Post* business section on 9 January 2000 reported that the number of criminal damage cases linked to debt collection in certain residential areas had soared by more than 50 per cent to 173 in 1999. It also reported that there were

---

[12] A useful source of information about Hong Kong are the annual yearbooks published by the Government Printer, the latest (covering 2004), being *Hong Kong 2005*. These contain lots of useful data, but the text is the official view. For a more critical view, but less data, there used to be the annual 'The Other Hong Kong Report' published by the Chinese University Press, Hong Kong.

Other useful factual information can be obtained from the websites of relevant Government Departments; for example, www.info.gov.hk/hkma (Hong Kong Monetary Authority), www.info.gov.hk/ird (Inland Revenue Department, for example for business registration figures), www.info.gov.hk/oro (Official Receiver's Office for insolvency statistics), www.info.gov.hk/cr (Companies Registry for company registration statistics, company charge registration statistics, etc.).

[13] Nearly half the then 615,000 businesses in Hong Kong employed fewer than ten staff (see *Sunday Post*, 13 June 1999).

about 20 credit-collection companies in Hong Kong, with new ones popping up every month. Business had grown four-fold in the past five years with the Asian financial crisis. This only deals with 'official' debt collection agencies. Of course, there is also criminal triad involvement. This may be cheaper and more effective than using debt-collection agencies. Embarrassing graffiti painted on the debtor's front door, threatening telephone calls, letters with the envelope clearly indicating a debt is being claimed, calling on the debtor at work and causing a scene are par for the course. If these tactics do not work, then tougher action may follow, for example, hanging the debtor from a building by his ankles (*Sunday Morning Post* 6 June 1999) or 'Two strangers cut my arm off, debtor tells jury' (*South China Morning Post* 5 August 1998).

On 29 July 2000 the Law Reform Commission's sub-committee on regulation of debt collection practices issued a Consultation Document proposing, *inter alia*, the creation of a new offence of harassment of debtors and relaxation of existing limitations under the Personal Data (Privacy) Ordinance on the collection and use of credit data by credit reference agencies. The Hong Kong Monetary Authority (HKMA) supported this latter proposal. The credit reference agency business is not as advanced in Hong Kong as in most developed countries and such agencies as exist tend to record only default and other 'negative' information. Banks have not been able to check how many credit cards a customer has and, as a result, many credit-risky customers have obtained additional cards and become over-extended. HKMA proposed separate plans to set up a commercial credit reference agency in Hong Kong.[14]

In any event Hong Kong has quite draconian enforcement of judgment procedures. Under Order 44A of the Rules of the High Court (RHC) a prohibition order can be obtained, even before the issue of the writ, to stop a debtor leaving Hong Kong. This is a modern version of the old writ of *ne exeat regno*. It is alleged to be justified because of Hong Kong's somewhat transient population. Oral examination under RHC Orders 48 and 49B is commonly used to enforce a judgment. The mere threat of being examined is valuable in itself, but, if the judgment debtor is not put off by that, he may be arrested under O 49B to secure attendance at the examination and a prohibition order may be made to prevent him absconding. There are also powers of imprisonment for failing to answer questions or to make full disclosure at the examination and for not paying where the court considers the judgment debtor has the means to satisfy the judgment or, where he does not have the means to pay the judgment in full, he fails to pay any instalment ordered to be paid by the court.[15]

---

14 For subsequent developments, see the reversal of Sakhrani J's decision (that the creditor doctor was not liable) by the Court of Appeal [2001] 1 HKLRD 736; the Code of Banking Practice 2001, Ch. 5 Recovery of Loans (available at www.info.gov.hk/hkma/eng/public/cbp_2001/cbp_eng.pdf); and the Law Reform Commissions's Report on The Regulation of Debt Collection Practices, July 2001 (available at www.hkreform.gov.hk).

15 On the details of debt enforcement see Heilbronn, G., Booth, C., and McCook, H.E., *Enforcement of Judgments in Hong Kong*, Butterworths Asia, 1998.

1.2 History, Sources and Philosophy of Insolvency Laws in Hong Kong

Imperial China did not have a system of insolvency law, but there was under the Penal Code a process for arrest and imprisonment of debtors,[16] not unlike that in early English law.[17] On the cession of Hong Kong Island in 1843 English bankruptcy law, which with the consolidation of earlier legislation in the Bankruptcy Act 1825 had become more sophisticated, applied to Hong Kong. There was, of course, no liquidation legislation or process in 1843 (there being no registered companies legislation until the 1844 legislation and no winding up procedures until the Joint Stock Companies Act 1856). The first local insolvency legislation was the Ordinance for the Relief of Insolvent Debtors in the Colony of 1846. This was not really bankruptcy legislation, though it allowed the property of an insolvent debtor to be taken and administered in a manner similar to bankruptcy. The first expressly bankruptcy legislation was the Bankruptcy Ordinance 1864, comprising 201 sections and 16 schedules and based on the Bankruptcy Act 1825 as subsequently amended. When the English legislation was again consolidated in 1883, this was followed by the Bankruptcy Ordinance 1891. The English Bankruptcy Act 1891 was replaced by the Bankruptcy Act 1914 and this was followed by the Bankruptcy Ordinance 1931. This latter Ordinance remained the bankruptcy law in Hong Kong until the 1996 amendments came into effect on 1 April 1998.

As with so much of Hong Kong's legislation the Bankruptcy Ordinance was a copy of the English legislation (so-called 'copycat' or 'Xerox' legislation[18]) with such amendments as were necessitated by the local organizational structure. But the 1931 legislation worked reasonably well, partly because there were not many bankruptcies in Hong Kong. Nevertheless with insolvency reform activity in other Common Law jurisdictions (especially Canada, UK and Australia) Hong Kong was being left behind. Also attitudes to bankruptcy had changed. The 1931 Ordinance reflected the 'criminal' policy basis reflected in the 1914 Act. Bankruptcy was to punish debtors, especially where, as in Hong Kong, it was virtually impossible to obtain a discharge from bankruptcy. Section 30(4)(a) of the 1931 Ordinance prevented discharge where the bankrupt's assets were valued at less than 50 per cent of his/her unsecured liabilities, unless he/she could prove circumstances for which he/she could not justly be held responsible. So one should not be surprised that in the period 1983 to 1992 only 25 discharge orders were made, while in the same period about 2,400 adjudication (bankruptcy) orders were made. For most bankrupts, bankruptcy was truly for life. In *Re Fung Hing Cheung Kenneth* [1995] 3 HKC 136, Waung J said at p. 140:

> The Bankruptcy Ordinance of Hong Kong is based on very old law going back into the last century where the harsh disapproval of bankruptcy by society was reflected in the severe restrictions on the court's power to grant absolute discharge. It is much to be regretted that

---

16 See Jamieson, G., *Chinese Family and Commercial Law*, 1970 Reprint (see note 4 above) p. 122.

17 See Holdsworth, W., *A History of English Law*, Methuen & Co Ltd, Sweet & Maxwell, 1982 reprint, Vol. iii, pp. 229–245, Vol. i, pp. 470–473.

18 See note 5 for copycating or 'xeroxing' English legislation.

> in respect of the law on bankruptcy, Hong Kong has fallen very much behind the rest of the civilized common law world …

By the time of that decision Hong Kong's insolvency law had already been under review since the topic had been referred to the Law Reform Commission of Hong Kong in September 1990. That review had been encouraged by the publicity engendered by the glaring lack of any effective corporate rescue procedure in Hong Kong during the mid-1980s shipping slump, when the former Chief Executive's shipping group, Overseas Oriental Container Line, and the associated corporate group run by Kenneth Fung and his father Sir Kenneth Fung very nearly failed. Also by 1990 the Official Receiver had his own agenda to make the bankruptcy procedure more efficient and cost-effective. Bankruptcy reform was the first stage of the Law Reform Commission's review and it published its Report on Bankruptcy in May 1995. This recommended reform of the bankruptcy law more or less in line with the bankruptcy provisions in the UK Insolvency Act 1986, with some reforms based on the Singapore Insolvency Act 1995 and the Australian Bankruptcy Act 1966. The recommendations were enacted in the Bankruptcy (Amendment) Ordinance, but the provisions did not come into effect until 1 April 1998, as there was a mammoth drafting task involved in the preparation of the Bankruptcy (Amendment) Rules 1998 and ancillary rules and orders. The delay was also partly caused by the need for the Law Department's Drafting Division to give priority to all the legislation necessary for the 'handover' in 1997.

The main reforms affected by the 1996 Amendment Ordinance were:

- the abolition of 'acts of bankruptcy'
- the introduction of the statutory demand, failure to pay being the main ground for a creditor's petition
- the tidying up of the qualifying conditions in respect of the debtor
- the abolition of the two-stage process of receiving order and adjudication order by a single stage bankruptcy order
- new provisions for the avoidance of antecedent transactions
- the introduction of a voluntary arrangement procedure as a substitute for and to avoid bankruptcy to replace the former compositions and schemes of arrangement which were not available until after a receiving order had been made, by which time a creditor would have invested so much time and expense that there was no inducement to save the debtor from bankruptcy
- the introduction of automatic discharge.

The latter reform and the introduction of the voluntary arrangement procedure are clear indications of the change of philosophy behind the reforms. Voluntary arrangements were to be encouraged, to avoid bankruptcy, but, if it could not be avoided, then early discharge would follow, if the debtor had acted reasonably, so he/she could start afresh unencumbered by past debts. How these reforms are working out will be discussed in section 1.3 below.

Bankruptcy reform was the first stage of the Law Reform Commission's Insolvency Review. Corporate rescue was chosen next, because the terms of the reference themselves specifically referred to Chapter 11 of the US Bankruptcy Code, and the deficiencies in the existing system in Hong Kong, made so obvious in 1985/86 in the slump in the shipping industry, were fresh in peoples' minds. Also, of course, the administration order procedure had been introduced in the UK by the Insolvency Act 1986 and Australia and Singapore were soon to follow a similar path. In Hong Kong the only alternatives to liquidation were a scheme of arrangement under section 166 of the Companies Ordinance (a common procedure under English-derived companies legislation, but not really suitable in an insolvency situation) or 100 per cent creditor approval to a voluntary debt rescheduling or other agreement.[19] Section 166 has rarely been used in Hong Kong in an insolvency situation, though it is commonly used for re-domiciling companies, reductions of capital, privatizations and other reorganizations. A s 166 scheme approved by a majority in number representing three quarters in value of the creditors or class of creditors will, if sanctioned by the court, bind *all* the creditors. But in the time it takes to hold a court-ordered meeting of creditors to approve a scheme and then to have the court sanction the scheme, a single recalcitrant creditor can petition the court for the winding up of the debtor company. In short, the main deficiency of s 166 is that there is no moratorium or stay of proceedings. There are other deficiencies such as the cost and the time the procedure takes.

In May 1995 the sub-committee on Insolvency of the Law Reform Commission published its Consultative Document on Corporate Rescue and Insolvent Trading and the response was generally supportive. The Law Reform Commission's Report, substantially reproducing the sub-committee's proposals, was published in October 1996. On corporate rescue the report recommended a process called 'provisional supervision'. The process assumed that in a typical case the board of directors of the relevant company would initiate it. The process would start, as would the moratorium, which would be fundamental to it, on the filing in the High Court Registry and the Companies Registry of a certified copy of the board resolution, an affidavit of the directors explaining the company's circumstances and the consent to act of the provisional supervisor. The usual supervisor would be an accountant or lawyer. There would be no need to go to court for an interim or other order. The initial moratorium period would be 30 days. A court order on summary application would be required for any extension or extensions, which could be up to a maximum period of six months from the commencement of the process. Any extension thereafter would require an affirmative resolution of a creditors' meeting. Major secured creditors, that is those with a charge over the whole or substantially the whole of the company's assets, could terminate the process by electing not to participate.

The task of the provisional supervisor would be to investigate the financial state of the company and decide if any of the 'relevant purposes' were capable of being

---

19 Sections 199(1)(e), (f), 237 and 254 of the Companies Ordinance give power to a liquidator to make arrangements with creditors. Sections 199(1)(e) and (f) are used, if at all, for compromising claims of individual creditors; s 237 is the power of a liquidator to accept shares, etc. of a purchaser company as consideration for the sale of property of the company in liquidation; and s 254 provides that an arrangement between a company about to be or in the course of being wound up and its creditors shall be binding on all creditors if acceded to by three quarters in number and value of the creditors. Since s 254 requires a greater majority than the three quarters in value of the creditors present and voting required under s 166, it is not surprising that s 254 is not used.

achieved. Relevant purposes included a more advantageous realization of the company's property than would be achieved on a winding up, the survival of the company and the whole or any part of its undertaking as a going concern and the more advantageous satisfaction in whole or in part of the company's debts or other liabilities. If the provisional supervisor decided that any of the relevant purposes was capable of being achieved, he/she would proceed to prepare a proposal for a voluntary arrangement, which, if completed, would be put to a creditors' meeting for approval or disapproval. If approved, the provisional supervision would terminate and the voluntary arrangement would take over. If disapproved (though there might be several intervening adjourned meetings and modifications of the proposal) the company would go into creditors' voluntary winding up. If the provisional supervisor was unable to formulate a proposal or decided that none of the relevant purposes were capable of being achieved, he/she would call a creditors' meeting and then (or at a subsequent adjourned meeting after intervening negotiations had failed to offer any hope of a proposal) the company would go into creditors' voluntary winding up. The process seemed to be effective, quick and as cheap as any such process could be.

But the Law Reform Commission's Report contained at least one recommendation that was to be the proposed process's downfall and that related to arrears of wages of employees. In 1985 the Protection of Wages on Insolvency Ordinance (PWOIO) had been enacted. This was a rather knee-jerk reaction of the Government to the downturn in the economy in Hong Kong in the early 1980s due to the uncertainty whilst Hong Kong's future was being discussed in the Sino-British negotiations of 1982–84. The negotiations were concluded with the signing of the Sino-British Agreement on 26 September 1984 and its ratification on 27 May 1985, by which time the economy had picked up. The PWOIO created the Protection of Wages on Insolvency Fund and provided for the payment of specified sums (which are increased from time to time) for arrears of wages, wages in lieu of notice and severance payment out of the Fund where a corporate employer is wound up or where an individual employer is made bankrupt. Upon payment, the Fund is subrogated to the workers' preferential rights under Companies Ordinance s 265 or Bankruptcy Ordinance s 38.[20] The payments out of the Fund are expressly stated to be *ex gratia*. Apparently, this was intended to cover the possibility of the Fund being unable to make the specified payments because it had been depleted.

When the Law Reform Commission (LRC) made its recommendation, in October 1996, that provisional supervision should be an additional triggering event for payment out of the Fund, the Fund was in a very healthy state. The Fund was originally subsidized by a grant from the Government and is funded by a levy (currently HK$600) payable by all businesses registerable under the Business Registration Ordinance when they pay their annual fee for their Business Registration certificate. There were 614,646 businesses registered under the BRO as at 31 March

20 The maximum entitlements under the preferential payments provisions are for arrears of wages HK$8,000, for wages in lieu of notice HK$2,000 and for severance payment HK$8,000. The equivalent maximum entitlements under the PWOIO are HK$50,000, $22,500 and $50,000 + 50 per cent of excess entitlements respectively.

1999.[21] When the Law Reform Commission's Report was published in October 1996 there had been comparatively few calls on the Fund since 1985 and it had built up to a substantial size.

It was apparent from soon after the publication of the Report that the board of the Fund, the unions and the relevant Government Departments were against the LRC's recommendation that provisional supervision should be a triggering event for a payment out of the Fund. There was a general consensus that some sort of rescue process was preferable to liquidation. The statistics given in the Law Reform Commission's Report as to the time it took for employees to receive their preferential payments in a liquidation were clear, for example, for 1994/95 it took an average of 2.88 years to pay an average dividend of 59.28 per cent of their entitlement. The Commission considered that provisional supervision must be the better option, because, in a recession, employees could not simply take their *ex gratia* payments under the Fund and get a job in another business in the next block. There would be no jobs to walk into and a workout under provisional supervision offered a realistic opportunity. But the protectionist attitude towards the Fund was surprisingly strong and by 1998, when the Asian financial crisis began to be felt, it was clear that the battle was lost. Rumours were spread that even with only liquidation or bankruptcy being the triggering events the Fund might be run down to a state such that payments could not be made.

When the Government published the Companies (Amendment) Bill 2000 on 7 January 2000, its position was made public. Provisional supervision, the provisions for which were to be a new Part IVB of the Ordinance, sections 168U to 168ZZA, could not take effect unless the company had established a trust account with an authorized banking institution for the exclusive purpose of providing money to pay all debts and liabilities owing under the Employment Ordinance to its employees and such account contained sufficient money to pay all those debts and liabilities or such debts and liabilities had been paid or the company had no such debts or liabilities.

This major change, in the opinion of insolvency practitioners, made the proposed process unworkable. Other clauses in the Bill relating to provisional supervision did not reflect the LRC's recommendations. For example, it had never been the intention that secured creditors should be prejudiced other than by delaying their enforcement rights. Under the Bill, if outvoted, they could be forced to take a 'haircut'. The banks became nervous. Other organizations came up with new objections to provisions, which had not been objected to at the consultation stage years before. For example, the Law Society suddenly decided that they did not like the virtual exclusion of the court! The Bill was given a hard time before the Legislative Council Bill Committee and in the business press. In consequence, the provisional supervision and the insolvent trading parts of the Bill were withdrawn on 26 June 2000. The Companies (Corporate Rescue) Bill 2001 was a slightly modified version of provisional supervision, but met similar objections and was allowed to lapse. To be realistic, provisional supervision is probably now a dead letter.[22] The insolvent

---

21 Figures for the last financial years reported in the Departmental Annual Report are available on the Inland Revenue Department's website, the address of which is shown at note 12.

22 In any event subsequent developments have reduced the need for a new corporate rescue regime. For the HKMA's 'Guidelines on the Hong Kong Approach to Corporate Difficulties', see text above, notes

trading provisions of the Bills were intended as a new section 295A *et seq* of the Companies Ordinance and to offer a liquidator a more effective civil compensatory remedy than that available under s 275 fraudulent trading. This provision was based partly on the UK Insolvency Act 1986 wrongful trading provisions and the Australian insolvent trading provisions. There appeared to be little or no objection to the insolvent trading provisions, though the extension of liability of so-called responsible persons beyond directors to senior managers had caused some comment. But the two major reform proposals were linked. Provisional supervision was to be the carrot to entice directors to seek a corporate rescue at an early stage and insolvent trading was to be the stick if they did not.

The final stage of the Law Reform Commission's Insolvency Review was its Report on the Winding-Up Provisions of the Companies Ordinance published in July 1999. The winding up provisions in the Companies Ordinance, except for a few amendments since, date from 1933 when the current Companies Ordinance came into force. The Ordinance copied, more or less, the English Companies Act 1929 and replaced the Companies Ordinance 1911 which had copied the English Act of 1908. In the past there had been a tradition of Hong Kong quite quickly following the English companies legislation consolidations. But this had not happened with the current ordinance. There were substantial amendments in 1984, which one commentator described as 'the great leap forward to 1948',[23] meaning that Hong Kong Company Law had been brought up to date as compared with the English Companies Act 1948, but these and other amendments, before and since, have not really affected the basic structure of the winding up provisions. So Hong Kong today is still basically working from the English Companies Act 1929.

The Law Reform Commission's Report contains little that is controversial. It contains some 160 proposals, most of which are of an administrative and technical nature intended to make the winding up process more efficient and time- and cost-effective. Some of the proposals mirror the recent changes in bankruptcy law. The major general proposals are as follows:

- There should be a separate Insolvency Ordinance, combining the Bankruptcy Ordinance and those provisions in the Companies Ordinance dealing with winding up, creditors' and members' voluntary winding up, receivership and disqualification of directors. Provisional supervision and insolvent trading, if and when enacted, should be included in such ordinance.[24]
- A licensed insolvency practitioner regime with two tiers should be established. 'Official liquidators' could act in all matters. 'Registered liquidators' could act in members' voluntary winding up and individual voluntary arrangements in bankruptcy.

26–28. And since *Re Keview Technology (BVI) Ltd* [2002] 2 HK LRD 290 the court has been willing, in appropriate cases, to give provisional liquidators appointed under s 193 of the Companies Ordinance power to seek to effect a corporate rescue.

23 See Bates, C., *The Companies (Amendment) Ordinance 1984 in Perspective*, Hong Kong Law Journal Ltd 1985, p. 1 (being a reprint of his two articles in (1985) 15 HKLJ). The 'leap forward' was, of course, a reference to Chairman Mao Tse-tung's great leap forward of 1958–59, i.e. the commune movement.

24 For similar thinking in Australia see (1999) 7 *Insolvency Law Journal* 4 (Keay).

- Provision should be made for the proper funding of the Official Receiver's Office, with various options being suggested. Recognition needs to be given to the changing nature of the role of the Official Receiver with less emphasis on the administration of estates of insolvent companies and more emphasis on his regulatory role.
- A Panel should be established to scrutinize disputed office-holders' fees.
- A provision similar to section 304 of the US Bankruptcy Code should be adopted to provide guidelines for the recognition of foreign insolvency proceedings. The Commission did not rule out the adoption of the UNCITRAL Model Law on cross-border insolvency, but did not want Hong Kong to be the first jurisdiction to adopt it. It preferred a 'wait and see' approach.

None of the broader policy recommendations in the Law Reform Commission's Report (such as those mentioned above) has yet been legislated. The Commission's Bankruptcy Report had not sought to set out any general philosophy for its proposed new bankruptcy law, though justifications for individual changes, such as in relation to discharge, were given. The Report on the Winding-Up Provisions does refer to the proper function of the insolvency provisions in the Companies Ordinance,[25] at its crudest as a waste disposal system for companies that have failed and as assisting in ameliorating the effect of economic downturns. The Report refers to, sets out and adopts the 'motherhood principles' for a modern insolvency law identified by the Australian Law Reform Commission's *General Insolvency Inquiry* (the *Harmer Report*), that is to provide a fair and orderly process for dealing with the affairs of insolvent individuals and companies, to provide an impartial, efficient and expeditious administration, and so on.

1.3 Key Insolvency Law Principles in Hong Kong

We now consider the key principles of the new Hong Kong bankruptcy law.

To encourage the avoidance of bankruptcy by the new provisions for voluntary arrangements The former composition and scheme of arrangement provisions only applied after a receiving order had been made, by which time it was too late and the petitioning creditor had incurred too much expense to make a rescue viable. In the event the new provisions were, at least initially, a failure. This is summed up in the heading to an article on bankruptcy in the *South China Morning Post* for 25 October 1999, 'Creditors snub voluntary repayment scheme as rates climb'. The article dealt with the increasing bankruptcy rates, mostly due to credit card defaults, and stated that over the 18 months since the new provisions came into effect only seven individual voluntary arrangements (IVAs) had been effected. A source from the Official Receiver's Office is cited as saying that the banks are not willing to enter into arrangements because they want to send out a warning to potential debtors. But the IVA figures have shown a modest increase in recent years.

---

25 See Ch. 1 of the LRC Report.

The banks' initial attitude to individual debtors is at odds with their attitude to corporate debtors. It may be that the failure to get the new corporate rescue process of provisional supervision on the statute book (discussed in section 1.2 above) and the banks' lack of support for that process was partly due to the fact that the banks had for several years had in place an informal process of corporate rescue. The Hong Kong Association of Banks (HKAB) published *Guidelines on the Hong Kong Approach to Corporate Difficulties* in April 1998 based on the Bank of England's London Approach.[26]

The underlying principles are support for the debtor company in difficulty and cooperation between all creditor banks in the form of a workout. The Hong Kong Monetary Authority (HKMA) published a revised version in November 1999.[27] The HKMA strongly supports the Guidelines and is prepared to act as a mediator if differences of views threaten the successful creation or execution of a workout.[28] The general perception amongst insolvency practitioners is that this informal process is working well.

To enable the bankrupt to obtain a discharge within a reasonable time so as to be able to start afresh We need to remind ourselves from time to time that, as section 32 of the Bankruptcy Ordinance states, discharge releases the bankrupt from all the bankruptcy debts, save those which are specified in the section. The new bankruptcy law provides in section 30 for the automatic discharge of a first-time bankrupt after four years, unless objection is made on any of the grounds specified in the section. The courts have indicated a fairly generous approach to discharge by putting quite a heavy burden on the objector.[29] However, there appears to be a feeling in the business community that the four-year automatic discharge rule is too generous.

To provide a timely and cost-effective procedure for collecting in the bankrupt's assets and paying the creditors Many of the technical amendments were intended to achieve this objective, such as providing a more realistic time frame for the debtor's statement of affairs, giving the Official Receiver the authority to extend time (rather than the court) and giving the Official Receiver authority to dispense with the statement of affairs.

The key principle of Hong Kong company liquidation law is:

- to provide a timely and cost effective procedure for collecting in the assets of the insolvent company and paying its creditors.

This goal has not always been achieved in the past. One of the special features of Hong Kong insolvency law was that until recently the Official Receiver's Office

---

26 On the London Approach see (1997) 6 *International Insolvency Review* 165 (Kent).

27 The revised Guidelines were published in the Hong Kong Monetary Authority's *Quarterly Bulletin* for November 1999. For the HKMA's website address see note 12.

28 See HKMA *Quarterly Bulletin* for February 2000 which is the text of a speech by David Carse, Deputy Chief Executive of the HKMA on the revised Guidelines. For an overview of the Guidelines see (1999) 15 *Insolvency Law & Practice* 128 (Bannister).

29 See *Re Hui Hing Kwok* [1999] 3 HKC 683.

(ORO) has had a virtual monopoly in insolvency work. The Official Receiver (OR) is a senior appointment made by the Chief Executive of the HKSAR under the Bankruptcy Ordinance.[30] The OR is the chief officer of the ORO, which is a separate department of the Hong Kong Government responsible to the Financial Secretary through the Financial Services Bureau.[31] Unfortunately the ORO, which derives its income from fees and percentages and, where necessary, from general Government revenue, has not been properly resourced in recent years. Between June 1992 and March 1999 the ORO had an operating deficit of HK$350 million.[32]

But the situation is already improving, at least as regards liquidations. In 1996, partly as a reaction to criticisms and also on the advice of an earlier organization and methods report on the Office, the then OR established two Administrative Panels of Insolvency Practitioners for the court winding up of companies and work was contracted out to qualifying firms. This informal procedure has been expanded over the intervening period and its success is the basis of the recommendation in the Law Reform Commission's Report referred to above, for any amendments to the winding up provisions of the Companies Ordinance to provide the legislative framework for a licensed insolvency practitioner regime.[33] The greater use of contracting out should, theoretically, allow the ORO more time for its monitoring role in liquidations. But this is unlikely to happen until the effects of the Asian financial crisis have worked their way out. The complaints of delay now generally relate to bankruptcy estates and this is because of the blow out in bankruptcy figures due to the increase in bankrupts' own petitions.

Many of the technical recommendations of the Law Reform Commission's Report on the Winding-up Provisions of the Companies Ordinance (the Report is referred to in section 1.2), which mirror those in the earlier Bankruptcy Report (which are now contained in the new bankruptcy legislation), will help to improve the liquidation process, when they are enacted. But a reduction in bankruptcy work, either by an improvement in the economy or by contracting out some of the larger bankruptcy work, will be required before the ORO can take up the greater monitoring role which the Law Reform Commission thought the ORO should play.

It is appropriate to mention here some of the key principles that the Law Reform Commission identified with regard to liquidation. The licensing of insolvency practitioners has already been mentioned. Where the court appoints a liquidator, provisionally, or otherwise, it will normally require that person to be suitably qualified. But there are no general statutory qualifications for liquidators in Hong

---

30 Bankruptcy Ordinance (cap 6) s 75. Section 2(1) of the Companies Ordinance (cap 32) defines 'Official Receiver' by reference to the Bankruptcy Ordinance.

31 The HKSAR Government is organized into bureaux and departments. The bureaux, each headed by a policy secretary, collectively form the Administration. There are 15 bureaux and 71 departments and agencies (examples of the latter are the Independent Commission Against Corruption and the Office of the Ombudsman).

32 See *South China Morning Post*, 28 June 2000, 'No takers for Official Receiver's job?' The position had been vacant since 1998. The ORO has been subject to criticism from various sources and the article refers to criticism from the Director of Audit, *inter alia*, for 'dragging its feet in handling insolvency cases and in the collection of debts'.

33 See Ch. 3 of the LRC Report 'Licensing of Insolvency Practitioners'.

Kong. The only provision in the Companies Ordinance requiring professional qualifications is section 228A. This special procedure (claimed to be unique to Hong Kong[34]) for voluntary winding up in case of a company's inability to continue its business, triggered off by the delivery to the Registrar of Companies of a winding-up statement signed by a director, was introduced in 1984 and requires the appointment of a provisional liquidator who, only since 1993, must be a solicitor or a professional accountant. Before 1993 there was no qualification requirement and therefore the procedure offered opportunity for abuse of the type recognized in *Re Centrebind Ltd* [1966] 2 All ER 889. But except for section 228A(3C) there are no qualification requirements set out in the Companies Ordinance. Of course, with the ORO contracting out more compulsory liquidation work to experienced practitioners, there is little likelihood of abuse, but it is still there for voluntary windings up. There is now sufficient insolvency work and sufficient experience in the legal and accounting professions to justify an insolvency practitioner regime.[35]

The change of role of the ORO from mostly administration to mostly monitoring had been a principal theme throughout the Law Reform Commission's Insolvency Review. This has been mentioned above. If it is to happen, it will require a major rethink on the funding of the ORO. The LRC's Report on the Winding-Up Provisions recommended use of part of the Business Registration fee (mentioned in section 1.2 in the context of the Protection of Wages on Insolvency Fund). If a fee is demanded on the start up and continuance of a business, it is not illogical to suggest that part of the fee should be used for the decent interment of such businesses. The same argument could be used, at least for corporate businesses, to claim some of the monies paid to the Companies Registry for the annual registration fee. The Registry, which is a trading fund within the terms of the Trading Funds Ordinance (cap 430), is expected to and does make a substantial profit. Another suggestion in the Report was to increase the rate of interest earned by the ORO on funds kept in the Companies Liquidation Account.[36]

Perhaps the 'hottest' topic in insolvency in Hong Kong, not just in recent years but ever, is that of liquidators' fees. The issue only arose after the Law Reform Commission sub-committee had published its Consultation Paper on the Winding-Up Provisions of the Companies Ordinance in April 1998. The issue had been brewing

---

34 In fact there is a somewhat similar provision in the Singapore Companies Act s 291. The Singapore section was drafted by Mr J.C. Finemore (draftsman of the 1961 Australian uniform legislation) for a bill which became the Malaysian Companies Act 1965 but without that section: see Woon & Hicks, *The Companies Act of Singapore*, note on s 291. There was one significant difference between the Singapore s 291 and s 228A. Under s 291 the directors could immediately appoint an 'approved liquidator', so there was some quality control.

35 On the recommendations for the licensing of insolvency practitioners, see Ch. 3 of the LRC Report. Some critics have suggested that this will create a new monopoly: see Mrs. Justice Le Pichon, and Ho, B.M., *Law Lectures for Practitioners 1999* HKLJ Ltd 78 at p. 121. And on the return of insolvency work to general practice, see Sir Gavin Lightman [1996] *Journal of Business Law* 113–126, at 117.

36 On the recommendations as to the role and funding of the ORO, see Ch. 5 of the LRC Report. The role of the official insolvency agency is under debate in other jurisdictions. For an entertaining argument for the abolition of the UK Insolvency Service, see Floyd, 'The Dinosaur Must Go – Do We Need an Insolvency Service?' (1999) 15 *Insolvency Law & Practice* 85 and the Deputy Inspector General's response at p. 90.

for some time and in England had come to a head with Ferris J's decision, delivered on 10 July 1997, in *Mirror Group Newspapers plc* v. *Maxwell*, subsequently reported in [1998] 1 BCLC 638. But before that decision there had been signs in the wind in England. In November 1995 Lightman J had given a pre-dinner talk to the Insolvency Lawyers Association, later published in the *Journal of Business Law* (1996, pp. 113–126), in which, in appropriately provocative and emotive language, he had dealt with the perception of excessive fees and how the problem might be remedied.[37] In 1997 Ferris J was appointed by the Vice-Chancellor (the head of the Chancery Division of the Supreme Court of Justice of England and Wales) to chair a Working Party on the Remuneration of Office-holders and certain related matters. The working party included the then Inspector General of the Insolvency Service (and his successor), the Registrar in Bankruptcy and a leading accountant and a leading solicitor insolvency practitioner.

In his judgment in the *Maxwell* case Ferris J was highly critical of the professionals involved. The case involved the receivership of the personal estate of the late Robert Maxwell. Mr. Maxwell's business and personal affairs were of extreme intricacy with alleged misappropriations of assets and a complex web of insolvencies, claims, cross-claims and other disputes. The receivers had been appointed in 1992 and by the time they applied for directions as to the payment of their fees in 1997, those fees, including their solicitors' fees and disbursements, amounted to £1.628 million. The net estate amounted to £1.672 million, though it was expected that the final figure might be higher. Ferris J referred to the concern voiced in the press about the unacceptably high level of costs in insolvency cases and to Lightman J's lecture. Ferris J gave a useful review of the fiduciary role of office-holders (that is receivers, provisional liquidators, liquidators, and so on) and their duty to account and to justify their remuneration. If time costing was used, the office-holder must do more than list the number of hours. Too much emphasis should not be placed on time. Time is only one of a number of factors. Remuneration should be a reward for value. Office-holders were expected to use commercial judgment and not act regardless of cost. As to the proper basis of determining the receivers' fees in the case before him, after rejecting time costing and other bases, he referred the receivers' bills to a court-taxing officer.

Ferris J's judgment in July 1997 had not impacted on Hong Kong when the sub-committee was reviewing the winding up provisions of the Companies Ordinance (notwithstanding the presence of some very experienced insolvency practitioners on the sub-committee). But the developments in England[38] had not

37 The talk was clearly intended to be provocative. The judge talked about the three Es (expertise, expedition and economy), 'bees in his bonnet' (p. 113) and gave some over-the-top examples of over-manning (pp. 116, 117). He suggested that office-holders should make prospective lawyers tender for work and hold 'beauty parades' to select the lawyers. Such out-of-court campaigning by judges does raise some serious constitutional issues.

38 Le Pichon J referred to another article by Lightman J in her judgment in *Peregrine (No. 1)*. The article was published in (1998) 19 *Co. Law.* 72. It was based on the 1997 Company Law Lecture Lightman J gave at the Institute of Advanced Legal Studies in London in December 1997, i.e. post *Maxwell*. Entitled 'Office Holders' Charges: Cost Control and Transparency', Lightman J summarized the lesson of *Maxwell* to be that in all decision-making an office-holder must transparently display the care and anxiety of a prudent

passed unnoticed by the new Companies and Bankruptcy judge,[39] Mrs. Justice Le Pichon, and she made full use of them when she gave the first of many reported judgments[40] in the Peregrine Group liquidation.

The Peregrine Group, which, for Hong Kong purposes,[41] consisted of Peregrine Investments Holdings Ltd, Peregrine Fixed Income Ltd and Peregrine Derivatives Ltd, was a Hong Kong success story. Started in 1988 with an initial capital of US$38 million by Philip Tose and Francis Leung Pak To, two well-known personalities in the financial industry in Hong Kong, within six years Peregrine was Hong Kong's premier investment bank and one of the largest in Asia. It was, its founders claimed, the financial bridge between China and the rest of the world at a time when China was looking to the outside world for funds for development. By early 1996 its capital had increased to US$2 billion and in 1996 the Group reported a pre-tax profit of HK$1.02 billion.

But by October 1997 the Group was in serious trouble. Peregrine Fixed Income Ltd had made an unsecured loan to a heavily indebted Indonesian taxi and bus company, inappropriately named Steady Safe, as part of a deal to underwrite a US$600 bond issue.[42] Hardly had the deal been set up when the Indonesian rupiah collapsed, losing 60 per cent of its value. The Thai baht had collapsed earlier after

---

businessman acting in his own affairs at his own cost and risk. He goes on to give suggestions as to how costs could be reduced; for example, Alternative Dispute Resolution, assignment of causes of action to outsiders.

39 There are no divisions in the High Court in Hong Kong, but there has been a dedicated judge for bankruptcy and compulsory winding up matters for the past 20 years.

40 The reported judgments are: on the basis of provisional liquidators' fees *Re Peregrine Investments Holdings Ltd* [1998] 2 HKLRD 670 [1998] 3 HKC 1 (hereafter '*Peregrine (No. 1)*'), on appeal [1999] 3 HKLRD 59, [1999] 3 HKC 291; on the basis of liquidators' fees *Re Peregrine Investments Holdings Ltd & ors (No. 2)* [1999] 2 HKLRD 666, [1998] 3 HKC 423 (hereafter '*Peregrine (No. 2)*'); on provisional liquidators' post-winding up order fees *Re Peregrine Investments Holdings Ltd (No. 4)* [1999] 2 HKLRD 722, [1999] 3 HKC 183 (where entitled *No. 3*); on taxation of fees *Re Peregrine Investments Holdings Ltd & ors (No. 5)* [2000] 1 HKLRD 157, [1999] 4 HKC 802 (where entitled *No. 4*) (hereafter '*Peregrine taxation*'); on unsuccessful application for conversion to creditors' voluntary winding up *Re Peregrine Fixed Income Ltd (in liq)* [1999] 2 HKLRD 653, [1998] 4 HKC 151; on application by the Financial Secretary for appointment of inspector into the affairs of Peregrine Fixed Income Ltd and Peregrine Investments Holdings Ltd *Financial Secretary* v. *Peregrine Investments Holdings Ltd (in liq) & ors* [1999] 2 HKLRD 691, [1999] 3 HKC 285; on unsuccessful application by Messrs Tose, Leung, Mercer and Wong, all four of whom were former directors of Peregrine Investments Holdings Ltd, and Messrs Tose and Leung, former directors of Peregrine Fixed Income Ltd, to inspect the file on the Financial Secretary's application for the appointment of an inspector *Re Peregrine Investments Holdings Ltd & anor (No. 3)* [1999] 2 HKLRD 686. In *Re Kansa General International Insurance Co Ltd* [1999] 2 HKLRD 429, [1999] 1 HKC 254 Le Pichon J stated the role of the creditors' committee to properly scrutinize the fees and expenses incurred by the liquidators prior to a section 166 scheme. The judge who ordered the pre-scheme fees to be taxed overruled the committee's agreement to an all-in fee. The liquidators' appeal against the judge's order was dismissed: [1999] 3 HKLRD 94, CA, [1999] 3 HKC 431.

41 Overall the Group comprised some 150 businesses in 15 countries including the US, UK, Japan, Singapore, Thailand and Indonesia.

42 For a detailed treatment of the collapse of the Peregrine Group see Srivastava, D.K., 'Peregrine's Fall from Rise: Misfortune, Mismanagement or Inadequacy of Law?' in (2000) 4 *Journal of Chinese and Comparative Law* (122–156).

it was de-pegged on 2 July 1997. The currency basket previously used had been approximately 80 to 90 per cent denominated by the US dollar. When the US dollar had strengthened against the Japanese yen from 1995 onwards the competitiveness of Thai exports abated and the Thai current account deficit widened substantially. The baht increasingly came under speculative attacks and the de-pegging was intended to stop that. The enormous reduction in the exchange rate following the de-pegging had devastating effects on the Thai economy.[43] With economies collapsing around the East Asian region, Japan in the doldrums, China having to pull back in its development programmes and Peregrine so exposed regionally, the end of Peregrine was probably inevitable.[44]

Winding up petitions were issued against the Hong Kong Peregrine companies at the beginning of January 1998. Trading in Peregrine shares was suspended on 8 January 1998. On 9 January 1998 restriction notices under ss 39 and 40 of the Securities and Futures Commission Ordinance were issued by the Securities and Futures Commission. Provisional liquidators of the three Peregrine companies were appointed in mid-January 1998. The terms of the order by which they were appointed provided for their remuneration to be calculated according to the standard hourly rates charged by Price Waterhouse fee earners. On 13 March 1998 the provisional liquidators, as was the practice in Hong Kong, submitted their and their solicitors' fees up to 15 February 1998, that is for the first month of their office, to the court for its approval. The fees were HK$27 million for the provisional liquidators, HK$13 million for Deacons and HK$7 million for Clifford Chance. Le Pichon J found the level of fees 'alarming'. At a preliminary hearing on 19 March 1998 she raised the *Maxwell* case with the provisional liquidators. They claimed that *Maxwell*, being a receivership, was distinguishable. The judge extracted from Lightman J's first article referred to above the public perception that liquidations can have 'all the appearance of "party-time" for the professionals involved'. Le Pichon J expressed disquiet about the possibility of overmanning and scepticism of apparent marathon feats with some fee earners averaging double-digit billable hours over a sustained period. Moreover the provisional liquidators' bills were insufficiently particularized. The hearing was adjourned to allow further information to be provided by the provisional liquidators and for their lawyers to address the issues raised by *Maxwell*. The court appointed an *amicus* to assist it.

The judge allowed the provisional liquidators, as a payment on account, 25 per cent of the fees sought. By the time of the adjourned hearing on 27 May 1998 the aggregate amount of fees and disbursements for which approval was sought was in the order of HK$76 million for the period of 63 days of the provisional liquidation up to the date of the winding up orders. The judge canvassed the lack of any statutory provision as to remuneration for provisional liquidators in the legislation,[45] compared

---

[43] For a detailed treatment of the collapse of the Thai economy, see Traisorat, K., *Thailand: Financial Sector Reform and the East Asian Crises*, Klewer Law International, 2000.

[44] Though some commentators suggest that had Hong Kong had a corporate rescue process (such as provisional supervision) in place by the start of 1998, some at least of the Hong Kong Peregrine companies might have been saved. For provisional supervision, see section 1.2 above.

[45] Companies (Winding-up) Rules r 28(3), which applied the same rate as when the Official Receiver was appointed provisional liquidator, did not apply where a winding up order was subsequently made.

the different situation in the UK and set out the *Maxwell* principles. In the light of those principles, the provisional liquidators' bills were inadequately particularized. Unfortunately Price Waterhouse's timekeeping system did not permit a fee earner to input a contemporaneous task for each unit of time. More details were required. Nor had the provisional liquidators scrutinized the solicitors' bills to the degree required. The provisional liquidators would have to file further evidence to justify their claims, which would be considered at a subsequent hearing, at which the provisional liquidators should make representations as to who should fix their remuneration – a Master under Order 36 r 1 of the Rules of the High Court, the registrar under the Companies (Winding-up) Rules r 6(a) or some expert appointed by the court to assist the judge. Pending the subsequent hearing, the judge increased the interim payment on account of the fees claimed to 33 per cent.[46]

In a subsequent hearing on 2 July 1998, *Peregrine (No. 2)*,[47] the provisional liquidators, who had by then become the liquidators, sought directions that the remuneration of the liquidators be such as might be agreed between the liquidators and the creditors' committee or in default of agreement on a percentage of assets realized or distributed basis as provided for in section 196(2) of the Companies Ordinance. The judge stated various matters to assist the committee in determining how the liquidators' remuneration should be fixed. *Inter alia*, she ordered that a time cost basis could be used, but referred to *Peregrine (No. 1)* as to the appropriate method and justification where the time cost basis was used.

In August 1998 the Ferris Report was published. It naturally tended to follow many of the views which the judge had expressed in *Maxwell* though in a more restrained manner. The Working Party categorically disclaimed that remuneration should be kept as low as possible. They accepted that besides the creditors' interest, there was the public interest. Office-holders had to investigate and this required properly qualified and experienced persons, who were entitled to expect reasonable remuneration. But proportionality, that is matching the regulatory requirements to the value of the assets, was another principle. It was impossible to prescribe a universal approach. Where a scale was used the onus was on the office-holder to justify more and on the creditors to justify less. Where a scale was not used, a *quantum meruit* (that is what the job was worth) approach should be used. The *Maxwell* principles should be adopted for recordkeeping by office-holders. A statement of practice should be adopted. An office-holder had a duty to satisfy him/herself as to the propriety and reasonableness of solicitors' and other bills. Taxation should be required if there were a suspicion of overcharging. Amendments to the English Insolvency Rules and scales were recommended. Remuneration on account should be provided for. There should be a Standing Consultative Committee to advise and assist the court. Despite its more moderate tone, the Report still emphasized value for money and proportionality.[48]

On a further application on 23 October 1998 Le Pichon J increased the interim payments for the solicitors' fees to 50 per cent. She expressed concern about the lack

46 For the full details, see *Peregrine (No. 1)*, reported as mentioned in note 40.

47 Reported as mentioned in note 40.

48 For a comment on the Report, see Nicholls, J., 'Holding on to your money – remuneration and how to keep it' (1999) 15 *Insolvency Law & Practice* 12 (in which *Peregrine* gets a very brief mention).

of effective opposition to the liquidators' application for a similar increase. She suggested that the Official Receiver should review the bills of the provisional liquidators, but he was unwilling to do so on the ground it was inappropriate, nor did his office have the resources, but if appointed by the judge he would require an independent third party with experience in insolvency matters to assist him.

On a directions hearing on 25 November 1998 Le Pichon J ordered that the Official Receiver should appoint such law costs draftsman as the Registrar of the High Court should approve to prepare a report for the purposes of taxation for submission to the court on the provisional liquidators' remuneration and their costs and disbursements. The judge also increased the interim advance of costs to the solicitors to 90 per cent subject to their giving bank guarantees in a form acceptable to the court, but allowed no increase to the provisional liquidators. This must have been the last straw for the provisional liquidators and they appealed the order.

On 12 January 1999 Chief Master of the Chancery Division, Master Hurst, delivered his assessment of the receivers' remuneration, costs and disbursements in the *Maxwell* case.[49] Master Hurst described his modus operandi as follows. He obtained the receivers' files, a detailed breakdown of hours spent, detailed summaries of tasks undertaken and other information. He applied the test of reasonableness under RSC O 62 r 12(1) and approached the task without using hindsight in accordance with the test in *Francis* v. *Francis & Dickerson* [1995] 2 All ER 836. The Master found that all the steps taken by the receivers, in the then state of their knowledge, were reasonable, the time taken was reasonable and there had been a proper level of delegation. He awarded the receivers 99 per cent of their claim for remuneration. As to the conduct of the receivership, the Master said:

> Having had the opportunity to consider all the written submissions and the papers supplied in support of the Receivers' bills, and having further had the opportunity to hear direct from Mr. Phillips and from Mr. Squires as to the work which they personally undertook I am satisfied that the conduct of this receivership was carried out with a high degree of skill and efficiency. Whilst the level of recovery of assets may appear disappointing when set against the total remuneration and disbursements claimed, the figures become far more acceptable and understandable when seen against the potential total asset recovery on behalf of the estate. In the event many assets which on the face of it appeared to be the personal property of Mr. Maxwell were either worthless, or, because of the immensely complex financial labyrinth which he had constructed, could not ultimately be recovered as personal property. I accept the general proposition that had the Receivers not investigated all leads in respect of the property potentially belonging to the estate, they would have been open to the severest criticism. During his lifetime Mr. Maxwell had portrayed himself as a man of immense wealth controlling a range of large multinational companies, which were themselves of great value. Subsequent investigations have shown that much of this was a façade and the Receivers or the Administrators could only establish the true ownership of assets after the most painstaking investigation.

On 27 May 1999 Le Pichon J gave judgment in *Peregrine (No. 4)*,[50] which dealt with the provisional liquidators' fees for, *inter alia*, the period between the making of the

---

49 *Mirror Group Newspapers plc* v. *Maxwell*, [1991] BCC 684.

50 Reported as mentioned in note 40.

winding up orders and their change of status to 'permanent' liquidators. She revisited part of her judgment in *Peregrine (No. 2)* and held that this was a matter for the court under its inherent jurisdiction, notwithstanding that the provisional liquidators' fees for the period between the winding up orders and their appointments as liquidators had been agreed by the committees of inspection (that is creditors' committees) and already paid in full, the necessary funds having been released from the Companies' Liquidation Account. She set aside the payments, did not allow any increase of the percentage for an advance to the provisional liquidators and ordered the Official Receiver to appoint a law costs draftsman to prepare a report for the purposes of taxation of the disbursements to solicitors (notwithstanding those costs had already been taxed, because the provisional liquidators had not opposed the solicitors' applications and the 'taxation' had been a charade).

On 15 July 1999 the Court of Appeal dismissed the provisional liquidators' appeal from Le Pichon J's orders of 25 November 1998. The judge did have jurisdiction to order the appointment of a law costs draftsman to assist the Official Receiver. As to whether she had exercised her discretion wrongly (as the provisional liquidators claimed), the Court would not, save in the most exceptional circumstances, interfere with case management directions. As to the requirement of bank guarantees for the interim payment to solicitors, this was unobjectionable. Mayo JA stated very clearly that it was the responsibility of the Official Receiver under s 204 of the Companies Ordinance (Control of Official Receiver over liquidators) to assume an active role in ensuring that bills or charges rendered by liquidators and their professional advisers are subjected to satisfactory scrutiny. If the Official Receiver finds that the resources available are inadequate for him/her to discharge his/her duties in a satisfactory manner, an application should, as a matter of urgency, be made to the relevant authorities to make good any deficiencies. The Court of Appeal confirmed the comprehensive control by the court of liquidators and liquidation proceedings in its decision handed down a couple of weeks later in *Re Kansa General International Insurance Co Ltd*.[51] If the court became concerned about the level of liquidators' fees or any other matter in a liquidation, the normal order would be addressed to the Official Receiver to fulfil his/her duties, but the court itself had jurisdiction to require the liquidator to submit to taxation.[52]

---

51 Reported as mentioned in note 40.

52 As regards liquidators CO s 196(2)(b) provides that, other than in the case of the Official Receiver, whose entitlement to remuneration and fees is laid down by the Companies (Fees and Percentages) Order, para 6 and Table B, liquidators' remuneration shall be by way of percentage or otherwise as is determined by agreement between the liquidator and the committee of inspection, where there is one, and where agreement is not reached or there is not a committee of inspection, as determined by the court. Where the remuneration is agreed between the liquidator and the committee, the Official Receiver may apply to the court for review of the remuneration pursuant to CO s 196(2A). Solicitors' and other professionals' fees are, generally, only allowed out of the assets of the company where they have been taxed and passed and allowed by the Registrar [of the High Court]: Companies (Winding-Up) Rules r 179(2). The Court of Appeal rejected the liquidators' argument that these provisions made up a complete legislative scheme, which excluded the court's inherent jurisdiction.

The latest reported case in the *Peregrine* saga is that relating to taxation,[53] where the Peregrine liquidators submitted for taxation their solicitors' bills of costs under r 179 of the Companies (Winding-Up) Rules. The bills of costs were prepared on a time basis. The Registrar reduced the hourly rates quite substantially. The liquidators objected and were unsuccessful in persuading the Registrar to review her ruling on the hourly rates and indicated that they would appeal. Therefore on 12 August 1999 Registrar Chu reduced her reasons into writing. She held that r 179 of the Companies (Winding-Up) Rules (Costs payable out of the assets required to be 'passed' by the Registrar) (see note 52) prevailed over the general costs rule O 62 r 29 of the Rules of the High Court. This was because the relationship between a liquidator and his/her solicitor was different from an ordinary solicitor and client relationship. A liquidator is not paying the solicitor out of his/her own resources, but from the funds and assets of the company. Before the liquidator's fees and disbursements could be allowed to come out of the estate, the liquidator was obliged to justify them. Where a liquidator had agreed with his/her solicitors as to the fees to be charged, he/she was contractually bound to honour that agreement.[54] That agreement did not bind the Registrar when considering the solicitors' bills under CWUR r 179(2). In reducing the hourly rates for which the estate should be responsible, the Registrar had compared the rates agreed with the normal hourly rates allowed by taxing masters that were set out in Law Society circulars. For example, the HK$1,750 hourly rate claimed by the solicitors for a particular trainee solicitor was well above the taxation range of HK$800–HK$1,000 and close to the rate of HK$2,000 allowed for newly admitted solicitors. There was nothing special in the work undertaken or the time spent on the work that justified the agreed rate. It was reduced to HK$1,000 per hour.[55]

No doubt there will be further litigation in the *Peregrine* saga. Le Pichon J has continued the debate extra-judicially in a *Law Lectures for Practitioners* in 1999[56] entitled 'Rethinking the Structure of Insolvent Liquidation' and in a Law Working Paper in the Faculty of Law at the University of Hong Kong Law Working Paper Series under the same title,[57] both in association with Betty M. Ho, an associate professor at the university. These texts cover the background to the *Peregrine* litigation, the existing law, the powers and duties of the participants and the court's control over remuneration. Then the texts look at the problem of overbilling by professionals in bankruptcy.[58] Reference is made to many books and articles on billing generally (mostly in the US) and in bankruptcy in particular. Appropriate reference is made to the tension between time and value. As to rethinking the future,

---

53 Reported as mentioned in note 40.

54 But in *Re First Bangkok City Finance Ltd & anor* [1989] 2 HKC 577, Jones J held that the solicitor's client was the company in liquidation, citing *Re National Life Insurance Co Ltd (in liq)* [1978] 1 WLR 45 and *Re Anglo-Moravian Hungarian Junction Rly Co, ex parte Watkins* (1875–76) 1 Ch. 130.

55 See further on *Peregrine taxation*, Srivastava, D.K and Sharma, C., 'Solicitor's Fees and Reimbursements: The Liquidator's Predicament' (2000) 29 *Asia Business Law Review* 58.

56 Wu, R., and Chan, F. (eds), *Law Lectures for Practitioners 1999*, Hong Kong Law Journal Ltd, 78–126. The late Peter Willoughby started this annual series of lectures, which subsequently results in the publication of the book of the lectures, in 1974.

57 Paper No. 25, June 1999.

58 Which, of course, in the US includes liquidation.

the authors clearly do not like the commonly used procedures of applications to the court for approval in advance for proposed steps by office-holders.[59] These are usually *ex parte*, unopposed and involve matters of commercial judgment that the court is ill-suited to determine. Similarly, the courts are not best suited for fixing and reviewing office-holders' remuneration, though they should be there as a last resort. The responsibilities of office-holders should be clarified. The Law Reform Commission, in recommending in its Report on the Winding-Up Provisions of the Companies Ordinance that the duties of liquidators should be spelt out in the legislation, had failed to identify to whom such duties should be owed. There was a conflict between the liquidator's duty to exercise commercial judgment and his/her duty to 'unearth' offences. The system should reward efficiency in recoveries for creditors. Theoretically, the creditors, who have the most to lose from incompetent administration by liquidators, should be the best monitors. The creditors' committee could be made an effective monitor on behalf of creditors. If they were suitably empowered and chose not to exercise their powers, then they would have only themselves to blame for expensive liquidations.

That brings us back to the 'problem'. Liquidations are inevitably going to involve expense. When the cost of the liquidation, or receivership as in *Maxwell*, eats up the bulk of the estate, the 'problem' is exacerbated. Of course, overbilling is not acceptable, but just because the costs of administration are high and not much, or even nothing, is left for the creditors, misconduct by office-holders is not necessarily indicated. *Maxwell*, where the costs claimed were eventually found to be justified, confirms that. But there is no way of controlling the ratio of liquidation costs to the balance left for creditors. A liquidator or other office-holder is entitled to reasonable remuneration for work done. The problem in winding up is that the liquidator's remuneration comes in priority to and at the expense of the creditors and others entitled to the net assets of the company. Often the costs of the liquidation eat up the whole estate. And often the administration of even a small estate may involve a great deal of work. Judges should not be 'startled' if the liquidator is to get, by way of remuneration, the bulk of the estate. They are entitled to be suspicious and to have the fees justified, but judges should realize that liquidators are *not* in competition with creditors. This was the mistake made by the sheriff in *Brownlie and Armstrong and Transitex (Ecosse) Ltd* (1984) 1 BCC 90, 047, when he said that one of the purposes of liquidation was to secure a fair distribution among the creditors and that that object was going to be entirely frustrated because of the large remuneration proposed for the liquidators. The liquidators' claim would be in direct competition with the claims of creditors. Lord Wheatley in the Court of Session said that the sheriff's approach was wrong and that the liquidators' claim was not in competition with the creditors. Though much has been made in *Peregrine* about the *Maxwell* judgment, nothing has been said about the almost total justification on taxation for the fees claimed. What appeared to the judge to be overbilling turned out to be nothing of the sort. And it is worth noting that the actual outcome of the *Maxwell* taxation is not mentioned in

59 See CO s 199(3) in Hong Kong. For a useful article on directions applications, see (1999) 7 *Insolvency Law Journal* 60 (Agardy, P.).

Le Pichon J's extra-judicial writing, though points from Master Hurst's reasons for assessments are mentioned.

One gets the impression from the various judicial opinions expressed in and out of court, that judges consider office-holders to be wimps, unwilling or unable to take commercial decisions on their own account and having to shield themselves behind court approvals. It is all very well exhorting office-holders to deploy commercial judgment and take decisions as a reasonably prudent person faced with the same circumstances in relation to their own affairs would, but this is a counsel of perfection. The reasonably prudent individual often takes professional advice, but in any event is not facing possible claims and litigation from dissatisfied creditors. The commercially right decision is not always obvious. The complexity of an investigation is not always apparent before it begins. Liquidators in Hong Kong do encourage creditors to undertake legal action themselves with the bait of indemnity for costs.[60] Far from encouraging liquidators to do things on their own initiative, the critical attitude of the judiciary is likely to lead to more applications to the court for directions[61] rather than fewer.

The Law Reform Commission in its Report on the Winding-Up Provisions of the Companies Ordinance,[62] made recommendations to deal with the problems that had arisen in *Peregrine*. First, it reviewed the current position as to office-holders' remuneration, as to which the legislation and rules were either silent or vague. Some guidelines were needed and an appropriate body was needed to review the fees of office-holders. By reference to the Ferris Report the LRC recommended that the Provisional Liquidator formula (the PL formula) under the UK Insolvency Rules be adapted, with the factors of time spent, complexity or otherwise, exceptional responsibility assumed, effectiveness of performance and value and nature of the property dealt with to be used in conjunction with each other, rather than as separate factors. In addition, the LRC recommended that the need for and desirability of investigatory work that may or may not lead to additional realizations should be taken into consideration. The LRC, while appreciating the Ferris Report's emphasis on value for money, considered that office-holders should not be prejudiced in terms of their remuneration if nothing ultimately materializes from the investigation or litigation.

The LRC also recommended the establishment of a Panel to scrutinize office-holders' fees. The Panel would be made up of suitably experienced persons, three of whom would sit on any case referred to it. The LRC had in mind, by way of analogy, the Inland Revenue Board of Review, which deals with tax appeals. A matter would

---

60 See CO s 265(5B), added in 1984 and derived from s 292(10) of the New South Wales Companies Act 1961. An example is *Re Intertrans Far East Ltd* [1994] 2 HKLR 331 where a creditor gave an indemnity for costs for litigation to the Official Receiver, when the latter had abandoned hope of recovery, and a substantial recovery was made. Rogers J (as he then was) awarded the relevant creditor a 15 per cent dividend and indicated that higher awards might be justified. He seemed eager to encourage creditors to come to the aid of liquidators. Assignment by liquidators to third parties of rights of action (see now *Norglen Ltd (in liq)* v. *Reeds Rains Prudential Ltd* [1999] 2 AC 1 HL, and (1997) 6 *Int Insolv Rev* 226 (Hede)) does not seem to occur in Hong Kong. In Australia see (2000) 8 *Insolv LJ* 70 (Britten-Jones).

61 See note 59.

62 See section 1.2 above of the text and Ch. 4 of the Report, 'Remuneration (Fees) of Office-holders'.

only be referred to a Panel in the event of dispute. The Court, the Official Receiver and office-holders would be able to refer matters to a Panel as of right. Creditors and others would need leave. A Panel's procedure would be inquisitorial. Charging a fee, similar to a taxation of legal fees, would cover the costs of running the system.

Pending any legislative changes, the High Court in 2004 (effective 3 May 2004) issued explanatory notes on how the existing law should be observed.[63]

The final issue arising out of the Report on the Winding-Up Provisions of the Companies Ordinance that will be mentioned here is that of cross-border insolvencies. Chapter 26 of the Report deals with the topic. As a major international business and finance centre with the majority of its listed companies incorporated offshore and many private companies also incorporated offshore (there are probably as many Hong Kong companies incorporated in the British Virgin Islands each year as are incorporated in Hong Kong), cross-border insolvency is a topic that can only increase in relevance and importance.

---

63 See Arboit, B., 'Liquidators' Remuneration in Hong Kong', in *Insol World*, Third Quarter 2004, 9–11.

Chapter 7

Insolvency Law in Vietnam

JOHN GILLESPIE*
Monash University, Melbourne

1 Introduction

Following *doi moi* (renovation) economic reforms in 1986, Vietnamese lawmakers began adopting laws suited to a mixed-market economy.[1] The transformation of socialist planning required an accompanying shift from administrative economic regulation to universal legislative norms and macro-economic levers. The new legislative framework, which included the Law on Business Bankruptcy 1993 (LBB) (*Luat Pha San Doanh Nghiep*), now replaced by the Bankruptcy Law 2004 (BL) (*Luat Pha San*), extensively relied on imported Western commercial laws.

The LBB failed to generate much support. From its commencement in 1994 until 2003 the courts received 152 petitions for bankruptcy, yet only 46 enterprises were declared bankrupt. The LBB was criticized by foreign investors for being inconsistent with international practice and by the Vietnamese business community for imposing foreign ideas and excessive 'state economic management'.[2] The Institute for Juridical Science at the Supreme People's Court drafted a new Bankruptcy Law with the following objectives:

- to harmonize the bankruptcy law with international protocols and treaty requirements;
- to improve the efficiency of bankruptcy procedures;
- to encourage more insolvent enterprises to use the law to resolve disputes with creditors;

---

* Professor, Department of Commercial Law and Taxation, Faculty of Business and Economics, Monash University, Melbourne. The author gratefully acknowledges the financial assistance of the Australian Research Council and the cooperation of Vietnamese judges, Ho Chi Minh City Justice Department Officials and Vietnamese law firms.

1 The Sixth National Congress of the Communist Party of Vietnam decided in 1986 that: '[t]he management of the country should be performed by law instead of simply by moral concepts. … It is necessary to systematically supplement and perfect the legal system so as to ensure that state machinery organizes and operates in accordance with the law.' Truong Chinh (1986), 'Introduction to the Political Report', Vietnam News Agency December 15, part 4.

2 See Author Unknown (2004), 'New Bankruptcy Law Thwarts Debt Asset Trading', *Thanh Nien*, 18 November, 3; Vu Long (2001), 'Alter Bankruptcy Law to Nab Company Bosses', *Vietnam Investment Review* 15 January, 5; Kim Chi (1998), 'Swimming Belly-Up', *Vietnam Economic News* (41), 18; Nguyen Quang Thai (1998), 'The Asian Monetary Crisis and Reforms of the Financial and Banking Systems in Vietnam', *Vietnam's Socio-Economic Development* (16) 10, 12.

- to allow parties other than creditors to participate in bankruptcy procedures;
- to give courts more flexibility in dealing with insolvent businesses.

The BL was enacted by the National Assembly on 15 June 2004 and commenced operation on 15 October 2004. This chapter explores the changes made by the BL to the LBB and more generally assesses the role of bankruptcy law in Vietnam's socio-legal landscape. To place bankruptcy law in context, it is necessary to trace the historical development of notions of debt and bankruptcy in Vietnam.

1.1 Borrowing Commercial Rules

1.1.1 Chinese legal borrowing For one thousand years (111 BC–938 AD) Chinese scholarship, political theories, religious values, family structures and bureaucratic practices indoctrinated and moulded, though never entirely supplanted, indigenous Vietnamese outlooks.[3] On gaining independence from the Chinese, the Vietnamese emperors applied a Sino-Vietnamese version of virtue rule *Li* (*Duc Tri*) and criminal rule *Fa* (*Phap Tri*). Confucianism replaced Buddhism as the state religion in the 15th century and by the time of the Nguyen Emperors in the 19th century, neo-Confucian morality supported by criminal law became the dominant legal ideology.[4]

Three aspects of pre-colonial or 'traditional' legality inform contemporary understandings of insolvency. One, people were not treated as legal equals. Society was divided roughly into the privileged imperial and mandarin families and unprivileged peasants, artisans and landless labourers.[5] In criminalizing breaches of Confucian morals and dispensing punishment according to social status, the primary function of imperial codes was to preserve hierarchical structures. Two, the Vietnamese legal codes were overwhelmingly preoccupied with top-down criminal sanctions, leaving horizontal debt transactions to village custom. State law only intervened on the rare occasions where commercial activities offended Confucian morality.[6] Imperial codes punished serious contractual fraud or duress that disrupted social order.[7] Interest rates for loans were capped at 2.5 or 3 per cent a month and total accrued interest could not exceed the principal debt.[8] The Le Dynasty in 1634 forbade the use of force to recover debts, violators were physically punished and their loans were cancelled.[9] A 30-year (20 years between relatives) limitation of action period

---

3 For a scholarly study of Vietnamese history, see Keith Taylor (1983), *The Birth of Vietnam*, University of California Press, Berkeley; Pham Diem (1995), 'A Brief Look at the Rule by Feudal China (from 179 BC to the Xth Century)', *Vietnam Law and Legal Forum* (1) (10), 28–29.

4 See Tran Thi Tuyet (1997), 'The Nguyen Dynasty and its Legislation in the First Half of the 19th Century', *Vietnam Law & Legal Forum* (3) (32) 24, 25.

5 See Yu Insen (1973), 'Law and Family in 17th and 18th Century Vietnam', PhD Thesis, University of Michigan, 67–8.

6 See Nguyen Ngoc Huy and Ta Van Tai (1986), 'The Vietnamese Texts', in M.B. Hooker (ed.), Vol. 1 *The Laws of Southeast Asia*, Singapore, Butterworths, 476–480.

7 Le Code, Articles 187, 190; Nguyen Code, Article 87.

8 Le Code, Article 587; Nguyen Code, 134.

9 See Ta Van Tai (1982), 'Vietnam's Code of the Le Dynasty (1428–1788)', *American Journal of Comparative Law*, 30 (3), 523, 529.

applied where creditors were state officials and debtors' assets were divided pro rata among creditors.[10]

Three, though superficially appearing to enforce private rights horizontally against other individuals, in practice imperial codes institutionalized and enforced Confucian morals. They were primarily concerned with legitimizing and protecting state, village and family hierarchies. For example, the state only became involved in the orderly distribution of debtors' estates to preserve the social entitlements of state officials and social order.

The political economy generated little demand for rights-based law. State monopolies tightly controlled urban trade and artisans were forced to practise their crafts in officially sanctioned trading streets (*phuong*).[11] In the villages, where most people lived, debt transactions were regulated by customary rules reflecting protean rituals, clan status and mystical beliefs.[12] Neo-Confucianism also generated moral obligations for sons to discharge their father's debts, even if this meant bonded labour.[13] Taken together, evidence suggests that creditor-debtor relationships were governed by personal and moral obligations that, in contrast to Western rights-based law, were situationally rather than universally valid.[14]

1.1.2 Colonial legal imports French colonial authorities established a system of legal pluralism in Vietnam that ensured imported French civil and commercial codes governing debt and bankruptcy primarily applied to Europeans.[15] By default the *Gia Long* Imperial Code and village customary practices continued to regulate informal credit among most rural Vietnamese.

---

10 Le Code, Articles 588, 592.

11 The legacy of this licensing system can be seen in the names of the 36 commercial streets in the ancient quarter of Hanoi – Paper Street, Fish Street, for example. See Nguyen Thua Hy (2002), *Economic History of Hanoi in the 17th, 18th and 19th Centuries*, National Political Publishing House, Hanoi, 78–101; Nguyen Duc Nhan (1984), 'Do the Urban Regional Management Policies of Socialist Vietnam Reflect the Patterns of the Ancient Mandarin Bureaucracy?', *International Journal of Urban Regional Research* (8) 74–75; Anthony Reid (1993), *Southeast Asia in the Age of Commerce 1450–1680*, Vol. II, Chiang Mai: Silkworm Books, 136–138.

12 *Dien*, an important rural commercial transaction, arose where A transferred land to B, in return for payment and an expectation of retransfer on repayment of the original payment. During the period of transfer B was entitled to enjoy profits from the land. Since the transaction transferred use and profit and not an outright alienation it did not generate debt obligations. See Henry McAleavy (1958), 'Dien in China and Vietnam', *Journal of Asian Studies* (17) 403, 405–411.

13 See generally Jamieson, N. (1993), *Understanding Vietnam*, Berkeley: University of California Press, 12–17.

14 The term *thao dang* is used to denote the situational validity of morals and rights. The word for rights, *quyen*, is derived from a Han (Chinese) word for balance. It emphasizes the oscillating nature of rights and their susceptibility to power. Rights ultimately belong to the powerful; there is no concept of natural rights in traditional Vietnam. Interviews with Hoang Ngoc Hien, Sociologist, Nguyen Du School of Creative Writing, Hanoi, April, September 1999.

15 See Hooker, M. (1975), *Legal Pluralism: An Introduction to Colonial and Neo-Colonial Laws*, Oxford: Clarendon Press, 226–230; Hooker, M. (1979), *A Concise Legal History of South East Asia*, Oxford: Clarendon Press, 156–160.

With the possible exception of a tiny urban Francophone elite, few Vietnamese had contact with, much less a detailed understanding of, the imported colonial rules governing debt and bankruptcy. Vietnamese were only peripheral to the colonial economy, contributing less than one per cent of invested capital and nine per cent of the workforce.[16] Few had any dealings with formal credit institutions. For example, Banque de L'Indochine, the colony's largest lender, invested most resources in international trade and neglected both expatriate and indigenous agriculture.[17] French legal influence further declined when many Vietnamese capitalists fled the North following communist victory in 1954.[18]

1.1.3 Importing socialist law Following the partitioning of the country in 1954, the Democratic Republic of Vietnam (DRV) gradually established a Soviet-inspired legal system.[19] The Republic of Vietnam in the South continued applying French colonial codes until reunification in 1975.[20] Thirty years of war impeded the development of legal institutions and jurisprudence in both the North and the South.

North Vietnamese lawmakers used the Soviet Union as an institutional model and source of legal ideology and statutory law. Thousands of Vietnamese were sent to the Eastern Bloc countries from the 1960s until 1990 to learn the skills needed to manage and implement the imported command economic system. Borrowed legal thought was derived from the Soviet doctrine of *sotsialisticheskaia zakonnost* (socialist legality), translated into Vietnamese as *phap che xa hoi chu nghia* (socialist legality). Socialist legality announced the three principles of socialist governance: the people as owners, the party as the leader, and the government as manager.[21]

---

16 See Chesneaux, J. (1955), *Contribution a l' Histoire de la Nation Vietnamienne*, Paris: Sociale, 74. It is estimated that at the height of the colonial economy in 1936 no more than 20,000 Vietnamese worked for French firms and approximately 3,000 Vietnamese owned private firms. See Dang Phong (1998), 'Vietnamese Economic Heritage from the French Colonial Period (1859–1945)', *Vietnam's Socio-economic Development* (16), 24–29.

17 See Wilson, J.S.G. (1957), *French Banking Structure and Credit Policy*, Cambridge Mass.: Harvard University Press, 108; Murry J.M. (1980), *The Development of Capitalism in Colonial Indochina* (1870–1940), Berkeley: University of California Press, 132–140.

18 See Dang Phong (1999), 'The Private Sector: In Vietnamese Industry from 1945 to the Present', in *Vietnam's Undersized Engine: A Survey of 95 Larger Private Manufacturers* (unpublished paper) Hanoi: Mekong Project Development Facility, 77.

19 See Ginsburgs, G. (1979), 'The Genesis of the People's Procuracy in the Democratic Republic of Vietnam', *Review of Socialist Law* (5) 187, 190–195.

20 See Vecchi, C. (1990), 'The Legal System of Vietnam', in Kenneth Redden (ed.), *Modern Legal Systems Cyclopedia*, 831.

21 For a comprehensive discussion of the Soviet legal theory taught to Vietnamese students in the former Soviet Bloc countries from the 1960s until 1990, see Jawitsch, L.S. (1981), 'The Essence of Law', in *The General Theory of Law*, 88–104. For a Vietnamese discussion of Soviet legal theory, see Hoang Hao (1987), 'Phap Luat va Kinh Te' ('Law and Economy'), *Tap Chi Cong San* (*Communist Review*), December, 24–28; Tran Duc (1987), 'Ve Cac Luat Kinh Te Trong Ithoi Ly Qua Do Len Chu Nhia Xa Hoi' ('Economic Laws in the Transition Period to Socialism') *Tap Chi Cong San*, May, 69–73. For a description of socialist legality in action, see Fforde, A. (1980), 'The Unimplementabily of Policy and the Notion of Law in Vietnamese Communist Thought', *Southeast Asia Journal of Social Science* (1) 60, 62–3.

The main focus of the socialist system was nationalization and 'sterilization' of the private sector. By 1960 the state proclaimed that the entire private sector was under state management.[22] Since capital was supplied by the state, central planning eliminated private debt from the formal, but not the informal, economy.[23] Although supply and distribution arrangements were formalized with contracts, these were essentially administrative directives used by central managers in line-ministries (*ho chu quan*) to implement production plans, and they did not create private debt obligations in the Western legal sense.[24] Bankruptcy and insolvency laws were unnecessary, as financial viability was not measured independently from state planning objectives.[25]

The doctrine of 'state economic management' (*quan ly Nha nuoc kinh te*) was imported into Vietnam to unify political and economic leadership in the state.[26] Devised in the Soviet Union to link state planning and economic production in command economies, it invested the state, as the sole owner of productive assets, with vertical control over economic production. Since law was only 'an important tool in the socialist state's management of society and economy'[27] the 'legal position of the parties in economic law [was] defined by their rights and obligations outlined by laws, plans, or economic contracts.'[28] In practice economic plans and administrative contracts drafted by line-ministries enjoyed an equivalent regulatory status to written laws.

1.1.4 Market-oriented legal reforms Most contemporary accounts of post-*doi moi* reforms portray the state as struggling to remain relevant by regulating the rapidly emerging market economy. Market mechanisms had now almost entirely supplanted command planning as the primary form of resource allocation. This devolution of decision-making power required laws that gave market players property and contractual rights. Legal reformers needed to establish a legal system that was capable of protecting commercial rights. To this end they introduced the *nha nuoc phap quyen* (or 'law-based state') doctrine, which called for stable, authoritative and compulsory law; equality of economic sectors before the law; the use of law to constrain and

22 See Pham Thanh Vinh (1965), 'The Obligatory Nature of Planning Targets', *Review of Contemporary Law* (12) 82, 84.

23 In practice an underground private economy coexisted with the command economy. Fforde, A. and de Vylder, S. (1996), *From Plan to Market: The Economic Transition in Vietnam*, Boulder: Westview Press, 58–59, 175–177.

24 As the sole owner of productive assets, the state monopolized control over economic production. Since law was only 'an important tool in the socialist state's management of society and economy', the 'legal position of the parties in economic law [was] defined by their rights and obligations defined by the law, the plan, or the economic contract'. Nguyen Nien (1976), 'Several Legal Problems in the Leadership and Management of Industry Under the Conditions of the Present Improvement of Economic Management in Our Country', *Luat Hoc* (*Jurisprudence*) April (14) 33, trans. JPRS 67995, 30 September, 34, 43.

25 See Duong Dan Hue and Nguyen Minh Man (1993), 'Some Issues on the Draft Bankruptcy Law', *Nha Nuoc va Phat Luat* (State and Law) (2), 39; Harmer, R. (1995), 'Insolvency Law Developments in Vietnam and China' (unpublished paper) Beijing: 14th Lawasia Biennial Conference, 3–4.

26 See Nguyen Nien, as note 24 above, 34–36.

27 Id. 36.

28 Id. 43.

supervise legal enforcement and a judiciary capable of resolving private, commercial disputes.[29]

In addition to proclaiming the 'law-based state', the Seventh Party Congress in 1991 also reaffirmed the long-standing socialist doctrine of *phap che xa hoi chu nghia* (socialist legality). Although the focus of the party and state has shifted from class struggle to economic development, the Marxist base (mode of production) determines the superstructure (ideals, culture and law) metaphor is still alive in the minds of central policymakers.[30] The purpose of law is accordingly to create a superstructure that reflects the 'will of the ruling class' (*y chi cua giai cap thong tri*) and its domination over the means of production. As a recent party communiqué confirms:

> The characteristics of our laws are different from those of bourgeois laws. Our laws are aimed at developing our nation in accordance with the socialist orientation while the laws of the bourgeois state are aimed at protecting capitalism.[31]

The role of law in Vietnam is uncertain. In the commercial arena pressure to regulate domestic entrepreneurs and harmonize laws to gain entry to market access treaties is producing a rights-based legislative framework, whereas party and state institutional relationships overwhelmingly conform to socialist legality (*phap che xa hoi chu nghia*). Although most command mechanisms have now been dismantled, 'state economic management' has migrated from production plans and supply contracts to market entry licences, prescriptive regulations and inspection regimes. The duty of 'unified management' inherent to 'state economic management' remains a central organizational principle.

The following discussion explores the ways in which socialist precepts and institutions undermine the market-orientated principles encoded in the Law on Business Bankruptcy 1993 and the new Bankruptcy Law 2004.

---

29 This new terminology first appeared in a speech made by Do Muoi at the 7th Party Congress in 1991. See Author Unkown (1992), *Sua Doi Hien Phap Xay Dung Nha Nuoc Phap Quyen Viet Nam Day Manh Su Nghiep Doi Moi* (*Amending the Constitution, Establishing a 'law based state' and Promoting Doi Moi Achievements*), Hanoi: The Gioi, 30, 32–3, 37.

30 Applying a historical-materialist analysis, society passes through various stages of development during its transition to advanced socialism. According to the Communist Party, the economy is currently traversing state-capitalism, where a dominant state sector coexists with private ownership. In this mixed economy, private ownership is tolerated provided it does not disrupt state economic management and 'collective mastery' – state and collective ownership.

31 Communist Party (1994), 'Resolution 7, Mid-term Congress Resolution, Part V', *Saigon Giai Phong* (*Saigon Liberation*), 19 March, 2; Vu Oanh (1993), 'Developing Combined Forces in Mass Motivation Work and Renovating the Work Content and Method of the Fatherland Front and Mass Organizations', *Nhan Dan* (*The People*), 23 December, 3; Do Phuong (1995), 'Party-State-Law', *Vietnam Law and Legal Forum* (1) (5), 3, 3–5; Do Muoi (1995), 'Building and Perfecting the State', *Vietnam Law and Legal Forum* (1) (6), 6.

1.2 Bankruptcy Principles

1.2.1 Imported bankruptcy principles Vietnamese writings about bankruptcy oscillate between advocating a rights-based regulatory approach and protecting the state benefit (the primary concern of socialist legality). At one end of the ideological spectrum, lawmakers recognize that credit is an essential ingredient of successful market economies and that the supply of investment capital depends on effective debt enforcement mechanisms.

Commentators identified the orderly regulation of market-exit mechanisms as one of the primary objectives of the BL and LBB.[32] Reflecting Western economic arguments, Duong Dang Hue, an influential member of both drafting committees, maintained that 'liquidating and dissolving inefficient enterprises paves the way for the more efficient enterprises to develop against strong competition.' Market economies, he surmised, require universal and systematic rules that reallocate resources into areas where they generate higher social returns. Bankruptcy rules, moreover, encourage business liquidity. Assets belonging to insolvent businesses are distributed in an orderly manner and when bankrupt enterprises are liquidated, their managers are prevented from incurring further debts for a prescribed period.

In drafting the BL, legislators imported the following bankruptcy principles from Western countries:

- most kinds of business enterprises (for instance state-owned enterprises (SOEs), private companies, private enterprises, foreign investment enterprises and cooperatives) are susceptible to bankruptcy;[33]
- creditors (and employees) may petition courts to bankrupt debtors (Articles 13, 14, BL);
- courts convene creditor conferences to prove claims in bankruptcy and determine whether to allow debtors to continue trading or declare them bankrupt (Articles 61, 64, BL);
- debtors may at any time propose schemes of arrangement (workouts) with creditors;
- bankruptcy assets are preferentially distributed to secured creditors (Article 33, BL); and
- bankrupt enterprises are liquidated.[34]

---

32 See Duong Dang Hue (2005), 'The Law on Bankruptcy with the Improvement of the Business Environment in Vietnam', *Democracy and Law* (3), 26–31; Hoang Minh Hieu (2004), 'On the Draft Law on Bankruptcy', *Tap Chi Nghien Cuu Lap Phap* (2), 64–71. For comments about the LBB, see Hue and Man, as note 25 above, 39.

33 Bankruptcy Law 2004, Article 2. Also see Decree No. 189 CP on Implementation of the Law on Bankruptcy 1994, Article 1.

34 Bankruptcy Law 2004, Article 86. For a discussion about business bankruptcy for the LBB, see Duong Dang Hue (1995), 'Main Contents of the Law on Business Bankruptcy', *Vietnamese Law & Legal Forum* (1) (11) 16; see Harmer R. (1994), 'Commercial and Bankruptcy Laws in Vietnam', in Graham Hassall and Truong Truong (eds), *Infractural Development and Legal Change in Vietnam*, Melbourne: Centre for Comparative Constitutional Studies, University of Melbourne, 68–70.

Imported Western principles were grafted onto a Vietnamese administrative structure that evinces 'state economic management' thinking:

- property owned by bankrupt enterprises automatically vests in state-controlled Property Management and Liquidation Teams (PMLTs) (*To Quan Ly va To Thanh Toan Tai San*) (Articles, 9, 10 BL);
- Property Management and Liquidation Teams realize bankruptcy assets (Article, 10 BL); and
- Property Management and Liquidation Teams distribute assets to creditors.

1.2.2 Bankruptcy as a 'state economic management' tool Contrasting with imported bankruptcy principles that presuppose resource allocation according to 'rational' self-interest and profit maximization, some government officials believe that bankruptcy regulations are primarily state management tools. In addition to protecting creditors' rights, the enactment and implementation of bankruptcy procedures gives state authorities powers to 'manage' the distribution of assets in bankruptcy and control market exist measures.[35] The 'state management' function of the BL is suggested by National Assembly debates that overwhelmingly focused on state management over insolvent SOEs (state-owned enterprises) and the subordination of creditors' rights to state economic policies.[36] In short, imported market-orientated bankruptcy principles were interwoven with 'state economic management' doctrines.

1.2.3 The central economic role of state enterprise SOEs are economically important. In 2000 they generated over 30 per cent of the GDP, compared to a mere eight per cent contributed by private enterprises.[37] But more significantly, they also play a pivotal role in legitimizing socialist ideology.[38] Though *doi moi* reforms recognized private ownership, party policy regards state ownership as the dominant economic force.[39] According to some commentators:

> the marriage of a private sector and a 'socialist orientation' is one of convenience, not true love. … The idea is that private sector development in Vietnam has traditionally occurred only as a compromise, needed to solve an immediate socioeconomic crisis rather than as a part of a comprehensive, long-term plan.[40]

---

35 Although realizing that there are substantial cultural and organizational impediments to the introduction of bankruptcy processes in Vietnam, Ronald Harmer, one of the principal foreign legal advisors to the bankruptcy law drafting committee, assumed the legal and economic converge would in time diminish these differences. See Harmer, as note 34 above. Also see Hue and Man, as note 25 above, 41.

36 See VNS (2004), 'NA Debates Draft Bankruptcy Law to Dispose of Failing Firms', Viet Nam News, 21 May, www.vietnamnews.vnagency.com.vn/2004-05/20/Stories/06.htm.

37 The statistics are based on figures published by the Vietnam General Statistical Office for 2000.

38 See (1999), 'Private Companies in Vietnam: A Survey of Public Perceptions', Hanoi: Mekong Project Development Facility, Paper No. 9, 15.

39 See Dan Duc Dam (1997), *Vietnam's Macro-Economy and Types of Enterprises: The Current Position and Future Prospects*, Hanoi: The Gioi, 121; Nguyen Van Huy and Tran Van Nghia (1996), 'Government Polices and State Enterprise Reform', in Ng Chee Yuen (ed.), *State-Owned Enterprise Reform in Vietnam*, 38–42.

40 As note 38 above, 15.

Although private production grew rapidly in the years following *doi moi*, state production grew more rapidly with the aid of state subsidies, market monopolies and foreign investment.[41]

Furthermore, the state uses SOEs to safeguard against the private sector 'moving in the wrong direction' (*check huong*) from socialism. This function is considered too complex and protean for static legislation and ad hoc bureaucratic discretion. State corporations (*tong cong ty*), which are conglomerations of SOEs operating in important economic sectors, have been formed to regulate aspects of the economy untouched by substantive law and macro-economic levers.[42] Contradicting constitutional changes in 2001 that reinforced the legitimacy of the private sector, the Commercial Law states that '[s]tate enterprises shall maintain their leading role in commercial activity and shall be one of the instruments of the State to regulate supply and demand and stabilize processes for the purposes of contributing to the implementation of the country's socioeconomic objectives.'[43]

In order to safeguard their pivotal economic and political role, the party and state resist market forces determining the bankruptcy of SOEs. Not only is bankruptcy perceived as a form of privatization, but the party-state needs to retain SOEs to confer legitimacy and relevancy to increasingly redundant socialist doctrines.[44]

1.2.4 Social obligations of enterprises Under the command economy, SOEs provided life-long employment, healthcare, subsidized housing, and retirement pensions to employees. They also organized community social, political and sporting

---

41 Although the Resolution of the 5th Plenum of the Party Central Committee in 2002 endorsed private sector development, it also reaffirmed the leading role of the state-owned sector. The Politburo quantified the level of SOE control of the non-farm GDP at 60 per cent or greater. See Politburo, as note above, 41; also see Mallon, R. (1998), 'Mapping the Playing Field: Opinions for Reducing Private Sector Disincentives in Viet Nam' (unpublished report), Hanoi: Swedish Embassy, 5; Mallon, R. (1996), 'State Enterprises in Viet Nam: Policy Developments, Attachments and Remaining Constraints' (unpublished report), Hanoi: Asian Development Bank, 12–16; Fforde, A. (1997), 'The Vietnamese Economy in 1996 – Events and Trends – The Limits of *Doi Moi*?', in Adam Fforde (ed.), *Doi Moi: Ten Years After The 1986 Party Congress*, Canberra: Research School of Pacific and Asian Studies, 154–155.

42 *Thong cong ty* (state corporations) are comprised of at least five SOEs operating in the same economic sector. Controlled by either central ministries or provincial peoples committees, *thong cong ty* are expected to coordinate the activities of member companies to increase market share, capital and competitiveness. In addition, they must 'limit both monopoly powers and disorderly competition'. This apparent contradiction is explained by the Vietnamese concept of competition. In the past, SOEs competed with each other to exceed planning targets – a form of 'socialist emulation'. Competition is still associated with socialist goals of 'mutual benefit' and 'cooperation'; 'disorderly competition' is accordingly market behaviour that disrupts state monopoly powers. State corporations encourage information and technology exchanges among SOEs and use import permits to fix domestic prices and suppress competition in the state sector. See Dam, as note 39 above, 167–169. In 1997 nearly 30 per cent of non-farm economic production came from state corporations.

43 Commercial Law 1997, Article 10. Also see Nguyen Van Dang (2001), 'Vietnam's Economic Renovation in Retrospect', *Cong San*, January.

44 For a detailed discussion concerning the compatibility of state enterprises and socialism, see Nguyen Ngoc Tuan (1993), 'Renovating the Enterprise Model in Our Country', *Tap Chi Cong San* (*Communist Review*), December, 29, 30–32.

activities.[45] Services were funded from enterprise profits and comprised the main source of social welfare for urban workers. Although *doi moi* reforms have removed many benefits, the perception remains that SOEs are more than profit-maximizers; they also owe extensive social and community obligations to employees and their families. This view is reinforced by the state's reluctance to develop a credible social safety net. More importantly, under a policy of 'socialization' (*xa hoi hoa*) it is progressively devolving responsibility for social welfare to local authorities and introducing a 'user pays' system to fund social services.[46] Social reliance on non-state sources of social welfare has forged a powerful alliance against bankruptcy between SOE employees and local government officials.

1.2.5 Moral property rights Bright-line legal distinctions in the BL, separating enterprise and employee ownership rights, define out of existence employee claims of moral rights in enterprise assets.[47] In response some employees frame their claims in Marxist ideological terms, asserting that assets were accumulated from the 'surplus value' of their labour.[48] Others refer to state regulations that vaguely declare 'entire people ownership' of SOE assets, but grant worker and management 'direct management and utilization of assets … for the development of production and business'. To put worker participation in context, until recently managers (in consultation with workers) distributed at least 35 per cent of retained profits for worker bonuses and social welfare payments.[49] Even though reforms have concentrated decision-making power in the hands of managers, employees and unions continue to regard workers as 'masters of the enterprises' exercising 'common property' rights over retained assets.[50] These sentiments have crystallized into moral principles that are invoked by trade unions in bankruptcy actions to oppose market forces redistributing 'common property' to 'outsiders'.

Surprisingly, workers in the private sector also assert moral claims over company assets. To some extent, these demands are ascribable to social expectations generated by the command economy. More recently, however, many employers have raised capital by borrowing directly from their employees.[51] These informal arrangements more closely approximate capital contribution and profit-sharing than loan agreements.

---

45 See Mallon (1996), as note 41 above, 17.

46 Resolution No. 90 CP on the Direction and Policy of Socialization of Education, Medical and Cultural Activities 1997. In essence the Resolution concedes that the state is unable to provide a full range of free social services and the public should accept responsibly for some of these activities.

47 Bankruptcy Law 2004, Articles 10, 36 (no distinction is made between state and private enterprise, although certain vital SOEs are granted immunity from creditors' actions). See Harmer, as note 34 above, 68–71; Lichtenstein, N. (1994), 'A Survey of Viet Nam's Legal Framework in Transition', Policy Research Working Paper 1291, World Bank, April, 37–40.

48 These comments are based on interviews with Nguyen Thi Duong, Civil Judgment Enforcement Department, Ministry of Justice, Hanoi, September 1999.

49 Decree No. 93-HDBT on Depreciation 1989 and Decree No. 195-HDBT on the Revaluation of State Enterprise Assets 1989.

50 See Mallon (1998), as note 41 above, 45.

51 See (1992), 'Small Enterprises in Vietnam' (unpublished report), Hanoi: International Labour Organization, 133.

For example, periodic interest payments are uncommon, and principal plus interest is usually only repayable when businesses are profitable. Employees asserting moral claims against their employers rarely comprehend abstract legal distinctions between company and personal assets embedded in the LB.

1.2.6 Loss of prestige Reforms designed to create independent self-governing SOEs have not severed the formal (policy direction) and informal (party and personal) bonds that closely link supervising authorities (line-ministries and peoples' committees) and SOEs.[52] As a consequence, the bankruptcy of SOEs damages the prestige and status of both SOE directors and supervising authorities.[53] In addition to 'loss of face' (*mat mat*), supervising authorities also lose access to the income produced by, and state subsidies granted to, SOEs.

In equating bankruptcy to death or incarceration, the public perceives the legal consequences of bankruptcy in emotional terms. Since there were no bankruptcies during the socialist period, some informants attribute social apprehension to a potent combination of neo-Confucian/traditional morality that makes debt repayment a yardstick of family status and integrity, and there are lingering memories of French colonial debtors' prisons and corporal punishment for defaulting debtors under the pre-colonial *Gia Long* penal code. Indeed, the Vietnamese word for debtor (*con no*) is considered a term of abuse by some. Others believe that bankruptcy is an 'ugly face' of capitalism that produces unemployment and economic waste and it does not belong in a socialist state. To varying degrees these cultural perceptions also inhibit bankruptcy in the private sector.[54]

Bringing together the themes discussed above, a powerful combination of political, regulatory, economic and cultural factors predispose the party-state against imported market-based bankruptcy principles. Though there is insufficient research to precisely ascertain the respective importance of these factors in Vietnam, studies of social attitudes to bankruptcy in China reveal that traditional neo-Confucian disdain for commerce and adversarial dispute resolution strongly inhibits the acceptance of bankruptcy.[55] Others believe that socialist ideology and pragmatic economic factors such as cost and time are the principal constraints. Despite convincing evidence that

---

52 *Luat Doanh Nghiep Nha Nuoc* (Law on State Enterprises) 2003. The employees of SOEs are still considered state civil servants and are under the direct supervision of SOE management, state-supervising authorities and, in important matters, the party. See Tran Tien Cung (1997), 'Restructuring of State-Owned Enterprise and Relations Between the State and State-Owned Enterprises in Vietnam', in John Gillespie (ed.), *Commercial Legal Development in Vietnam: Vietnamese and Foreign Perspectives*, Singapore: Butterworths, 377–378, 386–387.

53 See generally Nguyen Thanh Thuy (1997), 'Dispute Resolution and Enforcement of Economic Judgments in Vietnam', in John Gillespie (ed.), *Commercial Legal Development in Vietnam: Vietnamese and Foreign Perspectives*, Singapore: Butterworths, 195–207.

54 Interview, Nguyen Thi Duong, Expert, Civil Judgment Enforcement Department, Ministry of Justice, Hanoi, 27 September 1999.

55 See Tomasic R. and Little P. (1997), *Insolvency Law and Practice in Asia*, Hong Kong: FT Law & Tax Asia Pacific, 48–57; Asian Development Bank (1999), 'Law and Development at the Asian Development Bank', Manila: Asian Development Bank, 10–17; Harmer, R. (1996), 'Insolvency Law and Reform in the People's Republic of China', *Fordham Law Review* (64), 6.

insolvent SOEs absorb scarce state resources and slow down economic development, for a combination of ideological, moral and personal (frequently corrupt) reasons the party ensures that the bankruptcy of SOEs remains an administrative prerogative. At the same time, social stigma, cost and uncertainty erode private sector confidence in bankruptcy principles.

1.3 Regulating Bankruptcy

1.3.1 Statutory rule Though the precise relationship between law and commercial behaviour is poorly understood, some commentators maintain that legal frameworks have the capacity to shape commercial relationships.[56] Specific combinations of laws induce and maintain particular patterns of production. For example, resource allocation in capitalist economies relies on state support for horizontal property, contractual and business organizational relationships.[57] Bankruptcy law complements capitalist resource allocation, by allowing market-exit options to flexibly adapt to changing commercial opportunities.

Vietnam's legislative framework now includes most laws required to support market allocations. Laws, for instance, recognize state and private ownership of income producing assets and limited tenure over land.[58] Decree No. 165/1999/ND-CP on Secured Transactions 1999 permits pledges and mortgages over land use rights (*quyen su dung dat*) and buildings, and mortgages, pledges and guarantees over movables such as machinery, stock-in-trade, contractual rights and future property.[59] The Ordinance on Economic Contracts 1989 enables registered business entities (such as SOEs, companies and private enterprises) to invest resources to secure market opportunities and optimize competition.[60] Large-scale capital accumulation is made possible by the Enterprise Law 1999, because it permits entrepreneurs to select the most appropriate commercial vehicle (for instance, partnerships, private enterprises (unincorporated business associations), limited liability or joint-stock companies) for prevailing commercial conditions.[61] Finally, the Law on State-Owned

---

56 A full exploration of the relationship between law and development is beyond the scope of this chapter. The hypothesis used in this discussion assumes that states comprise not only laws, but also the behaviour of all officials formulating and implementing them. While not neglecting social influence on law formation, it is surmised that laws can instrumentally shape commercial behaviour. See generally Seidman, A. and Seidman, R. (1994), *State and Law in the Development Process*, London: Macmillan Press, 4–44; Sugerman, D. (1983), 'Law, Economy and The State in England, 1750–1914: Some Major Issues', in David Sugerman (ed.), *Legality, Ideology and the State*, London: Academic Press, 213, 223–230.

57 See Williamson, O. (1985), *The Economic Institutions of Capitalism: Firms, Markets, Relational Contracting*, London: Collier Macmillan, 68–75, 273–298. Weber concluded that 'modern capitalism prospers equally … under legal systems containing rules and institutions which considerably differ from each other at least from the juridical point of view.' See Weber, M. (1954), *Max Weber on Law in Economy and Society*, trans. Edward Shils and Max Rheinslein, Cambridge Mass.: Harvard University Press, 315; also see Habermas, J. (1973), *Legitimation Crisis*, trans. T. McCarthy, London: Heinemann, 53, 54.

58 Civil Code 1995, Articles 220, 241; Land Law 1998.

59 Civil Code 1995, Articles 77, 329, 346, 394–408; Nouel, Gide Loyrette (1999), 'The New Decree on Secured Transactions – "A Promising Reform"', *Vietnam Law and Legal Forum* (6) (64), 11, 11–12.

60 Ordinance on Economic Contracts 1989, Article 12.

61 Enterprise Law 1999, Articles 6, 26, 51, 112, 113.

Enterprises 2003 permits the state to participate, through wholly or partially owned commercial entities, in market activities.

The following discussion explores the tension in the BL between private rights to bankrupt debtors and state discretionary powers to preserve socio-economic policy. Naturally all states to some extent regulate resource allocation. But together with China, Vietnamese market-exit practices represent an extreme example of state regulation.[62]

1.3.2 Bureaucratic regulation The bankruptcy regime in Vietnam revolves around the twin legal doctrines of the 'law-based state' and 'socialist legality', by declaring that all economic sectors are treated equally. The BL proclaims the supremacy of the 'law-based state', but the enduring influence of 'socialist legality' is revealed in the preference shown for administrative rather than normative solutions to SOE insolvency. Facing immense ideological, economic and social pressures, the state has largely by-passed the BL and established the Central Steering Committee for Debt Solvency (an inter-ministerial body) to coordinate the liquidation of SOEs. This body equitizes (*co phan hoa*), as privatization is euphemistically called, and merges unprofitable SOEs.[63] Officials maintain that only state administrative bodies possess the regulatory skills and national focus needed to rehabilitate or wind up insolvent SOEs. They believe that provincial courts, which administer the BL, lack the macro-economic perspective required to engineer large-scale industrial restructuring.

Officials further believe that political processes provide the only effective remedies for politically generated economic problems. Consider the phenomenon of 'triangular' debt.[64] During the period of command regulation, compulsory production targets forced SOEs into complex, interlocking debt transactions. Enterprise A, for example, might acquire raw material from enterprise B on credit. At the same time, B may have obtained its own raw materials on credit from enterprise C, which in turn procured its raw materials on credit from enterprise A. Since these transactions were asymmetric, credits and debts could not be simply set-off. Funds were borrowed from state banks to make up credit shortfalls with little thought given to the underlying commercial feasibility of transactions.

The interlocking debt relationships were unstable and complex, since the bankruptcy of one enterprise quickly spread to other SOEs and state banks.[65] The government concluded that political solutions administered by the Central Steering Committee for Debt Solvency were required to unravel 'triangular' debts. This

---

62 For a comparative analysis of bankruptcy regulation in East Asia, see Tomasic and Little, as note 55 above.

63 See Hue and Man, as note 25 above, 40–42; (1994), 'Vo Van Kiet Attends Meeting on Debt Solvency', Hanoi, *Voice of Vietnam*, 22 March, 1994, trans. FBIS Daily Report East Asia Service 94–056, 23 March 1994, 58; for a case study, see Thuy, as note 53 above.

64 Interviews with Nguyen Tien Cung, Director Department of Enterprise Management Central Institute of Economic Management, Hanoi, July 1995, August 1996, October 1997, July 1998; Cung, as note 52 above, 393.

65 See Nguyen Ngoc Chinh (1998), 'City Man's SOS over Chain Reaction of Business Failures', *Vietnam Investment Review*, 16 August, 5.

thinking influenced the LBB, and to a lesser extent the BL. The LBB gave the courts and other state agencies extraordinary discretionary powers over every stage of bankruptcy. Modest reforms introduced in the BL, aiming to clarify and simplify bankruptcy procedures, have reduced, but by no means removed, state discretionary powers.

1.3.3 Courts In a radical departure from long-standing socialist management practices, the LBB shifted discretionary authority over enterprises from government authorities to economic courts (Article 4, LBB). The courts were, however, poorly prepared to resolve bankruptcy cases. Judges in economic courts were mostly drawn from state economic arbitration centres that were originally formed to administer production contracts in the command economy.[66] As market mechanisms began replacing central planning, economic arbitration became increasingly irrelevant and was eventually abolished in July 1994.[67] Economic courts during their first full year in 1995 heard 500 cases, a precipitous decline from over 3,000 cases considered by economic arbitrators in their final year of operation. The number of economic cases has remained at approximately this level.[68] As previously mentioned, from 1994 until 2003 only 152 bankruptcy petitions were lodged with the economic courts.

Various explanations are advanced for low litigation rates. As previously discussed, most cases involving insolvent SOEs never reach the courts and are processed administratively by the Central Steering Standing Committee for Debt Solvency. Those venturing inside courts complain that judges base their decisions on internal guidelines that are unavailable to creditors and debtors.[69] Litigants are likewise concerned that court proceedings will reveal commercially (and personally) damaging information; standards of proof are too onerous (in other words courts require formal documentation when none exists); and long procedural delays in

---

66 Arbitration functioned separately from the people's courts. See generally Pham Thanh Vinh, 'The Obligatory Nature of Planning Targets', *Review of Contemporary Law* (12) (1) 82, 89–99; Gillespie, J. (1991), 'Commercial Arbitration in Vietnam', *Journal of International Arbitration* (8) 25, 26–27, 55–56. Law Amending the Ordinance on the Organisation of the Supreme People's Court 1994, Articles 3–7. This transformation was not without its critics: see Hoang The Lien (1992), 'On the Model of Commercial Courts in Vietnam', *Nha Nuoc va Phap Luat* (State and Law) 3, 18.

67 According to State Economic Arbitration Statistics, 6,900 cases were filed in 1989, 4,202 in 1991, 1,648 cases in 1992, and rising to 3,200 in 1993–94.

68 During 1995, courts throughout the country heard 531 economic disputes and 22 petitions for bankruptcy. Most disputes related to economic contracts (sale-purchase, transport, construction, etc.) 74 per cent, companies 10 per cent, and finally foreign companies 12 per cent, divided into 202 economic contracts, 71 traded goods contracts, 27 transport contracts, 25 construction contracts, and 27 bankruptcy declarations, leaving 101 cases unaccounted for. See Ha Hung Cuong (1996), 'Resolution of Economic Disputes in Vietnam and the Accession to the 1958 New York Convention', in J. Gillespie (ed.) *Commercial Legal Development in Vietnam: Vietnamese and Foreign Commentaries*, Singapore: Butterworths, 163–164; (1996), 'Settlement of Economic Law Suits and Bankruptcy Declarations,' *Vietnam Law and Legal Forum* (2) (21), 11.

69 These views are based on interviews with private lawyers from Investconsult and Leadco, Hanoi, and IMAC, Ho Chi Minh City, from 2001–2005.

listing actions (over 12 months in Ho Chi Minh City) enable debtors to dispose of their assets.[70]

Negative public perceptions about the competency and impartiality of judges also discourage bankruptcy litigation. High on the list of concerns is a chronic shortage of experienced commercial judges.[71] Economic court judges were given only two weeks' bankruptcy training prior to the commencement of the LBB.[72] Before moving to the economic courts, state arbitrators successfully used administrative methods to resolve contract disputes in the command economy, but these techniques proved inappropriate in adversarial bankruptcy proceedings.[73] The low litigation rates imply that the public have not come to trust the courts to resolve commercial disputes.

In socialist legal theory law is considered a management tool (*cong cu quan ly*) to preserve the state's interest. Where the law is clear it must be followed. Where it is unclear, court officials are required to favour party-state interests. This institutional bias is manifested on the rare occasions where private creditors attempt to bankrupt SOEs. Instead of rejecting bankruptcy petitions outright, courts interminably delay proceedings in the expectation that creditors will either accept discounted settlements or abandon their claims entirely. This strategy is especially evident where foreign creditors have tried enforcing non-performing loans against SOEs. Vietnamese courts have responded to these claims with the same nationalistic zeal as their counterparts elsewhere in South East Asia.[74]

For their part, judges found the LBB inordinately difficult to implement. The Supreme Court has been unable to accumulate sufficient experience to formulate clear procedural guidelines. Without doctrinal signposts judges struggled to follow the basic procedural steps stipulated in the LBB and Decree No. 189 CP on the Implementation of the Law on Business Bankruptcy 1994 (DBB). In practical terms courts lacked the analytical tools needed, for example, to determine whether an act of

---

70 See Toa An Nhan Dan Toi Cao (2005), 'Bao Cao Tong Ket Cong Tac Nganh Toa An Nam 2004 va Phuong Huong Nhiem Vu Cong Tac Toa An Nam 2003' (Report on 2005 and the plan for 2004 Supreme People's Court), Hanoi. Also see Report (2003), 'Bankruptcy Law under Review', 10 *Vietnam Law and Legal Forum* (109), 17; Tran Van Su (1995), 'The People's Economic Court of Ho Chi Minh City: A Year of Establishment and Operation', *Tap Che Toa An Nhan Dan* (*People's Court Review*) (5), 2–3.

71 Statistics from the Ministry of Justice suggest an overall shortage of 1,714 judges. See Nguyen Tri Dung (1996), 'National Assembly Takes Tougher Measures to Restore Order', 11 November, 2.

72 See Fitzpatrick, Daniel and Alistair Wyvill (1995), 'Business Bankruptcy Seminars in Vietnam', *International Law News* (27) 23–27.

73 State economic arbitration personnel who were not directly engaged in company registration were transferred to the Supreme Court. Decision No. 355 (July 11, 1994) Prime Minister. See also Sidel, M. (1993), 'Law Reform in Vietnam: The Complex Transition from Socialism and Soviet Models in Legal Scholarship and Training', *UCLA Pacific Basin Law Journal* (11) 221, 223–228, 253–254; Quang Huong (1994), 'National Assembly Proceedings,' FBIS East Asia Service 94–210, 86, 31 October; Phan Van Thuyet (1996), 'Legal Framework and Private Sector Development in Transitional Economies: The Case of Vietnam', *Law and Policy Review in International Business* (27) (3), 541, 590.

74 See Quang Chung (2001), 'Unsolved Disputes', *Saigon Weekly Times*, 2 June, 28; Pauline, G. (1999), 'Corporate Rescue Regimes: Recent Developments in the Asia Pacific Region and their Implications', *INSOLE International Insolvency Review* (8), 3–25; Vatikiotis, M. (1998), 'Legal Hurdle: Under IMF Pressure, Thais Debate New Bankruptcy Law', *Far Eastern Economic Review*, 5 March, 54, 55.

bankruptcy had occurred or to distinguish genuine commercial transactions from unlawful preferential payments.

Convinced that private companies use bankruptcy to fraudulently avoid debts, courts routinely criminalized bankruptcy proceedings.[75] Security police (*canh sat dieu tra*), called in to investigate, evidently did not confine themselves to bankruptcy issues and routinely examined a broad range of economic offences.[76] Police used their extensive powers to seize records and arrest both debtors and creditors found breaching economic regulations.[77] Since it is virtually impossible to operate profitably without breaching some rules, debtors and creditors were understandably reluctant to commence bankruptcy proceedings.[78]

The BL has been in operation for too short a period to assess whether it has rectified the shortcomings with the LBB. There are, however, some reforms that may assist the courts:

- a simplified definition of bankruptcy that states any business that is unable to pay its due debts on demand to a creditor shall be deemed to have become insolvent (Article 3, BL);
- bankruptcy petitions must now provide documentary evidence supporting proofs of debt (Article 15, BL);
- judges are given more flexibility in deciding whether to initiate steps to allow insolvent enterprises to trade out of debt or to refer them to bankruptcy proceedings (Article 28, BL);
- procedures now clearly state that bankruptcy suspends civil judgment enforcement (Article 57, BL);
- the range of activities that are prohibited once a petition is accepted have been clarified (Article 31, BL);
- the range of assets that are subject to bankruptcy have been clarified (Articles 43–50, BL).

---

75 Courts can criminalize bankruptcy proceedings where they believe processes are used for 'objective' criminal purposes. Law on Business Bankruptcy 1994, Article 16 (2). See Le Dang Doanh (1994), 'The Bankruptcy Law in a Nutshell', *Vietnam Investment Review*, 20 February, 4. Informants give the case of the Kim Thoai Company in Can Tho Province that was bankrupted by the Can Tho provincial court in 1996. Creditors appealed the decision and the Supreme Court on reexamining the evidence found signs of criminality and transferred the case to the criminal court.

76 Interviews Do Cao Thang, Chief Judge Hanoi Economic Court, 10 March 2002; Vo Van Thon, Chief Civil Judgment Debt Enforcement Department, Ho Chi Minh City People's Committee, Hanoi, 24 February and 6 March, 2000.

77 These comments are based on discussions with Ho Chi Minh City-based private lawyers involved in bankruptcy transactions.

78 Tan Duc (1999), 'Bo Dieu 164 Cho Doanh Nhan Yen Tam Lam An' ('Revoke Article 164 to Make Businessmen Feel Assured in Doing Their Business'), *Thoi Bao Kinh Te Sai Gon* (*Saigon Economic Times*), 20 May, 11.

2 Enterprise Bankruptcy Rules

2.1 The Statutory Basis of Bankruptcy

2.1.1 The enactment of the Law on Business Bankruptcy The Central Institute of Economic Management in Hanoi began drafting the Law on Business Bankruptcy in 1991.[79] After considering many European, Asian and Australian bankruptcy laws,[80] the final draft borrowed heavily from the Chinese Bankruptcy Law 1986. Echoing the Chinese preoccupation with SOEs, Vietnamese officials primarily were concerned with state rather than private bankruptcies. Some thought '[l]oss making businesses [*sic*, SOEs] should be withdrawn from the market and this Law will help [do that] in a safe, legal way.'[81] Others speculated, rather implausibly, that '[t]his [*sic*, LBB], together with the establishment of the economic courts, will mean no more umbrellas, no godfathers but the law.'[82] The term 'umbrella' is a literal translation of the Vietnamese word '*o du*', which is a popular expression denoting the protection of incompetence or illegality by friends and relatives in the party-state. Departing from the Chinese model, from its inception the LBB applied to both state and private sector enterprises.

Five years after the LBB became operational on 1 July 1994, the Supreme People's Court was instructed to begin drafting a new law.[83] Ngo Cuong, the Deputy Director of the Institute for Judicial Science of the Supreme Court and a leading member of the drafting committee, concluded that the LBB was formulated in the early 1990s at a time when lawmakers knew little about the workings of market economies and the courts had no experience in settling bankruptcy cases. After reviewing bankruptcy cases, the committee decided that incomplete and fraudulent accounting records constituted the greatest hurdle to resolving cases. Committee members resolved that the new law must contain provisions that enabled judges to determine which debts arise from business activities, which debts arise from deliberate violations or illegal uses of enterprise assets and which debts are caused by external events. Finally, the committee simplified the rules, making it easier for creditors to bankrupt debtors. This modest shift away from the bureaucratic controls in the LBB

---

79 See Doanh, as note 75 above, 20; Tran Kim Hoa (1995), 'Some Issues on the Creation and Implementation of Enterprise Bankruptcy Law in Vietnam' (unpublished paper), Beijing: *14th Lawasia Conference*, 16 August, 2–3; Lay, J. (1994), 'The New Bankruptcy Law in Vietnam', *ICCLR* (11), 389.

80 Commentators indicate that the laws of China, Korea, Malaysia, Thailand, Singapore, Indonesia, Australia, New Zealand, Japan, the United States and France were considered. See Harmer, R. (1994), 'An Overview of Recent Developments and Future Prospects in Australia (With Some Reference to New Zealand and Asia)', in Jacob S. Ziegel (ed.), *Current Developments in International and Comparative Corporate Insolvency Law*, Oxford: Clarendon Press, 59.

81 Nguyen Tri Dung (1994), 'National Assembly Passes Bankruptcy Law', *Vietnam Investment Review*, 1 February, 2.

82 Ibid.

83 Interviews with Ngo Cuong, Deputy Director of the Institute of Judicial Science of the Supreme Court, Hanoi, March, April 2004, January 2005. Also see Report, as note 70 above, 17; Duong Dang Hue, as note 32 above, 26–28.

towards a more market-orientated approach to bankruptcy followed China's cautious experimentation with the Shenzhen Bankruptcy Regulations a decade earlier.[84]

Both the Enterprise Law 1999, which governs companies and private enterprises and the Law on State-Owned Enterprises 2003 provide that the BL is the sole source of bankruptcy rules in Vietnam.[85] However, the new BL does not apply to small-scale traders and individuals in the expectation that these entities would be regulated by amendments to the Civil Code.[86] Since the Civil Code has not been amended to regulate bankruptcy, an anomaly has arisen. Licensed enterprises can be bankrupted, but small-scale business entities registered under Decree No. 2 2000 escape bankruptcy even where both licensed and registered businesses conduct similar commercial activities.

2.1.2 Constitutional basis of the Bankruptcy Law Both the LB and LBB were enacted after the 1992 Constitution recognized the mixed market economy and state and private ownership of income-producing property.[87]

2.1.3 Bankruptcy utilization Prior to enacting the LBB, the government selected 315 hopelessly insolvent SOEs for expeditious bankruptcy.[88] For reasons previously considered, most of these enterprises were merged or liquidated by the Central Steering Committee for Debt Solvency. Contrasting with China, where over 2,000 SOEs have been bankrupt,[89] the number of bankruptcies in Vietnam has been extremely low. It is difficult to determine precise numbers since figures quoted are inconsistent. The Ministry of Justice reports the highest figures, with 21 cases heard by 1996,[90] just two cases in 1998, five cases in 1999 and 12 cases in 2000.[91] The courts report lower figures. The Chief Judge of the Ho Chi Minh City People's Court, Vietnam's most active commercial court, estimates that only ten bankruptcy cases have been heard in the South and doubts that the total number for the entire country

---

84 See Xianchu Zhang and Booth, C. (2001) 'Chinese Bankruptcy Law in an Emerging Market Economy: The Shenzhen Experience', 15 *Columbia Journal of Asian Law* 1; Cooper, P. and Zhang, J.M. (1996), 'Bankruptcy or Merger?', *China Trade Report* (36), 1–3; Chang, Ta-kuang (1987), 'The Making of the Chinese Bankruptcy Law: A Study in the Chinese Legislative Process', *Harvard International Law Journal* (28), 333–372.

85 Enterprise Law 1999, Article 113; Law on State Enterprises 2002, Article 22 (2).

86 Hoa, as note 79 above, 4–6.

87 Constitution 1992, Articles 15, 16 , 21, 58.

88 Dung, as note 81 above.

89 This statistic accounts for bankruptcies from 1986 until 1995. Since the rate of bankruptcy cases is increasing by over 100 per cent each year, it is expected that by the year 2000, over 5000 cases will have been decoded. See Li, S. (1995), 'Sessions of the Standing Committee on Insolvency Law Implementation of Bankruptcy Law in China: Difficulties and Prospects' (unpublished papers), Beijing: *14th Lawasia Biennial Conference*, 16 August, 2.

90 See 'Settlement of Economic Lawsuits and Bankruptcy Declarations', as note 68 above.

91 These statistics are based on interviews with Do Cao Thang, Chief Judge Hanoi Economic Court, 10 March 2002; informants suggest that no bankruptcy cases have been heard in Hanoi since 1997. See (2000), 'Five Companies Went Bankrupt Last Year', *Dow Jones Newswires*, 10 January.

is above 20.[92] Either way the bankruptcy of SOEs through the LBB has been a fringe phenomenon.

2.2 *Regulatory Institutions*

2.2.1 Courts The BL describes in considerable detail the administrative processes governing the two-tiered bankruptcy regime. The first phase involves court-based adjudication and the second phase regulates the recovery, management and distribution of assets. During the first phase, the economic divisions of provincial/city people's courts administer voluntary and involuntary bankruptcies (Articles 7, 8, LB). District-level courts have jurisdiction over bankruptcy petitions filed against cooperatives. After accepting bankruptcy petitions, courts are entitled to approve business reorganization plans, or issue 'bankruptcy declarations' (*pha san doanh nghiep trong*) that distribute assets and wind up insolvent enterprises (Articles 28, 61, LB).

Economic courts are only entitled to hear bankruptcies arising from 'economic contract' debts. When read together, Articles 1 and 2 of the Ordinance on Economic Contracts 1989 indicate that 'economic contracts' must be in writing and made between licensed business entities. The first stipulation means that debts based on informal family or revolving credit (*hui*) facilities cannot form the subject matter of bankruptcies. The second stipulation excludes 'household' enterprises registered under Decree No. 2 2000 and unregistered traders from participating in the bankruptcy regime.

In summary, courts are required to:

- collect materials supporting bankruptcy petitions;
- supervise the activities of Property Management and Liquidation Teams (PMLTs);
- preserve bankruptcy assets;
- organize and chair creditor meetings;
- temporarily or permanently suspend bankruptcy orders; and/or
- declare enterprises bankrupt.

2.2.2 Property Management and Liquidation Teams During the second phase, civil judgment enforcement departments in provincial/city justice departments (*so tu phap*) oversee bankruptcy administration. These bodies are attached to people's committees (local government), but are supervised by the Ministry of Justice (Article 9, LB). Civil judgment enforcement departments form PMLTs to preserve and manage bankruptcy assets (Article 10, LB). These bodies are dominated by state officials drawn from courts, people's committees, trade unions and state

92 Interviews with Phan Xuan Tho, Chief Judge Economic Court, Ho Chi Minh City People's Court, February 2000; Nguyen Thi Duong, Expert, Civil Judgment Enforcement Department, Ministry of Justice, Hanoi, September 1999. Unfortunately published statistics do not break down aggregate numbers into types of companies and forms of ownership. See 'Settlement of Economic Lawsuits and Bankruptcy Declarations', as note 68 above.

banks. In contrast, creditors and debtors are only entitled to one representative on PMLTs.

Property Management and Liquidation Teams make lists of available property, supervise and examine the use of property by insolvent entities, and propose emergency measures to preserve assets (Articles 10, 11, 53, LB). They also make lists of creditors and recover, sell and distribute bankruptcy assets.

2.3 Creditors' Petitions

2.3.1 Procedures Partially secured and unsecured creditors may petition courts to bankrupt enterprises that fail to repay loans within 30 days of them falling due (Articles 15–18, LB). Since their interests are presumed to be adequately protected, secured creditors are not permitted to petition for bankruptcy (Article 35, LB). As central players in the socialist-orientated economy, labour unions and employee associations may also petition for bankruptcy where enterprises fail to pay wages (Article 14, LB). Petitions must demonstrate that a demand for payment has been made and debt(s) are outstanding. Presumably to avoid wholesale bankruptcy of the numerous insolvent SOEs, there is no 'trigger' clause that creates 'automatic' acts of bankruptcy (Article 28, LB).[93]

2.3.2 Judicial powers and duties Judges are required to reject creditors' petitions that lack sufficient documentation to warrant relief (Article 28, LB). This typically occurs where proofs of debts have been inadequately documented. Despite a statutory obligation to provide reasons for dismissing petitions (Articles 28, 29, LB), informants report that in politically sensitive cases concerning SOEs courts, neither accept nor reject petitions, but instead leave them suspended for months.

More importantly, there are no automatic grounds for bankruptcy and courts have broad discretionary powers to reject petitions that fail to show enterprises have 'fallen into a state of bankruptcy' (Article 28, LB). Evidently, these powers were granted to assuage government concerns that 'automatic' bankruptcy triggers would compromise long-term business planing where companies sacrificed profits for market share and technological advantage.[94]

2.4 Debtors' Petitions

Where enterprises 'fall into the state of bankruptcy', owners or legal representatives are required to petition for bankruptcy (Article 15, LB). Petitions must:

- list creditors and outstanding debts;
- evaluate the causes of insolvency;
- describe the financial position of the enterprises six months prior to lodging the bankruptcy petition; and

93 See Lay, as note 79 above.

94 See Tran Minh Son (2004), 'Novelties in Bankruptcy Law', 10 *Vietnam Law and Legal Forum* (119), 16.

- contain financial and accounting records (Article 15, LB).[95]

2.5 Powers of Secured Creditors

2.5.1 Legislative sources The LB only generally outlines the powers available to secured creditors (Article 35, LB). It requires judges to 'prioritize the repayment of secured assets' and allow secured creditors to participate in bankruptcies where the value of secured assets is insufficient to discharge debts.

The Civil Code 1995 and Decree No. 165 ND-CP on Secured Transactions 1999 are, however, the main regulatory sources governing secured creditors. The Decree enables creditors holding mortgages and/or pledges over movables (present and future) and immovables to sell or foreclose in the event of bankruptcy.[96] The Decree No. 8 ND-CP on the Registration of Security Transactions 2000 further provides that before gaining priority over unsecured creditors, secured interests must be perfected by registration at the National Registration Office. Priority is determined by the date of registrations and lasts for five years. Once their interests are perfected, secured creditors have priority over unsecured creditors such as employees and tax authorities.

2.5.2 Practical difficulties with secured transactions One of the main difficulties with secured transactions is the uncertainty surrounding land use rights held by bankrupt enterprises. It is unclear, for example, whether the land rights contributed by SOEs to foreign joint ventures are revocable by bankruptcy actions. According to the Land Law 2003, land use leases revert to the state in the event of bankruptcy. This principle is also found in the LB (Article 40).[97]

Further undermining the usefulness of security interests, foreign creditors are not permitted to mortgage or pledge land use rights. Worse still, since state banks are entitled to set-off debts against bank account funds,[98] few recoverable assets are commonly available for secured, much less unsecured, private creditors.[99]

2.6 Creditors' Meetings

After satisfying itself that debtors have 'fallen into a state of bankruptcy', a court may postpone sequestration orders in favour of restoration orders (Article 68, LB). Courts then request debtors to present schemes of arrangement and/or business reconstructions to creditors' conferences (Article 64, LB). Creditors' conferences are composed of:

---

95 Ibid.

96 See Gide Loyrette-Nouel, 'The New Decree of Secured Transactions "A Promising Return"' (1999), 6 *Vietnam Law and Legal Forum* (64), 11–12; also see Skinner, S. (2000), 'A Small Step Forward, Two Giant Steps Back', *Vietnam Investment Review*, 21 February, 16–17.

97 Ibid.

98 Regulation on Short Term Credit 1994, Article 12.

99 See Kim Chi-My Hanh (1998), 'Protect Thyself', *Vietnam Economic News* (37), 18, 18–19.

- unsecured and partially secured creditors;
- owners or legal representatives of insolvent businesses; and
- labour representatives (Article 62, LB).

'Workout' or 'rescue' procedures in the LBB were loosely based on the French *Relative à la Prévention et au Réglement Amiables des Difficultés des Enterprise* (Act No. 85-98 for the Prevention and Amicable Settlement of Difficulties in Companies 25 January 1985).[100] But the provisions in the LB are much closer to Anglo-American practices (Article 69, LB).

Reconstruction proposals are required to include the following particulars:

- plans for the deferral, reduction, cancellation, purchase, or guarantee of debts; and
- solutions for restructuring business operations (including financial, management, technological and labour arrangements) to increase the capacity to service debts (Article 69, LB).

Courts are required to consider reconstruction proposals before they are submitted to a second creditors' conference for approval (Article 71, LB). Courts will not issue bankruptcy petitions until creditors have formally rejected reconstruction plans, giving debtors many opportunities to delay debt enforcement. For example, the approval of at least half of the creditors present (representing at least two thirds of the unsecured debt) is required to approve and reject reconstructions (Article 64, LB). During the currency of the reconstruction the debtor is treated as if it had not 'fallen into a state of bankruptcy' and directors and boards of management remain responsible for trading results (Article 77, LB).

Enterprises under reconstruction are given a maximum period of three years to regain solvency; if they fail, courts may issue sequestration orders and commence liquidation proceedings (Article 74, LB). In these circumstances bankruptcy assets are placed under the control of AMLTs (see below),[101] which administer both voluntary and involuntary bankruptcies.

3 Bankruptcy Regulation

3.1 Asset Recovery and Management

3.1.1 Powers and duties of Asset Management and Liquidation Teams (AMLTs)
The primary function of AMLTs is to safeguard bankruptcy assets (Article 10, LB).[102] Their main duties include:

---

100 See Ormesson D. *et al.* (1991), 'France', in L. Nelson (ed.), *Digest of Commercial Laws of the World*, New York: Oceana Publications, 104.

101 Law on Bankruptcy 2004, Article 10.

102 One of the leading drafters of the LBB erroneously asserted that 'in his relations with the Asset Management Team, the Judge has the decisive role'. See Hue, as note 32 above, 19.

- compiling inventories of bankruptcy assets;
- supervising, controlling and managing bankruptcy assets and, where necessary, requesting courts to take emergency measures to preserve assets; and
- testing the validity of creditors' proofs of debt.

Though analogous in some ways to trustees-in-bankruptcy in other jurisdictions, AMLTs do not act as receivers or managers for the bankrupt business.

3.1.2 Discovering assets Vietnam's cash economy frustrates the recovery of assets by AMLTs. Private business transactions in particular are predominantly conducted between family members or through networks comprising personalistic *tuong tro lan nhau* (mutual assistance) ties.[103] However strong its forces, the market economy has not destroyed communitarian, party, family and village affiliations, but rather it has accommodated them. Trust-based transactions rely on cash payments and are rarely formalized in writing.

Except where it is required by law, for example, the incorporation of companies,[104] businesses avoid banks. A business sector survey revealed that approximately 80 per cent of private enterprises relied on families and friends for finance.[105] There is little incentive to use alternatives to cash because cheques are only valid for 30 days, credit card transactions attract 4 per cent commission and electronic payment systems are embryonic. Finally, private companies rarely use accounting standards. The Law on Value Added Tax (VAT) 1997 may, however, induce more traders to keep paper records since numbered invoices issued by the government must be used to claim VAT paid on business-related goods and services (Article 11, VAT).

3.2 Debtors-in-Possession

The principle of 'debtors-in-possession', adopted by the LB, enables the owners and managers of insolvent enterprises to continue operating their businesses under the supervision of courts and AMLTs (Articles 10, 73, LB). The LB fails, however, to provide guidelines delineating the range of permitted activities. Economic court judges indicate that problems arise in the following areas:

---

103 Family and personal networks are highly secretive, designed to avoid government detection and gain competitive advantages over industry rivals. Interviews with Nguyen Trung Tuc, Director Industry Long Life Company, and Cong Ty Cong Nghiep Tuong Sinh, Chairman Viet-German Entrepreneurs Club, Hanoi, March, September 1999; Phan Van Hieu, Director Dainvest, Dia Hung Trading and Informatics Cong Ty, Hanoi, March 1999; Vu Duy Thai, Vice Chairman & Secretary The Hanoi Associations of Industry and Commerce, Hanoi, April 1999, February 2000; Nguyen Hoang Luu, Hiep Hoi Cac Doanh Nghiep Vua Va Nho Ha Noi, Hanoi Small and Medium Enterprises Council, General Secretary, Hanoi, April, October 1999, February 2000.

104 Enterprise Law 1999, Article 8.

105 See Webster, L. and Taussig, M. (1999), 'Vietnam's Undersized Engine: A Survey of 95 Larger Private Manufacturers' (unpublished paper), Hanoi: *Mekong Project Development Facility*, Discussion Paper No. 8, 32–35.

- the LB provides for the cancellation of leases where debtors are lessees, but makes no provision where debtors are lessors;
- though vaguely stipulating that during the bankruptcy period new debts arising from the business activities of the enterprise are to be settled under the court's supervision, the LB does not indicate whether debtors can raise finance to continue business operations.

3.3 Bankruptcy Declarations

Courts declare enterprises bankrupt where:

- debtors fail to rearrange enterprises in accordance with reconstruction agreements;
- debtors fail to comply with schemes of arrangement (Article 78, LB);
- creditors recommend immediate bankruptcy;
- enterprises are insolvent at the completion of reconstructions and/or schemes of arrangement; or
- enterprise owners abandon their businesses.

3.4 Effects of Bankruptcy

Once bankruptcy petitions are approved, court actions against insolvent enterprises are automatically 'stayed' and interest and principal payments on existing debts are frozen (Article 57, LB). The recently revised Civil Code now contains the procedures courts must follow in 'staying' debt recovery actions against insolvent enterprises. The Ordinance on Economic Contracts 1989 and Commercial Law 1997 do not contemplate bankruptcy.

The effects of bankruptcy on enterprise owners/managers are not particularly onerous. Chairpersons, general directors and board of management members are prohibited from holding similar positions for one to three years from the date of the bankruptcy declaration (Article 94, LB). This prohibition does not apply where:

- enterprises became bankrupt through force majeure;
- enterprise managers are not responsible for the bankruptcy;
- enterprise managers voluntarily petitioned for bankruptcy and paid all outstanding debts.

By allowing enterprise managers to escape punishment where insolvency is attributed to external forces (for example, force majeure), the law once again attempts to minimize the social stigma associated with bankruptcy.

3.5 Asset Recovery and Sale

3.5.1 Asset Management and Liquidation Teams Primary responsibility for recovering and realizing bankruptcy assets is devolved to AMLTs.[106] They are required to:

- receive assets surrendered to Asset Management Teams;
- recover assets, documents and accounting records belonging to bankrupt enterprises;
- detect and recover preferential payments (discussed below);
- freeze bank accounts;
- auction assets belonging to bankrupt enterprises;
- deposit auctioned proceeds in bank accounts established for that purpose; and
- distribute assets in accordance with court orders (Articles 10, 30, 44, LB).

3.5.2 What are bankruptcy assets? The definition of assets in the LB is primarily based on Anglo-American bankruptcy laws, but it also displays socialist property law influences. For example, land is not treated as a fixed asset and special provisions regulate assets advanced by the state to SOEs (Articles 36, 40, LB). Privately owned assets include those items familiar to Western creditors such as fixed and current assets, outstanding debts and loans, cash, company capital contributions, shares and other property interests. Assets belonging to SOEs and land use rights are considerably more difficult to ascertain. According to the Constitution 1992, SOE assets are owned by 'the people' and managed by SOEs on behalf of the state.[107] The Law on State-Owned Enterprises 2003 more precisely states that property under the management of SOEs, even assets technically owned by 'the people', are available to creditors.[108] '[C]apital is assigned by the State to enterprises to manage and use', together with powers that enable SOEs to borrow from, and give security interests to third party creditors. Only third party interests over 'important plant and equipment' requires the consent of state supervising authorities. In practice, this provision is frequently used to frustrate creditors. Fearing the loss of state assets, supervising authorities not infrequently pass regulations declaring certain SOE assets to be 'important plant and equipment'.

The rights of creditors to recover against debtors' land use rights (the highest form of land control) is equally controversial.[109] Improvements built upon land are available in bankruptcy, but uncertainty surrounds the substratum.[110] Local

---

106 Law on Bankruptcy 2004, Article 10.

107 Constitution 1992, Article 17. See Ngo Xuan Loc (1998), 'The Orientation of Renovation and Developing State-Owned Enterprises', *Tap Chi Cong San* (*Communist Review*) May, 17, 20–22; Beresford, M. (1993), 'Some Key Issues in the Reform of the North Vietnamese Industrial Sector', Canberra: Department of Social and Political Change, Australian National University, Working Paper No. 9, 7–8.

108 Also see Civil Code 1995, Articles 208–209.

109 The Civil Code suggests that only individuals and households may mortgage land use rights (articles 727–732).

110 Although Vietnamese law provides for outright ownership of houses and buildings, the Civil Code in articles 181, 205–207 does not authoritatively determine how such rights differ for land use rights.

government officials have an unfettered discretion over the transfer of commercial land use rights and as a corollary there is no guarantee that buildings owned by bankrupts are available to secured, much less unsecured, creditors. Adding to the impasse, receivership and mortgagee-in-possession rights are not recognized under Vietnamese law.

3.5.3 Asset valuation Under the LBB (Article 33) Asset Valuation Councils were formed to value bankruptcy assets. This role appears to have been transferred to the court in the LB (Article 38). How the courts will perform this onerous function has not been spelled out in the LB, and the details will presumably appear in a subsequent implementing decree. Asset Management and Liquidation Teams retain control over setting reserve prices for assets sold at public auctions (Article 10, LB).

3.6 Preferential Payments

Asset Management and Liquidation Teams may request courts to recover assets preferentially sold or transferred by debtors. Preferential payments are dispositions made within six months of the bankruptcy petition that satisfy one or more of the following criteria:

- conceal assets from creditors;
- pay debts prematurely;
- secure debts to defeat unsecured creditors;
- sell assets for less than their 'genuine value' (Articles 10, 43–45, LB).

As previously mentioned, one of the main difficulties facing bankruptcy courts and administrative bodies is distinguishing genuine commercial transactions from preferential dispositions. The LB prohibits and declares illegal all fraudulent conveyances or voidable transfers such as preferential mortgages and pledges and reductions or cancellations of debts (Article 43). But it lacks the guidelines judges require to differentiate preferential payments from *bona fide* transactions made in the ordinary course of business. Neither does it indicate whether *bona fide* purchasers of bankrupt assets take priority over unsecured creditors (Article 37). Finally, the LB penalizes directors and officials who have incurred debts knowing their enterprises were insolvent.

Worse still, some state authorities use administrative powers to gain preferential payments.[111] This typically occurs where people's committees stand to lose outstanding loan capital if the assets of bankrupt enterprises are distributed *pari passu* to competing unsecured creditors. Consider the case of the Long An Travel Agency, an insolvent SOE. During several years of trading the company accrued billions of dong (millions of dollars) in debts to 16 creditors. Trade creditors lodged a bankruptcy petition in the Vinh Long Provincial Court. Fearing substantial losses the Vinh Long People's Committee suggested that the Vinh Long Public Security Service arrest the Director of the Long An Travel Agency and sue him with the offence of

111 See Hoa, as note 79 above, 9–10.

'abusing trust to appropriate assets of the socialist republic and blockade the agency's assets.'[112] Evidently, the People's Committee was favoured with a preferential payment that went unchallenged by the court.

3.7 *Auctioning*

Bankruptcy assets are sold at state auction centres managed by judgment debt enforcement departments (Article 10, LB).[113] For a variety of cultural and economic reasons, auction centres have proved virtually unworkable.[114] First, auctioning is a relatively new concept in Vietnam and often fails to excite sufficient commercial interest to generate competitive bidding, resulting in sales well below market values. Second, the sale of real estate is especially difficult, since it is considered unlucky to live in houses previously owned by bankrupts. Third, agents acting for debtors sometimes disrupt actions by bidding over genuine purchasers, but later renege on their commitments. The penalty for failing to honour bids is only one per cent of the purchase price. Rather than selling on to the next highest bidder, new auctions are usually conducted months later, a practice that rewards collusive debtors with additional property rental. Fourth, vacant land cannot be transferred without the consent of housing and land departments and permission is rarely granted.

3.8 *Payment Priorities*

Secured creditors take priority over unsecured creditors in the distribution of bankruptcy assets. Unsecured creditors participate in the remaining assets (if any), in the following order:

- fees and expenses connected with bankruptcy proceedings;
- unpaid wages and employee entitlements;[115]
- unpaid taxes;
- pro rata distribution to other proved creditors according to the respective value of outstanding indebtedness (Article 37, LB).

Remaining assets are paid to enterprise members in proportion to their respective capital contribution (or share entitlement) or to the State Bank in the case of bankrupt SOEs.

---

112 Ibid.

113 Also see Decree No. 189-CP on Implementation of Law on Business Bankruptcy 1994, Article 34; Decree No. 86 CP on Property Auctioning 1996, Articles 1, 4–6.

114 See Thon, as note 76 above; interview with Hoang Tho Khiem, Director, Department of Civil Judgment Enforcement Management, Hanoi, February 2000.

115 See Labour Code.

4 Winding Up Procedures

4.1 Winding Up Private Companies and Enterprises

Private companies and enterprises are wound up in the following circumstances:

- business objectives have been completed;
- company members or proprietors of private enterprises pass termination resolutions;
- outstanding debts and labour obligations are settled;[116]
- membership drops below prescribed minimums for six consecutive months;
- government authorities withdraw certificates of business registration.[117]

Copies of termination resolutions/decisions must be circulated to the Business Registrar, creditors and other outstanding claimants. Notification must also be publicly posted at the enterprise's head office and published in local and national daily newspapers in three consecutive issues.

Enterprises are required to inform the Business Registrar, within six months of the termination resolution, whether outstanding obligations have been discharged. Dissolution may commence once the name of the enterprise is removed from the business registration book.

Where enterprises are unable to satisfy debtor claims they must petition for bankruptcy.[118] Given the uncertainty and delays surrounding bankruptcy proceedings, insolvent foreign investment enterprises usually 'disband' under administrative directions. According to Ministry of Planning and Investment sources, following the Asian financial crisis, more than 400 insolvent foreign-investment enterprises and thousands of domestic enterprises have 'disbanded' without petitioning for bankruptcy.[119]

4.2 Winding Up State-owned Enterprises

SOEs are liquidated where:

- business objectives have been completed;
- businesses have been making losses for protracted periods with little prospect of solvency;
- enterprises are unable to implement duties assigned by the state;
- the work of enterprises is no longer essential.[120]

---

116 Enterprise Law 1999, Article 112(1) (b–d).

117 Id. Article 111.

118 Id. Article 113.

119 See Vu Long, as note 2 above; Kim Chi, as note 2 above; Vision and Associates (2000), 'Legislation Muddles Liquidation Process', *Vietnam Investment Review*, 6 March, 16.

120 Law on State Enterprise 2002.

The state supervisory authorities that established SOEs in the first instance are responsible for deciding whether insolvent state enterprises should liquidate. Supervisory authorities must first gather, and then consider, advice given by AMLTs.[121] Once liquidation decisions are made, SOEs are either referred to the Central Steering Standing Committee for Debt Solvency or the economic courts for bankruptcy under the LB (Article 87).

4.3 Bankruptcy Liquidation

When civil judgment enforcement departments decide that all creditors' claims have been satisfied or that further action to recover assets is unwarranted, notification is sent to business registration authorities to strike the bankrupt enterprise from the Business Registry.[122]

5 Conclusion

Transplanted bankruptcy rules have so far failed to take root in Vietnam. Nowhere is this more convincingly illustrated than in the declining number of bankruptcy cases at the very time when market mechanisms are more deeply entrenched than ever before, and non-performing loans are proliferating.[123] Research data is insufficiently developed to reach definitive conclusions, but enough is known to speculate that this failure is partially ascribable to three facets of Vietnamese state and society.

First, Western bankruptcy norms were designed to address insolvency in advanced capitalist markets and they conflict with Vietnamese perceptions about affective socialist-oriented market economies. Western notions that market forces should determine bankruptcy presuppose a political economy characterized by legal equality and the devolution of economic decision-making from the state to private economic players. Although the 9th Party Congress in 2002 recognized private enterprise as 'an integral part of the national economy', there are few signs that the party accepts the principle that markets should determine bankruptcy. The party and state still actively use 'state economic management' powers to ensure that private rights (including creditors' rights) do not challenge the economic domination of SOEs. From a Vietnamese perspective, imported principles are not politically attuned to the social and economic problems of bankruptcy, and only administrative measures are considered sufficiently flexible to deal with these highly contextual issues. Official preference for situational discretion, rather than universal, normative solutions echoes pre-colonial techniques of commercial regulation. These deeply rooted attitudes will take much longer to change than government policy.

---

121 Id. Article 23.

122 The Business Registry is controlled by the Ministry of Planning and Investment and has offices in provincial/city people's committees. Enterprise Law 1999, Article 116; Law on State Enterprises 1995, Article 17.

123 See Ha Thang (2000), 'State Squares up to Growing Debt', *Vietnam Investment Review*, 6 March, 1, 4; Kim Diep (1997), 'Commercial Stock Banks Riddled with Bad Debt', *Vietnam Courier*, 5 October, 10.

Second, administrative structures in Vietnam differ significantly from those supporting Western bankruptcy laws. Although the LB gives courts more discretionary powers than the LBB, it still grafts market-based bankruptcy principles onto a 'state economic management' system originally designed to administer a Soviet-style command economy. Bureaucratic bodies such as AMLTs exercise broad discretionary powers over bankruptcy. In fact, most insolvencies involving SOEs bypass the courts entirely and are resolved administratively by the Central Steering Standing Committee for Debt Solvency.

Bureaucratic discretion is undoubtedly an effective mechanism for reconciling imported legal norms with local precepts and practices. But ad hoc administrative solutions produce situationally valid outcomes that have not generated the universal principles that judges and bureaucrats need to uniformly apply bankruptcy rules. Frustrated by the lack of workable guidelines, courts frequently use criminal proceedings to investigate preferential payments and fraudulent asset transfers. In the end, even the courts treat bankruptcy as an administrative exercise, and rarely use imported legal principles to adjust the interests of creditors and debtors.

Third, the market institutions and political economy that support bankruptcy practices in the West are either non-existent or function differently in Vietnam. For example, the Western notion that bankruptcy releases inefficient assets for more productive purposes has little resonance in an economy where the main purpose of production is to employ SOE workers or family members. Similarly, imported bright-line distinctions between enterprises and employees are subverted by entrenched local creeds such as moral property rights and the social obligations of SOEs. Finally, Vietnam lacks the market support agencies such as insolvency practitioners, auditors, receivers and auctioneers that make bankruptcy work in the West.

The LB forms part of a broader legal harmonization project. Proponents of transplanted legal development, such as the World Bank, United Nations Development Program and Asian Development Bank (ADB),[124] argue that as law becomes a more sophisticated regulator of commerce, it also becomes more remote from its host culture. In its extreme form, some postulate a future where a single translational jurisdiction emerges as national legal systems wither away.[125] It is a small step from this vision of global equivalence and convergence to the assumption that legal transplants no longer convey ideology and culture from one society to another, but rather are a series of technical adjustments between legal systems. The legal harmonization project has clearly influenced the LB, which, in line with Western facilitative legal systems, has begun shifting discretionary power from the government to the courts.[126]

---

124 For an example of the transplant model of law reform see UNDP (1999), 'Completion of Viet Nam's Legal Framework for Economic Development', Hanoi: UNDP Discussion Paper 2.

125 See generally Cappelletti, M. *et al.* (1986), 'Introduction', in Mauro Cappelletti *et al.* (eds), *Integration through Law: Europe and the American Experience.*

126 The ADB made the advance of a structural adjustment loan conditional on the enactment of a new bankruptcy law. Despite Vietnamese resistance that delayed signing for twelve months, the enactment of a new Bankruptcy Law, that reportedly will grant automatic liquidation of companies unable to repay debts within a prescribed time, is a release condition of the second tranche.

Working at the interface between imported laws, legal institutions and business practices, some multilateral donors,[127] bilateral donors[128] and researchers[129] believe that effective lawmaking must comprehend and accommodate differences in the ideological, institutional and cultural composition of donor and host countries. This nuanced approach to law reform rejects as simplistic the comparativist assumptions that legal systems in all societies face similar problems and legal drafters need only find external solutions to internal problems.[130] In order to make the LB more effective than its predecessor, judges and AMLTs should work hard to ensure that insolvency principles broadly reflect local market conditions.

127 See, for example, Webster and Taussig, as note 105 above; MPI-UNIDO, Research Report: Improving Macroeconomic Policy and Reforming Administrative Procedures to Promote Development of Small and Medium Enterprises in Vietnam, Hanoi (January 1999).

128 See, for example, Bring, O., Gunnarsson, C. and Mellbourn, A. (1998), 'Viet Nam: Democracy and Human Rights' (unpublished report), Swedish International Development Agency.

129 Bergling P. (1997), 'Theory and Reality in Legal Co-operation – the Case of Vietnam', in Per Sevastil (ed.), *Legal Assistance to Developing Countries*, Stockholm: Kluwer Law, 61–80; John Gillespie (1999), 'Law and Development in "The Market Place": An East Asian Perspective', in K. Jayasuriya (ed.), *Law, Capitalism and Power in Asia*, London: Routledge, 118–150.

130 See Zweigert, K. and Hein, K. (1987), *Introduction to Comparative Law* (2nd edn, trans. German edition by Tony Weir), Oxford: Clarendon Press, 36–48.

Chapter 8

Insolvency Law in Laos

TERRY REID
La Trobe University, Melbourne

1 Introduction

The Lao People's Democratic Republic has undergone a significant transformation in the past decade. The transformation has resulted in a shift from a centrally planned economy to a market-oriented economy. This has resulted in a major upheaval of not only the economy but also the legal system, with the latter providing the fundamental supporting structure to the new economic framework.

The most significant historical event in the recent history of Laos has been the implementation of the new economic mechanism (NEM). The NEM was the statement made by the government, which heralded in a raft of economic changes. It was clear that to ensure the transition from a planned to a market economy, the legal system would need to be completely overhauled. It was, in fact, a case of starting from scratch and developing new laws and principles at a rapid rate. The most important step was made in 1991 with the adoption of a new constitution.[1] The constitution was to provide the impetus for private sector investment and it provides a clear basis for the adoption of laws which will enhance the reform process.

The law-making structure attempts to establish a hierarchical arrangement. The constitution provides the base and is the supreme law of Laos. The National Assembly has the power under the constitution to make laws.[2] The President of the State is able to issue a state law between sessions of the National Assembly.[3] Such a law would then require ratification at the next session. The most common form of rule takes the form of a decree. The Council of Ministers, individual ministries or other agencies issue decrees.[4] They are issued and are considered a 'test-run' of a law. The decree has force, as if it were a law, and during the testing period, inconsistencies and loopholes are determined and opinion is gauged in order to produce a modified law that is effective in its application. Often decrees will continue in force for long periods of time without becoming laws. The potential problem of conflict has not been addressed in the constitution and does not appear to have manifested itself at this stage.

---

1 The National Assembly passed the Constitution of the Lao People's Democratic Republic on 14 August 1991.

2 Section IV, Articles 40–51.

3 Article 53.

4 Article 57.

Aside from the laws and decrees, agencies and ministries will draft and adopt their own regulations. These regulations allow for the practical implementation of the laws and decrees. They are intended to be operational in nature but this has generated some difficulties. Often regulations are drafted which conflict with the laws and there is no form of resolution of that conflict. Limitations and inconsistencies within the laws and decrees often hamper practices outlined in the regulations. Although regulations can be very helpful, they appear on occasion to be given only cursory consideration by the ministry or agency responsible for their implementation.

Of the above, only the laws and decrees are published and many are not translated or distributed to the public. Therefore, those wishing to access the current laws and decrees will find it difficult unless they seek assistance from local law firms.[5] The introduction of an Official Gazette was commenced in 1993. The objective was to publish the laws and decrees as they were passed in the Lao, English and French languages. The introduction added to the national dissemination of laws and decrees. The Swedish International Development Authority (SIDA) under the 'strengthening the rule of law project' supported the Official Gazette. Unfortunately a withdrawal of funding has brought a halt to the publication of the Gazette and after a few issues its future is in doubt.

A clear programme of laws and decrees has been established. Since 1990 a number of laws and decrees have been enacted which are of particular significance to the economy. These include the Contract Law,[6] Property Law,[7] Inheritance Law,[8] Insurance Law,[9] Labour Law,[10] the Code of Civil Procedure,[11] Business Law,[12] Secured Transactions Law,[13] Bankruptcy Law,[14] Decree on the Settlement of Economic Disputes[15] and Foreign Investment Law.[16]

It is clear from the preceding discussion that the legal framework in Laos is in its infancy. The laws/decrees are very new and a review of them reveals a very rudimentary structure. It is especially relevant to our discussion to highlight the absence of any well-developed jurisprudence. Given the early stages of the development this absence of jurisprudence is not surprising. The courts are finding it difficult to absorb the raft of new laws and decrees and at the same time are having to develop their own methods of legal reasoning. There has been a stark absence of training for the judiciary and this has also impeded the introduction of any jurisprudence. At this stage reliance is almost entirely on the written laws, and issues which arise on interpretation are still to be determined. As the courts come to grips

5 A handful of local law firms operate out of Vientiane.
6 Adopted 27 June 1990.
7 Adopted 27 June 1990.
8 Adopted 27 June 1990.
9 Adopted 29 November 1990.
10 No 24/PR adopted 21 April 1994.
11 Adopted 29 November 1990.
12 No. 3/94 adopted 18 July 1994.
13 No. 07/94 adopted 14 October 1994.
14 No. 06/94 adopted 14 October 1994.
15 No. 106/PM dated 15 July 1994.
16 Adopted 23 March 2001.

with interpretation and enforcement, there will still be a need to report their decisions so the law is able to develop in a formal manner.

The removal of the control economy and decision-making structure has required the Lao people to make huge adjustments and this has impacted on their traditional cultural values. The traditional manner of holding property has been on a collective basis and under the new regime there is a move to establish clear property rights, which will be upheld by the legal system. The establishment of property rights is taking time to achieve and often individuals will fall back on more traditional ways of doing things. Making a claim to the courts to enforce a property right is foreign to the traditional Lao culture and there is much reluctance to do this. The aid agencies that have supported financial sector reform in Laos have certainly impressed upon the banks the need to enforce their rights against individuals and using the court structure to do this. They have been encouraged to formalise arrangements with appropriate documentation and if there is a breach of agreement, then claims must be made to the courts to uphold the agreements, thus ensuring recovery of any outstanding loans and so on. The banks have not found the current system to be very supportive of their agreements with customers and invariably they are unable to enforce their rights. The courts find in favour of recalcitrant debtors on the basis that it would be unjust to disadvantage an individual or family in favour of a much larger and more powerful financial institution.

A common dilemma facing the supporters of the new legal framework and the drafters of new laws is the general resistance to change by the Lao people. It has already been stated that the shift to individual, enforceable property rights is proving difficult. There is a constant reference to the Lao way of doing things and this is proving to be a major stumbling block to the success of any reform.[17]

The Insolvency Regime

The insolvency regime in Laos is very rudimentary. As stated, there is a clear reliance on the passed laws and decrees and no jurisprudence to support these laws and decrees or to give some credibility and confidence in the system. The key laws and decrees which will be considered are the Bankruptcy Law, the Secured Transactions Law, the Business Law and the Decree regarding the Implementation of the Business Law. The provisions outline a very bare structure and individuals relying on them are finding that these provisions need constant revision and judicial interpretation which is not occurring at this stage.

As stated earlier, it is very difficult to obtain official translations of relevant laws and those conducting business in Laos rely heavily upon unofficial translations.[18]

---

17 There is little written on Lao customs and traditions; however, it would appear that Lao people are not motivated by an overriding desire to alter their position or to change their lifestyle in any significant manner. This impedes acceptance of new laws as there is no perceived need for them and therefore to comply with them seems pointless to the majority of Lao people.

18 This includes aid agencies. They have had many laws and decrees translated but these do not amount to official translations, as in most cases the government does not have the funding available to have all the laws translated. There is currently no central public repository of laws in Laos.

The substantive information provided in this chapter has been based on unofficial translations of the relevant laws and decrees.

The key law is the Bankruptcy Law and it has as its objective the overall promotion of investment in Laos and the assistance of socio-economic development.[19] It provides a regulatory base for the conduct of business, together with other relevant laws and decrees.[20] The Bankruptcy Law aims to protect creditors, debtor enterprises[21] and the government from companies who may be trading whilst insolvent and as such it provides for winding up and other methods of resolving difficulties a company may be experiencing.[22] It is rather difficult to find a precise definition of bankruptcy in the Law and it would appear that a bankrupt enterprise would be one which is unable to meet its financial commitments. This will arise out of an enterprise suffering losses and having utilised all available financial resources.[23] The Bankruptcy Law applies to all enterprises registered under Lao law[24] and both creditor and debtor enterprises have the right to file a petition for bankruptcy.[25]

There are no provisions under Lao law that deal with personal insolvency. All of the regulatory structures which have been put in place relate to the insolvency of enterprises as defined under the Business Law. There is an underlying theme in the constitution to protect workers and individuals and it will probably be some time before the government moves to introduce laws that cover personal insolvency issues.

2 Corporate Insolvency Rules

The Bankruptcy Law provides a range of options for creditors and debtors who wish to take some action regarding the solvency of a particular enterprise. As stated above, the action may be taken by a creditor or debtor by filing an appropriate petition. The options available under the Law are mediation, control of the enterprise assets and management of the affairs by an Assets Control Committee, reorganisation of the enterprise and a court judgment of bankruptcy and subsequent liquidation. Each of these mechanisms will be considered in the following discussion.

There is some evidence of the use of informal mechanisms to deal with an enterprise which may be having difficulty meeting its financial commitments. The

---

19 Bankruptcy Law, Section 1 (General Provisions) Article 1.

20 Above, page 272.

21 The law relating to the establishment of enterprise in Laos is the Business Law and the Decree regarding the Implementation of the Business Law. The broad categories of enterprise are: partnership companies (Business Law Articles 38–44), limited liability companies (Business Law, Articles 45–59) and public companies (Business Law Articles 60–76). There are also state-owned enterprises (Business Law Articles 77–87) and state mixed enterprises (Business Law Articles 88–94). The Bankruptcy Law does not contain a definition of enterprise and it is presumed that enterprise refers to those established under the Business Law. It should be noted that there are no instances of any state-owned enterprises being dealt with under the Bankruptcy Law.

22 Bankruptcy Law, Article 1.

23 Article 2.

24 Article 3.

25 Below at section 3.

reason for this is the lack of confidence in the courts to reach a solution that will be beneficial to the creditor. There is a great deal of nervousness by creditors who wish to enforce their rights under both the Bankruptcy Law and the Secured Transactions Law.[26] Often these informal methods are agreements that postpone payment or provide for additional security. In Laos there is a tendency to postpone payment rather than take action under the law. This is attributed to the general attitudes relating to loans and contractual obligations. There appears to be a clash between traditional Lao values and a new market-oriented commercialism.[27] There are obviously not a lot of benefits in postponing payment as it invariably will lead to the creditor being under more pressure and in most situations the debt will not be reduced or repaid.

There is no voluntary administration in Laos, as exists in some other jurisdictions, but there is a system of mediation, which has been created under the Bankruptcy Law.[28] This is seen as being a relatively positive feature of the Law as it supports traditional values and is intended to encourage individuals to use the Law to support what might otherwise be an informal method. The application to conduct a mediation is made by the enterprise, which is subject to the bankruptcy petition. The Law allows the court to determine, on the evidence provided, whether mediation is appropriate. The Law does not, however, provide the court with any guidelines as to the situations where mediation should be carried out. The primary objective of mediation is to try and establish a repayment programme which will have the effect of expediting a settlement of the debt between the petitioning creditor and the debtor enterprise.

The court will appoint mediators; no number is set down in the Law, nor are there criteria for selection of mediators. It is understood that the mediators will be prominent businesspersons or government officials with no interest in the transactions which affect the parties and who have no financial interests in the debtor or creditor. There is a sophisticated process, which exists under the Decree for Settlement of Economic Disputes, which provides for selection of mediators.[29] These provisions are not applied *mutatis mutandis* in the Bankruptcy Law. The mediation must be kept confidential and whilst the mediators are dealing with the matter all court proceedings relating to the bankruptcy petition will be suspended. The Law does not consider how any subsequent petition which may be lodged by another creditor will affect the mediation. It would be hoped that the fresh creditor would join the mediation process and be a party to any repayment scheme.[30] If an agreement is reached between the debtor and creditor the petition will lapse and the debtor will continue business as usual, adhering to the agreement. If the parties are unable to reach an agreement, the court will then consider the bankruptcy petition; this will also occur if there is an agreement and there is a failure on the part of the debtor to meet

---

26 Banks who have often, unsuccessfully, sought to enforce their rights as a secured creditor under both the Bankruptcy Law and the Secured Transactions Law raise this concern. The Secured Transactions Law is currently under revision.

27 As noted in the first part of this chapter.

28 Bankruptcy Law, Articles 12–13.

29 See Decree for Settlement of Economic Disputes, Article 22.

30 Bankruptcy Law, Article 12.

their obligations under the mediation agreement. An Assets Control Committee will at that time be appointed to control the assets of the debtor.[31]

3 Court-based Schemes of Administration, Reconstruction or Arrangement

Under Article 24, a creditors' meeting, which will be conducted as a duty of the court when determining a bankruptcy petition,[32] may propose to reorganise the enterprise.[33] The proposal to the court to reorganise shall be by agreement of creditors with not less than two thirds of the total outstanding debt.[34] At the creditors' meeting the enterprise representative[35] has an opportunity to convince creditors that reorganisation of the enterprise will be to their advantage[36] and any subsequent agreement to reorganise may be given court approval. If the court endorses the recommendation of the creditors' meeting for a reorganisation, it is the responsibility of the enterprise representative to draft the implementation plans, which will bring about the reorganisation.[37] The court may, at this stage, modify any proposal it has had placed before it and the enterprise representative will be forced to modify any plan to ensure it complies with the court order.

If the court approves the proposal for reorganisation, creditors will be obliged to comply with the proposal and there is an obligation placed on creditors under the Bankruptcy Law to supervise the reorganisation. This obligation has the potential to raise many problems; however, the intention is probably more one of assistance and cooperation rather than a policing of the reorganisation process.[38] The maximum term allowed for any reorganisation is two years and during this time the enterprise will have to be seen to be making progress in the reorganisation and meeting the objectives established under the reorganisation order.[39] The court reserves the right to cancel the order at any time it considers the order is not being complied with and the enterprise is not undergoing the reorganisation.[40]

To ensure the success of the reorganisation a number of changes may occur within the enterprise and these may be relatively cosmetic and allow for the legal support of

---

31 Article 13.

32 See Article 14.

33 Under Article 24, a creditors' meeting may propose that the court consider reorganisation of the enterprise, sale of the activities or bankruptcy and liquidation.

34 Article 25.

35 Throughout the Bankruptcy Law, there is common usage of the terms 'enterprise owner' or 'enterprise representative'. In many cases the bankruptcy petition against the enterprise will involve a one-person limited liability company which is a common business entity in Laos. The requirements of a one-person limited liability company are established under the Business Law, Articles 57–59.

36 The role of the enterprise representative is outlined in Article 23 of the Bankruptcy Law, which establishes the obligations of the debtor enterprise at a creditors' meeting.

37 Article 26.

38 Article 27.

39 Article 31.

40 Article 32, If an enterprise is adjudged bankrupt for failure to comply with a reorganisation order the creditors will assume all the rights set down under the bankruptcy provisions, see Articles 35–46.

the reorganised structure. For example a change to the Articles of Association may be required to ensure the new structure meets all legal requirements.[41] There are also provisions which relate to assets and capital of the enterprise. There is a blanket restriction on an enterprise transferring any of its assets which are essential to its business; court approval will be required if such assets are to be sold.[42] It may also be necessary to make changes to the capital structure of the enterprise following the order for reorganisation.[43] The increase in capital may be achieved by increasing the value of the shares, making a creditor a shareholder, increasing the total amount of shares or by loan. There is no reference to enterprises complying with the provisions in the Business Law which cover changes in structure but it is assumed that any such changes would be recorded with the appropriate government agency, thus complying with the Business Law.[44]

Under Section IV of the Bankruptcy Law, which covers enterprise reorganisation, there exist provisions relating to the sale of assets. These seem at odds with the reorganisation process. Article 33 states that an individual or business entity may at any time from the date of a court order, for the management or control of the debtor enterprise assets, submit a proposal for purchase of the assets.[45] There is a requirement that the court ensure that the purchaser is able to complete the transaction and if the sale is completed the purchaser is free to on-sell to another party.[46] As stated, this Article seems to run contrary to any agreement to reorganise. It is probably intended that a sale will only occur if there is agreement by all parties to the reorganisation or if the reorganisation process has failed and sale then becomes an option. To approve plans to sell after there has been agreement to reorganise would make reorganisation an unattractive and uncertain option.

4 Winding Up Procedures

In Laos there are a number of options available to courts when dealing with insolvent enterprises. The following are the options: mediation,[47] appointment of an Assets Control Committee,[48] reorganisation,[49] bankruptcy and appointment of a Liquidation Committee.[50]

---

41 Article 29 of the Bankruptcy Law. The requirements relating to an enterprise's Articles of Association are established under the Business Law, Article 27, and registration of the Articles is mandatory under the Decree regarding the Implementation of the Business Law dated 1 February 1996, Article 13.

42 Bankruptcy Law, Article 28.

43 Article 30.

44 The Business Law, Article 28. The changes to capital under the Bankruptcy Law mirror those outlined in the Business Law, Article 29.

45 This may include a portion of the assets; see Bankruptcy Law, Article 33.

46 Article 34.

47 As noted in the first part of section 2.

48 Bankruptcy Law Articles 15–18.

49 Articles 26–34.

50 Articles 35–46.

Bankruptcy Petitions

Under Section II of the Bankruptcy Law both creditors and debtors may file petitions for bankruptcy and there are strict provisions to be complied with in terms of the filing. A creditor is able to file a petition under Article 6. There is no standard form included in the Bankruptcy Law but the Article states that the petition must indicate the name and address of the creditor as well as the name and place of business of the debtor enterprise. The creditor must attach to the petition documentation that proves that there are obligations owed to the creditor, as well as demand notices, which have been forwarded and not complied with by the debtor. There is no stipulation on the number of demands sent or the form of such demands, but given the overall attitude of the courts to enforcement of obligations it would be reasonable to expect that considerable leeway has been given to the debtor with no results for the creditor. This general approach may change, as courts become more familiar with the Law and as attitudes change to debt and repayment in general. The creditor will pay any fees associated with the filing of the petition and these will be determined under the Law on Court Fees.

A debtor may also file a petition and the documentation which needs to accompany the request differs from that required of a creditor.[51] The request provides the name and location of the enterprise as well as the name and address of the owner or the representative of the enterprise. In most cases it will be the owner where it is a one-person limited liability company and a representative when there is more than one shareholder. The petition must have attached documentation which indicates the financial difficulties of the enterprise. These documents could include demand letters from creditors but must also include documents showing the enterprise has attempted to resolve its financial problems. This may include correspondence with financial institutions and so on. For companies with more than one shareholder there must be an attached memorandum of a general meeting which resolves to file a petition to have the enterprise adjudged bankrupt. A full schedule of assets and liabilities must be completed for the last two years. As with the creditor's petition, the debtor will pay any fees required, as established under the Law on Court Fees.

The court will accept petitions for bankruptcy when all the documentation has been submitted in accordance with the Law[52] and the person filing has standing to file.[53] Upon receiving a creditor's petition to sue, the court will inform the applicant creditor of its decision to consider the petition within seven days of receipt.[54] The court will also inform the debtor, attaching a copy of the creditor's petition. The debtor will have 15 days from receipt of the court notice to forward a report to the court outlining its ability to settle its debts. The court must have a full hearing to consider the petition within 30 days of its acceptance of the petition.

In the case of a debtor's petition, the court will decide within seven days whether to accept the petition for consideration. The court has a further seven days to inform all

---

51 Bankruptcy Law, Article 7.

52 Articles 6 and 7.

53 Article 8.

54 Article 10.

creditors in writing of the petition and its decision to consider the petition. As with the creditor's petition the full hearing must be heard within 35 days of the decision to accept the petition.

There exists a general liability for petitioners under the Law,[55] although its precise effect is a little unclear. If a petition to have an enterprise adjudged bankrupt does not have sufficient merit and the purpose of the petition is to cause harm to the debtor, the petitioner will be dealt with according to the law. The intention of this Article is to ensure frivolous or malicious petitions are avoided. There exists no penalty provision in the Law, which indicates how the petitioner will be dealt with according to the law. There is a strong possibility that the courts may exercise discretion in dealing with such a petition. There is a possibility that the courts view defendants in actions in a more favourable light than applicants in such situations as this seems to have some support in the constitution and according to identified practice.[56]

Consideration of the Petition

Section III of the Bankruptcy Law covers the process dealing with petitions. The mediation of such petitions has been considered earlier.[57] The court has imposed on it several rights and duties under the Law.[58] These duties include the collection of documents and any evidence necessary for consideration of the petition and the determination of temporary measures, which may assist in the protection of the debtor enterprise and the control of creditors' meetings. The court also has the jurisdiction to suspend, at any time, the consideration of the petition and when it reaches its decision it is able to announce the bankruptcy of the debtor, if it reaches such a decision. The court has a legal obligation to check on the activities of those appointed to manage or control the assets of the debtor.

The Bankruptcy Law does not provide for receivership in the traditional sense but it does allow for the control of assets by a committee known as the Assets Control Committee.[59] In many ways this committee operates as a receiver would in many common law jurisdictions. The court will give consent to the assets of the debtor being managed by the committee; the power to do this is not clearly outlined in the Law[60] and the pre-existing criteria which will give rise to the court making this decision are not clearly established. The decision to appoint an Assets Control Committee will be made by the court when it is considering the petition and provides a further option to assist the parties to resolve the financial difficulties of the debtor enterprise.[61]

---

55 Article 9.

56 The Constitution supports an approach which offers support for workers on the basis of general humaneness.

57 Articles 12–13 and above pages 274–275.

58 Article 14.

59 Articles 15–18.

60 Article 16 refers to the situation following the court's decision to allow control of the assets to the Assets Control Committee.

61 Although the court may appoint the committee following its deliberations on a petition, it may be requested by a creditors' meeting if that meeting is convened outside the jurisdiction of the committee

The Assets Control Committee is comprised of one employee of the court (as chairperson), a creditors' representative, a representative of the debtor enterprise, a trade union representative, a representative of the debtor enterprise's workers and an employee of a finance/accountancy firm.[62] It is interesting to note that two of the six members will be representatives of the workers. This is in line with the support for the workers of the state and supported by the constitution and the lenient line that the courts may take when considering the welfare of ordinary citizens in litigation.

Having approved of the composition of the committee the court requires the committee to report and take responsibility for its performance in dealing with the assets.[63] The debtor enterprise is able to continue trading under the supervision of the committee and the court. There are strict restrictions placed on the assets themselves.[64] Assets cannot be hidden or moved, they cannot be transferred or sold. There is also a requirement that if there is any unpaid capital registered against the company then the subscribers must pay the capital in full within 15 days of the receipt of a notice informing them of the appointment of an Assets Control Committee.

The overall objective of the committee is to manage the assets so as to provide for repayment of debts and a best-case scenario would be to allow the enterprise to trade out of its difficulties. There are clear rights and duties placed on the committee to ensure a responsible practice of trading and disposal. These consist of the following:

- keeping records and accounting for all of the debtor enterprise's assets
- inspection and control of the assets: there may be instances where the committee makes application to the court to assist in the protection of assets
- drawing up a list of creditors and debts outstanding
- making a media declaration announcing the control of the debtor enterprise's assets and advising a date and time whereby creditors are able to make claims for repayment of their debts.[65]

The expenses of the committee will be met by the debtor enterprise and, as stated, the committee will be responsible to the court for its handling of the assets.[66]

The assets, which will be controlled by the committee, include all of the assets of the debtor enterprise; the fixed and movable assets, which will include leased property, cash and assets contributed as capital and receivables.[67] Where the assets belong to an enterprise which is a partnership company or a one-person limited liability company, the committee shall exempt personal goods from control.[68] The

---

where there is a group representing at least a quarter of the total outstanding debts of the enterprise. See Article 20.

62 Bankruptcy Law, Article 15.

63 There does not exist in the Bankruptcy Law a description of the practical aspect of appointment of the committee. It may be a completely arbitrary process by the court, although it may solicit recommendations from various groups; this is unclear.

64 Bankruptcy Law Article 16.

65 Bankruptcy Law, Article 18.

66 Ibid.

67 Article 17.

68 Ibid.

definition of personal goods is not included in the Law; however, there exists a value limitation of Kip 200,000.[69] There exists no article, either in the Business Law or the Bankruptcy Law, which outlines the status of the board of directors or manager in respect of the assets once an Assets Control Committee is appointed. It is assumed that the judicial appointment of the committee would mean that it makes all decisions regarding the assets of the enterprise and the board may continue to exist but would be obliged to act according to directives issued by the committee on matters that concern the enterprise's assets.

Creditors' Meetings

A function of the Assets Control Committee is to call a creditors' meeting,[70] although creditors may also call a meeting if the number making the request total a quarter of the debts outstanding by the debtor enterprise. The notice of the meeting, together with the agenda, must be sent to all those participating at least three days before the meeting is scheduled. A meeting shall be held when over half of the creditors participating represent no less than two thirds of the total debt. It should also be noted that, in addition to creditors, other participants at a creditors' meeting include a representative of the debtor enterprise, a representative of the trade union and a representative of the enterprise workers.[71]

The primary objective of the creditors' meeting is to consider the adoption of any proposal to reorganise the enterprise and to inspect and submit opinions to the court regarding the division of the enterprise's assets where no reorganisation is agreed to.[72] A creditors' meeting may also be suspended where there are insufficient creditors to ensure a quorum,[73] or where there is a majority of the creditors present (provided they represent at least two thirds of the total amount of debt) that decide, by majority, to suspend the meeting.[74] It is a mandatory requirement under the Bankruptcy Law that a representative of the debtor enterprise be present at all creditors' meetings.[75] The representative's responsibility is to answer questions from all those authorised to attend the meeting, as well as explaining any proposals for reorganisation, mediation, or any other undertakings the enterprise is proposing. Following the creditors' meeting a recommendation may be put to the court and this may consist of a recommendation to reorganise the enterprise, sell the enterprise as a going concern or bankrupt and liquidate the enterprise.[76] Any agreement reached by the creditors' meeting shall only be effective if agreed by a majority of the representatives who

69 The kip is the unit of currency used in Laos and, at August 2005, 10,100 kip was equivalent to one US dollar. It should be noted that at the time the Bankruptcy Law was passed, one US dollar was equivalent to 500 kip.

70 Bankruptcy Law, Article 20.

71 Article 19.

72 Article 21.

73 See Articles 20 and 22.

74 Article 22.

75 Articles 19 and 23.

76 Article 24.

have no less than two thirds of the total debt.[77] A formal resolution must be passed; it appears on a strict interpretation of the Law that representatives will only be able to take part in a vote at a creditors' meeting if they can be defined as creditors. This makes it unclear as to the precise rights of the workers and trade union representatives. Presumably they will be able to vote if monies are owed to workers as creditors.

Bankruptcy

Following consideration of the petition, the court will adjudge an enterprise bankrupt in the following situations:

- there exist no plans for the reorganisation of the enterprise
- an enterprise representative is unable to meet its obligations at a creditors' meeting as set down in Article 23
- the creditors' meeting fails to accept any proposal by the enterprise to reorganise the enterprise
- the period for reorganisation has passed, the operations are still unprofitable and an application is made by the creditors for bankruptcy of the enterprise
- the enterprise is in breach of its reorganisation arrangement; the breach should be a serious one
- the owner of the enterprise cannot be located or is deceased and the successor either rejects the succession or no successor exists.[78]

The above indicate that failure to comply with any arrangements constitutes the main cause for the court adjudging an enterprise bankrupt. The grounds are set down in Article 35 and presumably the court will find that the enterprise is unable to meet its financial obligations as they fall due. The Law has provided ample opportunity to make alternative arrangements in the form of mediation, control by the Assets Control Committee and reorganisation. Failure to adopt an alternative will result in a declaration of bankruptcy by the court and subsequent liquidation. The court will make a formal notice and it becomes a document of public record.[79] The notice is recognised as the judgment of the court and it comprises the following details:

- the name of the court and judge
- the date and number of the petition

---

77 Article 25.

78 Article 35.

79 Article 35. There is an obligation on the court to publish, within ten days of the judgment, notice of the bankruptcy. See Article 43. This must be published for three consecutive days and must also be sent to the Office of Judgement Enforcement, all creditors and the owner(s) of the bankrupt enterprise, a financial/accountancy firm, trade union, the agency where the enterprise is registered, the banks, the trade and industry board and the economic police. It is unclear as to how this is operationalised. There are major problems with the distribution of notices and communication in general in Laos, and it is also a little difficult under the Article to ascertain precisely who it is that should be receiving the notice.

- the name and registration number of the enterprise[80]
- the date of bankruptcy
- the reasons for the bankruptcy
- the plan for distribution of the assets of the enterprise.

Under the latter requirement there are no formal provisions indicating how this will be achieved. As appointment of a Liquidation Committee follows the declaration of bankruptcy, the committee determines the distribution plan after it has had an opportunity to consider the position of the bankrupt enterprise.[81] There is a right to appeal the declaration of bankruptcy within 15 days of the court's decision.[82] This right will apply to creditors or the owners (or representatives) of the enterprise. The 15-day period does not commence until they have been notified. It is unclear as to how this will be determined. The infrastructure in Laos is extremely rudimentary and it may be very difficult for all affected parties to receive advice of judicial decisions.[83]

The Bankruptcy Law is silent on the effect of the bankruptcy on the enterprise. It would follow that as soon as the court issues the notice of adjudication of bankruptcy, the Liquidation Committee appointed under the Law by the court then handles all matters relating to the company. All powers of the board and managers as provided for in the Business Law will no longer be effective. All creditors will have had an opportunity to consider their options, as they will have been involved throughout the process through creditors' meetings. The Liquidation Committee acting under its jurisdiction contained in the Bankruptcy Law will then determine the rights of the shareholders.

Distribution of Assets

Following the collection and sale of the assets of the bankrupt enterprise, the Liquidation Committee shall distribute the proceeds according to the priority determined under Article 44. The priority is:

- workers' salaries
- government debts[84]
- secured creditors[85]
- unsecured creditors.

If there are insufficient monies available to repay all debts, each group will be repaid and if there is a shortfall for that particular group the monies will be distributed proportionately across the group. Following full distribution, any surplus remaining will be returned to the shareholders of the bankrupt enterprise. The distribution will

---

80 All enterprises are registered under the Business Law and provided with a registration number; see the Business Law, Articles 16–19 and Article 9 of the Decree regarding Implementation of the Business Law.

81 For a discussion of the Liquidation Committee, see below.

82 Article 37.

83 See note 79 above.

84 This is stated generally; it does not refer to taxes specifically but to any monies owed to the government.

85 See discussion below.

be on the basis of the profit distribution methods as described in the Articles of Association.

There is an obligation on the Liquidation Committee to make regular reports to the court, the creditors and to the enterprise owner or representative.[86] The creditors and/or the enterprise owner or representative will have a claim against the Liquidation Committee for any wrongful acts committed whilst carrying out the liquidation.[87]

5 Liquidators: Appointment, Powers and Duties

Following the declaration of bankruptcy, the court will appoint a Liquidation Committee, which will have the overall responsibility of managing the affairs of the bankrupt enterprise. Under Article 38 the Liquidation Committee will be comprised of the following:

- a representative of a financial/accountancy firm
- civil servants with the responsibility to ensure the court declaration is complied with; a civil servant will also act as chair of the committee
- a representative of a bank[88]
- a representative of the creditors
- a trade union representative
- a representative of the workers of the bankrupt enterprise
- a representative of the bankrupt enterprise.

The court appoints the committee and it can be seen that the composition is similar to the Assets Control Committee, with a strong workers' presence. The overall objective of the Liquidation Committee is to deal with the assets of the bankrupt enterprise. The rights and duties of the committee are set down in Article 39 as follows:

- to inspect the assets and liabilities of the enterprise
- to accept the transfer of all assets from the Assets Control Committee[89]
- to terminate any illegal contracts made by the enterprise[90]
- to collect all assets of the enterprise[91]
- to arrange for the auction of the enterprise's assets[92]

---

86 Bankruptcy Law, Article 46.

87 Ibid.

88 It is unclear as to how a bank representative will be selected. There is a two-tiered banking structure in Laos. The Central Bank, the Bank of the Lao PDR, has a supervisory function and there are also state-owned commercial banks and private banks.

89 This will be the case where assets have been previously managed by the Assets Control Committee; see Bankruptcy Law, Article 16.

90 See Article 47.

91 Article 41 provides an additional power to collect the assets which include land, houses, storage facilities, factories, vehicles, production equipment, stored goods and receivables.

92 See also Article 41. Note that auctions are a new type of sale forum in Laos; there is no formality to auction procedures and it may take some time for auctions to become commonplace.

- to distribute the assets amongst the creditors of the enterprise according to any priority established under law[93]
- to return any surplus after the sale of the assets to the shareholders of the Enterprise.

As with the Assets Control Committee, all expenses are met by the bankrupt enterprise.

In dealing with the assets, the Liquidation Committee has the jurisdiction to review all existing contracts and transactions. This is covered in Article 40 and is essentially a voidable preferences provision. It allows the committee to review all transactions, which are made prior to the court declaration of bankruptcy. The examples of preferences which will be examined and which may be set aside are discounted sales of assets, security provided over debts and signing contracts which have the effect of transferring ownership of assets into the names of relatives, friends or family. Assets leased to others will also fall into this category.

The bankrupt enterprise must cooperate fully with the Liquidation Committee to ensure the collection, sale and distribution of the assets proceeds without impediment. There are restrictions on the overseas travel of bankrupt debtors and the requirement of a deposit of security in the event that travel is undertaken.[94] This is an unusual provision in that it is unclear as to whom the travel restriction applies. It may be more relevant in situations where there has been a bankruptcy of a one-person limited liability company, a partnership or where there is a reliance on an enterprise representative.[95]

6 Enforcement of Securities over a Debtor's Assets in the Jurisdiction

In a developing jurisdiction, such as Laos, there are major difficulties with the enforcement of securities. The introduction of a new set of property rights takes time to be assimilated and it also takes some time for the courts to function at a level of confidence where rights will be recognised and where security holders will be able to rely on their documentation being upheld. This is a recognised difficulty and much funding has been channelled into rule of law projects. It is envisaged that future funding will be directed at supporting the training of the judiciary.

The Secured Transactions Law establishes the different types of security in Laos which will be recognised by the law and which can be relied upon. The three general types of security, in order of their priority are:

- security created by law
- security created by a court decision
- security created by a contract.[96]

93 See discussion below and the Bankruptcy Law, Article 44.

94 Bankruptcy Law, Article 42.

95 Under Article 42, if a debtor is likely to escape the jurisdiction, a restraining order may be granted to ensure this does not occur.

96 Secured Transactions Law, Article 3.

The above priority is important as secured creditors may find themselves in the unenviable position of being relegated by decisions a court may make. Security by law is defined as the assurance of a debt repayment as determined on the principles of humaneness and general national interest, such as debts arising from the labour of workers.[97] This would indicate that unpaid wages due to workers could be paid before a secured creditor. This being the case, the court may order the sale of the asset to pay the wages and any surplus would then belong to the security holder. As stated earlier, the Bankruptcy Law creates a security, which could be defined as a security by law. Under Article 44, government debts, such as taxes, take priority over secured debts. The secured creditor could then find the asset is sold and used to repay, in order of priority, worker wages, government taxes and finally the balance payable to the secured creditor. The chargeholder has an enforceable, contractual security yet the asset may be seized pursuant to a security created by law.

Taking priority over a secured creditor is a security created by a court decision. This is defined under the Secured Transactions Law as an assurance of debt repayment by a decision of the court or a decision of the Economic Dispute Resolution Tribunal, which has been certified by a court.[98] Under this type of security the court may seize or sequester an asset pending final judgment in a case or to enforce payment of a judgment. The difficulty which arises here is that often the assets which are subject to the seizure or sequestration order will be the subject of a charge and the chargeholder will lose priority.

The security created by contract will be the security that is utilised by a creditor wishing to secure the debt by taking a charge over an asset of the debtor enterprise. There are variations of this type of security. The Law provides rights to the security holder, which are common in most jurisdictions.[99] The security must be registered under the Decree on Registration of Documents.[100] Problems for a security holder arise in situations where a security may be terminated, namely:

- the creditors propose a termination of the registration
- the owner of the assets proposes to terminate the registration of the security if the security was made incorrectly
- a court orders that such a security be terminated.[101]

It is therefore possible for the security holder to lose priority if creditors decide that the registration should be terminated or if the court determines that the asset should no longer be subject to a charge. This highlights the pitfalls for a creditor wishing to secure its position in Laos under the law. The law in Laos is remarkably deficient in the area of enforcement of security and this is a common complaint from lenders when they seek to enforce their rights under their contractual securities. Nevertheless it is very clear in the case of insolvency of a debtor and under the Bankruptcy Law that

---

97 Secured Transactions Law, Article 5.

98 Article 6. The Office of Economic Dispute Resolution was established under the Decree regarding Resolution of Economic Disputes, No. 106/PM, 15 July 1994.

99 Secured Transactions Law, Articles 10–32.

100 Decree No. 52/PM/93, dated 13 March 1993.

101 Secured Transactions Law, Article 36.

the security will be valid. However, control of the asset will be lost to the Liquidation Committee and the secured creditor would only be repaid once the debts to workers and government debts are repaid.[102]

It is also worth noting that there is no legal recognition in Laos of the common floating charge security. Such securities are created and used rarely but they operate outside the law.[103] As there are no floating charges, the office of receiver does not exist in Laos.

7 Offences

One of the difficulties with the Bankruptcy Law is the absence of clear penalties to hand down. The Law establishes what constitutes a penalty, each being punishable under the Law without any prescribed penalty being attached. There are no monetary penalties included in the Bankruptcy Law but there exist general prohibitions on the holding of office.

Section VII of the Bankruptcy Law establishes the penalties. There is a general provision, which provides for the enterprise management to be dealt with if they deal with assets in a manner which would advantage certain creditors. If the Assets Control Committee, on examination of the affairs of the enterprise, finds that the enterprise management has hidden documents, manipulated accounts, moved or transferred assets, increased the debt of the enterprise, terminated or reduced its right to receivables or granted security over assets, then they will be guilty of committing an offence under the Bankruptcy Law and they will be dealt with according to the Law.[104] This Article relates to the period prior to the assets being controlled by the Assets Control Committee. It is presumed that the enterprise management must have intended to bring about any of the acts described and thus create a preference.

There is also a provision which deals with wrongful acts that are committed during the period; the assets are under the control of either the Assets Control Committee or the Liquidation Committee.[105] There is a prohibition on any further credit being obtained by the management of the enterprise during the control period. If the enterprise commits an act that amounts to it continuing to trade during a period when the assets are under control, then the management of the enterprise will be dealt with according to the Law. There is a mildly stated proviso in the Article which suggests that the consent of all creditors may make the acts of continued trading and obtaining additional credit lawful.[106]

Following an enterprise being adjudged bankrupt the manager and members of the board are prohibited from holding any similar office with any other enterprise for

102 Bankruptcy Law, Article 44.

103 The creation of a floating charge is permissible, as there is a good deal of flexibility granted under the Secured Transactions Law as to the form or structure of the contract. The enforceability of such arrangements is uncertain and if they provide for a receiver, there is little chance of this being upheld by the courts as the Bankruptcy Law will be strictly applied.

104 Article 47.

105 Article 48.

106 Ibid.

a period of three years from the date the enterprise has been adjudged bankrupt.[107] There are two exceptions to this prohibition; first, the members of a state enterprise which has been adjudged bankrupt and secondly, if a bankrupt enterprise filed its own petition and has been able to repay all of its outstanding debts.[108]

Under the Penalties Section of the Bankruptcy Law there are penalties provided if either the Assets Control Committee or the Liquidation Committee commits wrongful acts.[109] The court has the power to remove a member(s) of either committee if they have been seen to commit wrongful acts and they will then be replaced. There will also be personal liability in damages for the wrongful act. The Law is silent on what will constitute a wrongful act and it also does not establish how the court will identify a wrongful act. There is no indication as to who has standing to complain to the court of wrongful acts being committed by a member of the committees. It is thought that this Article will only be effective if the court, when reviewing a report of either committee, identifies acts of gross negligence which affect the interests of creditors and others affected by the bankruptcy.[110] In many situations where the Law is unclear, only clear statements by the courts and the development of jurisprudence in Laos will fill in the gaps.[111]

8 Rules regarding Cross-border Insolvency and Judicial Assistance to Foreign Insolvency Officials

Issues such as cross-border insolvency and judicial assistance for foreign insolvency officials are untested in Laos. The law is unclear how such matters will be dealt with. It is hoped that as part of a broad policy, the Lao courts will recognise foreign judgments and assist other jurisdictions in recovery of assets. With the law unclear it will depend very much on how the jurisprudence develops; this is of course the same situation as regards many of the 'grey' issues in insolvency law in Laos.

It is worth noting some of the mild references in the law to the importance of Lao law in determining validity. Under the Secured Transactions Law a foreign judgment will be binding in Laos provided that a Lao court certifies it.[112] This in itself is not a problem but there is, in the absence of any legal statement, no established practice surrounding the enforcement of the foreign judgment. The judgment will be recognised by the Court but it is uncertain as to its enforceability. Given that there are

107 Bankruptcy Law, Article 48.

108 There are some inconsistencies in the laws, which use terms which are not necessarily outlined in a related law or decree. For example, the Bankruptcy Law refers to Presidents of Enterprises, yet the Business Law is silent on the term President. It is assumed that the term President is referring to a manager or managing director under the Business Law. See Business Law Articles 40–42 (Partnership Company), 49–51 (Limited Liability Company), 58–59 (One-person Companies), 64–71 (Public Companies), 80–87 (State Enterprises), 89 (State Mixed Enterprises).

109 Bankruptcy Law, Article 50.

110 There does not exist in the Law the right of members to be indemnified.

111 The Bankruptcy Law also states that any person or enterprise representing them as a creditor of the bankrupt enterprise will be dealt with according to the law. See Article 51.

112 Secured Transactions Law, Article 37.

gaps surrounding the enforcement of local securities, it is not surprising that foreign judgments do not form any type of exception.

The Secured Transactions Law also makes reference to security being made in Laos.[113] There appears to be support for Lao law and the courts will therefore have comfort around documentation and security that originates in Laos. This is probably a realistic view, given the very early stages of development of not only the economy but also the supporting legal framework.

113 Article 20, which states that a contract securing immovable assets made outside Laos is not valid. To be valid the security must be made in Laos. This presumably means the documentation must be drafted, signed and registered in Laos.

Chapter 9

Thai Insolvency Law: One Step Towards the Development of the Legal Infrastructure for a Revitalised Economy

EUGENE CLARK
Charlotte Law School, North Carolina
and
SUTEE SUPANIT
Thammasat University, Bangkok

1 Introduction

1.1 Background

Thailand, known as the 'Fifth Tiger' through its strong economic growth in the 1980s, lost its way in the economic crisis of the late 1990s. However, since that time, Thailand has had a change of government and with it the political will to initiate long overdue changes. These changes have included significant legal reform, especially in the area of insolvency law. It is hoped that these legal reforms, coupled with political and administrative reforms, will go a long way towards reaffirming Thailand's attraction to foreign investors and increasing the odds that the Thai Tiger will regain its economic power. Culturally, these reforms are leading to the development of new economic values enforced by a group of Thai global professionals, exemplified by a specialised Bankruptcy Court and supported by the accounting and legal professions who appear likely to lead the way to a more market-oriented and globally competitive society.

1.2 Introduction to the Thai Legal System

Thailand is a country of approximately 60 million people, located in South East Asia. Although slowing down recently, it has enjoyed a rapidly developing and increasingly diversified economy. This includes major exports of technical goods such as computers, air-conditioners, integrated circuits, appliances, and other products to the US and European Union. Other major exports are mining products, processed food, jewelry and rice. While the major ethnic group are the Thai, the population also includes significant numbers of Chinese, Lao, Malay and Cambodians. The Chinese-Thai have been especially influential in business. Another major influence is religion with over 90 per cent of the population being Buddhist.

Modern Thailand's legal system dates from the reign of King Rama V and involves the adoption of the Romano-Germanic legal system with further adaptations in the form of localised codes which have drawn from a variety of legal sources, including Japan, Germany and the US (Hummel and Sethsathira, 1991).

Thailand has a constitutional monarchy led by HM King Bhumibol Adulyadei (Rama IX) who is also Commander-in-Chief of the military. Its legislature consists of a national assembly which in turn is divided into two Houses. The House of Representatives has 500 members, 100 of whom are from the election on a party-list basis and the remaining 400 from the election on a constituency basis. The term of the House of Representatives is four years. The Senate comprises 200 members elected by the people for a six-year term. The Senate is primarily a house of review and is confined to scrutiny or veto of legislation proposed by the House of Representatives.

The executive head of government is the Prime Minister. By virtue of the 1997 Constitution, the Prime Minister is appointed by the King upon the appointment of the House of Representatives. The Prime Minister must be appointed from members of the House of Representatives or persons who have been members of the House of Representatives. The Prime Minister presides over the 14 ministers of Cabinet. The Cabinet ministers include: Agriculture and Cooperative, Commerce, Defence, Education, Foreign Affairs, Finance, Industry, Interior, Justice, Labor and Social Welfare, Public Health, Technology and Environment. There are 35 ministers in total.

Government administration is part of a system made up of a central core (comprising approximately 80 departments), 76 provincial units and numerous local government units. Each province is divided into districts (*amphurs*) headed by a Chief District Officer (*Nai Amphur*). Districts in turn are comprised of sub-districts or communes (*tambols*) each representing about ten villages (*muban*). The leaders of *tambols* and *mubans* are elected under the supervision of a Provincial Governor. Local government units or authorities either report to central government directly or have government officials as their chairpersons. Examples are the Bangkok Metropolitan Administration (BMA) and the City of Pattaya. Typically, each city will have a mayor and city councilors who are elected (Halligan and Turner, 1995: 164–65).

The court system and independent judiciary play an important role in Thai society. Thailand's court hierarchy is comprised of a Supreme Court (*Sarn Dika*) which is the final court of appeal in all civil, bankruptcy, labor, juvenile and criminal matters. There is a middle-level Court of Appeal (*Sarn Uthorn*) and various lower courts which hear matters in the first instance (*Sarn Chunton*) and are divided into particular geographic areas (*Sarn Changvat*). In addition, there are a number of special courts; the Labor Court, the Tax Court, the Intellectual Property and International Trade Court, and the Bankruptcy Court.

The Thai judicial system has close links to the civil service system and government administration. The Ministry for Justice is responsible for the budget and general administration of the country's court system. Notwithstanding this 'link' with the government, the Thai judiciary has maintained its independence through the Thai Judicial Council, which is comprised of four government officials, four presiding judges elected by the total judiciary and four highly respected retired judges who are also elected (Halligan and Turner, 1995: 229).

In terms of its international linkages, Thailand is a member of the World Trade Organization (WTO), the Association of South East Asian Nations (ASEAN), the Asia-Pacific Economic Cooperation (APEC) group, and the East Asian Economic Caucus (EAEC). As a developing country, Thailand receives preferential treatment on tariffs as a member of the Generalized System of Preferences (GSP) established under the General Agreement on Tariffs and Trade (GATT) (now replaced by the WTO) (Anderson, 1997).

1.3 Recent Economic Events

Thailand experienced rapid economic growth during the 1980s and 1990s. Between 1985 and 1995, Thailand had an annual growth rate of 9.8 per cent while at the same time having low inflation of around 4.4 per cent per year (Falgui, 1997). Thailand experienced its highest rates of growth of 13.2 per cent, 12 per cent and 10.1 per cent in 1988, 1989 and 1990 respectively. However, by 1996 exports began to decrease and growth became stagnant. In July 1997, Thailand was forced to devalue the baht and the economy was in a steep dive from which it is now only just emerging (Webb, 1998).

Thailand's economy is heavily dependent on exports (Krnongkaew, 1993). Thailand's exports plummeted severely from 1996 through 1998. The Asian Development Bank attributed this slump in exports to several factors including tight monetary policies in other countries, the appreciation of the US dollar against the Japanese yen and a fall in the electronic sector. Thailand also had pegged its baht to the US dollar, but gave much higher interest rates. This attracted huge amounts of capital into Thailand and encouraged very active property development such as high-risk luxury hotels and high-rises. The Bank of Tokyo, Citibank, Sakura Bank and Hongkong & Shanghai Bank loaned a total in excess of US$10 billion (Einhorn and Corben, 1997). These poor loan decisions led to a troubled banking sector which resulted in the economic downfall.

In response, Thailand tried to stabilise its falling economy after 1992. Fiscal and economic controls were enacted in 1995 to slow down an overheated economy (Engardio, 1998). Controls were placed on foreign investments and limitations on the banking sector. In May 1997 the Bank of Thailand (BOT) placed strict restrictions on selling baht to foreign investors and prohibited sales to speculators. Banks were ordered not to buy back baht commercial paper from off-shore investors, again in an attempt to stabilise the currency (Dekle, Karchanasai and Hoontrakul, 2003).

Political corruption also played a role in worsening the economic crisis. This was especially so in the banking industry. The Bangkok Bank of Commerce (BBC) was plagued by scandal and mismanagement and the BOT Governor Vijit Supinit allegedly had close political ties to BBC's president, Krikkiat Vijit. The BBC was eventually suspended in 1996 after it posted losses of US$3 billion. Vijit resigned from the BOT in 1996, leaving the bank very weak. Critics suggest that the government did not act sooner because it was protecting Thai corporations which held large unhedged overseas loans.

These stories of corruption led to calls for amendments to the Constitution. Under former Prime Minister Anand Panyarchun, new strict guidelines were proposed which required mandatory disclosure of assets for public officials and formation of an independent body to crack down on corruption. But this was too little too late. In July 1997, the Thai government ended its defence of the baht and floated the currency and a necessary recession followed (Gonzalez, 1997).

The IMF offered to help matters in 1998 and this help was accepted, leading to a positive reaction on the Thai currency and stock markets. The IMF package required strict controls on the banking sector. These measures included allowing foreign banks to take a majority ownership and control of Thai banks and financial institutions. Two new regulatory bodies were also created. One was a company modeled after the US Resolution Trust Corporation, responsible for purchasing non-performing assets from financial institutions and auctioning them. The other body was to act as a super-agency to rehabilitate suspended companies. However, some have been critical of these measures, saying that the IMF has not been strong enough in requiring troubled economies such as Thailand's to implement sound economic policies (Simon, 1997; Bremmer, 1997).

The impact of the currency crisis and the emerging recovery is reflected in the official bankruptcy figures from the Ministry for Justice. During the economic crisis there were 2,886 bankruptcy cases in 1997 and 3,053 cases in 1998. However, this number dropped to 1,851 cases in 1999. There were 35 reorganisation cases in 1999.

1.4 Sources and History of Thai Bankruptcy Law

1.4.1 Constitutional basis The highest form of law in Thailand is the Constitution of 1997. With its civil law system, Thai law is derived from and found in codes or statutes. There are four major codes: the Penal Code, the Civil and Commercial Code, the Civil Procedural Code and the Criminal Procedural Code completed in 1934.

1.4.2 Civil and Commercial Code: Public Limited Companies Act Commercial transactions in Thailand are governed principally by the Civil and Commercial Code (hereinafter referred to as 'CCC'). Book I of the CCC ('General Principles') provides basic definitions and principles underlying commercial law transactions in Thailand. Book II, 'Obligation', covers the general provisions of contract law. The Thai laws governing companies are found in Book III, Title XXII of the Civil and Commercial Code of 1928 and the Public Limited Companies Act of 1992. The Civil and Commercial Code contains the provisions dealing with private limited companies and the Public Limited Companies Act regulates public limited companies. These laws cover all matters essential to companies. Book III of the CCC also includes the provisions governing 'Specific Contracts', including carriage of goods, mortgages, hire of services and so on. Other statutes or codes which relate to companies include the Revenue Act 1983, Bankruptcy Act 1940, the Anti-Monopoly Act, the Securities Exchange of Thailand Act 1974 and the Commercial Banking Act 1962.

1.4.3 Role of case law As noted above, the primary source of law is found in the legislation or codes governing companies. Reported court decisions do not constitute the law and there is no doctrine of precedent such as that found in common law countries. Prior cases, however, do provide useful examples of the provisions of law (Miller, 2000).

1.4.4 Origin of Thai insolvency laws Thailand has had its own insolvency regime since the Ayuthaya period in 843. Later the provisions relating to bankruptcy proceedings were incorporated in the Law Code of 1805 (the Law of the Three Great Seals). During 1868–1910, a time of expansion of trade and commerce, the Thai legal system was modernised along the line of Western laws (Wong, Phunsunthorn and Sucharitkul, 2000).

The first Bankruptcy Act was enacted in 1891, and it was replaced by the second Bankruptcy Act of 1909. The third Bankruptcy Act came into force in 1911 and was amended in 1927 and 1931 to keep pace with the changing conditions of trade and society in that period of time.

Thailand's present day insolvency regime is found in the Bankruptcy Act of 1940 (AI Chandler and Thong-Ek Law Offices Limited trans. 1998; available at http://www.bot.or.th/govnr/public/Act/Bkrup.Act.html). Thai bankruptcy law is largely based on the English system, but has been significantly modified to harmonise with Thailand's social and economic conditions. To a certain extent, the bankruptcy law in Thailand has been treated by the creditor as a debt enforcement. A bankruptcy petition is very often used by creditors to enforce the payment of a debt. With the view to strengthening the insolvency system, the new Bankruptcy Act of 1940 was promulgated to repeal and replace the Bankruptcy Act of 1911. It introduced a new principle, that is, the debtor will not be adjudged bankrupt immediately upon the presentation of a bankruptcy petition, but the court shall grant an order which has the effect of: (1) protecting the debtor and the debtor's estate from legal proceedings, and (2) taking away from the debtor the control over the debtor's property and placing it under the control of an officer of the court. This was designed to give an opportunity for the debtor to offer his or her creditors a composition. If the debtor fails to do so or the creditor refuses to approve the composition, the debtor shall be adjudged bankrupt.

In addition, the Bankruptcy Act of 1940 improved the methods of extracting money from recalcitrant debtors, of fairly dividing the proceeds amongst all debtors, and new procedures to ensure that all should be done without delay.

The Bankruptcy Act of 1940 was amended several times – in 1964, 1983, 1998, 1999 and 2000 (Dever and Vajassit). Further amendments are under consideration at the time of writing (The Asia Restructuring Group, 1998). The Bankruptcy Court Act, enacted on 8 April 1999, set up the Bankruptcy Court as a specialised court with a specialised legal procedure. The 1998 amendments introduced a reorganisation system to salvage failing companies. The amendment to the Bankruptcy Act, enacted on 21 April 1999, adjusted upwards the value of indebtedness in line with developments in the economy. It also sought to encourage debt restructuring for insolvent businesses and introduced an automatic discharge.

1.5 Insolvency Law Principles

Underlying most significant legislative regimes is a set of principles and policy objectives. Similarly, the new Bankruptcy Act seeks to enforce a number of ethical principles regarding insolvency contexts, especially in regard to companies (Fletcher, 1996: 613; Wood, 1995; Fletcher, 2005).

First among these principles is the belief that bankruptcy matters should be administered efficiently, effectively and fairly. This underscores the decision to establish a specialised bankruptcy court and new civil procedures to improve enforcement and fairness.

Another important principle is that it may often be in the best interests of an insolvent company, its shareholders and creditors to reorganise rather than to liquidate and dissolve. The new Bankruptcy Act thus contains new provisions which give the court greater options to get a company back on its feet.

Thirdly, Thai insolvency law also incorporates the principle of *pari passu* or equality of division among creditors; thus a particular class of creditors will share the remaining assets of the debtor which will be divided pro rata in proportion to the amount of the debt owed to them.

A fourth principle is that shareholders will not be liable for the debt of the company. In other words, Thai law recognises the separate legal personality of a company as a juristic person, a separate legal identity distinct from the legal identity of individual shareholders.

A fifth principle is that secured creditors are protected so that a bankruptcy will not generally affect the security interests created prior to the commencement of bankruptcy proceedings.

A sixth principle is that Thai law extends only to the territorial jurisdiction of Thailand. An insolvent debtor may be adjudged bankrupt by a court if the debtor is domiciled or carries on business (whether by the debtor themselves or their representative) in Thailand, at the time an application is made to adjudge such debtor as bankrupt, or in the previous year. A debtor is said to be 'insolvent' when the debtor's debts are greater than assets or over-indebtedness exists. Insolvency signifies the inability of the debtor to pay obligations as they fall due. The receivership of assets or a bankruptcy action is governed by Thailand's laws only to the extent of the assets of the debtor within Thailand. The receivership of assets or a bankruptcy action under the laws of other countries has no effect as to assets of a debtor in Thailand. Foreign creditors who are domiciled outside Thailand can claim for repayment of debts in the bankruptcy action in Thailand upon their compliance with the condition that creditors in Thailand are similarly entitled to claim for payment of debts in bankruptcy actions under the law and before the courts of the countries of which the foreign creditors are nationals.

A seventh principle of Thai Bankruptcy Law is that one regime should govern corporate and individual insolvency. The terminology of personal and corporate bankruptcy is indistinguishable. Therefore, when the debtor (personal or corporate) becomes insolvent, it might be adjudged bankrupt in order to collect all the debtor's assets and distribute them amongst the creditors.

2 Personal and Corporate Bankruptcy/Insolvency

2.1 The Regulatory Structures for the Control of Bankruptcy Proceedings

The bankruptcy court and official receivers play the most important part in controlling bankruptcy proceedings. The bankruptcy courts have sole jurisdiction to hear and decide bankruptcy cases. Before 1999, all bankruptcy cases resided in the jurisdiction of ordinary courts, which have jurisdiction to hear and decide general civil cases.

The bankruptcy court has the power to grant an absolute receivership order or interim receivership orders, to approve compositions, to declare a bankruptcy, or to dismiss the debtor from bankruptcy. In addition, the court controls and supervises the official receivers in performing their functions.

The official receivers are officials appointed by the Ministry of Justice. They are regarded as officials of the court. They are empowered to: (1) manage and dispose of the assets of the debtor, or do any necessary act to complete any pending business of the debtor; (2) collect and receive money or assets belonging to the debtor, or which the debtor is entitled to receive from others; (3) compromise, come to settlement, or file actions relating to the assets of the debtor.

The official receiver has the power to represent the debtor's estate and the debtor will lose the power to dispose of or manage its assets. The official receiver will investigate which assets are available for distribution to creditors. The receiver also chairs the meeting of creditors. Generally speaking, the official receiver is responsible for the administration and realisation of the assets and all other business of the debtor's estate and for dispersing the assets to the creditors and their representation before the court.

2.2 Initiation of Bankruptcy Proceedings

2.2.1 By a creditor or creditors Debtors are unable to petition themselves into bankruptcy. Only a creditor or creditors may file a bankruptcy action. A creditor may initiate a bankruptcy petition if the following conditions are satisfied: (1) the debtor becomes insolvent; (2) the debtor who is a natural person owes to one or several creditors who are the plaintiffs the amount of not less than one million baht, or the debtor who is a juristic person is indebted to one or several plaintiff creditors amounting to not less than two million baht; and (3) the said debts may be determined in a definite amount, irrespective of whether it becomes due for payment immediately or at a future date.

2.2.2 By a secured creditor A secured creditor may file a bankruptcy action against the debtor if, apart from the conditions mentioned above, the creditor is not the person prohibited from the enforcement for settlement of debts from the debtor's assets in excess of that placed as a security. The secured creditor must state in the plaint that if the debtor becomes bankrupt, the creditor is willing to waive the security for the benefit of all creditors, or make an appraisal of the security in the plaint of which, after the deduction of the obligation due to the creditor, the remainder will be a deficit of not less than one million baht for the debtor who is a natural person or two million baht for the debtor who is a juristic person.

2.2.3 By a liquidator In addition, the liquidator (of a registered or limited partnership, or company, or other juristic persons) must submit a petition to the court to have the company, limited partnership or other juristic person declared bankrupt if it appears that the capital money or the share money has been entirely spent, or the assets are insufficient to meet liabilities.

2.2.4 Hearing In hearing a bankruptcy action on the petition of the creditor, the court must consider the facts (determination of insolvency) as mentioned above. If the court finds them proved, the court shall order the debtor to be under an absolute receivership. If not proved, or the debtor gives evidence of ability to pay the debt in full, or if there are other grounds for not justifying the adjudication of the debtor as bankrupt, the court shall dismiss the petition.

The Bankruptcy Act provides a presumption that the debtor is insolvent where the debtor has committed the following acts:

1. If the debtor transfers assets or rights in management of the debtor's assets to other persons for the benefit of all the debtor's creditors within or outside Thailand.
2. If the debtor transfers or delivers the debtor's assets with dishonest or fraudulent intent, within or outside Thailand.
3. If the debtor transfers assets or creates any right over such assets which, if the debtor were a bankrupt, would be deemed as act of preference, within or outside Thailand.
4. If the debtor does any of the following acts in order to delay payment of his/her debt, or in order to prevent a creditor from receiving payment of the debt:
   - leaves Thailand, or, having previously left, remains outside Thailand
   - leaves the premises in which the debtor has resided, or hides him/herself in any premises, or absconds or leaves by other means, or closes the debtor's place of business
   - removes assets out of the jurisdiction of the court
   - consents to judgment ordering the payment of money which the debtor should not pay.
5. If the debtor has had an asset attached under a writ of execution, or there is no asset of any kind capable of attachment for payment of the debt.
6. If the debtor declares to the court in any action that the debtor cannot pay his/her debts.
7. If the debtor informs any of his/her creditors that the debtor cannot pay his/her debts.
8. If the debtor submits to any two or more of the debtor's creditors a proposal for composition of the debtor's debts.
9. If the debtor receives demand letters from a creditor not less than twice, at intervals of not less than 30 days, and the debtor does not pay the debt.

Thailand's Bankruptcy Law does not require that the debtor must commit the above acts in a certain period of time as a condition to file a bankruptcy action. When a creditor finds that the debtor has committed one of those said acts, the creditor is eligible to file a bankruptcy petition against the debtor. To prove that the debtor is insolvent, a creditor is required to prove that debts are greater than the debtor's assets.

2.3 Powers of Secured Creditors

Secured creditors are creditors who hold rights over the asset of the debtor in a mortgage, pledge or a right of retention; or a creditor possessing preferential rights in the nature of a pledgee. Creditors are able to execute an action against the said asset without resorting to bankruptcy.

2.4 Creditors' Meetings

Creditors' meetings are necessary in bankruptcy proceedings. In particular, the first meeting of creditors is designed to play the most important role in considering whether the debtor should be adjudged bankrupt. As soon as the absolute receivership order has been made, the official receiver shall call a general meeting of creditors as quickly as possible (referred to in the Bankruptcy Act as the 'first meeting of creditors') to consider whether a proposal for a composition shall be entertained or whether it is expedient that the debtor be adjudged bankrupt.

As a result of the first meeting of creditors, if the court finds that the creditors have passed a resolution that the debtor be adjudged bankrupt, or that creditors have passed no resolution, or that the creditors have not met at all, or that a composition is not accepted or approved, the court shall adjudge the debtor a bankrupt.

Other meetings of creditors are convened for the purpose of the administration of the official receiver, namely to approve the continuing of the debtor's business, or to approve the official receiver to act in relation to the following matters: (1) withdraw attachment of assets in a bankruptcy action; (2) transfer any assets other than by the method of a public auction; (3) surrender a right; (4) file or withdraw a civil action relating to assets in the bankruptcy case, or file or withdraw a bankruptcy case; (5) effect a compromise or submit a matter to arbitration; or (6) approve the selling of the debtor's assets other than at an auction.

3 Insolvency/Bankruptcy Procedures

3.1 Debtor's Control

Once an absolute receivership order or an interim receivership has been conferred by the court, the control of debtor's assets commences. The debtor shall deliver all the assets, seals, accounting ledgers, and documents relating to his or her assets and business in the debtor's possession to the official receiver. The debtor is prohibited from doing any act relating to the debtor's assets or the debtor's business, except if such act is done by order or approval of the court, the official receiver, the administrator of assets, or by resolution of creditors at a creditors' meeting.

The debtor must attend all meetings of creditors and reply to the questions of the official receiver or any creditor concerned with the debtor's business, assets or partnership. The debtor must undertake all acts relating to the debtor's business and assets, or to distribution of the debtor's assets amongst the creditors, as directed by the official receiver or ordered by the court. The debtor shall apply to the official receiver to fix a sum of money for expenses for the maintenance of the debtor and his/her family as may be proper to the debtor's condition in life: the official receiver permitting the debtor shall pay the sum from the money received by the debtor during the debtor's bankruptcy. The debtor shall send the balance of the money or assets to the official receiver within the period prescribed by the official receiver, together with a statement of receipts and expenditure.

On each occasion where the debtor is entitled to receive any assets, the debtor shall submit to the official receiver statements of receipts and expenditure every six months. The debtor shall not leave the country, except with the written permission of the court or the official receiver, and if the debtor changes address, the debtor must report the new address within a reasonable time in writing to the official receiver.

3.2 Collection of Information about Debtors

Under an absolute receivership, the debtor must proceed as follows. Firstly, within 24 hours from the time when the debtor has acknowledged an absolute receivership order, the debtor must take an oath before the official receiver, and submit an explanation, according to a printed form, stating whether or not the debtor is in partnership with any person; and, if so, the names and addresses of partners must be stated. Secondly, within seven days from the date the debtor has acknowledged such order, the debtor must take an oath before the official receiver, and submit an explanation regarding the debtor's business and assets, according to a printed form, showing the cause of insolvency, the debtor's assets and liabilities, the names, addresses, occupations of the creditors, the assets placed as security, as well as details of any assets which may be devolved in the future on the debtor, and the assets of spouses, including the assets of third parties which may be in the debtor's possession.

Moreover, information about the debtor may be collected in the investigation of the official receiver or the court. The court or the official receiver is empowered to issue a summons to the debtor, the debtor's spouse, or any person who has had or is suspected of having the debtor's assets in their possession, or who is believed to be indebted to the debtor, or is considered to be capable of giving information regarding the business or assets of the debtor, to appear for examination or investigation. The court is empowered to order that such a person produce documents or evidence in such a person's possession or control, which relates to the business or assets of the debtors. If such a person intentionally defies the summons or order, the court has power to issue a warrant for arrest of that person and to detain the debtor until the debtor complies with the order of the court or the official receiver (Kosolkitiwong, 2001).

3.3 Creditors' Claims

All unsecured creditors, including the petitioning creditor, shall file their claims with the official receiver within two months following the date of the order of absolute receivership. If a creditor fails to file the creditor's claim within this period of time, that creditor shall lose their right to enforce the creditor's debts forever. If the creditor resides outside the country, the official receiver may extend this period by not more than another two months.

The claim must be made in accordance with a printed form, with a statement showing details of the debt, the evidence of such debts and assets of the debtor held as security or which may be in the creditor's possession.

The creditor's claim for repayment of debt must be the debt incurred before the date on which the court ordered receivership of the assets, even if such debt may not yet be due or is subject to conditions. Unenforceable debts include a debt which the creditor allows the debtor to create when the creditor knows that the debtor is insolvent. In such event, the creditor is prohibited from filing a claim for repayment.

3.4 Proof of Debts

Two months following the date of the order of absolute receivership of assets, the official receiver shall promptly fix a date for a meeting of the debtor and all creditors to examine the claims for repayment of debts. In examining the claims for repayment of debts, whether such debts be judgment debts or not, the official receiver shall have the power to issue a summons to creditors, debtors, or other persons to appear for questioning as to the debts, and to report the official receiver's opinion and send the case file of such claims for repayment of debts to the court, together with a report as to whether any of the claims were contested or not.

Where any claim for repayment of debt is not disputed by the debtor, creditors, or the official receiver, the court may order the approval of repayment of the debt, unless there is any appropriate reason for any other order. If any claim for repayment of debt is disputed, the court shall hear the case and issue any of the following orders: (1) to dismiss the claim for repayment of debt; (2) to approve the repayment of the whole debt; (3) to approve the repayment of part of the debt.

3.5 Illicit Transfer of Property; Proof of Fraud; Discharge

There are two possibilities of illicit transfer of property recognised by the Bankruptcy Law. The first possibility is that a fraudulent disposition of property, transfer of property, or any acts affecting the property, performed or permitted to be performed by the debtor during one year prior to the application of bankruptcy, may be cancelled by order of the court on an application by the official receiver by way of motion. The second possibility is in the case of a preferential payment, transfer of property, or any acts done by the debtor, or permitted to be done, during the three months prior to an application to declare the debtor bankrupt and thereafter, with the wish to give undue preference to a creditor; the court is empowered to cancel such transfers or acts on the application of the official receiver by way of motion.

The Bankruptcy Act (No. 7) 2004, which came into effect in July of 2004, extends the three-year discharge rule for individual bankrupts to ten years upon evidence of dishonesty or fraud. The automatic discharge period may be extended to five years on the grounds of the person's previous bankruptcy within five years prior to the current proceedings. The court may also suspend the three-year discharge rule where a bankrupt fails to assist the receiver in collecting properties.

3.6 Rules for the Distribution of Assets of the Bankrupt

After the debtor has been adjudged bankrupt, the distribution procedure shall commence.

The official receiver shall realise all the debtor's assets seized by the official receiver and distribute the debtor's assets to all creditors who have filed claims for repayment of the debts. In distributing the assets amongst creditors, the expenses and debts shall be paid in the following order of priority:

1. administration expenses of a deceased debtor's estate
2. expenses of the official receiver in managing the debtor's assets
3. funeral expenses of a deceased debtor proper to his/her status
4. fees in collecting the assets of the debtor
5. fees of the petitioning creditor and counsel's fee, as the court or the official receiver shall prescribe
6. taxes which have become due for payment within six months prior to the order for receivership of the assets for work performed for the debtor as employer
7. other debts.

If the money is insufficient to pay any of the above in full, the creditors shall be paid *pari passu*. In the case where any debt in category 7 is required by law or by agreement that a creditor shall have the right to receive repayment only after other creditors have received repayment in full, the creditor shall remain entitled to a distribution of assets in accordance with the rights entitled to that creditor according to such law or agreement.

Generally, the property that secures a particular asset is not considered as part of the assets of the debtor that can be liquidated via bankruptcy proceedings. Thus, a secured creditor is able to enforce the security outside of bankruptcy proceedings. A discussion of creditors' rights against secured property is discussed below.

3.7 Composition

If the debtor wishes to avoid being adjudged bankrupt or to be discharged from bankruptcy, the debtor shall make a composition with creditors. Whenever the debtor desires to come to a settlement by repayment of debts in part or in any manner, the debtor shall submit a proposal for the composition of his/her debts in writing to the official receiver. This must be done within seven days from the date of submission of the debtor's explanation of his/her business and assets, or within such period as the official receiver shall prescribe.

The proposal for composition of the debts shall detail the contents of the composition, or the method of management of business or assets, and details of security, or the surety, if any. The official receiver shall call a meeting of creditors to consider and adopt a special resolution determining whether the proposal shall be acknowledged or not.

A special resolution requires a majority of creditors whose debts equal three quarters of the total debts of creditors present at the creditors' meeting in person or by proxy, and voting on such a resolution. The acceptance of the proposal for composition of debts by a special resolution of the meeting of the creditors shall not bind all creditors until the court issues an order approving the same. The composition accepted at a meeting of creditors and approved by the court shall be binding upon all creditors as regards debts for which claims for repayment may be made but shall not be binding upon any creditor as regards debts relating to taxes or land tax of the government or a municipality, or debts which have arisen through the dishonesty or fraud of the bankrupt.

4 Corporate Reorganisation

4.1 Background

In 1998 the Bankruptcy Act of 1940 was amended to incorporate a new procedure dealing with reorganisation of a debtor's operation, with a view to salvaging financially ailing companies that were economically viable. This new procedure is regarded as an alternative to liquidating a debtor's assets. The notion of this procedure is to bring in outside management for the failing companies for a period of five years, after which management returns to the previous directors. This procedure is provided for the debtors who are juristic persons only; it does not apply to business operations of individual debtors.

4.2 Out-of-court Restructuring

Borrowers and lenders agree on their own informal restructuring scheme to reformulate a loan repayment scheme regarding non-performing loans (NPLs). The legal basis of such informal schemes is a contract between the debtor and creditors. The Bank of Thailand, together with the Thai and Foreign Bankers' Associations and the Board of Trade, in 1999 created another form of binding framework for debtor-creditor and creditor-creditor agreements. It established the Corporate Debt Restructuring Advisory Committee (CDRAC) to facilitate and monitor such agreements. CDRAC has had a major impact since the end of September 2001, when the Central Bankruptcy Court had dealt with a total of 989 bankruptcy and business rehabilitation cases involving a total debt of 200.95 billion baht. CDRAC helped restructure 439,276 cases involving debts totaling 2.3 trillion baht (Business Monitor International, 2000).

Similarly, the Stock Exchange of Thailand established the SET-Rehabco Restructuring Process in 1999, following the suspension of a number of listed companies with balance sheet deficits. Upon meeting the restructuring requirements, the companies could have their suspension lifted.

Lastly, the government issued the Emergency Decree on Thai Asset Management Corporation (TAMC) in 2001. TAMC is managed by a Board of Directors appointed by the Minister of Finance and approved by the Council of Ministers. The TAMC seeks to address the high level of non-performing loans in both state-controlled and private financial institutions. In recent years the TAMC has focused more on medium size to small business. How effective the TAMC has been in addressing non-performing loans remains uncertain. The International Monetary Fund (2002), for example, has suggested a further strengthening of the banking system in Thailand by providing greater security to creditors.

The TAMC is a government entity owned entirely by the Financial Institutions Development Fund (FIDF). The TAMC is empowered to issue 170 billion baht ten-year notes guaranteed by the FIDF as payment for TAMC's purchase of non-performing loans of these financial institutions. The TAMC has the power to unilaterally amend loan terms, force debt-equity conversion, take assignments of debts, take transfer of shares or buy issued shares to increase the debtor's capital. In these circumstances, various provisions of the Civil and Commercial Code and the Public Company Limited Act are waived. As in the case of a court-supervised restructure, the TAMC approves a reorganisation plan. The TAMC, in other words, creates a reorganisation procedure separate from those provided for under the Bankruptcy Act. For a debtor to qualify under the TAMC:

- the debtor must be a limited company, a public limited company or a registered partnership
- TAMC must be a creditor and be owed more than 50 per cent of the debtor's total debt
- there must be evidence that the business can be carried on and its rehabilitation will benefit the national economy
- the debtor must consent and agree to be bound by the terms and conditions of business reorganisation under the TAMC Decree.

4.3 Court-supervised Restructuring: Initiation

The reorganisation's petition to the bankruptcy court can be initiated by:

1. a creditor(s) to whom the insolvent debtor owes not less than ten million baht
2. an insolvent debtor owing creditor(s) not less than ten million baht
3. certain government agencies such as the Bank of Thailand where the debtor is a commercial bank, a finance company, a finance and security company, or a credit finance company; the Office of the Securities and Exchange Commission where the debtor is a securities company, or the Department of Insurance where the debtor is an insurance against loss company, a life insurance company or the official authority that supervises the debtor as prescribed in the Ministerial Regulations.

The initiation of a petition for the reorganisation of the debtor's business may be done even though the debtor has been subject to a bankruptcy case. However, if the court in the bankruptcy case conferred an absolute order or the debtor has been liquidated for any reason, a petition to reorganise the debtor's business is not permitted.

The petition to the court shall:

1. state that the debtor is insolvent
2. list any creditor(s) to whom the debtor is indebted for a total amount of not less than ten million baht

3. state reasonable grounds for and the likely prospect of rehabilitation of the business
4. state the name and qualifications of the person who prepares the business reorganisation plan (the plan preparer) and
5. provide a letter of consent by the plan preparer.

The plan preparer may be a natural person, group of persons, the creditor or the debtor's executives. If the debtor is the petitioner, the list of all of its existing assets and debts, and the clear list of names and addresses of the creditors, must be annexed to the petition.

4.4 Court Hearing

After accepting the petition by the court order, the court shall proceed with the inquiry as a matter of urgency. If the creditor is the petitioner, the creditor shall send the copy of the petition to the debtor not less than seven days before the date of inquiry and the debtor shall also file a list of all the debtor's existing assets and debts and provide the court with a complete list of names and addresses of all creditors.

The debtor or the creditor may file an objection not less than three days before the date of the first inquiry. In the case of raising an objection against the plan preparer, the debtor or the creditor may nominate another person as the plan preparer. In nominating a person to be the plan preparer, a letter of consent from the nominated person shall also be submitted.

In considering the petition for rehabilitation, the court shall conduct an examination to ascertain the facts. If there are reasonable grounds for rehabilitating the business and the petitioner has filed the petition in good faith, the court shall give an order for business reorganisation or otherwise a dismissal of the petition. Where no objections against the petition are lodged, if the court thinks fit, it shall cancel the inquiry and grant an order for business reorganisation.

4.5 Stay of Proceedings

Once the reorganisation petition is ordered by the court, the order has the following effects:

1. There will be no resolution or order by the court to liquidate the company.
2. Secured creditors lose their rights to enforce their security over the company property.
3. Trade creditors, hire purchase and leasing creditors are unable to repossess any goods in the company.
4. No other proceedings, execution or other legal process may be commenced or continued. The Bankruptcy Act (s 16) provides for a party to apply to the Bankruptcy Court for an expedited hearing to receive evidence or testimony in question (s 16). The court also has the power to make orders to stop evidence being lost or destroyed (s 17).

4.6 Appointment of the Plan Preparer

The applicant of a reorganisation order is required to nominate a qualified plan preparer. If there is no objection by other creditors, the court shall appoint the nominated plan preparer. If there is an objection or the court is of an opinion that the person who is nominated by the petitioner is inappropriate, the court shall order a meeting of creditors for electing a suitable plan preparer. If the court is satisfied that the person who has been elected by the meeting of creditors is qualified to be the plan preparer, the court shall appoint that person.

4.7 Powers of the Plan Preparer

Upon the date of appointment, the plan preparer will assume the administration of the company. The plan preparer has authority in the management of company affairs, business and property, and will serve as an agent of the company. However, the court has power to give any directions regarding the management of the company.

4.8 Formulating a Reorganisation Plan

The plan preparer is entrusted with an important function of formulating a reorganisation plan within three months of the date of appointment. In essence, the reorganisation plan is broadly construed. At a minimum, the plan must contain the following as required by the law:

1. the reasons for reorganising the business
2. details concerning the assets, liabilities, and other binding obligations of the debtor at the time the court orders a business reorganisation
3. principles and methods for business reorganisation
   - steps in reorganising the business
   - payment of debts, extension of time of payment of debts, reduction of the debt, and classification of creditors
   - reducing and increasing capital
   - creating debt and raising funds, including sources of funds and any conditions relating to such debt and funds
   - managing and acquiring benefits from the assets of the debtor
   - conditions regarding payment of dividends and other benefits
4. redemption of collateral in the case where there are secured creditors and liabilities of a guarantor
5. ways to solve problems if there is a temporary lack of liquidity while implementing the plan
6. actions to be taken in cases in which a claim or debt is assigned
7. the name, qualifications and letter of consent of the 'plan administrator' and remuneration
8. the appointment of the plan administrator and the date of release from this position
9. time period for implementing the plan, which must not exceed five years (with a maximum of two one-year extensions)

10. the refusal of assets of the debtor or contractual rights, in the case of the assets of the debtor or contractual rights having obligations which exceed the benefits to be derived therefrom.

The plan must be submitted to the creditors within three months, though a maximum of two requests may be made for one-month extensions.

4.9 Creditors' Approval of the Plan

Upon receiving the draft plan, the official receiver shall convene a meeting of creditors to consider whether or not to accept the plan. Revisions of the plan can be made within fixed time periods. The meeting of creditors shall approve the plan by special resolution made by a majority of creditors (comprising at least three quarters of all creditors' total debts) who attend and vote at the meeting by each and every group of creditors, or by the creditors of at least one group of the creditors, and the total debt of the creditors who have approved the plan at the meeting of all groups of creditors must not be less than 50 per cent of the debt of the creditors who attend the meeting in person or by proxy at the creditors' meeting and who voted on such a resolution.

The classification of creditors shall be done in groups as follows:

1. each secured creditor having a secured debt of not less than 15 per cent of the total indebtedness for which a claim for repayment may be filed from the business reorganisation shall each be classed as a group
2. secured creditors not classified under (1) shall be classed as a group
3. unsecured creditors may be classified in several groups, where unsecured creditors whose claims or interests are identical or similar in material respects are in the same group
4. other creditors (subordinate lenders), who are required by law or by contract that they shall receive payment only after other creditors have received repayment in full, shall comprise one group.

The official receiver shall immediately report the creditors' acceptance or rejection of the plan to the court. Where the creditors have rejected the plan, the court shall call an urgent hearing. At the hearing, the court shall examine all evidence and decide whether to issue an order revoking the order of business reorganisation. If a bankruptcy case has been filed against the debtor before and the court considers it appropriate to adjudge the debtor as bankrupt, the petition for business reorganisation shall be dismissed and the suspended bankruptcy case shall proceed.

4.10 Court's Approval of the Plan

Where the plan has been accepted by the meeting of creditors, the official receiver shall report to the court as quickly as possible in order to ask the court if it approves the reorganisation plan. In this case the court shall fix a date for considering the plan on an urgent basis.

In considering the plan, the court shall consider the explanation provided by the official receiver and plan preparer and the objections of the debtor or the creditor who opposed the plan. The court shall issue an order approving the plan when the court is satisfied that if the implementation of the plan is successful, the result shall be that the creditors receive debt payments in amounts that are not less than the case where the court has adjudged the debtor a bankrupt.

Once the court has issued an order approving the plan, the court shall notify the plan administrator and the plan preparer as soon as possible. At the time that the plan administrator acknowledges the court's order, the rights and duties of the plan preparer shall immediately pass to the plan administrator (the person who manages the business and assets, or the debtor, according to the business reorganisation plan).

If the court issues an order not approving the plan, the court shall schedule a hearing to decide whether the debtor should be adjudicated as bankrupt.

4.11 Creditors' Claims

Creditors may file an application for repayment of debts as part of a business reorganisation if the obligation occurred before the court issued the order to reorganise the business, regardless of whether or not the debt has matured or is conditional. Creditors must file an application for repayment of debts along with a copy to the official receiver within one month after the order of appointment of the plan preparer. The official shall then send the copy of the application to the plan preparer without delay.

If there has been no objection from other creditors, the debtor, or the plan preparer to an application filed by any creditor for repayment of debts for business reorganisation, then the official receiver has the authority to authorise repayment of the debt unless there are reasonable grounds for ordering otherwise.

If any person opposes an application filed by any creditor for repayment of debts for business reorganisation, the official shall investigate the matter and issue one of the following orders: (1) to dismiss the application for repayment of debt; (2) to approve repayment of the debt in full; (3) to approve repayment of the debt in part. Any objections to the official receiver's order may be filed to the court within 14 days of learning of the order issued by the official receiver.

The plan approved by the court shall bind the creditors who may file application for repayment of debts for business reorganisation. If a creditor who is eligible to file an application for repayment of debt for business reorganisation does not file an application within the time limit, that creditor shall forfeit the right to receive payment of debt regardless of whether the business reorganisation of the debtor pursuant to the plan succeeds or not, unless (1) the plan provides otherwise; or (2) the court issues an order to cancel the business reorganisation order.

4.12 Termination of the Reorganisation

If the plan administrator feels that the reorganisation has been successfully completed pursuant to the plan, he/she shall report to the court and ask the court to order that the business reorganisation be terminated. In this case the court shall schedule a hearing. If it is found that the reorganisation has been successfully completed pursuant to the plan, the court shall order the reorganisation terminated without delay. But if it is found that the reorganisation has not been completed pursuant to the plan, the court shall order that the reorganisation be continued within the time period stipulated in the plan.

If the time limit for implementing the plan has expired but the business reorganisation has not yet been completed pursuant to the plan, the plan administrator shall report to the court within 14 days of the expiration of the time limit. The court shall schedule a hearing as soon as possible and notify the official receiver of the date and time of the hearing. The official receiver shall then notify the debtor and creditors at least three days in advance of the hearing. The court shall consider evidence in the file and listen to the statements given by the official receiver and creditors and the objections of the debtor. If the court deems it appropriate for the debtor to enter bankruptcy, it shall order the debtor to be under absolute receivership. However, if the court does not consider it appropriate to adjudicate the debtor to be bankrupt, the court shall order the reorganisation terminated.

4.13 The Court's Power

The Bankruptcy Court plays the most important part in controlling the reorganisation proceedings from beginning to end. The court shall consider whether to accept the petition for reorganisation or not. If accepted, the court shall proceed to make an inquiry to the petition and may issue an order for reorganisation or dismiss the petition.

After the reorganisation order has been made, the court shall appoint a plan preparer. In case the court is unable to appoint a plan preparer, it shall confer an order to repeal the previous order for reorganisation.

When the reorganisation plan formed by the plan preparer is passed by resolution at the creditors' meeting, the court shall consider whether to approve such plan. If the plan is not passed, the court shall set a hearing to consider whether the debtor be adjudged bankrupt. If the plan is approved by the court, the plan administrator shall implement the plan.

The court shall order the plan administrator to be removed from his/her position if the court finds that the plan administrator has failed to act in accordance with the plan or acts dishonestly. If failing to have a new plan administrator available, the court shall order an absolute receivership or give an order to repeal the previous order for reorganisation. If the plan has been implemented successfully, the court shall issue a terminating order.

4.14 The Role of the Official Receiver

The official receiver shall convene and chair the meeting of creditors when selecting the plan preparer, where the plan preparer nominated by the petitioner has not been approved by the court, when accepting the plan, and when selecting a new plan administrator. The official receiver has power to authorise the repayment of debt according to applications for repayment of debts for business reorganisation submitted by creditors, and has the power to manage the business and assets of the debtor temporarily during the time of selecting the plan preparer. To a certain extent, the official receiver shall get involved in all reorganisation proceedings, even in controlling the implementation of the reorganisation plan.

4.15 The Administration of the Debtor's Business

Where the court issues an order for reorganisation but has not yet appointed the plan preparer, the power and duties of the debtor's executive (the directors, managers or an authorised person who is empowered to operate the business of the debtor) in managing the business and assets shall cease.

The court shall appoint one or more persons to be the interim executive to manage the business and assets of the debtor under the supervision of the official receiver until a plan preparer is appointed. All legal rights of the debtor's shareholders shall be suspended, except the right to receive dividend, and such shall be vested in the interim executive or the official receiver as the case may be, until a plan preparer is appointed.

Upon acknowledgment of the order for reorganisation, the debtor's executive shall deliver the assets, seal, accounting ledgers and documents relating to the assets, liabilities and business of the debtor to the interim executive or the official receiver, as the case may be, as soon as possible. For this purpose, the interim executive or the official receiver is empowered to call upon any person who has in their possession the assets, seal, accounting ledgers and documents to deliver them to him.

When the court has appointed the plan preparer, the power and duties in managing the business and assets of the debtor and all legal rights of the debtor's shareholders, except the right to receive dividend, shall be vested in the plan preparer.

After the court has approved the plan, the rights and duties of the plan preparer shall immediately pass to the plan administrator.

If the court does not approve the reorganisation plan or terminates the reorganisation and orders an absolute receivership, the debtor goes into bankruptcy proceedings. When this happens, the creditors apply to the receiver for repayment. Creditors must file their claim within two months of the official publication of the absolute receivership, with the deadline extended to four months for foreign creditors. Upon filing all the claims, the receiver schedules a meeting to examine the claims of creditors. The court may approve claims not disputed by the debtor, receiver or other creditors. Upon approval of the claims, the receiver distributes the assets left after first paying fees and expenses. The bankrupt party must remain in bankruptcy for a period of three years.

In the event that the court has ordered the repeal of the reorganisation order, the responsibility for managing the business and assets of the debtor shall again devolve to the debtor's executive, and the debtor's shareholders shall again enjoy their legal rights. Where the order for the termination of the reorganisation has been made by the court, the debtor shall be free from all debt repayment which may be applied in the business reorganisation, and the debtor's executive shall again have the authority to manage the business operation and assets of the debtor. In such circumstances, the stay is lifted and all rights of shareholders and directors are reinstated. The debtor's shareholders shall again enjoy their legal rights. Secured creditors may then decide to foreclose on a debtor's assets.

4.16 Concurrent Application of Bankruptcy Proceedings in Reorganisation Proceedings

When the court has not approved the reorganisation plan, the court shall set a hearing to determine whether the debtor should be adjudged to be bankrupt. Where the court has removed the plan administrator and is unable to appoint a new one, if the court considers that the debtor should be adjudged bankrupt, the court shall issue an absolute receivership order at once. And in the case where the time limit for implementing the plan has expired, but the reorganisation has not yet been completed pursuant to the plan, if the court considers that the debtor should be adjudged bankrupt, the court shall issue an absolute receivership order. As the result of the court's order, proceedings shall shift from reorganisation proceedings to bankruptcy proceedings.

4.17 Appeals

Civil appeals regarding bankruptcy matters may be made to the Supreme (*Dika*) Court within one month from the date of judgment. The Bankruptcy Act (s 25) provides that the President of the Supreme Court shall establish a Bankruptcy Division to hear appeals from the Central Bankruptcy Court. The President of the Supreme Court, if he deems it appropriate, may have the General Assembly of the Supreme Court consider any point related to the bankruptcy case.

5 Creditors' Rights

5.1 Source of the Law

The Civil and Commercial Code (CCC) governs most aspects of the use of property to secure a debt. Both intangible and tangible property may be used to secure a debt. The major security arrangements used in Thailand are mortgage, sale with right of redemption, and hire purchase (Reid and Tomasic, 1997: 237).

5.2 Mortgage

Mortgages are dealt with in Title XII of the CCC. A 'mortgage' is defined in s 702 as 'a contract whereby a person, called the mortgagor, assigns a property to another person, called the mortgagee, as security for the performance of an obligation, without delivering the property to the mortgagee.'

Mortgages can apply to all immovables and movables such as ships or vessels of six tons or more, steam launches or motor-boats of five tons or more; floating houses, beasts of burden, and any other movables with regard to which the law requires a registration for that purpose (CCC, s 703).

Mortgage contracts must be in writing (s 713). A mortgage must be registered (s 714) and specify the property being mortgaged (s 704) and must contain, in Thai currency, either a certain sum or a maximum amount for which the mortgaged property is assigned as a security (s 708). If the property is subject to a condition, the mortgage of that property will be subject to the condition (s 706). One obligation may be secured by the mortgage of multiple properties (s 710).

A mortgage is security for the obligation and for interest, compensation in the case of non-performance of the obligation and costs of enforcement (s 715).

A mortgage extends to all things connected with the mortgaged property (s 718) with the exception of: (1) buildings constructed after the date of the mortgage unless there is a contract to that effect (s 719); (2) a mortgage on the building does not extend to the land it is on (s 720); and (3) fruits of the mortgaged property (s 721).

If mortgaged property is damaged so that the security becomes insufficient, the mortgagee may enforce the mortgage at once.

Where two or more persons have mortgaged their property as security for one obligation, and no order has been specified and one person has performed the obligation, the person who has performed the obligation or on whose property the mortgage has been enforced, has no right of recourse against the other mortgagors (s 725). Where an order has been specified, the payment of the mortgage by one of several mortgagors who have mortgaged their property to secure one and the same obligation, the release by the mortgagee of one of the mortgagors discharges the subsequent mortgagors to the extent of the injury suffered by them thereby (s 726).

A mortgage is enforced by notification to the debtor in writing demanding that the debtor perform their obligation within a reasonable time. If the debtor fails to comply, the mortgagee may initiate a court action for a judgment ordering the property to be sold at public auction (s 728).

A mortgage is extinguished by: (1) extinction of the underlying obligation; (2) release of the mortgage granted in writing; (3) the mortgagor being discharged; (4) the mortgage being removed; (5) auction sale of the mortgaged property by order of the court as a result of enforcement; and (6) foreclosure of the mortgage (s 744).

5.3 Pledges

A pledge is a 'contract whereby a person, called the pledgor, delivers to another person, called the pledgee, a movable property as a security for the performance of an obligation' (CCC, s 747). The law governing pledges is found in Title XIII of the CCC. Parties to a pledge may agree that the pledged property be kept by a third person (s 749).

If the pledged property is a right represented by a written instrument, the pledge is void unless such instrument is delivered to the pledgee and the pledge is notified in writing to the debtor of the right (s 750). If a named certificate for share or debenture is pledged, such pledge cannot be set up against the company or other third persons, unless the creation of the pledge is entered in the company's book in accordance with Title XXII of the CCC relating to the transfer of shares or debentures (s 754).

A pledgee is entitled to retain all pledged property until the pledgee has received full performance of the obligation and accessories (s 758). The pledgee is bound to keep the pledged property in safe custody and take due care of it (s 759). If, without the consent of the pledgor, the pledgee uses the property or lets a third party have custody of it, he is liable for the loss or damage of the pledged property, even if caused by *force majeure*, unless the loss or damage would have happened in any case (s 760).

To enforce a pledge, written notice must first be given to the debtor together with reasonable time to pay. If the debtor fails to comply, the pledgee is entitled to sell the pledged property, but only at public auction. The pledgee must notify the pledgor in writing of the time and place of the auction (s 764).

A pledge is extinguished when (1) the obligation secured is extinguished; or (2) when the pledgee allows the pledged property to return into the possession of the pledgor (s 769).

5.4 Sale with Right of Redemption

A sale with a right of redemption involves a contract of sale of collateral to the creditor with the right of the debtor to redeem the property upon the payment of the debtor's obligation (s 1299). If the property is not redeemed, the creditor becomes the owner. If it is redeemed, the ownership of the property is deemed never to have vested in the creditor. Where a sale with right of redemption involves immovable property, the security interest must be registered.

5.5 Conditional Sale

A conditional sale involves the sale of property where the seller gives the buyer credit on the basis that ownership of the property will not pass until the whole of the purchase price is paid. There is no system of registration for conditional sales (Reid and Tomasic, 1997: 239).

5.6 Charge

Immovable property may be subject to a charge entitling the beneficiary to a periodical performance out of such property or to a specified use and enjoyment of it (s 1429). Charges are dealt with in Title VIII of the CCC.

A charge may be created for either a period of time or for the life of the beneficiary. If no time is fixed it is presumed to last for the life of the beneficiary (s 1430). Unless otherwise provided in the contract creating it, a charge is not transferable even by way of inheritance (s 1431).

If the beneficiary of a charge fails to comply with any essential condition specified in the act creating the charge, the beneficiary's right may be terminated (s 1432).

If the owner of the property does not perform their obligations under the charge, the beneficiary may, in addition to remedies for non-performance, apply to the court to appoint a receiver to manage the property and perform the obligations of the owner, or order the property to be sold by auction and the beneficiary to be paid out of the proceeds. However, where the debtor puts up a security, the court may refuse to make an order to appoint a receiver or for an auction (s 1433).

5.7 Hire Purchase

A hire purchase agreement is a 'contract whereby an owner of a property lets it out on hire and promises to sell it to, or that it shall become the property of, the hirer, conditionally on his making of a certain number of payments' (s 572). Contracts of hire purchase must be in writing.

The hirer may at any time terminate the contract by redelivering the property at the hirer's expense to the owner (s 573).

The owner may terminate the hire purchase contract upon the default of two successive payments, or breach of any material part of the contract, in which case all previous payments are forfeited to the owner who is entitled to resume possession of the property (s 574).

5.8 Priority Rules

Priority rules can be quite complex in their application. Generally, secured debts will receive priority over unsecured ones. Competing security interests will have priority according to the date they were secured. Where the security interest must be registered, priority will be determined by the date of registration.

6 Cross-border Insolvency

Thai bankruptcy law recognises the principle of territory. Therefore, an insolvency decree only affects the assets of the debtor which are located within Thailand. Bankruptcy in another country does not extend to the properties of a debtor located in Thailand.

7 Further Legal Reforms

At the time of writing further reforms of the bankruptcy laws are being debated. These include measures to give greater protection to minor creditors; tougher provisions dealing with the case of debtor dishonesty; and greater powers regarding the seizure of assets hidden from the Bankruptcy Court.

The reforms leading to the establishment of the Bankruptcy Court with a specialised procedure and the amendments to the Bankruptcy Act must not be seen in isolation. They are part of an overall structural reform of the Thai legal system to bring it into line with the needs of a modern global economy. These reforms include the further reform of foreclosure laws, provisions of a regulatory framework for e-commerce, enhanced corporate governance standards, provision of greater protection of intellectual property rights, and a reform and greater use of competition law, especially removing the barriers to foreign ownership and participation in the Thai economy (Ministry of Finance, Thailand). These measures and improved economic performance will hopefully lead to a credit culture that is more conducive to direct foreign investment and a sustainable economic recovery.

7.1 Modified Civil Procedure

Other relevant legal reforms include Amendments to the Civil Procedure Code on petty cases to simplify court procedures involving small amounts (enacted 3 May 1999).

Stricter court enforcement has been brought about by the Amendment to the Civil Procedure Code on Execution of Judgment. This amendment, effective 3 May 1999, limits the court's discretionary power on rescinding auction sales to two reasons: (1) fraud among bidders and (2) officers' malfeasance. This is designed to stop attempts to prolong the sale and debt repayment process. A further tightening of the rules regarding defaults will come about by the proposed Amendment to the Civil Procedure Code on Default Judgment.

7.2 Corporatisation of State-owned Enterprises

Another important area of reform relates to state-owned enterprises. The purpose of this reform is to promote greater management efficiency and transparency, and to facilitate the privatisation process, thereby lessening the burdens to the government. Key areas targeted for corporatisation include the Petroleum Authority of Thailand, the Telephone Organization of Thailand and the Communication Authority of Thailand.

7.3 Reform of the Alien Business Act

The new Alien Business Act (effective mid-2000) was designed to lessen the restrictions applying to aliens (foreigners) operating businesses in Thailand. By allowing greater liberalisation in the job categories open to foreigners, it is hoped to promote capital inflows.

7.4 Banking Reform

New administrative arrangements are exemplified by the September 1999 Bank of Thailand notification to all commercial banks in Thailand. This places restrictions on the granting of credit facilities to or holding of shares in a debtor company in which a director or senior officer, with the rank of Senior Vice President or above, of the bank is one of the debtor company's directors. The purpose of the measure is to improve transparency and avoid conflicts of interest (Kamchadduskorn, 1999/2000).

7.5 New Competition Law

Thailand has also moved to enhance its attractiveness to investors by the promotion of open and fair competition. This is evidenced by the development of a modern competition regime through the Trade Competition Act 1999. Maximum penalties of three years' imprisonment and fines up to six million baht will give businesses strong encouragement to refrain from anti-competitive behavior (Chairprabba and Hancock, 1999/2000).

7.6 Act on Leasing of Property for Commerce and Industry

Effective since 18 May 1999, this Act extends the leasing period from 30 to 50 years, renewable for another 50. It also defines the leasing rights as an asset right which can be transferred from one party to another. These measures aim to attract long-term investment which requires large capital and a long breakeven period.

7.7 Amendment to the Land Code

This amendment allows foreign investors who bring in capital of at least forty million baht to own 1 rai (0.25 acres) of land for their residence. This is another measure to accommodate foreign investors who undertake substantial investment in Thailand.

7.8 Amendment to the Condominium Act

Enacted on 27 April 1999, this Act allows foreigners to own more than 49 per cent of the space of condominiums in Bangkok, municipal areas or local administration as specified by regulations, if the total space of the condominium is below five rais (1.25 acres). The purpose of this legislation is to attract foreign investment into the ailing real estate sector. However, foreigners will not be allowed to own more than 49 per cent of condominium developments outside the above areas.

7.9 Further Governance Reform

Thailand also needs further work on its corporate governance reform. This includes increased disclosure requirements, adoption of 'best international practice' in accounting standards, greater responsibility placed upon management to be proactive, limiting the use of stock options, stricter controls on the independence and accountability of auditors, tougher laws on fraud and corruption and greater transparency overall. A step in the right direction has been the disclosure since January 1999 by the Securities and Exchange Commission of information on companies failing to meet new corporate governance requirements, including:

- violating securities and exchange law, including delay in submitting reports, insider trading or suspension or revocation of licences;
- auditors, managers, financial advisers, fund managers who are on probation or whose licenses have been suspended or revoked;
- companies whose management or internal controls have failed.

(Stewart and Thompson, 2002; Thailand Securities Exchange Commission Action Plan 2005)

Most recently, the Thai Securities and Exchange Commission released its 2005 Action Plan which included the following:

2005 Action Plan

In December 2004, the SEC laid down its 2005 Action Plan focusing on the improvement of good corporate governance of Thai listed companies. The following are examples of actions included in the plan:

1. Improve good corporate governance of Thai listed companies on a par with international standards by:
   - Urging all Thai listed companies to comply with the SET's 15 CG principles
   - Promoting the good image of corporate governance of Thailand in the views of foreign investors
   - Building up better understanding among practitioners by introducing a 'Director's Handbook' that clearly prescribes roles and responsibilities of directors under the Thai law, and in accordance with best international practices, and by encouraging listed company directors to participate in the training courses organized by the Thai Institute of Directors Association (IOD)
   - Adopting a registration system for listed company directors and management, which will take effect from March 1, 2005, for the purpose of monitoring as well as imposing administrative sanction.

   (SEC News No. 11/2005 dated January 25, 2005)

2. Improve the quality of information disclosure by listed companies by:
   - Raising the quality of IPO companies by strengthening internal control standards and accounting practices
   - Preventing inappropriate connected transactions that take advantage of retail investors
   - Closely monitoring and strictly imposing sanctions in case of inappropriate action or misconduct of listed companies and company management.

3. Strengthen accounting standards and auditor practice by working closely with the Federation of Accounting Professions in raising the Thai accounting standards to be on a par with international accounting standards.

   (SEC News No. 8/2005, dated January 20, 2005)

4. Support whistle blowers in providing information on corporate fraud or embezzlement.

5. Enlarge the roles of institutional investors by requiring mutual funds to exercise proxy voting as well as make clear statements on proxy voting direction including investment policy in companies with a high standard of corporate governance.

8 Conclusion

Economic success in a global economy requires the development of a legal infrastructure which will give the world community confidence that the rule of law will prevail in a particular country and operate in a way which meets modern business expectations. The ability of a creditor to use the law to enforce its claim against an insolvent debtor reduces the risk of lending and thereby enhances the availability of credit and attracts further investment in Thai businesses. Good corporate governance in turn enhances the country's growth and international competitiveness. In this sense, Thailand's Bankruptcy Act, as recently amended and discussed in this chapter, will hopefully enable Thailand to proceed in the desired direction. It must also be realised that insolvency reform is but one component of good corporate governance. New laws, however, are ineffective unless they are enforced and seen to be enforced so that the rule of law replaces a past legacy of corruption and political interference. The eyes of the international community will watch with interest as Thailand proceeds with its reform agenda. If it succeeds, the Thai Economic Tiger will continue on its path to a healthy recovery.

References

Anderson, B.J. (1997), 'Thailand', in A. Gutterman and R. Brown (eds) *Commercial Laws of East Asia*, Hong Kong, Sweet & Maxwell Asia, pp. 559–61.

Asia Restructuring Group, The (1998), 'A Review of the 1998 Thai Bankruptcy Act', June, at http://cadwalader.com/resources/com/6-98.html.

Bremmer, B. (1997), 'Rescuing Asia', *Business Week*, 17 November, p. 116.

Business Monitor International (2000), 'The outlook for Thailand's pivotal TPI debt work out', *Asia Weekly Economic Alert*, Vol. 3, No. 23.

Chairprabba, C. and Hancock, J. (1999/2000), 'Thailand Report', *Asia Pacific Legal Developments Bulletin*, December/January, Vol. 14, No. 4, pp. 17–24.

Dekle, R., Karchanasai, C. and Hoontrakul, P. (2003), 'Credit Constraints, High Fixed Costs and the Asian Currency Crisis: Firm Level Evidence from Thailand', Paper presented for the Koc-Sabanci Conference in Macroeconomics, 18–19 August in Istanbul, Turkey, June 2003: http://www.usc.edu/dept/LAS/economics/event/content/dekle_thai.pdf.

Dever, E. and Vajassit, S., 'Amendment to Thai Bankruptcy Act (No 5) BE 2542', available at http://www.legal-ex.go.th/earticles1.htm.

Einhorn, B. and Corben, R. (1997), 'One Tired Tiger', *Business Week* (Intl Edition) 24 March, p. 22.

Engardio, P. (1998), 'Cleaning Up Thailand's Mess: The Long Struggle Ahead', *Business Week*, 12 October, at 120.

Falgui, R.G. (1997), 'Currency Crisis Puts ASEAN Scheme to the Test', *Business World* (Manila), 23 October.

Fletcher, I.P. (1996), *The Law of Insolvency*, 2nd ed, London, Sweet & Maxwell.

Fletcher, I.P. (2005), *Insolvency in Private International Law: National and International Approaches*, 2nd ed., Oxford, Oxford University Press.

Gonzalez, M. (1997), 'Thailand Tries to Recover', *Wall Street Journal*, 10 October, at 22.

Halligan, J. and Turner, M. (1995), *Profiles of Government Administration in Asia*, Canberra, AGPS.

Hummel, A.L. and Sethsathira, P. (1991), *Starting and Operating a Business In Thailand*, Singapore, Asia Books Co Ltd.

International Monetary Fund (IMF) (2002), 'IMF Warning: Corporate sector still needs help', *The Nation*, 31 August, http://www.nationmultimedia.com/.

Kamchadduskorn, C. (1999/2000), 'Directors of Banks/debtors face limits' *Asia Pacific Legal Developments Bulletin*, December/January, Vol. 14, No. 4, pp. 16–17.

Kosolkitiwong, P. (2001), 'Insolvency Law Reforms: Report on Thailand', Asian Development Bank Regional Technical Assistance Project No 5795-REG, at http://www.insolvencyasia.com/insolvency_law_regimes/thailand/index.html.

Krnongkaew, M. (1993), 'Poverty and Income Distribution', in Peter G. Warr (ed.), *The Thai Economy in Transition*, 401, pp. 535–36.

Miller, S. (2000), 'A New Era for Thailand's Bankruptcy Court?' available at http://www.hk-lawyer.com/2000-6/June00-43.htm.

Ministry of Finance, Thailand, Macroeconomic Framework and Policy, available at http://www.mof.go.th/ther_2/index_ther.html#1.

Reid, K. and Tomasic, R. (1997), 'The Philippines, Thailand and Vietnam', in Tomasic, R. and Little, P. (eds), *Insolvency Law and Practice in Asia*, Hong Kong, Pearson Professional Limited.

Simon, W.E. (1997), 'Abolish the IMF', *Wall Street Journal*, 23 October, at 18.

Stewart, G. Bennett and Thompson, A. (2002), 'A better governance system', *The Nation*, 14 October, at 6.

Thailand Securities Exchange Commission Action Plan (2005), at http://www.sec.or.th/en/cg/update/cg_update_e.shtml.

Webb, S. (1998), 'Asia's Financial Woes Becloud International Markets', *Wall Street Journal*, 2 January, at R1.

Wong, K., Phunsunthorn, C. and Sucharitkul, T. (2000), 'Problems and Promises: the Reform of Thai Bankruptcy Law in Wake of the Asian Financial Crisis', *Harvard Asia Quarterly*, Winter, at http://www.fas.harvard.edu/~asiactr/haq/200001/0001a004.htm.

Wood, P.R. (1995), *Principles of International Insolvency*, London, Sweet & Maxwell.

Chapter 10

Insolvency Law in Malaysia

BAHRIN (KAM) KAMARUL
University of Canberra

1 Introduction

1.1 Introduction to the Legal System and Local Legal Culture, Attitudes to Debt and Debt Enforcement

The Malaysian legal system is characterized as a pluralistic system. Its laws and legal institutions reflect various stages of Malaysian history and include the laws of pre-colonial Malaysia, the laws and institutions imposed by Britain during its period of colonization, and the laws of independent Malaysia.[1] Consequently Malaysian law has several sources. They include the following:

- the law of the Federal Constitution together with the constitutions of the 13 states comprising the federation;
- legislation enacted by the Parliament and State Assemblies under their respective powers;
- delegated legislation made according to powers conferred by Acts of Parliament or Enactments of State Assemblies;
- received principles of English law applicable to local circumstances;
- judicial decisions of the Supreme Court and High Courts;
- judicial decisions of the former Federal Court and Judicial Committee of the Privy Council;
- customs of the local inhabitants which have been accepted as law by the courts.

Muslim law is also a major source of Malaysian law but it is formally applicable only to Muslims and is administered by a separate system of shariah courts.[2]

Generally, Malaysian cultural attitudes to corporations in financial difficulty tend toward the denial or concealment of the fact that these corporations are in such difficulty rather than to admit it and to come to terms with it.[3] The multicultural environment of Malaysia, especially Chinese culture that emphasizes trust and family solidarity, has influenced these attitudes. But there are indications that financial rather

---

1 ASEAN Law Association, *ASEAN Legal Systems*, 1995, Singapore, Butterworths.

2 Wu, Min Aun, *The Malaysian Legal System*, 1990, Petaling Jaya, Malaysia, Longman.

3 Nathan, Rabindra, *Insolvency Law Reforms: Report on Malaysia* (www.insolvencyasia.com) Asian Development Bank.

than family and personal considerations are becoming the most important factors in the administration of insolvency in Malaysia.[4]

1.2 History, Sources and Philosophy of Insolvency Laws in Malaysia

The underlying philosophy of Malaysian insolvency law has been described as combining the elements of distributive, rehabilitative and penal philosophies.[5] The main objectives of corporate insolvency law of Malaysia are as follows: (1) to provide for rehabilitation where possible; (2) to ensure the preservation and ranking of secured creditors' rights and equal treatment of all other creditors where a company cannot be saved; and (3) to punish delinquent officers who have contributed to the insolvency. In the case of personal bankruptcy, on their discharge, the bankrupt is freed from all debts provable in bankruptcy and is also released from many civil liabilities attached to him or her as a bankrupt.

In practice, however, insolvency law has been described as having a bias towards the interests of creditors. The consensus among Malaysian practitioners of bankruptcy and insolvency law is that the law is both formally and practically concerned with the collection of debt and the protection of creditors.[6] As one local lawyer and advocate specializing in insolvency law stated:

> I have done quite a lot of recovery here, usually instigated by banks. Banks choose bankruptcy as a method of debt collection because the threat of insolvency is an effective tactic. Whilst not the fastest technique, it is a common and effective legal tactic in the recovery of debts. Banks see it as good management and there are no cultural reasons why this technique should not be used.

A local accountant commented that '[f]undamentally, insolvency law in Malaysia is designed to help creditors enforce their rights, recover their debts and protect their interests. Malaysia primarily has a creditor focused system.'

There are, however, indications of growing dissatisfaction with Malaysia's pro-creditor laws. In particular, there have been repeated calls for the introduction of an equivalent to the US Chapter 11 rescue procedures. For example, a senior government banker recalled that 'in the 1980s recession, a Chapter 11 equivalent was proposed but the banks were opposed to it and the proposal was not successful. The banks thought that the existing procedures were slow enough and that a Chapter 11 equivalent would make things even slower.' However, a leading local accountant was confident that 'changes will soon be made to reflect less creditor-friendly laws. These laws will support debtor rights and give debtors some control over the process.'

---

4 Tomasic, R. and Little, P. (eds) *Insolvency Law and Practice in Asia*, FT Law & Tax Asia Pacific, Hong Kong, 1997, p. 13.

5 Nathan, Rabindra *Insolvency Law Reforms: Report on Malaysia* (www.insolvencyasia.com) Asian Development Bank.

6 The statements quoted below are based on interviews with Malaysian bankruptcy and insolvency practitioners conducted by the author as part of a study of six East Asian insolvency law regimes in 1996. The study was funded by an Australian Research Council grant and has been reported in Tomasic, R. and Little, P. (eds) *Insolvency Law and Practice in Asia*, FT Law & Tax Asia Pacific, Hong Kong, 1997.

He added that when he commenced his career, 'receivership and liquidation were a matter of course. Now debtors are challenging this emphasis as they want a procedure that has a framework of negotiation with some control for debtors.'

1.3 Key Bankruptcy and Insolvency Law Principles in Malaysia

Bankruptcy and company law in Malaysia has been developed through the interaction and interdependence of case law that originated in England and Australia. Legislation dealing with personal bankruptcy consists of the Malaysian Bankruptcy Act 1967 and the Bankruptcy Rules 1969. They are modeled on English bankruptcy law. Similarly, the core company legislation in Malaysia, that is, the Companies Act 1965, is modeled on the English Companies Act 1948 and the Australian Uniform Companies Act 1961. Principles of common law that comprise English and Australian insolvency law are reflected in the Malaysian insolvency regime. In view of this historical relationship, English and Australian judicial pronouncements on the interpretation of company legislation are still highly persuasive in interpreting Malaysian company law, even though there is increasing divergence in Australian and English judicial attitudes to corporate governance.[7]

The broad aims of Malaysian corporate insolvency law are similar to the Australian and English equivalents. The purposes and principles of insolvency law in many different Western legal systems have been described in terms of such criteria as fairness, efficiency and impartiality.[8] The aims of Malaysian insolvency law are similar. They include the rehabilitation of debtors, fair and efficient distribution of debtors' assets to creditors, equality and impartiality of treatment of creditors, and the punishment of wrongdoers. The rehabilitative aim of the law manifests itself in section 176 of the Companies Act, which deals with the schemes of arrangements and in the Pengurusan Danaharta Nasional Berhad Act 1998. The recital to the latter statute *inter alia* states that its declared aim is to 'assist the business sector by dealing expeditiously with financially distressed enterprises'. Evidence of a distributive philosophy can be found in Part X of the Companies Act comprising sections 212 to 318 and in particular to Division 4 of Part X which deals with priorities. Provisions exist in the Act to punish wrongful trading and fraudulent trading and to punish non-compliance with the insolvency provisions.[9]

1.4 General Introduction to the Statutory, Regulatory and Judicial Approaches to Corporate Insolvency and Personal Bankruptcy Laws

The core of legislative regulation of personal bankruptcy in Malaysia consists of the Bankruptcy Act 1967 and the Bankruptcy Rules 1969. Company insolvency, on the other hand, is governed by the Companies Act 1965 (revised 1973), which came into

---

7 Arjunan, K., *Lipton & Herzberg's Understanding Company Law in Malaysia*, 1995, LBC Information Services, Sydney.

8 Tomasic, R. and Whitford, K., *Australian Insolvency and Bankruptcy Law*, 2nd Edition, 1997, Sydney, Butterworths, p. 4.

9 Nathan, Rabindra, *Insolvency Law Reforms: Report on Malaysia* (www.insolvencyasia.com) Asian Development Bank.

force on 15 April 1966, and the Companies Regulations 1966.[10] The Act is modeled on the English Companies Act 1948 and the Australian Uniform Companies Act 1961. As a result, judicial approaches to company law both in England and Australia have greatly influenced the development of legal principles of Malaysian bankruptcy and insolvency law.[11] A special insolvency process was established by the enactment of Pengurusan Danharta Nasional Berhad Act 1998. The relevant legislation for court-appointed receivers includes the First Schedule to the Courts of Judicature Act 1964 and Order 30 of the Rules of the High Court 1980.

2 Personal Insolvency Laws

2.1 Introduction to Personal Insolvency/Bankruptcy Laws in Malaysia

In Malaysia, personal bankruptcy is treated at law as separate from corporate insolvency and winding up. Legislation relating to personal bankruptcy is the enactment of the Malaysian federal Parliament exercising its power to make laws regarding 'civil and criminal law and procedure and the administration of justice'.[12] Bankruptcy and insolvency are matters that are listed under this heading of power granted to the federal Parliament. On the other hand, the power of the federal Parliament to make laws regarding 'incorporation, regulation and winding up of corporations' is listed under the 'trade, commerce and industry' heading.[13]

The main objects of bankruptcy are, first, to secure a just and equitable distribution of the debtors' available property among the creditors. Secondly, it relieves debtors from their debt and enables them to make a fresh start as soon as they are discharged by the court.

Recourse to formal proceedings under personal bankruptcy law in order to collect debt is not very high in Malaysia. The procedures are perceived to be highly costly and are subject to long delays. More often than not, the assets of the bankrupt prove to be insufficient to satisfy the debts. Consequently, creditors generally regard bankruptcy proceedings as an instrument of threat and a measure of last resort. Creditors prefer, instead, to collect personal debts through non-legal and informal means.[14]

2.2 The Regulatory Structures for the Control of Bankruptcy Proceedings

Bankruptcy proceedings in Malaysia are regulated legislatively by the Bankruptcy Act 1967, Bankruptcy Rules 1969, Bankruptcy (Costs) Rules 1969, Bankruptcy

---

10 *The Malaysian Companies Act*, MDC Sdn. Bhd, 1987, Kuala Lumpur, Malaysia.

11 Arjunan, Krishnan, and Low, Chee Kong, *Lipton & Herzberg's Understanding Company Law in Malaysia*, 1995, LBC Information Services, Sydney, Australia.

12 Ninth Schedule, Paragraph 4 (e) (i) of the *Malayan Federal Constitution* 1957.

13 Ninth Schedule, paragraph 8 (c) of the *Malaysian Federal Constitution* 1957.

14 This is the view expressed by several Malaysian lawyers and bankruptcy practitioners interviewed by the author in 1996.

(Fees) Rules 1969 and by the common law. Malaysian and Singaporean case law are relevant in determining the law of bankruptcy in Malaysia.

2.3 The Principal Institutions for the Application of these Laws

Formal bankruptcy proceedings are court-based procedures. The High Court is given comprehensive powers with regard to personal bankruptcy. On the adjudication of bankruptcy, the bankrupt's property is vested in the Official Assignee[15] who then has the duty of administering the assets of the bankrupt as well as undertaking the duty of investigating, reporting upon and conducting a public examination of the debtor.[16] With regard to the bankrupt's estate, the Official Assignee is under a duty to act as receiver and manager and raise money or make advances for the purposes of the estate. He or she is also obliged to conduct all meetings of creditors, and to report to the creditors as to any proposal that the debtor makes with respect to the mode of liquidating their affairs.[17]

Bankruptcy practitioners, drawn mainly from professional accountants, but also from lawyers, contribute to the bankruptcy process by advising and managing bankruptcy procedures, especially on behalf of creditors. They are involved mainly in facilitating the recovery of debts and sometimes in the negotiating of compromises and settlements of such debts. Special managers, with the powers of receivers, may be appointed by the Official Assignee to protect the estates of debtors against whom bankruptcy petitions have been lodged.[18]

2.4 General Powers of the Court in Bankruptcy Matters

The High Court of Malaysia has general jurisdiction over bankruptcy matters.[19] It is vested with the power to make a receiving order[20] and an adjudication of bankruptcy.[21] The court may adjudge the debtor bankrupt at the time of making a receiving order unless the debtor can show that they are in a position to offer a composition or make a scheme of arrangement satisfactory to their creditors. The Act also vests power in the High Court to decide all questions of priorities and all other questions whatsoever, whether of law or fact, which may arise in any bankruptcy case coming to it. It has power to decide on any matter that it deems is expedient or necessary to decide for the purpose of doing complete justice or making a complete distribution of property in any bankruptcy case.[22]

---

15 Under section 24(4), Bankruptcy Act 1967.
16 Section 72, Bankruptcy Act 1967.
17 Section 73, Bankruptcy Act 1967.
18 Section 12, Bankruptcy Act 1967.
19 Section 88, Bankruptcy Act 1967.
20 Section 4, Bankruptcy Act 1967.
21 Section 24, Bankruptcy Act 1967.
22 Section 91, Bankruptcy Act 1967.

2.5 Rules regarding Creditors' Petitions for Bankruptcy

A creditor is entitled to present a bankruptcy petition against a debtor. The requirements are, first, that the debt owing is a liquidated sum of more than RM10,000 payable either immediately or at a particular time in the future and, secondly, that an act of bankruptcy on which the petition is grounded has occurred within six months before the presentation of the petition.[23] A debtor has committed an act of bankruptcy in any one of the following circumstances:[24]

- if property is transferred to a trustee for the benefit of the creditors generally;
- if property is fraudulently transferred elsewhere;
- if the property transfer is void as a fraudulent preference when he or she is made a bankrupt;
- if with intention to defeat or delay creditors the debtor leaves Malaysia or stays out of Malaysia, does not attend their business or shuts down their business, or submits collusively or fraudulently to an adverse judgment or order for the payment of money;
- if an execution issued against the debtor has been levied by seizure of their property and the judgment, including costs, amounts to more than RM1,000;
- if the debtor files in the court a declaration of their inability to pay their debts or presents a bankruptcy petition against themselves;
- if notice is given to any of the creditors that payment of debts has been suspended or is about to be suspended;
- if the debtor makes an offer of composition with their creditors or a proposal for a scheme of arrangement which is not registered within 14 days;
- if the debtor does not comply with the Bankruptcy Notice which requires payment of the judgment debt; and
- if the sheriff or bailiff states that the debtor has no property liable to seizure.

2.6 Rules regarding Debtors' Petitions for Bankruptcy

A debtor may present their own petition. The petition must state that they are unable to pay their debts. The debtor's presentation itself is deemed to be an act of bankruptcy as a consequence of which the court is obliged to make a receiving order.[25]

When a receiving order is made the Official Assignee becomes the receiver of the debtor's property. No creditor has any remedy against the property or the debtor themselves and no creditor can sue or start any legal action except with the permission of the court. The receiving order does not deprive the debtor of the ownership of their property. They are only deprived of the possession and control of the property. The aim of the receiving order is to protect the debtor's property.

---

23 Section 5, Bankruptcy Act 1967.

24 Section 3, Bankruptcy Act 1967.

25 Section 7, Bankruptcy Act 1967.

2.7 *Powers of Secured Creditors*

A receiving order made by the court does not affect the rights of secured creditors. Secured creditors may realize or otherwise deal with their security.[26] Secured creditors may either rely on their security and not prove, or realize their security and prove for the balance, or surrender their security and prove for the whole debt, or estimate the value of their security and prove for the balance of their debt.[27] However, secured creditors shall not be entitled to any interest in respect of their debts after the making of the receiving order if they do not realize their security within six months from the date of the order.[28]

2.8 *Nature of Bankruptcy Petitions by Creditors and Debtors*

While the main aim of the debtor's petition is normally the protection of the debtor's property, the creditors' petition aims at ensuring control over the property and the person of the debtor. On the making of the receiving order against a debtor, the Official Assignee must take possession of all books of accounts and other papers and documents in the possession, custody or control of the debtor relating to their property or affairs. He or she may also take possession of all or any deeds, books, documents and other property of the debtor. After a receiving order has been made, a creditor may petition the court to have the debtor detained or, if the latter is not present, to be arrested and detained. Unless the debtor gives satisfactory security that they will not leave Malaysia without the approval of the Official Assignee, they may be imprisoned until the public examination.[29]

2.9 *Creditors' Meetings*

As soon as the receiving order is made, a general meeting of the creditors must be held. The meeting must consider whether a proposal for a composition or scheme of arrangements is to be accepted or whether it is expedient that the debtor be adjudged bankrupt. The meeting must also consider the issue of how to deal with the debtor's property.[30]

An adjudication order making the debtor bankrupt may be made by the court where the creditors, at their first meeting, resolve that the debtor be made bankrupt, or where a composition or scheme is not accepted or approved within 14 days after the examination of the debtor.

---

26 Section 8, Bankruptcy Act 1967.

27 As provided in Schedule C, Bankruptcy Act 1967.

28 Ibid.

29 Section 9, Bankruptcy Act 1967.

30 Section 15, Bankruptcy Act 1967.

3 Personal Bankruptcy Law Procedures

3.1 Controls Placed on Debtors once a Bankruptcy Petition has been Lodged

Several controls are placed on the debtor once a bankruptcy petition has been lodged against him or her. The court may cause the debtor to be arrested under a number of circumstances:

- if it appears that there is probable reason to believe that the debtor is in hiding or has absconded or is about to abscond with a view to avoiding payment of their debt or delaying or embarrassing proceedings of bankruptcy against them;
- if there is probable cause to believe that the debtor is about to remove his/her goods to prevent or delay the Official Assignee from seizing them;
- if there is probable ground for believing that the debtor has concealed or is about to conceal any goods, books, documents or writings that might be useful to the creditors in the course of the bankruptcy;
- failing to attend any examination ordered by the court.[31]

3.2 Collection of Information about Debtors and Examination of Debtors

A debtor, after a receiving order is made against him or her, is required to submit to the Official Assignee information regarding their affairs. The information must include a statement of assets, debts and liabilities. The debtor must also provide information regarding their creditors, the securities held by them and when these securities were created. To be provided as well is a statement of when the debtor last balanced their accounts and the amount of their capital at that time.[32]

When a receiving order is made, the Official Assignee applies to the court for a public examination of the debtor. The examination must be held as soon as possible after the submission of the debtor's statement of affairs and after the first meeting of the creditors. The debtor's conduct, dealings and property will be examined. The public examination may be dispensed with if a mental or physical disability makes the debtor unfit to attend.[33]

At the public examination, any creditor who has lodged a proof of debt may question the debtor on the latter's affairs and causes of their failure. The Official Assignee must participate in the public examination. The court may also question the debtor. The debtor must be examined under oath and he/she must answer all questions put by the court.[34] The court may adjudge the debtor bankrupt if a proposed composition or scheme is not accepted or approved within 14 days of the examination of the debtor.

---

31 Section 28, Bankruptcy Act 1967.
32 Section 16, Bankruptcy Act 1967.
33 Section 17, Bankruptcy Act 1967.
34 Ibid.

3.3 Rules regarding the Proof of Debts

Any creditor who wishes to share in the distribution of the proceeds of sale of the estate of the bankrupt must prove their debt to the satisfaction of the Official Assignee. All debts and liabilities, present or future, certain or contingent, to which the debtor is subject at the date of the receiving order are provable debts in bankruptcy.[35] Similarly, debts to which the debtor may become subject before their discharge by reason of any obligation incurred before the date of the receiving order are also provable in bankruptcy. Rules regarding the proof of debt are provided in *Schedule C* of the Act.

The rules provide that every creditor must prove their debt soon after the making of a receiving order. A debt may be proved by providing an affidavit verifying the debt to the Official Assignee. The affidavit must contain a statement of account showing the particulars of debt and must specify the vouchers, if any. The Official Assignee may ask for the vouchers. Every creditor who has lodged a proof is entitled to see and examine the proofs of other creditors.

The Official Assignee will examine every proof and the grounds for the debt and, in writing, admit or reject it or require further evidence in support of it. If a creditor's proof is admitted, the notice of dividend is sufficient notification to the creditor of the admission. If the proof is rejected, the creditor will be informed by the Official Assignee of the grounds of rejection. If the creditor is dissatisfied with the decision, the court may, on the creditor's application, reverse or vary the decision.

3.4 Orders which may be made in regard to the Property of the Debtor

Upon the making of the adjudication order, the property of the bankrupt immediately passes to and vests with the Official Assignee.[36] The Official Assignee takes the property subject to any liabilities attaching to it. The main duty of the Official Assignee is to realize the bankrupt's property and to distribute them to the creditors.[37] The debtor is under a duty to make full disclosure of their property and to deliver possession of their property to the Official Assignee.[38] If the debtor fails to perform these duties he/she is guilty of contempt of the court.[39]

Property is defined as including money, goods, things in action, land, every description of property, obligations and easements and every description of estate, interest and profit, present and future.[40] Property of the bankrupt refers only to property that is divisible. The property of the bankrupt comprises the following:

- all property belonging to the bankrupt at the commencement of the bankruptcy or acquired by them before their discharge;

---

35 Section 40, Bankruptcy Act 1967.
36 Sections 24 and 58, Bankruptcy Act 1967.
37 Section 62, Bankruptcy Act 1967.
38 Section 27, Bankruptcy Act 1967.
39 Section 28, Bankruptcy Act 1967.
40 Section 2, Bankruptcy Act 1967.

- the capacity to take proceedings for exercising all powers in respect of property as might be exercised by a bankrupt for their own benefit at the commencement of their bankruptcy or before their discharge; and,
- all goods, being at the commencement of bankruptcy, in the possession, order or disposition of the bankrupt, with the consent of the true owner under such circumstances that they are the reputed owner.[41]

However, the property of the bankrupt does not include trust property and articles excepted by the Act.

The court may issue a warrant for the seizure of a bankrupt's property. Any person acting under the warrant may break open any house, building or room of the bankrupt, where any of the latter's property is supposed to be. The court may also issue a search warrant to any police officer if it is satisfied that the property of the bankrupt is concealed in a place not belonging to him or her.[42] The Official Assignee may obtain from the court an order for the redirection to him or her by the postal authorities of all telegrams and post letters addressed to the debtor for a period of not more than three months.[43] This will enable the Official Assignee to secure information relating to the debtor's dealings that may not otherwise come to light.

3.5 Rules for the Distribution of the Assets of the Bankrupt

The debts of the bankrupt are ranked in an order of priority. The expenses of preservation and realization of the assets are ranked first. Second in priority are costs and charges of the bankruptcy proceedings. These include the expenses of the Official Assignee and costs of the petitioning creditor. Third in rank are pre-preferential debts such as funeral and testamentary expenses, and apprenticeship premiums and repatriation passage for an employee. Fourth in rank are the preferential debts. Preferential debts include:[44]

- all local rates and property taxes due within 12 months before the date of the receiving order;
- income tax assessed on the bankrupt, within a specified time of the receiving order;
- all wages and salaries of any clerk, servant, laborer or worker not exceeding RM1,000 for each;
- all amounts due in respect of contributions payable to provident funds by the bankrupt as employer in the last 12 months; and
- all amounts due in respect of workers' compensation accrued before the date of the receiving order.

41 Section 48, Bankruptcy Act 1967.
42 Section 56, Bankruptcy Act 1967.
43 Section 30, Bankruptcy Act 1967.
44 Section 43, Bankruptcy Act 1967.

The above debts rank equally between themselves and must be paid in full. If the property of the bankrupt is insufficient to meet the debts in full, they will abate in equal proportions between themselves. Only after full payment of preferential debts will the ordinary unsecured creditors be paid in full *pari passu*.[45]

3.6 Mutual Credit and Set-off

Where there are mutual creditors, mutual debts or other mutual dealings between a debtor and a creditor, an account of what is due from one party to the other will be taken. The sum due from one party must be set against any sum due from the other party and the balance of the account and no more must be paid on either side respectively. However, a person cannot claim the benefit of a set-off against the property of a debtor if he or she had, at the time of giving credit to the debtor, notice of an available act of bankruptcy committed by the debtor.[46]

The right of set-off is only allowed where the claims on each side result in pecuniary liabilities so that the account may be taken and the balance struck. Provided there is mutuality, all provable claims may be set-off. For it to be mutual, the debt must be due between the same parties and in the same right. But the right to set-off is not affected by the differences in the nature of the debt, so that a legal debt may be set-off against an equitable debt.

3.7 Discharge of Bankrupts

The bankrupt can apply to the court, at any time, for a discharge after the adjudication order. This is an order of release from bankruptcy.[47] A certificate discharging a bankrupt from bankruptcy may be issued by the Official Assignee after a period of five years from the date of the receiving and adjudication orders.[48]

On discharge the bankrupt is released from all debts provable in bankruptcy except any debt due to the federal or state governments, or any debt incurred by fraud or fraudulent breach of trust.[49]

4 Corporate Insolvency Rules

4.1 Introduction to the Different Corporate Insolvency Rules

Statutory and common law provide for several types of insolvency procedures that are administered by the courts. They include:

45 Section 43(4), Bankruptcy Act 1967.
46 Section 41, Bankruptcy Act 1967.
47 Section 33, Bankruptcy Act 1967.
48 Section 33A, Bankruptcy Act 1967.
49 Section 35, Bankruptcy Act 1967.

- private and court-appointed receivers;
- court-approved schemes of arrangements;
- the liquidation of corporate entities; and
- special administration by Pengurusan Danaharta Nasional Berhad (Special Asset Management Corporation).

Basically, there is no concept of judicial management in Malaysia. No form of Chapter 11 Bankruptcy, such as that which exists in the US, is available in the Malaysian legal system. The only real alternative to liquidation is a scheme of arrangement that is proposed pursuant to section 176 of the Companies Act.

4.2 Corporate Rescue and Informal Mechanisms for Dealing with Corporate Debtors

A workout of debt without resort to formal insolvency procedures is a process undertaken by creditors and the debtor for the restructuring of debt and the saving of the corporate debtor as an ongoing business. This commonly happens when a corporate debtor is unable to service a significant size of debt owed to a number of creditors (mostly bank or other financial institutions). But it may be of greater benefit to the debtor and creditors if the debt is restructured through a process of negotiation rather than resorting immediately to insolvency law. The corporate debts are altered, re-arranged or restructured through refinancing, security and other commercial techniques or the corporate debtor itself is restructured, to enable the servicing of the debt. It benefits all parties particularly if relatively more sophisticated refinancing and security techniques are available. The advantage to the creditors is that if the negotiation process breaks down, the legal insolvency process can be resorted to immediately.

A recent development in Malaysian insolvency law is the introduction of a framework and guidelines in the implementation of corporate workouts issued by Bank Negara Malaysia. Following the establishment of a Corporate Debt Restructuring Committee (CDRC) on 14 July 1998 Bank Negara Malaysia issued the framework and guidelines for CDRC-led and assisted workouts of corporate debts once an approach has been made to the CDRC by corporate creditors. The CDRC has a secretariat, the Bank Negara Malaysia. CDRC-assisted workouts are initiated by the corporate debtor applying to the CDRC for assistance.

The CDRC consists of a steering committee; a secretariat to coordinate and administer the workout; 'creditors' recognized by the CDRC; a creditors' committee; a lead creditor; and consultants. The guidelines limit CDRC-led workouts to cases where:

- the business of the corporate debtor is viable;
- the corporate debtor is not in receivership or liquidation;
- the total aggregate debt owing to more than one bank amounts to approximately RM50 million or more.

In assisting a corporate workout, the steering committee of the CDRC has several functions. It convenes meetings of the corporate debtor and the financial institutions;

ensures that deadlines are adhered to and mediates in disputes between financial institutions *inter se* or between financial institutions and the corporate debtor. The committee assists in disputes with foreign banks and expedites approvals or waivers (as the case may be) from regulatory bodies where possible. It assists in the appointment of a lead creditor and the selection of consultants.

In a workout regime, corporate debtors are required to provide information to the creditors and to undertake to operate the business only in the normal course of business, with transactions not falling within the ordinary course of business subjected to creditor approval before hand. Provisions are made for observers to be present at board meetings of the corporate debtor, on behalf of the financial institutions. The security rights of the financial institutions remain unaffected. New monies will, however, take priority over old. Debt trading is allowed but on condition that the restructuring is not affected. Creditors will be expected to agree to a standstill for a reasonable period of time and, during that time, to form a creditors' committee. Each creditor is expected to act in the best interests of the body of creditors as a whole. The creditors' committee should reflect the broad spectrum of creditors, and financial institutions with the largest exposure in each class of debt should be nominated as constituent members. A lead creditor is expected to be appointed and to manage and coordinate the workout with defined objectives in mind.[50]

4.3 Legally Prescribed Mechanisms of Voluntary Administration: Special Administration under the 1998 Act

It is neither usual nor customary for a corporate debtor to initiate negotiation towards an informal administration before formal insolvency procedures are commenced.[51] There is no provision for formal court-based insolvency administration as such under Malaysian law. There is, however, provision for special administration of insolvent corporations under the Pengurusan Danaharta Nasional Berhad Act 1998.

The aim of the special administration under the Pengurusan Danaharta Nasional Berhad Act 1998 is to assist in the survival of the company in financial difficulty as a going concern. For special administration by the corporation to be granted, it must be shown that it would serve the public interest. It should, in addition, serve either (1) the survival interest of the corporate debtor and the whole or any parts of its assets as a going concern, or (2) a more advantageous realization of the corporate debtor's assets than would be achieved on a winding up. The Act was enacted to enable the corporation to acquire non-performing loans and the underlying security rights from banks and other financial institutions, as part of a wider plan to recapitalize banks and financial institutions.

The Special Administrator cannot be appointed without the approval of the regulatory body concerned where a liquidator has already been appointed over the corporate debtor or where a scheme of arrangement has already been approved by the High Court in relation to the corporate debtor. Also, appointments over corporate

50 Nathan, Rabindra, *Insolvency Law Reforms: Report on Malaysia* (www.insolvencyasia.com) Asian Development Bank.

51 Ibid.

debtors whose businesses are regulated by one of several statutes will require the approval of the regulatory body concerned.[52]

4.4 Methods of Initiating Special Administration under the 1998 Act

Special administration under this legislation may be initiated by the Danaharta Corporation (the special asset management corporation set up under the Act) itself. The management of the corporate debtor may also request special administration. The board of directors of a corporate debtor can apply to the Corporation to appoint a Special Administrator under section 23 of the Act. The Corporation, through the 'Oversight Committee' set up under the act, may appoint the Special Administrator to administer the corporate debtor's affairs under section 24 of the Act. Only 'secured creditors' as defined in the Act have the right under section 46 to be consulted on a 'proposal' that is under consideration.

4.5 Effect of the Appointment of the Special Administrator on the Company

Once the Special Administrator is appointed, a moratorium takes effect during the first 12 months duration of the administration. During this period section 41 of the Act provides that in the case of a petition (voluntary or compulsory) to wind up, the corporate debtor is dismissed. No receiver, manager or provisional liquidator may be appointed except by one of the regulatory bodies named in the Act itself. Any application for a scheme of arrangement under section 176 of the Companies Act 1965 is immediately adjourned *sine die*. Any restraining order granted under section 176(10) is to be immediately discharged and set aside.

4.6 Powers, Liabilities and Qualifications of the Administrator and Duration of Administration

Only an approved auditor who, in the opinion of Danaharta Nasional Berhad, has the experience and is capable of performing the duties of a Special Administrator can be appointed a Special Administrator. The Administrator has the power to do all things that may be necessary for the management and realization of the assets and affairs of the corporate debtor. He/she can remove or suspend a director or appoint a person as director of the corporate debtor. The Administrator is given the power to take possession of, collect and get in assets of the debtor; sell or otherwise dispose of the assets; and raise or borrow money and grant security over the assets. He/she also has the power to bring or defend any action or other legal proceedings in the name of the corporate debtor. In addition, he/she has the power to use the common seal and power to do all acts and to execute in the name and on behalf of the corporate debtor any deed, receipt or other document. He/she also has the power to carry on the

---

52 They include the following legislation: Insurance Act 1996, Banking and Financial Institutions Act 1989, Securities Industry Act 1983, Futures Industry Act 1993, Securities Industry (Central Depositories) Act 1991, Offshore Banking Act 1990, and Islamic Banking Act 1983.

business of the debtor and draw, accept, make and endorse any bill of exchange in the name and on behalf of the corporate debtor.

The Special Administrator is under a duty to prepare a 'proposal' within the meaning of section 44 of the Act and submit it to the Danaharta Nasional Berhad. There is also a requirement to send to secured creditors of the corporate debtor the proposal and any modifications thereto for their consideration and approval.[53] Once a proposal is approved, the Special Administrator is under a duty to implement them,[54] and is also required to report any fraud, misfeasance or misconduct to any regulatory body concerned.[55] Under sections 13–17 of the Pengurusan Danaharta Nasional Berhad Act 1998, the Corporation may acquire the assets and liabilities of the corporate debtor under its administration. No proceedings and no execution or other legal process may be commenced or continued against any person acting as a guarantor of the corporate debtor's debt except with the consent of the administering Corporation.

4.7 Protection of Corporate Assets during Administration

During the period of administration under the Pengurusan Danaharta Nasional Berhad no steps may be taken to enforce a security, or execute upon a judgment or re-possess any asset or set-off any debt against the corporate debtor without the consent of the administering Corporation. Also, no legal proceedings may be commenced or continued and no execution or distress may be levied against the corporate debtor without the prior consent of the Administrator.

Under section 47(4) of the act, any asset of the corporate debtor that is the subject of a secured creditor's security can be dealt with by the Special Administrator once a proposal under section 46 has been approved and the manner of dealing is set out in the proposal.

4.8 Role of Creditors during Administration

Under sections 46 and 48 of the act, the Special Administrator is under a duty to send to the secured creditors of the corporate debtor the proposal and any modifications thereto. Only 'secured creditors' as defined in the Act have the right under section 46 to be consulted on the proposal. The creditors are to consider and approve of the proposal and of any modifications thereto. Once the creditors have given their approval, the Special Administrator is under a duty to implement the proposal.

4.9 Powers of the Courts and Termination of the Administration

Under the Act the Special Administrator will be liable for any willful misconduct and/or gross negligence under sections 28(4) and 66 of the Act. There are also individual

53 Sections 46 and 48, Pengurusan Danaharta Nasional Berhad Act 1998.

54 Section 47, Pengurusan Danaharta Nasional Berhad Act 1998.

55 Section 54, Pengurusan Danaharta Nasional Berhad Act 1998.

provisions whereby he/she commits an offence if he/she fails to comply with the particular provision in question.

There appears to be no express provision for termination of special administration. Even where a proposal has been rejected by the secured creditors or abandoned in its implementation, the Corporation may direct the Special Administrator to submit a new one. It also has the power to lift the moratorium under section 41. It may be safe to assume that once the moratorium under section 41 expires and is not renewed, then to all intents and purposes, the special administration is at an end.

5 Court-based Schemes of Administration, Reconstruction or Arrangement

5.1 Receivership

A receiver is a person 'who is appointed to collect and receive the debts and other property belonging to another person'.[56] In the case of a company, it enters receivership when a receiver is appointed in respect of some or all of its property. The appointment can be either private or court-based. The appointment of a receiver by debenture holders is, in practice, referred to as a 'private' or an 'out-of-court' appointment. The Act refers to such appointments as 'under an instrument'.

The court may appoint a receiver and manager if it considers it necessary or desirable to do so for the purpose of protecting the interests of persons to whom the person or company may be liable. An appointment of a receiver and manager is made by the High Court pursuant to the Rules of the High Court which give it power to appoint a receiver in all cases where it appears to be 'just and convenient'. This enables the court to appoint a receiver and manager in situations where, for example, the company defaults in the payment of a secured debt, or where the secured property is in jeopardy due to a threat of liquidation proceedings brought by the company's unsecured creditors. The court may also appoint a receiver where an application is made to the court to appoint a receiver on behalf of debenture holders or other creditors of a company that is being wound up by the court.[57]

Receiverships are governed by the Companies Act 1965.[58] Court appointments of receivers are made under the First Schedule to the Courts of Judicature Act 1964 read with Order 30 of the Rules of the High Court 1980. The Companies Act 1965 does not define the term 'receiver', but section 182 disqualifies certain persons from being appointed as a receiver of the property or part of the property of a company. The following persons are disqualified from appointment as receivers: (1) a corporation, (2) an undischarged bankrupt, (3) a mortgagee of any property of the company, (4) an auditor of the company or an officer of the company or of any corporation which is a mortgagee of the property of the company, and (5) a person who is not an approved liquidator or the Official Receiver.[59]

56 Ibid., p. 412.

57 Section 186, Companies Act 1965.

58 Part VIII, ss 182–192, Companies Act 1965.

59 Section 182, Companies Act 1965.

The appointment of a receiver and manager does not affect the legal personality of the company, nor does it displace the board of directors. It affects, however, the ability of the directors to exercise their powers of management of the corporation. The extent of the directors' disability depends on the powers of the receiver and manager as provided for by the debenture or by the court. Generally, the powers of a receiver and manager include the following matters:

- to enter into possession and take control of property of the corporation;
- to lease, let, hire or dispose of property of the corporation;
- to borrow money on security of property of the corporation; and
- to convert property of the corporation into money.

The primary duty of a privately appointed receiver and manager is to the appointing debenture holders, to get in the property charged, to manage the business of the company and ultimately to sell the charged property for the purpose of discharging the secured debt. A court-appointed receiver and manager also has a duty to be fair and impartial. He or she owes a fiduciary duty to those interested in the property, but is not regarded as an agent or trustee of those persons. Another duty is to exercise the power to sell the property in good faith and not to sacrifice the company's interests recklessly.

The directors, however, may initiate legal proceedings in the name of the company to challenge the validity of the debenture under which the manager was appointed. The directors continue to be responsible for the preparation and lodgement of annual returns, accounts and other financial statements. The status of the company as an entity remains unaltered on the appointment of the receiver and manager and the legal ownership of the company's property continues to vest with the company.

A privately appointed receivership normally ends when the receiver and manager achieve the objectives of the appointment. The appointment may also terminate and the receivership of the company be uplifted when the security is discharged and the debts of the receivership are paid. On termination of the receivership, the management of the company is returned to the directors of the company.

In the case of the court-appointed receiver and manager, who is regarded as an officer of the court, only the court can exercise control over him or her, including bringing the receivership to an end. This the court will do, at its discretion, when a case is made out, taking into account the achievement of the objectives of the receivership and considering the interests of the corporation and its creditors, as well as such other relevant and pertinent matters.

5.2 Schemes of Arrangements and Reconstructions

Proposals for schemes of arrangements are made when a company is in financial difficulty but its members and creditors consider there to be some advantage in the company continuing its business, rather than taking the drastic step of winding up the company. Part VII of the Companies Act 1965 (ss 176–181) enables the rights and liabilities of members and creditors of a company to be reorganized by a scheme of compromises or arrangement which complies with s 176. A proposal is first put by a company and its creditors, or any class of them, or between the company and its members, or any class of them. On application of the company, or a creditor, or a member of the company, a meeting of the company and its creditors or members will be ordered by the court.[60] The meeting may also be ordered on the application of the liquidator of the company. At the meeting the proposal will be considered. If the proposal is approved by a majority in number representing three quarters in value at the meeting of the creditors or members and subsequently approved by the court, the scheme binds the company, its creditors or members.[61]

An 'arrangement' is defined to include a reorganization of the share capital of a company by the consolidation of shares of different classes or by the division of shares into shares of different classes or by both these methods. A 'company' means any corporation or society liable to be wound up under the act.[62]

A 'moratorium' is one type of scheme. Its distinguishing feature is the deferment of payment for certain debts for a specific period of time. During the moratorium, the company's affairs are run by a scheme administrator or manager appointed by the creditors. Although the directors of the company remain in office, their functions are taken over by the scheme administrator, who exercises broadly defined powers including the selling of the company's business and, in some cases, the selling of members' shares. Provision for the appointment of an advisory committee to supervise the work of the administrator is usually made. Typically, the committee consists of creditor and member representatives, with creditor representatives being in the majority.

A 'compromise' is another type of scheme. Creditors agree to accept payment of less than the amounts they are owed in full satisfaction of their debts. On the payment of the compromised amount, the company is released from further obligation and is permitted to continue its business. In other compromise schemes the creditors may agree to convert their debts into shares in the company and release the company from its debt obligations.

Another scheme involves reorganizing the rights and liabilities of members, including a reorganization of share capital of a company by the consolidation of different classes of shares or by the division of shares into different classes or by both methods. In some schemes, the assets of one company controlled by shareholders are transferred to another company under the control of the same shareholders. It may involve a reconstruction of the company, in which shares in the original company are cancelled and the issue of shares of varying classes in a new company is made. Other schemes allowed under the legislation may involve an amalgamation or a takeover of a company.

5.3 Takeover Schemes

Company takeovers are governed by the Companies Act 1965 and the Malaysian Securities Commission Act 1993. A 'takeover' is defined as 'an acquisition of shares in a company which, when aggregated with shares already held by the acquirer, would

60 Section 176(1), Companies Act 1965.
61 Section 176, Companies Act 1965.
62 Section 176(11), Companies Act 1965.

give the acquirer the right to exercise or control the exercise of more than 33 percent of the voting right of that company.'[63]

The scheme for a takeover bid is not defined by the Companies Act but by the Code on Take-over and Mergers. Under the code the takeover procedures are as follows. Firstly, the offeror makes an offer to the board of the offeree or its advisers. If the offer is not made by the ultimate offeror, the identity of the person making the offer must be disclosed. The offeree obtains competent independent advice on the offer and informs the shareholders of the advice. When the offeree is reasonably confident that a firm offer will be made for its shares, it must make a public announcement in the newspaper. The offeree sends a copy of the press notice to its shareholders.

When a firm intention to make an offer is announced, the offeror must disclose:

- the terms of the offer;
- its identity;
- any existing holding in the offeree which it owns or over which it has control;
- any existing holding in the offeree which is owned or controlled by any person acting in concert with it; and
- any existing holding in the offeree in respect of which it has received an irrevocable undertaking to accept the offer.

The offeree must give shareholders all the facts necessary for the formation of an informed judgment as to the merits and demerits of an offer including:

- the shareholding of the offeree in the offeror;
- the shareholdings in the offeree and in the offeror in which the directors of the offeree are interested;
- the shareholdings in the offeree owned or controlled by the independent adviser to the offeree, if these shareholdings total 10 per cent or more of the offeree's equity share capital; and,
- whether the directors of the offeree intend, in respect of their own beneficial shareholdings, to accept or reject the offer.

6 Winding Up Procedures

Winding up is the process by which the life of a company is brought to an end. The major aims of winding up include the collection and realization of company assets and, out of the proceeds of such realization, first, the payment of creditors in a fixed order of priority and, secondly, the adjustment of rights of contributories among themselves.

63 Section 179(1), Companies Act 1965.

6.1 Introduction

The two modes of the winding up of a company are a compulsory winding up by the court, and a voluntary winding up which can either be a members' or a creditors' voluntary winding up.[64] The practical differences between compulsory and voluntary winding up are that the rules[65] impose more detailed requirements on the handling of funds by liquidators in a compulsory winding up. There is also more formality in the distribution of any surplus assets among the members. Insolvency is the most common reason for winding up a company.

6.2 Initiating Winding Up Proceedings: Powers of the Court and Powers of Creditors

A members' voluntary winding up is initiated by a special resolution of the company.[66] It happens at the expiration of the period fixed for the duration of the company by the memorandum or articles of association, or at the occurrence of an event at which the company is to be dissolved and the general meeting of the company has passed a resolution for a winding up.[67] A members' voluntary winding up proceeds only if the directors lodge a declaration of solvency and the company is in fact solvent.

A creditors' voluntary winding up is only appropriate when the company is insolvent. Where a members' voluntary winding up of a company has been initiated, but the directors do not make or lodge a declaration of solvency pursuant to s 257, the liquidation proceeds as a creditors' voluntary winding up. The Act recognizes that the creditors have a legitimate interest in the conduct of the liquidation and permits the creditors to appoint the liquidator where the members and the creditors have not appointed the same person.[68]

A members' voluntary winding up may be converted into a creditors' voluntary winding up even after the directors have made and lodged a declaration of insolvency. If a liquidator appointed by the members, during the course of the liquidation, forms the opinion that the company is unable to pay its debts in full within the period stated in the declaration of solvency, the liquidator is required to convene a meeting of creditors.[69] The liquidator is then required to lay before the creditors' meeting a statement of the assets and liabilities of the company, and they may then execute their right under s 259(2) to appoint a new liquidator.[70] From the date of the creditors' meeting, the liquidation proceeds as a creditors' voluntary winding up, whether or not the creditors appoint a new liquidator.[71]

A compulsory winding up may be made under an order of the court on the petition of any of the persons listed below:

---

64 Section 211, Companies Act 1965.
65 Companies (Winding-up) Rules, 1972, rule 65.
66 Section 254, Companies Act 1965.
67 Section 254, Companies Act 1965.
68 Section 259, Companies Act 1965.
69 Section 259(1), Companies Act 1965.
70 *Re Anrite Aviation Co Pte Ltd* (1990) 1 MSCLC 95, 424.
71 Section 259(3), Companies Act 1965.

- the company;
- any creditor, including a contingent or prospective creditor, of the company;
- a contributory or any person who is the personal representative of a deceased contributory or the trustee in bankruptcy or the Official Assignee of the estate of a bankrupt contributory;
- the liquidator appointed in a voluntary winding up;
- the Minister of Finance pursuant to section 205 of the Act or on the grounds specified in section 218(1)(d); and
- in the case of a company which is carrying on or has carried on banking business, the Minister for Finance; or in the case of a borrowing company licensed under the Borrowing Companies Act 1969, the Central Bank; or any two or more of those parties may also petition.[72]

The Act, however, provides that the company or any creditor or contributory may, where any action or proceeding against the company is pending, apply to the court to stay or restrain the proceedings accordingly and on such terms as it thinks fit.[73]

6.3 Grounds for Winding Up

The court may order the winding up of a company on one of 11 grounds listed under section 218(1). But the most common ones are the following:

- the company is unable to pay its debts;
- an inspector appointed under Part IX has reported that he/she is of the opinion that: (1) the company cannot pay its debts and should be wound up, or (2) that it is in the interest of the public, the shareholders or the creditors that the company should be wound up; or
- the court is of the opinion that it is just and equitable that the company be wound up.[74]

A company is deemed to be insolvent, that is, unable to pay its debts, if:

- the company fails to pay a debt after being served a 'statutory demand' for payment by a creditor;
- an execution or other process issued on a judgment, decree or order of any court in favor of a creditor of the company is returned unsatisfied in whole or in part; or,
- the court, after taking into account any contingent and prospective liabilities of the company, is satisfied that the company is unable to pay its debts.[75]

In this context, insolvency does not require proof that the company's liabilities exceed its assets. A company is insolvent if it is unable to pay its debts as they fall due.

---

72 Section 217, Companies Act 1965.

73 Section 222, Companies Act 1965.

74 Section 218 paragraphs (e) (g) and (i), Companies Act 1965.

75 Section 218(2), Companies Act 1965.

It requires an examination of the company's entire financial position and is not satisfied by evidence that merely suggests a temporary lack of liquidity.[76] A company is not regarded as being unable to pay its debt if, in the absence of any other proof of insolvency, it fails to pay the stated sum because it *bona fide* disputes the existence of the debt. Ordinarily, a *bona fide* disputed debt results in the dismissal of a winding up application provided that it is based on substantial grounds. The court also has the power to grant an injunction to prevent a creditor from filing a winding up application when its purpose is to induce the company to pay a genuinely disputed debt.

6.4 Effect of the Commencement of Winding Up upon the Company's Management

A compulsory winding up is deemed to commence at the time of the filing of the application for the winding up.[77] Any disposition of the company's property after commencement, other than one made by the liquidator, is void, unless the court orders otherwise. Creditors cannot enforce any judgment or orders they have obtained after the commencement of winding up. Nor can any legal proceedings be brought against the company without leave of the court. The commencement of winding up is also the relevant date for the purposes of determining which preferences are voidable and the validity of floating charges.[78]

After the commencement of winding up, the company is prevented from carrying on its business except for the purpose of winding up, even though the company continues to exist as a legal entity. The company's property continues to belong to it, but the powers of the company to deal with its property are severely limited. In a compulsory winding up, publication of the winding up also serves as a notice of dismissal of the company's employees, although this dismissal notice may be waived by the liquidator for employment contracts of limited periods. A receiver may be appointed by debenture holders notwithstanding that the company has commenced winding up. But, if the liquidator fails or refuses to cooperate in the delivery of possession to the receiver, the receiver must obtain leave of the court before venturing to take possession of the assets. The powers of a receiver and manager appointed prior to the commencement of winding up are restricted by the winding up, in that his or her authority to carry on a business as the agent of the company is revoked. But the power of the receiver and manager to retain and sell the secured assets is not affected by liquidation.

6.5 Creditors' Meetings

A meeting of creditors is required in a number of circumstances during a winding up. Where a members' voluntary winding up of a company has been initiated, but the directors do not make or lodge a declaration of solvency pursuant to s 257, the

---

76 *Sandell* v. *Porter* (1966) 115 CLR 666.

77 Section 219, Companies Act 1965.

78 Sections 223, 224, 225 and 226, Companies Act 1965.

company is required to convene a meeting of creditors for the day or the next day on which the members' resolution for a voluntary winding up is proposed. The creditors have the right to appoint a liquidator at that meeting.

If a liquidator appointed by the members, during the course of the liquidation, forms the opinion that the company is unable to pay its debts in full within the period stated in the declaration of solvency, the liquidator is required to convene a meeting of creditors.[79] The liquidator is then required to lay before the creditors' meeting a statement of the assets and liabilities of the company, and draw their attention to their right under s 259(2) to appoint a new liquidator.[80] From the date of the creditors' meeting, the liquidation proceeds as a creditors' voluntary winding up, whether or not the creditors appoint a new liquidator.[81]

In a creditors' voluntary winding up, a meeting of creditors at which the resolution is to be proposed must be held by the company. The directors of the company must provide to the creditors' meeting a full statement of the company's affairs showing the method and the manner in which the valuation of the assets was arrived at, together with a list of creditors and the estimated amount of their claim. The meeting may pass or postpone the passing of the resolution to wind up.[82]

Creditors have a limited right of participation in a liquidation process. Creditors can be appointed to a 'committee of inspection' under the Act.[83] Certain powers of the creditor can only be exercised with the consent either of the High Court or the committee of inspection. Creditors may also summon meetings of creditors to make their views known to the liquidator, and the liquidator is bound to have regard to their views.[84]

6.6 The Role of the Court in the Winding Up Process

The powers of the court with respect to winding up proceedings are extensive. They include:

- the power to stay winding up;[85]
- the discretion to settle the list of contributories and application of assets;[86]
- the discretion to order the payment of debts due by contributories to the company and the extent to which set-off is allowed, the power to make calls, the power to order to make payments into a bank money due to a company;[87]
- the discretion to make an appointment of a special manager;[88]

---

79 Section 259(1), Companies Act 1965.
80 *Re Anrite Aviation Co Pte Ltd* (1990) 1 MSCLC 95, 424.
81 Section 259(3), Companies Act 1965.
82 Section 260, Companies Act 1965.
83 Sections 241 and 242, Companies Act 1965.
84 Section 237, Companies Act 1965.
85 Section 243, Companies Act 1965.
86 Section 244, Companies Act 1965.
87 Section 245, Companies Act 1965.
88 Section 246, Companies Act 1965.

- the power to make an order to adjust the claims of creditors and the distribution of assets;[89]
- the discretion to order the inspection of books by creditors and contributories;[90]
- the power to summon persons connected with the company;[91]
- the power to order public examination of promoters, directors, etc;[92]
- the power to delegate some of the court's powers to a liquidator;[93] and
- the court may, for the purpose of ascertaining the wishes of creditors and contributories, direct that meetings of the creditors or contributories be called, held and conducted in such a manner as it directs, and may appoint a person to act as chair of any such meeting and to report the result of the meeting to the court.[94]

The conduct of liquidators in the winding up process is subject to the supervision and control of the court.[95] Dissolution of a company is granted by the court but it may also void such dissolution.[96]

6.7 Proof and Ranking of Claims by Creditors against the Company

If there are insufficient funds to pay all unsecured creditors, preferential creditors are paid according to their order of priority as follows:

1. the costs, charges and expenses of the winding up;
2. wages and salaries in respect of services rendered to the company by employees within a period of four months from the commencement of winding up of the company, with the priority only in respect of the first RM15,000 due to each employee;
3. all amounts due in respect of workers' compensation, where the liability arose before winding up;
4. all amounts due on or before winding up with respect to vacation leave accrued;
5. any contribution accruing over the past 12 months prior to the commencement of winding up to any employee superannuation or provident or such approved retirement benefit schemes under the federal law relating to income tax; and
6. priority is given to all federal taxes which have been assessed before the time fixed for the proving of debts has expired.[97]

---

89 Section 247, Companies Act 1965.
90 Section 248, Companies Act 1965.
91 Section 249, Companies Act 1965.
92 Section 250, Companies Act 1965.
93 Section 252, Companies Act 1965.
94 Section 289, Companies Act 1965.
95 Section 277, Companies Act 1965.
96 Section 307, Companies Act 1965.
97 Section 292, Companies Act 1965.

6.8 Set-off of Debts

The Companies Act 1965 incorporates the provisions of the Bankruptcy Act 1967 with regard to proof and the set-off of debts. The Bankruptcy Act provides that where there are mutual creditors, mutual debts or other mutual dealings between a debtor and a creditor, an account will be taken of what is due from one party to the other. The sum due from one party must be set against any sum due from the other party and the balance of the account and no more must be paid on either side respectively. But a person cannot claim the benefit of any set-off against the property of a debtor if he/she had, at the time of giving credit to the debtor, notice of an available act of bankruptcy committed by the debtor.[98]

The right of set-off is only allowed where the claims on each side are such which result in pecuniary liabilities so that the account may be taken and the balance struck. Provided there is mutuality, all provable claims may be set-off. For it to be mutual, the debt must be due between the same parties and in the same right. But the right to set-off is not affected by the differences in the nature of the debt, so that a legal debt may be set off against an equitable debt.

6.9 Voidable Transactions

Dispositions of the company's property made after the commencement of a compulsory winding up are void.[99] In some instances, liquidators of insolvent companies are able to recover dispositions of property, referred to as preferences,[100] made by the company before the commencement of winding up. Any transfer or assignment by a company of all its property to trustees for the benefit of all its creditors shall be void.[101] A floating charge on the undertaking or property of the company created within six months of the commencement of the winding up is invalid, unless it is proved that the company, immediately after the creation of the charge, was solvent.[102] The liquidator also has the right to recover in respect of certain sales to or by the company.[103]

6.10 Procedures for the Dissolution of the Company

Dissolution is the final stage of the winding up proceedings. The procedure depends on the type of winding up involved. In a compulsory winding up the liquidator may apply for an order of dissolution and that he be released when the winding up is completed.[104] More commonly, the company is dissolved by the Registrar of

98 Section 41, Bankruptcy Act 1967.

99 Section 293, Companies Act 1965.

100 Section 292, Companies Act 1965. This section incorporates s 53 of the Bankruptcy Act 1967.

101 Section 293(3), Companies Act 1965.

102 Section 294, Companies Act 1965.

103 Section 295, Companies Act 1965.

104 Section 240, Companies Act 1965.

Companies after due enquiry has been made to the liquidator as to whether there are reasons for the company to remain in existence.[105]

In a voluntary winding up, the company is automatically dissolved three months from the date of the final meeting of the company and its directors. This meeting considers the liquidator's account of how the winding up was conducted and the manner in which the assets of the company were disposed of and approves the report. The liquidator must lodge a final return to the Registrar and Official Receiver confirming that this meeting has been held and attach the final account.[106]

The court has the power, on the application of either the liquidator or any interested party, to declare that the dissolution of the company is void at any time within two years of the date of dissolution.[107]

7 Liquidators: Appointment, Powers and Duties

7.1 Appointment, Qualifications, Registration of Liquidators

A liquidator, who can appoint a 'special manager' to assist him, is appointed to administer the winding of a company. The liquidator or provisional liquidator must be an approved company liquidator within the meaning of section 8(3) of the Companies Act 1965. In order to be an 'approved company liquidator', the person has to be an approved company auditor and must have been approved of by the Minister of Finance. In a compulsory winding up, the Official Receiver is appointed by the court as provisional liquidator until an approved liquidator is put forward by either the meeting of the creditors and contributories or by the court. It is common for the Official Receiver to be appointed liquidator rather than a private insolvency practitioner.

7.2 Powers of Liquidators

A liquidator is regarded at law as agent of the company under liquidation. He/she has the usual powers of an agent to bind the company. But the Act sets out additional powers, which include the powers:

- to carry on the business of the company as far as is necessary for the beneficial winding up of the business;
- to pay any class of creditors in full, subject to priorities set in s 292;
- to make compromises with creditors and contributories with respect to their claims and liabilities;
- to bring or defend legal proceedings in the name of the company and to appoint a solicitor to assist;
- to sell or otherwise dispose of all or any part of the company's property;

---

105 Under Section 308, Companies Act 1965.

106 Section 272, Companies Act 1965.

107 Section 307(1), Companies Act 1965.

- to sign documents on the company's behalf and use its common seal for that purpose;
- to appoint an agent to do any business that the liquidator is unable to do, or that it is unreasonable to expect the liquidator to do in person; and,
- to do all other things as are necessary for winding up the affairs of the company and distributing its assets.[108]

Certain powers are also delegated to the liquidator to be exercised personally. These include powers with respect to:

- holding and conducting meetings to ascertain the wishes of creditors and contributories;[109]
- settling the list of contributories, rectifying the register of members where required and collecting and applying the assets;[110]
- the paying, delivery, conveyance, surrender or transfer of money, property or books to the liquidator;[111]
- making calls and adjusting the rights of contributories, subject to leave of the court;[112] and
- fixing a time within which debts and claims must be proved.

7.3 Duties of Liquidators

The liquidator is regarded as an agent of the company and therefore he or she owes fiduciary duties and duties of care to the company in the discharge of the function as liquidator. The specific duties of the liquidator include:

- the proper administration of a liquidator's general account;[113]
- the collection, preservation, realization, and distribution of the company's assets;[114]
- acquaintance with the company's affairs;[115]
- the reporting of breaches of the Act;[116] and
- effecting the dissolution of the company.[117]

In discharging these duties, a liquidator must act honestly and impartially, and strictly in accordance with the duties and obligations imposed on him/her by the Act.

In a winding up, the liquidator distributes the company's assets amongst its creditors. Creditors must prove their debts if they are to have any entitlement. Proof

108 Section 236, Companies Act 1965.
109 Section 237, Companies Act 1965.
110 Section 244, Companies Act 1965.
111 Section 245, Companies Act 1965.
112 Section 247, Companies Act 1965.
113 Sections 277 and 281, Companies Act 1965.
114 Sections 233, 231(1)(a), 236 and 292, Companies Act 1965.
115 Section 234(1)(2)(3), Companies Act 1965.
116 Section 235, Companies Act 1965.
117 Sections 239 and 240, Companies Act 1965.

of debts against the company being wound up is provided by s 291 of the Companies Act 1965 and is determined by reference to the provisions contained in the Bankruptcy Act 1967, as discussed above. Creditors' claims for damages against an insolvent company are confined to damages arising from a breach of contract, promise or breach of trust. Secured creditors, however, need not prove their debt. On default, secured creditors have the right to realize the secured assets. They are paid ahead of unsecured creditors. If the debts of secured creditors exceed the value of their security property, they may prove their debts, but they lose their security and rank equally with unsecured creditors.

The assets available for the liquidator to collect include:

- all property owned by the company at the date of commencement of the winding up;
- amounts due from contributories under s 214 of the Act;
- amounts recovered from creditors of the insolvent company who received preferential payment of their debts under sections 293 and 294 of the Act;
- excess profits from sales to or from the company recovered from persons connected with the company under s 295 of the Act; and
- payments to be made by officers of the company ordered to pay the company's debts under the fraudulent trading provisions under s 304 of the Act.

7.4 Status and Independence of Liquidators

A liquidator exercises the powers discussed above by authority of the court. In exercising these powers, he/she is, however, required to have regard to any directions given by the creditors, contributories or by a committee of inspection comprising representatives of creditors and members.[118] But a liquidator is not bound by these directions and may seek advice for directions in relation to any particular matter arising under the winding up.[119]

7.5 Powers of the Court in relation to Liquidators

The powers of the court in relation to liquidators are extensive. At any time after the presentation of a winding up petition of a company and before the making of a winding up order, the court may appoint the Official Receiver or an approved liquidator provisionally.[120] The provisional liquidator may exercise all the functions and powers of a liquidator as prescribed by the rules or by the court.

The court has the power to appoint a liquidator[121] or to remove and appoint another liquidator,[122] and to control the exercise of powers by the liquidator.[123] The court may, at any time, require a liquidator to answer any inquiry in relation to a winding up and

118 Section 237(1), Companies Act 1965.
119 Section 237(3), Companies Act 1965.
120 Section 231, Companies Act 1965.
121 Section 265, Companies Act 1965.
122 Section 266, Companies Act 1965.
123 Section 236, Companies Act 1965.

may examine him/her or any other person on oath concerning the winding up, and may direct an investigation to be made of the books and vouchers of the liquidator.[124]

If a liquidator does not faithfully perform their duties and observe all requirements or if any complaint is made by any creditor or contributory or by the Official Receiver, the court will inquire into the matter and take such action as it thinks fit.[125] The court is empowered to release the liquidator and dissolve the company.[126] Where an order is made that the company be dissolved, the company shall from the date of the order be dissolved accordingly.[127]

7.6 Reports by Liquidators

Liquidators are required to report to the court as to the amount of capital issued, subscribed, and paid up and the estimated amount of assets and liabilities of the company; also the causes of the company's failure if the company has failed; and whether any further inquiry into the affairs of the company is desirable. They may also report on any suspected fraud or concealment of information regarding the company's affairs by any officer of the company.[128]

7.8 Remuneration and Fees of Liquidators

A liquidator is entitled to receive such salary or remuneration by way of percentage or otherwise as determined by agreement between the liquidator and the committee of inspection, by a resolution passed at a meeting of creditors by a majority of not less than three quarters in value and one half in number of creditors, or by a court. The court may, on application of shareholders representing not less than 10 per cent of the company's issued capital, confirm or vary that salary or remuneration.[129]

8 Enforcement of Securities over a Debtor's Assets

Several types of securities are available under Malaysian law to secure borrowings by a corporation. They include:

- a registered charge over land under the National Land Code 1965;
- debentures containing fixed and floating charges over land and movable or personal property;
- legal and/or equitable mortgages of property of an intangible or personal nature;
- pledges of personal property;
- lien over land; and
- assignment of proceeds of contracts or other choses-in-action.

124 Section 277, Companies Act 1965.
125 Section 277, Companies Act 1965.
126 Section 239, Companies Act 1965.
127 Section 240, Companies Act 1965.
128 Section 235, Companies Act 1965.
129 Sections 232(3) and (4), Companies Act 1965.

Generally, the most common forms of securities are debentures containing fixed and floating charges over assets of the borrower company and registered charges over land.

Land that is subject to a statutory charge is sold by public auction. 'Registry title' land is sold through court proceedings that require a hearing before a judge where a sale will not be ordered if the charger can 'show cause to the contrary'. 'Land Office Title' or rural land is sold through quasi-judicial proceedings before a land administrator. Land that is not subject to statutory charge can be sold through a private treaty sale by a receiver, who will advertise the land for sale or put it out to tender.

Plant, machinery, vehicles and stock in trade can all be sold by private treaty or by public tender in the same way by the receiver. Proceeds of a contract, such as a building contract, that has been assigned to a lender, can be collected by the receiver or a court order can be obtained directing the debtor to pay the proceeds to the lender or the receiver.

Listed shares can be sold in the open market through a broker. These shares are now 'scripless' and are transferred electronically. Shares in private companies, which are not regulated by the electronic regime, can either be sold privately by the lender or the receiver (see below) using the power of attorney to complete the sale or be sold through the means of a charging order from the High Court.

8.1 The Position of Secured Creditors

Security over land typically takes the form of a debenture containing a fixed or floating charge over land or a statutory charge under the National Land Code 1965. This type of security is enforced mainly by the receiver and manager over the charged assets by first taking possession of the assets. The powers of the receiver and manager to sell such assets, however, are limited according to the recent *Kimlin Housing Development Sdn Bhd* case.[130] It was held that land subject to not only a fixed charge but also a statutory charge, could not be sold privately by the receiver using his power of sale under the debenture. The land must be sold by way of the mechanism laid down under the National Land Code 1965.

Assets such as plant, machinery and vehicles can be sold by the receiver and manager pursuant to the power of sale in the debenture. Shares that are the subject of a pledge or mortgage can be force-sold, the former in accordance with the provisions of the Contracts Act 1950 and the latter in accordance with the mortgage instrument.

8.2 The Appointment of Receivers and Managers of Property of a Debtor

A receiver or receiver manager is usually appointed by either debenture holders or by the court. The appointment of a receiver by debenture holders is, in practice, referred to as a 'private' or an 'out-of-court' appointment. The Act refers to such appointments as 'under an instrument'. It is usual for a debenture trust deed to provide for the appointment of a receiver and manager if the company defaults in its obligations

130 *Kimlin Housing Development Sdn Bhd (In Liquidation) (Receiver and Manager)* [1997] 2 MLJ 805.

under the debenture. It is, however, quite common that the debenture holders allow a receiver to be appointed in a variety of situations other than the company's default. Where the company ceases to carry on its business or is operating at a continued loss is one such situation. Where a person has filed an application to wind up the company is another typical situation. It also includes a situation where the company reduces its capital or the security created under the debenture is put at risk by a failure to maintain or insure it. The appointment of a receiver and manager must, however, comply strictly with the terms of the debenture and can only be appointed over the property secured by the debenture. The court may also appoint a receiver and manager if it considers it necessary or desirable to do so for the purpose of protecting the interests of persons to whom the person or company may be liable.

8.3 Powers and Duties of External Controllers, such as Receivers and Managers

Generally, the powers of a receiver and manager include the following:

- to enter into possession and take control of property of the corporation;
- to lease, let, hire or dispose of property of the corporation;
- to borrow money on security of property of the corporation; and
- to convert property of the corporation into money.

The primary duty of a privately appointed receiver and manager is to the appointing debenture holders, to get in the property charged, to manage the business of the company and ultimately to sell the charged property for the purpose of discharging the secured debt. A court-appointed receiver and manager also has a duty to be fair and impartial. He or she owes a fiduciary duty to those interested in the property, but is not regarded as an agent or trustee of those persons. Another duty is to exercise the power to sell the property in good faith and not to sacrifice the company's interests recklessly.

8.4 Effect of the Appointment of an External Controller

The appointment of a receiver and manager does not affect the legal personality of the company. Nor does it displace the board of directors. It affects the ability of the directors to exercise their powers of management. The extent of the directors' disability depends on the powers of the receiver and manager as provided for by the debenture or by the court.

9 Offences

9.1 Insolvent Trading Rules

Non-payment of debts by corporate debtors does not generally result in any form of civil or penal sanction. However, it is an offence for an officer of a company to knowingly contract a debt on behalf of the company if, at that time, he has no reasonable or probable ground of expectation, after taking into consideration other liabilities, if any, of the company at the time, of the company being able to pay the debt.[131] The penalty for this offence is imprisonment for one year or a fine of RM5,000.

It is also an offence if, within the 12 months before the commencement of the winding up of the company, an officer obtains on credit, for or on behalf of the company, under the false pretence that the company is carrying on its business, any property which the company does not subsequently pay for.[132]

9.2 Other Insolvency-related Offences by Corporate Controllers

The act provides for offences with regard to the conduct of officers of a company that is designed to frustrate the liquidator. Offences by officers of the company in the course of winding up include:

- concealment from the liquidator of any property (movable or immovable) of the company; and non-delivery of all movable and immovable property of the company in their custody or under their control that is required to be delivered up to the liquidator; and
- non-delivery of all books and papers under their control that are required to be delivered to the liquidator.[133]

It is an offence if proper books were not kept by the company throughout the period of two years immediately preceding the winding up of a company.[134] It is also an offence to destroy, mutilate, alter or falsify any books, papers or securities or make any false or fraudulent entry into any register or book of account or document of a company being wound up.[135]

9.3 Other Relevant Corporate Law Offences

The Act provides for a general fraudulent trading provision. In the course of the winding up of a company, any business of the company that is carried on with intent to defraud creditors of the company is an offence punishable by three years' jail or a fine of RM10,000.[136]

It is an offence for a person to give or offer to give valuable consideration to any member or creditor of a company with a view to securing their own or another person's appointment or nomination as a liquidator. To offer inducement to prevent another person from being nominated or appointed a liquidator of a company is also an offence.[137]

---

131 Section 303(3), Companies Act 1965.
132 Section 300, Companies Act 1965.
133 Section 300(1)(a) and (b), Companies Act 1965.
134 Section 303, Companies Act 1965.
135 Section 302, Companies Act 1965.
136 Section 304, Companies Act 1965.
137 Section 301, Companies Act 1965.

10 Rules regarding Cross-border Insolvency and Judicial Assistance to Foreign Insolvency Officials

10.1 Broad Policy on the Recognition of Foreign Judgments and Court Orders

There is a policy of non-discrimination as to recognition of claims of foreign creditors and local creditors under Malaysian law. Claims by foreign creditors are not subject to particular rules in relation to priority of payment. These creditors do not have to satisfy special or additional rules for their claims to be admitted. There is a requirement, however, under the Exchange Control Act 1953, that in taking out the proceeds of a claim when it is satisfied, the foreign creditor must have the approval of the Controller of Exchange Control. In practice this is rarely refused.

10.2 Procedures for the Assistance of Courts in Foreign Jurisdictions

The High Court is empowered to act in aid of and be auxiliary to the courts of the Republic of Singapore or any designated country having jurisdiction in bankruptcy and insolvency so long as the law thereof requires its courts to act in aid of and be auxiliary to the courts of Malaysia.[138] At the request of a court of the Republic of Singapore or other designated countries, the High Court will give effect to its orders in bankruptcy and insolvency. In doing so, the High Court will have regard to the rules of private international law.

References

Allan, David E., Hiscock, Mary E. and Roebuck, Derek (1980), *Credit and Security in West Malaysia*, St Lucia, Australia: University of Queensland Press.

Ariff, Mohamed (1991), *The Malaysian Economy: Pacific Connections*, Singapore: Oxford University Press.

Arjunan, Krishnan and Low, Chee Kong (1995), *Lipton & Herzberg's Understanding Company Law in Malaysia*, Sydney: LBC Information Services.

ASEAN Law Association (1995), *ASEAN Legal System*, Singapore: Butterworths Asia.

Attorney-General's Department, Australia (1994), *Legal Services Country Profile: Malaysia*, Canberra: Attorney General's Department.

CCH Asia Ltd (1995), *Guide to Company Law in Malaysia and Singapore*, 3rd ed., Singapore: CCH Asia Ltd.

Gomez, Edmund Terence (1994), *Political Business: Corporate Involvement of Malaysian Political Parties*, Townsville, Australia: James Cook University of North Queensland.

Ibrahim, Ahmad and Joned, Ahilemah (1987), *The Malaysian Legal System*, Kuala Lumpur, Malaysia: Dewan Bahasa dan Pustaka.

138 Section 104, Bankruptcy Act 1967.

Ismail, Muhd Salleh and Saha, Dhevan Meyanathan (1993), *The Lessons of East Asia: Malaysia*, Washington, DC: World Bank.
Kahn, Noel S. and Wah, Francis Loh Kok (eds) (1992), *Fragmented Vision: Culture and Politics in Contemporary Malaysia*, North Sydney: Allen & Unwin.
Malaysian Institute of Accountants (1995), *Annual Report and Accounts*, Kuala Lumpur, Malaysia: Institut Akauntan Malaysia.
Nathan, Rabindra (1999), *Insolvency Law Reforms: Report on Malaysia* (www.insolvencyasia.com), Asian Development Bank.
Means, Gordon P. (1991), *Malaysian Politics: The Second Generation*, Singapore: Oxford University Press.
Simone, Vera and Feraru, Anne Thompson (1995), *The Asian Pacific: Political and Economic Development in a Global Context*, New York: Longmans.
Tan, Yew Hock (1985), *The Malaysian Company Director*, Kuala Lumpur: Heinemann (Malaysia) Sdn Bhd.
Tomasic, Roman and Little, Peter (1997), *Insolvency Law and Practice in Asia*, Hong Kong: FT Law & Tax Asia Pacific.
Wong, Kim Fatt (1988), 'Winding Up a Company on Inability to Pay Debts', 3 *Malayan Law Journal*, i.

Chapter 11

Insolvency Law and Institutions in Indonesia

DAVID K. LINNAN
University of South Carolina

Indonesia's legal system is built upon a foundation of Dutch colonial law. Substantively speaking, since the late 1980s most Indonesian economic law has moved away from older civil law models as part of legal modernization efforts. Bankruptcy, however, is exceptional to the extent that Indonesia's Law No. 4/1998 as amended in minor ways and restated as Law No. 37/2004 on bankruptcy currently in force still lies close to Dutch models. Law No. 4/1998 was produced under IMF conditionality in the form of an emergency regulation (Perpu No. 1/1998, affirmed by the Indonesian parliament as Law No. 4/1998) early in the Asian Financial Crisis, based upon revisions to the 1906 colonial law, then following a relatively contentious six-year trial of the new bankruptcy law, largely minor amendments were made. Law No. 37/2004 contains two basic insolvency approaches reaching back to Dutch law: liquidation in bankruptcy and a weak voluntary debt compromise procedure.

The intent behind Law No. 4/1998 was arguably more to prod debtor-creditor negotiations outside of court rather than to channel bankruptcy proceedings through judicial institutions. A largely hidden debate among Indonesian elites was conducted concerning corporate workouts, but in the end Law No. 37/2004's minor amendments to clarify definitions (for example, debt) and to counter the tactical use of bankruptcy in broader disputes involving financial sector companies was the end result of six years' effort. Indonesian insolvency practice never quite resolved the carnage wrought by the Asian Financial Crisis, while judicial insolvency proceedings have decreased over time. Six years into the process the accompanying banking crisis is still felt. The common strategy among many indebted enterprises long remained waiting out private creditors, or seeking special treatment via the political process (particularly vis-à-vis government creditors, especially the Indonesian Bank Restructuring Agency or IBRA, discussed below, as the Resolution Trust Corporation-style agency charged with resolving the banking crisis). Successful corporate workouts were largely voluntary and were motivated by certain debtors' desire to regain speedy access to international capital markets. Otherwise, controlling shareholders typically waited out creditors, eventually purchasing corporate debt at substantial discounts, following which formal reorganizations typically left controlling shareholders in a strong position. This second reform of Indonesian insolvency law resulting in Law No. 37/2004 has already been followed by rumblings of a third reform. Given the six-year period necessary to pass the very modest changes in Law No. 37/2004, however, a new round of statutory amendments seems unlikely through the medium term. Difficulties with Indonesian insolvency practice typically reflect larger problems with the Indonesian legal system rather than substantive insolvency law concerns. The weakness of judicial insolvency proceedings is visible in the statistics that in the commercial court's first five years of operation (September 1998–December 2003), 353 bankruptcy petitions were filed, of which only 114 (32 per cent) were granted, 205 (58 per cent) were declined or refused, settlement was reached on 24 (7 per cent) and 10 (3 per cent) turned into the voluntary debt compromise track.

Background and Law Reform Efforts

The modern experience of Indonesian insolvency law unfolds against the background of the Asian Financial Crisis in parallel to the large-scale challenges of a banking crisis and depressed economic conditions. Indonesian law recognizes that both individuals and juridical persons may be debtors, but the overwhelming majority of modern insolvency proceedings in the wake of the Asian Financial Crisis involve corporate debtors. Thus, we treat personal insolvency as bankruptcy or liquidation proceedings against business debtors. Thereafter, Indonesian corporate insolvency proceedings are treated more against the background of the voluntary debt compromise prong of Law No. 37/2004 since only the rarest Indonesian corporate debtor seeks liquidation. Given significant transaction costs, consumer bankruptcy is theoretically possible but non-existent in practice. Even small businesses fall below the necessary economic threshold for formal insolvency proceedings, and small business workouts, often involving individuals, have occurred on a significant scale only on the basis of summary workout programs conducted under the sponsorship of the Jakarta Initiative discussed below.

Law No. 4/1998 is best understood as a reaction to problems with insolvency-related judicial and administrative institutions under the Dutch colonial 1906 *Faillissements Verordnung*. The 1906 statute already incorporated a predecessor of the current two-prong system of liquidation in bankruptcy and voluntary debt compromise, but did so within the context of civil servant insolvency administrators (in the *Balai Harta Peninggalan* or BHP) and the ordinary courts. From an Indonesian viewpoint, the chief innovations under Law No. 4/1998 involved the creation of entirely new commercial courts (*Pengadilan Niaga*) and the opening of bankruptcy administration to the private sector by providing for the new positions of bankruptcy receivers (*kurator*) and voluntary debt compromise administrators (*pengurus*) registered with the state. Reworking the institutions was intended to inject commercial sophistication into insolvency proceedings, since *kurator* and *pengurus* would be drawn from accounting firms and the sophisticated commercial bar alongside the BHP. The new commercial courts intended also to create a cadre of judges familiar with sophisticated commercial problems while attempting to rise above perceived general problems with existing Indonesian courts. No formal doctrine of precedent applies in Indonesia as a civil law jurisdiction; however, following suggestions more generally to improve transparency in the courts, Law No. 4/1998 provided for the publication of insolvency law opinions for the first time, and Law No. 37/2004 allows for dissenting opinions.

Intentions to inject commercial sophistication were not immediately successful despite intensive IMF-sponsored training for the initial cohort of commercial court judges, *kurator* and *pengurus*. At the judicial level there were three difficulties. First, the initial cadre of commercial court judges was recruited from the existing judiciary and so were civil servants without any significant prior business experience. Second, provision was made for the appointment of special ad hoc judges in insolvency proceedings, for example from the commercial bar. However, commercially sophisticated ad hoc judges were not appointed in the first few years. Third, following Indonesian judicial management practice, most of the initial cadre of commercial court judges, who received significant training, have been rotated on to other judicial assignments. Not all were replaced as caseloads decreased, while the new commercial court judges did not receive the same level of training. At the trial level, the problem was that, early on, judicial decisions made it difficult to open bankruptcy or debt reorganization proceedings with the result that *kurator* and *pengurus* commercial skills rarely came into play.

Indonesia admittedly suffers rule of law problems. Corruption, alongside weak legal institutions, leads to low expectations generally when creditors assert substantive legal rights in a judicial forum. The best known example may be the Manulife case involving a bankruptcy proceeding against the local partner (*Dharmala Sakti Sejahtera* or DSS) of Canadian insurer Manufacturers Life Insurance Company (Manulife), which proceeding aimed at the planned sale in bankruptcy court to Manulife of DSS's 40 per cent share in the profitable insurance joint venture constituting Manulife's Indonesian operations (*Asuransi Jiwa Manulife Indonesia* or AJMI, ownership of which originally included Manulife with 50 per cent, DSS with 40 per cent and the World Bank-affiliated International Finance Corporation or IFC with 10 per cent) (Linnan, 2002).[1]

This would appear to be a case in which the Indonesian legal system was successfully dealing with DSS's insolvency through the new commercial court system on the bankruptcy liquidation track under Law No. 4/1998. However, when the bankruptcy sale was scheduled to be conducted, the representative of an offshore company (Roman Gold Assets Limited) appeared claiming that the AJMI shares to be sold in bankruptcy had been sold by the debtor previously under an undisclosed power of attorney empowering yet another offshore company (Harvest Hero International Limited) to sell DSS's 40 per cent AJMI stake. Thus, the alleged new owner of the shares challenged the power of the bankruptcy court to dispose of the property, saying DSS no longer owned the shares This led to an abridged sale with proceeds paid into an escrow account, followed by a challenge triggering an extremely aggressive police investigation (including the incarceration of a local AJMI executive and the *kurator* in the DSS bankruptcy proceedings plus related investigation of commercial court personnel including judges). In the course of this case, it was alleged that Manulife was complicit with the commercial court in what was claimed to be fraudulent negotiation of the shares in the joint venture company

1 David Linnan, 'Manulife Indonesia: A Meditation on Three Mythologies', in *Communities in Southeast Asia: Challenges and Responses* (H. Lansdowne, P. Dearden and W. Neilson, eds) University of Victoria, BC, 2002.

via the bankruptcy auction. The police then went on first to freeze and then to transfer the bankruptcy sale funds from the escrow account into a police account as material evidence without clear legal authority, which chain of events was regarded as unusual even by local legal practitioners. This left DSS's creditors, including IBRA, holding approximately 38 per cent of DSS's debt, with nothing to show for their prosecution of the entire case through the official insolvency system except a perceived attack on the bankruptcy system itself via the criminal justice system. Subsequently, the Indonesian Capital Markets Supervisory Agency or *Bapepam* investigated the alleged share transfer on the basis that DSS as a public company failed to comply in a number of significant ways with capital market regulations and company law principles, if indeed it executed a secret power of attorney and sold its AJMI shares.

The Manulife case was raised in high-level discussions between the Canadian and Indonesian governments, and apparently was also addressed in Indonesia's periodic IMF discussions and with the IFC. The Canadian investor essentially claimed that the undisclosed prior sale was a fraudulent device by which the insolvent debtor intended to retain control of its assets (the issue is who controls the mysterious Roman Gold claiming to have acquired the 40 per cent AJMI stake which was the subject of the bankruptcy sale). The case is regarded as emblematic for rule of law problems hindering the foreign investment necessary to general economic recovery as well as the new insolvency system created under IMF conditionality.

The perceived problem with Manulife and similar cases is that, just when creditors believed the Indonesian insolvency system envisioned under Law No. 4/1998 was finally beginning to function, more general rule of law problems emerged, including perceived attacks on the insolvency system itself. The Manulife case is exceptional for its perceived rawness and police involvement, but is not extraordinary to the extent that analogous claims of fraudulent debtor behavior were raised by the IFC in on-going insolvency proceedings in which it was a creditor of Panca Overseas Finance. In the *Panca Overseas* case, the IFC had organized creditor voting, hoping to defeat a debtor proposal under the voluntary debt compromise track provided for under Law No. 4/1998 in favor of liquidating Panca Overseas. However, shortly before the required vote of creditors in the debt compromise proceedings, a hitherto unknown group of creditor claims was registered with the commercial court under the aegis of the same mysterious offshore company, Harvest Hero, alleged to have acted under the undisclosed power of attorney in the Manulife case. As a result of the late 'discovered' creditors, the debtor secured the necessary votes to have its voluntary debt compromise proposal approved over IFC objections. Creditor claims were written down under the debt compromise to approximately 16 per cent of the original indebtedness, which recovery is less than would have been achieved in liquidation according to the IFC. The Supreme Court (*Makamah Agung*) on review of the *Panca Overseas* case unhelpfully opined that the IFC's fraudulent debt challenge could not be brought before the commercial court handling the insolvency proceedings without a prior criminal judgment, an insurmountable burden in practice given general rule of law problems.

Final insolvency law background is provided by a quick review of bankruptcy law reform efforts on-going since 1998. Second round reform efforts followed automatically from the Indonesian executive's promise to the parliament (*Dewan Perwakilan Rakyat* or DPR) in August 1998 to bring a wholly new bankruptcy statute to the DPR for debate within a year as a condition of its approval in transforming into Law No. 4/1998 the emergency insolvency regulation promulgated in early 1998 under IMF conditionality at the height of the Asian Financial Crisis.

The revisions under discussion in the period 1998–2004 were in the form of two separate draft laws produced by teams working separately in the Ministry of Justice, one a limited revision of Law No. 4/1998 (the so-called *RUU Tentang Kepailitan* or draft law concerning bankruptcy) and the other a broader revision in the form of a company reorganization law, the conceptual father of which is American insolvency law's Chapter 11 proceedings (the so-called *RUU Tentang Restrukturisasi Utang dan Perseroan* or draft law concerning debt and corporate restructuring). Only the limited revision made it out of the Ministry, but the other draft's existence illustrates a sense of unfinished business on the reorganization side. The relatively minor changes discussed under advanced drafts of the bankruptcy law as a revision to Law No. 4/1998 surprised those who expected broad changes, either because of a perception that the initial law was IMF-imposed (hence presumed unsatisfactory to Indonesians) or because the insolvency system still was not functioning well. The discussed changes which were enacted in Law No. 37/2004 are focused on (1) standardizing certain key terms such as creditor, debt and debtor to overcome confusion and inconsistent definitions given by courts since the 1998 enactment, (2) voting and related changes to secured creditor rights under the voluntary debt compromise procedure, and (3) refining the trigger mechanism for bringing a bankruptcy proceeding, concerning which there had been repeated inconsistent judicial decisions. The discussed changes under the draft debt and corporate restructuring law were much broader, since they would reorient corporate reorganizations away from the relatively weak voluntary debt compromise proceeding under Law No. 4/1998 towards proceedings involving full-fledged recasting of a debtor's capital structure, probably oriented in Indonesian eyes towards preserving viable businesses for employment purposes. However, the addition of secured creditor voting rights on a voluntary debt compromise under Law No. 37/2004, discussed subsequently, will arguably discourage reorganizations in encouraging secured creditors more often than not to vote against them.

Now that Law No. 37/2004 has finally been passed, there are again two competing visions of further amendments being quietly mooted, but substantial change seems unlikely through the medium term. As part of court reform, there is some sentiment on the part of donors and the Indonesian Supreme Court or *Makamah Agung* supporting a package of highly technical amendments to various statutes focused on jurisdiction, procedure and the reconciliation of separate laws on personal and real property security (fixtures). The competing, academic vision is focused again on better implementation of workout principles, targeting valuation approaches and economic feasibility as necessary elements of any reorganization plan. They mirror the broader legal reform issue of whether Indonesia requires new laws versus better implementation of those already on the books.

As a formal matter, Law No. 37/2004 concerning bankruptcy continues to be available to individuals and companies, but for cost reasons only large-scale commercial insolvencies are practical so that workouts are the real concern. The draft law on debt and corporate restructuring under discussion in the period 1998–2004 contemplated that the restructuring would be accomplished under an initiative to be approved by the commercial court, but following an independent team of consultants' study of restructuring's feasibility. The emphasis was on process, and the draft law did not completely articulate standards for judging a restructuring. The older Dutch law approach focuses on procedure rather than substantive concepts, while underlying assumptions about economic organization are not necessarily shared by modern Indonesian law. Perhaps not surprisingly, there is still no Indonesian consensus on insolvency law's purpose even following two rounds of bankruptcy law reform. General workout negotiations through non-judicial institutions and rule of law concerns probably will continue to loom larger in creditor eyes than substantive insolvency rules.

Non-judicial Insolvency Institutions

Indonesia is a developing country with a strong tradition of managing economic concerns bureaucratically. This found expression under Indonesian insolvency practice in the idea that, alongside new commercial courts with bankruptcy jurisdiction created under Law No. 4/1998, there were at least two further institutions of significant importance. The first important non-judicial insolvency institution was the *Prakarsa Jakarta* or Jakarta Initiative, a government-sponsored voluntary debt restructuring forum following the London approach, set up in November 1998 and closed in December 2003. Most large-scale voluntary restructurings were accomplished via the Jakarta Initiative, which facilitated the restructuring of 102 significant companies with distressed debts totalling US$26.91 billion. Total Indonesian corporate debt owed to offshore and domestic creditors was estimated at US$120 billion at the Asian Financial Crisis' commencement, of which half was distressed, illustrating the Jakarta Initiative's relative success as compared to judicial proceedings. As initially conceived, the Jakarta Initiative incorporated the following aspects of the London approach, viewed as an international best practice standard for negotiated workouts: (1) a troubled enterprise's major creditors agree to a temporary standstill while they form a creditors' steering committee; (2) the debtor and the steering committee both appoint insolvency practitioners to review the enterprise's business prospects; (3) the creditors and enterprise work together to determine whether and how to rescue the enterprise; and (4) contractual rights are recognized generally, but any additional funding is given a priority over existing indebtedness. Unlike the London approach, the Jakarta Initiative includes an active role for government.

Senior Jakarta Initiative staff initially came out of the Ministry of Finance, although foreign insolvency professionals were also retained early on as workout mediators and trainers. The initial head of the Jakarta Initiative wore two hats as, simultaneously, the head of the Jakarta Initiative and of *Bapepam* as capital markets supervisory agency, while his successor was a long-serving ministry official and former *Bapepam* head. From that position, it is easy to understand how the Jakarta Initiative negotiated a variety of waivers with the Jakarta Stock Exchange to avoid potential delisting of participating listed company debtors. It also procured special tax regulations to change then-current Indonesian tax law requiring that debt forgiveness be treated as income, as well as generally securing advantageous regulatory treatment for business combinations in the workout context. These represent the carrots, while the government's stick was also prominent in provision under the Jakarta Initiative for the Indonesian Attorney General himself to initiate bankruptcy proceedings against debtors not acting in good faith once they entered the Jakarta Initiative.

Among other activities, the Jakarta Initiative organized special summary workout programs in major cities under which private sector Indonesian accountants were contracted and trained quickly as insolvency mediators. On roadshows at significant commercial centers, they were generally successful in disposing of a large number of small business insolvencies via quick marshalling of assets and liabilities under summary reorganization plans, with small to medium-sized business debtors and their creditors being given a chance to resolve issues on the spot. By several years into the crisis, however, smaller business reorganizations under the Jakarta Initiative's sponsorship were completed.

The second important non-judicial insolvency institution was the *Badan Penyehatan Perbankan Negara* or Indonesian Bank Restructuring Agency (IBRA), created as a special agency in January 1998 along the lines of the US Resolution Trust Corporation and closed in early 2004. IBRA was created to manage the large number of failed Indonesian banks and to collect on defaulted loans in the wake of the larger Asian Financial Crisis. Almost half of Indonesia's private domestic banks (72) were either closed or taken over by the government, while the major state banks were typically recapitalized with government bonds, followed by partial privatization.

IBRA was also assisted by some donor-funded foreign insolvency professionals, but, much more so than the Jakarta Initiative, was staffed with Indonesian financial professionals from the private sector. In practice insolvency institutions overlapped, since IBRA acted like a debtor-guarantor in dealing with creditors of failed financial institutions, while at the same time it might appear as a significant creditor in judicial proceedings or voluntary restructurings under the Jakarta Initiative. Similarly, Bank Indonesia (BI) as central bank made significant liquidity loans as lender of last resort to banks early in the Crisis, which funds were often misused by recipients funneling them through to their affiliated corporate groups, leaving the central bank a large-scale creditor of the related banks and, indirectly, of the major domestic corporate groups. Responsibility for dealing with these debts moved from BI to IBRA over time.

Concerning amounts and levels of recovery in bank restructurings, in the period 1999–2003 IBRA disposed of 192.26 trillion IDR in principal amount of loans for proceeds of 45.67 trillion IDR (23.75 per cent recovery rate), while during the same period it sold equity securities (pledged assets) originally valued at 42.451 trillion IDR for 19.710 trillion IDR (46 per cent recovery). Recovery rates decreased over time, and at termination IBRA still held substantial assets so that ultimate recovery rates are hidden, but employing a US$1=10,000 IDR exchange rate over this very volatile period, the most substantial part of IBRA disposals amounted to loans in principal amount of US$19.226 billion sold for US$4.567 billion, and equities originally valued at US$4.245 billion for US$1.971 billion. One notable peculiarity was that, during the Financial Crisis, a blanket guarantee was issued not only on bank accounts, but also on bank debt owed to third parties generally (that is, interbank obligations as well as bonds issued by banks). The blanket guarantee is being phased out in favor of deposit insurance with a 100 million IDR ceiling (circa US$10,000) by March 2007, but the newer deposit insurance system has already been criticized as still based upon ideas about certain banks being too large to fail.

Early on, IBRA appeared to exercise its full powers acting through other government agencies. For example, from time to time the Indonesian government acted instrumentally by threatening criminal prosecution of major 'uncooperative debtors', or for violation of prudential banking regulation, both as an apparent matter of creditor strategy and under the terms of various IMF letters of intent (establishing a system for the Attorney General to pursue uncooperative debtors). This apparent criminalization of insolvency problems has doctrinal precedents given Indonesia's civil law tradition, but more properly reflects how the Indonesian government itself is constrained by the limitations of its weak legal institutions. The government's relatively high profile as creditor was not matched by IBRA success as a creditor in judicial proceedings. Typically IBRA's share of unsecured debt exceeded one third of the total in major insolvency proceedings, giving it a de facto veto over composition plans under applicable voting rules. It was relatively more successful in securing concessions from other creditors in Jakarta Initiative proceedings where it used its veto power to increase government recoveries over private creditors.

IBRA as creditor itself often acted on behalf of the government, but it was not a truly independent agency as that term is understood internationally. Formally speaking IBRA had broad powers, including those of extra-judicial execution, under Government Regulation No. 17/1999, but, given political pressure and a revolving door at IBRA's senior management level, over time it often appeared as an orphan within government and subject to conflicting demands. For example, IBRA's basic mandate was repair of the banking system, but at the same time its asset disposition plans were a major revenue source for the national budget, and IBRA was often treated by multilateral institutions as though it were the chief locus for insolvency policy as opposed to the commercial court or DPR. IBRA's ultimate problem as creditor was that, for much of the period 1998–2004, it was precluded by political pressures from accepting realistic recovery rates (with negative effects on commercial negotiations and increasing losses over time as its assets aged). IBRA was criticized for a lack of transparency, but special institutions created for oversight (initially the Financial Sector Policy Committee, consisting of economic ministers and senior officials, later the IBRA Oversight Committee including senior figures from outside government) as well as parliamentary committee oversight were often perceived as meddling on political grounds.

Judicial Bankruptcy or Liquidation Procedures

Under Article 2 of Law No. 37/2004, a debtor having two or more creditors and failing to pay at least one matured and payable debt can be declared bankrupt through a commercial court decision, either upon his own petition or at the request of one or more creditors, or upon the request of the public prosecutor in the public interest. (Note that this does not require a finding of technical insolvency, which facilitated from time to time the tactical use of bankruptcy in ordinary commercial law disputes.) Jurisdiction lies in the responsible court with jurisdiction for the debtor's domicile (with the current complication being that the new commercial courts mandated by Law No. 4/1998 were being rolled out in different geographic areas over time, pending which jurisdiction remained in its Jakarta branch, with only recently a small

Surabaya commercial court being added and small courts planned to be added also in Semarang, Medan, and Ujung Pandang, all based upon Presidential Decree No. 97/99), or most recent legal domicile in the event that the debtor has left Indonesia. Domicile for legal entities is specified in their articles of incorporation. If the debtor is a partner of a firm, jurisdiction lies in the court responsible for the legal domicile of the firm's office. If the debtor is not domiciled in Indonesia but conducts business or a profession there, jurisdiction lies in the court responsible for the legal domicile of the Indonesian office through which such business or profession is conducted. The only significant restraints are that, if debtors are married, their spouse must approve the petition if there is mingled property, and BI or *Bapepam*, respectively, must petition if the debtor is a bank or capital markets participant (including securities companies, exchanges, and clearing and settlement entities). The new law addressed concerns about the tactical use of bankruptcy in the insurance industry by specifying that the Minister of Finance must petition if the debtor is an insurance or reinsurance company, pension fund, or state-owned enterprise operating in the public interest, of which its whole capital is owned by the government and is not divided into shares. The SOE addition in particular may raise theoretical concerns in areas like infrastructure project finance, given that utility off-take guarantors will typically be SOEs.

Application for liquidation in bankruptcy must be decided within 60 days of its filing, subject to an accelerated appeal to the Supreme Court, which must be decided no later than 68 days following the lower court opinion. If the petition is admitted the judicial order will name both the receiver and a supervising judge. Subject to special rules for agricultural liens, a bankruptcy filing normally suspends secured creditors' rights to enforce their security for up to 90 days from the date of a decision declaring bankruptcy to enable the receiver to continue the debtor's business, provided that reasonable protection is provided for creditor interests. Secured creditors may petition to reduce the 90-day period or alter its conditions, which petition must be decided within ten days taking into consideration: (1) the elapsed period of deferment; (2) protection of creditor and third party interests; (3) the possibility of compromise; and (4) the deferment's impact on the debtor's business and settlement of the bankrupt estate.

Concerning creditors' joint action, the court may in its decision to admit a bankruptcy petition form a provisional creditors' committee to advise the receiver, and must upon completion of verification of claims offer creditors the option of forming a permanent creditors' committee. The creditors' committee consists only of unsecured creditors, subject to the idea that secured creditors may seek unsecured status for the amount of their claims exceeding collateral value. Only unsecured creditors are entitled to participate in the creditors' committee. Law No. 4/1998 contained no provision for representation of, or negotiations among, differing classes of creditors, but as discussed subsequently such distinctions have now been introduced under Law No. 37/2004 specifically for approval of a voluntary debt compromise in the form of a secured creditor class vote.

The supervising judge determines the day, date, time and place of the initial meeting of the creditors' committee, which must be held within 30 days of the decision to admit the petition to bankruptcy, with provision for registered letter or courier notice to creditors. Subsequent meetings can be called on his/her own initiative on a date, time and place to be determined by the supervising judge, or whenever a reasonable request is made to him/her by the creditors' committee or at least five creditors who represent one fifth of the acknowledged or conditionally verified claims. The normal rule is that decisions are taken by a simple majority of creditor votes cast, with creditors entitled to vote once their claims are provisionally verified (but subsequently discussed rules also require approval of debt compositions by two thirds of represented claims, since Law No. 37/2004 classes votes separately of secured and unsecured creditors in a voluntary debt compromise). The committee may require inspection of books and documents relating to the bankruptcy, which the receiver is obliged to provide to the committee. There are a variety of provisions requiring or enabling the receiver to consult the creditors' committee, but the receiver is not bound by their advice. In the case of disagreement between the creditors' committee and receiver, provision is made for a three-day postponement of the receiver's action to enable the creditors' committee to seek a binding decision from the supervising judge.

Concerning restraints on debtors, following commencement of bankruptcy the debtor is prohibited from leaving his domicile without the supervising judge's permission and is required to appear before the supervising judge, receiver, or creditors' committee to provide information if summoned. In the case of juridical persons, the board of directors and commissioners are required to appear. Formally, the debtor must be placed in custody, with or without bail, if the bankrupt person fails without good reason to perform these duties. This criminal sanction in bankruptcy proceedings is claimed as a longstanding matter of civil law doctrine. There have been occasional threats by the government to invoke such criminal sanctions for unresponsive debtors; however, the draconian provisions are not applied in current practice. Once the receiver is appointed, he/she must immediately take possession of all documents, monies, jewellery, stocks and other valuable papers comprising the bankrupt estate. As soon as possible, he/she must proceed with an inventory of the bankrupt estate and produce a statement of the nature and amount of its assets and liabilities, the names and addresses of the creditors and the amount of each creditor's claim. The inventory and statement are available for public inspection at the receiver's office. The receiver may also open all letters and telegrams sent to the bankrupt debtor.

Concerning verification of claims, within 14 days of the time the declaration of bankruptcy becomes final (that is, taking into account possible appeals), the supervising judge establishes the time limit for the submission of claims and the date, time and venue for the creditors' meeting to verify claims. However, the time limit for submission of claims is not absolute to the extent special provision is made for submission of claims up to two days prior to the verification meeting under certain circumstances, with further special allowance made for creditors unable to submit claims sooner by reason of distant domicile. Provision is made for direct notice to all known creditors plus newspaper announcement.

Claims are filed with the receiver by showing an invoice or other written statement indicating the nature and amount of such claim, accompanied by documentary evidence plus a statement whether the creditor claims secured status, a right of retention, or agricultural liens. The receiver in turn consults the bankrupt's records and may require provision of further documentation or inspection of the creditor's original documentation. The receiver then prepares lists of claims that are approved, provisionally acknowledged, or disputed (including grounds for dispute). The receiver also discloses in the said lists his/her opinion of whether individual claims are preferred or secured, or whether retention rights exist (disputes solely concerning priority or retention rights result in a claim's provisional acknowledgement). The lists are available for examination in the receiver's office for seven days prior to the verification meeting. The receiver must also notify in writing all known creditors, including those whose claims he/she rejects, of the lists' availability, whether the debtor has filed a composition with the receiver, and must invite them to the verification meeting.

The verification meeting itself is presided over by the supervising judge, who reads the lists of provisionally acknowledged and disputed claims, and such creditors may submit requests for further clarification from the receiver and otherwise argue their case, while the receiver may require affirmation of claims under oath. The bankrupt debtor (its directors if the bankrupt is a juristic person) must appear in person at the verification meeting, while creditors may appear in person or by proxy (power of attorney). Provision is made for the adjournment and continuation of the meeting within eight days without further notice. Acknowledgement of a claim in the minutes of the meeting, including under bearer instruments (with each admitted claim being considered a separate creditor, important for voting purposes), is conclusive absent fraud. Disputed claims not settled at the meeting are referred by the supervising judge to a judicial hearing. Once verification is completed, the receiver's report, together with minutes of the verification meeting, is filed with judicial authorities and is made available to interested parties at the receiver's office.

Provision is made for the debtor to offer a composition to all creditors through pre-verification meeting filings with the receiver and court (similar voluntary debt settlement provisions are discussed subsequently). The composition proposal may be heard at the verification meeting itself if timely filed, but would more typically be heard separately to enable creditors time to study such an offer. If the composition proposal is filed at least eight days before the verification meeting, announced as available for public inspection, and sent to provisional creditors' committee members, the receiver and creditors' committee must submit written opinions on the composition proposal at the verification meeting subject to the supervising judge's postponing it under a variety of circumstances to a subsequent meeting to be held within three weeks. Ultimately, the composition proposal is subject to approval by more than half the number of unsecured creditors attending the creditors' meeting holding at least two thirds of the unsecured claims represented at the meeting, plus since Law No. 37/2004's passage, an additional similar class vote of secured creditors. Only those unsecured creditors whose claims are admitted, or are provisionally admitted, count for voting purposes.

Following creditor approval, the composition proposal still must be ratified in judicial proceedings. Judicial ratification must be refused if the assets of the bankrupt's estate considerably exceed the sum agreed to in the draft composition, or if performance of the composition is insufficiently assured, or if fraud, unfair means, or unfair preference among creditors are involved. The judicial decision on ratification may be appealed on an accelerated basis to the Supreme Court. Once ratification of the composition becomes final, the receiver must account to the debtor before the supervising judge and release to the debtor all goods, monies, books and documents in the bankrupt estate. However, release of the bankrupt's estate is subject to the receiver's obligation to retain all its monies and goods unless and until either adequate security is provided by the debtor, or any amounts payable to verified creditors under an admitted priority right plus the costs of the bankruptcy have been paid. If the debtor fails to comply with the ratified compromise any creditor may request dissolution of the composition, and the debtor bears the burden of proving compliance. Judicial dissolution of a composition results in formally reopening bankruptcy proceedings, including the new naming of a receiver and supervising judge, although provision is made where possible for reappointment of those who served in the original bankruptcy.

If at the verification meeting no composition is offered, or if the offered composition or its ratification is rejected, the bankrupt estate is insolvent at law. At this point attention turns to maximizing the value of the estate (that is, liquidating assets versus continuing the business and trying to sell it as a going concern) and a plan of distribution. The receiver or a creditor can propose continuation of the business subject to discussion by creditors at the verification meeting, or another creditors' meeting to be held promptly under a variety of circumstances. Approval is required by more than half of all admitted or provisionally admitted unsecured claims represented. Nonetheless, at the request of the receiver or any creditor the supervising judge may order continuation of the business to cease. However, continuation of the business is only a maximization of value issue with certain complications for secured creditors, since all assets of the bankrupt estate may thereafter be sold by the receiver in a public sale, or sold privately with the supervising judge's permission. The receiver may use the bankrupt's services in the asset disposition for compensation to be determined by the supervising judge.

The receiver also prepares a plan of distribution describing income and expenditures of the bankrupt estate, including bankruptcy administration costs, creditor names and verifications with distribution amounts, all to be ratified by the supervising judge. The distribution plan approved by the supervising judge is available at court and in the receiver's office, while the receiver arranges for newspaper announcements. The time period for inspection commences upon publication of approval in the *State Gazette*. During this period any creditor may oppose the distribution plan by filing a petition (including his reasons) with the court, and the objecting petition will be attached to the distribution plan. The supervising judge will then convene a hearing on the distribution plan at which written reports of the receiver and supervising judge must be submitted, and any creditor may submit reasons for or against the distribution plan. The court is required to issue its decision as soon as possible, and expedited appeal lies to the Supreme Court for the receiver or any creditor. Special cost and filing provisions apply to petitions challenging the plan of distribution only to seek verification of a creditor's claim.

Once the plan of distribution is final, the supervising judge will order payments to admitted creditors whenever there are sufficient funds available. Unsecured creditors receive a percentage as determined by the supervising judge, while secured creditors receive proceeds from their security up to the amount of their claim to the extent they have not already executed against the property itself. If secured creditors' security is not sold, or if the proceeds are less than their claim, then the secured creditors will be granted a percentage of the distribution which is the same as the unsecured creditors in proportion to the shortfall. General costs of the bankruptcy are apportioned over the entire estate, except collateral executed on by secured creditors.

Regarding improper transfers of property by the debtor, following Dutch law's *actio Pauliana*, Law No. 37/2004 provides for the debtor's legal acts to be invalidated and for the clawback of assets under circumstances roughly equivalent to fraudulent transfer principles in Anglo-American bankruptcy proceedings via Indonesian Civil Code section 1341. Transfers may be set aside if debtors knew or should have known they would harm creditors' interests, and contracts may be voided if debtor obligations greatly exceed those of the other party to the contract. Acts may also be voided if they constitute a payment of, or provision of security for, a debt not yet due and payable, as may contracts with related entities and family members. However, in practice the *actio Pauliana* has not been employed even where its use appears justified.

Separate and apart from Supreme Court review at various points in the process on an interlocutory basis, cassation to a special insolvency chamber generally is available: (1) if, within a time period of 180 days from the commercial court decision, new written evidence is discovered which, if known previously, would have resulted in a different decision; and (2) for a major error in the application of the law on petition within a time period of 30 days from the commercial court decision. Beyond cassation, Indonesian civil procedure also recognizes a procedure for the Supreme Court to re-examine the correctness of its own decisions. Supreme Court review is the rule for contentious insolvency proceedings, so that commercial court judgments are often subject to serial challenges after becoming final.

Judicial Debt Moratorium or Voluntary Debt Compromise Procedures

The second prong of Law No. 37/2004 provides for a voluntary debt compromise procedure, in theory to be completed within 270 days of the debt payment moratorium's commencement if not earlier terminated, with provision for automatic conversion into liquidation proceedings if a debt compromise does not achieve the requisite approval of creditors. (But in practice the 270-day statutory limit has been exceeded.) The voluntary debt compromise procedure is formally the predominant judicial channel for corporate workouts, and takes precedence over bankruptcy proceedings, but more often than not simply represents the path of insolvent debtors faced with an imminent bankruptcy petition. In current practice more willing or more solvent debtors, with good prospects of reaching agreement with their creditors, gravitated to negotiations and the Jakarta Initiative as a non-judicial workout forum. The voluntary debt compromise procedure remains problematic to the extent that it provides formally only for debt reductions or reschedulings rather than, for example, recasting debtor capital structures under debt for equity swaps. Thus it may be useful for the equivalent of prepackaged bankruptcies involving the ratification of agreements reached outside judicial proceedings. However, it is generally unsuitable for forcing an unwilling corporate debtor to reorganize because, absent prior agreement, the only thing that can be forced is a debt haircut.

A debtor (and since Law No. 37/2004 creditors and where appropriate BI, *Bapepam* and the Minister of Finance where only those agencies could petition for bankruptcy) who is unable, or expects that they will be unable, to continue paying their debts which have matured and must be paid may request a moratorium on the repayment of these debts, with the general intention of presenting a composition proposal that includes an offer to pay all or part of their debts to creditors. The appropriate party petitions the commercial court for a temporary moratorium on debt repayments, accompanied by a composition proposal, and the documentation is available for public inspection at the court. The court must issue an order naming a supervising judge and administrator, who effectively manages the business together with the debtor. Thereafter, in the period 1998–2004, much of the debt compromise procedure followed that under Law No. 4/1998's liquidation prong, *mutatis mutandis*, but creditor voting and ultimately secured creditors' position theoretically has changed significantly under Law No. 37/2004.

Law No. 37/2004's amendments include a new Article 281(1) provision requiring that a voluntary debt compromise plan be approved by both more than one half of the unsecured creditors who hold at least two thirds of the unsecured debts represented at the meeting, *and* by more than one half of the secured creditors attending who hold at least two thirds of the secured debts represented at the meeting. Article 281(2) goes on to say that secured creditors who vote against the plan will receive compensation in the amount of the lesser of the secured debt or the value of the security (presumably so that the property in which they hold their security interest stays in the debtor's continuing business, but for technical reasons the provision may also lead to valuation disputes between secured creditors and debtors/administrators). Article 286 states that the voluntary debt compromise so approved binds all creditors excepting those who voted against the plan under Article 281(2). The practical problem is that these provisions may be interpreted potentially to undercut security interests while incentivizing secured creditors to vote against voluntary debt compromises. This problem has been recognized, but one year after Law No. 37/2004's passage it has not been addressed by clarifying regulations or other approaches common to civil law jurisdictions.

In theory, secured creditors who vote in favor of a plan presumably will insist that principal amounts or interest rates on their debt might be reduced, but that they retain their security. However, all secured creditors, whether or not represented at the meeting, will be bound by the plan's terms unless they positively vote against it. So there is a potential issue with plan terms which might interfere with the security of non-voting secured creditors. On the other hand, if a secured creditor has any qualms about the plan and a debtor's prospective financial performance, he/she must vote against the plan to be bought out in theory under Article 281(2). However, the mechanism for buying out secured creditors who vote against the plan is unclear, since most assume that debtors will have insufficient cash for these purposes. There have been suggestions ranging from third-party bridging loans, to secured creditors voting in favor of the plan being required effectively to buy out secured creditors voting against the plan, to installment buy-out payments from the debtor (but the secured creditor voting against the plan is presumably now rendered an unsecured creditor because his original security interest is assumed lost if that property is necessary to the debtor's continued operation). Ultimately, the new buy-out rules are commercially and practically difficult to implement.

The practical effect may be that only prepackaged reorganizations are now likely to be approved, since it seems unlikely to expect a debtor's plan to be approved absent good future business prospects and willing creditors. The ultimate result of new rules chiefly workable for prepackaged reorganizations may be to de-emphasize the commercial court's role in reorganizations and to correspondingly increase the practical role of extra-judicial institutions prospectively.

The underlying distinctions between the voluntary debt compromise and bankruptcy procedures are inherent in the assumption that the business may continue for the longer term in the debtor's hands but that operations may be recast, requiring provisions dealing with executory contracts, ordinary course legal proceedings and sharing of operational authority between the debtor and administrator. Thus, once the court admits the moratorium petition a debtor may terminate employees, with their salaries and related expenses becoming debts of the estate, and a debtor-lessee may terminate a lease before its expiration on the earlier of a customary notice period or the period for which rent has been prepaid. For executory contracts, the counterparty may request assurances of continued implementation from the administrator. If the administrator affirms the executory contract security must be offered, and if the contract is disallowed the counterparty's claim is converted into an unsecured debt. Concerning litigation, the debt moratorium itself suspends enforcement of attachments, and any payments to creditors during the period of suspended payments must be pro rata. On-going proceedings will not be halted unless they concern a claim for payment of a debt acknowledged by the debtor, but the debtor may not become involved in new litigation as plaintiff or defendant without the administrator's cooperation.

Concerning the debtor's general authority to operate the business, during the period of the debt moratorium the debtor may not, without the authorization of the administrator, take any management actions or transfer rights to any part of its assets. Obligations of the debtor arising after commencement of the debt moratorium which are undertaken without the administrator's authority may only be imposed on the debtor's estate to the extent it benefits it. The debtor may obtain third-party loans, but only to increase the value of the business's assets and only under the administrator's authority and, if security is required, with the supervising judge's approval. The same rules apply for secured creditors *mutatis mutandis* under the debt moratorium procedure as under the bankruptcy procedure. During the period of the debt suspension the administrator is liable for the conduct of the debtor's business and must prepare and file quarterly reports of the debtor's condition with the court. In practice, however, administrators have not been proactive, instead largely acquiescing in the decisions of debtor management representing controlling shareholders.

In debt suspension proceedings the court is required to appoint a creditors' committee so long as the debt involved is substantial or complex, or if requested by the unsecured creditors holding half that debt. As in liquidation proceedings, the creditors' committee arguably represents only unsecured creditors without provision for voting by others. The administrator is required to receive and consider creditor committee recommendations.

The debtor's debt moratorium petition includes a list of assets and liabilities alongside a list of creditors. The administrator is required to prove up the list of creditors similarly to liquidation proceedings. However, future claims are contemplated as part of the permanent debt moratorium. Claims with an uncertain due date or for periodic payments will be valued as of the suspension of payments date, as will those which would become payable within one year, with claims payable after one year being valued as of one year following the suspension date. Upon the administrator's request, the supervising judge may also hear witnesses or commission experts to clarify the suspension of obligations.

The ultimate goal of the debt compromise proceeding is that the debtor's proposed composition plan be approved at a meeting of creditors by respective class votes of unsecured and secured creditors by at least one half of the class creditors present at the meeting and holding two thirds of the class debt represented. Failing that approval, the proceeding is automatically converted into a liquidation proceeding. Following creditor approval, the composition proposal still must be ratified in judicial proceedings. Judicial ratification must be refused if the debtor's estate is much larger than the sum agreed to in the draft composition, or performance of the composition is insufficiently assured, or if fraud, unfair means, or unfair preference among creditors is involved, or if fees and expenses incurred by the administrator and experts have not yet been paid or no security for payment has been given. If the court refuses to ratify the composition, it is obligated in the same decision to declare the debtor bankrupt. Under Law No. 4/1998, in practice there were problems with so-called fictive creditors as in the *Panca Overseas* case previously discussed (with secured creditors' voting under Article 281 of new Law No. 37/2004 intended to address that problem, even while it created new issues previously discussed). Judges themselves seem disinclined to exercise any economic judgment concerning composition proposals, since plans have been approved even where the enterprise does not appear economically viable post composition.

Secured Creditors under Indonesian Law

Indonesian law follows Dutch and the civil law more generally in emphasizing possession and the theory of *in rem* rights defining property rights as a relationship between a person and a thing (under Indonesian Civil Code Article 1131 *et seq*). This differs from common law concepts such as equitable versus legal ownership, and rights of security are themselves property rights under the Indonesian approach. As a result of the theoretical property construct a creditor need not necessarily approach a court for execution, since he is just taking possession of a property interest he already owns. This insight helps in understanding the traditional odd position of secured creditors in Indonesian bankruptcy. On the one hand, they seem stepchildren since they did not have any legal right to participate in creditors' committees or any vote on a debt composition except to the extent the value of debts owed them exceeds the value of their security. However, this has all been called into question by Articles 281 and 286 of Law No. 37/2004, which may be interpreted to displace Civil Code security rights in voluntary debt compromise proceedings.

Applicable Articles 56–57 of Law No. 37/2004 discuss the rights of a secured creditor in terms of enforcement as if there were no bankruptcy and provide only for a temporary stay of their rights to enforce the security of 90 days in a bankruptcy proceeding and during the term of a provisional debt repayment moratorium. Thus, subject to the new Article 281(2) provision for buy-outs of secured creditors voting against voluntary debt compromise plans, execution is permitted typically at some point between 90 and 270 days depending upon the kind of proceeding in question. For these purposes execution may represent a removal of the property without judicial proceedings. However, the bankrupt estate is entitled in turn to value realized on security above the value of the related debt and permission is necessary to conduct private sales which, at the same time, may result in higher prices but also offer opportunities for collusion affecting price.

Concerning general types of security, we shift into general legal issues outside insolvency. Mortgages of real property are common in Indonesia and are governed by Mortgage Law No. 4/1996 which requires for a mortgage: (1) an agreement to that effect, (2) a mortgage deed and (3) registration of the mortgage in land records. The 1996 Mortgage Law changed prior law and thereby created pitfalls, since pre-1996 Indonesian law encouraged creation of mortgage deeds without recordation until needed for execution. Compliance with the new statute was not widespread at the outset of the Asian Financial Crisis, casting doubt on the validity of mortgages given unrecorded mortgage deeds. Pledges are recognized for security in tangible and intangible personal or movable property under the Indonesian Civil Code, empowering a pledgee to seek recourse against the assets in the event of a breach or non-performance by the pledgor of its obligations under a loan agreement. Under traditional law pledged tangible assets are required to be in the possession of the pledgee or a third party, while third-party notice was required for a pledge of intangible assets. Beyond the Indonesian Civil Code concepts, caselaw also recognized a form of fiduciary ownership without any public registration, typically by deed of assignment, to avoid onerous statutory requirements of notice and transfer of possession. Foreseeably, problems for creditors arose with *bona fide* purchasers without knowledge from the pledgor still in possession, with specific outcomes differing depending upon the exact kind of personal property. Most recently, Fiduciary Transfer Law No. 42/1999 provides for a registration system to give effective notice, but requires a written agreement in the form of a notarial deed, basically covering all types of movable property plus property that might be considered fixtures or similar real property in a common law jurisdiction (for example, buildings where the underlying land is owned by another which places the property outside the Mortgage Law No. 4/1996). Fiduciary Transfer Law No. 42/1999's registration system has been incomplete in practice, so those newer principles of security in movable property are unevenly applied in practice. There are also practical problems in terms of Law No. 4/1996 and Law No. 42/1999 containing what are interpreted as conflicting provisions, thus accounting for the post-Law No. 37/2004 initiatives for further technical amendments.

Insolvency and Criminal or Civil Liabilities of Management

Articles 396–405 of the Indonesian Criminal Code set forth several criminal offenses relevant to bankruptcy which are mostly applicable to business entities. The director of a bankrupt company may be jailed for up to 16 months: (1) for activities contrary to the company charter which cause substantial losses; or (2) if he fails to prepare and maintain proper records as required under the law; or (3) if he borrows money on onerous terms to delay the bankruptcy, knowing that even then the bankruptcy cannot be avoided. A director or commissioner may be jailed for up to seven years if he has fraudulently impeded creditors' rights: (1) by transferring assets without consideration or below value; or (2) by recording non-existent liabilities, failing to record assets or revenues; or (3) by favoring certain of the company's creditors. Imprisonment for up to 5½ years is possible for anyone who presents a fraudulent bankruptcy claim to the receiver, or who fraudulently accepts property of the bankrupt or payment of a claim, knowing that the debtor is insolvent, and so deprives other creditors of their lawful claim. There are also criminal sanctions applicable to both creditors and debtors for secret agreements offering special inducements to accept compositions. While the above criminal offenses exist in theory, they have not been applied in modern practice.

Civil liability of company management may exist under various provisions of Indonesia's 1995 Company Law. The beneficiary of company law's liability provisions is normally a shareholder or the company itself, but in theory these rights may be available for recovery under the bankrupt's estate. Indonesian company law employs a dual board system of directors (analogous to officers in most common law jurisdictions) and commissioners (analogous to directors in most common law jurisdictions). The most relevant provision is that all directors are jointly and severally liable for losses resulting from an insolvency if the insolvency occurs because of the fault or negligence of the board of directors and the company's assets are not sufficient to cover losses resulting from the insolvency.

Rules regarding Cross-border Insolvency

Law No. 37/2004 is inconsistent to the extent that it seems to adopt a universal theory of bankruptcy for actions commenced in Indonesia, requiring receivers also to investigate the existence of possible foreign assets. Further, offshore actions by individual creditors are discouraged by Law No. 37/2004's provisions that creditors must pay into the debtor's estate recoveries from assets outside Indonesia made by them or their assignees if they did not have a pre-existing security interest and if such claims are paid following commencement of Indonesian insolvency proceedings. However, a bankruptcy declared outside Indonesia does not theoretically affect the assets of the insolvent party within Indonesia. Under Indonesian civil procedure, foreign judgments can be enforced only upon the basis of a treaty, of which there are currently none for these purposes. Thus, it may be necessary to commence bankruptcy proceedings within Indonesia to reach assets here separate and apart from the foreign proceedings, while it may also be possible to attach assets within Indonesia despite on-going foreign bankruptcy proceedings.

Given general rule of law difficulties, such theoretical possibilities have not been pursued in practice. However, the issue is visible in the major international debt restructuring of foreign-listed Asia Pulp & Paper (APP, from Indonesia's Sinar Mas Group), given its significant Jakarta-listed operating subsidiaries with their own differing circles of creditors and public shareholders in Indonesia. IBRA was involved in the pending APP debt restructuring by virtue of its parallel status as a significant creditor of numerous APP-affiliates through control of a Sinar Mas-affiliated bank (*Bank Internasional Indonesia* or BII). IBRA also guaranteed BII obligations to prevent wider banking system problems, reprising its problematic status simultaneously as creditor and guarantor visible in purely domestic insolvencies.

APP's operations are spread across Indonesia, India, Mainland China and Singapore, with current attention focused on see-saw attempts of certain creditors to displace management in Singapore proceedings, while APP management continues to reformulate settlement offers in an attempt to gather necessary creditor approvals, which would ultimately affect debts of its Indonesian subsidiaries. However, APP as a transnational insolvency proceeding is more properly viewed currently as a problem of Singaporean rather than Indonesian law.

Chapter 12

Insolvency Law in Singapore

VICTOR YEO* and PAULINE GAN**
Nanyang Technological University

1 Introduction

1.1 Singapore's Legal System and Culture

The origins of Singapore's legal system may be traced to the days when the island was a British colony. Singapore's laws are therefore strongly rooted in the English common law tradition.[1] Moreover the environments in which these laws operate – the judicial system, court structure and governmental and administrative institutions – were all likewise modelled on their English counterparts.

Notwithstanding the strong influence of the English common law, Singapore's legal system, like those of many former colonies, has evolved and developed along an increasingly independent path. The growth and development of an indigenous legal system has been particularly evident in the last 15 years or so, even as the nation as a whole has striven to define itself and establish its own identity in the international arena.[2]

1.2 History, Sources and Philosophy of Singapore's Insolvency Laws, Attitudes to Debt and Debt Enforcement

Given this historical background, it is hardly surprising that Singapore's insolvency laws are modelled primarily on English insolvency laws and influenced, in part, by those of other Commonwealth jurisdictions such as Australia. Singapore has separate regimes for personal and corporate insolvency. Personal insolvency laws are

---

* Associate Professor, Head, Division of Business Law, Nanyang Business School, Nanyang Technological University, Singapore.

** Assistant Professor, Division of Business Law, Nanyang Business School, Nanyang Technological University, Singapore.

1 For further reading on the history and development of Singapore law, see generally, Michael Rutter, *The Applicable Law in Singapore and Malaysia: A Guide to Reception, Precedent and the Sources of Law in the Republic of Singapore and the Federation of Malaysia*, Singapore, Malayan Law Journal, 1989 and Andrew Phang, *The Development of Singapore Law: Historical and Socio-Legal Perspectives*, Singapore, Butterworths, 1990.

2 See further, Philip Pillai, *State Enterprise in Singapore: Legal Importation and Development, Singapore*, Singapore University Press, 1983 and Lau Kok Keng *et al.*, 'Legal Crossroads: Towards a Singaporean Jurisprudence' (1987) 8 *Singapore Law Review* 1–31.

contained in the Bankruptcy Act (Cap 20) while most of the rules of procedure and other such matters are contained in subsidiary legislation, the most important of which are the Bankruptcy Rules. Corporate insolvency laws and procedural rules are to be found in the Companies Act (Cap 50) and the Companies (Winding up) Rules.

English bankruptcy legislation was first received into Singapore in 1848. Significant changes were made to the bankruptcy laws by Ordinance II of 1888 but thereafter, save for some minor amendments, the bankruptcy law of Victorian England was applied in Singapore for more than a hundred years. After Singapore achieved independence and as it developed into the thriving financial and business hub that it is today, it became increasingly clear that the laws relating to personal insolvency were archaic, outdated and out of step with the realities of modern-day commercial life. When Parliament embarked on a review of Singapore's bankruptcy laws in the early 1990s, many felt that reform was long overdue.

The Bankruptcy Act of 1995 came into force on 15 July 1995.[3] Further amendments to the Bankruptcy Act were made in 1999,[4] in line with the Singapore government's efforts to encourage entrepreneurship by cultivating a calculated risk-taking culture and fostering a climate of greater tolerance of failure. The changes aim to promote the use of alternatives to bankruptcy, to facilitate earlier discharge from bankruptcy in appropriate circumstances, and to enable bankrupts to continue to be economically productive during bankruptcy.

Singapore's Companies Act, which was first enacted in 1967, is based on the Malaysian Companies Act of 1965, which, in turn, was based on the Uniform Companies Act 1961 of Victoria, Australia. This Victorian legislation itself had been based on earlier English legislation. Like its personal insolvency laws, therefore, Singapore's corporate insolvency laws are modelled on the English system.

Unlike its personal insolvency laws, however, Singapore's corporate insolvency laws have not been the subject of as many widespread changes in recent times. The most important recent amendment relating to corporate insolvency was the introduction of a scheme of corporate rehabilitation known as judicial management, which was introduced by the Companies (Amendment) Act 1987. When the government embarked on a review of the country's insolvency laws in the early 1990s, it was decided that no major reform of the corporate insolvency legislation would be undertaken for the time being as, according to the Minister for Law, they appeared to 'have worked fairly well'.[5]

---

3 The proposal for revision of Singapore's bankruptcy laws was first mooted in 1989. The Bankruptcy Bill was read for the first time in Parliament on 25 July 1994 and the second reading of the Bill was on 25 August 1994. It was then referred to a Select Committee, which presented its Report on 7 March 1995. The Bill was read for the third time and passed on 23 March 1995. Professor S. Jayakumar, Minister for Law, in his speech to Parliament, said that the intention was to 'introduce legislation to improve administration of the affairs of bankrupts and protect creditors' interests without stifling entrepreneurship'. Parliament: Parliamentary Debates Vol. 63, no. 2, 25 July 1994, col. 123.

4 Initial amendments were effected in July 1999 and further amendments came into effect *vide* Act No. 37 of 1999 in September 1999. (There have been subsequent amendments since then, but these are not substantive and are primarily consequential amendments arising from amendments to other statutes relating to arbitration, stamp duties, and so on.)

5 Supra note 3, at col. 400.

In December 1999, however, the Company Legislation and Regulatory Framework Committee (CLRFC) was appointed by the Ministry of Finance, the Attorney-General's Chambers and the Monetary Authority of Singapore to embark on a comprehensive review of Singapore's company law and regulatory framework. As part of its work, the Committee reviewed the nation's insolvency laws and made several proposals, including the introduction of a separate omnibus legislation for personal as well as corporate insolvency, a review and refinement of existing rescue options for ailing companies and the improvement of training and accreditation procedures for insolvency practitioners.[6] At present, only broad recommendations have been made and the exact scope and extent of the changes to Singapore's insolvency regime remain to be seen.

The history and development of Singapore's insolvency laws, both corporate and personal, indicate a gradual shift in attitude towards insolvent debtors. The early paradigm of insolvency law in Singapore was strongly pro-creditor. Attitudes have changed somewhat in recent times. While it would be an overstatement to say that the country's insolvency laws have become pro-debtor, they have certainly moved along a continuum towards a slightly more pro-debtor stance. There now appears to be a more sympathetic attitude towards insolvent debtors and recognition of the fact that they are not always to blame for business failure. A press statement announcing the 1999 amendments to the bankruptcy regime had this to say:

> ... the bankruptcy regime seeks to provide assistance to persons who fall into dire financial straits due to normal business risks, as opposed to malpractice or mismanagement, and to provide adequate opportunities to restructure their debts, so as to enhance the prospects for settlement of debts to creditors' satisfaction without resort to bankruptcy. Declaring them bankrupt will be a last resort and even in that event, they will be given early opportunities to restart new businesses afresh. *Falling into bankruptcy should also not be seen as a stigma, since failure is part of normal business risk* [emphasis added].[7]

This change in attitude is part of an overall government initiative to shift the economy towards a more knowledge-based one and to encourage entrepreneurship, particularly in the high-technology sector.[8]

1.3 Key Insolvency Principles

The Bankruptcy Act provides several ways in which insolvent individuals may be dealt with. These include voluntary arrangements, compositions or schemes of arrangement and bankruptcy. The provisions for voluntary arrangement provide a

---

6 The Company Legislation and Regulatory Framework Committee Report is available at http://www.mof.gov.sg/cor/clrfc.html.

7 Insolvency & Public Trustee's Office press statement, 'Changes to bankruptcy regime to cultivate a calculated risk-taking culture and foster a climate of greater tolerance for failure', Annex A para 2, reproduced at http://www.minlaw.gov.sg/ipto.

8 This initiative, named Technopreneurship 21, or T21 for short, is spearheaded by the T21 Ministerial Committee led by Singapore's Deputy Prime Minister Dr Tony Tan. The initiative aims to cover four main areas which it feels are critical for the technology sector to flourish – education, facilities, regulation and financing.

regime under which an insolvent debtor may avoid bankruptcy by coming to an agreement with his creditors. In addition, the Bankruptcy Act provides an avenue for a debtor, against whom a bankruptcy order has already been made, to make a proposal to his creditors for a composition or scheme of arrangement. If the proposal is accepted by the creditors, the bankruptcy order is annulled. Bankruptcy proceedings are commenced by way of a petition, which may be filed by a creditor or creditors, or by the debtor himself. The Bankruptcy Act also contains various provisions that enable the assets available for distribution among creditors to be maximised. These include provisions which deal with unlawful dispositions of property by the bankrupt and the avoidance of extortionate credit transactions. The Act sets out rules for the proof of debts and establishes a scheme for the orderly distribution of the bankrupt's assets among his creditors. Finally, the Act also provides for an end to bankruptcy through annulment or discharge. These and various other key bankruptcy principles will be dealt with in greater detail in sections 2 and 3 of this chapter.

Insolvent corporate debtors are dealt with in various ways under the Singapore Companies Act. Judicial management is the scheme by which insolvent companies may seek refuge from their creditors, avoid liquidation and attempt to rehabilitate their business. The Companies Act also provides for compositions and schemes of arrangement between a company and its creditors. Liquidation may take one of two forms – voluntary liquidation or liquidation by the court. Solvent companies may voluntarily liquidate by a members' voluntary winding up while insolvent companies must do so by a creditors' voluntary winding up. As is the case with personal insolvencies, the Act also deals with the avoidance of unlawful dispositions of property by the company and provides a scheme by which creditors may share in the assets of the liquidated company. Sections 4, 5 and 6 of this chapter contain a more detailed discussion of the law relating to corporate insolvencies.

2 Personal Insolvency Laws

2.1 Introduction

In the ten years between 1988 and 1997, the number of new bankruptcy orders made in Singapore remained steady at an average of about 1,500 per year. In 1998, the number increased to 2,841 and in 1999 there were 3,094 new bankruptcy orders made. Except for a small dip in 2000 the upward trend continues, with 3,588 bankruptcy orders made in 2002.[9] Efforts are being made, however, to enable bankrupts to emerge from bankruptcy sooner and increase the number of discharges.

---

9 Insolvency & Public Trustee's Office, 'Bankruptcy Orders & Discharges', Graphical Statistics at http://www.minlaw.gov.sg/ipto.

2.2 Regulatory Structures and Principal Institutions for Bankruptcy Proceedings

The office of the Official Assignee, which is part of the Insolvency and Public Trustee's Office of the Singapore Ministry of Law, is the main administrative body in charge of bankruptcy proceedings in Singapore. Section 18 of the Bankruptcy Act describes the three main functions of the Official Assignee's office, namely, to act as interim receiver of a debtor's property;[10] to act as receiver and trustee of the bankrupt's estate and to act as trustee of the estate of a deceased debtor in bankruptcy. As administrator of the bankruptcy estate it is also charged with the duty of investigating a bankrupt's conduct while he/she remains bankrupt. The duties of the Official Assignee include adjudication of creditors' claims, payment of dividends and applying to the High Court for a bankrupt's discharge.

In situations where bankrupts are unable to make full payment of their debts, the Official Assignee's office also acts as mediator between the bankrupt and their creditors. This is in order to promote earlier discharges for bankrupts and earlier settlement and repayment of creditor claims. For this purpose, the Official Assignee's office has set up a Bankruptcy Mediation Unit[11] to assist bankrupts and their creditors to arrive at a mutually acceptable debt settlement agreement. Often, parties begin mediation as soon as the bankruptcy order is made.

With the coming into effect of the 1995 amendments to the Bankruptcy Act, it is now also possible for private trustees to be appointed to administer bankrupts' estates.[12] The main intention behind the introduction of private trustees in bankruptcy was to encourage creditors to take a more active role in the administration of bankruptcy estates.[13] Only a handful of appointments of private trustees have been made since the introduction of the legislation, usually in cases where there are substantial assets or where, in the opinion of the petitioning creditor, there is a need for greater scrutiny and investigation of the bankrupt's financial affairs and antecedent transactions.[14]

2.3 Powers of the Courts

Singapore does not have a specialist insolvency court dealing exclusively with insolvency matters. Bankruptcy proceedings are heard in the High Court.[15] Generally, the High Court has the power to decide all questions of law or fact which may arise in any bankruptcy case coming within its cognisance. It has power to make orders for

---

10 Under section 73 of the Bankruptcy Act, the court may appoint the Official Assignee as interim receiver of the debtor's property at any time after the presentation of the bankruptcy petition and before the making of the bankruptcy order. The purpose of such appointment is to protect and preserve the debtor's property pending the hearing of the bankruptcy petition.

11 See generally, Insolvency & Public Trustee's Office, 'Mediation in Individual Insolvency', supra n. 7.

12 Section 33 of the Bankruptcy Act.

13 See speech by the Minister of Law at the Second Reading of the Bankruptcy Bill, supra n. 3 at col. 402.

14 Kala Anandarajah *et al.*, *Law and Practice of Bankruptcy in Singapore and Malaysia*, Singapore, Butterworths, 1999 at 125–127.

15 Section 3 of the Bankruptcy Act.

committal against defaulting persons[16] and to make orders for arrest and seizure in appropriate circumstances.[17] Section 10 of the Bankruptcy Act further provides for a District or Magistrate's Court to have criminal jurisdiction to hear and determine offences under the Bankruptcy Act and related rules, and to impose the full penalty and punishment in respect of such offences. Orders made in bankruptcy matters are subject to appeal in the same manner as orders of the High Court are appealable in other matters.[18]

2.4 Duties of Bankruptcy Practitioners

Both lawyers and accountants are qualified to act as nominees in voluntary arrangements[19] and as private trustees in bankruptcy.[20] However, lawyers involved in insolvency practice in Singapore tend to confine themselves strictly to the legal aspects of insolvency, leaving the business and administrative aspects to the accountants.

The nominee's role is to assess the debtor's proposal for a voluntary arrangement and to form an opinion as to whether a creditors' meeting should be called to consider the proposal.[21] This opinion is presented to the court in the form of a report. The nominee is then responsible for summoning the creditors to a meeting to consider the proposal[22] and, if the creditors accept the proposal, implementing the terms of the voluntary arrangement.[23]

The trustee in bankruptcy is controlled generally by the court and, in specific circumstances, by the creditors and/or the Official Assignee. Subject only to these controls, he/she has the discretion to act in the day-to-day administration of the bankrupt's estate. Section 36 of the Bankruptcy Act provides for the private trustee in bankruptcy to have all the functions and duties of the Official Assignee and to exercise all the powers of the Official Assignee. The duties of the trustee in the administration of the bankruptcy estate include:

- taking over custody, control and management of the bankrupt's property;[24]
- realisation of the bankrupt's property;[25]
- investigation into the bankrupt's conduct and affairs leading to the insolvency;[26]
- investigation of the bankrupt's assets and antecedent transactions;[27]
- monitoring the bankrupt's conduct during the bankruptcy;

---

16 Section 6 of the Bankruptcy Act.
17 Section 9 of the Bankruptcy Act.
18 Section 8 of the Bankruptcy Act.
19 Section 46 of the Bankruptcy Act.
20 Section 34 of the Bankruptcy Act.
21 Section 49 of the Bankruptcy Act.
22 Section 50 of the Bankruptcy Act.
23 Section 55 of the Bankruptcy Act.
24 Section 107(1) of the Bankruptcy Act.
25 Section 111(a) of the Bankruptcy Act.
26 Section 21(1)(a) & (b) of the Bankruptcy Act.
27 Sections 97–106 of the Bankruptcy Act.

- adjudication of claims filed against the bankruptcy estate;[28]
- assisting the bankrupt in putting forward debt settlement proposals to the creditors;[29]
- distribution of assets to creditors;[30] and
- filing, supporting or opposing applications for annulment or discharge of the bankrupt.[31]

A private trustee in bankruptcy is also subject to certain additional duties such as the duty to report to the Official Assignee every six months,[32] to pay all monies received by him into a prescribed bank account[33] and generally to cooperate with the Official Assignee.[34]

Certain other powers may only be exercised by the private trustee with the sanction of the court, or the creditors' committee or, where there is no creditors' committee, by the Official Assignee. These include carrying on the business of the bankrupt so far as it is necessary for its beneficial winding up,[35] compromise with debtors of the bankrupt[36] and division of property in its existing form to creditors when it cannot be advantageously sold.[37] Certain powers of the Official Assignee may not be exercised by the private trustee at all. These include the power to administer oaths,[38] the power to impound the bankrupt's passport or other travel document[39] and to discharge a bankrupt by certificate.[40]

2.5 Voluntary Arrangements in Bankruptcy

It is, of course, always open to a debtor to seek an informal, private arrangement for settlement of debts with his creditors. Informal measures to reach a compromise with creditors are often unsuccessful for the following reasons. First, pending agreement, creditors are free to proceed with individual efforts at recovering their claims. Secondly, only creditors who have agreed to a proposal for compromise are bound by it.

With the introduction of court-supervised voluntary arrangements to the bankruptcy regime in Singapore in 1995, the debtor is now offered valuable respite or breathing space from individual creditor action, pending the consideration by his/her creditors of a proposal for compromise. Section 45(1) of the Bankruptcy Act provides

28 Sections 87–94 of the Bankruptcy Act.
29 For example, under section 95 of the Bankruptcy Act.
30 Sections 117–122 of the Bankruptcy Act.
31 Sections 123–126 of the Bankruptcy Act.
32 Rule 55 of the Bankruptcy Rules.
33 Section 37(1) of the Bankruptcy Act.
34 Section 39(3) of the Bankruptcy Act.
35 Section 112(a) of the Bankruptcy Act.
36 Section 112(f) of the Bankruptcy Act.
37 Section 112(1) of the Bankruptcy Act.
38 Section 24 of the Bankruptcy Act.
39 Section 116 of the Bankruptcy Act.
40 Section 125 of the Bankruptcy Act.

that any insolvent debtor who intends to make a proposal to their creditors for a composition or scheme of arrangement (henceforth referred to in this section as a voluntary arrangement) may apply to the court for what is known as an interim order.[41] The interim order is effective for an initial period of 42 days,[42] subject to extensions by the court. While it is in effect, no bankruptcy petition may be presented, nor any other proceedings or legal process commenced or continued against the debtor or his property without leave of court.[43] In fact, once an application for an interim order has been filed, and pending the making of the order, the court may, in its discretion, stay any action, execution or legal process against the debtor.[44]

A debtor wishing to apply for an interim order must first prepare a proposal for the nominee, who has to give his/her consent to act in the supervision and implementation of the voluntary arrangement.[45] Rule 68 of the Bankruptcy Rules enumerates a number of matters that should be dealt with in the proposal. These include a statement of the bankrupt's assets and an estimate of their value; the nature and amount of his/her liabilities; the proposed duration of the voluntary arrangement; the proposed dates of distributions to creditors and estimated amounts to be paid; if the debtor has any business, the manner in which it is proposed to be conducted during the course of the arrangement, details of any further credit facilities intended to be arranged for the debtor and how such facilities are to be repaid.

Once the nominee has consented to act, the application for the interim order may be filed.[46] Notice of the hearing of such an application must be given to any creditor who has presented a bankruptcy petition against the debtor and the proposed nominee.[47] In order for the court to make an interim order, it must be satisfied that the debtor intends to make a proposal for a voluntary arrangement and that no previous application for an interim order has been made in the 12 months immediately preceding the application.[48] If these conditions are satisfied, the court may make an interim order if it deems it appropriate to do so for the purposes of facilitating the consideration and implementation of the debtor's proposal.

Upon the making of the interim order, the court also fixes a date for the consideration of the nominee's report.[49] In the report the nominee is required to state whether, in his/her opinion, a meeting of the debtor's creditors should be called

---

41 Because of the use of the word 'may' in relation to an application for an interim order as opposed to the word 'shall', it has been suggested that the making of an interim order may not be a necessary prelude to a binding voluntary arrangement. However, for various reasons, the preferred view is that an interim order is a necessary step in the process. For a discussion of the opposing views, see supra n. 14 at 28–29.

42 Section 45(4) of the Bankruptcy Act. Under the 1995 version, the initial period of the interim order was 28 days. This was amended in September 1999 to allow more time for the debtor to put up a proposal and increase the chances of success of a voluntary arrangement.

43 Section 45(3) of the Bankruptcy Act.

44 Section 47 of the Bankruptcy Act.

45 Section 46 of the Bankruptcy Act.

46 Application is by way of originating summons supported by affidavit – rule 71(1) of the Bankruptcy Rules.

47 Rule 72(1) of the Bankruptcy Rules.

48 Section 48(1) of the Bankruptcy Act.

49 Rule 73(1) of the Bankruptcy Rules.

to consider the proposal and, if so, the date, time and place for the proposed meeting.[50] To enable the nominee to prepare his/her report the debtor must provide the nominee with a statement of affairs and a document setting out the terms of the proposed voluntary arrangement.[51]

Where a nominee has reported to the court that a meeting should be called, section 50 of the Bankruptcy Act provides that the nominee shall, unless the court otherwise directs, summon a meeting of creditors to consider the debtor's proposal. The meeting must be held not less than 14 days and not more than 28 days from the date of the filing of the nominee's report[52] and creditors[53] must be given not less than 14 days' notice of the meeting.[54] At the creditors' meeting the creditors may approve, by special resolution[55] and with or without modification, the debtor's proposal for a voluntary arrangement. There are several restrictions on the matters which may be approved by creditors at the meeting. For example, secured creditors and preferential creditors are afforded special protection and their rights may not be altered or affected unless their concurrence is obtained.[56] The meeting may also not approve a proposal with any modifications unless the debtor has consented to such modification.[57] A proposal for voluntary arrangement which has been approved by the requisite majority of creditors is binding on the debtor and on every person who had received notice and was entitled to vote at the creditors' meeting, whether or not such person was present or represented at the meeting.[58] The ability to bind dissenting creditors greatly enhances the likelihood of success of the voluntary arrangement.

The Bankruptcy Act does make provision for persons[59] dissatisfied with the outcome of the creditors' meeting to apply to court for a review of the decision of the meeting. The grounds for review are, first, that the voluntary arrangement unfairly prejudices the interests of the debtor or any of the creditors or, secondly, that there has been some material irregularity at or in relation to the meeting.[60] The powers of the court in such a situation include the ability to revoke or suspend any approval given at the meeting or to direct that a further creditors' meeting be summoned to consider a revised proposal or, in the case of a material irregularity, to reconsider the debtor's original proposal.[61]

50 Section 49 of the Bankruptcy Act.

51 Section 49(2)(a)–(c) of the Bankruptcy Act.

52 Rule 81 of the Bankruptcy Rules.

53 These include every creditor named in the debtor's statement of affairs and every other creditor whom the nominee is otherwise aware of – section 50(2) of the Bankruptcy Act and rule 81(2) of the Bankruptcy Rules.

54 Rule 81(2) of the Bankruptcy Rules.

55 Defined in section 2 of the Bankruptcy Act as a majority in number representing three quarters in value of the creditors present (personally or by proxy) and voting.

56 See sections 51(4) and (5) of the Bankruptcy Act.

57 See sections 51(2) and (3) of the Bankruptcy Act.

58 Section 53 of the Bankruptcy Act.

59 The debtor or nominee or any person entitled to vote at the creditors' meeting.

60 Section 54 of the Bankruptcy Act.

61 Section 54(2) of the Bankruptcy Act.

The responsibility for supervising the implementation of the voluntary arrangement lies primarily with the nominee. If the debtor or any creditor is dissatisfied with the nominee in the latter's supervision of the implementation of the voluntary arrangement, he/she may apply to the court for a review of the relevant act, omission or decision.[62] The court is empowered to confirm, reverse or modify any act or decision of the nominee and to give such directions to the nominee or make such order as it thinks fit. In addition the nominee may themselves apply to court for directions in relation to any matter arising out of the voluntary arrangement.[63]

A voluntary arrangement comes to an end either because it has failed or upon its successful implementation. A voluntary arrangement may fail at various stages. It may be that, upon scrutiny of the debtor's proposal, the nominee reports to the court that it cannot succeed and that a creditors' meeting should not be called. In practice this seldom happens because, in almost all cases, the nominee is actively involved in helping the debtor prepare the proposal. The second situation in which a voluntary arrangement might fail is if the proposal does not receive the support of the requisite majority at the creditors' meeting. What invariably follows in this case is the expiry of the interim order, whereupon the moratorium on creditor action is lifted and any creditor may file a bankruptcy petition or proceed with other legal action against the debtor. A voluntary arrangement may also fail because the debtor fails to comply with its terms. Section 56 of the Bankruptcy Act provides that where a debtor fails to comply with his obligations under the voluntary arrangement, the nominee or any creditor bound by the arrangement may file a bankruptcy petition against the debtor.

The happiest outcome of a voluntary arrangement is its successful implementation and completion. Upon completion of the voluntary arrangement, the nominee is required to file with the court and send to all creditors bound by the arrangement a notice that the arrangement has been fully implemented.[64] The effect of the completion of a voluntary arrangement is to extinguish or reduce the debtor's liabilities in accordance with the arrangement.

2.6 Jurisdiction of Courts to Hear Bankruptcy Petitions

A bankruptcy petition may only be presented in the Singapore High Court if the court has jurisdiction to hear the petition against the debtor. In the case of an individual debtor, jurisdiction may be founded upon one of the following facts :

- the debtor is domiciled in Singapore;
- the debtor has property in Singapore;
- the debtor was ordinarily resident in Singapore at any time within the period of one year immediately preceding the date of the presentation of the bankruptcy petition; or

62 Section 55 of the Bankruptcy Act.

63 Section 55(3) of the Bankruptcy Act.

64 Rule 90 of the Bankruptcy Rules.

- the debtor carried on business in Singapore at any time within the period of one year immediately preceding the date of presentation of the bankruptcy petition.[65]

The Singapore courts do not assert bankruptcy jurisdiction against foreign debtors who are neither present nor have property in Singapore. In such cases, it is unlikely that any assets may be recovered for creditors and it would therefore be an unnecessary waste of the Official Assignee's time and resources.

2.7 Creditors' Petitions

Provided that the court has jurisdiction to hear the bankruptcy petition against the debtor, such petitions may be presented by a creditor, by a nominee of a voluntary arrangement or any person bound by such arrangement,[66] or by the debtor himself. In the case of a creditor's petition, the following conditions[67] must be satisfied. Firstly and quite obviously, a debtor-creditor relationship must exist, that is to say, the petitioner must be a creditor. Secondly, the amount of the debt (or the aggregate amount of the debts[68]) must amount to not less than S$10,000[69] or such other sum as the Minister may prescribe. Thirdly, the debt (or each of the debts, as the case may be) must be for a liquidated sum, payable immediately. Fourthly, the debtor must be unable to pay his debts and finally, if the debt was incurred outside Singapore, it must be payable by virtue of an award or judgment enforceable by execution in Singapore.

A creditor may rely on one of several presumptions[70] in order to establish that the debtor is unable to pay his debts. The court will presume inability to pay debts if a statutory demand is served on the debtor and the debtor fails to comply with the demand or apply to court to set the demand aside. The presumption will also be raised if execution is issued against the debtor in respect of a judgment debt and is returned wholly or partly unsatisfied. Finally, a debtor may be presumed to be unable to pay his debts if it is shown that he has departed from or remained outside Singapore with the intention of defeating, delaying or obstructing a creditor in the recovery of a debt.

At the hearing of a creditor's petition for bankruptcy, the court must be satisfied that the substantive grounds for the presentation of a bankruptcy petition have been established. In addition, section 65(1) of the Bankruptcy Act requires the court to be satisfied that, since the presentation of the bankruptcy petition, the debt upon which the petition is founded has not been paid, secured or compounded and, where the

65 Section 60(1) of the Bankruptcy Act. See also section 60(2), which deals with the jurisdiction of the court where a petition is presented against a debtor firm, as opposed to an individual debtor.

66 When the debtor has failed to comply with his obligations under the voluntary arrangement, a bankruptcy petition may be presented against him. See section 56 of the Bankruptcy Act.

67 Section 61(1) of the Bankruptcy Act.

68 A single creditor may aggregate several debts or two or more creditors may aggregate their debts and present a bankruptcy petition jointly or collectively.

69 The minimum debt under the Bankruptcy Act immediately prior to the coming into effect of the 1995 amendments was S$500. This was increased to S$2,000 in 1995 and further increased to $10,000 with effect from 3 July 1999. The rationale for the increase was apparently to prevent persons from being made bankrupt in respect of small claims and to encourage creditors to resort to other alternatives in such cases.

70 Section 62 of the Bankruptcy Act.

debtor is absent from the hearing, that the petition has been duly served on him. Section 65(2) of the Bankruptcy Act further affords the court the discretion to dismiss a bankruptcy petition in various circumstances; for example, where it is satisfied that the debtor has made an offer to secure or compound the petitioning creditor's debt, the acceptance of which would have required the dismissal of the petition, and the petitioning creditor has unreasonably refused[71] the offer; or where it is satisfied for other sufficient cause that no order should be made.

2.8 Debtors' Petitions

A debtor may present a bankruptcy petition against himself.[72] The grounds for the presentation of a bankruptcy petition prescribed under section 60 of the Bankruptcy Act and enumerated above must be satisfied before a bankruptcy order may be made. The debtor must also satisfy one of the conditions establishing the jurisdiction of the court in respect of a debtor under section 61 of the Act. The court hearing a debtor's petition will not make a bankruptcy order unless it is satisfied that the debtor is unable to pay his/her debts.[73] If the petition is one that is presented against a firm by some, but not all, of the partners of the firm, a bankruptcy order will not be made unless the court is satisfied that notice of the petition has been served in the prescribed manner on each of the partners who did not join in the petition.

2.9 Bankruptcy Petitions when a Voluntary Arrangement is in Place

When a debtor who is bound by a voluntary arrangement defaults in his/her obligations under the arrangement, the Bankruptcy Act provides that the nominee or any person bound by the arrangement may present a bankruptcy petition against him/her. The court will not make a bankruptcy order on such a petition unless it is satisfied: (1) that the debtor has failed to comply with his obligations under the arrangement; or (2) that the statement of affairs or other documents supplied by the debtor, or otherwise made available by the debtor to his creditors at or in connection with a meeting summoned under Part V of the Bankruptcy Act, either contained information which was false or misleading in any material manner or contained material omissions; or (3) that the debtor has failed to do all such things as may, for the purposes of the voluntary arrangement, have reasonably been required of him by the nominee.[74] The procedure in such cases follows essentially that of a creditor's bankruptcy petition, subject to specified modifications.[75]

---

71 An offer is unreasonably refused if no hypothetical reasonable creditor would have refused the debtor's offer in the circumstances of the case *Re a Debtor (No 32 of 1993)* [1995] 1 All ER 628.

72 However, since it is possible that the debtor may be using the process as a shield to protect themselves against their creditors, the court has the discretion to refuse to make a bankruptcy order on a debtor's petition to prevent abuse.

73 Section 67(1) of the Bankruptcy Act.

74 Section 66 of the Bankruptcy Act.

75 For details of the differences, see supra n. 14 at 111–112.

2.10 Rights of Secured Creditors

Upon the making of the bankruptcy order, the Official Assignee is constituted receiver of the bankrupt's property and all such property vests in the Official Assignee and becomes divisible among the creditors.[76] However, section 76(3) of the Bankruptcy Act provides that nothing in the section shall affect the right of a secured creditor[77] to realise or otherwise deal with their security in such manner as they would have been able to realise or deal with it had the section not been enacted. Hence property subject to the rights of secured creditors are taken out of the general body of assets available for distribution to the creditors, unless the secured creditor voluntarily surrenders the security for the benefit of the general property of creditors. If the amount realised upon sale of the security is insufficient to satisfy the debt, the secured creditor may file a proof of debt for the balance and will rank as an unsecured creditor for the amount of such balance.

2.11 Creditors' Meetings

Creditors of a bankrupt, being the persons most likely to be affected by the manner in which a bankruptcy estate is administered, are entitled to be involved in and kept informed of the process of administration. To this end the Bankruptcy Act provides that the Official Assignee may, at any time after the making of a bankruptcy order, summon a creditors' meeting.[78] Creditors holding claims amounting to one quarter in value may also compel the Official Assignee to summon a creditors' meeting by making a request in writing to the court to direct him/her to do so.[79] Creditors' meetings are required to be conducted in accordance with prescribed rules, which are contained in rules 151–166 of the Bankruptcy Rules. These rules deal with procedural matters such as the period of notice, quorum and voting at meetings.

The creditors may also resolve, by ordinary resolution,[80] to appoint a committee of creditors to advise the Official Assignee on matters relating to the administration of the property of the bankrupt.[81] The committee should consist of not more than three persons.

76 Section 76(1)(a) & (b) of the Bankruptcy Act.

77 A 'secured creditor' is defined, for the purposes of the Bankruptcy Act, as a person holding a mortgage, charge, pledge or lien on or against the property of the debtor or any part thereof as security for a debt due to him/her from the debtor.

78 Section 79(1) of the Bankruptcy Act.

79 Section 79(2) of the Bankruptcy Act.

80 Section 2(1) of the Bankruptcy Act defines an 'ordinary resolution' as one which has been passed by a majority in value of the creditors present personally or by proxy at a meeting of creditors and voting on the resolution.

81 Section 80(1) of the Bankruptcy Act.

3 Personal Insolvency Procedures

3.1 Controls Imposed on Bankrupts

The freedom of an individual is considerably curtailed once a bankruptcy order has been made against him or her. The Bankruptcy Act, as well as several other statutes, imposes a number of restrictions and disabilities upon bankrupts. Recently, however, steps have been taken to ameliorate the harshness of these restrictions and disqualifications, particularly where it is felt that they unnecessarily hamper bankrupts' ability to remain economically productive during the period of their bankruptcy.

Immediately upon the making of a bankruptcy order, all property belonging to the bankrupt vests in the Official Assignee.[82] Since the bankrupt no longer owns the property, he/she may not make any effective transfers of such property. In fact, pursuant to section 77 of the Bankruptcy Act, any disposition of property made by the bankrupt between the presentation of the bankruptcy petition and the making of the bankruptcy order is void, unless made with the consent of, or subsequently ratified by, the court.

A bankrupt is also disqualified from acting as a trustee or personal representative in respect of any trust, estate or settlement, unless leave of court has been obtained.[83] Section 131(1)(a) of the Bankruptcy Act further stipulates that an undischarged bankrupt is incompetent to maintain any legal action (other than an action for damages for personal injury) without the sanction of the Official Assignee. By virtue of section 131(1)(b), he/she cannot leave Singapore or remain or reside outside Singapore without the permission of the Official Assignee. To this end the Official Assignee is empowered, if it is deemed fit, to impound the bankrupt's passport or other travel document or issue a direction to the Controller of Immigration to take measures to prevent the bankrupt from leaving the country.[84]

Previously, an undischarged bankrupt was prohibited from acting as a director or from directly or indirectly taking part or being concerned in the management of any company, unless leave of court had been granted.[85] A similar restriction applied with regard to the management by a bankrupt of businesses[86] registered under the Business Registration Act.[87] However, with effect from September 1999, the Official Assignee has been empowered to grant leave for bankrupts to act as directors or to manage companies and businesses.

A bankrupt may also be disqualified from practising their profession. For example, under the Legal Profession Act (Cap 161), an undischarged bankrupt may not practise as an advocate and solicitor in Singapore. Other professions which have similar restrictions include public accountants or tax consultants under the Accountant's

---

82 Section 76(1)(a) of the Bankruptcy Act.

83 Section 130 of the Bankruptcy Act. Contravention of the section is an offence and renders the bankrupt liable on conviction to a fine of not more than S$5,000, imprisonment of not more than one year, or both.

84 Sections 116(1) and (4) of the Bankruptcy Act.

85 Section 148(1) of the Companies Act (Cap 50).

86 Sole proprietorships or partnerships.

87 Section 22(1) of the Business Registration Act (Cap 32).

Act (Cap 2A), architects[88] and surveyors.[89] A bankrupt also faces restrictions in employment – unless certain approvals are granted, he or she may not be employed in a solicitor's firm or in a public accountant's practice.

Finally, Singapore's Constitution prohibits an undischarged bankrupt from being elected or continuing to hold office as a Member of Parliament.[90]

3.2 Collection of Information about the Bankrupt

The bankrupt must provide the Official Assignee with a statement of affairs within 21 days (or longer, if the Official Assignee grants an extension) from the making of the bankruptcy order.[91] The statement of affairs should contain, *inter alia*, particulars of the bankrupt's assets, creditors, debts and other liabilities. The bankrupt is also required to submit, once every six months, an account of all moneys and property which have come into their hands for their own use during the preceding six months (or such other period specified by the Official Assignee) and pay over to the Official Assignee so much of such moneys and property as have not been expended in the necessary expenses of maintenance of himself and his family.[92]

The Bankruptcy Act contains several provisions regarding the examination of the bankrupt. The court may, upon an application by the Official Assignee or any creditor who has tendered proof, summon the bankrupt to appear before it to be examined under oath as to his affairs, dealings and property under section 83 of the Bankruptcy Act. The section also empowers the court to summon other persons, such as the bankrupt's spouse, to be examined if it appears to the court that such persons would be able to give information concerning the bankrupt, or their affairs, dealings and property. Section 129 of the Bankruptcy Act, which stipulates the duties of a bankrupt, obliges the bankrupt to attend at such time and place as may be stipulated by the Official Assignee to be examined as to their affairs, dealings and property and the causes of their failure. Further, the bankrupt is also under a duty to attend meetings of creditors and to submit to examination at such meetings.

Other duties enumerated in section 129 of the Bankruptcy Act include:

- making discovery of and delivering all his/her property to the Official Assignee;
- delivering all books, records and documents relating to his/her property and affairs to the Official Assignee;
- assisting the Official Assignee in making an inventory of his/her assets; and
- making disclosures to the Official Assignee of certain prescribed dispositions of property and providing relevant details regarding the same.

---

88 Section 27(1)(h) of the Architect's Act.

89 Section 25(1)(h) and section 10 of the Land Surveyors Act (Cap 156).

90 Article 45 of the Constitution.

91 Section 81 of the Bankruptcy Act.

92 Section 82 of the Bankruptcy Act.

3.3 *Rules regarding Illicit Transfers of Property by the Bankrupt*

If a bankrupt had, within a period of five years prior to the bankruptcy order, entered into a transaction at an undervalue then, provided he/she was insolvent[93] at the time or became insolvent as a result of the transaction, the Official Assignee may make an application to the court to restore the parties to their original position.[94] A transaction at an undervalue is defined in section 98(3) of the Bankruptcy Act as a gift or a transaction in which the bankrupt received no consideration; or a transaction in consideration of marriage; or a transaction in which the bankrupt received consideration the value of which was significantly less, in money or money's worth, than the value of the consideration he/she provided. If the transaction at an undervalue was with an associate[95] of the bankrupt, the insolvency requirement is presumed to be satisfied unless the contrary is shown.

The Official Assignee may also seek to avoid a payment or other transaction on the grounds that it is an unfair preference.[96] The following requirements must be met:

- the preference has been given by the debtor to a creditor, surety or guarantor for any of his/her debts or other liabilities;
- the preference has the effect of putting the person in a better position than he/she would have otherwise been, in the event of the debtor's bankruptcy, had the preference not been granted;
- the debtor was influenced, in giving the preference, by a desire to produce that effect (in the case of an associate, such intention is presumed);
- the preference must have been given within two years prior to the bankruptcy (where the preference is made in favour of an associate) and within six months (where the person to whom the preference has been given is not an associate); and
- the debtor must have been insolvent at the time of the transaction or become insolvent as a result of it.

3.4 *Orders regarding the Property of the Bankrupt*

The powers of the court to make orders under sections 98 and 99 of the Bankruptcy Act, which deal with transactions at an undervalue and unfair preferences respectively, are very wide. In addition to the general power to 'make such order as it thinks fit for restoring the position to what it would have been if [the bankrupt] individual had not entered into the transaction', section 102 of the Act lists specific orders that may be made. The list includes an order requiring any property transferred as part of the undervalued transaction or in connection with the preference to be vested with the Official Assignee and also an order requiring any property which

93 Section 100(4) of the Bankruptcy Act defines insolvency as: (1) inability to pay debts as they fall due; or (2) where the value of the debtor's assets is less than the amount of his/her liabilities.

94 Section 98 of the Bankruptcy Act.

95 An 'associate' is defined in section 101 of the Bankruptcy Act and includes the bankrupt's spouse, relative or partner.

96 Section 99 of the Bankruptcy Act.

represents the application of sale proceeds of the property transferred to be vested with the Official Assignee. An order may affect the property of any person whether or not he/she is the person with whom the bankrupt entered into the undervalued transaction or to whom the bankrupt gave the unfair preference. However, section 102(2) protects the interests of third parties in two circumstances. First, the order cannot prejudice any interest in property acquired from a person other than the bankrupt which was acquired in good faith, for value and without notice of the relevant circumstances.[97] Secondly, the order must not require a person who received a benefit from the transaction or unfair preference in good faith, for value and without notice of the relevant transaction to pay any money to the Official Assignee, except where he/she was a party to the undervalued transaction or the preference was made to him/her at a time when he/she was a creditor of the bankrupt.

3.5 Rules regarding Proof of Debt

Section 87 of the Bankruptcy Act provides that demands in the nature of unliquidated damages arising otherwise than by contract, promise or breach of trust are not provable in bankruptcy. Hence a tort claim for unliquidated damages, for example, would not be provable in bankruptcy. Further, the section also provides that a person who had notice of the presentation of a bankruptcy petition may not prove under the bankruptcy any debt or liability contracted by the bankrupt after the date of having received such notice. Save the foregoing, any debt or liability to which the bankrupt is subject at the bankruptcy order or to which he/she may become subject before discharge by reason of any obligation incurred prior to the bankruptcy order is provable.[98]

Where, before the commencement of bankruptcy, there have been any mutual credits, mutual debts or other mutual dealings[99] between a bankrupt and any creditor, the debts or liabilities to which each party is entitled as a result of such mutual dealings shall be set off against each other and only the difference is provable as a debt in bankruptcy.[100]

The mode of proving debts, the right of proof by secured creditors, and rules regarding the admission and rejection of proofs by the Official Assignee are contained in the Bankruptcy Rules and must be observed. Proofs of debt must be filed in the prescribed form.[101]

The Official Assignee is required to examine every proof and the grounds of the debt, and either admit or reject the same, in whole or in part, or require further

---

97 The 'relevant circumstances' are defined in section 102(4) of the Bankruptcy Act.

98 Section 87(3) of the Bankruptcy Act.

99 Before a set-off is possible, there must be mutuality of debts. In *Good Property Land Development Pte Ltd (in liquidation)* v. *Societe Generale* [1996] 2 SLR 239, it was held that two conditions must be satisfied: firstly, that each claimant is personally liable for the debt he/she owes the other claimant and, secondly, that each claimant must beneficially own the claim which is owed to him/her by the other claimant, such ownership being clear and ascertained without inquiry. See further Anandarajah *et al.*, supra n. 14 at 347–349.

100 Section 88 of the Bankruptcy Act.

101 Form 23 of the Bankruptcy Rules.

evidence to support it.[102] He/she is further required to put in writing any such admission, rejection or request for further evidence. Where a creditor is dissatisfied with the decision of the Official Assignee in rejecting the former's proof, the court may, on the application of the creditor, reverse or vary the decision of the Official Assignee.[103]

3.6 Rules regarding the Distribution of the Assets of the Bankrupt

Section 78(1) of the Bankruptcy Act provides that the property of the bankrupt divisible among his/her creditors shall comprise:

- all property belonging to, or vested in, the bankrupt at the commencement of bankruptcy or which is acquired by or devolves on him/her before discharge; and
- the capacity to exercise and to take proceedings to exercise all powers over or in respect of such property as might have been exercised by the bankrupt for his/her own benefit.

However, the following are excluded from the definition of divisible property in section 78(1): property held by the bankrupt on trust for any other person; the tools of his/her trade; clothing, bedding, furniture, household equipment and provisions as are necessary for satisfying the basic domestic needs of the bankrupt and his/her family; and property of the bankrupt which is excluded under any written law.[104] The latter category would include the bankrupt's Housing Development Board flat, pursuant to section 51(3) of the Housing and Development Board Act (Cap 129).

From the property of the bankrupt divisible among his/her creditors, the Official Assignee must make payment to the creditors in accordance with the prescribed order of payment under the bankruptcy laws. Secured creditors would, more often than not, choose to realise their security and satisfy their claims out of the proceeds of sale of the secured asset. They would, however, be entitled to claim out of the bankruptcy estate for any outstanding balance after realisation of the secured asset, provided the relevant rules as to proof of debt have been complied with. Section 90 of the Bankruptcy Act specifies certain creditors who shall be paid in priority to other creditors.[105]

All debts in the same class rank equally among themselves and the debts in each class are to be paid in full before the debts in each subsequent class are paid, unless the property of the bankrupt is insufficient to pay that class in full, in which case the creditors in that class shall take rateably. These preferential debts must be paid before any dividend is payable to ordinary creditors, who rank equally, or *pari passu*, among themselves.

---

102 Rule 197 of the Bankruptcy Rules.

103 Rule198(1) of the Bankruptcy Rules. Any application to court must be made within 21 days from the day of rejection of the proof and served personally on the Official Assignee.

104 Section 78(2) of the Bankruptcy Act.

105 These are similar to those specified in section 328 of the Companies Act and have been listed in section 6.8.2 of this chapter.

If there is any surplus remaining after payment in full to the debtor's creditors, and all costs, charges and expenses of the bankruptcy proceedings, this shall be payable to the bankrupt unless the Official Assignee applies for an order not to pay the surplus to him/her.[106] This would arise in a situation where there is an order made for confiscation of the proceeds of a crime against the bankrupt.

3.7 Creditors of the Debtor and Debt Agreements and their Termination

In the course of administration of bankruptcy, a bankrupt may choose to make a proposal to his/her creditors for a composition in satisfaction of the debts due to them under the bankruptcy, or a scheme of arrangement of his/her affairs.[107]

With effect from September 1999, the procedure for putting forward a scheme of arrangement or composition has been amended so that creditors may approve the proposal in writing as an alternative to summoning a creditors' meeting. Even in the case where a meeting of creditors is called, any creditor who has proved their debt may assent to or dissent from the proposal by letter to the Official Assignee. The creditors must, in either case, be notified of the general terms of the proposal and be provided with a report by the Official Assignee. The introduction of the procedure for approval or voting in writing makes it more convenient for creditors to consider and vote for or against the bankrupt's proposal.

The scheme or composition must be approved by special resolution which is now defined, for the purposes of the relevant section, to mean, where a meeting of creditors is called, a resolution passed at such meeting by a majority in number holding at least three quarters in value of the creditors who have proved their debts, taking those creditors who do not attend as having voted in favour of the resolution. Likewise where approval in writing is sought, a special resolution is one which is approved in writing by a majority in number and at least three quarters in value of creditors who have proved their debts, taking those creditors who fail to assent to or dissent from the proposal as having assented to it. The new definition of 'special resolution' in this section should be contrasted with the general definition under section 2(1) of the Bankruptcy Act, where creditors who fail to attend or vote are not taken into account.

Under the newly added section 95A of the Bankruptcy Act, the Official Assignee may, when a composition or scheme has been approved by creditors, annul the bankruptcy order by certificate. The composition or scheme is not binding on creditors unless the bankruptcy order is so annulled.

3.8 Termination of Bankruptcy – Provisions for Annulment or Discharge

An annulment of a bankruptcy order effectively wipes the slate clean and puts the bankrupt in the same position as if no bankruptcy order had been made against him/her. The court may annul a bankruptcy order on one of the following grounds: (1) that the bankruptcy order ought not to have been made; (2) that the bankrupt has

---

106 Section 122 of the Bankruptcy Act.

107 See generally section 95 of the Bankruptcy Act.

settled all his debts in full; or (3) that the distribution of assets ought to be under Malaysian bankruptcy law.[108] In addition, with the introduction of the new section 123A in September 1999, the Official Assignee may annul a bankruptcy order by certificate when a composition or scheme of arrangement has been accepted by the requisite majority of the bankrupt's creditors, as described in the foregoing section.

One of the main reforms introduced by the 1995 Bankruptcy Act was to enable bankrupts to obtain discharges more easily. Prior to 1995, the only avenues available to bankrupts for discharge were by full settlement of their debts or by proposing a composition or scheme of arrangement acceptable to their creditors. The 1995 Bankruptcy Act introduced what the Minister for Law called a 'more practical and pragmatic regime' for discharge.

The provisions for discharge that were introduced included a more simplified regime for discharges by the court and a new scheme for discharge by certificate of the Official Assignee. Under section 125 of the Act, the Official Assignee may issue a certificate of discharge to bankrupts who have been in bankruptcy for at least three years and whose debts do not exceed S$500,000. A bankrupt who does not qualify for discharge by certificate of the Official Assignee may apply to the court for discharge.[109] The provisions for discharge by the court make a distinction between two broad categories of cases. In the first category are cases in which the bankrupt has committed one or more of the offences stipulated or whose conduct is regarded as blameworthy in some specified manner.[110] In such cases, the court must refuse to discharge the bankrupt or otherwise make the order for discharge subject to certain conditions. In the second category are cases where no offences have been committed or where the bankrupts have not conducted themselves in a blameworthy manner. In such cases, the court is empowered to order an absolute discharge or may order a discharge subject to conditions. An order for discharge releases the debtor from all their provable debts in bankruptcy except debts which are preserved under the Act.

4 Corporate Insolvency Rules

4.1 Introduction

The legislative provisions dealing with corporate insolvency may be found in Parts VII, VIII, VIIIA, and X of the Companies Act as well as in the related portions of the Companies Regulations and the Companies (Winding up) Rules. At the time of writing, an initiative to consolidate and refine Singapore's insolvency legislation was under way.[111]

A company facing insolvency faces two options. It can attempt to survive by using various mechanisms to deal with its creditors or be content with its fate and allow

108 Section 123 of the Bankruptcy Act.

109 See generally section 124 of the Bankruptcy Act.

110 See further section 124(5) of the Bankruptcy Act. These include insolvent trading, rash speculations and extravagant living, fraud, and so on.

111 See paragraph 1.2 in the text above.

itself to be dissolved. The course of action that is ultimately taken depends on two interrelated factors: the probability of the company surviving as a going concern and the extent to which the company's creditors wish to pursue their claims. The major processes that may be brought into operation in cases of insolvency are:

- compositions and arrangements with creditors;
- judicial management; and
- voluntary or court-ordered winding up.

The CLRFC has recommended the introduction of company voluntary arrangements modelled after the UK Insolvency Act 1986 as another alternative.

We shall discuss compositions and arrangements in this section and leave the topics of judicial management and winding up to subsequent sections in this chapter.

4.2 Compositions and Arrangements with Creditors

Companies facing insolvency are free to enter into some form of compromise arrangement with each and every one of their creditors individually. Such arrangements may be privately arranged or court sanctioned.

4.2.1 Privately arranged schemes It is open for the company to attempt to enter into a scheme with its creditors privately and without the assistance of the court. In this event, the company will have to secure the agreement of all its creditors to the arrangement. A deed between the company, its creditors and the creditors *inter se* reflecting the arrangement is usually executed. As can be imagined, obtaining the agreement of all affected creditors is not an easy task. The creditors at the meeting have to be satisfied that there are no other creditors who may take action that may jeopardise their interests. They also face the added risks and difficulties associated with having to enforce the arrangement should one of their number act in contravention of it. Secured creditors are also usually not very willing to assent to any arrangement whereby their ability to enforce their security is delayed and where the assets secured face the risk of depreciation or dissipation.

4.2.2 Court-sanctioned schemes of arrangements To address some of the difficulties arising out of private schemes, the legislation provides for court-sanctioned schemes of arrangements. The company, the liquidator or any of its creditors may apply to the court for an order that a creditors' meeting be convened for the purpose of considering any proposed compromise or arrangement between the company and its creditors or any class of creditors.[112] The method of summoning the meeting is at the discretion of the court. The usual method is through the sending of a notice of the meeting to the company's creditors and the taking out of an advertisement giving notice of the meeting. The company must make available sufficient information that explains the effect of the proposed compromise or arrangement on the various

112 Section 210 of the Companies Act.

classes of creditors.[113] The compromise or arrangement will be binding on the creditors, the liquidator, the contributories and the members, as the case may be, if a majority in number and representing three quarters in value of the creditors or class of creditors present and voting at the meeting agree to it and it is subsequently approved by order of the court.[114] Although the court has full discretion as to whether or not to grant its approval and to subject the scheme to any alterations or conditions as it thinks just, it will usually not interfere with the decision of the meeting so long as the requisite majority has agreed to the scheme and the scheme appears to be *bona fide*. The order must be lodged with the Registrar and takes effect on the date of its lodgement or at such other earlier date as is specified in the order.

5 Judicial Management[115]

5.1 Nature of Judicial Management

Judicial management was introduced into the Singapore legislation in 1987. Its introduction was in response to the recognition that there was a need for the legislative framework to provide viable companies facing cash flow difficulties with a reasonable chance of rehabilitation. Another of its intended functions was also to enable insolvent companies to be liquidated in a more orderly fashion.[116] Underpinning the process is the appointment of an independent and impartial person (the 'judicial manager') to take over the management of the company from its directors. The judicial manager's mission is to achieve one of the following objectives:

- to rehabilitate the company and achieve its survival or the survival of part of its undertaking as a going concern;
- to obtain a court-sanctioned scheme of arrangement; or
- to achieve a more advantageous realisation of the company's assets than would be effected should the company be wound up.

5.2 Initiating the Judicial Management Process

A judicial management petition may be brought by the company (pursuant to a members' resolution), its directors (pursuant to a board resolution) or its creditors (including contingent and prospective creditors) either together or separately. The application may be initiated only where the company or a creditor considers that the company is or will be unable to pay its debts.[117] In addition, the applicant must show

113 Section 211 of the Companies Act.

114 Section 210(2) of the Companies Act.

115 See Part VIIIA of the Companies Act and Part V of the Companies Regulations.

116 *The Singapore Economy: New Directions*, Report of the Economic Committee (Ministry of Trade and Industry, 1986).

117 The presumptions of insolvency relating to court winding up as provided under section 254(2) of the Companies Act apply in cases of judicial management as well.

that there is a reasonable probability of rehabilitating the company or of preserving its business, or part of its business, as a going concern or that the interests of creditors would be better served than if a winding up were to take place.[118] The court may make a judicial management order if it is satisfied that the company is or will be unable to pay its debts and it considers that the making of the order would be likely to achieve one or more of the objectives set out above. In addition, it is open to the court to make an order if it would be in the public interest to do so.[119] Whether or not an order is finally made, however, is generally at the discretion of the court.

The legislation compels the court to dismiss the application where a receiver and manager has been appointed over the whole or substantially the whole of the company's property under a debenture of a company secured by a floating charge. The application must similarly be dismissed if it is opposed by a person entitled to appoint such a receiver and manager.[120] A judicial management order is also not to be made against a company after it has gone into liquidation or against a bank, finance company or insurance company registered under their respective governing Acts.[121] However, these provisions do not preclude the court from making a judicial management order if it considers that the public interest so requires.

5.3 Effect of a Judicial Management Order

From the moment a petition for a judicial management order is presented to the making of the order, its dismissal, or, where the order is granted, throughout the judicial management process, no resolution may be passed or order made for the winding up of the company. Neither can any steps be taken to enforce any security over the company's property except with the leave of the court. The same applies to the repossession of goods pursuant to any hire purchase agreement, equipment leasing agreement or under a retention of title clause. No other proceeding, execution, distress or other legal process may be commenced or continued against the company or its property without the leave of the court.[122]

Upon the making of a judicial management order, any receiver or manager is to vacate office and any petition for winding up of the company is to be dismissed.[123] The affairs, business and property of the company are placed under the management of the judicial manager. The judicial manager takes over all the powers conferred and the duties imposed on the directors.[124] In effect, the directors' powers of management are suspended for the duration of the order.

---

118 Section 227A of the Companies Act.

119 Section 227B(10)(a) of the Companies Act. *Re Cosmotron Electronics (Singapore) Pte Ltd* [1989] 2 *Malaysian Law Journal* 11.

120 Section 227B(5) of the Companies Act.

121 Section 227B(7) of the Companies Act.

122 Section 227C of the Companies Act.

123 Section 227D(1) of the Companies Act.

124 Section 227G(2) of the Companies Act.

5.4 *The Judicial Manager*

5.4.1 Appointment The applicant for an order for judicial management must nominate an approved company auditor,[125] who is not the company's auditor, to be the judicial manager.[126] Where it is the company who has made the nomination, the creditors (comprising a majority in number and value) of the company may oppose the nomination through a court application. The court may in such instances invite the creditors to nominate the judicial manager and adopt their nomination instead. Although the provisions in the Companies Act provide for a single judicial manager to be appointed, it is generally accepted that joint appointments may be made. This is often done in practice.

5.4.2 The judicial manager's duties and powers The main duty of a judicial manager is to attempt to achieve the purpose stated in the judicial management application. Once the appointment is made, judicial managers have to give notice of the judicial management order to the public, the company and all creditors of which they are aware.[127] They have an initial period of 60 days, or such longer period as the court may allow, to prepare and send to the company's creditors a proposal stating whether, and if so, how these purposes may be achieved. A meeting of creditors must then be convened to consider the proposals. The judicial manager must report the result of the meeting to the court and give notice of the result to the Registrar. If the meeting approves the proposals, the judicial managers then have the duty to manage the company in accordance with the proposals.[128]

To assist judicial managers in fulfilling their duties, they are given very broad powers. These are listed in the Eleventh Schedule of the Companies Act and correspond to the judicial managers' obligation to do all things necessary for the management of the affairs, business and property of the company.[129] These powers must be exercised in furtherance of the purposes that the judicial management order seeks to achieve. In addition, the company has to furnish the judicial managers with a statement of affairs showing, *inter alia*, the particulars of the company's assets, debts and liabilities, and the details of its creditors and the securities held by them.[130] Officers, promoters and employees of the company are also statutorily bound to provide the judicial managers with such information as the judicial managers may reasonably require for the performance of their duties.[131]

5.4.3 Liabilities of the judicial manager Judicial managers are deemed to be agents of the company. They are also personally liable on any contract entered into by them in the carrying out of their functions unless such liability has been expressly

---

125 An approved company auditor is a person who has been approved by the Minister of Finance to act as such pursuant to section 9 of the Companies Act.

126 Section 227B(3) of the Companies Act.

127 Section 227K of the Companies Act.

128 Sections 227M to 227P of the Companies Act.

129 Section 227G(3)(a) of the Companies Act.

130 Section 227L of the Companies Act.

131 Section 227V of the Companies Act.

disclaimed through a notice to the other party. The same applies to contracts entered into by the company and adopted by the judicial managers. They are, however, entitled to be indemnified in respect of such liability as well as to have their remuneration and expenses defrayed out of the company's property in priority to all other debts.[132] The provisions relating to personal liability of judicial managers do not extend to rent under leases held by the company at the time of the appointment.

5.4.4 Vacation of office[133] Judicial managers hold office until the judicial management order is discharged. The court may, however, remove them from office. The main event that may precipitate a removal is where the creditors or members petition for the removal on the grounds that the company's affairs are being managed in an unfair or prejudicial manner.[134] Judicial managers may also, upon such conditions as are imposed by the court, resign from their office by giving notice of the resignation to the court. Where a judicial manager ceases to be an approved company auditor, he or she must vacate office.

5.5 Protection of Corporate Assets during Judicial Management

One of the main reasons for the appointment of a judicial manager is to impose a moratorium against creditors from enforcing their rights against the company's assets. As mentioned in section 5.3 above, the moratorium takes effect from the time the application is made to the court for an appointment of a judicial manager. Judicial managers have the power to consent to the lifting of the moratorium in respect of any proceeding or legal process.[135]

Judicial managers also have the power to dispose of secured assets. Where the assets are secured by a floating charge, they may be disposed of at the judicial managers' discretion. The floating charge holder must be given the same priority in respect of any property of the company that represents the property disposed of as that in respect of the disposed property itself.[136] For all other forms of secured assets, the judicial managers have to satisfy the court that the disposal of the assets would be likely to promote one or more of the purposes specified in the judicial management order. On being so satisfied, the court may by order authorise the judicial manager to dispose of the assets on condition that the net proceeds of the disposal are to be first applied towards discharging the sums secured by the security.[137]

5.6 Role of Creditors

Although the moratorium imposed on creditors' claims by a judicial management order affects their rights somewhat, the creditors also stand to gain from a successful

132 Section 227I of the Companies Act.
133 Section 227J of the Companies Act.
134 See section 227R of the Companies Act.
135 Section 227D of the Companies Act.
136 Section 227H(1) and (4) of the Companies Act.
137 Section 227H(2) and (5) of the Companies Act.

judicial management. Provision is thus made for the creditors to participate in the judicial management process.

It is open for creditors to oppose the making of a judicial management order through the filing and service of an affidavit stating the grounds for the opposition of the petitioner.[138] An opposition may succeed where it is shown that the making of the order is unlikely to achieve its stated purpose[139] or is an abuse of the process of the court or lacks *bona fide*.[140] It may also be opposed by a person who has appointed or is entitled to appoint a receiver or manager of the whole or substantially the whole of the company's property.

In an application brought by the company, the creditors' role in the appointment of the judicial manager is limited to the opposition of the company's nomination. They may make their own nomination only if invited by the court to do so and only where the opposition is made by a majority in number and in value of all the company's creditors.[141]

Once a judicial management order is made, the judicial managers must present their proposals to a meeting of creditors within 60 days (or such longer period as the court may allow) of the making of the order. The procedure for the calling and conduct of creditors' meetings is provided for by rules 54 to 77 of the Companies Regulations. The proposal must be approved by a majority in number and value of the creditors present and voting. Only creditors whose claims have been accepted by the judicial managers may vote.[142] Secured creditors can exercise their voting rights only in relation to the unsecured balance of the debt owing unless they surrender their security.[143] Creditors may decide to modify the proposals and to approve the proposals subject to the modifications. All modifications, however, must receive the consent of the judicial managers. Alternatively, the creditors may refuse to accept the proposals.

Apart from just considering the propriety of the proposals, creditors may take a more active role in monitoring the conduct of the judicial managers. They are entitled, once they have approved the proposals, to establish a committee of creditors to monitor the manner in which the judicial management is conducted by requiring the judicial managers to attend before the committee and to furnish it with such information relating to the judicial management as it may require.[144] In addition, creditors and members may seek redress should they feel that the affairs of the company are managed by the judicial manager in a manner that is unfairly prejudicial to their interests.[145] The court is given wide powers to make orders to remedy the situation if this is proven.

---

138 Rule 37 of the Companies Regulations.

139 *Re Cosmotron Electronics (Singapore) Pte Ltd* [1989] 2 MLJ 11.

140 Ibid. See also *Re Genesis Technologies International (S) Pte Ltd* [1994] 3 Singapore Law Reports 390.

141 Section 227B(3)(c) of the Companies Act.

142 Section 227N of the Companies Act.

143 Rule 74 of the Companies Regulations.

144 Section 227O of the Companies Act.

145 Section 227R of the Companies Act.

5.7 Powers of the Court

As may be seen from the preceding discussion, the court has broad discretionary powers in relation to the making of the judicial management order, the appointment of the judicial managers, the conduct of the judicial managers and the making of orders affecting the moratorium imposed pursuant to the order. In addition to these powers, the court is given specific powers to assist the judicial managers in the performance of their duties. These include the power to make orders against any contributory or member, trustee, banker, agent, officer or any person who has previously held office as receiver or receiver and manager of the company's property for the seizure and delivery of property, books, papers or records to the judicial manager.[146] The court may summon persons whom the court thinks are capable of giving information concerning the company's property or affairs (including its officers, debtors and creditors) to appear before it and to require such persons to furnish an affidavit containing an account of his or her dealings with the company.[147] It is also open to the court to release the judicial managers from any liability in respect of any act or omission by them in the management of the company or otherwise in relation to their conduct as judicial managers. This power may only be exercised where the liability does not arise from either a misapplication or retention of money or property of the company or in cases where their liability arises as a result of negligence, default, misfeasance, breach of trust, or breach of duty in relation to the company.

5.8 Termination of the Judicial Management

Termination of the judicial management may come about in one of several ways. First, where it appears to the judicial managers that the purpose or purposes specified in the judicial management order have been achieved or are incapable of being achieved, the judicial managers must apply to the court for the judicial management order to be discharged. The court, after considering the application, may discharge the order.[148] Secondly, the court may discharge the order where creditors decline to approve the judicial manager's proposals.[149] Finally, a judicial management order may be discharged pursuant to a petition made under section 227R of the Companies Act asserting that the affairs of the company are being managed by the judicial manager in a manner that is prejudicial to the creditors or members.[150]

---

146 Section 227U of the Companies Act.

147 Section 227W of the Companies Act.

148 Section 227Q of the Companies Act.

149 Section 227N(4) of the Companies Act.

150 Section 227R(3)(d) of the Companies Act.

6 Winding Up Procedures[151]

6.1 Introduction to the Range of Winding Up Procedures

The Singapore Companies Act provides that the winding up of a company may either be voluntary or by the court.[152] Voluntary winding up may either take the form of a members' voluntary winding up or a creditors' voluntary winding up. Where a company is wound up because it is insolvent, it generally proceeds by way of a winding up by the court. In some instances, it proceeds as a creditors' voluntary winding up.

6.2 Initiation of Winding Up Proceedings

A company may be wound up voluntarily if it so resolves by special resolution.[153] The winding up will proceed as a members' voluntary winding up where the company's directors have made a statutory declaration to the effect that they have made an inquiry into the affairs of the company and have formed the opinion at a directors' meeting that the company will be able to pay its debts in full within a period not exceeding 12 months after the commencement of the winding up.[154] In the absence of such a declaration, the winding up will proceed as a creditors' voluntary winding up.

Where the liquidator appointed by the company for the purpose of a members' voluntary winding up comes to the opinion that the company will not be able to pay or provide for the payment of its debts in full as declared by the directors, he or she will have to call for a meeting of the company's creditors. A statement of the company's assets and liabilities will be presented to the creditors who will then be given the option of appointing another person to take over the liquidation of the company. The winding up will proceed thereafter as a creditors' voluntary winding up.[155]

In a creditors' voluntary winding up, the directors are obliged to call for a creditors' meeting. The notice for calling the meeting must be sent out simultaneously with the notice for the company meeting at which it is proposed to resolve that the company be wound up.[156] It must be sent to the creditors at least seven days prior to the date of the meeting and should have accompanying it a statement showing the names of all creditors and the amounts of their claims. The meeting must be convened at a time and place that is convenient to the majority in value of the creditors. At the meeting, the creditors may nominate a liquidator. Should this nomination be different from that of the company, the creditors' nomination shall, subject to a court order to the contrary, take precedence.[157] Creditors may also appoint a committee of inspection to monitor the liquidator's performance of his or her responsibilities.[158]

---

151 Winding up procedures are governed primarily by Part X of the Companies Act and the Companies (Winding Up) Rules.

152 Section 247 of the Companies Act.

153 Section 290 of the Companies Act.

154 Section 293(1) of the Companies Act.

155 Section 295 of the Companies Act.

156 Section 296 of the Companies Act.

157 Section 297 of the Companies Act.

158 Section 298 of the Companies Act.

A winding up by the court may be initiated through a petition by the following persons, regardless of whether or not it is in the process of being wound up voluntarily:[159]

- the company;
- any creditor (including a contingent or prospective creditor);
- a contributory or his/her legal representative;
- the company's liquidator;
- a judicial manager appointed to manage the affairs of the company; or
- the Minister of Finance, in specified instances.

The court is given very broad powers in relation to the conduct of the winding up petition.[160] Its discretion extends to ordering the winding up, dismissing the petition, adjourning the hearing and the making of an interim or other order that it thinks fit. The only restriction placed on the court by the legislation is that it cannot refuse to make a winding up order solely because of any of the following grounds:

- that the assets of the company have been mortgaged to an amount equal to or in excess of those assets;
- that the company has no assets; or
- where the petition is brought by a contributory, that there will be no assets available for distribution amongst the contributories.[161]

The common thread that runs through the grounds listed above appears to be that the court should not refuse to make a winding up order purely because it does not think that the winding up order would bring any monetary benefit to the petitioner.

6.3 Grounds for Court-ordered Winding Up

The circumstances in which the court may order a winding up are specified in section 254(1) of the Companies Act. The situation that is most relevant in cases of insolvency is reflected in section 254(1)(e) which provides that a court may order a winding up where 'the company is unable to pay its debts'. The petitioner bears the burden of proving, to the satisfaction of the court, that the company is unable to pay its debts. There is no restriction on the method by which a petitioner can go about proving this. In theory, a company is unable to pay its debts where its total liabilities exceed its total assets (sometimes referred to as the 'balance-sheet test'). This is one of the two tests accepted for determining insolvency. The other test is whether the company is able to pay its debts as and when they fall due (that is, the 'cash-flow' test).[162] In assessing the situation, the court must take into account the contingent and

159 See section 253 of the Companies Act.

160 See section 257 of the Companies Act.

161 Section 257(1) of the Companies Act.

162 *Re Great Eastern Hotel (Pte) Ltd* [1988] SLR 841.

prospective liabilities of the company.[163] The legislation provides for two additional instances where a company is deemed to be unable to pay its debts.[164]

First, a company is deemed to be unable to pay its debts where it is shown that the company is indebted to a creditor for a sum exceeding S$10,000 and the creditor has served on the company a demand requiring the company to pay the sum due, and the company has for three weeks thereafter neglected to settle the debt to the satisfaction of the creditor. There is no prescribed form for the demand save that it be signed by the creditor or by his authorised agent. The demand should also be served by leaving it at the company's registered office.[165] The debt must be a liquidated sum and should not be in respect of a claim that is genuinely disputed by the company.[166] There should also not be in existence a genuine cross-claim against the creditor.[167]

Secondly, a company is deemed to be unable to pay its debts where any execution or other process issued on a judgment in favour of a creditor is returned unsatisfied, whether in whole or in part.

6.4 *Effect of Commencement of Winding Up*

A voluntary winding up commences upon the passing of the resolution by the company that it be wound up. In the case of a winding up by the court where a winding up order is made, the winding up will be deemed to have commenced at the time of the presentation of the petition for the winding up and not on the date the order is made. This is so unless a resolution for the voluntary winding up of the company has been passed prior to the presentation of the petition, in which case, the commencement of the winding up will be deemed to have commenced at the time of the passing of the resolution.[168] The effect of relating the date of commencement of a court winding up to the date of the petition is, in a sense, paradoxical as one would have to wait until the winding up order is made before one can confirm that a company has in fact been wound up. Yet, the winding up is deemed to have taken place at the time of the petition, which may have been filed weeks or months earlier. This poses some practical difficulties regarding the status of the company between the time of the petition and the order for winding up.

6.4.1 Effect on company's management Winding up often proceeds in conjunction with the appointment of a liquidator, or in the case of winding up by court, a provisional liquidator. In general, the liquidator takes over the powers of the company's directors once he or she is appointed. There are, however, subtle differences in relation to this depending on the type of winding up. In a members' voluntary winding up, the liquidator or the company in general meeting, with the liquidator's consent, is able to approve the continuance of the directors' powers.[169]

---

163 Section 254(2)(c) of the Companies Act.
164 Section 254(2) of the Companies Act.
165 *Pac-Asian Services Pte Ltd* v. *European Asian Bank AG*, [1987] SLR 1.
166 *Re Mechanised Construction Pte Ltd* [1989] SLR 533.
167 *Malayan Plant (Pte) Ltd* v. *Moscow Narodny Bank* [1980–81] SLR 8.
168 Section 255 of the Companies Act.
169 Section 294(1) of the Companies Act.

Where the winding up proceeds as a creditors' voluntary winding up, the committee of inspection or, where no such committee is established, the creditors may approve the continuance of the directors powers.[170]

The legislation does not state categorically that the powers of the directors cease upon the appointment of a liquidator in a court-ordered winding up. It is, however, generally accepted as a matter of law and practice that all the powers of the directors vest in the liquidator or the provisional liquidator upon their appointment subject to any directions given by the court.

6.4.2 Effect on other creditors' claims Creditors' claims will be affected where a company is wound up only where the company is insolvent. In light of this, the legislative provisions dealing with the effect of winding up on other creditors' claims generally apply to winding up by the court and creditors' voluntary winding up. For example, no action or proceeding may be proceeded with, except by leave of court after a winding up order has been made, or where a provisional liquidator has been appointed,[171] or upon commencement of winding up in a creditors' voluntary winding up.[172] Prior to a winding up order being made or a provisional liquidator being appointed in a court-ordered winding up, the company or any creditor or contributory may apply to the court to stay or restrain further proceedings in any pending action or proceeding. It is also provided that any attachment, sequestration, distress or execution put in force against the company after the commencement of winding up by the court or the commencement of a creditors' voluntary winding up is void.[173]

Where execution has been issued against the goods or land of the company or where the creditor has attached a debt to the company's assets, the creditor is not entitled to retain the benefit of the execution or attachment against the liquidator unless the execution or attachment has been completed prior to specified dates. For winding up by the court, the date is that of the presentation of the petition. For voluntary winding up, the date is that of the passing of the resolution to wind up the company unless the creditor has had notice of the meeting at which it has been proposed to wind up the company, in which case, the date is that on which the creditor was so notified. The court has the power to allow creditors to keep any benefit of such execution or attachment as it deems fit.[174] Any assets of the company that are in the possession of the bailiff, and which are affected by the rule, will have to be delivered to the liquidator. The bailiff is, however, entitled to charge the assets with the costs of the execution.[175]

6.4.3 Effect on members' rights Any transfer of shares or alteration in the status of members purportedly made after the commencement of a winding up by the court is void unless there is a court order to the contrary.[176] In the case of a voluntary winding

170 Section 297(1) of the Companies Act.
171 Section 262(3) of the Companies Act.
172 Section 299(2) of the Companies Act.
173 Sections 260 and 299(1) of the Companies Act.
174 Section 344 of the Companies Act.
175 Section 345 of the Companies Act.
176 Section 259 of the Companies Act.

up, transfers of shares made after the commencement of the winding up are void unless sanctioned by the liquidators. Any alteration of the status of members made after the commencement of the winding up is also void.[177]

Where a company is wound up because it is insolvent, every past and present member of the company is liable to contribute to the assets of the company to an amount sufficient for payment of the company's debts and liabilities, including the costs and expenses of winding up.[178] This general rule is subject to exceptions. For companies limited by shares, no member is required to contribute any sum in excess of the amount of any unpaid shares of which he or she is liable to the company. In companies limited by guarantee, the contribution is limited to the amount undertaken. Past members are not required to contribute where they have ceased to be members for one year or more before the commencement of winding up or in respect of any debts or liability contracted after they have ceased to be members. In addition, a past member is not liable to make contribution unless it appears to the court that the existing members are unable to satisfy the contributions required by them.

Finally, the common law rule that members are entitled to treat as a debt a dividend that has been declared is superseded by section 250(2)(g) of the Act which provides that any sum due to members in their capacity as members by way of dividends, profits or otherwise are not to be treated as debts of the company for the purpose of a competing claim between the members and other creditors.

6.5 Creditors' Meetings

A creditors' meeting may be convened at various points in time during the winding up process. In situations where the winding up is initiated as a creditors' voluntary winding up, such a meeting is convened immediately after the company meeting at which the resolution to wind up the company is passed. Where the winding up is initiated as a members' voluntary winding up and subsequently 'converted' into a creditors' voluntary winding up, the creditors' meeting is convened by the liquidator once he or she has formed the opinion that the company is insolvent.[179] The main purpose of these initial meetings is to decide on who should act as liquidator. Subsequent meetings are called primarily to allow the liquidator to report on the progress of the liquidation to the members and creditors. Where the voluntary winding up extends for more than one year, the liquidator is obliged to summon a general meeting to present an account of his/her acts and dealings and the conduct of the winding up.[180]

The general procedure for creditors' meetings in court winding up is prescribed in rules 106 to 141 of the Companies (Winding up) Rules. It is the liquidator who arranges for such meetings to discuss the progress of the liquidation and to seek the creditors' views[181] or to arrange for a compromise.[182] Creditors do, however, have the

177 Section 292(2) of the Companies Act.

178 Section 250 of the Companies Act.

179 Section 295 of the Companies Act.

180 Section 307 of the Companies Act.

181 Rule 112 of the Companies (Winding up) Rules; section 273 of the Companies Act.

182 Section 272 of the Companies Act.

power to direct the liquidator to summon a general meeting either through a resolution to that effect or, if they hold 10 per cent or more in value of the debts owed by the company, through a request in writing. In such a case, it is the party requesting the meeting who will have to bear the cost of convening the meeting.[183] The court may also order meetings for the purposes of ascertaining the wishes of the contributories and creditors.

The procedure for the conduct of meetings is largely subject to the law of meetings. The quorum for a creditors' meeting is three, except where there are fewer than three creditors, in which case all the creditors must be present for a quorum.[184] Resolutions are carried where the majority in number and value of the creditors present and voting either personally or by proxy vote in favour of the resolution.[185] Creditors generally do not have any voting rights in relation to contingent or unascertained debts.[186] Secured creditors are only entitled to vote in relation to the unsecured portion of their debt unless they intend to surrender their security.[187] Minutes of the meeting together with a record of the contributories and creditors present must be kept.[188]

6.6 Committees of Inspection

Because of the sheer number of creditors and members that are likely to be affected in an insolvent winding up, the law has in place a mechanism for these creditors and members to be represented by a committee referred to as a 'committee of inspection'. In a creditors' voluntary winding up, the creditors may appoint a committee of inspection consisting of not more than five persons. Where such a committee is appointed, the company may subsequently in general meeting appoint up to five other persons to act as members of the committee. The creditors, however, retain the power to resolve that all or any of the persons appointed by the company ought not be members of the committee of inspection. In the face of such a resolution, the relevant persons shall not be qualified to act as members of the committee in the absence of a court direction to the contrary.[189]

In a court-ordered winding up, the liquidator has the discretion to initiate the appointment of a committee of inspection. Any creditor or contributory may also request that the liquidator summon separate meetings of the creditors and contributories for the purposes of determining whether such persons require the appointment of a committee to act with the liquidator and, if so, who the members of the committee should be.[190]

The proceedings of committees of inspection are the same regardless of the method of their appointment.[191] The liquidator or any member of the committee may

---

183 Rule 117 of the Companies (Winding up) Rules.
184 Rule 123 of the Companies (Winding up) Rules.
185 Rule 119 of the Companies (Winding up) Rules.
186 Rule 125 of the Companies (Winding up) Rules.
187 Rule 126 of the Companies (Winding up) Rules.
188 Rule 130 of the Companies (Winding up) Rules.
189 Section 298 of the Companies Act.
190 Section 277 of the Companies Act.
191 See sections 278 and 298(3) of the Companies Act.

call for a meeting. Actions are taken in line with the decision of the majority of the committee's members. The committee, however, cannot act unless a majority of the committee is present.

6.7 The Role of the Court in the Winding Up Process

The court does not play a major role in the majority of winding up proceedings apart from the hearing and granting of a petition in a court winding up. At times, its assistance may be sought by various parties to resolve issues arising from the winding up or to protect the rights and interests of affected parties. Examples include the appointment and removal of a liquidator,[192] the monitoring of the liquidator's performance of his or her duties,[193] the granting of leave for other actions or proceedings to be proceeded with or commenced against the company after the commencement of winding up,[194] and the making of orders to stay or restrain pending proceedings against the company.[195] In addition, the legislation provides the court with other general powers in court winding up.[196] These include broad powers to:

- stay winding up proceedings;
- settle a list of contributories, collect assets of the company and apply the assets in the discharge of the company's liabilities;
- order the payment of debts due by contributories and allow any relevant set-off;
- make calls on the contributories for payment of money;
- fix a date for creditors to prove their debts;
- order an inspection of the company's books and papers;
- summon persons connected with the company and examine such persons on oath concerning the company's property;
- order a public examination of promoters and directors of the company; and
- arrange for the arrest of contributors and directors who are likely to abscond.

The court may delegate some of these powers to the liquidator who shall then perform these duties as an officer of the court and subject to the court's control.[197]

6.8 Proof of Debts and Ranking of Claims by Creditors against the Company

6.8.1 Proof of debts One of the main functions of a liquidator is to determine the amount of debt owed by the company being wound up. The mechanism that assists the liquidator in this function is that of requiring the company's creditors to lodge a proof of debt with the liquidator. All claims against the company, whether present or contingent, ascertained or sounding only in damages, are provable against the

---

192 See, for example, sections 267, 268, 301 and 302 of the Companies Act.
193 See, for example, sections 273(3), 274, 313 and 318 of the Companies Act.
194 Section 262(3) and 299(2) of the Companies Act.
195 Section 258 of the Companies Act.
196 These are set out in Part X, Division 2, subdivision (4) of the Companies Act.
197 Section 288 of the Companies Act.

company. Where the debt is unascertainable at the time that it is to be proved, the creditor is to provide a just estimate of the value of the debt or claim.[198] All unsecured claims and debts must be proved in accordance with the procedure laid down unless the court (in the case of a court winding up) directs that the debts of any creditors or class of creditors are to be admitted without proof.[199] Secured creditors may realise their security to satisfy any debt and need not prove for their debts except where the proceeds of their realisation are insufficient to satisfy the debt. In this case, they need only to prove for the balance of the amount owing as unsecured creditors.

The procedure for proving debts is found in the Companies (Winding Up) Rules and the Bankruptcy Rules.[200] The process is initiated by the liquidator through a notice given by way of an advertisement in the *Government Gazette* and a major newspaper for creditors to prove their debts within a fixed time. The liquidator also has to send individual notices to all persons claiming to be creditors and whose claims have not been admitted or, in a winding up by the court, to every person mentioned in the statement of affairs as a creditor who has not proved his/her debt.[201] Creditors thereafter prove their debts by sending to the liquidator a statutory declaration in the prescribed form verifying the debt.[202] The liquidator will then examine each proof of debt lodged and accept or reject the proof in writing. Where the proof is rejected, the liquidator must provide the grounds for the rejection to the creditor in writing.[203] Such a creditor may apply to the court for a review of the liquidator's decision.[204]

6.8.2 Ranking of claims Ranking of claims only becomes a substantive issue where a company is insolvent. Secured creditors generally have priority to the assets that have been given as security against all unsecured creditors. The next in line are the 'preferred creditors'. These include those involved in the liquidation of the company (that is, liquidators, auditors and lawyers), the company's employees and the tax authorities. Their claims, in order of descending priority, are:[205]

1. The costs and expenses of the winding up, including the taxed costs of the petitioner, the remuneration of the liquidator and the costs of audits carried out
2. All wages and allowances due to employees up to a maximum of an equivalent of five months' salary or $7,500, whichever is lower, per employee
3. Amounts due to employees as retrenchment benefits or other payments under any contract of employment or award up to a maximum of an equivalent of five months' salary or $7,500, whichever is the lesser, per employee
4. All amounts due in respect of workmen's compensation

---

198 Section 327(1) of the Companies Act.

199 Rule 78 of the Companies (Winding up) Rules.

200 This is theoretically applicable in cases of insolvent winding up by virtue of section 327(2) of the Companies Act. In practice, it is the Companies (Winding up) Rules that are generally followed.

201 Rule 91 of the Companies (Winding up) Rules.

202 Rules 79 to 83 of the Companies (Winding up) Rules.

203 Rule 92 of the Companies (Winding up) Rules.

204 Rule 93 of the Companies (Winding up) Rules.

205 Section 328 of the Companies Act.

5. Amounts due in respect of payments required under the Central Provident Fund Act (Cap 36) relating to employee superannuation for the 12 months next before, on or after the commencement of winding up
6. All remuneration payable to employees in respect of unconsumed vacation leave
7. Tax.

Claims in the same category rank equally. Should the funds available be insufficient to meet the claims of all persons in any category, the funds are to be distributed to the claimants in that category in proportion to the debt owed to each claimant.[206] Where the assets of the company are insufficient to meet the claims of parties making claims under categories (1), (2), (3), (5) and (6) above, these claims are to have priority over the claims of the holders of floating charges and are to be paid out of any property comprised in or subject to that charge.[207]

Once the claims of the secured and preferred creditors have been satisfied, the balance of any assets may then be applied to satisfy the claims of unsecured creditors and the unsecured portions of the claims of secured creditors on a *pari passu* basis.

6.9 Set-off of Debts

The rules governing the setting-off of debts in cases of corporate insolvency are found in section 88 of the Bankruptcy Act (Cap 20)[208] and are similar to those relating to individual bankruptcy. The section requires the company and all creditors with whom the company has mutual dealings to set-off all mutual credits, debts or dealings against each other. Only balances in favour of the creditors are provable debts. The set-off is mandatory. In order to determine the balance due, an account should be taken. The date of the account should relate back to the date of commencement of the winding up.[209] Debts that are not provable in a winding up (for example, unliquidated claims in tort) cannot be set-off against a company that is in liquidation. In addition, debts or liabilities that arise as a result of an obligation incurred at a time when the creditor had notice that there was a pending winding up petition against the company cannot be set-off against sums owing to the company.[210]

6.10 Effect of Winding Up on Specified Transactions

6.10.1 Undervalued transactions and unfair preferences[211] Where a company is wound up, the court may, upon the application of the liquidator, require that certain transactions be nullified and order that the parties' pre-transaction position be restored. The situations where such an order may be made are where it is deemed that

---

206 Section 328(3) of the Companies Act.
207 Section 328(5) of the Companies Act.
208 Made applicable by section 327(2) of the Companies Act.
209 *Good Property Land Development Pte Ltd* v. *Societe Generale* [1996] 2 SLR 239.
210 Section 88(2) of the Bankruptcy Act.
211 Governed by section 98 of the Bankruptcy Act read in conjunction with section 329(1) of the Companies Act and the Companies (Application of Bankruptcy Act Provisions) Regulations.

the company has entered into an 'undervalued transaction' or where the company has given an 'unfair preference'.

A transaction with another party is at an undervalue where the company makes a gift to that person or where the transaction is entered into on terms that provide for the company to receive no consideration, or where the value of the consideration provided by that party is significantly less than the value of the consideration provided by the company.[212] The court shall not make an order affecting such a transaction where it is satisfied that the transaction was entered into in good faith and where there is a belief that the transaction was for the benefit of the company. A company is taken to have given an unfair preference to its creditors or guarantors where it does anything or suffers anything to be done which has the effect of putting such persons into a position which, in the event of the company's winding up, would be better than the position they would have been in if that thing had not been done.[213] It must also be shown that the company, in giving the preference, was influenced by a desire to produce this effect.[214]

Only transactions entered into and preferences given within a specified time are affected. In the case of undervalued transactions, the specified time is five years from the date of the presentation of the winding up petition. For unfair preferences, the specified time is two years prior to the date of presentation of the winding up petition where the preference is given to a person who is connected to the company[215] and six months from that date for all other cases.[216] In addition, the transactions or preferences are only affected where the company was insolvent at the time of the transaction or preference, or became insolvent consequent to the entering into of the transaction or the granting of the preference in question.[217]

6.10.2 Effect on security Winding up proceedings generally do not affect the rights of secured creditors or the security they hold. It is usual, however, for creditors to reserve the right in their security documentation to enforce their security upon there being a petition filed against the company. In addition, floating charges on the undertaking or property of the company that are created within six months of the commencement of the winding up of the company are invalid for the purposes of securing sums advanced prior to the grant of the charge unless it is proved that the company was solvent at the time the charge was created. The floating charge, however, is valid to secure the amount of any cash paid to the company at the time of or subsequent to its creation in consideration for the charge together with interest on the amount at a statutory rate of 5 per cent per annum.[218]

---

212 Section 98(3) of the Bankruptcy Act.

213 Section 99(3) of the Bankruptcy Act.

214 Section 99(4) of the Bankruptcy Act.

215 For a definition of 'person connected with the Company', see regulation 2 of the Companies (Application of Bankruptcy Act Provisions) Regulations read together with regulations 4 and 5 of the said Regulations and section 101 of the Bankruptcy Act.

216 Section 100(1) of the Bankruptcy Act.

217 Section 100(2) of the Bankruptcy Act.

218 Section 330 of the Companies Act.

6.10.3 Transactions with directors or director-related companies Section 221 of the Companies Act allows the liquidator to recover money in respect of sales to or by the company that were for a cash consideration but were at an undervalue where the transaction takes place within the two years prior to the commencement of winding up. The provision only affects transactions with persons who were directors of the company at the time the transaction took place or companies who shared a director with the insolvent company at the time of the transaction. The amount recoverable is, in the case of an undervalued acquisition by the company, that by which the cash consideration for the acquisition exceeded the value of the property, business or undertaking. In the case of an undervalued sale by the company, the amount recoverable is the amount by which the property, business or undertaking exceeds the cash consideration given.[219]

6.11 Dissolution

Dissolution of insolvent companies takes place either pursuant to liquidation proceedings or through a 'striking-off' action.[220]

6.11.1 Dissolution pursuant to liquidation In voluntary liquidation, the liquidator has to present an account showing how the winding up has been conducted as well as how the property of the company has been disposed of to a general meeting of the company and, in the case of a creditors' voluntary winding up, to a meeting of the creditors as well. This has to be done as soon as the affairs of the company are fully wound up. The liquidator then has to lodge with the Registrar and the Official Receiver a return relating to the holding of such a meeting and of its date together with a copy of the account within seven days after the meeting is held. The company is deemed to be dissolved on the expiration of three months after the lodging of the return. The court may, however, defer this date upon the application of the liquidator or of any other person who appears to be interested in the matter.[221]

In court-ordered winding up, dissolution takes place through an application by the liquidator for a court order. Such applications are made when the liquidator has realised the property of the company and has distributed a final dividend to the creditors or contributories or where the liquidator has either resigned or has been removed from his/her office.[222] The dissolution takes effect on the date the court makes the dissolution order.[223] The liquidator is then obliged to lodge a copy of the order with the Registrar and with the Official Receiver within 14 days of the making of the order.

The court may upon the application of the liquidator or any interested party make an order declaring the dissolution to have been void so long as the order is made

219 Section 331 of the Companies Act.

220 It is also possible for a company to be dissolved as a result of a group reconstruction, merger or acquisition. See section 212 of the Companies Act.

221 See section 308 of the Companies Act.

222 Section 275 of the Companies Act.

223 Section 276 of the Companies Act.

within two years after the date of the dissolution. Such an order must be lodged with the Registrar and with the Official Receiver by the applicant within seven days.[224]

6.11.2 Striking-off by the Registrar The Registrar is empowered to strike off defunct companies from the Companies Register where there is reasonable cause to believe that the company is not carrying on business or is not in operation.[225] A notice must be sent to the company informing it of the Registrar's intention to strike off the company. The company is given one month to respond to the notice and to show cause why it should not be struck off. In the absence of such a response, the Registrar will send another notice informing the company that it will be struck off the Register and dissolved on the expiration of three months from the date of the notice. The company will be struck off upon the expiration of the three months. In practice, the Registrar will only proceed with a striking-off where the company does not have any assets or liabilities or where the assets are disposed of and the liabilities written off or time-barred. In addition, the directors must not have any outstanding Registry summonses. The company must also not have any outstanding Registry penalties or liabilities with the Inland Revenue Authorities. It must also not have any outstanding charges in its charge register and must not be involved in any legal proceedings. An application may be made to the court to have the company restored to the Register any time within 15 years after its name has been struck off upon the applicant satisfying certain prescribed conditions.[226]

7 Liquidators

7.1 Appointment of Liquidators, their Qualifications and Registration

In a winding up by the court, the liquidator is appointed by the court. He/she may either be the Official Receiver or any approved company auditor who has also been approved to act as a liquidator pursuant to section 9(3) of the Companies Act. In a members' voluntary winding up, the liquidator is appointed by the company in general meeting.[227] The liquidator appointed in a members' voluntary winding up need not be the Official Receiver or an approved company auditor. In the case of a creditors' voluntary winding up, the company will nominate a liquidator at the meeting at which the resolution for winding up is passed and the creditors may also nominate a creditor at the creditors' meeting. If the company and the creditors nominate different persons, the creditors' choice will prevail but if the creditors do not nominate a liquidator, then the person nominated by the company becomes the liquidator.[228] The CLRFC has recommended widening the range of qualified insolvency practitioners to include finance and other professionals, as well as the

224 Section 343 of the Companies Act.
225 Section 344 of the Companies Act.
226 See section 344(5) of the Companies Act.
227 Section 294(1) of the Companies Act.
228 Section 297(1) of the Companies Act.

establishment of an insolvency practitioners' association that would be responsible for the accreditation of insolvency practitioners, continuing education and the setting of professional standards.[229]

Section 11(4) of the Companies Act stipulates that a person may not be appointed liquidator unless he/she has consented in writing to act as liquidator. The Act also provides that he/she may not consent if the person subject to any of the disqualifications set out in section 11(1), which are as follows:

- he/she is not an approved liquidator;
- he/she is indebted to the company or a related corporation in an amount exceeding S$2,500;
- he/she is an officer of the company, a partner, employer or employee of an officer of the company, or a partner or employee of an employee of an officer of the company;
- he/she is an undischarged bankrupt;
- he/she has assigned his/her estate or made an arrangement with his/her creditors under any law relating to bankruptcy; or
- he/she has been convicted of an offence involving fraud or dishonesty punishable with imprisonment of three months or more.

However, in the case of a members' voluntary winding up the disqualifications in the third point above do not apply. This is also the case in a creditors' voluntary winding up if a resolution to that effect is passed by a majority in number and value of the creditors.[230]

7.2 Powers and Duties of Liquidators

Upon a winding up order being made, the liquidator is entitled to take into custody or under his/her control all property to which the company is entitled.[231] He or she has various discretionary powers, which are enumerated in section 272(2) of the Companies Act. These include the power to bring and defend actions in the name and on behalf of the company, to compromise debts, to sell the assets of the company and generally to do all things which may be necessary for the winding up of the affairs of the company and distributing its assets. Other powers of the liquidator are exercisable only with the authority of the court or the committee of inspection. These include carrying on the business of the company so far as is necessary for its beneficial winding up; paying off any class of creditors in full (except preferred creditors as prescribed under section 328 of the Companies Act) and appointing a solicitor to assist in liquidation duties.[232]

In the case of a voluntary winding up, the liquidator need not seek the approval of the court to carry on the business of the company, but may do so only so far as is

---

229 See CLRFC Report Recommendation 4.3.
230 Section 11(2) of the Companies Act.
231 Section 269(1) of the Companies Act.
232 Section 272(1) of the Companies Act.

necessary for its beneficial winding up.[233] He/she is entitled to exercise all the discretionary powers granted to a liquidator in a court winding up and, in the case of powers requiring court sanction, may exercise those powers provided that he/she obtains the approval of a special resolution of the company in a members' voluntary winding up or the creditors in a creditors' voluntary winding up.[234]

The Act assists the liquidator in his/her efforts to gather information about the company, its property and its financial position by allowing the examination of various persons. The court may summon any officer of the company, any debtor, any person who has or is believed to have the company's property in their possession and any person whom the court feels is capable of giving information concerning the formation, trade dealings, affairs or property of the company and examine such person under oath.[235] Such person may also be required to produce any books, papers and documents in their custody relating to the company. Further, pursuant to section 286 of the Companies Act, where the liquidator has reported to the court that, in his/her opinion, a fraud has been committed or some material fact has been concealed by any person in the promotion of the company or by any officer, or that an officer has failed to act honestly or diligently or has been guilty of some impropriety or recklessness, the court may order the public examination of such person.

The liquidator's primary responsibilities are to take into his/her custody and control all the property of the company, realise such property and distribute the proceeds among the creditors according to the scheme of priority prescribed by law. The Companies Act and the Companies (Winding up) Rules prescribe other more detailed duties and responsibilities of the liquidator. These include the submission of reports and accounts as described in section 7.5 below, the maintenance of a special bank account for payment of moneys received, and the keeping of proper books in which entries or minutes of meetings shall be made.

7.3 Status, Independence, and so on of Liquidators compared with the Powers of the Court

Where the Official Receiver is appointed liquidator in a winding up by the court, the Minister exercises overall control over the Official Receiver and Assistant Official Receivers who are concerned in the liquidation. Section 266 of the Companies Act provides that the Minister shall take cognisance of their conduct and, if they fail to perform their duties and observe all the requirements of the law, or if any creditor or contributory makes a complaint, the Minister is required to inquire into the matter and take such action as he/she deems expedient.

Where a person other than the Official Receiver is appointed liquidator in a court winding up, the Official Receiver has the task of overseeing the due performance of the appointee's duties.[236] The Official Receiver may make inquiries into the appointee's conduct in the proper case and may apply to examine the liquidator under

233 Section 292(1) of the Companies Act.

234 Section 305(1) of the Companies Act.

235 Section 285 of the Companies Act.

236 Section 265 of the Companies Act.

oath concerning the winding up or direct an investigation of the liquidator's books and vouchers. Section 264(2) of the Companies Act obliges the liquidator to give the Official Receiver such information and such access to facilities for inspecting the books and documents of the company, and generally such aid as may be required for enabling the Official Receiver to perform his/her duties.

In addition the liquidator is required, in administration and distribution of the assets of the company, to have regard to any directions given by resolution of creditors and contributories or by the committee of inspection, if any.[237] He/she may also apply to the court for directions as to any matter that may arise in the winding up. Subject to the foregoing, the Companies Act stipulates that the liquidator shall use his/her own discretion in the management of the affairs and property of the company and the distribution of its assets.

In every mode of winding up the court shall take cognisance of the conduct of the liquidator. If he/she fails to perform his or her duties faithfully or to observe the prescribed requirements or if any creditor or contributory makes a complaint, the court is required to inquire into the matter and take such action as it deems fit. If, in the opinion of the Registrar of Companies or the Official Receiver, there has been misfeasance, neglect or omission on the part of the liquidator, the court may order the liquidator to make good any loss and also make such other order as it deems fit. The liquidator may also be required to answer any inquiry relating to the winding up and, for this purpose, may be examined under oath.[238]

7.4 Suspension or Removal of Liquidators

A liquidator may be removed by the court on cause shown.[239] Cause may be shown in cases where the liquidator is unfit to act, either because of their personal character or because they are in a position of conflict of interest due to their connection with other parties, or because of the circumstances they may be involved or mixed up in.[240]

7.5 Reports of Liquidators

In a winding up by the court the liquidator is required to submit a preliminary report to the court (or, if the liquidator is not the Official Receiver, to the Official Receiver) as soon as practicable after the receipt of the company's statement of affairs.[241] The report should contain information as to the capital of the company, its assets and liabilities, the causes for the company's failure and whether, in the liquidator's opinion, further inquiry is desirable as to any matter relating to the promotion, formation or failure of the company or the conduct of its business. He/she may also, if deemed appropriate, make further reports to the court or the Official Receiver, as the case may be.

---

[237] Section 273 of the Companies Act.

[238] Section 313 of the Companies Act.

[239] In the case of a court winding up, pursuant to section 268(1) of the Companies Act and, in the case of a voluntary winding up, under section 302 of the Companies Act.

[240] See generally, Walter Woon, *Company Law*, Singapore, Sweet & Maxwell, 1997 at 706–707.

[241] Section 271 of the Companies Act.

In the case of a voluntary winding up, the liquidator is required, if the winding up continues for more than one year, to summon a general meeting of the company (in the case of a members' voluntary winding up) and of the company and the creditors (in the case of a creditors' voluntary winding up) at the end of the first year to lay before the meeting an account of his/her acts and dealings and the conduct of the winding up in the preceding year.[242] Thereafter, he/she is required to summon such a meeting at the end of each succeeding year or not more than three months thereafter.

A liquidator in any winding up is also required to file six-monthly accounts of their receipts and payments and the status of the winding up with the Registrar of Companies and the Official Receiver.[243]

7.6 Remuneration and Fees of Liquidators

The remuneration of liquidators is provided for under section 269 of the Companies Act. Such remuneration may be determined by agreement between the liquidator and the committee of inspection (if any);[244] or failing such agreement or where there is no committee of inspection, by a resolution passed by a majority in number and at least 75 per cent in value of the creditors at a creditors' meeting;[245] or failing that, by the court.

8 Enforcement of Securities over Debtors' Assets in Singapore

8.1 Position of Secured Creditors

The law relating to security for debt is well developed and firmly established in Singapore. Creditors may require and obtain various forms of security in order to protect themselves against the risk of non-payment or default by the debtor. These security interests include mortgages and charges (both fixed and floating), guarantees, and so on. In addition, third parties may make use of quasi-security devices such as retention of title clauses and hire purchase or leasing arrangements to protect their interests.

Secured creditors are generally able to enforce security interests to the fullest extent allowed by law and in contract, and such rights are generally protected and preserved in the event that the debtor becomes insolvent. However, secured creditors may, in some cases, be required to stay their hand if the law deems it necessary in order to provide an insolvent debtor with the opportunity to come up with a viable plan for rehabilitation of its business and to avoid bankruptcy or liquidation. The extent to which the law sanctions the postponement of, or interference with, secured creditors' rights in the event of voluntary arrangements, schemes of arrangement

242 Section 307 of the Companies Act.

243 Section 317 of the Companies Act.

244 Members of the company holding not less than 10 per cent of the issued capital of the company may apply to the court to vary the determination and the court may either do so or confirm it.

245 In such a situation, the liquidator is entitled to apply to the court, who may either vary the determination or confirm it.

or composition and in judicial management have been described previously in this chapter.

8.2 Appointment of Receivers and Managers of Property of a Debtor

The right of a creditor to appoint a receiver or a receiver and manager over the property, assets and undertaking of a debtor is a valuable security right. In Singapore, receivers, or receivers and managers, may be appointed privately pursuant to a right granted under an instrument, or by the court pursuant to certain statutory provisions.

Statutory provisions which provide for the right or power to appoint a receiver include the Conveyancing and Law of Property Act (Cap 61), which stipulates that a mortgagee of land under a mortgage made by deed may appoint a receiver of the income from the mortgaged property if the mortgage moneys have become due.[246] Also, the Companies Act provides that the trustee for debenture holders may apply to court for an order to appoint a receiver where he/she considers that the assets of the borrowing company are insufficient to discharge the principal debt as and when it falls due, or when the company has failed to comply with an order made by the Minister under section 101(2).[247] Other more general provisions which empower the court to appoint a receiver are contained in the Civil Law Act (Cap 43) and the Supreme Court of Judicature Act (Cap 322).

Contractual rights to appoint a receiver are usually contained in a debenture document. The event(s) which will trigger the right to appoint a receiver, and the powers of a receiver so appointed, would depend on the terms of the debenture. If it is necessary to realise the debtor's business as a going concern, then a receiver and manager, as opposed to a receiver, may be appointed. While a receiver's duty is simply to get in the assets subject to the charge, a receiver and manager is empowered to run the company's business, undertaking or a part thereof for a limited period with a view to realising it as a going concern.

8.3 Effect of Appointment of an External Controller of Assets

The appointment of a receiver or a receiver and manager does not affect the existence of the company. At the end of a receivership, the company still exists and may continue its business, at least in theory. The reality, however, is that in most cases, liquidation is the next step after a company has undergone receivership.

The effect of receivership on the powers of the board of directors depends on the scope and extent of the receivership. Where a receiver is appointed over a specific asset or class of assets, then the powers of the company and its directors to deal with that asset or class of assets are suspended. However, the company may carry on business and utilise the assets not covered by the receivership and the powers of the directors to govern the company are preserved, at least insofar as those other assets are concerned. However, where a receiver and manager are appointed over the whole or substantially the whole of the company's assets and undertaking, then the powers

246 Section 24 of the Conveyancing & Law of Property Act.

247 See generally, section 101 of the Companies Act.

of the directors are suspended for the duration of the receivership. Nonetheless, they are not discharged and retain residual duties and powers, insofar as these do not affect the receiver and manager's power over the assets and undertaking of the company. For example, directors may, in the proper case, commence action on behalf of the company without obtaining the consent of the receiver.

When a receiver or manager has been appointed, section 222(1) of the Companies Act requires that the fact must be stated on every invoice, order for goods or business letter, being a document on which the name of the company appears, issued by the company, the receiver or the liquidator. The appointment of a receiver also has the effect of crystallising a floating charge. Thereafter it ceases to be a floating charge and is fixed on the assets so that the company may thereafter no longer deal with such assets, except subject to the charge.

8.4 Powers and Duties of the External Controller

A receiver appointed by the court is not an agent of any person, but is an officer of the court. A receiver appointed privately pursuant to a debenture is, in the absence of any provision to the contrary, an agent of the debenture holder. However, most debentures stipulate that the receiver shall act as agent of the company. This is significant because, as agent of the company, the company would be liable for any debts incurred by the receiver. A receiver appointed by the court is personally liable for debts incurred by him. However, he or she is entitled to be indemnified out of the assets of the company. Further, under section 218(1) of the Companies Act, it is provided that a receiver (whether appointed by the court or otherwise) is, notwithstanding any agreement to the contrary but without prejudice to their rights against the company or any other person, liable for debts incurred by them in the course of the receivership for services rendered, goods purchased or property hired, leased, used or occupied. If the receiver is an agent of the debenture holders, it would follow that they should be liable to indemnify him or her. Nonetheless, as a precaution, receivers often require their appointers to expressly grant them an indemnity before consenting to accept the appointment.

A receiver's primary duty is to the debenture holder who appointed him/her and not to the company. His/her obligation, therefore, is to safeguard the debenture holder's interests and he/she is not obliged to act in the company's interests in this regard. Certain fiduciary duties are nonetheless owed to the company; for example, the receiver must not put themselves in a position where their personal interests conflict with that of the company. In handling the company's assets, he/she must exercise the same degree of diligence and care that a person in the conduct of their own affairs would exercise. In addition, a receiver and manager other than one appointed by the court is an officer of the company pursuant to the definition of 'officer' in section 4(1) of the Companies Act. The receiver and manager are therefore subject to all liabilities and duties of an officer of the company as specified in the Companies Act. However, a receiver may apply to the court to be excused from liability in respect of negligence, default, breach of duty or breach of trust under section 391(1) of the Companies Act. The court may excuse the receiver if he/she acted honestly and reasonably and it is fair to excuse him/her having regard to all circumstances.

A receiver who has misapplied or retained or become liable or accountable for any money or property of the company or who has been guilty of any misfeasance or breach of trust or duty against the company may be compelled by the court to repay or restore the money or property with interest or to contribute such sums to the assets of the company by way of compensation, pursuant to section 227(2) of the Companies Act.

9 Offences

The legislative regime governing offences in cases of insolvency are targeted primarily against 'officers' of the company.[248] Such persons include directors, corporate secretaries, receivers and managers appointed pursuant to debentures, liquidators and any person employed by the company in an executive capacity.[249]

9.1 Fraudulent and Wrongful Trading

Where it is established, either in the course of winding up or in any proceedings against the company, that the business of the company has been carried on with intent to defraud creditors or for any other fraudulent purpose, every person who was knowingly a party to the carrying on of the business is taken to be guilty of an offence. The offence carries a fine not exceeding $15,000 or imprisonment for a term not exceeding seven years, or both.[250] Such a person may also be held personally responsible for all or any of the debts or other liabilities of the company as the court directs.

It is also an offence for an officer of a company to knowingly be a party to the contracting of a debt by the company in situations where such an officer had no reasonable or probable ground of expectation, at the time the debt was contracted, of the company being able to repay the debt.[251] Such action may be taken against the officer either in the course of the company's winding up or in cases where proceedings have been brought against the company. The penalty for the offence is a fine not exceeding $2,000 or a term of imprisonment not exceeding three months. In addition, where a person has been convicted of such an offence, the court, on the application of the liquidator, a creditor or a contributory of the company, may declare that the person be personally responsible for the payment of the whole or any part of the contracted debt.[252]

---

248 See Part X, Division 4, Subdivision (4) of the Companies Act.

249 The definition of 'officer' is found in section 4 of the Companies Act.

250 Section 340(1) read together with section 340(5) of the Companies Act.

251 Section 339(3) of the Companies Act.

252 Section 340(1) of the Companies Act.

9.2 Other Insolvency-related Offences

Corporate directors and other officers owe an array of statutory duties that carry penal sanctions if not performed satisfactorily. It is often the case that these offences only come to light when the company is facing winding up proceedings and the liquidator looks into the affairs of the company. The procedure for the prosecution of delinquent officers is provided for in section 342 of the Companies Act.

In addition to these statutory duties, there are other criminal provisions that are more closely related to the winding up process. To assist the liquidator in performing his/her duties, the legislation makes it an offence if any past or present officer or contributory of the company either hinders the liquidator or fails to adequately assist the liquidator in specified circumstances. For a conviction to be secured, it must generally be shown that such a person had an intention to defraud or mislead or otherwise acted fraudulently.[253] There is also a specific criminal provision in section 338 against the destruction, mutilation, alteration or falsification of corporate records with the intent to defraud or deceive any person. Where it is found that proper books of accounts are not kept, every officer in default is also liable for an offence unless the officer shows that he or she acted honestly and that, in the circumstances in which the business of the company was carried on, the default was excusable.[254]

10 Rules regarding Cross-border Insolvency

10.1 Recognition of Foreign Judgments

A foreign judgment will generally be recognised by the Singapore courts as a debt owed to the judgment creditor by the judgment debtor. The foreign judgment creditor will therefore have to initiate an action for the debt and prove his case in accordance with the procedures of the Singapore courts. A local court will recognise the foreign judgment as a debt where it is shown that the judgment is final and conclusive as between the parties, it is for a fixed sum of money that is not in the form of a tax or a penalty and has been granted by a court of competent jurisdiction. A summary procedure is often used and a local judgment will usually be granted unless it is shown that:

- the foreign judgment was not given by a court of competent jurisdiction;
- the foreign judgment was obtained by fraud; or
- the foreign judgment was in respect of a claim that is contrary to public policy in Singapore (for example, a gambling debt).

Upon obtaining judgment on the debt, the judgment may be enforced in any way permitted in Singapore, including bankruptcy or insolvency proceedings.

---

253 Section 336 of the Companies Act.

254 Section 338 of the Companies Act.

The need to commence a fresh action on the judgment as a debt may be dispensed with should the judgment originate from countries that fall under the Reciprocal Enforcement of Commonwealth Judgements Act (Cap 264)[255] and the Reciprocal Enforcement of Foreign Judgements Act[256] (Cap 265). Foreign judgments from the designated countries will be treated as if they originated from the Singapore courts if they are registered with the High Court. Enforcement and bankruptcy or insolvency proceedings may be proceeded with once the foreign judgment has been properly registered.

10.2 Procedures for Assistance of Courts and Parties in Foreign Jurisdictions

Section 151 of the Bankruptcy Act 1995 provides that the High Court of Singapore and its officers are to act in aid of and be auxiliary to the courts of Malaysia and any designated country[257] in all matters of bankruptcy and insolvency so long as there is a reciprocal arrangement existing between the respective countries. The section empowers the High Court to exercise the same powers of the court of the country making a request for aid in regard to any order being made by such a court. In addition, an agreement has been entered into between Singapore and Malaysia for the reciprocal recognition of the official assignees appointed by each government.[258]

Where a foreign company doing business in Singapore is liquidated or dissolved in its place of incorporation or origin, notice of the liquidation and, when a liquidator is appointed, notice of such appointment must be lodged with the Registrar in Singapore within one month.[259] The foreign liquidator has the same powers and functions of a local liquidator until a liquidator for Singapore is appointed. Generally, only assets that are situate in Singapore may be realised by the liquidator. Sums recovered and realised may only be passed on to the foreign liquidator for distribution outside of Singapore after paying any debts and satisfying any liabilities incurred in Singapore by the foreign company in the absence of a court order to the contrary. Where a foreign company has been wound up so far as its assets in Singapore are concerned and there is no liquidator for the place of its incorporation, the liquidator in Singapore may apply to the court for directions for the purposes of disposing the net amount recovered.

---

255 The relevant countries whose judgments come under this Act are Australia, Brunei, Hong Kong, India (except the states of Jammu and Kashmir), Malaysia, New Zealand, Pakistan, Papua New Guinea, Sri Lanka, the United Kingdom and the Windward Islands.

256 To date, this Act is applicable only in relation to judgments from Hong Kong, Special Administrative Region, People's Republic of China.

257 To date, no other country has been designated under the provision.

258 Declaration under section 152(1) of the Bankruptcy Act for the Reciprocal Recognition of Official Assignees, 1 February 1950.

259 Section 337 of the Companies Act.

11 Conclusion

Much of Singapore's insolvency law is still rooted in the laws that were put in place at the time when the country was still part of the British Empire. Developments made in the UK and other Commonwealth countries have been, and continue to be, continuously tracked and considered for implementation locally. The local courts also continue to take serious consideration of case law from these countries and have followed or approved the cases in the appropriate circumstances. At the same time, the law in some areas (such as those reflected in the recent changes to the Bankruptcy Act) have been developed to specifically cater to domestic policies and needs. This pattern of management of the insolvency laws is likely to continue, with an added focus on developments in the US, as Singapore continues in its quest to be a world-class global centre for corporate and financial activity.

Chapter 13

The Corporate Insolvency System of the Philippines: Experience and Reforms

CESAR L. VILLANUEVA[1]
Ateneo de Manila Law School

Since the onset of the Asian financial crisis of 1997, the Philippines has become fully aware of the need to put into place clear and effective statutory rules on corporate insolvency that would be consistent with the country's existing institution on credit transactions, with a responsive judicial or quasi-judicial system that will oversee the enforcement proceedings.

This chapter therefore looks into the Philippine experience in the ongoing efforts to set up a corporate insolvency system that meets international standards and is also responsive to the local setting.

The Philippine Scenario

The Philippine corporate insolvency system has for almost a century operated on very tenuous legal bases: (1) an antiquated 1906 Insolvency Act,[2] which essentially provides for simple suspension of payments and corporate liquidation resulting from insolvency, with no provisions on corporate rehabilitation or restructuring; and (2) the 1980 amendment[3] to Presidential Decree No. 902-A (PD 902-A), which recognized

---

1 B.Sc., LL.B., LL.M., FAICD. The author is the Associate Dean for Faculty and Academic Affairs of the Ateneo de Manila Law School, where he is also a Professorial Lecturer in the courses on *Sales* and *Corporate Law*. He is a member of the Corps of Professorial Lectures and Chairman of the Commercial Law Department of the Philippine Judicial Academy. He has authored the following books: *Commercial Law Review*, *Law on Sale*, and *Philippine Corporate Law*. He is a Senior Partner in the law firm of Villanueva, Gabionza & De Santos, 20/F Antel Corporate Center, 139 Valero Street, Salcedo Village, Makati City. For queries: cvillanueva@vbglaw.com.ph.

2 Republic Act No. 1956.

3 Presidential Decree No. 1758, which amended Section 5 of Pres. Decree No. 902-A, provided that the Securities and Exchange Commission shall have

> original and exclusive jurisdiction to hear and decide cases involving … d) Petitions of corporations, partnerships or associations to be declared in the state of suspension of payment in cases where the corporation, partnership or association possesses property to cover all of its debts but foresees the impossibility of meeting them when they respectively fall due or in cases where the corporation,

in very sketchy provisions the jurisdiction of the Philippine Securities and Exchange Commission (SEC), acting as a quasi-judicial body, to hear petitions for corporate suspension of payments and rehabilitation.

The Insolvency Act does not provide for corporate rehabilitation and its automatic stay provisions do not effectively cover actions on enforcement by secured creditors. Considering the state of economic development in the Philippines where most of the important assets of corporate business enterprises are subject to mortgage, the filing of insolvency proceedings merely covers the liquidation of remaining assets for the benefit of unsecured creditors, while secured creditors pursue separate foreclosure proceedings. In addition, the Insolvency Act does not grant a discharge to a corporate debtor. As a result, the legislation is rarely invoked, and has effectively fallen into disuse.

On the other hand, the remedy of corporate rehabilitation under PD 902-A was very unfamiliar to the Philippine jurisdiction at the time the amendment was introduced in 1980, and the lack of adequate provisions to support the process prevented its application on a pervasive basis. Most of the major gaps in the law (that is, the standing of who can avail and the issue of joinder of corporate officers bound personally to corporate debts, coverage of the stay order, the standing of creditors on the approval of the corporate plan, the ability to cram down a rehabilitation plan, and so on) had to be worked out through tedious, case-by-case decisions rendered by the Supreme Court from appeals coming from petitions being processed by the SEC. That meant that the whole framework upon which creditors and corporate debtors would be able to find comfort and familiarity with the rehabilitation proceedings took a process of almost 20 years. It was only the demands of the 1997 Asian financial crisis which forced the SEC to finally exercise its rule-making powers and issue in December 1999 the SEC Rules of Procedure on Corporate Recovery.

Unfortunately, by July 2000, the Securities Regulation Code[4] was enacted into law, which effectively removed from SEC's jurisdiction petitions for corporate suspension of payments and rehabilitation and transferred them to the regular trial courts (that is, the Regional Trial Courts). The Supreme Court, through its Philippine Judicial Academy, had to undertake a training of selected judges who were designated to hear petitions for corporate rehabilitation, and also promulgated the Interim Rules of Procedure on Corporate Recovery, which improved on the SEC Rules.

The Philippine corporate bankruptcy system has been rather spotty, and has tended to be a 'patch-up' job. The imperatives of globalization, the need of the country to attract foreign investments as one of the key components to economic development, as well as the experience and continuing repercussions of the 1997 Asian financial crisis, have all crystallized the need to overhaul the Philippine corporate bankruptcy system in order to comply with international standards.

---

partnership or association has no sufficient assets to cover its liabilities, but is under the Management Committee created pursuant to this Decree.

4 Republic Act No. 8799.

The Constitutional and Substantive Law Setting

Economic and Social Values

The economic and constitutional history of the country would show that when it comes to business and property rights, Philippine society has always sought to strike a balance between the free enterprise system and a paternalistic or socialistic system. This ambivalent stance finds its best manifestation in the various provisions of the Philippine 1987 Constitution itself. Although the Constitution would protect property and life under the due process clause,[5] and declares that '[t]he State recognizes the indispensable role of the private sector, encourages private enterprise, and provides incentives to needed investments',[6] it aims to provide nevertheless for the 'social function' of private property and enterprise ownership, thus:

> … The use of property bears a social function, and all economic agents shall contribute to the common good, individuals and private groups, including corporations, cooperatives, and similar collective organizations, shall have the right to own, establish, and operate economic enterprises, subject to the duty of the State to promote distributive justice and to intervene when the common good so demands.[7]

Sanctity of Contracts and Contractual Commitments

Since the 1935 Constitution, Philippine society has constitutionally sanctified the binding effects of contracts between the parties and prohibits the passage of any law, rule or regulation impairing the obligation of contracts, now embodied in Section 10, Article III of the 1987 Constitution. The purpose of the non-impairment clause

> … is to safeguard the integrity of valid contractual agreements against unwarranted interference by the State. As a rule, they should be respected by the legislature and not tampered with by subsequent laws that will change the intention of the parties or modify their rights and obligations. The will of the obligor and the obligee must be observed; the obligation of their contract must not be impaired.[8]

The sanctity of contractual commitments is likewise emblazoned in basic provisions of the Civil Code, which requires that contracts shall 'bind both contracting parties, and its validity or compliance cannot be left to the will of one of them',[9] and from the moment of their perfection 'the parties are bound not only to the fulfillment of what has been expressly stipulated but also to all the consequences which, according to their nature, may be in keeping with good faith, usage and law'.[10] Contracts 'shall

---

5 Section 1, Article III (Bill of Rights), Philippines Constitution.

6 Section 20, Art. II (Declaration of Principles and State Policies), Philippine Constitution.

7 Section 6, Art. XII (National Economy and Patrimony), Philippine Constitution.

8 Cruz, *Constitutional Law*, Central Lawbook Publishing Co., Inc., 1980 edition, p. 192.

9 Article 1308, Civil Code of the Philippines.

10 Article 1315, ibid.

be obligatory, in whatever forms they may have been entered into, provided all the essential requisites for their validity are present'.[11]

Philippine Corporate Set-up and the Business Judgment Rule

On the other hand, the 'business judgment rule' has always been a tenet in Philippine corporate law that recognizes corporate power and competence to be within the board of directors. Under this doctrine, courts and administrative bodies exercising quasi-judicial powers are enjoined from supplanting the discretion of the board on administrative matters as to which they have legitimate power of action; and contracts which are *intra vires* entered into by the board are binding upon the corporation and will not be interfered with unless such contracts are so unconscionable and oppressive as to amount to a wanton destruction of rights of the minority.[12]

Courts and other administrative bodies having jurisdiction over corporations generally would not interfere in the judgment or business decisions of the board, nor will they substitute their wisdom for that of the board. Under Section 23 of the Corporation Code,[13] the contract of the State with corporations, their investors, and the public at large who must deal with the corporation, is that the 'corporate powers' are vested in the board, and generally no courts or other tribunal would overturn or interfere with the judgment and decisions of the board, and the management appointed by the board.

Courts and other tribunals are wont to override the business judgment of boards mainly because courts are not in the business of running businesses, and the *laissez-faire* rule or the free enterprise system prevailing in our social and economic set-up dictate that it is better for the State and its agencies to leave business to the businesspeople. This is especially so since courts and administrative bodies are ill equipped to make business decisions. More importantly, the prevailing social contract in the corporate setting on the power to decide the course of corporate business enterprise is vested in the board and not with the courts or other quasi-judicial bodies.[14]

Hierarchical System of Claims against the Business Enterprise

In the hierarchical test of priority, creditors have, by express statutory provisions, and common law application, always been preferred to the business assets on which they

---

11 Article 1356, ibid.

12 *Gamboa* v. *Victoriano*, 90 SCRA 40 (1979).

13 Batas Pambansa Blg. 68.

14 Section 23 of the Corporation Code of the Philippines provides that

> Unless otherwise provided in this Code, the corporate powers of all corporations formed under this Code shall be exercised, all business conducted and all property of such corporations controlled and held by the board of directors or trustees to be elected from among the holders of stocks, or where there is not stock, from among the members of the corporation, who shall hold office for one (1) year and until their successors are elected and qualified.

have extended credit, as against the equity holders, whether they be sole proprietors, partners[15] or shareholders.[16]

People who make equity placements in corporations expect that their returns shall be tied up with the successes or losses of the corporations. Therefore, when placing their investments they are willing to take a risk by twisting the management's style of operating the affairs of the corporation. Since the return of the equity investors is intricately woven into the business affairs of the corporation, they are reciprocally given a voice or a say in management in the sense that they would be entitled to participate in the election of the board of directors, and also to cast votes on certain corporate structural matters in those instances enumerated by law when stockholders have a ratificatory vote on management action.

To a corporation, the advantage of equity investment is the absence of 'carrying cost', since the corporate enterprise is not bound to pay any return on the investment unless there is profit, and even then, the board of directors is generally granted large business discretion to determine when to declare such return in the form of dividends. The corporate enterprise has the flexibility of declaring dividends in the form of stock dividend which does not drain the finances of the enterprise, and yet allows the stockholders to 'cash in' on the stock dividends by selling them in the open market.

An equity investment in a corporate enterprise is generally non-withdrawable for so long as the corporation has not been dissolved.[17] This assures the corporate enterprise and its managers that they will have such resources at their disposal so long as the corporate enterprise remains a going concern.

On the other hand, a creditor of the corporation only looks at the financial condition and operation of the corporation as a means of gauging the ability of the corporation to repay the loan principal and accumulated interests at the specified period. But a creditor puts no stake on the operations of the corporation, and therefore the contractual obligation of the corporate enterprise to pay the stipulated return (interest) remains binding even when the operations are incurring losses. Since the relationship is essentially contractual in a loan placement with a corporation, the creditor has every right to demand the payment of the placement upon its maturity.

Consequently, the expected return between the two types of 'investments' would be different. In a loan placement in a corporation, since the investors place no stake in the results of the operations, they can only demand the stipulated fixed return of their investment even if, by the use of the borrowed funds, the enterprise is able to reap huge profits. In the case of equity investors, since they have placed their stake in the results of operations, they generally participate in all income earned by the venture.

This difference in legal motivation and risk assumption factors between a debt investor and an equity investor also dictates the legal preference in payment from corporate properties of the former as compared to the latter. Since debt investors place no stake in the corporate operations and their rights are based on contract, then

---

15 Article 1839(2) of the Civil Code provides priority payment from partnership assets to those owing to creditors other than partners before any payment may be made to the partners.

16 Section 122 of the Corporation Code embodies the 'trust fund doctrine' and provides that 'no corporation shall distribute any of its assets or property except upon lawful dissolution and after payment of all its debts and liabilities'.

17 Section 122, Corporation Code.

the corporate venture must, in the case of insolvency, devote and prefer all corporate assets towards the payment of its creditors. On the other hand, since the equity investors clearly undertook to place their investment to the risk of the venture, they can receive a return of their investment only from the remaining assets of the venture, if any, after the payment of all liabilities to creditors.

Types of Bankruptcy Proceedings

Suspension of Payments Proceedings

This is Spanish in origin, copied from the provisions of the Spanish Code of Commerce. In unclear cases, we would go back to the Spanish authorities. Under the Philippine Insolvency Law,[18] a corporation 'possessing sufficient property to cover all [its] debts ... but foresees the impossibility of meeting them when they respectively fall due, may petition that [it] be declared in the state of suspension of payments by the court'.[19]

The automatic stay order is effective only for three months, within which period the petitioner should be able to obtain approval from its creditors of the scheme of repayment of obligations.

Insolvency Proceedings

Insolvency proceedings work under the premise that the debtor has neither cash nor property of sufficient value to pay all the debts. There are two types of proceedings covered by the law:

- *voluntary insolvency*, when it is the debtor who files the petition for insolvency; and
- *involuntary insolvency*, when it is the creditors who ask for the declaration of the debtor's insolvency.

Whether the insolvency proceedings are voluntary or involuntary, the Insolvency Act recognizes that the purpose is not to distort nor amend property and contractual rights and obligations, but to provide for an orderly means by which the claims against the business enterprise may be satisfied in line with the underlying hierarchical rules on claims. That is the reason why the stay order does not cover secured creditors, who are given the right to pursue separate foreclosure proceedings on the properties mortgaged.

---

18 Act No. 1956, as amended.

19 Section 2, The Insolvency Law.

Rehabilitation Proceedings

In the Philippine setting, 'rehabilitation' is taken as 'a continuance of corporate life and activities in an effort to restore and reinstate the corporation to its former position of successful operation and solvency'.[20]

Rehabilitation under PD 902-A is deemed to be vested with 'public interests' and is resorted to not only for the benefit of creditors but for other stakeholders affected by the corporate enterprise. Thus, the Philippine Supreme Court has held that:

> Rehabilitation of a financially distressed corporation benefits its employees, creditors, stockholders and, in a larger sense, the general public. And in considering whether to rehabilitate or not, the SEC gives preference to the interest of creditors, including employees [because] shareholders can recover their investments only upon liquidation of the corporation, and only if there are assets remaining after all corporate creditors are paid.[21]

Interim Measures taken in the Field of Corporate Rehabilitation

Since the economic and financial circumstances prevailing after the 1997 Asian financial crisis did not permit waiting for Congress to pass a modern bankruptcy law, several sectors in Philippine society answered the need to 'improvize' by establishing an interim framework for a corporate rehabilitation system based on the country's SEC experience. The plan of action basically followed two routes: (1) 'judicial legislation', and (2) judicial specialization and training in corporate rehabilitation.

Using its powers under Subsection 5.2 of the Securities Regulation Code to designate the Regional Trial Court (RTC) branches to exercise jurisdiction over corporate cases,[22] and its power under Section 5(5) of Article VIII of the Philippine Constitution to promulgate rules of procedure, the Philippine Supreme Court took the lead by:

- designating the most qualified RTC judge or judges in each of the regional districts of the Philippines to be the 'commercial law judges', to hear and decide corporate

---

20 *Ruby Industrial Corp.* v. *Court of Appeals*, 284 SCRA 445, 90 SCAD 407 (1998).

21 *Rubberworld (Phils.), Inc.* v. *NLRC*, 305 SCRA 721, 105 SCAD 485 (1999).

22 Subsection 5.2 of the Securities Regulation Code reads:

> The Commission's jurisdiction over all cases enumerated under Section 5 of Presidential Decree No. 902-A is hereby transferred to the Court of general jurisdiction or the appropriate Regional Trial Courts; provided that the Supreme Court in the exercise of its authority may designate the Regional Trial Court branches that shall exercise jurisdiction over these cases. The Commission shall retain jurisdiction over pending cases involving intra-corporate disputes submitted for final resolution which should be resolved within one (1) year from the enactment of this Code. The Commission shall retain jurisdiction over pending suspension of payments/rehabilitation cases filed as of 30 June 2000 until finally disposed.

cases, including petitions for corporate suspension of payments/rehabilitation;[23] and

- promulgating in December of 2000 the Interim Rules of Procedure on Corporate Rehabilitation, which were largely based on and an improvement on the SEC Rules on Corporate Recovery.

Under the auspices of the Philippine Judicial Academy (PHILJA), which is the judicial education arm of the Supreme Court, the designated commercial law judges underwent extensive training on the various aspects of corporate rehabilitation and exposure to 'law and economics', to enable them to read financial statements and understand accounting, economic, banking and commercial concepts. With funding from the Asian Development Bank, and in partnership with the Asian Institute of Management, the judges went through three-phase training modules on the management, financial and legal aspects of corporate rehabilitation or restructuring. Several sessions were also spent by the judges in familiarizing themselves with existing jurisprudence governing Section 5(d) of PD 902-A, as well as the mechanics and rationale of the various provisions of the Interim Rules of Procedure on Corporate Rehabilitation.

The salient features of the Interim Rules of Procedure on Corporate Rehabilitation are as follows:

1. The proceedings are mandated to be *in rem*: through compliance with publication requirements, the results of the proceedings are binding on creditors and other affected persons even when they do not participate in the proceedings.
2. The proceedings are declared to be 'summary', 'non-adversarial', and 'technology friendly' such that pleadings that unduly delay (motion to dismiss/reconsideration, motion for bill of particulars, and so on) are prohibited. Causes of actions and oppositions are based on affidavits attaching actionable documents when necessary. Service of pleadings may be effected by fax or e-mail.
3. The proceedings are strictly 'time-bound'. The whole process cannot exceed 18 months.
4. The orders of the courts are immediately executory, even on appeal, unless enjoined by the Court of Appeals or the Supreme Court.

In addition, the Interim Rules contained 'assertive provisions' to enhance the possibility for rehabilitation of the corporate debtor, which items were not covered by the substantive provisions of Section 5(d) of PD 902-A, namely:

1. An expanded definition of 'claims' subject to the stay order to cover 'claims or demands of whatever nature or character against the debtor or its property, whether for money or otherwise'
2. Express prohibitions against withholding of supply of goods and services to the corporate debtor

---

23 Administrative Order No. 00-11-03-SC.

3. Provision for the payment of administrative expenses
4. Provision for relief to secured creditors whenever they have no 'adequate protection'
5. Empowerment of the court to approve the rehabilitation plan over the opposition of the majority of the creditors, and absence of provision for the classification of creditors.

Among some of the Philippine corporate practitioners, the Interim Rules are thought to constitute a bold move on the part of the Supreme Court given that some of the provisions are considered substantive law, and beyond the scope of the procedural power of the Supreme Court. Some sectors even consider the key provisions of the Interim Rules, such as the 'cram down' power of the courts, to lack a substantive law basis and constitute 'unlawful taking' in the contravention of the constitutionally protected property rights of secured creditors. The cram down power is understood to be the power of the rehabilitation court to impose, by way of judgment approving the terms of the rehabilitation plan, the provisions in the plan that affect creditors. The judgment can even be imposed against creditors who have not agreed to the said terms of settlement in the voting session called for the purpose of discussing the terms of the plan.

Two years after the promulgation of the Interim Rules, the expected rise in corporate rehabilitation cases, brought about by the continuing financial and economic difficulties being experienced in the Philippines, has not eventuated. The following reasons have been attributed to the limited resort to the Interim Rules:

1. The 'innovative' provisions are really 'untested' and practitioners are not quite certain how much 'control' they can retain over the proceedings after filing a petition. Basic familiarity with the operation of the various provisions of the Interim Rules should see developments similar to the SEC's initial jurisdiction over corporate rehabilitation cases: slowly through the growth of Supreme Court decisions interpreting and implementing the Interim Rules, commercial practitioners should gain enough confidence within the 'workings' of the corporate rehabilitation under the Interim Rules and more readily seek to involve those provisions;
2. The 'substantive' provisions of the Interim Rules present a strong basis by which approved rehabilitation plans may be overturned on the basis of constitutional issues raised with the Supreme Court. This results in a great deal of uncertainty on whether the funds and resources spent on a corporate rehabilitation process might be wasted.

Nevertheless, the Interim Rules, together with the relevant jurisprudential pronouncements of the Supreme Court covering rehabilitation proceedings falling under Section 5(d) of PD 902-A, provide for the existing legal framework of the Philippine corporate rehabilitation system.

Proposed Corporate Recovery and Insolvency Act

Under the aegis of the Capital Market Development Council, bills have been introduced in both the House of Senate and House of Representatives of the Philippine Congress for what initially was called the Corporate Recovery Act. This draft legislation was designed to cover only corporate rehabilitation, leaving the Insolvency Law intact.

The bill has been under scrutiny in the Economic Committee of the House of Representatives, but has received little attention in the Senate. The current version of the bill is dubbed as the 'Corporate Recovery and Insolvency Act', a consolidate law governing the entire bankruptcy field for corporate debtors, thereby intended to effectively supplant the Insolvency Act and Section 5(d) of PD 902-A on matters covering corporate suspension of payment, rehabilitation, and liquidation.

A paper was read by Congressman Oscar Moreno, who heads the Economic Committee of the House of Representatives, in which he reported on the salient features of the current version of the bill. These are summarized below.[24]

1. Speedy and efficient rehabilitation
   - A maximum of 18 months is allowed from the date of filing for the court to approve a rehabilitation plan; otherwise, the proceedings are converted to dissolution and liquidation
   - The court must find that there is 'substantial likelihood of rehabilitation'; otherwise the suspension order automatically expires 90 days from the date of filing.
2. Consolidation of all legal proceedings and stay on enforcement of claims
   - The suspension order also stays the enforcement of all claims against the debtor in order to preserve the assets of the debtor
   - All legal proceedings by and against the debtor are consolidated upon the issuance of the commencement order
   - All other proceedings are stayed (except those which were filed on appeal at the CA or SC prior to the commencement date, or those filed at specialized courts/quasi-judicial agencies).
3. New money
   - Super-priority status is accorded to money given by third parties to the debtor to keep it operational and help it achieve rehabilitation; as such, new money creditors are entitled to priority in payment and preferred even over secured obligations.
4. Management-in-place; powers and duties of rehabilitation receiver
   - The task of the rehabilitation receiver is limited to overseeing and monitoring the operations of the debtor while the proceedings are pending

---

[24] Congressman Moreno read the paper at the Second Forum for Asian Insolvency Reforms (FAIR), held at the Shangri-La Hotel, Bangkok, Thailand, on 16–17 December 2002, and sponsored by ADB, OECD and AusAid.

- The receiver only gains control and takes over the management of the company with the written consent of the debtor and the general unsecured creditors' committee.

5. Creation of commercial courts
   - Establishment of commercial courts with exclusive and original jurisdiction over rehabilitation and insolvency cases and other commercial disputes is proposed in order to promote expertise in, and hopefully expedite, the adjudication of cases in commercial law.
6. Adjustment and balancing of rights
   - Relief from the enforcement of claims against the debtor, including judgment claims
   - Relief from interest upon commencement of proceedings
   - Right to terminate contracts with limited liability: the debtor is given 60 days from the commencement date to confirm or terminate contracts, after which all contracts are deemed terminated; debtor's liability arising from such termination is limited
   - Right to contract post-commencement loans, upon recommendation of receiver and subject to the approval of the court.
7. Iron-clad rule/global filing
   - Each entity in a group of companies is treated as a separate legal entity, and therefore the remedies that accrue to the debtor company do not extend to other members in the group
   - However, the proposed law allows global filing in specific cases, such as where there was actual commingling of assets and liabilities prior to filing; and the debtor and related entity/ies have common creditors and it would be more convenient to treat them together rather than separately.
8. Remedies of debtor and bundle of rights therein
   - Suspension of payments – enables the debtor to postpone payments for 90 days from the commencement date, and thereafter expires automatically; election of this remedy forfeits access to other relief within one year from the commencement date so as to prevent abuse by the debtor
   - Pre-negotiated rehabilitation – provides for the debtor to work out extra-judicially a rehabilitation plan with its creditors, and for the relief of suspension of claims against it while the rehabilitation plan awaits judicial approval; upon approval, all creditors are bound
   - Court-supervised rehabilitation – the debtor enjoys the suspension of claims against it while a rehabilitation plan is drafted under court supervision; support by majority vote of creditors to plan binds all, otherwise the plan is converted to liquidation
   - Liquidation and dissolution.
9. Definition of creditor and equality of creditors
   - All creditors, whether secured or unsecured, are prohibited from enforcing their claim once the debtor undergoes rehabilitation
   - While the proposed law seeks to equalize creditors, the creation of distinct classes or sub-groups among them is allowed for purposes of decision-making
   - Creditor Government Financial Institutions (GFIs) are similarly bound by the rehabilitation proceedings.

10. Cram down
    - Proceedings bind all creditors to a decision supported by more than half of them, and in the process repeals the provision in the Insolvency Act which allows certain secured creditors to stay away from and not be bound by the results of negotiations and proceedings for the rehabilitation of the debtor.
11. General unsecured creditors' committee
    - The committee is intended to give voice to unsecured creditors; the committee is granted certain powers, such as that of vetoing petitions for post-commencement financing requested by the rehabilitation receiver, to protect the interests of creditors without the benefit of security.
12. Right to initiate involuntary proceedings
    - Creditors with total claims equivalent to PHP 1 million, or 25 per cent of the total paid-up capital or partners' contributions, whichever is higher, are allowed to initiate involuntary proceedings when there is, or at least there exists the imminent possibility of, default in payment by the debtor.
13. Creditors' rights
    - Creditors are to be served notice of pleadings against the property of, and claims against, the debtor
    - The commencement order is required to be published in a newspaper of general circulation
    - Court appointment of a rehabilitation receiver requires nomination by and support of 50 per cent of secured and unsecured creditors
    - Adequate protection – creditors are given the right to petition the court for any of the following steps: (1) an order to the rehabilitation receiver to take reasonable steps to prevent the depreciation of its property in possession of the debtor, or to allow the foreclosure of the property; (2) the conveyance of a lien or ownership interest in a substitute property of the debtor; (3) the conveyance of a lien on the residual funds from the sale of encumbered property; or (4) the sale or disposition of the property
    - The court is empowered in cases where adequate protection over a property securing a creditor's claim is lacking, to order the debtor to make arrangements to insure the property, provide additional or replacement security, make payments, or allow the enforcement of a security claim against the debtor
    - Right against solidary guarantors, third party/accommodation mortgagors – creditors are allowed to proceed against solidary guarantors or third party/accommodation mortgagors, except when the property subject of the third party accommodation mortgage is necessary for the rehabilitation of the debtor. Solidary guarantors are those who are liable primarily with the principal obligor (that is, corporate debtor) on the corporate debts.
14. Preference of credits
    - Administrative expenses – reasonable and necessary expenses incurred in connection with and for the rehabilitation of the debtor, or those incurred in the ordinary course of business after the filing of the petition; administrative expenses are preferred over all other credits; they are exempt from the stay/suspension order

- Taxes – there exists a strong lobby for the government to waive documentary stamp tax, capital gains tax and withholding taxes on, as well as interest on late payment of taxes by, companies undergoing rehabilitation.

15. Conformity with international standards and best practices
    - Specialized liquidation and rehabilitation for financial institutions under receivership established by state-funded or state-mandated insurance system – generally governed by relevant legislation but proposed legislation to apply suppletorily (that is, the deficiencies of the former)
    - Cross-border insolvency – representatives of a foreign corporation under insolvency proceedings in foreign countries are allowed to seek a judicial order stopping Philippine creditors from acting unilaterally with respect to assets located in the Philippines: this is, however, made subject to the principle of reciprocity
    - Directors' and officers' liability – directors and officers who cause, authorize or directly participate in the disposition of property fraudulently, or in a manner grossly disadvantageous to debtor and/or creditor, or those who conceal from creditors, or embezzle or misappropriate any property, are made liable for double the value of the property, or the amount of the transaction involved, whichever is higher.

Special Purpose Vehicle (SPV) Act of 2002

In December 2002, the Republic Act No. 9182 was enacted into law providing a limited period of five years for the Philippine financial sector to dispose of their non-performing assets (NPAs) under the concept of 'true sale' to special purpose vehicles (SPVs) organized for such purposes.

The Act grants both tax and registration incentives during the window period for availment.

In March 2004, a companion Securitization Act was enacted into law by Congress as Republic Act No. 9267, which has become the basis for the asset-backed securities system of the Philippines.

Allied Developments

In the drive to overhaul the corporate and financial sectors of the Philippine economy, particular agencies have promulgated rules on corporate governance to improve the overall investment climate in the Philippines.

The SEC promulgated the Code of Corporate Governance[25] governing listed and public companies in the Philippines. The Code defines 'corporate governance' as 'a system whereby shareholders, creditors and other stakeholders of a corporation ensure that management enhances the value of the corporation as it competes in an increasingly global market place'.

---

25 SEC Memorandum Circular No. 2, series of 2002.

The Code not only institutionalizes the duties and responsibilities of the board of directors and management to promote transparency in corporate operations and finances, improve on the rights of minority shareholders, expand the duties of directors and officers to other stakeholders other than just the stockholders, but also ensures the long-term prospects of public corporations.

The *Bangko Sentral ng Pilipinas* (Central Bank of the Philippines) has also issued circulars[26] putting together a code of governance for directors and officers of banking institutions. The circulars not only expressly expand the constituencies of bank directors beyond the stockholders, but also detail the specific duties and responsibilities to ensure that directors assume primary responsibility in corporate governance.

A similar code of corporate governance is currently being prepared to govern government-owned and controlled corporations (GOCCs).

Conclusions

The Philippine experience with the specialized jurisdiction of the SEC, which has been transported to specially designated commercial courts, has allowed a realization of the following advantages:

1. A specialized court system in a given jurisdiction allows systematic and well-focused development and evolvement of both procedural and substantive components of insolvency proceedings.
2. Various stakeholders in the enterprise are encouraged to properly evaluate the various alternatives available to them.
3. The development of auxillary support systems that would allow a more efficient approach to insolvency proceedings are encouraged.

The historical developments in the Philippines show how both the substantive basis insolvency law and the court system designated to handle such a system would prove critical in evolving a truly responsive and efficient insolvency system. Thus:

1. There must be a reasonable comprehensive substantive statutory basis (that is, a comprehensive Bankruptcy Code) underpinning the bankruptcy system of a given jurisdiction, and laying down the jurisdiction and powers of the specialized court.
2. There must also be accompanying or integrated remedial or procedural provisions governing such proceedings, with appropriate laws setting up the procedure and requirements for insolvency proceedings.
3. There must be in place a system of professional managers and a pool of experts as auxiliary supports to such a specialized court system.

---

26 BSP Circular No. 283, series of 2001; BSP Circular No. 296, series of 2001.

Insofar as the Philippines is concerned, the following would be the major hurdles that must be overcome so that a corporate insolvency regime that would adhere to international standards could be implemented within the local setting:

1. State commitment to use its various departments to enact a responsive Bankruptcy Code
2. The hefty financial costs involved in setting up a specialized court system, and hiring competent judges/hearing officers
3. Upgrading of the commercial law system
4. Appropriate orientation or re-orientation of the community to such a system within its cultural setting.

Chapter 14

Insolvency Law in New Zealand

THE HON JUSTICE PAUL HEATH

High Court of New Zealand

Introduction

Introduction to the Legal System

New Zealand is a unitary State with a unicameral Parliament. Its legal system has developed from the Westminster Parliamentary democracy model and many of its laws have been inherited from the UK. In terms of insolvency law, it is fair to describe New Zealand law as largely pro-creditor in emphasis.

Most of the jurisdiction in insolvency[1] law is vested in the High Court of New Zealand which is a superior court of record with inherent jurisdiction. Some aspects of insolvency law are dealt with by Associate Judges of the High Court but, generally, jurisdiction is exercised by judges of that court. There are appeals to the Court of Appeal and, with leave, to the Supreme Court of New Zealand.

All legal systems are required to deal with the situation which arises when a debtor is unable to pay his or her debts. In New Zealand, where the debtor is a corporate entity, the assets are sold and the proceeds distributed among its creditors rateably in accordance with the statutory priorities. The company is then dissolved. The law is more merciful to an individual; the individual's property is sold and the proceeds distributed rateably among his or her creditors. But, in due course, the individual will be discharged from bankruptcy and permitted to resume a normal life freed from the burden of past debts.[2]

History of Insolvency Laws in New Zealand

The first insolvency statute in New Zealand was the Imprisonment for Debt Ordinance of 1844. That statute made it possible for the court to grant relief to persons who had been imprisoned for debt but who had become indebted without fraud or gross or culpable negligence on their part.[3] While the ordinance allowed such persons

---

1 In New Zealand, the term 'insolvency' denotes a state of things rather than a status, whereas the term 'bankruptcy' denotes the status of a person who has been adjudged bankrupt by the High Court.

2 *Laws NZ Insolvency* (Butterworths, Wellington, 1994) para. 2. Adapted from the observations of Sir Donald Nicholls VC in *Re Paramount Airways Limited* [1992] 3 ALL ER 1(CA).

3 *Laws NZ Insolvency* para. 4; Imprisonment for Debt Ordinance 1844 (Gazette, 1844, No. 7 (25 June) p. 130), Preamble.

to be released from imprisonment, it continued to require their estates to remain liable for satisfaction of their debts.[4]

The next substantive piece of legislation was the Debtors and Creditors Act 1862 which repealed the Imprisonment for Debt Ordinance 1844 and its amendments.[5] The debtor was entitled, with the concurrence of one or more creditors to the extent of not less than £50, to apply by petition to a judge of the Supreme Court of New Zealand for sequestration of his or her estate for the benefit of creditors and for relief under the provisions of the Act. However, the Act did not apply to a debtor who was a prisoner in custody.[6] This statute was the first attempt in New Zealand to enact a coherent system of realisation of assets of a debtor for the benefit of the general body of creditors.

Subsequently, more detailed provisions were enacted by the Bankruptcy Act 1867, the Bankruptcy Act 1892,[7] the Bankruptcy Act 1908 and the Insolvency Act 1967. This last Act remains in force and regulates the law of insolvency so far as individual debtors are concerned.[8]

Company law also developed from the UK statutes with liquidation rules dominating the landscape. Until the company law reform package of 1993, the Companies Act 1955 (which was based on the UK Companies Act 1948) governed all insolvency procedures affecting companies. In essence, liquidation was the main remedy although there were also provisions enabling applications to be made for 'schemes of arrangement' under s 205 of the 1955 Act.

Under the Companies Act 1993 the primary focus is still on liquidation although there are provisions contained in Parts XIV and XV of the Act which enable compromises with creditors to be struck and, in certain circumstances, for the court to impose an amalgamation, reconstruction or compromise arrangement.[9]

Core Insolvency Law Principles

The core principle of insolvency law in operation in New Zealand is the *pari passu* rule which requires the proceeds of sale of assets of an insolvent entity to be distributed rateably among its creditors in accordance with statutory priorities.[10] The *pari passu* rule was enshrined as a rule of public policy by the House of Lords in *British Eagle International Airlines Limited* v. *Compagnie Nationale Air France*.[11] In New Zealand, the majority of our Court of Appeal approved Professor Goode's proposition that the principle of *pari passu* distribution was 'the most fundamental

---

4 Imprisonment of Debt Ordinance 1844, Preamble.

5 *Laws NZ Insolvency* para. 5.

6 *Laws NZ Insolvency* para. 5.

7 After Parliamentary inquiries into the operation of the bankruptcy laws: see Heath, Paul, *Insolvency Law Reform: The Role of the State* [1999] New Zealand Law Review 569 at 572–578 for more details.

8 *Laws NZ Insolvency* para. 6.

9 Companies Act 1993, Parts XIII, XIV and XV.

10 Generally, see Goode, Roy A., *Principles of Corporate Insolvency Law* (Sweet & Maxwell, London, 1990) p. 59 and *Priority Debts in the Distribution of Insolvent Estates: An Advisory Report to the Ministry of Commerce* (NZLC SP2, October 1999).

11 [1975] 2 ALL ER 390 (HL).

principle of insolvency law' in *Attorney-General* v. *McMillan & Lockwood Limited*.[12] The *pari passu* rule is reinforced by a number of provisions which enable either the Official Assignee (as trustee in bankruptcy of an individual's bankrupt estate) or a liquidator to recover monies paid preferentially to creditors prior to the commencement of the bankruptcy or liquidation.[13]

Another core principle of insolvency law in New Zealand is that secured creditors stand outside the bankruptcy/liquidation regime and are entitled to realise their security to pay debts owed to them. They will be entitled to prove their claims in the bankruptcy or liquidation only to the extent of any shortfall after disposition of assets which are subject to the charge.

Approach to Regulation and Statutory Interpretation

The New Zealand approach is one of 'light-handed regulation'. This approach endeavours to provide incentives for voluntary compliance with statutory requirements.

There is no provision in New Zealand law to require insolvency practitioners who act as liquidators or trustees to be licensed or registered. And, in the area of personal bankruptcy, only the Official Assignee, a salaried State servant, is entitled to act as a trustee in bankruptcy.

As in England, there is no common law of bankruptcy. All insolvency law concepts are derived from statute.

The general approach to statutory interpretation in New Zealand is a purposive approach. The Interpretation Act 1999 applies to all statutes and provides, in s 5:

1. The meaning of an enactment must be ascertained from its text and in the light of its purpose.
2. The matters that may be considered in ascertaining the meaning of an enactment include the indications provided in the enactment.
3. Examples of those indications are Preambles, the analysis, a table of contents, headings to Parts and sections, marginal notes, diagrams, graphics, examples and explanatory material, and the organisation and format of the enactment.[14]

Personal Insolvency Laws

Background

Bankruptcy, in New Zealand, is the name given to the form of proceeding whereby a debtor who has committed certain acts and defaults is divested of his or her property so that the person in whom it is vested can distribute the proceeds of sale rateably

---

12 [1991] 1 NZLR 53 (CA) at 58.

13 Insolvency Act 1967 ss 54, 56, 57; Property Law Act 1952 s 60; Companies Act 1993 ss 293, 294 and 296. See the discussion on antecedent transactions in the next section of this chapter.

14 See also, *Mangin* v. *Commissioner of Inland Revenue* [1971] NZLR 591 (PC) at 594.

among the debtor's creditors according to statutory priorities.[15] The property is vested in an officer of the court, the Official Assignee. Once a debtor has been discharged from bankruptcy, the debtor is discharged from liability for payment of all debts provable in the bankruptcy except for certain statutory exceptions.[16] However, even after discharge, the Official Assignee must continue to deal with assets vested in him or her by the statute.

Nothing in the Insolvency Act 1967 affects the ability of a secured creditor to realise or otherwise deal with his or her security in the same manner as he or she would have been entitled to realise and deal with it had the Insolvency Act not been passed.[17] In addition, nothing in the Insolvency Act affects the rights of local authorities to recover judgment for rates.[18] Further, nothing affects the provisions of the Joint Family Homes Act 1964, the general objectives of which are to promote the unity of marriage by true co-ownership of the matrimonial home and to afford that home some protection against the winds of financial adversity.[19]

The Official Assignee is entitled to avail himself or herself of all rights and remedies provided by any other act or rule or law in addition to rights and remedies provided by the Insolvency Act 1967.[20]

Principal Institutions

In order for a creditor to obtain an order for adjudication against a debtor who is an individual, it is necessary to bring a petition before the High Court of New Zealand.[21] The court has discretion to make an order of adjudication.[22] The court must be satisfied that an act of bankruptcy has been committed.[23]

The Official Assignee was created as a public official to supervise and administer bankrupt estates when the Bankruptcy Act 1892 was passed. The Official Assignee's present function under the Insolvency Act 1967 is to hold the bankrupt's property, to turn it into money and to distribute it to creditors in accordance with statutory priorities. A number of ancillary powers are given to the Official Assignee to carry out those general functions.[24]

---

15 *Laws NZ Insolvency* para. 7; Insolvency Act 1967 s 42.

16 Insolvency Act 1967 s 114.

17 Insolvency Act 1967 s 3(3).

18 Ibid. s 3(1).

19 *Laws NZ Insolvency* para. 14; Insolvency Act 1967 s 3(2). See also *Official Assignee* v. *Lawford* [1984] 2 NZLR 257 (CA) at 260–261 and *Official Assignee* v. *Noonan* [1988] 2 NZLR 252 (CA) at 255–256.

20 Insolvency Act 1967 s 3(4).

21 Ibid. s 23.

22 Ibid. s 26.

23 For a discussion of acts of bankruptcy see *Laws NZ Insolvency* paras 29–67. In general, available acts of bankruptcy can be characterised as follows: (1) dispositions of property to trustee for benefit of creditors; (2) fraudulent disposition of property; (3) absconding debtors; (4) bankruptcy notices (based on judgment debt); (5) suspension of debt; (6) return of *nulla bona* on execution; (7) removing or concealing property or failing to account for trust money.

24 Insolvency Act 1967 s 71.

Powers of the Court to make Orders of Adjudication

The High Court can adjudge a debtor bankrupt when the debtor has been proved to have committed an act or acts of bankruptcy and the debt owed to the creditor remains unpaid at the date of the hearing. The debt must be at least $200.[25] The act of bankruptcy must have been committed either before or after incurring the debt but in any event within three months before the filing of the petition.[26] The debt must be a liquidated sum payable either immediately or at some certain future time.[27] It is unnecessary for the debt on which the petition is based to be a judgment debt but if it is not, the court must be satisfied that the debt remains owing at the time of the hearing.[28]

The High Court retains a discretion to order adjudication even if all of the allegations set out in the creditor's petition are proved.[29] In considering whether to make an order of adjudication, the court must take into account the wishes of the petitioning creditor, other creditors who wish to be heard, and the debtor. Other creditors must be heard because all creditors must be treated fairly and equally in bankruptcy as opposed to execution. The court will also take into account whether the adjudication would be conducive or detrimental to commercial morality and the interests of the general public. The term 'commercial morality' has been interpreted as comprehending conduct on the part of the bankrupt which involves fraud and dishonesty as well as recklessness and gross negligence; putting the matter in another way, the court can consider whether the debtor has been guilty of undesirable commercial behaviour.[30] Finally, the court has a discretion to refuse to adjudge a debtor bankrupt if such an order would be pointless.[31]

On appeal, the Court of Appeal will not usually interfere with the High Court's exercise of discretion to make an order of adjudication unless the Presiding Judge erred in principle, took into account irrelevant considerations, disregarded relevant considerations or was plainly wrong.[32]

When may a Debtor File for Bankruptcy?

A debtor may present his or her own petition to the High Court to adjudge himself or herself bankrupt. On filing such a petition the debtor is deemed to be adjudged bankrupt with the same consequences in all respects as if the court had made an order adjudging him or her bankrupt.[33] Such an adjudication in bankruptcy is binding on all persons but does not affect the ability of a third party to seek an annulment of the bankruptcy.[34]

---

25 Insolvency Act 1967 s 23(a).

26 Ibid. s 23(b).

27 Ibid. s 23(c).

28 *Ronaldson* v. *Dominion Freeholds Limited* [1981] 2 NZLR 132 (CA).

29 Insolvency Act 1967 s 26(1); generally, *Laws NZ Insolvency* para. 98.

30 *Re Anderson* (High Court, Hamilton B 213/89, 14 April 1992, Penlington J).

31 *Re Fidow (A Debtor)* [1989] 2 NZLR 431.

32 *Re Young* (Court of Appeal, CA 337/92, 7 December 1992).

33 Insolvency Act 1967 s 21; *Laws NZ Insolvency* para. 81.

34 Insolvency Act 1967 ss 30, 119; *Harding* v. *Hooper* (1869) 1 NZCA 315.

Role of Creditors

The creditors do not play a major role in the bankruptcy process. It is open, but not usual, for creditors to elect a creditors' committee to assist the Official Assignee.[35] Meetings of creditors can be called throughout the administration by the Official Assignee. The Official Assignee must call a meeting of creditors when required to do so by one quarter in value of the creditors who have proved their debts. In other cases, the Official Assignee has discretion to call a meeting of creditors when he or she thinks fit.[36]

Controls on Debtors Adjudged Bankrupt

Bankrupts are prohibited from entering business on their own account during the currency of the bankruptcy. The exception to this is where the Official Assignee or the High Court gives permission for that person to be involved in business.[37] Neither may a bankrupt take part in the management of any company, either directly or indirectly, except with the consent of the Official Assignee or the High Court.[38] Similarly, no undischarged bankrupt may be engaged in the management or control of any business by or on behalf of the following persons without leave of the Official Assignee or consent of the court: the bankrupt's husband or wife; a lineal ancestor or descendant of the bankrupt; the wife or husband of such an ancestor or descendant; a brother of the bankrupt, the wife of such a brother, a sister of the bankrupt, and the husband of such a sister.[39]

The purpose of these restrictions is not to penalise the bankrupt but to protect members of the public who might have dealings with the bankrupt if he or she were free to carry on business or take part in the management of any company either on his or her own behalf or on behalf of a family member.[40]

The High Court has the power to issue warrants to seize any part of the bankrupt's property in the custody or possession of the bankrupt or any other person.[41] Furthermore, the Official Assignee may apply to the court for an order redirecting postal articles addressed to the bankrupt.[42] It is an offence for an undischarged bankrupt to leave New Zealand without first having obtained the consent of the Official Assignee or the High Court. In exercising the discretion to permit overseas travel, the Official Assignee must have regard to the interests of the bankrupt's creditors as well as the bankrupt himself or herself.[43]

---

35 Insolvency Act 1967 s 41(1) and *Laws NZ Insolvency* para. 128.

36 Generally, *Laws NZ Insolvency* para. 123; Insolvency Act 1967 s 36.

37 Insolvency Act 1967 s 62.

38 Ibid. s 62(1)(a).

39 Insolvency Act 1967 s 62(1)(b).

40 *Laws NZ Insolvency* para. 222. See also, *Ramsay* v. *Sumich* [1989] 3 NZLR 628 and *Re Focas* (1993) 6 NZCLC 68,417 which deal with analogous provisions under previous company law.

41 Insolvency Act 1967 s 65.

42 Ibid. s 67.

43 *Murray* v. *Official Assignee* (High Court, Hamilton B 318/92, 9 September 1992, Penlington J).

The Official Assignee has the power to examine on oath in private the bankrupt about his property; also, the Official Assignee can examine any other person known or suspected to have in his or her possession property of the bankrupt, or known or suspected to have in his or her possession any book, paper or document relating to the affairs or property of the bankrupt, or any person whom the Official Assignee thinks is capable of giving information concerning the bankrupt.[44] The power to examine is to enable the Official Assignee to obtain information and to be as fully informed as possible in respect of a property and transactions of the bankrupt. It is, in part, a recognition that in many cases information as to the bankrupt's affairs and dealings will be incomplete.[45] In addition, an examination can be conducted before a District Court Judge or another Official Assignee.[46] While this evidence will be admitted in civil proceedings, it cannot be admitted in criminal proceedings brought against the bankrupt unless the prosecution is for perjury arising out of the evidence.[47]

Further, there is power for the Official Assignee to require a public examination of a bankrupt. Usually, a public examination is held if there are elements of fraud or reckless commercial behaviour involved.[48]

Collection and Use of Information about Debtors

When a person has been adjudged bankrupt, the bankrupt or any person who has lodged a proof of debt (or any solicitor or accountant acting on behalf of such a person) is entitled to inspect and copy (1) the bankrupt's books of account; (2) the bankrupt's answers to prescribed questions and his or her statement of affairs; (3) all proofs of debt; and (4) the minutes of any creditors' meeting and the record of any examination of the bankrupt.[49]

Subject to those express powers, there are limits on the extent to which information can be collected about a debtor in New Zealand. Those limits arise from the privacy principles enshrined in the Privacy Act 1993.[50] In essence, unless there is consent from the debtor, the collection of personal information is limited to publicly available information. Where an agency collects personal information directly from the individual, they must (*inter alia*) take sufficient steps to ensure that the individual is aware of the fact that the information is being collected, the purpose for which the information is being collected and the intended recipients of the information. Furthermore, information concerning the identity of the agency collecting the

---

44 Insolvency Act 1967 s 68; *Laws NZ Insolvency* para. 227.

45 *Re Smith (A Bankrupt)* [1992] NZFLR 241 (CA).

46 Insolvency Act 1967 s 68(2). Usually an examination before a District Court Judge will be held if issues of relevance arise which require rulings to be backed by coercive powers.

47 Ibid. s 70.

48 Ibid. s 69.

49 Ibid. s 131.

50 Privacy Act 1993, s 6; in particular, see Information Privacy Principles 1, 2 and 11 set out in s 6. The Information Privacy Principles are set out in New Zealand Law Commission's report *Electronic Commerce Part 2: A Basic Legal Framework* (NZLC R58) para. 172 available at http://www.lawcom.govt.nz under 'Publications'.

information and the consequences which may flow from collection must also be disclosed.

Antecedent Transactions

Under bankruptcy law there are five main provisions under which the Official Assignee can seek to recover monies paid to persons prior to bankruptcy in an endeavour to redistribute those funds among all creditors. They are the provisions relating to voidable gifts,[51] voidable preferences,[52] voidable securities,[53] fraudulent conveyances[54] and dispositions between legally married persons.[55] Where a disposition has been made from one partner to another, the only provision under which the Official Assignee can act to recover that disposition is the provision contained in s 47 of the Property (Relationships) Act 1976 as that Act comprises a code for proceedings involving spouses and *de facto* partners and/or their respective assignees.[56]

The periods during which antecedent transactions may be attacked by an Official Assignee vary. In the case of a voidable gift there is a two-year period which can be extended to five years if it can be proved that the donor was insolvent at the time that the gift was made.[57] Voidable preferences may be attacked where one creditor has been preferred over another when the debtor has an intention to prefer and the transaction occurred within two years of bankruptcy.[58] A security may be attacked in a period of one year prior to bankruptcy.[59] However, if intention to prefer can be proved, a charge entered into between one and two years from bankruptcy can be attacked as a voidable preference under s 56 of the Insolvency Act 1967.

In the case of fraudulent conveyances there is no time limit because reliance is placed on fraudulent conduct.

In the case of dispositions between legally married persons, there is a two-year time limit within which to bring a claim. The claim can be brought where the effect is to prefer the spouse over creditors. If there are elements of fraud involved there are no time constraints upon the making of an application to avoid a disposition made between spouses.[60]

---

51 Insolvency Act 1967 s 54.

52 Ibid. s 56.

53 Ibid. s 57.

54 Property Law Act 1952, s 60.

55 Property (Relationships) Act 1976, s 47.

56 *Official Assignee* v. *Williams* [1999] 3 NZLR 427 (CA). In that case, the Court of Appeal held that any proceedings to set aside antecedent transactions brought under the Insolvency Act 1967 had to be decided as if raised in proceedings brought under the Property (Relationships) Act 1976. See also s 4(4) Property (Relationships) Act 1976.

57 Insolvency Act 1967 s 54.

58 Ibid. s 56.

59 Ibid. s 57.

60 Property (Relationships) Act 1976, s 47.

Proof of Claims

Only debts which are provable in bankruptcy can form the basis of a valid claim to share in the proceeds of sale of the bankrupt's property.[61] All debts and liabilities, present or future, certain or contingent, to which a bankrupt is subject at the time of his or her adjudication are debts provable in the bankruptcy unless expressly excluded.[62]

Debts which are not provable in bankruptcy comprise (*inter alia*) fines or penalties imposed following a conviction or on a discharge of an offender without conviction, claims which should not be admitted for public policy reasons, claims barred by the Limitation Act 1950, double proofs and claims against minors.[63] Similar rules apply to liquidations.[64]

Role of the Court

The Official Assignee, as a trustee in bankruptcy, can apply to the High Court for directions in relation to the way in which he or she should act.[65] The High Court also entertains applications by affected persons to review decisions made by the Official Assignee.[66]

Save for the power to give directions to the Official Assignee, the court acts in an adjudicatory role and does not play any part in the administration of the bankruptcy.

Rules for Distribution of the Assets of a Bankrupt

The rules for distribution of the proceeds of sale of assets of a bankrupt are set out in s 104 of the Insolvency Act 1967. The general thrust of the priorities can be summarised as follows.

First, administration costs will be paid. Second, the costs incurred by a petitioning creditor in procuring the order for adjudication will be paid. Payments such as wages (up to a limit of $6,000 in the case of any one claimant), PAYE and GST deductions will also be paid.[67]

Other priority payments include monies payable to the Commissioner of Inland Revenue in respect of deductions made from money payable to a liable parent under the Child Support Act 1991 and certain compensation for lay-by sales where the goods are not available to deliver to the purchaser.

In a recent publication, the New Zealand Law Commission divided priorities into three main categories: (1) employee-related claims; (2) revenue-related claims; and

---

61 Insolvency Act 1967 s 2, definition of 'debt provable in bankruptcy' or 'provable debt'.

62 Ibid. s 87(1).

63 *Laws NZ, Insolvency* para. 351.

64 Companies Act 1993 ss 302–313.

65 Insolvency Act 1967 s 85.

66 Ibid. s 86.

67 PAYE means 'pay as you earn' and is tax deducted at source from an employee; GST is goods and services tax which is in the form of a value added tax.

(3) miscellaneous claims. The bulk of priorities refer either to employee-related or revenue-related debts.[68] Again, similar rules apply to liquidations.[69]

Discharge from Bankruptcy

A person will be bankrupt in New Zealand for three years from the date of bankruptcy unless earlier discharged by the court. On a hearing of an application for discharge the court will decide whether the conduct of the bankrupt justifies the discharge being withheld or made conditional or suspended. After the three-year period a bankrupt will be discharged unless there is an objection to discharge lodged by the Official Assignee, in which case it is necessary for a public examination of the bankrupt to be held.[70]

On an application for discharge from bankruptcy it is necessary for the Official Assignee to prepare and file in the High Court a report which deals with the following points: (1) the affairs of the bankrupt; (2) the causes of the bankruptcy; (3) the manner in which the bankrupt has performed duties imposed upon him under the Insolvency Act 1967 or obeyed orders of the court; (4) the bankrupt's conduct both before and after the bankruptcy; and (5) any other fact, matter or circumstance which would assist the court in making its decision.[71] The Official Assignee performs a role akin to that of a guardian of the public interest on an application for discharge.

Arrangements Outside Bankruptcy

Part XV Insolvency Act 1967: Proposals A debtor may, prior to being adjudged bankrupt, put a proposal to creditors which, if accepted by requisite majorities and by the court, will be treated as a full and final settlement with creditors and will avoid the need to go through the bankruptcy process.[72]

A proposal to creditors may include any or all of the following:

- an offer to assign all or any of the insolvent's property to a trustee for the benefit of creditors;
- an offer to pay debts by instalments;
- an offer to compromise debts at less than 100 cents in the dollar;
- an offer to pay debts at some future time; and
- any other offer which satisfies all of the insolvent's debts.[73]

In order to accept a proposal there must be a majority in number and three quarters in value of those creditors who are present and voting. Some creditors can vote through

---

68 New Zealand Law Commission, *Priority Debts in the Distribution of Insolvent Estates: An Advisory Report to the Ministry of Commerce* (NZLC SP2, October 1999) at chapters 4, 5 and 6. Available at http://www.lawcom.govt.nz under 'Publications'.

69 See the next section of this chapter.

70 Generally, see *Laws NZ Insolvency* paras 410–426.

71 Insolvency Act 1967 s 109(2).

72 *Laws NZ Insolvency* paras 449–475.

73 Insolvency Act 1967 s 140.

representatives or by voting letter.[74] All debts which are preferential on bankruptcy must also be paid preferentially in a proposal.[75]

The court will generally approve a proposal if creditors have agreed to it and the requisite majorities have been attained. However, the court does possess a discretion to refuse the proposal which has, in some cases, been exercised on the grounds that the public interest demands a bankruptcy.[76] Once the court has approved the proposal, no creditor whose debt is provable under the proposal can take any action against the insolvent in respect of that debt while the proposal remains in force.[77]

Part XII Insolvency Act 1967: Compositions A person who has already been adjudged bankrupt can apply to the court to annul that bankruptcy if the creditors agree to a composition during the course of the bankruptcy. The composition is effected under Part XII of the Insolvency Act 1967.[78]

The court has discretion to refuse to approve a composition even though the statutory majorities have been attained at a meeting held for that purpose. Like a proposal, the requisite majorities have been attained if there is a resolution decided by a majority in number and three quarters in value of those creditors personally present and voting on the resolution. But it is clear that in respect of a composition the court can consider whether there has been any misconduct which would justify the court in refusing, qualifying or suspending a bankrupt's discharge from bankruptcy; if there was such conduct, the court could refuse to make an order annulling the bankruptcy or giving effect to the composition.[79]

Applications to approve compositions are rarely made. Generally, once a person has been adjudged bankrupt, the administration of assets will take place under the bankruptcy regime. In practice, there needs to be a compelling reason to justify the additional expense of calling meetings of creditors to have assets administered, sometimes by a private trustee, through the composition process.

Corporate Insolvency Law

Background

As a result of what is called, colloquially, the 1993 Company Law Package there has been a radical change in emphasis in company law in New Zealand. For insolvency law purposes, it is important to note that the Companies Act 1993 tends to require less court involvement than had been the case under the Companies Act 1955. Also, there are flexible mechanisms under which companies can reach binding agreements with creditors which allow for less than 100 cents in the dollar to be paid.

---

74 Ibid. s 142(3).
75 Ibid. s 143(4).
76 For competing views on the role of the court in this regard, see *Laws NZ Insolvency* para. 467.
77 Insolvency Act 1967 s 144(1)(a).
78 *Laws NZ Insolvency* paras 433–448.
79 Generally, *Laws NZ Insolvency* para. 436.

Unless stated otherwise, the High Court of New Zealand has jurisdiction to deal with insolvency issues affecting bodies corporate. Like the bankruptcy jurisdiction, powers of the High Court are exercised either by Judges or Associate Judges of the High Court. The venue for any High Court hearing will, generally, be the High Court registry closest to the registered office or principal place of business of the company.

Liquidation Provisions

The liquidation provisions are set out in Part XVI of the Companies Act 1993.

A liquidation is commenced by the appointment of a liquidator.[80] A liquidator may be appointed in one of three ways:

- by special resolution of those shareholders entitled to vote and voting on the question;
- by the Board of the company on the occurrence of an event specified in the company's constitution; or
- by the High Court on the application of the company, a director or shareholder of the company, a creditor of the company, the registrar of companies or any other entitled person.[81]

The Official Assignee can be appointed by the court to act as liquidator of a company. However, the Official Assignee may be appointed under a special resolution passed by shareholders if only he or she has exercised voting rights attaching to shares in the company which are held either by a person who has been adjudged bankrupt or by another company of which the Official Assignee is liquidator.[82]

The High Court can appoint a liquidator if:

- it is satisfied that the company is unable to pay its debts;[83]
- the company or the Board of Directors of the company has persistently or seriously failed to comply with the Companies Act 1993;[84]
- the company has failed to comply with s 10 of the Companies Act 1993;[85] or
- it is just and equitable that the company be placed in liquidation.[86]

Generally, the liquidation of a company will commence on the date on which the liquidator is appointed.[87]

---

80 Companies Act 1993 s 241(1).

81 Ibid. s 241(2).

82 Ibid. s 241(3).

83 Ibid. s 241(4)(a). A shorthand method of proving inability to pay debts is provided by the statutory demand procedure to which ss 287–291 of the Companies Act 1993 refers.

84 Ibid. s 241(4)(b).

85 Ibid. s 241(4)(c); s 10 sets out the essential requirements of a company which are that it must have a name, one or more shares, one or more shareholders having limited or unlimited liability obligations of the company and one or more directors.

86 Ibid. s 241(4).

87 Ibid. s 241(5).

Once a liquidator has been appointed a meeting of creditors is usually summoned at which the meeting can resolve to appoint a person as liquidator of the company in place of any liquidator appointed. The right to appoint a person as a replacement liquidator arises only in relation to voluntary appointments by directors or shareholders; where a liquidator has been appointed by the court, the meeting of creditors can only resolve to apply to the court for the appointment of a liquidator in place of the appointed liquidator.[88]

Once a liquidation has commenced the liquidator has custody and control of the company's assets. The directors remain in office but cease to have the powers, functions or duties previously conferred upon them. No proceedings may be commenced or continued against the company or in relation to its property and neither may any enforcement proceeding be taken in relation to property of the company unless the liquidator agrees or the High Court otherwise orders. No shares in the company can be transferred after liquidation unless the High Court orders otherwise. No alteration can be made to the rights or liabilities of shareholders of the company. The constitution of the company cannot be altered. No shareholder can exercise powers under the constitution or under the Act except for the purposes of the liquidation provisions of the Act.[89] But nothing affects the rights of a secured creditor to take possession of and realise or otherwise deal with property of the company over which that creditor has a charge.[90]

The principal duty of a liquidator is to take possession of, protect, realise and distribute the assets or the proceeds of the realisation of the assets of the company to its creditors in accordance with the provisions of the Act. Where surplus assets remain, they are to be distributed to shareholders as specified in the Act. The liquidator is to perform that duty in a reasonable and efficient manner.[91]

The liquidator also has certain duties in relation to the provision of public notice of his or her appointment, the date of commencement of the liquidation and the place to which inquiries should be directed by creditors or shareholders and in relation to the sending to known creditors and filing with the Registrar of Companies reports in relation to the affairs of the company.[92] In that regard, it is important to note that where the Official Assignee has been appointed as liquidator of the company by the court and the company has no assets available for distribution to creditors, the Official Assignee is not required to take any steps without the consent of the Minister of the Crown who is for the time being responsible for the administration of the Companies Act if to do so would, or would likely, involve the incurring of any expense.[93] But the same rules do not apply to private liquidators who can only decline to carry out duties under the Act if it is in relation to property that is subject to a charge.[94] Liquidators must have regard to the views of creditors and shareholders when performing their duties.[95]

88 Ibid. s 243(6) and (7).
89 Ibid. s 248(1).
90 Ibid. s 248(2). See also s 305.
91 Ibid. s 253.
92 Ibid. s 255.
93 Ibid. s 254(b).
94 Ibid. s 254(a); see also s 305 of the Act.
95 Ibid. s 258.

In order to carry out the functions and duties of a liquidator under the Companies Act 1993 the liquidator has all the powers necessary to carry out those functions and duties and those powers which are expressly conferred by the Act. Without limiting those powers, the liquidator does have all of the powers set out in the Sixth Schedule to the Act.[96]

Every document entered into, made or issued by a liquidator of the company must state in a prominent position that the company is in liquidation.[97]

Corporate Rescue Provisions

Under Part XIV of the Companies Act 1993 a company may enter into a compromise with its creditors. For this purpose the term 'compromise' includes any arrangement which cancels all or part of the debt of the company or varies the rights of its creditors or returns of a debt or relates to an alteration of the company's constitution which affects the likelihood of the company being able to pay a debt.[98] The term 'creditor' includes both a person who, in the liquidation, would be entitled to claim that a debt is owing and a secured creditor. The person who puts forward the proposal is known as a 'proponent'.[99]

Before a proponent can make a proposal it must have reason to believe that the company is or will be unable to pay its debts.[100] Unless the contrary is proved, a company is presumed to be unable to pay its debts if:

- it has failed to comply with a statutory demand for payment of the debt (on the basis of which a liquidation proceeding may then be issued); or
- execution has been issued against the company in respect of a judgment debt and has been returned unsatisfied in whole or in part; or
- if a person entitled to a charge over all or substantially all of the property of the company has appointed a receiver under the instrument creating the charge.[101]

A creditor or shareholder of the company may propose a compromise with the leave of the High Court. Otherwise, the proponent must be the Board of Directors of the company or a receiver appointed in relation to the whole or substantially the whole of the assets and undertaking of the company or a liquidator of the company.[102] If a compromise is to be approved by creditors or a class of creditors at a meeting, it must be passed by a majority in number representing 75 per cent in value of those creditors or class of creditors voting in person or by proxy in favour of the resolution.[103]

There are no general moratorium provisions contained in Part XIV of the Act. Indeed, there is no power whatsoever to affect the rights of secured creditors while

96 Ibid. s 260.
97 Ibid. s 259.
98 Ibid. s 227.
99 Ibid. s 227.
100 Ibid. s 228(1).
101 Ibid. s 287.
102 Ibid. s 228(1).
103 Ibid. s 230(1) and Fifth Schedule, cl 5(2).

the compromise is being considered.[104] But the High Court can make an order that proceedings in relation to any debt owing by the company be stayed or that a creditor refrain from taking any other measure to enforce payment of a debt owing to the company during a period specified in the order and beginning not earlier than the date on which notice is given of the proposed compromise and ending not later than ten working days after the date on which notice was given of the result of the voting on it.[105]

If creditors agree with the proposal, no court order is required to give effect to the compromise. But if the statutory majorities are not attained, approval from the court will be necessary. However, in no circumstances will creditors who have not been given notice of the compromise be bound by it.

If a resolution proposing a compromise is put to the vote of more than one class of creditors, it is presumed, unless the contrary is expressly stated in the resolution, that the approval of the compromise by each class is conditional on the approval of the compromise by every other class voting on the resolution.[106]

Powers are vested in the High Court to vary a compromise or to make orders in anticipation of, or on, liquidation to the extent (if any) to which the compromise will continue in effect and be binding on a liquidator.[107]

Part XV of the Companies Act 1993 was introduced after Select Committee hearings. Part XV is brief and applies to any 'arrangement', 'amalgamation' or 'compromise' with creditors affecting equity and debt investments. Part XV of the Act can be brought into play by an application to the High Court by a company or any shareholder or creditor of the company. Such an application can seek an order that 'an arrangement or amalgamation or compromise shall be binding on the company and on such other persons or classes of persons as the court may specify' and 'any such order may be made on such terms and conditions as the court thinks fit'.[108]

An application can be made under Part XV even though it may have been possible to effect the arrangement compromise or amalgamation under Parts XIII or XIV of the Act.[109]

The threshold test has already caused a divergence of views between two differently constituted divisions of the New Zealand Court of Appeal. Both cases arise out of the insolvency of *Suspended Ceilings (Wellington) Limited.*

The *Suspended Ceilings* case involved an attempt by the debtor company to impose upon a single creditor (the Commissioner of Inland Revenue) a compromise (to which the Commissioner did not agree) which would have resulted in the Commissioner reducing a debt of over $1m (which would have ranked on liquidation as a preferential debt) to a debt of approximately $400,000 with further interest or penalties being foregone. Repayment was to be made at a rate of $7,500 per month.

On its first visit to the Court of Appeal, the case involved an appeal from an Associate Judge who had held that the term 'compromise' had a limited meaning

104 Ibid. s 232(2).
105 Ibid. s 232(1).
106 Ibid. s 230(3).
107 Ibid. s 233.
108 Ibid. s 236(1).
109 Ibid. s 238.

which precluded the court from entertaining the application. The Court of Appeal disagreed with that view.[110] The effect of the Court of Appeal's decision was to permit the bringing of an application under Part XV to bind a single creditor even though that single creditor did not agree to the compromise in question. As Thomas J pointed out in the second *Suspended Ceilings* case (which went to the Court of Appeal after the Associate Judge had rejected the substantive application),[111] an interpretation that Parliament did not intend the unilateral proposal to be made was precluded by the earlier decision of the court. In the second *Suspended Ceilings* case the majority (Henry and Keith JJ) inclined to the view that an applicant should at least satisfy the court that it would be unreasonable not to make the order sought while Thomas J preferred a formula invoking concepts of equity and justice. Thomas J preferred a conclusion resting on the objective of protecting the interests of the company and the creditors involved which would lie more easily with other functions vested in the court under the Companies Act 1993 which required those interests to be safeguarded.

While the court may make an order under Part XV of the Act it is almost inconceivable that the court would impose a compromise on creditors without the statutory majorities under Part XIV being met unless the case involved so called 'tainted votes'.[112]

As a matter of practice it is usual for the debtor to approve the full terms of any reorganisation plan before the plan is put to creditors or to the court. While it is not mandatory for a company to propose an independent trustee or scheme administrator this will, usually, be done. Occasionally, there will be provision for the appointment of a committee of creditors to oversee administration of the scheme.

Priorities

Under the liquidation provisions of the Companies Act 1993, those debts to be paid in priority to unsecured debts of the company are set out in the Seventh Schedule.

Similar debts to those which are granted priority on bankruptcy are afforded priority in liquidation although there are some anomalies. The anomalies relate not only to the priority in which the debts will be paid but also to the type of debt.[113]

Statutory Management and Judicial Management

Statutory management is not a form of insolvency regime brought into action by either debtor or creditor. It is imposed upon a body corporate by Order in Council

---

110 *Suspended Ceilings (Wellington) Limited* v. *Commissioner of Inland Revenue* [1995] 3 NZLR 143 (CA).

111 *Suspended Ceilings (Wellington) Limited* v. *Commissioner of Inland Revenue* [1997] 8 NZCLC 261,318 (CA).

112 Compare *Re Farmers' Co-Operative Organisation Society of New Zealand Limited* [1992] 1 NZLR 348 with *Whiteman* v. *UDC Finance Limited* [1992] 3 NZLR 684 (CA).

113 Generally, see New Zealand Law Commission, *Priority Debts in the Distribution of Insolvent Estates: An Advisory Report to the Ministry of Commerce* (NZLC SP2, October 1999) at paras 4–7 (incl). This report is available at http://www.lawcom.govt.nz under the heading 'Publications'.

made by the Governor General on the advice of the Minister of Commerce given in accordance with a recommendation made by the Securities Commission.[114]

The Securities Commission cannot make a recommendation unless it is satisfied on reasonable grounds that it is desirable to subject the company to statutory management because it is operating fraudulently or recklessly, or for some other reason it is necessary to preserve the interests of its members or creditors. Alternatively, a recommendation can be made if it is required by the public interest or it is required to enable the affairs of the corporation to be dealt with in a more orderly or expeditious manner.[115]

A different form of statutory management is in place to deal with systemic problems caused by the insolvency of a financial institution: reference is made to the Reserve Bank of New Zealand Act 1989. Both forms of statutory management curtail absolutely the ability of creditors to enforce rights which they may otherwise have against the company in question (including rights of set-off) without leave from the court or the permission of the statutory manager.

There is a further regime known as 'judicial management' which applies to life insurance companies. The appropriate Minister of the Crown is empowered to apply to the High Court for the appointment of a judicial manager where it appears that there is a likelihood that the company is or will be unable to meet any of its liabilities to policyholders. A moratorium is imposed upon proceedings against the company together with a prohibition against removal of its assets.[116]

Judicial management is, as its name suggests, invoked by judicial decision rather than by executive order as is the case under the Corporations (Investigation and Management) Act 1989 or the Reserve Bank of New Zealand Act 1989. The latter Act applies only to banks registered under that Act.

Role of Insolvency Practitioners

Both the Official Assignee and private insolvency practitioners have a role to play in corporate insolvencies.

There is no regulatory or licensing framework for insolvency practitioners in New Zealand. However, there are restrictions upon appointment as a liquidator.[117] Generally, as long as the proposed liquidator is a natural person, is more than 18 years old, has no conflict of interest and is not otherwise barred from being a director or involved in the management of a company, that person can be appointed as a liquidator. Similar provisions apply to the appointment of receivers under the provisions of a floating charge and to receivers appointed by the court or under some other form of security.[118]

---

114 Corporations (Investigation and Management) Act 1989 s 38.

115 Ibid. s 39. See also *McDonald* v. *Australian Guarantee Corporation (NZ) Limited* [1990] 1 NZLR 227.

116 Life Insurance Act 1908 ss 40A(2), 40B and 40C.

117 Companies Act 1993 s 280.

118 Receiverships Act 1993 s 5.

Role of the Court

As with the administration of bankruptcy, the court has, by and large, an adjudicatory function. There is a power for the liquidator to apply for directions.[119]

There is also a more general supervisory jurisdiction over liquidators vested in the High Court.[120]

Termination of Insolvency Procedure

In the case of a bankruptcy of an individual, termination of the procedure is brought about by an order for discharge, although the assets which are vested in the Official Assignee remain for distribution among creditors.

In a company situation, the liquidation can be terminated by order of the court if circumstances justify that course of action.[121] The court must be satisfied it is just and equitable to terminate a liquidation. Where an application is made to terminate a liquidation, the liquidator must, if required by the court, furnish a report to the court with respect to any fact or matters relevant to the application.[122]

Antecedent Transactions

Antecedent transactions which are capable of attack on company liquidation are similar to those in bankruptcy except that the provisions for the voidable gifts do not apply and the test for voidable transactions (compared with voidable preferences under the bankruptcy legislation) is premised upon 'preferential effect' rather than an 'intention to prefer'.[123] Procedures to avoid charges are also contained in the 1993 Act.[124] Furthermore, it is possible to obtain orders for the pooling of assets of related companies or for contributions to be made by one company to the other where the companies are related.[125] Also, there are more general provisions to set aside securities involving related parties[126] and to enable recovery of transactions which have occurred for inadequate consideration.[127]

In the case of a voidable transaction the time limit is a period of two years before the commencement of the liquidation, but there is a restricted period in which the onus of proof on questions of solvency and whether the transaction was in the ordinary course of business is reversed.[128]

---

119 Companies Act 1993 s 284(1)(a).
120 Ibid. s 284.
121 Ibid. s 250.
122 Ibid. s 250(3).
123 Ibid. s 292.
124 Ibid. s 283.
125 Ibid. s 271.
126 Ibid. s 299.
127 Ibid. ss 297 and 298.
128 Ibid. s 292(2), (5) and (6).

Offences and Director Liability

Director Liability

In the case of corporate reorganisations it will remain open to the scheme managers, suing through the company, to take action against directors for breaches of duties owed by directors to the company. In liquidation proceedings the liquidator can take action for pre-existing breaches of duties by directors through the summary remedy provided by s 301 of the Companies Act 1993.

The Companies Act 1993 aims to specify in greater detail the types of duties owed by directors to companies. However, the legislation falls short of a codification of directors' duties and (to the extent that enacted duties are not co-extensive with duties at common law or in equity) it will still be possible to sue directors for duties which they owed to the company at common law or in equity.[129]

It is doubtful whether causes of action available only upon liquidation could be maintained by the company through scheme managers if liquidation has not occurred. Specifically, the ability of a liquidator to sue officers of the company for failure to keep accounting records only arises in a liquidation.[130] However, it appears to be reasonably clear that breaches of duties set out in the Companies Act 1993[131] would be actionable by the company or by a liquidator. Those duties include:

- the duty to act in good faith and in the best interests of the company;[132]
- the exercise of powers in relation to employees;[133]
- the requirement to exercise powers for proper purposes;[134]
- the need to comply with the Companies Act and the constitution of the company;[135]
- the requirement not to trade in a reckless manner;[136] and
- the duty to take reasonable care.[137]

---

129 This appears to be the effect of the incorporation into the liquidation provisions of the Companies Act 1993 (s 301) of the former s 321 Companies Act 1955: *Benton* v. *Priore* [2003] 1NZLR 564. In *Grayburn* v. *Laing* [1991] 1 NZLR 482 at 491 Gallen J held that the words 'guilty of any negligence default or breach of duty or trust in relation to the company' as used in s 321 of the 1955 Act (and as continued to be used in s 301 of the 1993 Act) were co-extensive with duties owed to the company at common law or in equity.

130 Companies Act 1993, s.300.

131 Ibid. ss 131–138.

132 Ibid. s 131.

133 Ibid. s 132.

134 Ibid. s 133.

135 Ibid. s 134.

136 Ibid. s 135.

137 Ibid. s 137.

Disqualification Provisions

Both the Registrar of Companies and the High Court have powers in relation to the disqualification of directors.[138] The Registrar's ability to prohibit people from being involved in the management of the company is, as one would expect, more circumscribed than is the power of the court and relates to circumstances in which a director has been involved in companies which have been placed in liquidation or have otherwise not met their obligations in full.[139] Procedures are set out in the statute to ensure that the principles of natural justice apply.[140]

Criminal Offences

There are also criminal sanctions for breach of certain obligations by directors under the Companies Act 1993 and otherwise. Offences and penalties are provided for under the Companies Act 1993.[141] Directors can be made liable for certain environmental damage.[142] Directors may also be liable under occupational health and safety legislation.[143] They will also be personally liable for some taxation debts if the company cannot pay.[144]

Cross-border Insolvency

Personal Insolvencies

In all matters of bankruptcy, the High Court must act in aid of and be auxiliary to any court of any Commonwealth country other than New Zealand which has jurisdiction in bankruptcy. An order of a Commonwealth Court requesting aid is sufficient to enable the High Court to exercise such powers in regard to the matters specified in the order as the Court may have exercised in respect of the matter had it arisen within its own jurisdiction.[145] Further, if it thinks fit, the High Court may also exercise these powers at the request of a court in any country that is not a Commonwealth country. It would appear that in deciding whether to exercise that discretion, the Court should take into account the nature of the insolvency regime intended to be enforced and any relevant matters of public policy.[146]

---

138 Ibid. ss 383 and 385.

139 Ibid. s 385.

140 Ibid. s 385.

141 Ibid. ss 373–386.

142 Resource Management Act 1991 s 340(3). See also *Laws NZ Resource Management* paras 295 and 299.

143 Health and Safety in Employment Act 1992 ss 49 and 50.

144 For example, Income Tax Act 1994, s HK 11(3) and (4).

145 Insolvency Act 1967 s 135(1).

146 Ibid. s 135(2). Compare *Re Bank of Credit and Commerce International SA* [1993] BCC787 and *Re Dallhold Estates (UK) Pty Ltd* [1992] BCC 394.

A New Zealand Court is not likely to limit the phrase 'jurisdiction and bankruptcy' to jurisdiction of an identical scope to that administered in New Zealand. Rather, the term 'bankruptcy' is likely to be interpreted as a class of judicial or administrative process dealing with insolvent persons as opposed to the personal condition of the insolvency.[147]

Although the power to act in aid of and be auxiliary to a request from a court of a Commonwealth country is expressed through the use of the word 'may', it is likely that this provision will be interpreted as a mandatory requirement given that the comparable Australian statute has been similarly interpreted.[148]

The doctrine of relation back does not apply with regard to a foreign bankruptcy; similarly, a foreign country's doctrine of relation back will not apply with regard to a bankruptcy in New Zealand.[149]

Corporate Insolvencies

New Zealand courts have not yet had to grapple with difficulties arising out of the placement of a company into some form of insolvency administration by a foreign court; particularly when that order is designed to facilitate rescue of a corporation which has assets in New Zealand. It is likely that in approaching any such issue New Zealand courts will have regard to established principles of private international law; in that regard a company is deemed to be domiciled in the country under whose law it is incorporated.[150]

Unlike the Insolvency Act 1967 (which expressly takes companies outside of the scope of the Insolvency Act 1967[151]) the Companies Act 1993 does not include any provision giving power to the High Court to act in aid of and be auxiliary to any overseas court which has jurisdiction in bankruptcy matters. However, the 1993 Act does give an express power to the High Court to entertain an application for the liquidation of the assets in New Zealand of an overseas company in accordance with the liquidation provisions of the Companies Act 1993 but subject to modifications and exclusions set out in the Ninth Schedule to the Act.[152] Further, with regard to a

---

147 See *Re Bolton* [1920] 2 IR 324 and *Re A Debtor Ex Parte Viscount of the Royal Court of Jersey* [1980] 3 ALL ER 665.

148 Compare *Ayres* v. *Evans* (1981) 39 ALR 129 (Full Court of the Federal Court of Australia) with *Re Beadle* (High Court Auckland B116/80, 1 September 1980, Barker J). Query whether public policy would require aid to be declined if the sole purpose of seeking aid was to enforce a foreign revenue claim: see generally *Government of India* v. *Taylor* [1955] AC491 and *Peter Buchanan Ltd* v. *McVey* [1955] AC516n. Note that in *Ayres* v. *Evans* (1981) 39 ALR 129 the Federal Court of Australia granted a request for aid from the High Court of New Zealand in a case where the indirect consequence of that was the indirect enforcement of significant revenue claims of New Zealand. See also *Re Tucker Ex Parte Bird* [1988] LRD (Comm) 995.

149 *Galbraith* v. *Grimshaw* [1910] AC508 at 510 and 511. See also *Re Beadle (No.2)* (High Court Auckland B 116/80, 14 June 1982, Vautier J).

150 *Dicey and Morris's Conflict of Laws* (12th Edition and 1994 Supplement), Rule 154 at page 1103. See also Brown, David, *Corporate Rescue: Insolvency Law in Practice* (John Wiley & Sons, 1996) at 723.

151 Insolvency Act 1967 s 168.

152 Companies Act 1993 s 342(1) read in conjunction with the Ninth Schedule.

foreign company on the overseas register in New Zealand, it may be possible to get an order to assist a foreign administrator under Part XV of the Companies Act 1993.[153]

In relation to corporate insolvencies, it is likely that New Zealand courts will apply established rules of comity.[154] Nevertheless, the absence of a provision akin to the bankruptcy order in aid procedure leaves a lacuna in existing New Zealand law.

Future Developments

The New Zealand Law Commission recommended in February 1999 that New Zealand adopt the UNCITRAL Model Law on Cross-Border Insolvency.[155] In coming to that conclusion, the Commission emphasised the increasing need to develop laws which are effective in the global market of which New Zealand is part while noting that the Model Law's option of deference to a local proceeding was a political necessity accepted to accommodate concerns about potentially over-intrusive foreign proceedings dominating local insolvency systems. Reference was also made to the fiscal need for such legislation, for example, the likely reduction of transaction costs and promotion of trade and capital flows, thereby improving the economic well-being of the New Zealand economy. The ability to deal more effectively with cross-border fraud perpetrated by electronic means was also considered.[156]

---

153 Ibid. s 235, definition of 'company'.

154 Generally, see *Hilton* v. *Guyot* 59 US 113 (1895) (Supreme Court of USA) as applied in New Zealand in *Fournier* v. *The Ship 'Margaret Z'* [1997] 1 NZLR 629 and *Turners & Growers Exporters Limited* v. *The Ship 'Cornelis Verolme'* [1998] 2 NZLR 110.

155 New Zealand Law Commission, *Cross-Border Insolvency: Should New Zealand Adopt the UNCITRAL Model Law on Cross-Border Insolvency?* (NZLC R52, February 1999); available at http://www.lawcom.govt.nz under the heading 'Publications'.

156 Ibid. para. 112.

Chapter 15

Insolvency Law in Australia

ROSALIND MASON
University of Southern Queensland

1 Introduction

1.1 Introduction to the Australian Legal System

The Australian legal system derives from the UK with relatively recent recognition of a place for Aboriginal customary law. Australia is a common law country and so the sources of law include both general (judge-made) law and statute. It is a federation with law-making power distributed between the Commonwealth (federal Parliament) and six states and two internal self-governing territories.[1]

Upon European settlement in 1788, the continent was regarded, as a matter of law, as a settled not conquered or ceded colony, and so English law was the received law of the land. During the 19th century, although the UK retained certain law-making power,[2] the colonies gradually developed their own legislatures and court systems. Eventually six colonies were established, each with a Constitution granting plenary power to make laws for the peace, order and good government of their relevant jurisdictions. They joined together as a federation on 1 January 1901 with the Commonwealth Parliament being granted specific powers under the Commonwealth Constitution. The states' plenary powers continue to the extent they are not overridden by the Commonwealth Constitution. Where the Commonwealth and the states exercise concurrent legislative powers, then Commonwealth legislation overrides to the extent of any inconsistency.[3]

The Australian legal culture bears many similarities to other common law jurisdictions. There are well-established court systems at federal, state and territory levels with a well-established independent legal profession from whom judges are drawn. The federal system of government means that there are federal and state

1 The internal territories are the Northern Territory and the Australian Capital Territory. The external territories, Cocos (Keeling) Islands, Christmas Island and Norfolk Island, are not dealt with in this chapter.

2 Both the UK's power to pass paramount force legislation and the right of appeal from Australian courts to the Judicial Committee of the Privy Council ceased at different stages for the Commonwealth and the States. An important final step was the Australia Act 1986 (Cth) and its complementary UK and state legislation.

3 Section 109 Commonwealth Constitution.

court hierarchies, exercising federal and state jurisdiction. Cross-vesting legislation permits limited cross-vesting of jurisdiction.[4]

Australians' attitude towards debt appears to have undergone a change since World War II. The amount of consumer debt, for example, has increased markedly over the past four decades.[5] While debt enforcement through the enforcement of judgments against debtors' assets is taken seriously, some avenues for the amelioration of debt recovery in respect of consumer credit have been introduced in the Consumer Credit Code.[6]

Another change in attitude is evident in the change in focus from the liquidation of the debtor's assets for prompt distribution among creditors to insolvency administrations which aim at resolving creditors' claims without resorting to liquidation, particularly where this may permit continuation of the debtor's business. This reflects a movement from the traditional pro-creditor stance to a more debtor-oriented approach to debt enforcement.

1.2 History, Sources and Philosophy

Australian insolvency laws have their origin in English bankruptcy and corporate insolvency law. However, as early as 1823,[7] legislation was passed for the colony of New South Wales and Van Diemens Land (Tasmania) to provide relief for insolvent debtors and in 1841,[8] provision was made for debtors resident in the colony to assign their estate and effects to trustees for the benefit of all their creditors.[9] Later in the same year,[10] New South Wales introduced a collective bankruptcy administration. By the end of the century, all colonial bankruptcy legislation[11] was substantially based on the English Bankruptcy Acts of 1869 and 1883.[12]

---

4 Jurisdiction of Courts (Cross-vesting) Acts 1987 and Corporations Acts 1990, as interpreted in *Re Wakim ex p. McNally* (1999) 163 ALR 270; 31 ACSR 99, allow grants of jurisdiction which include Federal Court to Supreme Courts, and state, internal territory and external territory Supreme Courts to Supreme Courts. (For further details, see R. Mortensen (1999), *Private International Law*, Butterworths, Sydney, pp. 34 – 40.)

5 *Reserve Bank of Australia Bulletins*. For a comparison between bankruptcy rates and consumer credit through personal loans, see J. Kumar, R. Mason and D. Ralston, 'Consumer Bankruptcies: Causes and Implications for the Credit Industry' (1998) 17 (3) *Economic Papers* 18, 23.

6 Sections 66 and 70 Consumer Credit Code (Consumer Credit (Queensland) Act 1994 (Qld). See R. Mason, 'Consumer Bankruptcies: An Australian Perspective' (1999) 37 *Osgoode Hall Law Journal* 449.

7 4 George IV c. 96 s 22 (1823). There were numerous similar acts passed to relieve honest debtors in respect of execution of debts which they were unable to pay and to discharge them from imprisonment following disclosure and seizure of their estate: 2 William IV No. 11 (1832); 5 William IV No. 4 (1834); 6 William IV No. 18 (1836); 2 Victoria No. 14 (1838); 4 Victoria No. 24 (1840).

8 5 Victoria No. 9 (1841) s 33.

9 Imprisonment for debt was finally abolished in 1843: 7 Victoria No. 19 (1843) s 26.

10 The Insolvency Act 1841 (5 Victoria No. 17) provided for the appointment of Commissioners of Insolvent Estates.

11 Bankruptcy Act 1898 (NSW); Insolvency Act 1915 (Vic); Insolvency Act 1876 (Qld); Bankruptcy Act 1892 (WA); Insolvency Act 1886 (SA); Bankruptcy Act 1870 (Tas).

12 The Bankruptcy Act, 1869 (32 & 33 Victoria c. 71) and Bankruptcy Act 1883 (46 & 47 Victoria c. 52).

Upon federation, constitutional power to legislate with respect to 'bankruptcy and insolvency' was conferred on the Commonwealth.[13] It first exercised this power with the enactment of the Bankruptcy Act 1924 (Cth) and subsequently with the current Bankruptcy Act 1966 (Cth). This has undergone substantial amendment since its commencement in 1968.

The development of the law of corporate insolvency is closely connected to the evolution of corporations, in particular the concept of limited liability and the extension of corporate personality to joint-stock companies.[14] It is also related to the law of personal insolvency in that bankruptcy concepts have consistently been included in corporate insolvency legislation, although in recent years there has been an increasing divergence between the two.[15]

Although each of the colonies introduced their own companies acts at various times, by the end of the 19th century all had adopted legislation based on the English Companies Act 1862.[16] Following federation, the Commonwealth Parliament was granted power to make laws with respect to 'foreign corporations, and trading or financial corporations formed within the limits of the Commonwealth'.[17] Nevertheless the federal Parliament did not exercise its general powers in this regard and so state companies legislation continued to apply.

Attempts at standardisation of corporate regulation were made when the Australian states each passed largely uniform legislation, first in the Companies Code of 1961 and then in the Companies Act of 1981. The first attempt at the Commonwealth passing a national Corporations Law 1989 was successfully challenged on constitutional grounds in *The State of New South Wales* v. *The Commonwealth of Australia*.[18] The High Court held that the Commonwealth had no power to legislate on the act of incorporation itself, rather only in respect of trading and financial corporations already formed within the Commonwealth. To overcome this problem, each state and internal territory passed its own Corporations Act with a uniform Corporations Law as a schedule thereto.[19] The Corporations Law commenced operation in 1991, with the insolvency provisions being significantly amended in 1993.

In 1999 the cross-vesting scheme between state and federal courts, which was an intrinsic part of the cooperative scheme, was held by the High Court to be constitutionally invalid in so far as it attempted to cross-vest state jurisdiction in the federal courts.[20] Soon afterwards another High Court decision[21] raised concerns

---

13 Section 51(xvii) Commonwealth Constitution.

14 A. Keay (1999), *McPherson, The Law of Company Liquidation*, 4th edn, LBC Information Services, Sydney, pp. 11–12.

15 A. Keay (1999), 'The Unity of Insolvency Legislation: Time for a Re-think?' 7 *Insolvency Law Journal* 4.

16 25 & 26 Vict c 89.

17 Section 51(xx) Commonwealth Constitution. Also relevant is the trade and commerce power in s 51(i) Commonwealth Constitution.

18 (1990) 169 CLR 482.

19 For more details on Australian company law, see K. Whitford, 'Corporations Law in Australia', in R. Tomasic (ed.) (1999), *Company Law in East Asia*, Ashgate, Dartmouth.

20 *Re Wakim: Ex parte McNally* (1999) 163 ALR 270.

21 *R* v. *Hughes* (2000) 171 ALR 155.

about the continued viability of the cooperative scheme in so far as it involved Commonwealth officers and authorities[22] performing functions conferred under state law. After a period of significant uncertainty that was adversely affecting national commerce and foreign investment, agreement was finally reached between the various governments to put national corporations' regulation on a firmer constitutional foundation. Through state referral powers to the Commonwealth,[23] comprehensive federal legislation was passed in the form of the Corporations Act 2001 (Cth) and Australian Securities and Investments Commission Act 2001 (Cth).[24]

Thus Australian insolvency law is primarily found in the federal Bankruptcy Act 1966 (Cth) for personal insolvency and the Corporations Act 2001 (Cth) for corporate insolvency law. Another source is case law on these statutes. For personal bankruptcy, the federal court system is the essential source of case law.[25] In the corporate arena, relevant case authorities derive from the state and territory Supreme Courts, as well as the federal system. Case law is also relevant to corporate receiverships, which administrations largely derive from judge-made law with some legislative measures. There are also numerous other laws which may interact with insolvency law and affect the outcome of insolvency administrations, for example contract law, property and security law and family law; however, these are not dealt with in this chapter.

There is no stated underlying philosophy of insolvency laws in Australia. Perhaps it can best be seen as a regulatory system which seeks to balance the competing interests of debtors, creditors and the community.[26]

1.3 Key Insolvency Law Principles

In the 1980s, the Australian Law Reform Commission[27] conducted a wide-ranging General Insolvency Inquiry which resulted in a report generally known as the Harmer Report. During its investigations, the Commission identified the certain principles which it considered should guide the development of modern insolvency law in general and its specific recommendations in particular.

---

22 For example, the Australian Securities and Investment Commission.

23 Section 51 (xxxvii) Commonwealth Constitution.

24 The states agreed to refer powers to the Commonwealth to enact the Corporations Bill 2001 and the Australian Securities and Investments Commission Bill 2001 in so far as they contained matters that are included in the legislative competence of the states. They also referred power to make express amendments to the Corporations Act or the ASIC Act in relation to the formation, corporate regulation and the regulation of financial products and services. The references last for five years but may be terminated earlier or may be extended by proclamation.

25 Yet in *Sutherland* v. *Brien* [1999] NSWSC 155; 149 FLR 321 the New South Wales Supreme Court exercised jurisdiction to determine claims to a fund held in a trust account, even though the legal issue for determination required construction and application of s 120 Bankruptcy Act.

26 Report of the Insolvency Law Review Committee, *Insolvency Law & Practice*, Cmnd. 8558 (UK) para. 182. Australian law and practice likewise reflect this. For a discussion of principles of corporate insolvency law, see R. Tomasic and K. Whitford (1997), *Australian Insolvency and Bankruptcy Law*, 2nd edn, Butterworths, Sydney, chapter 1.

27 http://www.alrc.gov.au/.

The Harmer Report states that the 'fundamental purpose of an insolvency law is to provide a fair and orderly process for dealing with the financial affairs of insolvent individuals and companies'.[28]

Concepts of a 'fair' process include participation by both debtor and creditors; identification of property which 'should' be divisible among creditors; that there be equal sharing between (like) creditors; and that the individual insolvent eventually be discharged from (most) financial liabilities and obligations.

'Orderliness' is reflected in the aims of participation by debtors and creditors with the least possible delay and expense and of impartial, efficient and expeditious insolvency administrations. There should also be a convenient means of collecting or recovering divisible property. Insolvency law should, so far as it is convenient and practical, support the commercial and economic processes of the community. As far as possible and practical, it should also harmonise with the general law. Where there is a cross-border insolvency, then insolvency law should enable ancillary assistance in the administration of an insolvency originating in a foreign jurisdiction.

In June 2004, the Parliamentary Joint Committee on Corporations and Financial Services[29] released its report, *Corporate Insolvency Laws: a Stocktake*, following an enquiry into the operation of Australia's corporate insolvency laws. In the Committee's view, the foremost objective of an insolvency regime is 'to promote and maximise trust and confidence in the operation of insolvency law on the part of the community in general and the business and corporate sector in particular'.[30]

1.4 Statutory, Regulatory and Judicial Approach

Australia's bifurcated approach to regulation of personal insolvency and corporate insolvency is reflected not only in its legislation and court systems but also in the relevant regulatory bodies and the fact that different federal government departments have responsibility for policy and law reform. The regulatory body for personal insolvency is the Insolvency and Trustee Service Australia (ITSA), and for corporate insolvency, the Australian Securities and Investments Commission (ASIC). Ministerial responsibility for personal bankruptcy is vested in the Attorney-General and the Minister for Justice, with ITSA located within the Attorney-General's Department.[31] The Minister responsible for corporate governance policy, including corporate insolvency, is the Treasurer.[32]

28 Australian Law Reform Commission 1988, *Report No. 45: General Insolvency Inquiry*, vol. 1, Australian Government Publishing Service, Canberra, Paragraph 33 (Harmer Report).

29 The Parliamentary Joint Committee on Corporations and Financial Services was established under the corporations legislation with duties that include inquiring into and reporting on the operation of the corporations legislation as well as into any question in connection with its duties that is referred to it by a House of the Parliament: s 243 Australian Securities and Investments Commission Act 2001 (Cth).

30 http://www.aph.gov.au/senate/committee/corporations_ctte/ail/report/ail.pdf at p. xxix.

31 http://www.itsa.gov.au.

32 http://www.treasury.gov.au/ The aim of the government's Corporate Law Economic Reform Programme (CLERP) is to bring a stronger economic focus to corporate law and regulation.

The statutory approach to personal bankruptcy law has been one of increasing regulation in an attempt to clip the wings of 'high-flying' debtors whose financial misfortunes do not necessarily affect their lifestyle[33] while introducing measures such as debt agreements in response to the increase in estates with relatively few assets and liabilities.[34] There has also been a move towards 'streamlining' the administrative dimension to bankruptcy.[35]

The Insolvency and Trustee Service Australia (ITSA) regulates bankruptcy matters within Australia. Not only does it advise government on policy and law reform but it also regulates trustees and administers the vast majority of bankruptcy estates. The Official Trustee, through the Official Receivers, administers approximately 90 per cent of bankruptcies.[36] Private sector registered trustees or debt agreement administrators administer the remaining bankruptcies as well as Part X arrangements and Part IX debt agreements between debtors and their creditors.

As bankruptcy is a federal matter, one court system deals with bankruptcy matters. The Federal Court and Federal Magistrates Court have exclusive jurisdiction under the Bankruptcy Act. The judicial approach is a purposive approach to statutory interpretation (as for corporate insolvency law discussed below).

The statutory approach to corporate insolvency law is uniform throughout Australia with commencement of the Corporations Act 2001. The Corporations Act has been undergoing significant reform in recent years as part of the government's Corporate Law Simplification and subsequent Company Law Economic Reform Programme (CLERP) agendas. This has only affected corporate insolvency law in a minor way as the last substantial reform was introduced in 1993. The Parliamentary Joint Committee has recommended reform of corporate insolvency laws.[37]

The regulatory authority appointed in respect of corporate insolvency matters is the Australian Securities and Investments Commission (ASIC). Its relevant responsibilities include the maintenance of company records, the receipt of reports from insolvency administrators and the registration of company liquidators. It also has power to conduct investigations where it has reason to suspect that there may be relevant breaches of the Corporations Act.[38]

The judicial approach to corporate insolvency law is the same as that for any legislation; that is, the purposive approach is adopted.[39] A first instance judge deciding a matter under the Corporations Act 2001 which creates a national scheme

---

33 For example, the Bankruptcy Act Amendment Act 1991 (Cth), which largely commenced from 1 July 1992, granted trustees wider investigative and recovery powers and introduced a stricter income contribution scheme during bankruptcy.

34 Part IX Bankruptcy Act 1966 (Cth) introduced in 1996.

35 The Bankruptcy Legislation Amendment Act 1996 (Cth) abolished the office of Registrar of Bankruptcy within the Federal Court and permitted debtors' petitions to be presented to the Official Receiver, who is also the trustee for the majority of estates.

36 Inspector-General in Bankruptcy 2004, *Annual Report on the Operation of the Bankruptcy Act 2003–2004*, p. 7.

37 See note 29 of this chapter.

38 Section 13 Australian Securities and Investments Commission Act 2001 (Cth).

39 Section 15AA Acts Interpretation Act 1901 (Cth). This is mirrored in state acts.

of regulation will follow the decision of a court exercising coordinate jurisdiction, unless plainly wrong.[40]

2 Personal Insolvency Laws

2.1 Introduction

Australia's personal insolvency laws are essentially contained in the Bankruptcy Act 1966 (Cth). Despite its title, the Act provides not only for bankruptcy or sequestration of personal debtors' estates, but also for arrangements into which debtors may enter with their creditors to compromise or discharge their liabilities outside bankruptcy. Where a creditor has obtained a judgment against a debtor, then the usual provisions for enforcement of a judgment debt may apply, such as the garnishee of a debtor's wages or execution against a debtor's assets; however, these are individual creditor remedies and this chapter concentrates on collective administrations.

Over the past 15 years, there has been a marked increase in the number of bankruptcies in Australia. A slight decline since the peak in 1998–1999 has been offset by an increase in Part IX debt agreements; and recent changes to Part X arrangements may also affect the number of bankruptcies. By far the greatest increase has been in the number of consumer, as opposed to business-related, bankruptcies. In 2004–2005 there were approximately four times as many consumer bankruptcies as business-related administrations. There has also been a marked increase in the proportion of voluntary debtor-initiated administrations. In 2004–2005, 94 per cent of the total of 20,501 bankruptcies arose from debtors' petitions and 6 per cent were based on creditors' petitions.[41]

2.2 Regulatory Structures

Voluntary bankruptcy petitions are presented to the Official Receivers and creditors' involuntary petitions are presented to the Federal Court or the Federal Magistrates Court[42] for determination on the granting of a sequestration order. These courts may also determine disputes that arise during the course of bankruptcy and insolvency administrations. A trustee's administration of a bankruptcy may be supervised by the Court and/or by creditors.[43]

---

40 *Gebo Investments (Laburn) Ltd* v. *Signatory Investments Pty Ltd* [2005] NSWSC 544 at [24] per Barrett J referring to a decision of the Supreme Court of Queensland.

41 Inspector-General in Bankruptcy 2004, *Annual Report on the Operation of the Bankruptcy Act 2003–2004*, p. 7.

42 Sections 30–31 Bankruptcy Act 1966 (Cth). Registrars may exercise delegated judicial power to make sequestration orders.

43 Sections 134, 178–179 Bankruptcy Act 1966 (Cth). Also, the Inspector-General in Bankruptcy may takes steps to have a private trustee's registration terminated: ss 155H–J Bankruptcy Act 1966 (Cth).

The Inspector-General in Bankruptcy[44] has the general administration of the Bankruptcy Act and other powers and functions conferred by the Act.[45] For example, the Inspector-General may make such inquiries and investigations as he or she thinks fit with respect to the administration of, or conduct of a trustee in relation to, bankruptcy and insolvency administrations under the Act.[46]

2.3 Principal Institutions

Of primary importance to the application of the bankruptcy and insolvency laws are the courts. The Federal Court and the Federal Magistrates Court have exclusive jurisdiction 'in bankruptcy' which is defined broadly.[47] Even though their jurisdiction is 'exclusive of the jurisdiction of all courts other than (a) the jurisdiction of the High Court under s 75 of the Constitution or (b) the jurisdiction of the Family Court under section 35 or 35A', bankruptcy matters may still arise in other courts.[48]

In appropriate cases the Supreme Courts of the States and the Northern Territory may be able to deal with bankruptcy matters under the Jurisdiction of Courts (Cross-Vesting) Act 1987.[49] Trustees may take action in Magistrates Courts, District or County Courts or Supreme Courts as courts of competent jurisdiction for the recovery of debts from bankrupts and other persons.[50] In addition, a State or Territory Court of summary jurisdiction may try summarily a bankruptcy offence that is punishable by fine only.[51] The Family Court has jurisdiction in bankruptcy where a trustee is a party to property settlement or spousal maintenance proceedings[52] as well as jurisdiction to hear matters transferred to it by the Federal Court or the Federal Magistrates Court.[53]

Upon a sequestration order being made, the property of a bankrupt vests in a trustee in bankruptcy to be administered in accordance with the Bankruptcy Act. That trustee may be either a (private sector) registered trustee or the Official Trustee. Registered trustees are individuals with the prescribed qualifications, experience, knowledge and abilities necessary to obtain registration from the Inspector-General.[54]

---

44 Appointment by the Attorney-General: Section 16 Bankruptcy Act 1966 (Cth).

45 Section 12 Bankruptcy Act 1966 (Cth). For example, the Inspector-General is responsible for the operation of the National Personal Insolvency Index: Bankruptcy Regulation 13.

46 Section 12(1)(b) Bankruptcy Act 1966 (Cth).

47 Section 27(1) Bankruptcy Act 1966 (Cth). Also see *Forshaw* v. *Thompson* (1992) 35 FCR 329 at 334 per Lockhart J.

48 *Sutherland* v. *Brien* [1999] NSWSC 155; 149 FLR 321 where Austin J (NSW Supreme Court) exercised jurisdiction to determine claims to a fund held in a trust account, even though the legal issue for determination required construction and application of s 120 Bankruptcy Act.

49 Explanatory Memorandum to Bankruptcy Legislation Amendment Bill 1996, paragraph 81.

50 Actions pursuant to s 139ZG, ss 139ZL(10), 139ZQ(8) and 161B(2) Bankruptcy Act 1966 (Cth).

51 Section 273 Bankruptcy Act 1966 (Cth); *R* v. *Ward* (1978) 140 CLR 584.

52 Section 35 Bankruptcy Act 1966 (Cth).

53 Section 35A(3) Bankruptcy Act 1966 (Cth).

54 Applications are made to the Inspector-General for determination by a Committee comprising the Inspector-General, an officer of the Department and a registered trustee chosen by the Insolvency Practitioners Association of Australia: s 155(2) Bankruptcy Act 1966 (Cth). Bankruptcy Regulation 8.02(1) prescribes the necessary qualifications, experience, knowledge and abilities for registration.

A registered trustee who has consented to act[55] may be appointed when the sequestration order is made or subsequently during the bankruptcy administration.[56]

The Official Trustee is the trustee of any estate for which a registered trustee has not consented to act or in which, at any time, there is no registered trustee.[57] The Official Trustee is a body corporate[58] which acts through the Official Receiver for the relevant Bankruptcy District when it is a trustee of an estate.[59] Currently each state and internal territory comprises a Bankruptcy District.[60]

2.4 Powers of the Courts

Petitions for voluntary bankruptcy are presented to the Official Receiver so that the court's role is limited at the time of initiation of proceedings. The Official Receiver must seek court directions if there is a creditor's petition pending against a group of debtors that includes the debtor against whom the debtor's petition is presented.[61] Otherwise the Official Receiver should not refer a petition to the court for its consideration.[62]

Creditors' petitions are determined by the court, with a Registrar exercising judge-delegated power.[63] Even where a creditor proves the necessary elements for a sequestration order,[64] the court has a discretion whether to make the order.[65] The court may adjourn or dismiss the petition. The creditor may also seek leave to withdraw the petition, although the court considers the interests of all creditors.[66]

2.5 Duties of Bankruptcy Practitioners

The duties of a trustee in bankruptcy derive both from statute as well as general law. The Bankruptcy Act[67] contains a non-exhaustive list of duties as follows:

---

55 Section 156A Bankruptcy Act 1966 (Cth).

56 Section 157 Bankruptcy Act 1966 (Cth).

57 Section 160 Bankruptcy Act 1966 (Cth).

58 Section 18 Bankruptcy Act 1966 (Cth).

59 Section 18(8) Bankruptcy Act 1966 (Cth). Officers may assist the Official Receiver in the performance of such functions: s 15 Bankruptcy Act 1966 (Cth).

60 *Commonwealth of Australia Gazette* No. GN 38, 29 September 1993. Section 5AA Bankruptcy Act 1966 (Cth) identifies the place of origin of bankruptcy and insolvency matters.

61 Section 55(3B) Bankruptcy Act 1966 (Cth). This applies whether the group are joint debtors or members of a partnership.

62 *Official Receiver* v. *Walia* (1997) 79 FCR 299. If a debtor's petition complies with the requirements of s 55(2) and is not the subject of a reference under s 55(3B) the debtor is entitled to be made a bankrupt and no question can arise that requires the consideration of the court. If the presentation of the petition is an abuse of process the court has power to annul the bankruptcy under s 153B Bankruptcy Act 1966 (Cth).

63 Order 77 rule 7 Federal Court Rules; Rule 20.00A Federal Magistrates Court Rules.

64 Section 52 Bankruptcy Act 1966 (Cth).

65 For example, it may be established that the debtor can pay the petitioning creditor's debt but chooses not to. *Sarina* v. *Council of the Shire of Wollondilly* (1980) 48 FLR 372. This reflects the significance a sequestration order has for a debtor's status: *Russell* v. *ANZ Banking Group Ltd* (1987) 14 FCR 72 at 75.

66 Section 47 Bankruptcy Act 1966 (Cth); *Re Hood* [1971] ALR 151.

67 Section 19 Bankruptcy Act 1966 (Cth).

- A trustee is to determine whether there is any realisable property or any property available because of voidable transactions and take appropriate steps to recover it.
- The trustee is to notify creditors of the bankruptcy, report to creditors within three months of the date of bankruptcy on the likelihood of a dividend and provide information to creditors upon reasonable request.
- The trustee is to take whatever action is practicable to ensure that the bankrupt discharges all his or her duties under the Act.
- A trustee is also to consider whether the bankrupt has committed any offences against the Act and, if so, refer any evidence of such offence to the relevant law enforcement authorities.
- Trustees are to administer the estate as efficiently as possible by avoiding unnecessary expense and to exercise their powers[68] and perform their functions in a commercially sound way.

Other statutory duties of a trustee include taking possession of the bankrupt's property;[69] convening of meetings of creditors upon proper request;[70] declaring and distributing dividends among creditors as expeditiously as possible; and fulfilling administrative duties with respect to records, accounts and so on.[71]

The general law relating to trustees governs trustees in bankruptcy except in so far as their position is modified by the provisions of the Bankruptcy Act or other statutes.[72] Accordingly a trustee in bankruptcy owes fiduciary duties to the creditors of the bankrupt and to the bankrupt him- or herself.[73]

2.6 Creditors' Petitions for Bankruptcy

A creditor may present a petition where a debtor has committed an act of bankruptcy at a time when the debtor had a relevant jurisdictional connection with Australia.[74] The Bankruptcy Act lists a number of acts of bankruptcy; however, the one most commonly relied upon is that of failure to comply with a Bankruptcy Notice.[75] Other

---

68 For example, a trustee has powers of investigation of the bankrupt's affairs (s 19AA) and the general powers listed in s 134 Bankruptcy Act 1966 (Cth).

69 Section 129 Bankruptcy Act 1966 (Cth).

70 Section 64 Bankruptcy Act 1966 (Cth).

71 Sections 169–174 Bankruptcy Act 1966 (Cth).

72 *Re Ladyman* (1981) 38 ALR 631, 643 approved by the Full Federal Court in *Adsett* v. *Berlouis* (1992) 37 FCR 201 at 209.

73 *Fuller* v. *Wily* (No. SG 34 of 1995 FED No. 523/96 Bankruptcy; Full Federal Court, Sheppard, Spender and Hill JJ, 28 June 1996), paragraph 58.

74 Section 43 Bankruptcy Act 1966 (Cth). Section 45 deals with petitions against partnerships and s 46 with petitions against joint debtors who are not partners.

75 Section 40(1)(g) Bankruptcy Act 1966 (Cth). A creditor who has obtained a final judgment or order, the execution of which has not been stayed and which is for the sum of at least A$2,000, applies to the Official Receiver for the issue of a Bankruptcy Notice. Section 41: The notice, which is to be in the prescribed form, claims the debt is due and payable and requires the debtor within a certain time (usually 21 days) either to pay the amount or to make arrangement to the creditor's satisfaction for settlement of the debt. Because of the significance of failure to comply with a Bankruptcy Notice, there are a number of Bankruptcy Regulations (4.01–4.04) which deal with applications for their issue, the necessary form, their service and

acts of bankruptcy include certain acts done with the intent to defeat or delay creditors, failure of an execution process, and signing an authority to commence proceedings aimed at arriving at an arrangement with creditors outside bankruptcy.

A creditor may not present a petition against a debtor unless the debtor has committed the act of bankruptcy on which the petition relies within six months before the presentation of the petition and the debtor owes the petitioning creditor(s) a liquidated debt of at least A$2,000, payable either immediately or at a certain future time.[76]

At the hearing, the court shall require proof of the matters stated in the petition, service of the petition and the fact that the debt is still owing before it may make a sequestration order against the debtor's estate.[77] Alternatively at the hearing of the petition, the court may adjourn or dismiss the petition. The creditor may also seek leave to withdraw the petition.[78]

2.7 Rules regarding Debtors' Petitions for Bankruptcy

A debtor seeking voluntary bankruptcy must present a petition accompanied by a statement of affairs to the Official Receiver.[79] The Official Receiver must reject the petition if the debtor does not have a relevant connection with Australia at the time of presentation.[80] The Official Receiver may reject the petition if it does not comply substantially with the approved form, is not accompanied by a statement of affairs or the statement of affairs is considered by the Official Receiver to be inadequate.[81] The Official Receiver may also reject the petition if it appears that if the debtor did not become a bankrupt, the debtor would be likely to be able to pay all the debts in the statement of affairs and the debtor is unwilling to pay or is a repeat bankrupt.[82] The Official Receiver must accept a debtor's petition unless rejecting it on these grounds or unless a court directs the Official Receiver to reject it.[83] Prior to accepting the petition, the Official Receiver must give the debtor prescribed information about bankruptcy and its alternatives.[84]

---

so on. Although personal service is no longer required (Bankruptcy Regulation 16.01), it is preferable: M. Murray (2005), *Keay's Insolvency:Personal and Corporate Law and Practice*, 5th edn, Lawbook Co., Sydney [3.225]. Bankruptcy Notices are not open to public inspection unless a creditor's petition is presented based on failure to comply with it (Bankruptcy Regulation 4.03).

76 Section 44 Bankruptcy Act 1966 (Cth).

77 Section 52 Bankruptcy Act 1966 (Cth).

78 Section 47 Bankruptcy Act 1966 (Cth).

79 Section 55 Bankruptcy Act 1966 (Cth). Section 56A deals with petitions by partnerships and s 57 with petitions by joint debtors who are not partners.

80 Section 55(2A) Bankruptcy Act 1966 (Cth).

81 Section 55(3) Bankruptcy Act 1966 (Cth).

82 Section 55(3AA) Bankruptcy Act 1966 (Cth).

83 Section 55(4) Bankruptcy Act 1966 (Cth). Where a creditor's petition is pending against a group of debtors of whom the debtor is one, the Official Receiver must refer the petition to the court for direction whether to accept or reject it: s 55(3B) Bankruptcy Act 1966 (Cth).

84 Section 55(3A) Bankruptcy Act 1966 (Cth).

2.8 Secured Creditors

A secured creditor may present a creditor's petition if the debt owing exceeds the value of the security, at least to the extent of A$2,000.[85] However, if it does not, then the secured creditor may only present, or join in presenting, a petition if he or she states in the petition that he or she is willing to surrender the security for the benefit of the creditors generally in the event of a sequestration order being made against the debtor.[86]

2.9 Nature of Bankruptcy Petitions by Creditors and Debtors

The petition by a creditor (or creditors jointly) must be in the prescribed form, if any.[87] A creditor's petition must be verified by affidavit of a person who knows the relevant facts.[88] Five modes of service for a petition are available: post or courier service; document exchange; leaving at the last-known address; personal delivery or, in certain circumstances, facsimile or other electronic transmission such as electronic mail.[89]

A debtor's petition presented to the Official Receiver is to be in accordance with the approved form[90] and accompanied by a statement of affairs as well as a copy thereof.[91]

Bankruptcy Regulation 4.11 states that, at the time of presentation of the debtor's petition, the Official Receiver must give the debtor information about alternatives to and consequences of bankruptcy, sources of financial advice and guidance to persons facing or contemplating bankruptcy, and information about the debtor's right to choose administration either by a registered trustee or the Official Trustee, and a statement about certain acts of bankruptcy. The Official Receiver must not accept a debtor's petition unless the debtor has given a signed acknowledgment that the debtor has received and read the prescribed information.[92]

If the debtor wishes a registered trustee to act as the trustee in bankruptcy, then he or she must obtain the written consent of such a trustee[93] and file it with the Official Receiver at the same time as filing the debtor's petition.[94]

In certain circumstances, a debtor may present a Declaration of Intention to Present a Debtor's Petition that introduces a seven-day moratorium for certain enforcement processes and remedies by creditors.[95] This is intended to minimise the chance of mistaken and unintended bankruptcies. A debtor is disqualified from

---

85 Section 44(2) Bankruptcy Act 1966 (Cth).
86 Section 44(3) Bankruptcy Act 1966 (Cth).
87 Section 47(1A) Bankruptcy Act 1966 (Cth).
88 Section 47(1) Bankruptcy Act 1966 (Cth).
89 Bankruptcy Regulation 16.01.
90 The approved form for a debtor's petition is ITSA Approved Form 6.
91 Section 55(2) Bankruptcy Act 1966 (Cth).
92 Bankruptcy Regulation 4.11(3).
93 Section 156A Bankruptcy Act 1966 (Cth).
94 Bankruptcy Regulation 4.12.
95 Sections 54A–54L Bankruptcy Act 1966 (Cth).

presenting a Declaration in a number of circumstances, such as where a creditor's petition has been presented and served on the debtor and before the sequestration order is made or the petition is withdrawn, dismissed or lapsed.[96] The presentation of a Declaration is itself an act of bankruptcy.[97]

2.10 Creditors' Meetings

Once a bankruptcy has commenced, the trustee may convene a creditors' meeting at any time.[98] A meeting must be convened whenever the creditors so direct by resolution or whenever the trustee is so requested in writing either by at least one quarter in value of the creditors or by less if the creditor(s) has lodged with the trustee sufficient security for the cost of holding the meeting.[99]

The typical reasons for calling meetings are:

> ... to give reports, seek the meeting's sanction for a course of action or realisation of property, seek information or assistance in relation to the administration of the estate, seek indemnities from creditors in order to allow the trustee to pursue a course of action, such as litigation, or seek approval of the trustee's remuneration.[100]

3 Personal Bankruptcy Law Procedures

3.1 Controls Placed on Bankrupts

Once a debtor becomes a bankrupt upon the making of a sequestration order, the person's status remains that of an undischarged bankrupt until discharge.[101] (An order may be annulled in certain circumstances.[102])

While an undischarged bankrupt, controls are placed over the person and property of the bankrupt. Unless excused by the trustee or prevented by illness or other sufficient good cause, a bankrupt must give to the trustee all books relating to his or her examinable affairs.[103]

The bankrupt must also attend the trustee or creditors' meetings whenever reasonably required and provide information required by them about his or her conduct and examinable affairs including any material changes.[104] The bankrupt must

---

96 Section 54B Bankruptcy Act 1966 (Cth).

97 Section 40(1)(da) Bankruptcy Act 1966 (Cth).

98 Section 64(2) Bankruptcy Act 1966 (Cth).

99 Section 64(1) Bankruptcy Act 1966 (Cth).

100 M. Murray (2005), *Keay's Insolvency: Personal and Corporate Law and Practice*, 5th edn, Lawbook Co., Sydney [6.75].

101 Section 149 ff Bankruptcy Act 1966 (Cth).

102 Section 74 ff and section 153A ff Bankruptcy Act 1966 (Cth).

103 Section 77(a) Bankruptcy Act 1966 (Cth). This also refers to surrender of the bankrupt's passport, if any. This includes books of any 'associated entities' such as companies, partnerships, trusts: s 5(1) Bankruptcy Act 1966 (Cth).

104 Section 77(b)–(d) Bankruptcy Act 1966 (Cth).

execute documents and generally assist in the realisation of property, as well as disclose after-acquired property.[105] The bankrupt must generally aid to the utmost of his or her power in the administration of the estate.[106]

3.2 Collection of Information about Debtors; Examination of Debtors

The bankrupt may be required to attend before the Official Receiver to give evidence and produce books.[107] The bankrupt may also be examined before the court or the Registrar about the bankrupt's examinable affairs.[108] The examinee's privilege against self-incrimination may be abrogated.[109]

The Official Receiver (accompanied by a registered trustee where relevant) is entitled at all reasonable times to full and free access to all premises and books for any purpose of the Act and to take copies from books or, if this is not reasonably practicable or is an unreasonable intrusion on the occupier's affairs, to remove relevant books.[110]

The trustee may investigate the bankrupt's conduct and examinable affairs and the bankrupt's books, accounts and records so far as they relate to the bankruptcy.[111] For the purposes of such an investigation, the trustee or Official Receiver may require in writing that a person produce specified books or classes of books of an associated entity of the bankrupt which are in his or her possession. These are to be, in the investigator's opinion, relevant to the investigation.[112] The person may be required to explain to the best of his or her knowledge and belief any matter about the compilation of the books or to which the books relate.[113]

3.3 Offshore Collection of Information

If the Official Receiver has reason to believe that information relevant to the examinable affairs of a bankrupt is known by a person outside Australia or recorded in a book which is outside Australia, or books relevant to the examinable affairs of a bankrupt are outside Australia, the Official Receiver may give an offshore information notice to a person requesting that they give the information or produce the books or copies thereof.[114] Failure to comply with such a notice affects admissibility of the information or books in proceedings for the recovery of amounts payable by the bankrupt or third parties under the income contribution scheme.[115]

---

105 Section 77(e)–(f) Bankruptcy Act 1966 (Cth).
106 Section 77(g) Bankruptcy Act 1966 (Cth).
107 Section 77C Bankruptcy Act 1966 (Cth).
108 Section 81(1) Bankruptcy Act 1966 (Cth).
109 Section 81(11AA) Bankruptcy Act 1966 (Cth).
110 Section 77AA Bankruptcy Act 1966 (Cth).
111 Section 19AA Bankruptcy Act 1966 (Cth).
112 Section 77A Bankruptcy Act 1966 (Cth).
113 Section 77A(3) Bankruptcy Act 1966 (Cth).
114 Section 81A Bankruptcy Act 1966 (Cth).
115 Section 81G; sections 139ZG–ZL Bankruptcy Act 1966 (Cth).

If the trustee or Official Receiver otherwise requires information which is outside the jurisdiction, then alternative means of obtaining it may be by calling upon the bankrupt's general duty to assist the trustee. Alternatively, the trustee or Official Receiver may seek the aid and assistance of a foreign court.[116]

3.4 Rules Regarding the Proof of Debts

The trustee is required with all convenient speed to declare and pay dividends from the estate amongst creditors who have proved their debts.[117] The debts provable in a bankruptcy are all debts and liabilities, present or future, certain or contingent, to which a bankrupt was subject at the date of the bankruptcy or to which he or she may become subject before his or her discharge by reason of an obligation incurred before the date of the bankruptcy.[118] This includes sums payable under a maintenance agreement or maintenance order before the date of the bankruptcy.[119]

Claims for unliquidated damages are not provable unless they arise by reason of a contract, promise or breach of trust.[120] Generally penalties or fines imposed by a court in respect of an offence against a law are not provable.[121] Other non-provable debts include a civil penalty under the Corporations Act 2001 (Cth); and an order under a proceeds of crime act.[122] Where a debt is subject to a contingency or is otherwise of uncertain value, the trustee shall make an estimate of the debt or liability.[123]

Before declaring dividends, the trustee must give written notice thereof to anyone known to the trustee who claims or might claim to be a creditor and who has not lodged a proof of debt. The creditors are to be given a reasonable time in which to lodge proofs of debt.[124]

A creditor shall not be taken to have proved a debt until a proof of debt lodged by him or her in respect of that debt has been admitted.[125] A proof of debt must set out particulars of the debt, be in accordance with the approved form,[126] specify any vouchers by which the debt can be substantiated and state whether or not the creditor is a secured creditor.[127] A creditor may, with the consent of the trustee, amend a proof of debt.[128]

---

116 See discussion below on s 29 Bankruptcy Act 1966 (Cth).

117 Section 140 Bankruptcy Act 1966 (Cth).

118 Section 82(1) Bankruptcy Act 1966 (Cth).

119 Section 82(1A) Bankruptcy Act 1966 (Cth).

120 Section 82(2) Bankruptcy Act 1966 (Cth).

121 Section 82(3) Bankruptcy Act 1966 (Cth).

122 Subsection 82(3AA) (3AB) (3A) and (3B) Bankruptcy Act 1966 (Cth).

123 An appeal lies to the court from such an estimate: subsections 82(4) and (5) Bankruptcy Act 1966 (Cth).

124 Sections 140 and 145 Bankruptcy Act 1966 (Cth).

125 Section 83 Bankruptcy Act 1966 (Cth). The provisions on admission or rejection of proofs are found in sections 102–106 Bankruptcy Act 1966 (Cth).

126 ITSA Approved Form 8.

127 Section 84(2) Bankruptcy Act 1966 (Cth).

128 Section 98 Bankruptcy Act 1966 (Cth).

3.5 Illicit Transfers of Property, etc. of the Bankrupt

The property available for distribution in respect of provable debts includes the property vested in the bankrupt at the commencement of the bankruptcy.[129] As the bankruptcy may commence before the actual date of the sequestration order, the doctrine of relation back may result in property being 'clawed back' into the estate.

In the case of a creditor's petition, the bankruptcy commences at the time of the commission of the earliest act of bankruptcy committed by the bankrupt within the period of six months immediately preceding the date on which the creditor's petition was presented.[130] In the case of a debtor's petition, the bankruptcy may commence at various times on or before the presentation of the petition depending on the circumstances.[131] Certain dealings with the debtor during the relation back period are protected under the Act.[132] For example, a transaction entered into before the date of bankruptcy in good faith and in the ordinary course of business is protected.

The bankrupt's divisible property also includes any property acquired between commencement of the bankruptcy and the bankrupt's discharge.[133] In addition, it includes the capacity to exercise and take proceedings for exercising all such powers in, over or in respect of property exercisable by the bankrupt between commencement and discharge.[134]

Property vested in the trustee under the associated entity provisions and money paid to the trustee under the associated entity provisions are also included in the bankrupt's estate.[135] Some bankrupts are required to contribute funds based on their income.[136] Typically this does not apply unless a bankrupt (with no dependants) earns approximately A$37,000 after tax.

Proceeds of execution levied against the debtor's property within six months prior to the presentation of the petition may be recovered from the executing creditors or from sheriffs and courts.[137] Property may also be clawed back into the estate under the

---

129 Section 116 Bankruptcy Act 1966 (Cth).

130 Section 115(1) Bankruptcy Act 1966 (Cth). This is subject to special rules where the time for compliance with the Bankruptcy Notice was extended (s 115(1A) Bankruptcy Act 1966 (Cth)) or the sequestration order was made following a composition or arrangement with creditors or a personal insolvency agreement (s 115(1B) Bankruptcy Act 1966 (Cth)).

131 These include whether the court directed the Official Receiver to accept the petition, whether any creditors' petition was pending, and whether the debtor committed any acts of bankruptcy prior to the presenting of any petition (s 115(2) Bankruptcy Act 1966 (Cth)).

132 Sections 123–124 Bankruptcy Act 1966 (Cth).

133 Section 116(1)(a) Bankruptcy Act 1966 (Cth).

134 Section 116(1)(b) Bankruptcy Act 1966 (Cth).

135 Subsections 116(1)(c)–(d) and sections 139D–139EA Bankruptcy Act 1966 (Cth).

136 Sections 139J–139ZI Bankruptcy Act 1966 (Cth).

137 Sections 118–119A Bankruptcy Act 1966 (Cth).

voidable transaction provisions. These include undervalued transactions,[138] transfers to defeat creditors[139] and voidable preferences.[140]

The estate does not include exempt property, such as household property, property used to earn income and specific life assurance and superannuation funds.[141]

3.6 Orders in regard to the Property of the Debtor

Although a trustee may institute proceedings in the court to recover property void against him or her, a more economical and efficient avenue may be via administrative means. The Official Receiver may require a person by written notice to pay to the trustee an amount equal to the money or the value of the property received.[142] An amount payable to the trustee pursuant to such notice is recoverable by the trustee as a debt by action against the person in a court of competent jurisdiction.[143] Refusal or failure to comply with the notice is an offence.[144] The notice may be set aside by order of a court if it is satisfied that the relevant provisions do not apply on the basis of the alleged facts and circumstances contained in the notice.[145]

3.7 Rules for the Distribution of the Assets of the Bankrupt

While a key principle of Australian insolvency law is the *pari passu* distribution of assets to creditors,[146] the Act does contain rules on distribution which accord a special place to secured creditors and priority to certain classes of unsecured creditors.

A secured creditor may choose from four options:

1. He or she may choose not to participate in the bankruptcy as a secured creditor's right to realise or otherwise deal with the security is not affected by the bankrupt's property vesting in the trustee.[147]
2. A secured creditor may surrender the security and prove for the whole of the debt.[148]
3. A secured creditor may realise the security and prove for the balance, if any, outstanding.[149]

---

138 Section 120 Bankruptcy Act 1966 (Cth). The Bankruptcy Legislation Amendment (Anti-Avoidance) Act 2006 has recently amended this section, for example, introducing a rebuttable presumption of insolvency where there has been a failure by the bankrupt in keeping books, accounts and records.

139 Section 121 Bankruptcy Act 1966 (Cth). The Bankruptcy Legislation Amendment (Anti-Avoidance) Act 2006 has recently amended this section.

140 Section 122 Bankruptcy Act 1966 (Cth).

141 Section 116(2) Bankruptcy Act 1966 (Cth).

142 Sections 139ZQ–139ZT Bankruptcy Act 1966 (Cth).

143 Section 139ZQ Bankruptcy Act 1966 (Cth).

144 Section 139ZT Bankruptcy Act 1966 (Cth).

145 Section 139ZS Bankruptcy Act 1966 (Cth).

146 Section 108 Bankruptcy Act 1966 (Cth).

147 Section 58(5) Bankruptcy Act 1966 (Cth).

148 Section 90(2) Bankruptcy Act 1966 (Cth).

149 Section 90(3) Bankruptcy Act 1966 (Cth). That is, unless a trustee is satisfied that the realisation has not been effected in good faith and in a proper manner.

4. A secured creditor may estimate the value of the security and prove for the balance due after deducting that estimated value.[150]

Priority creditors are:

- the costs and expenses (including the trustee's remuneration) of the bankruptcy administration;
- the remuneration and costs of a controlling trustee where a Part X arrangement has been unsuccessfully initiated or commenced, then terminated and the debtor made bankrupt;
- certain liabilities of a Part X arrangement or composition or scheme of arrangement terminated within two months of the bankruptcy;
- capped amount for wages and leave payments of employees;
- priorities in favour of a creditor or groups of creditors agreed by special resolution at a meeting of creditors.[151]

The court also has a discretion to give an advantage to a creditor, for example where one has agreed to indemnify the trustee for legal costs associated with recovery of property for the estate.[152]

3.8 Creditors Agreements with the Debtor

A debtor may seek to enter an arrangement with his or her creditors in order to avoid bankruptcy. There are essentially three categories for such arrangements under the Act:

1. A debtor who is already bankrupt may seek to enter a composition or scheme of arrangement with his or her creditors and have the bankruptcy annulled.
2. A debtor with few assets and liabilities and low income may seek to enter into a debt agreement with his or her creditors.
3. A debtor with sufficient assets available may initiate the more complex personal insolvency agreement with his or her creditors.

3.9 Composition and Scheme of Arrangement

A Part IV Division 6 composition or scheme of arrangement is initiated by a bankrupt lodging with the trustee a written proposal setting out the terms of the proposed composition in satisfaction of his or her debts or scheme of arrangement of his or her affairs as well as particulars of any sureties or securities forming part of the proposal.[153] The trustee then calls a meeting of creditors and sends them the proposal and a report indicating the trustee's view on whether it would benefit the bankrupt's

---

150 Section 90(4) Bankruptcy Act 1966 (Cth). The trustee may redeem the security for the estimated value: s 91 Bankruptcy Act 1966 (Cth).

151 Section 109 Bankruptcy Act 1966 (Cth).

152 Section 109(10) Bankruptcy Act 1966 (Cth).

153 Section 73(1) Bankruptcy Act 1966 (Cth).

creditors generally.[154] If the creditors accept the proposal by special resolution, the composition or scheme is binding on all the creditors in respect of their provable debts.[155] The bankruptcy is annulled on the date of the special resolution.[156]

3.10 Debt Agreements

A Part IX debt agreement may be proposed by debtors to their creditors with few assets and liabilities and a low annual net income.[157] Certain debtors are disqualified from proposing a debt agreement, for example one who has been a bankrupt within the last ten years.[158]

A debtor initiates a debt agreement by giving a written proposal and a statement of affairs to the Official Trustee.[159] The proposal must:

- identify the property it deals with;
- specify how it is to be dealt with; and
- authorise a specified person (such as the Official Trustee, a registered trustee or another person) to deal with the specified property in that way.[160]

The Official Receiver processes the proposal either by calling a meeting of creditors or seeking their views in writing.[161] Following acceptance of a debt agreement and its details being entered on the National Personal Insolvency Index, the debtor is discharged from provable debts[162] and certain creditor action is prevented.[163]

Debt agreements may be varied.[164] They are terminated in five circumstances:

- upon discharge of the obligations under it;[165]
- upon the debtor submitting a proposal for its termination;[166]
- upon a court ordering its termination (for example because of default);[167]
- upon a special resolution to that effect by a meeting of creditors;[168] or
- upon the debtor becoming a bankrupt.[169]

---

154 Subsections 73(2)–(2A) Bankruptcy Act 1966 (Cth).

155 Section 75 Bankruptcy Act 1966 (Cth).

156 Section 74(5) Bankruptcy Act 1966 (Cth).

157 These amounts are indexed. See http://www.itsa.gov.au which, at the time of writing, states the current maximum amount for assets and liabilities is approximately A$73,200 and the after tax income would be approximately A$54,900.

158 Section 185C(4) Bankruptcy Act 1966 (Cth).

159 Sections 185C–D Bankruptcy Act 1966 (Cth).

160 Section 185C(2) Bankruptcy Act 1966 (Cth).

161 Section 185A Bankruptcy Act 1966 (Cth).

162 Section 185J Bankruptcy Act 1966 (Cth).

163 Section 185K Bankruptcy Act 1966 (Cth).

164 Section 185M Bankruptcy Act 1966 (Cth).

165 Section 185N Bankruptcy Act 1966 (Cth).

166 Section 185P Bankruptcy Act 1966 (Cth).

167 Section 185Q Bankruptcy Act 1966 (Cth).

168 Section 185QA Bankruptcy Act 1966 (Cth).

169 Section 185R Bankruptcy Act 1966 (Cth).

3.11 Personal Insolvency Agreements

A Part X personal insolvency agreement is commenced by a debtor signing an s 188 authority to a trustee to call a meeting of the debtor's creditors and to take control of the debtor's property.[170] The debtor must also give to the controlling trustee a statement of affairs and a proposal for a Part X arrangement.[171] When notifying the creditors of the meeting, the controlling trustee must provide a report about the debtor's affairs and state his or her opinion on whether the creditors' interests would be better served by accepting the proposal or by the bankruptcy of the debtor.[172]

Creditors accept a proposal for a personal insolvency agreement by special resolution passed at a creditors' meeting. A personal insolvency agreement may be set aside by the court as unreasonable, non-compliant or based on false or misleading information.[173] It may also be terminated by the trustees, the creditors, court order or occurrence of a terminating event.[174] Personal insolvency agreements may also be varied by creditor resolution or by the trustee.[175]

4 Corporate Insolvency Rules

4.1 Introduction

There are a number of insolvency administrations available in respect of companies under Australian law. As occurs with personal insolvency, there are terminal and non-terminal administrations. The former is a liquidation or winding up of a company, which normally results in its deregistration. This may be initiated voluntarily by the members and/or the creditors of the company[176] or involuntarily by court order.

Non-terminal administrations can be further divided into those which are in the interests of the creditors as a whole (schemes of arrangements or deeds of company arrangement) or administrations in the interests of the secured creditor which initiated them (receiverships).

An 'interim form' of administration introduced for insolvent companies in 1993 is the voluntary administration. This commences a moratorium on creditor action while a registered liquidator manages the company until a meeting of creditors decides between a deed of company arrangement, liquidation or the return of the company to management by the directors.

---

170 Section 188 Bankruptcy Act 1966 (Cth).

171 Sections 188(2C) and 188A Bankruptcy Act 1966 (Cth).

172 Section 189A Bankruptcy Act 1966 (Cth).

173 Section 222 Bankruptcy Act 1966 (Cth).

174 Sections 222A–222D Bankruptcy Act 1966 (Cth).

175 Section 221A Bankruptcy Act 1966 (Cth).

176 A creditors' voluntary liquidation applies to insolvent companies. Members' voluntary liquidation is only available for a solvent company.

4.2 Corporate Rescue and the Use of Informal Mechanisms

In the later 1980s, the Harmer Report promoted a corporate rescue culture, stating:

> Constructive or creative insolvency is not a myth. However, it requires suitable procedures that encourage and offer a reasonable prospect of achieving that result. A constructive approach to corporate insolvency requires the preservation, if practical and possible, of the property and business of the company in the brief period before creditors are in a position to make an informed decision. This assists in an orderly and beneficial administration, whether creditors decide to wind the company up or accept a compromise.[177]

The Report recommended the introduction of a new regime capable of swift implementation; as uncomplicated and inexpensive as possible; and flexible, providing alternative forms of dealing with the financial affairs of a company. This recommendation was adopted with the introduction of the voluntary administration.

Companies facing financial stress and their creditors may nevertheless seek private informal arrangements in order to resolve the debtor's difficulties.[178] In order to be binding on creditors, such arrangements should be by way of deed under seal. Advantages of these arrangements include the lack of adverse publicity, which may affect market confidence in the debtor's business, and their flexibility. They may allow for more creative solutions than formal arrangements, which may need to implement statutory priorities. Nevertheless, their major disadvantage is that they are not binding on creditors without each creditor's agreement and a single dissenting creditor may jeopardise the arrangement. Also if there is a subsequent liquidation, then certain payments may be set aside[179] or the directors may be liable for insolvent trading during the term of the arrangement.[180]

4.3 The Nature of Voluntary Administration

The voluntary administration scheme achieves the necessary moratorium on creditor action while permitting an independent insolvency practitioner to take over from the directors as the company's management and make an assessment of the company's circumstances. Meanwhile, management can investigate the possibilities for rescuing the business, or viable parts thereof.

Section 435A states that the object of Part 5.3A of the Corporations Act is:

> to provide for the business, property and affairs of an insolvent company to be administered in a way that:
>
> (a) maximises the chances of the company, or as much as possible of its business, continuing in existence; or

177 Australian Law Reform Commission 1988, *Report No. 45: General Insolvency Inquiry*, vol. 1, Australian Government Publishing Service, Canberra, paragraph 53, pp. 28–29.

178 See M. Murray (2005), *Keay's Insolvency: Personal and Corporate Law and Practice*, 5th edn, Lawbook Co., Sydney, [18.45].

179 For example, as unfair preferences under s 588FA Corporations Act 2001 (Cth).

180 Section 588G Corporations Act 2001 (Cth).

(b) if it is not possible for the company or its business to continue in existence – results in a better return for the company's creditors and members than would result from an immediate winding up of the company.

4.4 Methods of Initiating Voluntary Administration Schemes

One of the features of the voluntary administration scheme is that it can be initiated quickly, inexpensively and without court intervention. Directors of companies are also encouraged to consider initiating a voluntary administration as soon as the company appears to be insolvent through provisions dealing with directors' liability for insolvent trading and for unremitted tax deductions.[181]

A voluntary administration may be initiated in one of three ways:[182]

1. The most common method is by resolution of the board of directors that, in the opinion of the directors voting, the company is insolvent or is likely to become insolvent at some future time and an administrator should be appointed.[183]
2. A liquidator or provisional liquidator may appoint an administrator by writing.[184] This may occur, for example, where the company is insolvent yet part(s) of its business could be realised more beneficially if continued as a going concern for a period of time before being sold.
3. A chargee of the whole or substantially the whole of the company's property may in writing appoint an administrator if the charge has become or is still enforceable.[185]

4.5 Effect of the Appointment of an Administrator

Upon appointment, the administrator takes control of the company's business, property and affairs. The administrator may perform any function and exercise any power of the company or any of its officers if the company had not been under administration.[186] While doing so, the administrator acts as the company's agent.[187] While the officers are not removed from their positions, they may only exercise their powers with the written consent of the administrator.[188]

During the administration, only the administrator can deal with the company property. Transactions and dealings with company property are void unless entered

---

[181] See insolvent trading defences in s 588H(5) and (6) Corporations Act 2001 (Cth) and potential responses by directors to receipt of an estimate of liability of a company to remit tax deductions in order to avoid personal liability attaching in s 222AOB Income Tax Assessment Act 1936 (Cth). There is also a moratorium on enforcement of directors' guarantees during a voluntary administration: s 440J Corporations Act 2001 (Cth).

[182] See s 435C Corporations Act 2001 (Cth) on when the administration commences.

[183] Section 436A Corporations Act 2001 (Cth).

[184] Section 436B Corporations Act 2001 (Cth).

[185] Section 436C Corporations Act 2001 (Cth).

[186] Section 437A Corporations Act 2001 (Cth).

[187] Section 437B Corporations Act 2001 (Cth).

[188] Section 437C Corporations Act 2001 (Cth).

into by, or with the prior written consent of, the administrator or entered into under a court order.[189] The voluntary administration commences a moratorium on creditor action.

4.6 Powers, Liabilities and Qualifications of the Administrator and Duration of the Administration

The administrator may carry on the company's business and manage its property and affairs. The administrator may terminate or dispose of all or part of the business and may dispose of any property.[190]

The role of the administrator is to investigate the company's business, property and affairs and financial circumstances and to form an opinion on each of three matters: whether it would be in the creditors' interests for the company to execute a deed of arrangement, to be wound up or for the administration to end.[191]

The administrator must also call at least two creditors' meetings. The first meeting is to be held within five business days of the commencement of the administration[192] for the purpose of allowing the creditors to determine whether to appoint a committee of creditors and, if so, to select the members.[193]

The second meeting is to be held within five business days after the convening period which will ordinarily be 21 days from the commencement of the administration.[194] This convening period may be extended by the court[195] and meetings may also be adjourned from time to time, but not more than 60 days after the first day on which the second meeting was held.[196] This limit may be extended by court order.[197]

Prior to the second meeting, the administrator is to advertise the meeting in relevant newspapers and send notices to creditors accompanied by a report on the company and a statement of the administrator's opinion on the three options on which the creditors may vote. If a deed of company arrangement is proposed, then the administrator is also to send a statement setting out details of the proposed deed.[198]

An administrator is liable for debts incurred in the course of the administration for services rendered, goods bought or property hired, leased, used or occupied.[199]

189 Section 437D Corporations Act 2001 (Cth).

190 Section 437A Corporations Act 2001 (Cth). Where the property to be disposed of is subject to a lease or a charge the administrator must obtain the written consent of the lessor or chargee or the leave of the court: s 442C Corporations Act 2001 (Cth).

191 Section 438A Corporations Act 2001 (Cth).

192 Section 436E(2) Corporations Act 2001 (Cth).

193 Section 436E(1) Corporations Act 2001 (Cth).

194 Section 439A Corporations Act 2001 (Cth).

195 Section 439A(6) Corporations Act 2001 (Cth).

196 Section 439B Corporations Act 2001 (Cth).

197 Section 447A Corporations Act 2001 (Cth). See *Cawthorn* v. *Keira Constructions Pty Ltd* (1994) 12 ACLC 396; 13 ACSR 337 on the breadth of the s 447A discretion, albeit one which is to be exercised as an integral part of the legislative scheme provided for by Part 5.3A: *Australian Memory Pty Ltd* v. *Brien* (2000) 200 CLR 270; 74 ALJR 991.

198 Section 439A Corporations Act 2001 (Cth).

199 Section 443A Corporations Act 2001 (Cth).

However, an administrator has a right to be indemnified out of company property for these debts[200] and for his or her fixed remuneration.[201]

An administrator must be a registered liquidator.[202] A person is disqualified from acting as an administrator if relevantly connected with the company[203] or an insolvent under administration.[204]

4.7 Protection of Assets during Administration

There are restrictions on a company being wound up during an administration. It can not be wound up voluntarily unless under the specific provision for transition to a creditors' voluntary winding up.[205] Court winding up applications are to be adjourned if the court is satisfied that it is in the creditors' interests that the administration continue rather than the company be wound up.[206]

Legal proceedings, winding up proceedings and execution against company property cannot be commenced or proceeded with.[207] In particular, a person cannot enforce a charge[208] on the property of the company nor can owners or lessors take possession of, or otherwise recover, property, unless with the administrator's written consent or the leave of the court.[209]

4.8 Role of Creditors during Administration

At the first meeting of creditors, the creditors may decide to appoint a committee of creditors and select its members.[210] The functions of the committee are to consult with the administrator about the administration and to receive and consider administrator's reports. Except to the extent that they may reasonably require the administrator to report to the committee, the creditors are not to give directions to the administrator.[211]

---

200 The s 443D indemnity extends to liabilities under ss 443A, 443B and 443BA Corporations Act 2001 (Cth).

201 Section 443D Corporations Act 2001 (Cth). The administrator is accorded certain priority in this indemnity: s 443E Corporations Act 2001 (Cth).

202 Section 448B Corporations Act 2001 (Cth). Also see sections 1279 and 1282 Corporations Act 2001 (Cth).

203 Section 448C Corporations Act 2001 (Cth). For example, a person who is a partner or employee of an auditor of the company or a related body corporate is disqualified: s 448C(1)(f) and s 448C(3) Corporations Act 2001 (Cth).

204 Section 448D Corporations Act 2001 (Cth).

205 Sections 440A(1) and 446A Corporations Act 2001 (Cth).

206 Section 440A(2) Corporations Act 2001 (Cth).

207 Sections 440A, 440D and 440F Corporations Act 2001 (Cth). Legal proceedings are stayed except with the written consent of the administrator and a court may grant leave to continue such proceedings as well as an enforcement process.

208 That is, except for the brief window of opportunity afforded a chargee of an enforceable charge over all or substantially all of the company's property during the first ten days of the administration: s 441A Corporations Act 2001 (Cth).

209 Sections 440B–440C Corporations Act 2001 (Cth).

210 Section 436E(1) Corporations Act 2001 (Cth).

211 Section 436F Corporations Act 2001 (Cth).

The role of the creditors at the second meeting is to determine whether the company is to execute a deed of company arrangement, the company is to be wound up, or the administration is to end and the company be returned to the directors' management.[212]

4.9 Powers of the Courts in relation to Administration and the Administrator

A court is not necessarily involved in voluntary administrations. Its role is supervisory with wide-ranging powers to facilitate the objects of the voluntary administration procedure. In particular, the court has a general power 'to make such order as it thinks appropriate about how [Part 5.3A] is to operate in relation to a particular company'.[213]

For example, in respect of the administrator, the court may declare whether or not the purported appointment is valid[214] and give direction to the administrator about a matter arising in connection with the performance or exercise of any of the administrator's functions or powers.[215]

4.10 Termination of the Administration

An administration is terminated by various events.[216] Normally it is terminated following the creditors resolving that a deed of company arrangement be executed, that the administration should end or that the company be wound up. It may also terminate because the convening period ends without a second meeting being called or without an application that the convening period be extended.

4.11 Other Related Matters

One of the possible outcomes of a voluntary administration is that creditors approve the execution of a deed of company arrangement by the company and the deed administrator. The creditors are bound by the deed during the period between the meeting and the actual execution.[217]

The Corporations Act contains very few requirements of the deed which increases the flexibility of this option. It must specify:

- the administrator;[218]
- the property available to pay creditors' claims;
- the nature and duration of any moratorium period;
- the conditions if any for the deed to come into or continue in operation;
- the circumstances in which the deed terminates;

---

212 Section 439C Corporations Act 2001 (Cth).
213 Section 447A Corporations Act 2001 (Cth).
214 Section 447C Corporations Act 2001 (Cth).
215 Section 447D Corporations Act 2001 (Cth).
216 Section 435C Corporations Act 2001 (Cth).
217 Section 444C Corporations Act 2001 (Cth).
218 Normally, although not necessarily, the voluntary administrator becomes the deed administrator.

- the order for distribution of proceeds from realisation of the property; and
- the day on or before which admissible claims must have arisen.[219]

A deed may be varied during its operation.[220] A deed will terminate if the court so orders,[221] if the creditors so resolve, or if the circumstances in the deed providing for its termination exist.[222]

5 Court-based Schemes of Administration, Reconstruction or Arrangement

5.1 Schemes of Arrangement

Another form of insolvency administration which enables a debtor company to enter into a binding arrangement with its creditors is the scheme of arrangement. This administration differs from the Part 5.3A deed of company arrangement in that it is not preceded by a voluntary administration and the court plays an important role in the process of scheme approval.

The scheme is initiated by the company preparing a proposal (possibly in consultation with its major creditors) as well as an explanatory statement of the proposal which includes a report of the affairs of the company.[223] Copies of these are to be delivered to the ASIC at least 14 days before the first court hearing.[224]

The company applies to the court to approve the convening of a meeting of creditors, or classes of creditors,[225] to consider the proposal.[226] If the court approves the meeting, it is convened with 14 days' notice to creditors. At the meeting, the proposal must be accepted by a majority in number of the creditors present and voting,[227] being a majority whose debts or claims against the company amount in the aggregate to at least 75 per cent of the total amount of the debts or claims of the creditors present and voting.[228]

If the proposal is accepted, the company must then seek court approval of the scheme.[229] Matters considered by the court include issues of public policy and commercial morality, so that even though the necessary majority of creditors approve the scheme, the court may nevertheless not sanction it where it believes that in the

---

219 Section 444A Corporations Act 2001 (Cth).

220 Section 445F Corporations Act 2001 (Cth).

221 Section 445D Corporations Act 2001 (Cth).

222 Section 445C Corporations Act 2001 (Cth).

223 Section 412 Corporations Act 2001 (Cth).

224 Section 411(2) Corporations Act 2001 (Cth).

225 The applicant must decide whether the interests or rights of creditors or members are such that separate meetings are necessary. Examples of creditors who have been held to be in different classes are secured and unsecured creditors, and partly secured and unsecured creditors: see R. Tomasic and K. Whitford (1997), *Australian Insolvency and Bankruptcy Law*, 2nd edn, Butterworths, Sydney, pp. 145–147.

226 Section 411(1) Corporations Act 2001 (Cth).

227 In person or by proxy.

228 Section 411(4) Corporations Act 2001 (Cth).

229 Section 411(4) Corporations Act 2001 (Cth).

circumstances a winding up with the liquidator's broader powers of investigation would be preferable.[230]

Following court approval, the company must file the order of the court with the ASIC, upon which the scheme becomes effective.[231] The scheme is then carried into effect and terminates in accordance with its terms, if the company is wound up, or if a court approves a subsequent scheme[232] or declares that the scheme has been terminated by creditors.[233]

6 Winding Up Procedures

6.1 Introduction

A company may be wound up either voluntarily or involuntarily. Voluntary winding up is available both for solvent and insolvent companies. A solvent company may be wound up through a members' voluntary winding up,[234] for example where a member of a corporate group has served its useful purpose. An insolvent company may be wound up through a creditors' voluntary winding up.[235]

Both solvent and insolvent companies may be wound up compulsorily. A court may order that a company be wound up in insolvency[236] or on a number of general grounds, including oppression of members, failure of the substratum and so on.[237]

The rest of this chapter will concentrate on winding up in insolvency.

6.2 Initiation of Winding Up Procedures

An application may be made to the court to wind up a company in insolvency by the company, a creditor (including secured and contingent or prospective creditors), a contributory, a director, a liquidator or provisional liquidator of the company, the ASIC and the Australian Prudential Regulatory Authority.[238] The court has a discretion whether to order a winding up.[239]

---

230 *Re Brian Cassidy Electrical Industries Pty Ltd* (1984) 9 ACLR 140.

231 Section 411(10) Corporations Act 2001 (Cth).

232 *Re Gasweld Pty Ltd* (1986) 4 ACLC 560.

233 *BTS Bearings Pty Ltd* v. *Transmission Supplies Pty Ltd* (1983) 1 ACLC 923.

234 Sections 491–495 Corporations Act 2001 (Cth).

235 Sections 496–499 Corporations Act 2001 (Cth).

236 Section 459A Corporations Act 2001 (Cth).

237 Section 461 Corporations Act 2001 (Cth).

238 Section 459P(1)(g) Corporations Act 2001 (Cth): a prescribed agency may apply to the court. Under Corporations Regulation 5.4.01, the Australian Prudential Regulatory Authority (APRA) is currently the only prescribed agency for winding up applications. APRA regulates banks, insurance companies and superannuation funds, credit unions, building societies and friendly societies. Leave of the court is required by a contingent or prospective creditor, a contributory, a director and the ASIC: s 459P(2) Corporations Act 2001 (Cth).

239 Sections 459A and 461 Corporations Act 2001 (Cth) state that a court 'may' order the winding up.

6.3 Grounds for Winding Up

Keay has summarised five broad grounds on which a company can be wound up in insolvency:[240]

1. the company is proved to be insolvent after application is made to the court under s 459P;[241]
2. an application is made to the court pursuant to s 260, s 462 or s 464 and the court determines that the company is insolvent;[242]
3. where the creditors of a company subject to voluntary administration resolve that it be wound up;[243]
4. where a company fails to execute the instrument providing for a deed of company arrangement within 21 days of the meeting of creditors after the creditors resolve to accept the deed;[244]
5. where the creditors of the company resolve that a deed of company arrangement be terminated.[245]

A company is insolvent where it is not 'able to pay all [its] debts as and when they become due and payable'.[246] For applications under sections 234, 459P, 462 or 464, there is a rebuttable presumption that the company is insolvent if, during or after the three months ending on the day when the application is made:

- the company failed to comply with a statutory demand;
- execution of certain judgment debts was returned unsatisfied;
- a receiver or receiver and manager was appointed under a floating charge granted by the company; or
- a person entered into possession or was appointed to enter into possession of property for the purpose of enforcing a change.[247]

The most common ground is failure to comply with a statutory demand which requires a due and payable debt by the company to the creditor of at least the statutory minimum, currently A$2,000.[248] A demand must be in the prescribed form[249] and satisfy the formal requirements of s 459E(2). Following service of the demand, the

---

240 See M. Murray (2005), *Keay's Insolvency: Personal and Corporate Law and Practice*, 5th edn, Lawbook Co., Sydney [11.75].

241 Section 459A Corporations Act 2001 (Cth).

242 Section 459B Corporations Act 2001 (Cth).

243 Subsections 446A(1)(a) and (6) Corporations Act 2001 (Cth).

244 Sections 446A(1)(b), 444B(2)(a) and s 446A(6) Corporations Act 2001 (Cth).

245 Sections 446A(1)(c), 445E and 446A(6) Corporations Act 2001 (Cth).

246 Section 95A Corporations Act 2001 (Cth).

247 Section 459C Corporations Act 2001 (Cth).

248 Section 459E(1) Corporations Act 2001 (Cth).

249 Form 509H.

company has 21 days to meet the terms of the demand or apply to the court to set it aside.[250]

6.4 Effect of the Commencement of Winding Up

Upon winding up, the directors' powers to manage the company are suspended[251] although they do not lose office.[252] The directors and secretary are required to prepare a report as to the affairs of the company within 14 days of the winding up order, unless the time period is extended by the liquidator.[253] The officers of the company are required to cooperate with the liquidator and to attend meetings with the liquidator and of creditors, to give information and to deliver up all company books.[254]

Unlike bankruptcy, a winding up order does not effect a transfer of legal ownership of company property to the liquidator.[255] The liquidator exercises statutory powers to identify, recover and realise company property and distribute the proceeds in accordance with the Corporations Act.[256] The liquidator must also make certain reports to the ASIC on the company's failure and the affairs of the company.[257]

A winding up order effects a moratorium on proceedings against the company or execution of process except with court leave.[258] Secured creditors' rights to deal with their security are not affected.[259] Transfers of shares or alterations in the status of members after the commencement of a winding up are void, unless the court otherwise orders.[260]

---

250 Grounds for setting aside include that the amount in fact owed is less than the statutory minimum or that there is a defect in the demand which would cause substantial injustice if the demand were not set aside: s 459H and s 459J Corporations Act 2001 (Cth). The company may not oppose a winding up application based on the failure to comply with the statutory demand if the company could have relied on the ground in an application to set the demand aside unless the court grants leave, which it may only do if it is satisfied that the ground is material to proving the company is solvent: s 459S Corporations Act 2001 (Cth).

251 Section 471A Corporations Act 2001 (Cth).

252 *Aloridge Pty Ltd* v. *West Australian Gem Explorers Pty Ltd* (1996) 22 ACSR 484 at 486.

253 Subsections 475(2) Corporations Act 2001 (Cth).

254 Section 530A Corporations Act 2001 (Cth).

255 It remains vested in the company unless the liquidator seeks a vesting order: s 474(2) Corporations Act 2001 (Cth).

256 Section 477 Corporations Act 2001 (Cth). A liquidator may also carry on business so far as is necessary for the beneficial disposal or winding up of the business: s 477(1)(a) Corporations Act 2001 (Cth).

257 Section 476 Corporations Act 2001 (Cth) and a report is required under s 533 Corporations Act 2001 (Cth) where it appears an offence or misfeasance may have been committed in connection with the company or the company may be unable to pay its unsecured creditors more than 50 cents in the dollar.

258 Section 471B Corporations Act 2001 (Cth).

259 Section 471C Corporations Act 2001 (Cth).

260 Section 468(1) Corporations Act 2001 (Cth).

6.5 Creditors' Meetings

A liquidator has a discretion whether to convene creditors' meetings.[261] He or she may also be required to convene such a meeting when so requested in writing by at least 10 per cent in value of the creditors or contributories.[262] Additional meetings are required in a creditors' voluntary winding up:

- when advised of the members' resolution to wind up;[263]
- annually during the liquidation;[264] and
- once the company's affairs are fully wound up.[265]

A liquidator may consider it prudent and proper to call a creditors' meeting to report on:

> ... aspects of the investigations; the realisation of substantial assets and how the realisation should occur; obtaining approval for initiating litigation or initiating extensive investigation procedures; seeking of financial indemnification and seeking financial information concerning the company's business dealings etc which may facilitate the liquidator's investigations.[266]

6.6 Role of the Court in the Winding Up Process

During the liquidation, the liquidator may seek directions from the court.[267] The court may supervise the liquidator's exercise of his or her statutory powers[268] and has a general supervisory power.[269] Persons who are aggrieved by acts, omissions or decisions of the liquidator may appeal to the court and seek appropriate orders or directions.[270]

6.7 Proof and Ranking of Claims by Creditors Against the Company

The debts and claims admissible in a winding up are those payable by and against the company,[271] being debts or claims the circumstances giving rise to which occurred

---

261 Subsections 479(2) and 506(1)(b) Corporations Act 2001 (Cth).

262 Subsection 479(2) Corporations Act 2001 (Cth).

263 Sections 496–497 Corporations Act 2001 (Cth).

264 Section 508 Corporations Act 2001 (Cth).

265 Section 509 Corporations Act 2001 (Cth).

266 See M. Murray (2005), *Keay's Insolvency: Personal and Corporate Law and Practice*, 5th edn, Lawbook Co., Sydney [15.50].

267 Section 479 Corporations Act 2001 (Cth). P Agardy (1999), 'Applications by Insolvency Practitioners to the Court for Directions' 7 *Insolvency Law Journal* 60.

268 Section 477 Corporations Act 2001 (Cth).

269 Section 536 Corporations Act 2001 (Cth).

270 Section 1321 Corporations Act 2001 (Cth).

271 Present, future, certain or contingent, ascertained or sounding only in damages.

before the relevant date.[272] The relevant date in a compulsory winding up where there are no prior insolvency administrations is the date of the court order.[273]

A liquidator may require a debt or claim to be proved formally, otherwise the creditor may choose to claim formally or to prove in some other way, subject to the requirements of the regulations relating to informal proof of debts and claims.[274]

A secured creditor has similar options in respect of proving in the liquidation as those described above in a bankruptcy.[275]

Except as otherwise provided in the Corporations Act, all debts and claims are to rank equally and if the company's property is insufficient to meet them all, then they shall be paid proportionately.[276] In summary, priority payments relate to costs and expenses relating to the liquidation (and prior voluntary administration, if any), employee entitlements[277] and indemnifying creditors.[278] Employee entitlements comprise wages, superannuation contributions, leave and retrenchment payments, in that order, and are capped in respect of excluded employees such as directors and their families.[279]

6.8 Set Off of Debts

Where there have been mutual credits, mutual debts or other mutual dealings between a company that is being wound up and a person seeking to have a debt or claim admitted against the company, an account is to be taken of what is due from one party to the other. The sum due from one is to be set off against the sum due from the other and only the balance is admissible to proof or is payable to the company as the case may be.[280]

The important aspect to set off is establishing the mutuality of dealings – for example this does not occur where a company acts as trustee of a trading trust and owes moneys in its role as trustee to another party which itself owes money to the company for a transaction entered by the company in its own right.

6.9 Voidable Transactions

The property available to a liquidator for distribution comprises the property of the company on the date of the winding up order (including choses-in-action), after-acquired property, property recoverable by avoidance of pre-liquidation transactions

272 Section 553 Corporations Act 2001 (Cth).
273 Section 513A Corporations Act 2001 (Cth).
274 Section 553D Corporations Act 2001 (Cth). (See Corporations Regulation 5.6.49 on formal proofs of debt.)
275 Section 554E Corporations Act 2001 (Cth).
276 Section 555 Corporations Act 2001 (Cth).
277 Sections 556 and 560 Corporations Act 2001 (Cth).
278 Section 564 Corporations Act 2001 (Cth).
279 Subsections 556(1)–(2) Corporations Act 2001 (Cth).
280 Section 553C Corporations Act 2001 (Cth).

and compensation recoverable by the liquidator from company officers. The liquidator may also disclaim onerous property.[281]

Transactions which may be avoided under Division 2 of Part 5.7B are unfair preferences; uncommerical transactions; unreasonable director-related transactions; and unfair loans. In order to establish either unfair preference or uncommerical transaction, it is necessary to establish that at the time of the relevant transaction, or as a result of it, the company was insolvent.[282] There are certain presumptions which may assist in proving insolvency in recovery proceedings, such as the company's failure to keep proper financial records.[283]

The additional elements to establish that there has been an unfair preference are that:

- the company and the creditor are parties to the transaction;
- the transaction results in the creditor receiving more in respect of an unsecured debt than would have been received if it were set aside and the creditor required to prove in a winding up; and
- the transaction occurred within a relevant time period.[284]

For an uncommercial transaction, in addition to it being an insolvent transaction, it is necessary to establish that a reasonable person in the company's circumstances would not have entered into the transaction having regard to the potential benefits and detriments to the company.[285] It is also necessary to establish that it occurred within a relevant time period.[286] Unreasonable director-related transactions are those in favour of a director or close associate where a reasonable person in the company's circumstances would not have entered into it having regard to the potential benefits and detriments to the company. It need not be an insolvent transaction but must have occurred within a relevant time period.[287]

An unfair loan is one in which the interest on, or other charges in relation to, the loan were extortionate when the loan was made.[288] There is no restricting time period for unfair loans.

---

281 Section 568 Corporations Act 2001 (Cth).

282 Section 588FC Corporations Act 2001 (Cth).

283 Section 588E Corporations Act 2001 (Cth).

284 Sections 588FA and 588FE Corporations Act 2001 (Cth). The relevant period is during six months ending on the relation back day (in a typical liquidation, the date of filing the application) or after the filing date and before the day the winding up commences. Where a related entity was a party to the transaction, then the relevant period is during the four years ending on the relation back day. If the company became a party to the transaction for the purpose of defeating, delaying or interfering with the rights of creditors on a winding up, then the relevant period is during the ten years ending on the relation back day.

285 Section 588FB Corporations Act 2001 (Cth).

286 Section 588FE Corporations Act 2001 (Cth). That is during two years ending on the relation back day (in a typical liquidation, the date of filing the application) or after the filing date and before the day the winding up commences. Similar provisions to those for unfair preferences extend this to four years for related entities, that is during four years of the relation back day or after the filing date and before the day the winding up commenced.

287 Section 588FDA Corporations Act 2001 (Cth).

288 Section 588FD Corporations Act 2001 (Cth).

A court is not to make an s 588FF order in respect of voidable transactions where parties to the transaction or others have good defences under s 588FG that refer to matters such as receiving benefits in good faith, not suspecting the company was insolvent and so on.

6.10 Deregistration and Reinstatement

A liquidator[289] may apply to the ASIC for the deregistration of a company where certain circumstances are satisfied.[290] If the ASIC is not aware of any breaches of the relevant procedure,[291] then it must give notice of the proposed deregistration on the ASIC database and in the *Commonwealth Government Gazette*. Two months after the *Gazette* notice, the ASIC may deregister the company. The ASIC must give notice of the deregistration to the applicant or person nominated for its receipt in the application for deregistration.

The ASIC may itself decide to deregister a company in a number of situations. Some of these are where the company is being wound up and the ASIC has reason to believe that:

- the liquidator is no longer acting;
- the company's affairs have been fully wound up and a return that the liquidator should have lodged is at least six months late; or
- the company's affairs have been fully wound up in insolvency under Part 5.4 and the company has no property or not enough property to cover the cost of obtaining a court order for the company's deregistration.[292]

In these circumstances, the ASIC must give notice of the proposed deregistration to the company, the company's liquidator if any, the company's directors, on the ASIC database and in the *Gazette*. Two months later, the ASIC may deregister the company.[293]

The ASIC must deregister a company if the court orders the deregistration when also ordering the release of the liquidator.[294]

A deregistered company may be reinstated by the ASIC upon it being satisfied that it should not have been deregistered or upon a court ordering a reinstatement.[295]

---

289 As also may the company, a director or a member of the company: s 601AA(1) Corporations Act 2001 (Cth).

290 Section s 601AA Corporations Act 2001 (Cth). That includes that all the members of the company agree to the deregistration; the company is not carrying on business and is not a party to legal proceedings.

291 Subsections 601AA(1)–(3) Corporations Act 2001 (Cth).

292 Subsection 601AB(2) Corporations Act 2001 (Cth).

293 Subsection 601AB(3) Corporations Act 2001 (Cth).

294 Subsection 481(5)(b) Corporations Act 2001 (Cth). In a voluntary liquidation, see s 509 Corporations Act 2001 (Cth) concerning court orders for deregistration.

295 Section 601AH Corporations Act 2001 (Cth).

7 Liquidators: Appointment, Powers and Duties

7.1 Appointment of Liquidators, Qualifications, Registration, etc.

Under a creditors' voluntary winding up in which a creditors' meeting immediately follows the members' meeting, if the creditors nominate a liquidator, that person shall be the liquidator. However, if they do not, the person nominated by the company shall be the liquidator.[296] Where different persons are nominated, a director or member may apply to the court within seven days of the creditors' nomination, for an order directing that the company's nominee be liquidator instead of, or jointly with, the creditors' nominee.[297]

Under a compulsory winding up, the applicant for the winding up order must lodge the written consent of an official liquidator before the hearing. The court makes the appointment as a separate order to the order that the company be wound up.[298]

There are two categories of liquidator: registered liquidators and official liquidators. Official liquidators are registered liquidators who are recognised by the ASIC as suitable for appointment by courts in compulsory liquidations.

To become a registered liquidator, a person applies to the ASIC.[299] They must satisfy this body that they have appropriate professional or tertiary qualifications in accountancy; that they have experience in connection with the winding up of bodies corporate; and that they are capable of performing the duties of a liquidator and are otherwise a fit and proper person to be registered as a liquidator. ASIC Policy Statement 40 sets out the relevant experience criteria.

To become an official liquidator, there is no prescribed method for registration. Section 1283 states that the ASIC may register as an official liquidator a natural person who is a registered liquidator.

7.2 Liquidator's Powers

The Corporations Act confers both original and delegated powers on liquidators.[300] Original powers are expressly provided, primarily in s 477, and delegated powers are those which are conferred on the court but the exercise of which is delegated to the liquidator under the rules or regulations.[301]

A liquidator's statutory powers include:

---

296 Subsection 499(1) Corporations Act 2001 (Cth).

297 Subsection 499(2) Corporations Act 2001 (Cth). Where a creditors' voluntary liquidation arises out of a members' voluntary liquidation, then the creditors may appoint another liquidator instead of the liquidator appointed by the company: s 496(5) Corporations Act 2001 (Cth).)

298 *Re National Safety Council of Australia (Victoria Division)* (1989) 15 ACLR 355; 7 ACLC 602.

299 Sections 1279 and 1282 Corporations Act 2001 (Cth).

300 A Keay (1999), *McPherson, The Law of Company Liquidation*, 4th edn, LBC Information Services, Sydney, pp. 333–343.

301 For example, s 488 Corporations Act 2001 (Cth).

- to carry on the company's business;[302]
- to pay in full any class of creditors;
- to make compromises with creditors (subject to requirements in s 477(2A) for approval over a certain amount);
- to compromise claims upon the company;[303]
- to dispose of the company's property;
- to bring or defend legal proceedings in the name of and on behalf of the company and to appoint a solicitor to assist in his or her duties;
- to appoint agents to do any business the liquidator is unable to do; and
- generally to do all such other things as are necessary for winding up the affairs of the company and distributing its property.[304]

In the exercise of these powers conferred by s 477, the liquidator is subject to the control of the court and a creditor may apply to the court with respect to their exercise or proposed exercise.[305] A liquidator may apply to the court for directions in relation to any particular matter arising during a winding up.[306]

The powers of a voluntary liquidator are set out in s 506 and include all the powers conferred on a court-appointed liquidator.

In identifying and taking possession of company property for the purposes of realisation and distribution in payment of provable debts, a liquidator has certain powers of investigation, such as access to books and examination of relevant witnesses.

Officers have a duty to deliver the company's books to the liquidator[307] and the liquidator has the power to demand company books and records.[308] A liquidator may also apply to the court for a warrant to search for and seize property or books of the company in the possession of a person who has concealed or removed them.[309]

Officers must also attend on the liquidator and give information about the company's business, property affairs and financial circumstances and attend creditors' meetings as reasonably required.[310] There is a general obligation on officers to help a liquidator in the winding up and in the exercise of their functions and powers.[311]

A liquidator has power to apply for a court summons to examine an officer or provisional liquidator under s 596A.[312] A broader category of person may be

302 That is, to the extent necessary for its beneficial disposition: s 477(1)(a) Corporations Act 2001 (Cth).

303 Subsection 477(1) Corporations Act 2001 (Cth).

304 Subsection 477(2) Corporations Act 2001 (Cth).

305 Subsection 477(6) Corporations Act 2001 (Cth).

306 Subsection 479(1) Corporations Act 2001 (Cth).

307 Section 530A Corporations Act 2001 (Cth).

308 Section 530B Corporations Act 2001 (Cth).

309 Section 530C Corporations Act 2001 (Cth).

310 Subsection 530A(2) Corporations Act 2001 (Cth).

311 Subsection 530A(3) Corporations Act 2001 (Cth).

312 'Officer' is defined in s 9 Corporations Act 2001 (Cth). It includes a director or secretary of the corporation or a 'shadow or *de facto*' director.

examined under s 596B if the court exercises its discretion to summons them. These may include those who have taken part in or been concerned in, or may be able to give information about, the company's examinable affairs. 'Examinable affairs' are broadly defined under s 9 and include the management and administration of the company.

7.3 Duties of Liquidators

Duties are imposed on a liquidator by the general law as well as statute.[313] The general duties include fiduciary duties owed to the company, its creditors and members as well as a duty to exercise care and skill[314] and a duty to use his or her own discretion in the administration of the winding up. The fiduciary duties impose obligations to act honestly, to avoid conflicts of interest and to act impartially.

Specific statutory duties include a duty to ascertain and collect the company's property and apply it to discharging the company's liabilities.[315] Liquidators have a duty to investigate and report to the ASIC on the company. Within two months of appointment, he or she is to report on:

- the share capital, if any;
- the estimated amounts of assets and liabilities;
- the causes of the company's failure; and
- whether in his or her opinion an inquiry is desirable into the company's promotion, formation, insolvency or the conduct of the company's business.[316]

If it appears to a liquidator that an offence or misfeasance may have been committed in connection with the company or the company may be unable to pay its unsecured creditors more than 50 cents in the dollar, then the liquidator has a duty to report further.[317]

There is also a duty to keep proper books and accounts[318] and to retain them normally for a period of five years after deregistration.[319]

7.4 Status, Independence, etc. of Liquidators

In describing the unique status of a liquidator, the court has stated:

> The office of a person appointed liquidator to a corporation does not fit any precise legal category or classification, which defines the rights and liabilities, attaching to that office. It

---

313 For a more comprehensive discussion of these duties, see A. Keay (1999), *McPherson, The Law of Company Liquidation*, 4th edn, LBC Information Services, Sydney, pp. 290–297; 357–393.

314 *Sydlow Pty Ltd (in liq)* v. *T G Kotselas Pty Ltd* (1996) 20 ACSR 47.

315 Subsection 478(1) Corporations Act 2001 (Cth).

316 Section 476 Corporations Act 2001 (Cth).

317 Section 533 Corporations Act 2001 (Cth).

318 Section 531 Corporations Act 2001 (Cth).

319 Section 542 Corporations Act 2001 (Cth).

is a hybrid composite with elements of fiduciary, trustee, agent, officer of the corporation and (in some instances) 'officer' of the court.[320]

As an officer of the court, the liquidator is not a servant in the sense that he or she can be directed in a manner which is at variance with his or her statutory duties, but rather that he or she is the representative of the court and entrusted with its reputation for the impartial and proper dispatch of duties.[321]

A liquidator must act independently and this is underpinned by the fiduciary duty to act impartially. In *Gooch's Case*,[322] the Court stated it was 'of the utmost importance that the liquidator should … maintain an even and impartial hand between all individuals whose interests are involved in winding up. He should have no leaning for or against any individual whatever.'

7.5 Powers of the Court in relation to Liquidators

Where it appears to a court that a liquidator is not faithfully performing his or her duties or observing requirements of the court or the Corporations Act, the court may inquire into the matter and take such action as it thinks fit.[323] The court may require a liquidator to answer inquiries about the winding up, examine a liquidator on oath and direct an investigation into the liquidator's books.[324]

In the case of a compulsory liquidation where the liquidator is appointed by the court, he or she is an officer of the court and as such is 'subject to the control and direction of the court'.[325]

A person aggrieved by any act, omission or decision of a liquidator may appeal to the court in respect thereof. The court may confirm, reverse or modify the act or decision or remedy the omission and make such orders and give such directions as it thinks fit.[326]

7.6 Liquidators' Suspension or Revocation

A court may remove a liquidator where cause is shown[327] and the court is satisfied that the removal would be conducive to the better conduct of the liquidation and it is for the general advantage of the creditors.[328] This may occur, for example, where there has been a breach of duty, an appearance of partiality or of conflict of duty.

---

320 *Sydlow Pty Ltd (in liq)* v. *T G Kotselas Pty Ltd* (1996) 20 ACSR 47 at 52 (Tamberlin J).

321 *Re Timberland Ltd; Commissioner for Corporate Affairs* v. *Harvey* (1979) 4 ACLR 259 at 286.

322 *Re Contract Corporation (Gooch's Case)* (1871) 7 Ch App 207 at 211.

323 Subsection 536(1) Corporations Act 2001 (Cth).

324 Subsection 536(3) Corporations Act 2001 (Cth).

325 M. Murray (2005), *Keay's Insolvency: Personal and Corporate Law and Practice*, 5th edn, Lawbook Co., Sydney, [10.115].

326 Section 1321 Corporations Act 2001 (Cth).

327 Section 473 Corporations Act 2001 (Cth).

328 *City & Suburban Pty Ltd* v. *Smith* (1998) 28 ACSR 328 at 336.

A liquidator's registration may be cancelled or suspended for a specified period, in certain circumstances.[329] These include the person ceasing to be a resident of Australia, and failure adequately or properly to carry out or perform his or her duties as a liquidator.

7.7 Reports by Liquidators

As outlined above, a liquidator has a duty to report under s 476 and where s 533 applies.

7.8 Remuneration and Fees of Liquidators

A liquidator is entitled to receive remuneration as agreed between the committee of inspection and liquidator or, if there is no agreement or no committee, then by resolution of the creditors or, if none, by the court.[330]

There is no fixed method of calculating a liquidator's remuneration. From 1 July 2000, the Insolvency Practitioners Association of Australia (IPAA) has proposed a Statement of Best Practice Remuneration.[331] It recommends that, in most insolvency appointments, fees be fixed upon a basis of time spent at the level appropriate to the work performed.

A liquidator's costs and expenses are the first priority for distribution, with remuneration a subsequent priority.[332] A liquidator has an equitable lien over the company's property for costs, expenses and remuneration as long as a court of equity would feel it were conscionable.[333]

8 Enforcement of Securities over a Debtor's Assets

8.1 Secured Creditors and Protection of their Property Interests

Sykes provides a general definition of a security as:

> an interest vested in a person called 'the creditor' in certain property owned by another called 'the debtor', whereby certain rights are made available to the creditor over such property in order to satisfy an obligation personally owed or recognised as being owed to the creditor by the debtor or some other person.[334]

Thus in the event of default by the debtor, the creditor has not only a right to sue for default under the terms of their contract, but also an interest in the property of

329 Section 1292 Corporations Act 2001 (Cth).
330 Subsection 473(3) Corporations Act 2001 (Cth).
331 See http://www.ipaa.com.au/.
332 Subsections 556(1)(a) and (de) Corporations Act 2001 (Cth).
333 *Re Biposo Pty Ltd (No 4)* (1995) 14 ACLC 78; (1995) 124 FLR 385.
334 E.I. Sykes and S. Walker (1993), *The Law of Securities*, 5th edn, Lawbook Co., Sydney, p. 12.

the debtor or some other person. Security interests may essentially arise by four methods:

- by transfer of title (legal mortgage);
- by agreement (equitable mortgage and equitable charge);
- by possession (pledge); and
- by operation of law (lien).[335]

Of particular relevance to insolvency administrations are the mortgage and the charge because of the remedies available for enforcement. A mortgagee may enter into possession of the property, for example in the case of land, in order to lease it. Where the debtor is a company and the mortgagee (or an agent on its behalf) enters into possession of a company's property, then the mortgagee or agent is subject to the obligations discussed below which are imposed by the Corporations Act on a 'controller'.[336] (This is in addition to any obligations arising under property and security law.)

The charge is of particular relevance to insolvency administrations of companies. This is because a debtor company may grant a creditor a fixed and/or floating charge over its property. The contract which grants a charge typically includes the right to appoint a receiver (or a receiver and manager where the charge is over a company's whole assets and undertakings) of the property.

A receiver or other controller of property of a company can be appointed either privately or by a court. Private appointments derive from the contractual relationship between the company and its creditor.[337] Court appointments are made pursuant to (1) a court's inherent jurisdiction or express power where it 'appears to the court to be just and convenient that the order should be made' or (2) general statutory provisions in order to preserve assets.[338]

Although private appointments are made by a secured creditor on the basis of a security document, the Corporations Act does regulate such administrations, such as the appointee's powers and duties. The legislation refers to a 'controller', which means in relation to the property of a company:

- a receiver or a receiver and manager of that property; or
- anyone else who (whether or not as agent for the corporation) is in possession, or has control, of that property for the purpose of enforcing the charge.

This chapter refers only to private appointments in order to enforce a security over a debtor's local assets. Unless otherwise stated, the term receiver includes receiver and manager.

335 S. McCracken and A. Everett (2004), *Everett and McCracken's Banking and Financial Institutions Law*, 6th edn, Lawbook Co., Sydney, chapter 16.

336 S. McCracken and A. Everett (2004), *Everett and McCracken's Banking and Financial Institutions Law*, 6th edn, Lawbook Co., Sydney, [17.01]–[17.06].

337 R. Tomasic and K. Whitford (1997), *Australian Insolvency and Bankruptcy Law*, 2nd edn, Butterworths, Sydney, p. 22.

338 Such as s 1323 Corporations Act 2001 (Cth).

8.2 Appointment of Receivers and Managers

The power to appoint a receiver to deal with the assets of the debtor company is ancillary to the secured creditor's proprietary interest in the assets.[339] That is, the debtor grants a charge[340] over the assets to the creditor and typically provides in the document the events of default upon which the creditor may exercise its proprietary rights. The mode of private appointment of a receiver depends on the terms of the security documentation which must be strictly followed.[341]

The receiver or person in possession to enforce a charge must lodge notice of the appointment with the ASIC within seven days.[342]

8.3 Powers and Duties of a Receiver

Specific powers may be granted in the security documentation to a receiver or mortgagee in possession. In addition, but subject to any limiting provisions in the instrument of appointment, the Corporations Act grants a receiver general and specific powers.[343] These include the power:

- to enter into possession and take control of the company's property in accordance with the terms of the appointment
- to deal with such property in a number of specific ways[344]
- to realise the property
- to carry on any business of the company[345]
- to engage solicitors and other professional advisers and
- to appoint an agent to do any business that the receiver is unable to do, or that it is unreasonable for the receiver to do in person.

The duties of a receiver derive from the debenture, the appointment document, the Corporations Act and general law.[346] A receiver owes duties not only to the appointing secured creditor but also to the debtor company.

The receiver's main responsibility is to realise the assets of the company which are the subject of the charge for the benefit of the debenture holder.[347] In *Expo International Pty Ltd* v. *Chant*,[348] the following major duties were identified:

339 *Re Geneva Finance Ltd* (1992) 7 ACSR 415 at 427.

340 Section 9 Corporations Act 2001 (Cth).

341 M. Murray (2005), *Keay's Insolvency: Personal and Corporate Law and Practice*, 5th edn, Lawbook Co., Sydney, [19.70].

342 Section 427 Corporations Act 2001 (Cth).

343 Section 420 Corporations Act 2001 (Cth).

344 For example, lease, grant options over, borrow money on its security, insure or repair the property.

345 There is also a power to engage or discharge employees on the company's behalf.

346 M. Murray (2005), *Keay's Insolvency: Personal and Corporate Law and Practice*, 5th edn, Lawbook Co., Sydney, [19.205].

347 *Gomba Holdings UK Ltd* v. *Homan* [1986] 3 All ER 94 at 97.

348 *Expo International Pty Ltd* v. *Chant* [1979] 2 NSWLR 820; 4 ACLR 679.

- to exercise his or her powers in good faith
- to act strictly within the conditions of appointment and
- to account to the debtor company for any surplus after discharging the chargee's security.

An important statutory duty of the receiver when exercising the power of sale is to take all reasonable care to sell the property for not less than market value or (in its absence) the best price that can be reasonably obtained having regard to the circumstances existing when the property is sold.[349] This is in addition to the statutory duties placed on officers (which includes receivers and managers)[350] such as to act in good faith in the best interests of the corporation and for a proper purpose.[351]

There are also specific statutory duties in respect of filing and serving notices of appointment,[352] obtaining a report as to affairs from the directors and company secretary,[353] reporting to the ASIC on possible offences by the directors and others[354] and lodging reports and accounts with the ASIC.[355]

8.4 Effect of Appointment of a Receiver

In *George Barker (Transport) Ltd* v. *Eynon*[356] the court held the appointment of a receiver by a debenture holder did not end the life of the company:

> The company is, so to speak, anaesthetised but the receiver may carry on the business on its behalf. The legal persona of the company will continue to subsist until liquidation, and the company in the case of most successful receiverships may be restored to full conscious activity when the anaesthetic is no longer applied after the debts owing to the debenture holders have been paid.

The authority and management powers of company officers are superseded[357] although they retain residual powers and duties.[358] The property of the company does not vest in the receiver, rather control over it passes to the receiver. There is no automatic moratorium on legal proceedings by and against the company; however, the property against which execution of any judgment may be levied may be limited.

The appointment of a receiver does not automatically terminate pre-receivership contracts.[359] Such a contract may terminate because of a specific term or its continuation being inconsistent with the existence of the receivership. If a receiver

---

349 Section 420A Corporations Act 2001 (Cth).

350 Section 9 Corporations Act 2001 (Cth).

351 Section 181 Corporations Act 2001 (Cth).

352 Sections 427 and 429 Corporations Act 2001 (Cth).

353 Section 429 Corporations Act 2001 (Cth).

354 Section 422 Corporations Act 2001 (Cth).

355 Section 432 Corporations Act 2001 (Cth).

356 [1973] 3 All ER 374 at 380.

357 *Hawkesbury Development Co Ltd* v. *Landmark Finance Pty Ltd* (1970) 92 WN (NSW) 199 at 209.

358 For example, the power to challenge the appointment of the receiver and to file returns.

359 *Re Diesels & Components Pty Ltd* (1985) 9 ACLR 825; 3 ACLC 555.

repudiates a contract, then the company may be liable in damages because of the actions of its agent. As the company is probably insolvent, this is unlikely to concern a receiver, unless because of the particular circumstances, the court awards an equitable remedy of injunction or specific performance instead of damages.[360] Employment contracts would fall within these general principles.[361]

9 Offences

9.1 Insolvent Trading

Insolvency not only concerns debtors and their creditors but also involves the public interest. This is reflected in the fact that in many administrations there is a requirement upon the insolvency administrator to investigate the past conduct of the debtor and, in the case of a corporate debtor, its officers. A company's insolvency may also signify that compensation is recoverable from company officers for the benefit of creditors and that past debtor or officer conduct is liable for prosecution as an offence.

A significant implication of a company trading whilst insolvent is that the directors may become personally liable for the debts so incurred. The relevant circumstances are where:

- a person is a director when a company incurs a debt;
- the company is insolvent at that time or becomes insolvent because of the debt; and
- there are reasonable grounds for suspecting that the company is or would so become insolvent.[362]

By failing to prevent the company incurring the debt, the director contravenes the Corporations Act if they are aware at that time that there are grounds for so suspecting the company's insolvency or a reasonable person in a like position in a company in the company's circumstances would be so aware.

Contravention may result in a civil penalty order to compensate the company for the damage suffered.[363] An offence is committed where the failure to prevent the company incurring the debt was dishonest.[364]

Available defences are that at the time the person had reasonable grounds to expect (as opposed to suspect) and did expect that the company was solvent.[365] A director

360 *Re Diesels & Components Pty Ltd* (1985) 9 ACLR 825; 3 ACLC 555.

361 *Griffiths* v. *Secretary of State for Social Services* [1974] QB 468 at 485–486 refers to termination occurring where there is a sale of the business; a new service contract is entered into with the employee which is inconsistent with the old; and the role and functions of the receiver are inconsistent with the continuation of the employee's services.

362 Section 588G Corporations Act 2001 (Cth).

363 Sections 1317E and 1317H Corporations Act 2001 (Cth).

364 Subsection 588G(3) Corporations Act 2001 (Cth).

365 Subsection 588H(2) Corporations Act 2001 (Cth).

may have a defence where he or she had reasonable grounds to believe and did believe that a competent and reliable person was responsible for providing information on the company's solvency and that the other person was fulfilling that responsibility and expected on the basis of that information that the company was solvent and remained so after the incurring of the debt.[366]

Other defences are that the director for good reason was not part of the management at that time;[367] and that the director took all reasonable steps to prevent the company incurring the debt.[368] A specific example is to act to appoint a voluntary administrator.[369]

9.2 Other Insolvency-related Offences by Corporate Controllers

A director may be subject to penalties where the company has failed to remit tax instalments to the Tax Commissioner and where the director has not caused the company to act to remit the amounts due; to enter into a payment agreement; to initiate a voluntary administration; or to initiate a winding up.[370]

9.3 Other Relevant Corporate Law Offences

Additional offences connected with liquidation are for an officer to:

- fail to disclose or to deliver up company property
- fraudulently deal with the company's books
- fraudulently obtain property for the company on credit or dispose of company property obtained on credit
- fraudulently make a material omission in a report as to the company's affairs
- prevent the production of the company books to the liquidator
- falsely deal with the company's books or
- fraudulently obtain the consent of creditors.[371]

10 Rules Regarding Cross-border Insolvency

10.1 Introduction

Australia has adopted a generally pragmatic approach to cross-border insolvency issues. There is a willingness to exercise jurisdiction over an insolvent debtor where

366 Subsection 588H(3) Corporations Act 2001 (Cth).
367 Subsection 588H(4) Corporations Act 2001 (Cth).
368 Subsection 588H(5) Corporations Act 2001 (Cth).
369 Subsection 588H(6) Corporations Act 2001 (Cth).
370 Section 222AOB Income Tax Assessment Act 1936 (Cth).
371 Section 590 Corporations Act 2001 (Cth).

there is a relevant connection with the jurisdiction.[372] This approach accords with Australia's generally broad approach to jurisdiction.[373]

Where there are foreign insolvency proceedings, both the Bankruptcy Act and the Corporations Act provide avenues for aiding and assisting such proceedings in response to a request from a relevant foreign court. Australian courts have often extended comity to foreign proceedings[374] although there have been exceptions.[375]

10.2 Procedures for the Assistance of Courts in Foreign Jurisdictions

The Corporations Act provides that the court shall act in aid of, and be auxiliary to, courts with jurisdiction in external administration matters which are from prescribed countries.[376] These countries are the Bailiwick of Jersey; Canada; Papua New Guinea; Malaysia; New Zealand; Singapore; Switzerland; the UK and the US.[377] In the case of requests from courts from other countries, the court has a discretion whether to assist.[378]

The relevant procedure requires the following:

1. A request for assistance must be made to an appropriate Australian court by a foreign court.
2. The requesting court must have jurisdiction in external administration matters, that is winding up or insolvency.[379]
3. The request must relate to an external administration matter.
4. If the requesting court is from a prescribed country the Australian court 'shall' assist (otherwise it 'may' assist).
5. In responding to the request, the Australian court may exercise such powers with respect to the matter as it could exercise if the matter had arisen within its own jurisdiction. Thus, although the Australian court is required to assist the relevant court from a prescribed country, the type of assistance given appears to be a matter of discretion for the Australian court.

---

372 Bankruptcy: section 43 and subsections 55(2A) and 57(2A) Bankruptcy Act 1966 (Cth) refers to a debtor's connection by way of personal presence; ordinary residence; dwelling house or carrying on business. Liquidation: jurisdiction to wind up a foreign company may be exercised under s 583 and s 601CL which refer to connections such as registration and carrying on business. For more detail on this issue, see A Keay (1999), *McPherson, The Law of Company Liquidation*, 4th edn, LBC Information Services, Sydney, pp. 685–689.

373 *Oceanic Sun Line Special Shipping Co Inc* v. *Fay* (1988) 165 CLR 197; *Voth* v. *Manildra Flour Mills Pty Ltd* (1990) 171 CLR 538.

374 *Smith* v. *Australian Securities Commission* (1995) 13 ACLC 511.

375 In *Rolfe* v. *Transworld Marine Agency Company NV* (1998) 28 ACSR 117, the Federal Court of Australia proceeded to judgment in Australia rather than acceding to the request from the Belgian court to stay local proceedings and transfer local funds to the foreign trustees.

376 Section 580 Corporations Act 2001 (Cth).

377 Corporations Regulation 5.6.74.

378 Section 580 Corporations Act 2001 (Cth).

379 On the basis of the very wide terms of this definition, it may be assumed that these are to be given a wide interpretation: G. Sutherland (1998), 'Issues in Cross-Border Insolvency Law in Australia' 12 (2) *Commercial Law Quarterly* 7 at 11. However, see *Re AFG Insurances* (2002) 20 ACLC 1588.

Conversely, a relevant Australian court may request a foreign court to act in aid of, or be auxiliary to, an Australian external administration matter.[380]

10.3 Other Rules that may Apply to Foreign-based Assets

Where the company's property is in a foreign jurisdiction, however, the liquidator's ability to identify, to take into custody or under control and to realise the assets depends upon the extent to which the liquidator is able to do so unchallenged as agent for the company[381] and upon whether creditors or others are taking action in the foreign jurisdiction against the debtor company and its assets.

The private international law issue that this raises is the extent to which a foreign court will recognise and enforce an Australian court order to wind up a company and appoint the liquidator. This is a matter for the foreign jurisdiction. The issue may arise where the Australian liquidator has seized assets (or attempted to do so) and been challenged in the foreign court or where the Australian liquidator has instituted foreign court proceedings on behalf of the company, which action is challenged. Thus the preferred approach may be for the Australian liquidator[382] to obtain an order from an Australian court requesting the assistance of a foreign court.

---

380 See *Re Dallhold Estates (UK) Pty Ltd* (1991) 6 ACSR 378; *Joye* v. *Beach Petroleum NL* (1996) 20 ACSR 525.

381 *Re Timberland Ltd; Commissioner for Corporate Affairs* v. *Harvey* (1979) 4 ACLR 259; also s 471A Corporations Act 2001 (Cth).

382 Section 581 Corporations Act 2001 (Cth) or in the case of an Australian bankruptcy trustee, under s 29 Bankruptcy Act 1966 (Cth).

Chapter 16

Culture, Insolvency and Legal Orientalism in Asia: Reaching for Goering's Revolver

TIM LINDSEY[1]
University of Melbourne

Whenever I hear the word culture ... I release the safety-catch of my Browning.[2]

So often 'culture' is the tag given by law reformers – particularly foreigners introducing a new law into an Asian jurisdiction – for the reasons why their new, imported law does not work. The instrumentalist view of law reform turns on an implicit equation of 'statute + institution = change'. When the equation fails and a legal transplant fails to take root, the explanations usually given include 'lack of commitment', 'lack of local ownership', 'local legal traditions', 'local political opposition', 'lack of local support', 'sabotage' and so on. All of these fall under the rubric of 'local legal culture'. This is an experience common in insolvency law reform in Asia for many decades[3] but has recently been particularly marked in explanations for the difficulties faced by insolvency reform in Indonesia, China and Thailand.

'Culture' in the world of Asian legal transplantation can, however, become a grab-bag of everything the foreign law reformers do not know or are unable to find out about the target jurisdiction: local ideas about law, local legal theory, the practical operation of the local legal system or political issues impinging on the operation of the local legal system. In many cases, 'culture' embraces everything encountered by foreign law reformers short of formal 'black letter law' (which is usually used to mean any or all of statutes, reported judicial decisions and formal legal institutions).

Implicit in this is the notion that foreign legal culture is unmanageable, beyond the logic of global 'best practice' law reform. There is even often an assumption, sometimes made express, that although 'legal culture' issues are what usually

---

1 Professor of Asian Law, Director, Asian Law Centre, Deputy Director, Centre for the Study of Contemporary Islam, Associate Dean, Faculty of Law, The University of Melbourne, Barrister-at-Law, Victorian Bar.

2 *Wenn ich Kultur hore ... entsichere ich meinen Browning!* The phrase is from Hanns Johst's 1934 play *Schlageter* (Act 1, Scene 1) but is commonly, if incorrectly, attributed to Hermann Goering, as 'Whenever I hear the word "culture" I reach for my revolver'.

3 For accounts of reforms, see Lindsey (1998); Lindsey and Taylor (2000); Linnan (2000b); Tomasic *et al.* (1996); Tomasic and Little (1997); Tomasic and Kamarul (1999), Tomasic (2000).

determines the success or failure of legal transplants in Asian countries, legal culture is somehow mysterious and inaccessible as well as inherently inadequate or even a- or im-moral: just 'not worth knowing about'. In other words, the 'legal culture' of developing states that obstructs the reforms offered by developed states is seen as something inherently different or alien to the culture of developed states.

The difference, or alterity, of Asian legal cultures is often emphasised and exaggerated – and thus represented as something inherently threatening and negative. This is done at the expense of attention to the often very considerable similarities between Western legal systems and many aspects of Asian legal systems. These similarities mostly arise from the longstanding colonial transfer of elements of Civil Law, Common Law or Socialist Law models derived ultimately from Western Europe, albeit delivered via former colonies such as the US, Canada, Australia or, in the case of Marxism, via the USSR and China (Hiscock, 2000). And all this, of course, ignores the fact that Western legal systems are saturated with informal 'cultural' influences just as much as are Asian systems or indeed any legal system, anywhere (Freidman, 1994).

In other words, asserting legal culture in Asia as the chief reason for the failure of commercial law transplants from developed countries inevitably involves a caricaturing of Asian legal cultures that ultimately stems from Western Orientalist traditions.

Legal Orientalism

This 'Orientalising' of Asian legal cultures reflects closely the broader paradigm that Said (1978) identified in Western writing about Asia: interwoven themes of opacity, seductiveness, immaturity and immorality seen as constituting the essence of the 'Orient'. In its legal form, this Orientalism often becomes a demonising of the local 'Asian' legal culture (as immature, primitive, backward, subjective and irrational) and a concomitant valorising of Western laws (as developed, modern and advanced, objective and rational) (Taylor, 1997: 49).

Frankenberg (1997: 259) has identified this dichotomy as hegemonic and ethnocentric and reflecting an assumed superiority of Western ideas of law. Labelling this 'legocentrism' (at 260) Frankenberg claims (at 264) that most legal transplanters

> ... remain smugly united in 'belief in ... the unity of legal systems constituting the "Western" system', and in the hope for a 'common order underlying the diversity of law' or a 'planetary system of justice'. In a legal world so constructed and defended one is tempted to believe that paradise is near ... No wonder then that the comparativist praises the superiority – and with it the authority – of his home law ...

Thus legal Orientalism creates an uncritical assumption of the superiority and effectiveness of Western models among legal transplanters from foreign jurisdictions. At its extreme, the consequences of this can be as farcical as they are destructive. Witness, for example, the Australian law firm that drafted a law based on Australia's federal model for Vietnam, a unitary state made that way through a long war in which Australia participated, albeit on the other side.

At a less direct, but perhaps more destructive level, another unfortunate consequence of legal Orientalism is that the 'demonising' of Asian legal cultures exaggerates the importance and influence of local Asian opponents of law reform. These are typically members of the political elite who seek to use claims of cultural incompatibility to resist reforms that might threaten their political position.[4] They usually suggest that real reform is inappropriate for their country and thus impossible. Accepted by reformers, this claim can justify the marginalising of local reformers as irrelevant or quixotic. This has been a consistent pattern in Southeast Asian law reform, where foreign aid programmes – including insolvency law reform programmes in Indonesia – until recently ignored NGOs, consistently the most effective regional advocates for law reform (Neilson, 2000: 24–6; Lev, 2000: 84–5), because it was felt, generally incorrectly, that political elites better represented the local legal culture (Lindsey, 2001).

The Elusiveness of 'Culture'

Why are legal cultures Orientalised in Western readings of Asian legal systems? One answer is the relative lack of detailed knowledge in the West of both the substance and the operational intricacies of most Asian legal systems. In this, legal scholarship lags well behind other disciplines that have been active in Asian studies since last century, for example, history, political science and anthropology (Taylor, 1997: 51–5). An obvious necessity is for an increase in interdisciplinary studies in designing legal transplants for Asian jurisdictions (Lindsey, 1997: 109–10).

The slipperiness of the term 'culture' and its ability to evade simple definition is another reason for its unpopularity with the agencies that drive most inter-jurisdictional law reform in Asia, particularly multilateral donor and lending aid agencies, such as the International Monetary Fund (IMF), the World Bank, the Asian Development Bank (ADB) and the United Nations Development Program (UNDP), as well as the bilateral aid agencies active in law reform, such as USAID. The solution is much less clear because the problem is so conceptually confused.

The standard dictionary definition of 'culture' – for example, that of the Oxford dictionary – relates largely to the arts and restricts it to 'the intellectual side of civilisation'. This is obviously too vague to be useful in the context of law. What is usually intended by the term 'legal culture' is something that draws on anthropological reading. So, Hildred and Clifford Geertz (1975: 2–3) describe culture as 'ideas, beliefs and values' that form a 'conceptual framework' or 'pattern'. Bateson (1972), following Malinowski, has developed the theme of the pattern so far as to argue that it is fallacious even to classify the components of a society's 'patterns' or 'frameworks' – traits of a 'culture' – into categories such as economic, religious, political (and, it follows, legal) subcultures. This is because in 'real' everyday life all these categories overlap and partake of shared motivations and functions. Bateson argues that these categories are therefore, at best, abstractions for the purpose of convenience in describing societies. To ascribe them independent reality as discrete aspects of a society is a 'fallacy of misplaced concreteness' (Bateson, 1972: 37–8).

---

4 These issues are considered in more detail below under 'Asian Values'.

The significance for legal scholarship of culture as a broad panoply of complex and interacting, even competing, values and ideas, many with legal implications, has been accepted slowly. There is now, however, an acknowledgment, albeit sometimes grudging, that comparative law – whether as scholarship or as a tool for cross-jurisdictional law reform – must consider cultures as well as rules and institutions. However, the dilemma of how to deal with subject matter so unamenable to definition, and so hard to categorise, remains largely unresolved. Bateson's notion that culture cannot, ultimately, be subdivided is one resisted at all levels of analysis: scholarship, policy and aid delivery.

Some examples of the problems which comparative legal theory has had in coming to terms with the inherent intricacy of legal culture are now considered briefly. These are important, because these theoretical positions have directly informed the practical implementation of law reform in Asia, particularly in the field of commercial law.

Locating Legal Culture in Legal Systems

Much comparative law thinking on legal culture can trace its pedigree to Ehrlich's sociological distinction between the 'law in books' (Weber's norms sanctioned by state authorities) and the 'living law'. Originating from his study of the Austro-Hungarian empire, Ehrlich's notion was that it is social behaviour rather than the 'compulsive norms of the state' which dominate (Ehrlich, 1936; Antons, 1997: 417–18; Tan, 1997: 4). His idea of the 'living law' has been expressed in many different ways by later theorists, for example by Katz and Katz (1975) as 'law without law' in their analysis of the Indonesian legal system; or by Hiscock as 'soft law', as opposed to formal 'hard law' (Hiscock, 1995; 2000).

Similarly, writing on Japan, Chiba (1984; 1989) proposed an analytical model of legal culture that is largely an elaboration on Ehrlich's basic dichotomy. He proposes three basic competing sources of legal culture. Again, each might be seen as a subset of the 'law in books' versus 'living law' dichotomy: official versus unofficial law; indigenous law versus transplanted law; and legal rules versus legal postulates.

The problem with analysis of the sort advocated by Ehrlich and Chiba is that although they recognise 'living law' as important, they define it by contrast to 'black letter' or formal law – the two are causally distinct. Likewise their analysis relies on the notion that 'living law' influences a 'neutral' formal law: it either positively supports and supplements it, or opposes, modifies and even undermines it, wholly, or in part (Tan, 1997:7). As they suggest, it is important to acknowledge that informal law and legal practices can play as important role in legal activity as formal laws. In some cases, for example, Indonesia, they may even play a more important role than formal law (Katz and Katz, 1975; Lindsey, 1997; 1998; 2000; 2001). But this should not obscure the fact that both formal and informal law are products of broader, overarching and diverse cultures, made of many competing and overlapping nominal subcultures and 'cultural traits'. Statutes are therefore as much a product of culture as is informal legal behaviour. Thus, those who prepare and pass rules are influenced in doing so by the 'living law' or may well pass their 'law in books' regulations in the expectation that the 'living law' will modify them. Likewise, the application of the 'living law' is equally influenced by the formal legal culture that exists at any given time.

The sharp distinction between formal and informal law is therefore hard to maintain in the reality of everyday 'doing law' and the attempt to maintain the distinction by attempting to isolate bits of actions or decisions as solely 'living law' or 'formal' law is usually impossible.

Insolvency: Untangling Korobkin's Web of Values?

This notion of legal culture as a complex, conflicted and diverse part of broader cultures is not restricted to contemporary comparative theory. It is also found in contemporary theorising on insolvency law. It is interesting to see the same issue being fought out in a more circumscribed battleground.

The equivalent of 'black letter' formalism in insolvency theory is the economic, or 'creditors' bargain', theory of Baird and Jackson (1984). This views insolvency law as essentially a process to distribute the assets of bankrupt businesses among creditors with maximum efficiency, thus maximising '... the social product available to all parties in a particular case while at the same time ensuring an efficient national economy by weeding out weak, inefficient firms' (Delaney, 1989: 643–4). Jackson (1986) argues that insolvency processes exist only to solve the problem of the 'common pool' of assets that arises when a debtor becomes insolvent. Assuming creditors to be rational, wealth-maximising individuals, insolvency laws seek to set up the best system for ordering the distribution of the (usually) inadequate pool, on the basis that it gives the maximum return possible to each creditor by ensuring they act together to preserve or maximise the overall value of the pool (Jackson 1986: 15). Relying on the contractarian approach of Rawls, Baird and Jackson justify the insolvency process on the grounds that it is what risk-adverse creditors with no knowledge of their position in the nominal 'queue' for the assets (that is, their relative rights as fixed by the legal remedies available *outside* insolvency law, for example, contract, torts, and so on) would agree to in advance of bankruptcy, were there hypothetically a negotiation between creditors: the imagined 'creditors' bargain'. On this view, insolvency laws are rational, neutral, objective and efficient.

Critics such as Carlson (1987) have objected to this model principally on the grounds that it lacks realism. It assumes that 'hard laws' operate in a vacuum, used by purely rational players. Legal culture – 'living' or 'soft law' – seems to have no place. Carlson notes, for example, that the 'creditors' bargain' does not assert that any person has actually consented to be bound by insolvency law. Instead a hypothetical essence of human personality (Carlson, 1987: 1343) is presented and it is claimed that this essential personality *would* consent to the systems offered by insolvency law in the imagined negotiation proposed. Another way of expressing this essence is to describe it as a generalised, Platonic picture of ideal responses to insolvency, 'stripped of all historical knowledge' (Carlson, 1987: 1344).

Carlson suggests in reply that in the 'real world' few creditors are, in fact, ignorant of their place in the 'queue' (that is, completely unaware of their legal rights to the debtor's assets). Few creditors therefore have great interest in maximising the hypothetical 'common good' of fellow creditors, for example by not enforcing secured rights (1987: 1345). Likewise, there is no room in Jackson's analysis for the vengeful or greedy creditor who has no concern at all for the common pool and, in the case of the former, may not actually be concerned to obtain assets at all, preferring rather to punish the debtor by other means, such as humiliation or harassment. Both of these are, of course, familiar figures for insolvency practitioners.

To reframe Carlson's argument in terms of the legal culture discourse, he is arguing that insolvency law must be read in terms of complex legal and other cultures that determine individual responses to the allocation of wealth in a society.

This point is made explicit in Korobkin's criticism (1991) of Jackson. He proposes an alternative analysis of insolvency law, which he describes as 'values-based'. He sees insolvency law as aiming to deal with the broad implications of the 'problem of financial distress' (Korobkin, 1991: 765) rather then focusing solely on the narrow formal issues of distribution among creditors. He argues that insolvency creates a 'community' of parties affected by the debtor's problems, which includes creditors but extends also to a broader, perhaps even unlimited, group which might include employees, managers, the public, and so on. The conflicts that arise within this community might involve disagreements between moral, political, personal and social values, as well as economic interests (ibid.), thus acknowledging both the vengeful creditor and, presumably, even the sympathetic judge.

In other words, Korobkin's insolvency system is seen in terms of legal culture, locating 'the law in books' in a web of broader 'living law' and non-legal cultural influences. Thus insolvency law becomes not an economic process formalised by laws but '... a forum in which competing and various interests and values accompanying financial distress may be expressed and sometimes recognised' (Korobkin, 1991: 766).

Korobkin's critique is therefore valuable as a gloss to the discussion on legal culture above, because it demonstrates the truth both of Ehrlich's warning that law is not merely 'black letter', and Bateson's claim that subcultures do not exist independently of each other and of broader 'culture'. Insolvency law will always involve cultural issues both explicitly legal in nature and others that reach beyond the 'law', even if only because it deals with the critical issue of the distribution of wealth in society. Insolvency therefore sits at the interface of law, business, social policy, economics, politics, morality and personality: a typically tangled mix of shame, litigation, greed, rehabilitation and other powerful human motivators.

These are not merely theoretical issues. Much has been written on the failure of the bankruptcy reform process in Indonesia.[5] These critiques identify the potent cultural brew which faced the International Monetary Fund (IMF)'s reform programme introduced in 1998: economic nationalism, intensified by the economic crisis then at its height; hostile local commercial traditions; popular fear of the judicial process; profound institutional incompetence and corruption; lack of experience of insolvency and so forth (Linnan, this volume; Linnan, 2000a; Lindsey, 1998; Lindsey and Taylor, 2000).

Against this was set a conditionality-driven[6] reform project that its proponents saw as based on distinctly Jacksonian criteria, as is evident from the IMF's own account of insolvency law.

---

5 For detailed bibliographies, see the reference lists in each chapter of Lindsey (2000).

6 Conditionality in law reform refers to the process by which loans from aid agencies are made conditional on the recipient state's compliance with detailed reform programmes: see Neilson (2000) for a detailed account of the issues raised by conditionality.

> ... [B]ankruptcy law conditions debtor-creditor relations, establishing their respective rights, determining the allocation of the related risks and thereby the risks of the enterprise ... A first objective is to establish a system for the allocation of risk among participants in the market economy that is predictable, equitable and transparent. For predictability, the relevant risk allocation rules must be readily identified in the legal process and must be applied consistently. Equitable treatment requires, for example, sharing among all creditors, and the prevention of fraud and favouritism. ... A second objective of bankruptcy law is to protect and maximise value for the benefit of all interested parties (and the economy in general) ... (Holder, 2000: 45).

That such a Jacksonian transplantation effort would fail could surely never be in doubt from Carlson or Korobkin's perspectives.

So: why the formalist approach to reform in Asia, after the best part of a century since Ehrlich identified the importance of informal laws? Why is recognition of the complex cultural 'web' of Korobkin and Bateson, among others, so frequently absent when internationally-supported law reform projects are designed for Asia?

Applying the 'Cultural Web' to Law Reform in Asia

The problem for agencies trying to draft and implement concrete programmes for what is, in effect, social engineering – using law as a 'kind of lever' (Lindsey and Taylor, 2000) – is that the broad definition of 'legal culture', however accurate it may be, is protean, evasive and unwieldy. This is especially true where the legal reform proposed involves insolvency.

From the usual instrumentalist perspective of many of the international reform agencies, Bateson and Korobkin's approaches are, in a sense, meaningless. The approach of these theorists could make 'culture' simply 'what people do' or even 'what people think'. Are law transplanters required to grasp the whole of social frameworks and patterns of legal behaviour before they can introduce a new bankruptcy law or an anti-monopoly jurisdiction? If they are to abstract a legal 'set' from the web of culture for convenience, how is it to be selected? If this selection would be as arbitrary as Bateson suggests, will it be of any use? Can legal culture be dealt with usefully at all?

The answer is that somehow it must, as it inevitably affects law reform projects, whether or not it is recognised and even if it is rejected. Kahn-Freund's view (1974) that most legal transplants fail because of political differences between donor and recipient countries nicely summarises what makes this approach to legal culture so difficult for aid agencies. It forces recognition that law reform will inevitably involve the far more threatening realm of local politics, amongst other issues. It is often difficult to win support for an aid project if its 'political' nature is obvious.

The fact is, however, that almost all legal transplants, and many comparative legal projects, under the rubric of 'governance' are, as Frankenberg (1997: 261) argues, 'not only academic projects but also political interventions'. It is therefore impossible to do much in the way of law reform, particularly insolvency law, if the political nature of the exercise is not accepted. To ignore this is to court failure, as in the case of the collapse of the World Bank's judicial reform project in Peru in 1998, in the face of sustained opposition from the government (LCHR, 2000).

Governance: Law and Development Redux?

These issues underscore the controversy legal culture has attracted for cross-jurisdictional law reform, especially in relation to development assistance from developed to developing countries. The history of the 'Law and Development' approach to cross-jurisdictional law reform and legal culture is illuminating. As a specific school of thought pertaining to legal transplantation, it has been discredited for some time. Ironically, although its proponents paid scant attention to legal culture, one consequence of the fall from scholarly grace of 'Law and Development' has been a tainting of 'legal culture' as a legitimate field of enquiry, both for scholars and law reformers.

The 'Law and Development' movement turned on the Weberian notion that introducing selected rules and institutions from developed 'rule of law'[7] systems (and, in particular, American interpretations of democracy and due process) would kick-start the 'inevitable' evolution of authoritarian states in developing countries to become liberal democracies (Franck, 1972). Often linked to the Western anti-communist agenda of the Cold War (Trubeck and Galanter, 1974), 'Law and Development' enjoyed brief success but was aggressively attacked in the mid-1970s by the Critical Legal Studies school and some host governments, for being ethno(Western)centric, simplistic and neo-colonialist (Tamanaha, 1995). These criticisms were often justified, given the failure of various, somewhat evangelic and ill-conceived 'Law and Development' programmes in the 1970s.

The problem for 'culture' was that it was implicitly central to the 'Law and Development' movement, however small a role it seemed to play on the surface. Underlying the movement was the idea that Western democratic 'legal culture' embodied in the Trojan horse of transplanted laws and institutions could act as a sort of 'germ', infecting its host with liberal democracy (Franck, 1972; Merillat, 1966: 71–8; Lindsey, 2001). In fact, the outcome was sometimes the reverse. In many cases, the local culture swallowed colonies of foreign democratic infections whole – statutes, training courses, study tours and institutions gone, with barely a trace (Watson, 1996a; 1996b; Burg, 1977; Merryman, 1977).

The common conclusion was that legal importing programmes of 'Law and Development' did not work or at least could not on their own deliver a liberal-democratic market-capitalist transformation. This led to a distrust of legal transplantation and thus, by extension, 'legal culture' discourse among many comparative lawyers. At its extreme, some scholars went so far as to say that '[a]t best, what can be displaced from one jurisdiction to another is, literally, a *meaningless* form of words' (Legrand, 1997: 120). The consequences were strongly felt among international development agencies, which Neilson has described as openly deriding legal development proposals in Asian countries in the 1980s (Neilson, 2000: 16–27). With legal transplants marginalised as development assistance, the issue of determining the role culture played in them naturally lost relevance.

---

7 On the different meanings of 'rule of law' see Lindsey (1999) on 'rule of law' and *negara hukum* in Indonesia; and Clark (1999) on the development of the concept and competing accounts.

This is not to say, however, that law reform does not have a role in the transformation of such states. Obviously it does. Any shift from authoritarianism to more open and democratic models must result in some change to the legal system, just as would a shift in the opposite direction. It is also possible – although hotly debated – that the introduction of institutions and laws that tend to support such open and democratic models may be not just consequences of a change towards openness but may also be capable of provoking or completing it, to some extent, at least.

After a lull of twenty years or so, aspects of the 'Law and Development' theory have been revived under the aegis of 'Governance', sometimes necessarily in an opaque, even covert fashion, given the taint still borne by 'Law and Development' itself. The basic motivator here is an awareness that development projects in almost every sector are usually stymied by the absence of proper mechanisms for accountability and transparency in counterpart governments, that is, 'rule of law'. 'Governance' appears to answer long-standing concerns that assistance to Asian states that lack the 'rule of law' has often been unproductive or unsustainable, given that so much money and effort was lost through corruption before the crisis and then by the collapse of state systems in the face of the crisis. Its answer is to re-attempt the 'Law and Development'-style projects but with a 'rule of law', 'anti-corruption' and 'democratisation' gloss, often through conditionality.

This policy shift is, in part, a response to the end of the Cold War and diminishing international resistance to the US-led argument (articulated with, perhaps premature, fervour by Fukuyama (1992)) that there is no alternative for developing countries to 'adoption of a democratic market model of state, economy and society' (Neilson, 2000: 17; Rose, 1998: 136). This is why Frankenberg (1997: 260) describes contemporary legal transplanters as

> … the juridic midwives of capitalism. It is their task to establish a rule of law that secures civil rights, facilitates investment, and complies with the demands of a globalised economy. They, incidentally, reinvent comparative law as 'governance', … in societies that are 'in transition'.

This 'end-of-history' triumphalism sits, however, a little uneasily with another motivation for the rise of 'Governance': a sense among many aid agencies that their avoidance of 'rule of law' reform left them out-of-step with reform movements in recipient countries. 'Governance' allows them to answer the criticism that the 'de-ideologised' programmes that allowed these agencies to work with authoritarian and corrupt governments, such as that of Soeharto in Indonesia, amounted to complicit support for oppressive regimes. To this extent, 'Governance' is also a response to the economic crisis that hit many Asian countries from 1997 and the legal and political reforms that it provoked. Aid agencies are now embarrassed to find themselves struggling to catch up with a reform agenda that they assumed was unachievable, because 'local culture' (as manipulated by the former elite) was previously accepted as making it impossible.

The rationale of some new 'Governance' legal assistance programmes therefore sometimes closely follows the logic of 'Law and Development' and their objectives are often strikingly similar: deliver 'rule of law' and democracy through legal transplantation. In other, arguably more effective, incarnations, 'Governance' reform breaks free from its 'Law and Development' past and appears as less rigidly committed to US and common law ideas of 'rule of law'. Instead it focuses on how to locate and use compatibilities in the legal cultures of donor and recipient to build legal institutions and systems that allow diverse participation and strengthen civil societies – with an acceptance that the outcome may not necessarily precisely fit Western models. Of course, these also often involve liberal, 'rule of law' aspirations but need not do so exclusively – or at least not to the same, uncritical and rigid level of the 1970s.

The danger for 'Governance' is that whatever the fate of 'Law and Development', the underlying problem of any programme involving the transplantation of laws – that is, any attempt to deliver cultural change in legal systems – remains the same: 'culture' is hard to locate and even harder to manipulate for actors outside it (for example, foreign law reformers). Legal cultural change is therefore a crucial part of any legal reform programme, but it will always remain an unpredictable tool for those who see it as a merely utilitarian instrument rather than, in reality, the whole of the task.

Reverse Orientalism: Reform and Asian Values

These problems which 'culture' poses for law reform are not restricted to Western legal evangelists seeking to 'save' Asia. Asian readings of Asian cultures also frequently obstruct legal reform imports from West to East. As suggested above, the 'Asian values' polemic – which assumes an incompatibility between Asian cultures and Western values – is often used to argue that legal models from developed countries cannot work in Asian societies. A puerile vision of a 'clash of civilisations' (Huntington, 1993) is usually called upon to prove that they will never take root. The argument, put most prominently by Dr Mahathir of Malaysia and Lee Kuan Yew of Singapore, and less publicly by Soeharto in Indonesia, has been summarised (Inoue, 1998: 65–6) as follows:

> ... Asia has its own cultural essence, fundamentally different from that of the West; and ... this essence penetrates all Asian societies and their history so that they constitute a uniform and perennial cultural whole despite their phenomenal differences and constant changes. This dualism enables Asian advocates to charge Western concerns about human rights with cultural imperialism and to make the cultural relativist response: Asia will go its own way.

In this sense, 'Asian values' as applied to legal reform is really a variation on Western legal Orientalism because it assumes that East and West are legally inherently 'different', except that here Asians are adopting the dualism of Western Orientalism for different purposes, valorising the East.

Tatsuo Inoue has disputed these claims on several grounds; first, because the 'Asian values' argument is usually used to justify 'a system of economic freedom without political liberties' (Inoue, 1998: 59), also described by Jayasuriya (1999) as 'economic constitutionalism'. This rhetoric is relied upon by elites in East Asia[8]

---

[8] See for example, Mahathir Mohamad and Ishihara Shintaro's *The Asia That Can Say No*.

to insulate government and the economy from politics and opposition; to justify government by political and business elites; and to allow the development of what are, in effect, one-party systems despite their democratic shells and rhetoric (as in Singapore, Malaysia and, until recently, Indonesia).

The irony here is that if this 'Asian values' claim was accurate, there would be little need to assert it to justify acting against domestic opposition, because there would be no opposition – society would be unified in support for one, authoritarian government. Obviously, however, it is inaccurate. In every Asian society there are groups who oppose the legal and political paradigms asserted by the government or who fiercely contest dominant 'patterns and frameworks' of values and ideas or even just modify or reinterpret them. As Reid (1998) has demonstrated, most Asian societies (with the obvious exception of Japan) are notable for a significant diversity of ethnicity, with each group influenced by differing historical, intellectual and philosophic traditions. Yet these are rolled into mega-categories like 'Asian', 'Chinese' or 'Indonesian' both by much Western legal analysis and by regional Asian chauvinists.

Orientalism in its 'Asian values' incarnation is thus a tool wielded by ruling elites for obvious political purposes, rather than something somehow inherent in the world views of Asians.

Secondly, Inoue (1998: 61) identifies the elevation of state sovereignty to the level of sanctification as a key component of the 'Asian values' paradigm. As embodied in the 1993 Bangkok Declaration, this is the notion that sovereignty demands that states be immune from interference in their 'internal affairs' by other states, particularly as regards human rights. It is ironic that here East Asian states are relying on a doctrine that is, itself, fundamentally non-Asian. 'In origins and evolution, sovereignty is definitely a Western concept, and was not shared by other regions until this century.'[9] Inoue argues that, in fact, the idea of the integrity of the sovereignty of states has always been tied to, and qualified by, limits on state power. The development of the modern state since the British and French revolutions has always involved supposed liberation of subjects from the arbitrary power of rulers. Thus the modern idea of state sovereignty in fact *implies*, rather than excludes, protection of human rights, because '... such a formidable leviathan as the sovereign state should be allowed to exist only in so far as human rights are its creator and master' (Inoue, 1998: 62–3).

Thirdly, central to the 'Asian values' argument is the 'evolutionist' view that rights and democratic systems are luxuries and cannot be delivered until economic rights are delivered: subsistence via development. Demands for rights are therefore morally 'bad' because they obstruct economic development, which must be protected from politics and criticism (Jayasuriya, 1999). Against this, Inoue points out that, historically, the conferral of civil and political rights in fact often preceded social and economic rights or 'second generation rights' (Inoue, 1998: 64). In fact, few East Asian developing states have been able to deliver lasting social and economic rights – as the economic crisis demonstrates – perhaps because of the absence of civil and political rights which provide checks and balances that might restrain corruption

---

9 Richard Falk, 1993, 'Sovereignty', in Joel Kreiger (ed.) *The Oxford Companion to Politics of the World*, Oxford University Press, 851, cited in Inoue (1998: 61).

and allow a more lasting and equitable distribution of the fruits of development. Certainly this argument explains much about Indonesia's sudden collapse in 1997, after three decades of both economic growth and political repression. It also raises the question of when 'subsistence' is sufficiently secure for other rights to be permitted. Surely Singapore, for example, has reached that point and can now afford to modify its one-party, intrusive model of social control?

Finally, Inoue identifies the gross distortions of history and contemporary reality necessary to maintain the extreme Hegelian dualism that underlies 'Asian values': the trope of denial of individualism in Asia and assertion of its 'stagnancy' and unchanging communitarian nature, versus the idea of Western individualism and constant change or 'instability'. In fact, no legal culture – nor, indeed, any culture – is monolithic or static – much to the contrary.

Bateson (1972: 38), for example, reminds us that cultures compete, interact and overlap within larger national cultures and even between individuals to form those 'national' cultures.

> [W]e should consider under the head of 'culture contact' not only those cases in which contact occurs between two communities with different cultures and results in a profound disturbance of the culture of one or both groups; but also cases of contact within a single community ... contacts between groups of individuals with different cultural norms of behaviour in each group.

For example, in the case of 'Indonesian' insolvency culture, is the behaviour in issue in fact characteristic of the ethnic Chinese minority who exercise a disproportionate influence on economic activity and control many – perhaps most – of the large debtors and creditors? How useful is it to call it 'Chinese', given that their dominance of *konglomorat* or large company groups may have now led supposed *peranakan* (ethnic Chinese) business attitudes to become sectoral rather than ethnic?[10] Or is the behaviour to be described as 'Javanese', given that the Javanese are the largest ethnic group in the archipelago and dominate politics? Pemberton (1994) has shown that under Soeharto aspects of traditional Javanese culture were appropriated to produce a Java-centric official culture that 'muffled' and smothered the expression of other ethnic characteristics and critical expression of political and religious ideas (Geertz, 1990; Lindsey, 1995). Or is this commercial behaviour better identified with other ethnic groups also seen as disproportionately active in politics and business, for example, the Bataks of mid-Northern Sumatra or the Minangkabau of Western Sumatra who are noted for their supposedly more 'aggressive' and 'forthright' approach to business? Or is the behaviour typical of any of the other 300 (Geertz, 1963) or so ethnic groups – and cultures – to be found in the archipelago?

Turning now to the question of whether cultures are static, even legal cultures as ancient as Southeast Asian *adat* (traditional customary law), so often described as being an obstacle to modernity (Alisyabana, 1966; Haverfield, 1999), are in fact inherently dynamic. The essence of *adat* is, in fact, procedural rules rather than substantive laws. The manner in which decisions are made is ultimately

---

10 I am indebted to Jeremy Mulholland for this insight.

more important than the content of the decisions. This ensures that mechanisms for flexibility of response are retained (Hooker, 1978; Haverfield, 1999) as social conditions change. As the traditional Minangkabau proverb has it (Haverfield, 1999):

> If the river is in spate, the washing place is shifted
> With a change of rajah comes a change of *adat*.[11]

Equally, there can be no doubt that cultures in Asia have changed significantly in response to globalisation, by which I refer specifically to electronic communication technology, increased travel, rapid international capital flow and the penetration of foreign investment. The significant increase in foreign investment in Indonesia under Soeharto has led to an opening of Indonesian business culture beyond the restrictions of pre-existing ethnicity to absorb international attitudes to business, predominantly from the US and Japan (Taylor, 1999).

Thus, when a business person decides to negotiate rather than litigate, it is probably impossible to determine with precision and certainty to what extent this is because of the influence of traditional Javanese values, traditional Chinese family ethics, or a decision driven by international business culture which sees law as an inappropriate form of dispute resolution, or simply a purely rational wealth-maximising decision to avoid an expensive process. Indeed the person him or herself may well not be able to answer. The project of unravelling complex cultural constructs in Indonesian business is thus probably an impossible one (which is why the *Doing Business in ...* books are rarely of much use). Rather than trying to pick a dominant culture or unpack complex moments of (sometimes unconscious) commercial decision-making, it may be more productive to accept that business cultures in Indonesia today – like most urban cultures – are mestizo cultures undergoing rapid and constant change and are therefore not amenable to generalisation or stereotyping. In other words, the role that 'culture' plays in any transaction – whether commercial, political or intellectual – must be understood or predicted (if that is possible) in the specific context of that transaction, as well as the broader society or societies in which it takes place, rather than attributed to simplistic historical or ethnic traditions.

In criticising the stereotyping inherent in the dualism of Asian values, Inoue (1998: 67–79) also demonstrates that communitarianism of course exists in the West and is indeed a basic part of liberal democratic principles and the idea of civil society itself (Inoue, 1998: 73–4; Sandel, 1982). He likewise identifies 'individualist' strands in Asia within major traditions such as Islam and Confucianism and points out that these two traditions themselves are part of competing value systems within individual states, Indonesia and Malaysia for example, as part of a matrix of diversity common in East Asia. He also points to 'individualism' within diverse social groups within East Asian states (not least of which are political opposition groups), as well as within individuals.

Inoue concludes (1998:79):

---

11 J.F. Holleman, *Van Vollenhoven on Adat Law*, 1981, cited in Haverfield (1999).

> [i]ndividualism is not alien to Asia ... There are perhaps no pure individualists nor pure communitarians either in the West or Asia. The two orientations are competing within us, although we may differ from each other and change ourselves in the way we strike a balance.

The Reasonable Man versus the Cultured Man?

Thus, legal Orientalism – whether imposed by the West in its representations of 'Asia as travesty' or self-assertively wielded by Asians to represent 'Asia as righteous' – inflates the authority of culture to a supreme position within states. It suggests that legal and commercial decisions, like most other decisions with legal implications, are determined almost entirely by pre-existent monoliths of nationally-held values and ideas conferred at birth and confirmed by the experience of citizenship of an Asian state. This overstatement of culture is, in fact, tied to the law reformer's common problem of ignoring culture, identified in the opening of this chapter. This is because by generalising local culture into an immutable, overwhelming elemental force, it is seen as something that cannot be overcome or even understood by the foreigner. There is thus no reasonable alternative to ignoring 'culture' when delivering law reform projects.

The key flaw in this 'culture'-based analysis of commercial legal behaviour is an underlying assumption that culture-driven behaviour is not rational. On this view, 'culture' is determined almost exclusively by ethnic, religious or traditional values, implicitly at odds with 'modern' post-industrial society and 'rational' wealth-maximising business behaviour. Legal Orientalism would therefore have it that disputants choose not to pursue a legal remedy, for example bankruptcy litigation, because it offends a set of values shared by members of their ethnic or national group. Implicitly, these values are a set, definable series of attitudes and traditions that are inflexible, uniform and irrational. The end result then is that the Indonesian failure to use insolvency law, for example, is considered to have been an irrational product of local cultural aversion to litigation, an obstacle to development, and something that is thus morally 'bad' but beyond the reach of rational, 'rule of law' reform.

Taylor and Pryles (1997) reflect on the work of Haley (1978) and others (Ramsayer, 1988) on low Japanese use of litigation to resolve commercial disputes. They argue that behaviour seen to demonstrate the tradition-rooted (and thus implicitly 'irrational') nature of Japanese legal culture – for example, dislike of courts – can also be explained as a rational, wealth-maximising response to shortcomings in the litigation system. They follow the line of relational contract theorists such as McNeill and Linzer (Linzer, 1989) who have demonstrated that a dislike of courts as a mechanism for commercial dispute resolution is not unique to Asia and is, in fact, common in the US and other Western jurisdictions. Likewise, Asian businesses sue debtors – including other Asians – in jurisdictions where there are functioning court systems that allow for efficient, reliable and transparent debt recovery, for example, Australia, the US or (Asian) Singapore. The point here is that 'litigation aversion' is not an irrational 'Oriental' peculiarity, fixed and incapable of change, but a rational response across many different cultures to similar features of courts: their cost, the time they take, the public nature of their proceedings, the uncertainty they deliver and so on.

If this is the case, then individual creditors' decisions to avoid litigation in an Asian system without a functioning judicial system might be influenced by either traditional legal cultures or might be a rational profit-maximising decision to avoid pointless and expensive litigation – or both. The point is that the two are not incompatible. Indeed, 'traditional' cultural values may well adapt to suit the needs of 'rational' wealth maximisation. As the model of *adat* dynamism suggests, it would be hard to imagine these values lasting long if they did not. Put another way, rational behaviour in a fixed set of circumstances can easily be seen as a 'cultural' response because it is the common response. So where does 'reason' end and 'culture' take over? The question is, in a sense, pointless. If a culture is dynamic and responds to changing circumstances, then (regardless of any judgement that may be made about the rationality or otherwise of the religious, spiritual, philosophic or historical ideas underpinning it) it is to that extent not irrational, as it is capable of adapting to suit immediate needs.

Culture and Reason in Reading Indonesian Insolvency Reforms

It is worth now considering Indonesia's insolvency reforms in more detail, as a case study.

It cannot be disputed that prior to 1998 insolvency litigation was rarely used in Indonesia (Linnan, this volume; Linnan, 2000a; Lindsey, 1998) and even since the 1998 reforms, it remains relatively neglected by Indonesian creditors and debtors. The question is whether there are explanations for this that extend beyond 'culture'? The most obvious explanation, as with Japan, is inadequacies in the judicial process.

It is now widely accepted that the chief source of problems in Indonesia's dysfunctional judiciary lie with its judges (Lev, 1999; 2000). Their relatively poor legal skills and dishonesty are widely criticised. The judiciary is seen as 'auctioning off' decisions, creating 'mafia justice' (*mafia peradilan*) (Happy *et al.*, 2000). The word *hakim* (judge), jokes Bismar Siregar, a former judge himself, is short for *hubungi aku kalau ingin menang* (contact me if you want to win) (*Tempo*, 2000). The Indonesia Supreme Court has been plagued by a series of corruption scandals since the mid-1980s, including the notorious 'Golden Key' fraud case, the Gandhi Memorial School affair and the Manulife insolvency case. Post-Soeharto decisions to acquit highly connected members of the former New Order elite facing charges – for example, in relation to the Bank Bali scandal – have increased popular disgust with the courts.

In April 2000, a lawyer, Kamal Firdaus, played a recording to the Jakarta press in the presence of Supreme Court Justice and Secretary General, Pramono, in which a Supreme Court clerk, Anhar, demanded bribes. He:

> ... could be heard advising Mr Firdaus by phone that it was not the amount that counted in winning his case, but whether he offered more money to the court than his opponent. 'If you give us 50 million rupiah but your opponent gives us more, then the case will be won by your opponent ...' Mr Anhar also told Mr Firdaus to 'hurry up' and place money into a Bank Central Asia account that he said was his wife's, if he wanted to speed up the case, which had dragged on for five years (*The Straits Times*, 2000).

Likewise, almost 36 per cent of the complaints received by the newly established National Ombudsman Council in its first year of operation related to judicial corruption. Businessman Djohan Taniwidjaya, for example,

> … lodged a complaint with the [C]ouncil alleging a substitute registrar at the Supreme Court in August 1999 had asked him for a RP 200 million payoff if he wanted to win his land dispute case, Djohan claimed the registrar told him the money would be given to several justices … the female registrar gave him a time limit of one month to deliver the money, after she returned from visiting her children who were studying overseas (*Jakarta Post*, 2000a).

Clearly, corruption in the judiciary reached such proportions that it came to define that institution. This is true of most other legal institutions, including, most notably, the *Kejaksaan Agung* (Attorney General/Public Prosecutor's Department) and the police.

As I have argued elsewhere (Lindsey, 1999; 2000), 'rent-seeking' and extra-legal payments became pervasive under the New Order, because the state depended on these systems to function. In other words, a 'black' system evolved that shadowed the 'official' state and allowed it to appear to be functioning. In some cases this 'shadow' system was relatively benign in Indonesia, filling gaps in state structures via fixers and political influences and providing de facto 'social safety nets' by supplementing income. In the case of the legal system, however, the influence of the shadow system was predominantly malign.

The examples given above date from 2000, the second full year after Soeharto's resignation. Since then there have been continued initiatives for reform to the Indonesian system, particularly the Constitution; a marked increase in the rhetoric of reform within the Supreme Court since a new reform-minded Chief Justice, Professor Bagir Manan, was appointed; and corruption convictions for former New Order luminaries such as Tommy Soeharto (the former President's son). Despite these hopeful signs, however, the New Order 'shadow' system remains substantially in place five years after Soeharto's fall, although corruption is now far more subject to scrutiny and corruptors perhaps more circumspect than before (Lindsey, 2001; Lindsey and Dick, 2002).

One consequence of the continuing dysfunction of the judiciary and the consequent effective non-availability of litigation to private citizens is the dominance of relational contracting and informal alternative dispute resolution models (Taylor, 1999) in all transacting. The long-standing Indonesian combination of a corrupt and incompetent judiciary and long-established alternative models of dispute resolution – albeit unreliable and uncertain in nature – created patterns of practice that tended to avoid litigation. Thus if commercial practice is a culture, then avoidance of litigation has become the dominant Indonesian debt recovery mode and, to that extent, part of Indonesian legal 'culture'. The point is, however, that the practice is not followed simply because it is 'the culture'. Rather it has become, or been confirmed, as part of culture – a pattern or framework of values and ideas – because it is practical to do so, adapting, as does *adat*, to changing circumstances. In other words, 'culture' here is, as is so often the case, rational. An 'en-cultured' person, that is, a person acting within the web of values constituting his or her Asian culture, may well also be the rational 'reasonable man'. This is significant because this analysis suggests that whatever their present litigation-averse behaviour, Indonesian creditors might well choose to use courts to recover debts if the courts ever did become available as a sensible means of debt recovery.

If correct, these conclusions have important consequences for insolvency reform. First, they suggest that law reform *is* worth doing because perceived 'local culture' barriers are not unsurmountable obstacles to litigation as a dispute resolution mechanism because 'legal culture' is not an impermeable, unshifting wall of alterity. Although complex, it is usually amenable to rational analysis. Secondly, however, they also suggest that reform will not work – creditors will not, for example, litigate to recover debts in Indonesia – unless there is reform to the entire judicial system and thus a basic shift in debt recovery culture. In other words, there must be a realistic alternative available if 'culture' is to change and relational contracting transmute into classic or 'hard' contracting.

This has not happened in Indonesia, where insolvency was treated by the formal reform programme initiated by the IMF as something discrete from judicial reform, which was seen as 'too hard'. The result was that rational business people in Indonesia saw no reason to abandon established and effective relational alternatives and return to the courts, which had proven their dysfunction over some four decades and which were therefore regarded as a last resort in local business culture (Linnan, this volume; Linnan, 2000b; Lindsey, 1998). Unfortunately, foreigners frequently identified this outcome as simply a fixed and irrational Indonesian 'cultural' preference. Consequently reformers were left scratching their heads, disgusted that culture-bound recalcitrant Indonesians refused to take the option of a world best-practice insolvency system inserted into Indonesia (and its dysfunctional judicial system) by the foreign reformers.

Legal Models for Cultural Complexity

This recognition of Asian diversity and the complexity of its cultures underpins Said's argument that, by exaggerating and generalising selected perceptions of Asia to create an idealised, seductive but corrupt and immoral 'other', Western literature has ignored complex and diverse realities of Asian societies, with consequent damage to the West's ability to deal with those societies. Asian cultures must be understood in their own, complex (but often rational) terms and not as manifestations of a mysterious (and irrational) 'Oriental' alterity.

Lawrence Freidman (1994) has offered a model for understanding legal culture that 'transcends national boundaries' (Taylor and Pryles, 1997: 18). Freidman is attempting to create a model that looks at law and culture without emphasising nationality or ethnicity as key determinants. His analysis, basically following Ehrlich, Chiba *et al.* divides legal systems into institutions (structure), laws (substance) and legal culture. He posits as the key to comparative analysis the emergence of a global legal norm of modern legal culture that is characterised by:

- a process of rapid change;
- dense legal regulation of almost every facet of commercial and private life;

- popular acceptance of law as a legitimate instrument for allocating resources and a simultaneous explosion in 'rights' and 'entitlements';
- rising individualism – more willingness to 'access justice', either individually or as part of a horizontally linked interest group;
- globalisation – the gradual convergence of legal culture, particularly in commercial settings (Taylor and Pryles, 1997: 18).

The problems with Freidman's model are, however, obvious. First, the approach of separating out culture as values and attitudes from institutions and rules is, for the reasons put above in relation to Ehrlich and Chiba, artificial and thus misleading. Secondly, Freidman is ultimately chiefly concerned with whether 'non-modern' legal cultures can be made 'modern'; and to what extent a 'modern system' requires transplantation of his modern legal culture. His modern legal culture is essentially Western and is based on the dichotomy of this new hegemonic super-culture against increasingly irrelevant 'others', that is, most of Asia beyond Japan. To this extent it does not give sufficient weight to the inherent diversity of legal cultures and the resilience of non-modern legal cultures, for example, *syari'ah* (Islamic law) in Malaysia and Indonesia, which has its own, divergent modernisation process, with very different goals to those of Freidman's global legal culture.

So, where does this leave cultures that are a complex mixture of traditional and modern (as most are)? Will their trajectory necessarily be the same as the global paradigm? Assessing Asian legal cultures on their approximation of the hegemonic global ideal effectively returns us to the legal transplanters' 'Orientalism' identified above.

One approach that tries to deal with the diversity of legal systems and the intermeshed nature of culture, institutions and rules is that of Zweigert and Kotz (1985), who base their analysis on 'legal style'. They look to historical background and development; dominant and characteristic modes of thought; distinctive institutions; legal sources and how they are dealt with; and ideology. On these bases they classify legal systems into groups, or families. Again, however, the problem remains that the ultimate aim of generalising the legal systems of states – and thus, the legal cultures within them – forces oversimplification and, inevitably, the impossibility of any real consideration of how legal cultures operate in everyday legal activities. Further, the groups Zweigert and Kotz propose are, in the end, highly Euro-centric in nature (Tan, 1997: 4).

Ugo Mattei offers a more sophisticated model that deals more effectively with some of these problems. He would look at a legal transplant in terms of the changes it produces within the recipient society. His focus is on the way diverse legal cultures operate, contending and overlapping within legal systems and the broader cultures of which they are a part. In other words, Mattei's analysis of legal culture turns on operational practice, rather than 'stage of development' (Freidman) or extent of contest between formal and informal law (Ehrlich, Chiba); or how style allows classification into a 'family' or supposedly similar systems. Mattei's model assumes the conflation of culture and other elements of legal systems. He argues that it is the method of operation of a legal system that is the key to understanding it.

> … [The] simple idea behind it – not completely new in comparative circles – is that in all societies there are three main sources of social norms or social incentives which affect an individual's behaviour: politics, law and philosophical or religious tradition (Mattei, 1997: 12).

His taxonomy proposes three categories that would cut across the Common/Civil/Socialist models usually adopted by comparative lawyers by focusing on the patterns that drive day-to-day operations of 'systems of control' (his broad definition of 'law'), within a given state: Professional, Political and Traditional. 'Professional law' embraces both functioning common law and civil law systems as aspects of Western legal tradition. This tradition is, in turn, seen as embodied by two key concepts:

> … the separation between law and politics and the separation between law and religious and/or philosophical tradition … in law the lawyer is the main actor; in politics, the politician is the main actor; and in religion, the priest is the main actor (Mattei, 1997: 22, 27).

By contrast, in 'Political law' systems the political and the legal cannot be formally separated. Of course, the two are always linked to some extent, even in a professional system: politicians make laws; laws regulate political conduct; and the practice of law always has political connotations, especially where the state is a party. Mattei accepts this. His argument rather is that in his 'Political law' system autonomous spheres for law and politics do not exist at all. This means that:

> … law in the professional term of the word is not absent, but it is extremely marginalised and weak before other sources of social rule-making (mainly political power) … the outcome of litigation depends on 'who is who' in the political world … in the rule of political law, there is not such a thing as formal law binding on government. Governments may make efforts to comply (e.g. in order to pay lip service to the western-centric requirements of international financing institutions), but the surrounding circumstances and the need to keep power … do justify the disregard for formal law. In the everyday working rule of law such a non-formalised model of decision making based on political power flavours the whole of the legal system. As it has been pointed out by the late Professor Schlesinger: 'when men rather than law govern, people usually find it more prudent to seek a powerful human protector than to stand on legal rights against the state' (Mattei, 1997: 28–9).

Thus, Mattei's reading of 'politics' is a broad one and it is based on the notion of 'power', rather than being tied to the institutions of politics – government, parliament and so on – alone. 'Politics' in this sense would extend, for example, to 'legal culture' and 'other forms of social regulation'.

It is also important in understanding Mattei's categories to understand that they are not exclusive.

> In each legal system, where one pattern is hegemonic, the other two do not disappear. They will play a larger or smaller role depending on the scope of the alternative forms of social control left by the hegemonic pattern. Occasionally non-hegemonic patterns will determine certain legal outcomes in an unofficial, cryptic way … (Mattei, 1997: 14).

Thus, a 'legal system never corresponds perfectly with a legal pattern' (Mattei, 1997: 15). Patterns will co-exist, perhaps in different sectors or at particular times in particular circumstances. Mattei also recognises that the hegemonic pattern may, in fact, be replaced; in particular by legal transplants, which usually seek to insert professionalism into a traditional or political legal system.

In the last of Mattei's patterns, 'traditional', he includes Islamic law, Hindu law and 'other Asian and Confucian conceptions of law' (Mattei, 1997: 39). Of all his categories, this is the least clearly enunciated and it reflects his apparent interest in African, rather than Asian, legal systems.[12] Essentially, however, it refers to a '... very important, hegemonic, sphere of legal relationships governed by informal or non-professional institutions: religion ... and traditional philosophic-behaviour' (Mattei, 1997: 39). The test here is not the absence of law or legal institutions but the presence of certain of what he calls 'working rules', in particular (to select a few):

> ... a reduced role played by lawyers with respect to other individuals entrusted with the resolution of social disputes (mediators, wise men, religious authority); forced [W]esternisation and consequent hurried incorporation of professional models; ... a high rate of survival of very diversified local customs; disparate sources of law in the countryside and in urban contexts (Mattei, 1997: 39).

Perhaps the most significant aspect of the traditional pattern is in the 'supernatural rhetoric of legitimisation': 'It is a very strong, very ancient and respected rhetoric, that may successfully compete with both that (recent) of democracy and that (much less symbolic) of the political contingency' (Mattei, 1997: 40).

Applying Mattei

So, to turn again to Indonesia, Mattei's classifications suggest a strongly Politically patterned legal system.[13] Within this pattern, we can also locate vestigial Professional sectors (for example, Jakarta's commercial advisers and some of the legal NGOs) and a more significant Traditional sector, *adat* and *syari'ah*. Both of these sectors leach into the Political at different times and to different extents, for example, in dispute resolution (Taylor and Pryles, 1997) and, less commonly, into the Professional pattern, for example, in marriage law (Butt, 1999) or land disputes (Fitzpatrick, 1999). Insolvency regulation, however, while it may be expressed in 'Professional' terms, for example by reference to the Dutch or other Western models or through statutes, is almost always ultimately played out in the Political sector.

This analysis is useful to understanding why the insolvency law transplantation has failed in Indonesia, because the basic framework of insolvency law in most East Asian countries was derived from the West and can thus be seen as a transplant. What Mattei's model tells us is that what reformers seek to do is to transform a Political

---

12 Mattei in fact at first uses the highly contested and problematic term 'Oriental' (at 35) to describe these systems before acknowledging that the geographic label is not sufficiently 'indicative of the system's structural nature'. I would argue, per Said, that the label is, in fact, positively misleading and unhelpful as it is redolent of the same Western-centrism he seeks to avoid.

13 Although Mattei appears to consider the traditional law pattern more dominant in 'China and in other Asian countries' (1997: 33).

pattern of legal operations into a Western-style Professional pattern by inserting discrete units of professional law. Underlying the reformers' programme is a fundamentally instrumentalist approach that views reform statutes modelled on Western precedent as legal 'viruses', positive contagions that will multiply and 'infect' an entire system with 'professionalism', transforming it. As Mattei acknowledges, this 'Western' virus could be an import or a local product, because he allows for transplants without a donor country, that is, transplants between sectors within the one country. Because on Mattei's analysis the real issue is the pattern of legal behaviour, rather than the laws themselves, the 'virus' approach rarely works in reality, unless the patterning of the entire legal system has changed.

Mattei's framework helps us gloss Kahn-Freund's concerns about the essentially political nature of legal transplants by providing a much broader definition of 'political'. On Mattei's analysis, without political shift in a recipient country away from the Political pattern of law, legal transplants from a Professional system – whether transplants or originating from within – are usually doomed to failure because the entirety of the Political pattern militates against implementing Professionalism, in however discrete or limited a form. To continue the medical metaphor, the body politic will muster all its resources to reject the transplant, often with dire consequences for the body politic itself.

Mattei's focus on what happens to law within a society or culture, rather than on comparing cultures and analysing them by the nature of legal exchanges between them, suggests one implicit difference between 'Law and Development' and the 'Governance' approach. The latter tends to have more interest in internal change, with transplantation as just one tool, albeit the most important one. While 'Law and Development' was primarily concerned with using transplants to force change – that is, it relied on cultural generalisation – 'Governance' tends to take a more sophisticated approach to the complexity of local cultures.

Conclusion: Uncultured Comparativists?

This may suggest a step in the direction Frankenberg (1997) advocates for future legal transplantation and comparativist understandings of legal cultures. Frankenberg proposes a departure from the assumption that developing and transitional country legal systems will be reformed simply by being remade in Western form. This rejects the idea that the solution for Asian legal dysfunction is the injection into a matrix of demonised and stereotyped ideas known as 'Asian legal culture' of a set of idealised but contested ideas known as 'Western legal culture', suspended in a blend of institutions, statutes and education. The result is so often like the IMF exercise in Indonesia of creating a new bankruptcy court (the *Pengadilan Niaga* or Commercial Court): it might have been better if nothing (at least in the medium term) had been done at all (Lindsey, 1998; Breitzke, 2000; Linnan, 2000a).

Rather, Frankenberg (1997: 259) calls for a recognition of Western legal systems not as objectives on an idealised path of a global legal evolution but as culturally specific constructs which are thus tools, rather than objectives, of cross-jurisdictional law reform:

> 'Escape attempts' from Western law's overpowering and ethnocentric everyday are bound to fail, unless comparativists realise that the everyday is shaped and dominated by a grid of concepts, research techniques, professional ethics, and politics by which the prevailing culture imposes on the individual scholar its canons of how legal scholarship is to be conducted ... Only after such a deconstructive move – after breaking down the conceptual repression – will the entire world, including her own, appear as a foreign land. When she returns to her native country, she will find it strange; when she reenters the citadel of law, she will find it even more strange. The recognition of the law school as an exotic place, and of traditional comparative legal work as an exotic practice, might be the first step toward a new approach to comparative law.

So what role, then, for culture in this 'exotic', albeit Western, academy? Do we adopt the solution of Daniel Lev, a leading American scholar of Indonesian law, who bans his students from using the word 'culture' because it is usually code for something else – politics, religion or ethnicity, for example? This is surely the scholarly equivalent of reaching for Goering's revolver, but it does have the advantage of forcing precision and more careful analysis of legal transplants and 'local culture' in comparative legal studies and cross-jurisdictional law reform. This is particularly important in the case of insolvency, because, in any society, this area of law will always straddle a complex and volatile cultural interface of law, politics, economics and the global distribution of wealth.

References

Alisyabana, Sutan Takdir, 1966, *Indonesia: Social and Cultural Revolution*, Oxford University Press, Singapore.

Antons, Christoph, 1997, 'Indonesian Intellectual Property Law in Context', in Veronica Taylor (ed.), 1997, *Asian Laws Through Australian Eyes*, LBC Information Services, North Ryde, Sydney, 401–423.

Baird, Douglas and Thomas Jackson, 1984, 'Corporate Reorganisations and the Treatment of Diverse Ownership Interests: a Comment on Adequate Protection of Secured Creditors in Bankruptcy', 51 *University of Chicago Law Review* 97.

Bateson, Gregory (1972, Chandler Publishing) 1973, *Towards an Ecology of Mind*, Granada Publishing, London.

Breitzke, Paul, 2000, 'Securitisation and Bankruptcy in Indonesia: Theme and Variations', in Tim Lindsey (ed.), *Indonesia: Bankruptcy, Law Reform and the Commercial Court*, Desert Pea Press, Sydney.

Burg, Elliot M., 1977, 'Law and Development: A review of the literature and a critique of "Scholar in Self-Estrangement"', *The American Journal of Comparative Law*, Vol. 25, 492–530.

Butt, Simon, 1999, 'Polygamy and Mixed Marriage in Indonesia: The Application of the Marriage Law in the Courts', in T. Lindsey (ed.), *Indonesia: Law and Society*, Federation Press, Sydney, 122–144.

Carlson, David, 1987, 'Philosophy in Bankruptcy', 85 *Michigan Law Review*, 1341.

Chiba, Masiji, 1984, 'Cultural Universality and Particularity of Jurisprudence', in M.L. Marasinghe and W.E. Conklin (eds), *Essays on Third World Perspectives on Jurisprudence*, Malayan Law Journal, Singapore.

Chiba, Masiji, 1989, *Legal Pluralism: toward a general theory through Japanese legal culture*, Tokai University Press, Tokyo.

Clark, David, 1999, 'The Many Meanings of Rule of Law', in Kanishka Jayasuriya (ed.), *Law, Capitalism and Power in Asia: the Rule of Law and Legal Institutions*, Routledge, London and New York.

Delaney, Kevin J., 1989, 'Power, Intercorporate Networks, and "Strategic Bankruptcy"', 23 *Law and Society Review*, 643.

Ehrlich, Eugen (trans. W.L. Moll), 1936, *The Fundamental Principles of the Sociology of Law*, Harvard University Press, Cambridge.

Fitzpatrick, Daniel, 1999, 'Beyond Dualism: Land Acquisition and Law in Indonesia', in T. Lindsey (ed.), *Indonesia: Law and Society*, Federation Press, Sydney, 74–95.

Franck, Thomas, 1972, 'The New Development: Can American Law and Legal Institutions Help Developing Countries?', *Wisconsin Law Review*, No. 3, 762–801.

Frankenberg, Gunter, 1997, 'Stranger than Paradise: Identity and Politics in Comparative Law', *Utah Law Review*, No. 2, 257–274.

Freidman, Lawrence, 1994, 'Is There a Modern Legal Culture', *Ratio Juris*, 7, 117–131.

Fukuyama, Francis, 1992, *The End of History and the Last Man*, Free Press.

Geertz, Clifford, 1990, '"Popular Art" and the Javanese Tradition', *Indonesia*, 50, 77.

Geertz, Hildred, 1963, 'Indonesian Cultures and Communities', in Ruth McVey (ed.), *Indonesia*, Yale University, New Haven.

Geertz, Hildred and Clifford Geertz, 1975, *Kinship in Bali*, University of Chicago Press, Chicago and London.

Haley, John O., 1978, 'The Myth of the Reluctant Litigant', 4 *Journal of Japanese Studies*, 359.

Happy, S., A.K. Arif and I.G.G. Maha Adi, 2000, 'The Door isn't yet shut for Benjamin', *Tempo* (trans. Helen Pausacker with Tim Lindsey) 5 March 2000, 60.

Haverfield, Rachel, 1999, '*Hak Ulayat* and the State: Land Reform in Indonesia', in T. Lindsey (ed.), *Indonesia: Law and Society*, Federation Press, Sydney, 42–73.

Hiscock, Mary, 1995, 'Changing Patterns of Regional Law Making in Asia', 5 *Australian Journal of Corporate Law*, 367.

Hiscock, Mary, 2000, 'Remodelling Asian Laws', in T. Lindsey (ed.), *Indonesia: Bankruptcy, Law Reform and the Commercial Court*, Desert Pea Press, Sydney, 28–43.

Holder, W.E., 2000, 'Indonesian Bankruptcy Reform: The IMF Approach', in T. Lindsey (ed.), *Indonesia: Bankruptcy, Law Reform and the Commercial Court*, Desert Pea Press, Sydney, 48–51.

Hooker, M.B., 1975, *Legal Pluralism: An Introduction to Colonial and Neo-Colonial Laws*, Clarendon Press, Oxford.

Hooker, M.B., 1978, *Adat Law in Modern Indonesia*, Oxford University Press, Kuala Lumpur.

Huntington, S., 1993, 'The Clash of Civilisations', 72 *Foreign Affairs*, No. 3.

Inoue, Tatsuo, 1998, 'Liberal Democracy and "Asian Values"', in Morigiwa Yasutomo (ed.), *Law in a Changing World: Asian Alternatives*, Frans Steiner Verlag, Stuttgart.

Jackson, Thomas, 1986, *The Logic and Limits of Bankruptcy Law*, Harvard University Press.

Jakarta Post, 2000, 'Jakarta judges moved around in major govt shift', 20 April.

Jakarta Post, 2000a, 'Businessman reports graft in Supreme Court', 28 April.

Jakarta Post, 2000b, 'Four new commercial courts to be opened next week', 3 May.

Jayasuriya, Kanishka, 1999, 'The Rule of Law and Governance in the East Asian State', *The Australian Journal of Asian Law*, Vol. 1, No. 2.

Kahn-Freund, Otto, 1974, 'On the Uses and Misuses of Comparative Law', *The Modern Law Review*, Vol. 37, 1–27.

Katz, June and Ronald Katz, 1975, 'The New Indonesian Marriage Law: A Mirror of Indonesia's Political, Cultural and Legal Systems', *American Journal of Comparative Law*, 653.

Korobkin, Donald, 1991, 'Rehabilitating Values: A Jurisprudence of Bankruptcy', 91 *Columbia Law Review*, 717.

LCHR (Lawyers Committee for Human Rights), 2000, *Building on Quicksand: the Collapse of the World Bank's Judicial Reform Project in Peru*, http://www.lchr.org.pubs/Perubuilding.htm.

Legrand, Pierre, 1997, 'The Impossibility of Legal Transplants', *MJ*, Vol. 4, 11–124.

Lev, Daniel, 1999, 'Between State and Society: Professional Lawyers and Reform in Indonesia', in T. Lindsey (ed.), *Indonesia: Law and Society*, Federation Press, Sydney, 227–246.

Lev, Daniel, 2000, 'Comments on the Course of Law Reform in Modern Indonesia', in T. Lindsey (ed.), *Indonesia: Bankruptcy, Law Reform and the Commercial Court*, Desert Pea Press, Sydney, 74–93.

Lindsey, Tim, 1995, 'Concrete Ideology: Taste, Tradition and the Javanese Past in New Order Public Space', in Virginia Hooker (ed.), *Culture and Society in New Order Indonesia*, Oxford University Press, Kuala Lumpur.

Lindsey, Tim, 1997, 'Paradigms, Paradoxes and Possibilities: Towards Understandings of Indonesia's Legal System', in Veronica Taylor (ed.), *Asian Laws Through Australian Eyes*, LBC Information Services, Sydney.

Lindsey, Tim, 1998, 'The IMF and Insolvency Law Reform in Indonesia', 34(3) *Bulletin of Indonesian Economic Studies*, 199–124.

Lindsey, Tim, 1999, 'Indonesia's *Negara Hukum*: Walking the Tightrope to the Rule of Law', in Damien Kingsbury and Arief Budiman (eds), *Democracy in Indonesia: the Crisis and Beyond*, Monash Asia Institute/Centre for Southeast Asian Studies, Clayton.

Lindsey, Tim, 2000, 'Black Letter, Black Market and Bad Faith: Corruption and the Failure of Law Reform', in Chris Manning and Peter van Dierman (eds), *Indonesia in Transition*, CSEAS, Singapore, 278–292.

Lindsey, Timothy, 2001, 'Abdurrahman, the Supreme Court and Corruption: Viruses, Transplants and the Body Politic in Indonesia', in Arief Budiman and Damien Kingsbury (eds), *Rethinking Indonesia*, Routledge, London.

Lindsey, Tim and Howard Dick (eds), 2002, *Corruption in Asia: Rethinking the Governance Paradigm*, Federation Press, Sydney.

Lindsey, Tim and Veronica Taylor, 2000, 'Rethinking Indonesian Insolvency Reform: Contexts and Frameworks', in T. Lindsey (ed.), *Indonesia: Bankruptcy, Law Reform and the Commercial Court*, Desert Pea Press, Sydney, 2–14.

Linnan, David, 2000a, 'Bankruptcy Policy and Reform: Reconciling Efficiency and Economic Nationalism', in T. Lindsey (ed.), *Indonesia: Bankruptcy, Law Reform and the Commercial Court*, Desert Pea Press, Sydney, 94–113.

Linnan, David, 2000b, 'Indonesian Law Reform, or "Once More Unto the Breach": A Brief Institutional History', Vol. 1, *Australian Journal of Asian Law*, 1.

Linzer, Peter, 1989, 'Uncontracts: Context, Contorts and the Relational Approach', in Linzer (ed.), *A Contracts Anthology*, Andersen Publishing.

Mattei, Ugo, 1997, 'Three Patterns of Law: Taxonomy and change in the world's legal systems', *American Journal of Comparative Law*, Vol. 45, 5–44.

Merillat, H.C.L, 1966, 'Law and Developing Countries', *The American Journal of International Law*, Vol. 60, 71–78.

Merryman, John H., 1977, 'Comparative Law and Social Change: On the Origins, Style, Decline and Revival of the Law and Development Movement', *The American Journal of Comparative Law*, Vol. 25, 457–491.

Neilson, William, 2000, 'Reforming Commercial Laws in Asia: Strategies and Realities for Donor Agencies', in T. Lindsey (ed.), *Indonesia: Bankruptcy, Law Reform and the Commercial Court*, Desert Pea Press, Sydney, 15–27.

Pemberton, John, 1994, *In the Subject of 'Java'*, Cornell University Press, Ithaca and London.

Ramsayer, J.M., 1988, 'Reluctant Litigant Revisited: Rationality and Disputes in Japan', 14 *Journal of Japanese Studies*, 111.

Reid, Anthony, 1998, 'Political Tradition in Indonesia: The One and the Many', *Asian Studies Review*, Vol. 22:1, 23–28.

Rose, Carol, 1998, 'The "New" Law and Development Movement in the Post-Cold War Era: A Vietnam Case Study', 32 *Law and Society Review*, 93–140.

Said, Edward, 1978, *Orientalism*, Penguin, London.

Sandel, Charles, 1982, *Liberalism and the Limits of Justice*, Cambridge University Press, Cambridge.

Straits Times, 2000, 'Judge's Verdict for Sale? Indonesia's Supreme Court embarrassed by Tape' (no author), April 14.

Tamanaha, Brian Z., 1995, 'The Lessons of Law-And-Development Studies', *The American Journal of Comparative Law*, Vol. 89, 475.

Tan, Poh-Ling (ed.), 1997, *Asian Legal Systems; Law, Society and Pluralism in East Asia*, Butterworths, Adelaide.

Taylor, Veronica (ed.), 1997, *Asian Laws Through Australian Eyes*, LBC Information Services, North Ryde, Sydney.

Taylor, Veronica, 1999, 'The Transformation of Indonesian Commercial Contracts and Legal Advisers', in T. Lindsey (ed.), *Indonesia: Law and Society*, Federation Press, Sydney, 279–290.

Taylor, Veronica, and Michael Pryles, 1997, 'The Cultures of Dispute Resolution in Asia', in Michael Pryles (ed.), *Dispute Resolution in Asia*, Kluwer Law International, The Netherlands.

Tempo, 2000, 'The Biggest Mafia or the Highest Court?', Opinion No. 04/XXIX/27 (editorial – trans. Simon Butt with Tim Lindsey) March–April 2000.

Tomasic, Roman, 2000, 'Asia-Pacific Law Reforms: Directions for Indonesia', in T. Lindsey (ed.), *Indonesia: Bankruptcy, Law Reform and the Commercial Court*, Desert Pea Press, Sydney, 114–124.

Tomasic, Roman *et al.*, 1996, 'Insolvency Law Administration and Culture in Six Asian Legal Systems', 6 *Australian Journal of Corporate Law*, Desert Pea Press, Sydney, 211–288.

Tomasic, Roman and Bahrin Kamarul, 1999, 'The Rule of Law and Corporate Insolvency in Six Asian Legal Systems', in Kanishka Jayasuriya (ed.), *Law, Capitalism and Power in Asia: The Rule of Law and Legal Institutions*, Routledge, London, 151.

Tomasic, Roman and Peter Little, 1997, *Insolvency Law and Practice in Asia*, FT Law and Tax, Hong Kong.

Trubeck, David and Marc Galanter, 1974, 'Scholars in Self-Estrangement: Some Reflections on the Crisis in Law and Development Studies in the United States', *Wisconsin Law Review*, No. 3, 1085–1086.

Watson, Alan, 1996a, 'Aspects of the Reception of Law', *The American Journal of Comparative Law*, Vol. 44, 335–351.

Watson, Alan, 1996b, 'Legal Transplants and Law Reform, *The Law Quarterly Review*, Vol. 92, 79–84.

Zweigert, K. and Kotz, H., 1985, *An Introduction to Comparative Law*, Clarendon, Oxford.

Chapter 17

Cross-border Insolvency in East Asia: Formal and Informal Mechanisms and UNCITRAL's Model Law

ANGUS FRANCIS
Griffith University

Introduction

Interest in cross-border insolvency has increased with the rise in economic interdependence and the associated legal risks involved in international transactions.[1] There is growing awareness that current insolvency regimes are inadequate to deal with the growth in global trade and investment.[2] International and regional organizations have focused their attention on formulating official and unofficial legal mechanisms to deal with the complex jurisdictional and enforcement issues that arise in cross-border insolvencies. Organizations such as the Asian Development Bank have been particularly active in promoting reform initiatives in insolvency regimes in East Asia following the Asian financial crisis.

The first section of this chapter provides a brief overview of cross-border insolvency, including the principles of private international law that have evolved in response to the particular issues raised in many international insolvencies. In the second section, the national approaches of jurisdictions in East Asia are considered. The third section focuses on some of the more notable cross-border insolvencies that have impacted on jurisdictions in East Asia. The final section considers in more

---

1 The annual average rate of global direct investment increased approximately threefold between 1980 and 1990: Bureau of Industry Economics (1995), *Investment abroad by Australian companies*, Report 95/19 Canberra: AGPS, 3.

2 The Guide to the Enactment of the UNCITRAL Model Law on Cross-border Insolvency states (at para. 13):

> The increasing incidence of cross-border insolvencies reflects the continuing global expansion of trade and investment. However, national insolvency laws have by and large not kept pace with the trend, and they are often ill-equipped to deal with cases of a cross-border nature. This frequently results in inadequate and inharmonious legal approaches, which hamper the rescue of financially troubled businesses, are not conducive to a fair and efficient administration of cross-border insolvencies, impede the protection of assets of the insolvent debtor against the dissipation and hinder maximization of the value of those assets (UNCITRAL, *Model Law on Cross-border Insolvency with Guide to Enactment*, A/CN.9/442).

detail the international and regional initiatives taken to foster domestic reform in the regulation of cross-border insolvency.

1 A Brief Overview of Cross-border Insolvency

Cross-border insolvency, an incident of international trade and investment, has a correspondingly long lineage (although the commercial form of the debtors and creditors may have changed).[3] As Fletcher states, 'since the medieval period in Europe, at the very latest, the phenomenon of cross-border insolvency has been an aspect of commercial experience posing special challenges for lawyers and courts alike'.[4] Nadelmann refers to the 'economic shock-waves' caused by the failure of the Ammanati Banking House of Pistoia in 1302.[5]

A company incorporated in one jurisdiction may incur liabilities and acquire assets in foreign jurisdictions in the course of trade and investment. Cross-border insolvency may occur, for instance, where an insolvent debtor has assets in more than one state, or where creditors are not from the state where the insolvency proceedings are taking place.[6] Cross-border insolvency can apply to individuals or corporations. This chapter focuses on the particular issues raised by the cross-border insolvency of corporations.[7]

Cross-border insolvencies can give rise to many issues relating to jurisdiction and enforcement. For instance, in a local winding up these issues may concern:

- the liquidation order (for example the jurisdiction of the local court to liquidate a foreign corporation);
- the identification of the estate (for example the examination of company officers outside the jurisdiction);
- the realisation of assets (for example the sale of real property in another jurisdiction);
- the avoidance of pre-administration transactions (for example preference transactions which partially occurred outside the jurisdiction);

3 Fletcher, I. (1994), 'Harmonization of Jurisdictional and Recognitional Rules: The Istanbul Convention and the Draft EEC Convention', in Ziegel, J. (ed.), *Current Developments in International and Comparative Corporate Insolvency Law*, Oxford: Clarendon Press, 709 at 709.

4 Fletcher, I. (1994), 'Harmonization of Jurisdictional and Recognitional Rules: The Istanbul Convention and the Draft EEC Convention', in Ziegel, J. (ed.), *Current Developments in International and Comparative Corporate Insolvency Law*, Oxford: Clarendon Press, 709 at 709.

5 Nadelmann, K. (1994), U. Pa. L. Rev. 58, 58–9, cited in Fletcher, I. (1994), 'Harmonization of Jurisdictional and Recognitional Rules: The Istanbul Convention and the Draft EEC Convention', in Ziegel, J. (ed.), *Current Developments in International and Comparative Corporate Insolvency Law*, Oxford: Clarendon Press, 709 at 709.

6 United Nations Commission on International Trade Law, *Model Law on Cross-border Insolvency with Guide to Enactment*, A/CN.9/442 at 15. See generally Smart, P. (1991), *Cross-border Insolvency*, London: Butterworths.

7 For a discussion of globalisation in the context of individual bankruptcy, see Mason, R. (1997), 'Globalisation of Bankruptcy Practice – An Australian Perspective', 5 *Insolvency Law Journal*, March 1997, 12.

- distribution to creditors (for example adjudication upon a foreign creditor's claim which is based upon events in another jurisdiction);
- dissolution (for example determination of the local effect on assets of a foreign dissolution of a foreign corporation); and
- recognition of foreign proceedings and the foreign liquidator when a foreign administration has already commenced.[8]

An example of cross-border insolvency may arise in circumstances where a company incorporated in Taiwan suffers financial difficulties subsequent to borrowing funds through the Taipei branch office of a Singaporean bank to purchase property in Hong Kong. The company instigates insolvency proceedings in Taiwan's civil court.[9] The question is how to reconcile the competing interests attached to the assets and liabilities in the different jurisdictions. Inevitably, this raises difficult questions of law, practice and administration.[10]

The major complication in cases of cross-border insolvency is the difference between the form and implementation of national insolvency laws.[11] These differences are the more acute because of the strong influence of political, social, economic and cultural factors in national insolvency regimes.[12] Complications are not surprising given that the international trade and investment giving rise to more cross-border insolvencies necessarily involves movement across national frontiers that are politically, economically, and legally defined.[13]

National insolvency regimes are still the only formal option for resolving cross-border insolvency.[14] It cannot be assumed that insolvency proceedings initiated in a particular jurisdiction automatically extend to the company's assets in other jurisdictions. Domestic legal institutions in common and civil law countries have traditionally resolved jurisdictional issues in accordance with principles of private international law. The principles of private international law (or conflict of laws) govern the existence of a foreign element in local litigation.[15] The word

---

8 The Australian Law Reform Commission (1996), *Legal Risk in International Transactions*, Canberra, Australian Government Publishing Service, ALRC 80, Ch 4, 13–14.

9 For example, under Article 282 (reorganization) of Taiwan's Company Law 1929. See Tomasic, R. and Francis, A., 'Taiwan', in Tomasic, R. and Little, P. (eds) (1997), *Insolvency Law and Practice in Asia*, Hong Kong: FT Law & Tax Asia Pacific.

10 Crutchfield, P. (1996), *Extraterritorial and International Aspects of Corporate Voluntary Administrations: A Case Study*, a paper delivered at the Business Law Education Centre Eighth Annual Insolvency Masterclass, June 1996, 289 at 289.

11 Fletcher, I. (1999), *Insolvency in Private International Law*, Oxford: Clarendon Press, at 4.

12 Fletcher, I. (1999), *Insolvency in Private International Law*, Oxford: Clarendon Press, at 4. Ziegel also notes the particular susceptibility of insolvency laws to changes in business conditions and economic and social values: Ziegel, J. (ed.) (1994), *Current Developments in International and Comparative Corporate Insolvency Law*, Oxford: Clarendon Press ('Current Developments'), at xxi.

13 Hiscock, M. and Allan, D. (1998), 'Australian legal services – exportable global commodities?', 72 *Australian Law Journal* 101–108, at 101.

14 Fletcher, I. (1999), *Insolvency in Private International Law*, Oxford: Clarendon Press.

15 Sykes, E. and Pryles, M. (1987), *Australian Private International Law* (2nd ed), Sydney: The Law Book Company Limited, at 1.

'international' refers to the international or foreign element in litigation and does not indicate that the relevant rules are universal.[16]

The preliminary issues in formal cross-border insolvency proceedings are jurisdictional: firstly, which national law will govern the insolvency (choice of law), and secondly, which judicial institutions in one or more countries will manage the process (choice of forum).[17] There are three generally identifiable approaches to determining choice of law and choice of forum issues in an international insolvency:[18]

1. The universalist approach: the courts and laws of one jurisdiction have exclusive authority over the insolvency of a debtor, and all creditors must pursue their claims in that jurisdiction.
2. The territorial approach: each jurisdiction manages the assets within its own territory according to its own laws, and the representatives of creditors outside the jurisdiction are not recognized.
3. The mixed approach: courts of each jurisdiction have authority over the assets in their territory but acknowledge the interests of foreign creditors and aim to cooperate with courts in other jurisdictions.

The territorial approach can lead to 'an international "grab", with each country claiming plenary power over assets located in that country and ignoring what rulings other countries may have made'.[19] The application of the universal approach, on the other hand, means that a single insolvency proceeding affects assets and liabilities in all jurisdictions.[20] There are also permutations of each.[21] The mixed approach is a move toward the cooperative concurrent handling of cross-border insolvency.[22]

The rules of private international law developed in each jurisdiction to overcome differences in insolvency law regimes have paradoxically inspired further diversity in the national systems of private international law.[23] International efforts to harmonize rules of private international law in the area of cross-border insolvency have been relatively unsuccessful to date. The only multilateral agreements or treaties

---

16 Sykes, E. and Pryles, M. (1987), *Australian Private International Law* (2nd ed), Sydney: The Law Book Company Limited, at 1–2.

17 Westbrook, J. and Trautman, D. (1994), 'Conflict of Laws: Issues in International Insolvencies', in *Current Developments*, at 657.

18 Woloniecki, J. (1986), 'Cooperation Between National Courts in International Insolvencies: Recent United Kingdom Legislation', 35 *International and Comparative Law Quarterly* 644, at 644 cited in Hon. Mr Justice Farley (1996), 'A Judicial Perspective on Cross-border Insolvencies and Restructurings', *International Business Lawyer*, May 1996, 220.

19 Westbrook, J. and Trautman, D. (1994), 'Conflict of Laws: Issues in International Insolvencies', in *Current Developments*, at 655–656.

20 Westbrook, J. and Trautman, D. (1994), 'Conflict of Laws: Issues in International Insolvencies', in *Current Developments*, at 656.

21 Wood, P. (1995), *Principles of International Insolvency*, London: Sweet & Maxwell, at 228.

22 The advantages and disadvantages of this approach are discussed in LoPucki, L. (1999), 'Cooperation in International Bankruptcy: A Post-Universalist Approach', 84 *Cornell Law Review* 3, 697 at 742–759.

23 Fletcher, I. (1999), *Insolvency in Private International Law*, Oxford: Clarendon Press, at 6.

dealing with cross-border insolvency are at the regional level in Europe[24] and Latin America.[25]

The United Nations Commission on International Trade Law promulgated a Model Law on Cross-border Insolvency in 1997 ('The Model Law').[26] The Model Law was selected as the appropriate vehicle due to the reluctance of states to enter into bilateral or multilateral conventions in the area of cross-border insolvency.[27] The modified universalist approach, which is endorsed by the Model Law, has gained momentum with the Model Law's incorporation in the new Chapter 15 of the United States Bankruptcy Code, reflecting similar developments in the European Union.

Due to the complexities associated with reconciling national insolvency regimes, debtors and creditors also resort to informal mechanisms to resolve international insolvencies. These informal practices involve self-help measures allowing the debtor and creditors to achieve a solution to the corporation's insolvency without recourse to formal legal institutions (legislation, courts or administrative agencies).[28]

The importance of cross-border insolvency lies in the nexus between it and trade and investment. As one commentator has noted, 'just as automotive enthusiasts rarely rave about radiators, bankruptcy is not often a major topic in the discussion of development and globalization – until the engine boils over'.[29] Cross-border insolvency law and practice facilitates trade and investment. Joseph Stiglitz, a former Senior Vice President and Chief Economist of the World Bank, ranks bankruptcy laws alongside limited liability as the keystones in the development of modern capitalism.[30]

2 National Insolvency Regimes

Jurisdictions in East Asia have adopted, to a degree, approaches to resolving jurisdictional and enforcement issues in cross-border insolvency that have emerged out of common law and civil law principles of private international law. Malaysia, Thailand, Singapore, New Zealand, Australia and Hong Kong inherited a common law legal system, while Indonesia, the Philippines, Korea, the People's Republic of China, and Taiwan inherited a civil law system.[31] Each jurisdiction has quite

---

24 The *European Convention on Insolvency Procedures* adopted in November 1995 (entered into force on 1 May 1996) and the Convention between Denmark, Finland, Iceland, Norway, and Sweden regarding bankruptcy of 7 November 1933 (the *Nordic Bankruptcy Convention*).

25 *The Montevideo Treaties* of 1889 and 1940 and *the Bustamante Code of the Havana Conference* of 1928.

26 Discussed further infra.

27 UNCITRAL, *Model Law on Cross-border Insolvency with Guide to Enactment*, A/CN.9/442.

28 The Asian Development Bank, *Insolvency Law Reform in the Asian and Pacific Region*, April 1999, a report of the ongoing technical assistance for Insolvency Law Reform (TA No. 5795-REG), Section VI.

29 Westbrook, J. (1998), 'Universal Priorities', 33 *Texas International Law Journal* 1, 27.

30 Stiglitz, J. (1998), *The Role of International Financial Institutions in the Current Global Economy* (a speech given to the Chicago Council on Foreign Relations on 27 February 1998).

31 Tomasic, R. and Little, P. (eds) (1997), *Insolvency Law and Practice in Asia*, Hong Kong: FT Law & Tax Asia Pacific; Hussain, Q. and Wihlborg, C. (1999), *Corporate Insolvency Procedures and Bank Behaviour: A Study of Selected Asian Economies*, a working paper of the International Monetary Fund: WP/99/135.

different approaches to cross-border insolvency, reflecting the influences of local and imported law.

In the People's Republic of China, for instance, the development of Chinese private international law has corresponded with the rapid growth of international economic relations between the PRC and other jurisdictions and the increase in cases with cross-border legal issues.[32] Substantive Chinese principles of private international law, developed to adjudicate cases with a foreign element (*shewai*), have typically followed principles of reciprocity and been guided by international custom and practice.[33]

A strict version of the territorial approach was traditionally evident in Japan.[34] The Japanese Bankruptcy Law and Reorganization Law stated that bankruptcy and reorganization procedures in foreign jurisdictions were not effective over property in Japan, and, conversely, that Japanese insolvency procedures did not cover property in foreign jurisdictions.[35] Japanese courts were therefore reluctant to act on behalf of international creditors.[36] Some commentators, however, did point to Japanese assistance in the Bank of Credit and Commerce International and Barings Bank cases.[37] The Japanese court accepted a petition for the 'special liquidation' proceeding in respect of the Bank of Credit and Commerce International's Japanese branch.[38] Giving further impetus to a modified universalist approach, in November 2000 Japan passed the Law relating to Recognition and Assistance for Foreign Insolvency Proceedings (Law No. 129 of 2000), which entered into force in April 2001. The Japanese law is based on the UNCITRAL Model Law with various changes.

Under the Statute of Conflict of Laws operating in Taiwan, foreign insolvency procedures are not recognized where assets are located in Taiwan. Article 8 of the Draft Bankruptcy Law of the People's Republic of China also provides for a territorial approach.[39] Territorial approaches have also traditionally been followed

---

32 Zheng, H. (1988), *China's Civil and Commercial Law*, Singapore: Butterworths, 199.

33 Li Shuangyuan (1986), 'Woguo Guoji Sifa Lilun Yanjiu He Lifa Gongzuozhong De Jige Wenti' [Several Issues in the Research and Legislation of Private International Law in China], *Forum of Law and Politics* 3, 66, cited in Zheng, H. (1988), *China's Civil and Commercial Law*, Singapore: Butterworths, 199.

34 Hamano, T. (1999), 'Japan', in Giovanoli, M. and Heinrich, G. (eds), *International Bank Insolvencies: A Central Bank Perspective*, The Hague: Kluwer Law International, 117–140, 124.

35 Article 3 of the Bankruptcy Law and Article 4 of the Company Reorganization Law, cited in Hamano, T. (1999), 'Japan', in Giovanoli, M. and Heinrich, G. (eds), *International Bank Insolvencies: A Central Bank Perspective*, The Hague: Kluwer Law International, 117–140, 124.

36 Taniguchi, Y. (1987), 'International Bankruptcy and Japanese Law', 23 *Stanford Journal of International Law* 449.

37 Miyake (1996), 'Japanese International Insolvency: The Problem of Territoriality', *International Business Lawyer* 238.

38 Kanda, H. (1999), 'Cushioning the Effects of Bank Insolvencies', in Giovanoli, M. and Heinrich, G. (eds), *International Bank Insolvencies: A Central Bank Perspective*, The Hague: Kluwer Law International.

39 Tomasic, R. (1998), 'Draft Bankruptcy Law of the PRC', 9 *Australian Journal of Corporate Law* 211, 230. The only national law on insolvency in the PRC applies only to state-owned enterprises: State-Owned Enterprises Bankruptcy Law (1986). In accordance with article 67 of the Constitution of the PRC (1982), the laws of the PRC consist of the Constitution, laws, administrative regulations, and local regulations. Local regulations on insolvency include the Rules of the Shenzhen Special Economic Region on Enterprise Bankruptcy (1994), and the Rules of the Guangdong Province on Company Bankruptcy (1993). The

in Korea[40] and Thailand.[41] In Thailand, under the Conflict of Law Act and the Bankruptcy Act, B.E. 2541 foreign insolvency proceedings or administrators were not recognized or enforced in Thailand nor were foreign proceedings recognized as having any effect on property situated in Thailand.[42]

The Hong Kong Companies Ordinance provisions relevant to the area of cross-border insolvency provide for the winding up of foreign companies but effectively leave the issues of jurisdiction and enforcement to the courts. In exercising their discretion in this regard, Hong Kong courts have followed the lead of the English common law in adopting a version of the universal approach that allows for international cooperation. The general rule for liquidations in Hong Kong is that foreign liquidators, if recognized in their own jurisdiction, will be recognized under Hong Kong law.[43]

Australia[44] and New Zealand[45] have also followed the lead of English developments. Australia, for example, draws upon its English common law heritage in allowing judges to assist foreign representatives appointed under foreign proceedings recognized in Australia. The case law principles of cooperation were introduced into Australia's Corporations Law in 1992 as sections 580 and 581.[46]

Formal mechanisms for cross-border insolvencies have been relatively untried in many jurisdictions in East Asia due to the reluctance of creditors and debtors to resort to formal mechanisms for resolving insolvency generally – a result of the particular historical, social and economic factors surrounding insolvency in the respective jurisdictions.[47] However, recently reported cross-border insolvency cases in the region include: *Equiticorp Industries Group Limited (In Statutory Management)* v. *The Crown*;[48] *Ting* v. *Chen*;[49] *Bank of Credit and Commerce International (Overseas)*

Liquidation Measures for Foreign Investment Enterprises (1996) do not apply to insolvent companies. If a foreign investment enterprise's assets are insufficient to satisfy its liabilities, the liquidation committee must apply to the People's Court for a declaration of bankruptcy: Hong, A. and Kelly, K. (1998), 'Liquidation of FIEs in China', 15 *East Asian Executive Reports* 1, 15.

40 Legal Office, Bank of Korea (1999), 'Korea', in Giovanoli, M. and Heinrich, G. (eds), *International Bank Insolvencies: A Central Bank Perspective*, The Hague: Kluwer Law International, 141–149, 147.

41 Gibbons, D. (1996), 'Bankruptcy in Thailand', 11 *Commercial Law Bulletin* 4, 50 at 52.

42 Bankruptcy Act, s 177.

43 *Irish Shipping* [1985] HKLR 437, discussed in Booth, C. (1997), 'The Effect of 1997 on Hong Kong's Law of Transnational Corporate Insolvency', 7 *Australian Journal of Corporate Law* 206. Also see generally: Gannon, S. and Kemp, K. (1999), 'Hong Kong', in Giovanoli, M. and Heinrich, G. (eds), *International Bank Insolvencies: A Central Bank Perspective*, The Hague: Kluwer Law International, 67–93, 80–85.

44 Fletcher, I. (1999), *Insolvency in Private International Law*, Oxford: Clarendon Press, 171.

45 New Zealand Law Reform Commission (1999), *Report No 52: Cross-border Insolvency: Should New Zealand adopt the UNCITRAL Model Law on Cross-border Insolvency?*, tabled 18 February 1999.

46 Fletcher, I. (1999), *Insolvency in Private International Law*, Oxford: Clarendon Press, 211.

47 Tomasic, R. and Little, P. (eds) (1997), *Insolvency Law and Practice in Asia*, Hong Kong: FT Law & Tax Asia Pacific; Hussain, Q. and Wihlborg, C. (1999), *Corporate Insolvency Procedures and Bank Behaviour: A Study of Selected Asian Economies*, a working paper of the International Monetary Fund: WP/99/135.

48 (No 2) [1996] 3 NZLR 685; (No 51) [1996] 3 NZLR 690; (No 47) [1998] 2 NZLR 481.

49 [1998] 3 H.K.C. 119 (CA(HK)).

Ltd (In Liquidation) v. *Bank of Credit and Commerce International (Overseas) Ltd Macau Branch (In Liquidation)*;[50] and *Re China Tianjin International Economic and Technical Cooperative Corp.*[51]

Self-help measures have traditionally been widely employed in domestic insolvency cases in many of the jurisdictions in the region, such as Indonesia, Malaysia, Taiwan, Hong Kong and the People's Republic of China.[52] However, concerns over the effectiveness of these processes in a number of jurisdictions in the region have been expressed before and after the Asian financial crisis.[53] There are indications that recourse to informal processes in the region is less likely where foreign creditors are involved.[54]

The use of self-help measures is not peculiar to jurisdictions in East Asia. The concept of the informal workout has emerged in other regions, notably the US and the UK (the 'London Approach').[55] Initiatives have recently been undertaken in Indonesia, Malaysia, Korea, Thailand and Singapore to promote the use of a supervised informal workout.[56] The Indonesian, Malaysian and Korean approaches each provide for state institutional support and facilitation.[57] It remains to be seen to what extent these initiatives offer models for successfully resolving instances of cross-border insolvency.

The initial premises of informal mechanisms include an effective sanction that if the informal process fails there can be quick and efficient resort to formal mechanisms.[58] Imported insolvency laws in many jurisdictions in the region have failed to date to provide an effective avenue for enforcing rights in insolvency.[59] Foreign investors and financiers who 'tumbled over one another in the race to invest and provide finance' in the 'tiger' economies now 'struggle with the economic consequences as they seek to stabilise or redeem the investments or recover the loans and the debts'.[60] A part of the challenge is so-called 'dead letter' insolvency laws.

---

50 [1997] H.K.L.R.D. 304.

51 [1995] 1 H.K.C. 720.

52 Tomasic, R. and Little, P. (eds) (1997), *Insolvency Law and Practice in Asia*, Hong Kong: FT Law & Tax Asia Pacific.

53 Tomasic, R. and Little, P. (eds) (1997), *Insolvency Law and Practice in Asia*, Hong Kong: FT Law & Tax Asia Pacific; Hussain, Q. and Wihlborg, C. (1999), *Corporate Insolvency Procedures and Bank Behaviour: A Study of Selected Asian Economies*, a working paper of the International Monetary Fund: WP/99/135.

54 Tomasic, R. and Little, P. (1998), 'Corporate Insolvency and Selp-help in Six Asian Legal Systems', 6 *Insolvency Law Journal*, 61.

55 The Asian Development Bank, *Insolvency Law Reform in the Asian and Pacific Region*, April 1999, a report of the ongoing technical assistance for Insolvency Law Reform (TA No. 5795-REG), 32.

56 The Asian Development Bank, *Insolvency Law Reform in the Asian and Pacific Region*, April 1999, a report of the ongoing technical assistance for Insolvency Law Reform (TA No. 5795-REG), 32.

57 The Asian Development Bank, *Insolvency Law Reform in the Asian and Pacific Region*, April 1999, a report of the ongoing technical assistance for Insolvency Law Reform (TA No. 5795-REG), 32.

58 The Asian Development Bank, *Insolvency Law Reform in the Asian and Pacific Region*, April 1999, a report of the ongoing technical assistance for Insolvency Law Reform (TA No. 5795-REG), 29.

59 See generally Tomasic, R. and Little, P. (eds) (1997), *Insolvency Law and Practice in Asia*, Hong Kong: FT Law & Tax Asia Pacific.

60 Harmer, R. (1998), 'Book Review: Insolvency Law and Practice in Asia', 6 *Insolvency Law Journal* 209.

Parties to cross-border insolvencies in other regions are becoming increasingly involved in the development of formal procedures for resolving instances of cross-border insolvency. An example is the use of protocols to coordinate procedures between courts in different jurisdictions. North America has led the way in this regard, with the Canadian case of *Re Philip Services Corp.* being an example.[61] The parent company, a Canadian publicly traded company, filed for protection in Canada (under the amended Companies' Creditors Arrangement Act 1985) and Chapter 11 of the US Bankruptcy Code.[62] The parties and courts developed a protocol that sought to facilitate both Canadian and US plans for restructuring of the company.[63] The use of protocols in East Asia has not been widespread. In the recent liquidation of Peregrine Investments Holdings Ltd (discussed further below) a protocol was developed to ensure cooperation between the courts and administrators in Hong Kong and Bermuda.

The courts in the North American cases ensured that these protocols did not diminish either the court's independent jurisdiction over the subject matter of the proceedings or the sovereignty of either country.[64] For example, Blair J in *Re Philips Corp.* held that comity and international cooperation does not require a court to cede authority over the process and application of substantive laws of its own jurisdiction whenever a conflict arises.[65]

Jurisdictions in East Asia are being encouraged to move toward the UNCITRAL Model Law as a part of the general movement to reform insolvency laws.[66] There were examples of insolvency law reform prior to the Asian financial crisis.[67] Domestic reform has been further encouraged by regional and international state and non-state forums responding to the crises – and the worldwide recessions of the 1980s – with calls for greater transparency, accountability, and domestic responsibility.[68] An example of domestic reform is Thailand's new Bankruptcy Act in 1998.[69] An effective insolvency regime is seen as an essential mechanism for preventing and restricting another financial crisis.[70] A formal framework to deal with cross-border insolvency is perceived to be an integral part of this regime.[71]

---

61 August 27, 1999, (Ont. S.C.J.), unreported.

62 Caplan, L. and Reyes, T. (1999), 'Recent Developments in Restructuing', 12 *Commercial Insolvency Reporter* 7.

63 *Cross-border Insolvency Protocol for Philip Services Corp., Philip Services (Delaware), Inc. and Certain Wholly-Owned Subsidiaries*, reported in August 27, 1999, (Ont. S.C.J.), unreported, 3.

64 *Re Philips Corp.* August 27, 1999, (Ont. S.C.J.), unreported, at 6.

65 *Re Philips Corp.* August 27, 1999, (Ont. S.C.J.), unreported, at 14.

66 Hussain, Q. and Wihlborg, C. (1999), *Corporate Insolvency Procedures and Bank Behaviour: A Study of Selected Asian Economies*, a working paper of the International Monetary Fund: WP/99/135.

67 Harmer, R., 'Bankruptcy Law Reform in the Asia Pacific Region', a paper presented at the *Asia Pacific Law Forum Conference*, University of Canberra, 8–9 February 1996.

68 *Possible future work on insolvency law*, a report of the United Nations Commission on International Trade Law: A/CN.9/WG.V/WP.50.

69 Kitipong Urapeepatanapong (1998), 'New Bankruptcy Act to boost Thai economy', 17 *International Financial Law Review* 4, 33.

70 *Possible future work on insolvency law*, a report of the United Nations Commission on International Trade Law: A/CN.9/WG.V/WP.50.

71 *Possible future work on insolvency law*, a report of the United Nations Commission on International Trade Law: A/CN.9/WG.V/WP.50.

3 Cross-border Insolvencies Impacting on East Asian Jurisdictions

There have been a number of high-profile cross-border insolvencies impacting on jurisdictions in East Asia. The complexity of these cases partly reflects the growing range and scope of products offered in global financial markets.

Peregrine Group – Hong Kong

On 13 January 1998, provisional liquidators were appointed to the Peregrine group following the presentation of winding up petitions in respect of Peregrine Investments Holdings Limited, Peregrine Derivates Limited and Peregrine Fixed Income Limited ('PFIL'). The Peregrine group was reputed at the time to be the largest investment bank in the region outside Japan. The group collapsed with estimated liabilities of US$4.5 billion. The three major operating arms of the group were Peregrine Investments Holdings Limited, Peregrine Derivatives Limited, and PFIL. The court wound up the companies on 18 March 1998.

There had been considerable public concern in Hong Kong over the collapse. The Financial Secretary successfully applied to the court for a declaration that the affairs of Peregrine Investments Holdings Ltd and PFIL be investigated by an inspector to be appointed by the Financial Secretary under s 143(1)(a) of the Companies Ordinance (Cap 32).[72] The official report into the causes of the insolvency was expected shortly at the time of writing. In 1998 the Hong Kong Court of First Instance rejected an application for a court order that the compulsory winding up of PFIL be converted into a creditors' voluntary winding up. The grounds included that the court was not willing to divest itself of the control of the liquidation in circumstances where the collapse of PFIL was a matter of public concern 'affecting as they do Hong Kong's standing as a financial centre'.[73]

A substantial portion of the group's assets and liabilities involved unsettled derivatives transactions undertaken by PFIL. PFIL was the largest operating arm of the Peregrine group. These derivative transactions included more than 2000 swaps, forwards, options and other products, transacted with close to 300 counterparties. The transactions had a total notional value greater than US$15 billion and represented total debtor and creditor positions of approximately US$1.5 billion and US$1 billion respectively.

The majority of these transactions were carried out under International Swaps & Derivatives Association (ISDA) Master Agreements. The majority of these agreements were subject to English law. Most of Peregrine's ISDA agreements provided for the automatic termination of the derivative transactions on the commencement of liquidation of the Peregrine group. The sudden collapse of the Peregrine group inevitably resulted in a number of issues in relation to the default and automatic termination terms of the agreements. The liquidators of the Peregrine group negotiated settlements of these agreements with PFIL's numerous counterparties outside Hong Kong.

---

72 *Re Peregrine Investments Holdings Ltd (In Liq) & Anor* [1999] 3 HKC 285.

73 *Re Peregrine Fixed Income Ltd (In Liq)* [1998] 4 HKC 151, per Le Pichon J at 160.

In addition, as the agreements were subject to English law, the liquidators sought clarification from the English High Court on the issue of whether (and to what extent) the credit standing of a counterparty to a terminated transaction under an ISDA Master Agreement should be taken into account in valuing the terminated transaction. This valuation issue, also impacting on Peregrine Investments Holdings Limited and Peregrine Derivatives Limited, had a large effect on the number and value of ISDA creditors of PFIL. The decision of the English High Court on 18 May 2000 effectively rejected significant discounting of ISDA claims on the basis of credit standing.

Many of the PFIL assets recovered have been from US and European investment bank counterparties to derivative contracts. Future payouts to creditors will also depend on recovering from debtors in Indonesia (where PFIL's exposure was estimated at US$1.1 billion) and Thailand (where PFIL's exposure was estimated at US$300 million). In particular, the liquidators have had difficulty in recovering from Steady Safe, the Indonesian taxi firm to which PFIL had an exposure of US$265 million.

Other cross-border elements in the liquidation of the group include the protocol between liquidators in Hong Kong and Bermuda approved by the courts in the respective jurisdictions in December 1999. The protocol prevented separated liquidations being carried out in each jurisdiction in respect of Peregrine Investments Holdings Ltd.

Kunnan Enterprises Ltd – Taiwan

Kunnan Enterprises Ltd, a company incorporated in Taiwan, was the manufacturer of the Pro-Kennex tennis racquet. The company entered into reorganization proceedings under Taiwan's Company Law. Creditors of the company included a number of professional tennis players claiming amounts owed under endorsement contracts for the racquet. The players sued Kunnan Enterprises Ltd for damages in the US District Court in Washington DC in late 1995.[74]

Kunnan filed a separate Section 304 petition in the US Bankruptcy Court.[75] This petition could be filed on behalf of a company undergoing liquidation or reorganization in a foreign jurisdiction. The US bankruptcy judge exercised considerable discretion in providing relief to aid the foreign proceedings. Kunnan was successful and the court ordered a permanent injunction against the continuation of the US District Court action, effectively requiring that the players and other creditors of Kunnan pursue their claims through the reorganization process in Taiwan. In *Re Kunnan*, the US Bankruptcy Court held that reorganization procedures of Taiwan were consistent with the principles of fairness and due process and did not cause undue prejudice or inconvenience to the creditors involved.

---

74 *Paul Haarhuis & Others* v. *Kunnan Enterprises Ltd*, Case No. 95-1967 (TPJ).

75 *In re Kunnan Enterprises Ltd*, Case No. 97-0630 (U.S. Bankr. D.C.)

The Linter Litigation – Australia

The Linter Group was an Australian group of companies. The group's principal business was the manufacture and distribution of clothing. In May 1988 the group required funds to pay for the acquisition of a large number of companies featuring well-known Australian clothing brand names. The group decided to raise funds in the US through a subordinated debenture issue. Linter Textiles Corporation issued a prospectus in New York offering debentures maturing in October 2000 and carrying 13.75 per cent interest. The prospectus issue raised US$200 million.

The Linter Group collapsed in 1990 with an estimated deficiency of A$550 million. The Linter Group was put into receivership. At the outset the receivers sought a scheme of arrangement between the companies and their respective creditors but subsequently sold each of the businesses and brand names. US debenture holders and Australian and foreign banks bore the main loss.

In 1991 and 1992 the companies were put into liquidation, the liquidators holding the proceeds of the sale of the businesses (about A$400 million). The breakdown of the group led to a number of proceedings in Australia and the US, including:

- proceedings in Australia to determine whether the subordination was effective in the winding up of the Linter companies under Australian law;[76]
- proceedings in the US (New York) by the debenture holders against certain banks and professional advisers;
- proceedings in Australia by the US debenture holders and also by some banks against other banks and professional advisers;[77]
- proceedings in Australia by the liquidators of Linter to recover property of Linter paid in breach of directors' duties;[78] and
- proceedings in Australia to determine the distribution of the A$400 million held by the liquidators from the sale of the businesses.[79]

Guangdong International Trust and Investment Corp. – People's Republic of China

On 16 January 1999 the Guangdong International Trust and Investment Corporation (GITIC) sought protection from its creditors under the People's Republic of China State Enterprise Bankruptcy Law 1986. GITIC, the PRC's second largest trust and investment company, was established in 1980 as the main fundraising arm of the Guangdong provincial government. GITIC is the biggest bankruptcy in the history of the PRC. GITIC has total liabilities of US$4.37 billion. Foreign creditors are owed US$3.7 billion. This is the first time that the PRC Bankruptcy Law has been used in

---

76 *United States Trust Co of New York & Others* v. *Australia and New Zealand Banking Group Limited & Others* (1995) 37 NSWLR 131.

77 *Allstate Life Insurance Co & Others* v. *Australia and New Zealand Banking Group Limited & Others* (No 19) (1995) 134 ALR 187.

78 *Linter Group Ltd* v. *Goldberg & Others* (1992) 7 ACSR 580.

79 *United States Trust Co of New York & Others* v. *Australia and New Zealand Banking Group Limited & Others* (1993) 11 ACSR 7.

the insolvency of a major financial institution or for a debtor with significant foreign liabilities.

The People's Bank of China announced the closure of GITIC on 6 October 1998. The announcement stated that 'overseas liabilities registered with the foreign exchange administration authorities and the legal principal and interest of deposits of domestic natural persons shall have priority for repayment'.[80] There was no mention of the PRC Bankruptcy Law. The announcement provided that all creditors' claims against GITIC were to be entrusted to the Bank of China, which would register the claims between 6 October 1998 and 6 January 1999. Furthermore, the announcement stated that the securities trading business of GITIC would be transferred to Guangfa Securities.

At the expiration of the period for registering claims, creditors of GITIC were notified of a creditors' meeting to be held in Guangzhou on 10 January 1999. There was a separate location for foreign and domestic creditors. At these meetings it was announced that GITIC (including certain subsidiaries) was to be put into bankruptcy under the PRC Bankruptcy Law. There was to be an official liquidation committee comprising the People's Bank of China, GITIC, the Guangdong provincial government, the Bank of China, Guangfa Securities, a PRC law firm, and Peat Marwick Huazen.

At the first joint meeting of creditors of GITIC, convened at the Guangdong Higher People's Court in Guangzhou on 22 April 1999, the liquidation committee announced that GITIC had liabilities of RMB (renminbi) 36.165 billion (US$4.37 billion). This exceeded its assets by a shortfall of RMB 14.694 billion (US$1.77 billion). GITIC was also announced to have 105 domestic subsidiaries and 135 overseas subsidiaries.

Foreign creditors of GITIC had been relying on the previous practice of the PRC authorities to ensure the payment of foreign creditors in full. However, Article 37 of the PRC Bankruptcy Law provides that the order of priority in the insolvency of a state-owned enterprise is wages and labour insurance, taxes, then unsecured creditors. The PRC Bankruptcy Law does not contain any provisions for priority of payment to foreign creditors.

Representatives of foreign creditors have expressed the following concerns with the insolvency process of GITIC:

1. There was no opportunity given to creditors to make representations at the hearing of the Guangdong Higher People's Court which oversaw the first creditors' meeting.
2. Any challenge of the transfer of GITIC securities trading business to Guangfa Securities under Article 35 of the PRC Bankruptcy Law (a general avoidance provision for acts during the six months prior to bankruptcy which include private distributions or gratuitous transfer of property) would be unlikely to be endorsed by the liquidation committee given that a representative of Guangfa Securities is on the committee.

---

80 Cited in Chang, T. (1999), 'The East is in the Red', *International Finance Law Review*, March 1999 (http://www.coudert.com/practice/thered, accessed 25 August 2000, 1–6, 2).

3. The dominance and composition of the liquidation committee raises conflict of interest concerns, for example, the Bank of China is one of the largest creditors of GITIC.
4. Foreign creditors were relying on so-called comfort letters from the Guangdong provincial government that it would ensure the necessary support for the repayment of principal and interest, whereas the Notice of the State Council Regarding the Strengthening of Control over the Borrowing and Using of International Commercial Loans, issued on 12 January 1989, clearly states 'no governmental agency or institution shall provide foreign exchange guarantees to any foreign party'.[81]

4 Regional and International Developments

There is no formal avenue for recognizing insolvency administrations across multiple borders in East Asia. Parties to a cross-border insolvency primarily rely on the goodwill of the courts and the individuals within the court systems to cooperate and facilitate the development of protocols. Reports by the Asian Development Bank (ADB)[82] and the International Monetary Fund recommend that jurisdictions in East Asia adopt the UNCITRAL Model Law.[83]

This Model Law was formulated through discussion with insolvency professionals (represented by the International Association of Restructuring, Insolvency and Bankruptcy Professionals (INSOL) and Committee J (Insolvency) of the Section on Business Law of the International Bar Association (Committee J), judges, judicial administrators, and government officials.[84]

The Model Law, it is said, implements a cooperative or mixed approach to cross-border insolvency. The approach underlying the Model Law, its supporters maintain, is to overcome difficulties in choice of law and choice of forum issues by encouraging coordination of concurrent proceedings. On the other hand, critics of

---

81 Cited in Chang, T. (1999), 'The East is in the Red', *International Finance Law Review*, March 1999 (http://www.coudert.com/practice/thered, accessed 25 August 2000, 1–6).

82 The ADB consists of member states (both regional and non-regional). In accordance with the Agreement establishing the Asian Development Bank (done at Manila on 4 December 1965), the ADB is controlled by its member states through a Board of Governors and Board of Directors.

83 The Asian Development Bank, *Insolvency Law Reform in the Asian and Pacific Region*, April 1999, a report of the ongoing technical assistance for Insolvency Law Reform (TA No. 5795-REG); Hussain, Q. and Wihlborg, C. (1999), *Corporate Insolvency Procedures and Bank Behaviour: A Study of Selected Asian Economies*, a working paper of the International Monetary Fund: WP/99/135.

84 This included three Colloquium and four two-week sessions of the Working Group on Insolvency. The colloquiums included the UNCITRAL-INSOL Colloquium on Cross-border Insolvency held in Vienna from 17 April to 19 April 1994, the UNCITRAL-INSOL Judicial Colloquium on Cross-border Insolvency held at Toronto from 22 to 23 March 1995, and the UNCITRAL-INSOL Multinational Judicial Colloquium on Cross-border Insolvency held at New Orleans from 22 to 23 March 1997 (see UNCITRAL, *Model Law on Cross-border Insolvency with Guide to Enactment*, A/CN.9/442, at 16 and ff 3,4,5,6).

the Model Law argue that it endorses a universalist approach, which will simply encourage strategic forum shopping.[85]

The ADB Regional Technical Assistance for Insolvency Law Reform project covers Korea, Japan, Taipei, China, Hong Kong, Singapore, Indonesia, Malaysia, Thailand, India, Pakistan, and the Philippines. A Symposium on Insolvency Law Reforms, held as a part of this project in January 1999, highlighted the absence in these jurisdictions of cross-border insolvency provisions which encouraged a mixed cooperative approach. Further, the ADB noted in the subsequent report (April 1999) that it did not appear that any of the economies were contemplating the adoption of the Model Law.[86]

As noted above, Japan has now adopted a modified or amended version of the Model Law.[87] There are also indications that certain jurisdictions in the region, notably Australia and New Zealand,[88] are considering implementing the Model Law. The Hong Kong Law Reform Commission has recommended a 'wait and see' policy toward the implementation of the Model Law.[89] The Commission did recommend, however, that an equivalent to s 304 of the US Bankruptcy Code – reflecting a mixed cooperative approach – be incorporated into Hong Kong's Companies Ordinance and Bankruptcy Ordinance.[90]

There have been few attempts at bilateral cooperation in this area amongst jurisdictions in East Asia. An example of bilateral reform initiatives in the area is the Closer Economic Relations Trade Agreement (1983) and Memorandum of Understanding on the Harmonisation of Business Law (1988) between Australia and New Zealand.[91] The Australian Law Reform Commission Report on Legal Risk in International Transactions recommended that an advisory committee report on the potential for judicial cooperation between Australian and New Zealand courts on cross-border insolvencies.[92]

As noted, regional and international efforts in the regulation of cross-border insolvency are presently concentrated on the Model Law. The Model Law was developed by a Working Group of UNCITRAL composed of 36 member states elected by the General Assembly of the United Nations – including China, Fiji,

---

85 Lo Pucki, L. (2005), 'Global and out of control?', 79 *American Bankruptcy Law Journal* 79–103; Lo Pucki, L. (2005), 'Universalism unravels', 79 *American Bankruptcy Law Journal* 143–167.

86 The Asian Development Bank, *Insolvency Law Reform in the Asian and Pacific Region*, April 1999, a report of the ongoing technical assistance for Insolvency Law Reform (TA No. 5795-REG).

87 'Japan to Install Cross-border Insolvency Regime', *Jiji Press Ticker Service*, 22 February 2000.

88 New Zealand Law Reform Commission (1999), *Report No 52: Cross-border Insolvency: Should New Zealand adopt the UNCITRAL Model Law on Cross-border Insolvency?*, tabled 18 February 1999.

89 The Law Reform Commission of Hong Kong (1999), *Report on the Winding-up Provisions of the Companies Ordinance.*

90 The Law Reform Commission of Hong Kong (1999), *Report on the Winding-up Provisions of the Companies Ordinance*, 213.

91 Barker, I. and Beaumont, B. (1992), 'Trans-Tasman Legal Relations – Some Recent and Future Developments' 66 *Australian Law Journal* 566 cited in Wyatt, A. and Mason, R. (1998), 'Legal and Accounting Regulatory Framework for Corporate Groups: Implications for Insolvency in Group Operations', 16 *Company and Securities Law Journal*, 448.

92 Australian Law Reform Commission (1996), *Report No 80: Legal Risk in International Transactions*, Australian Government Publishing Service: Canberra.

India, Japan, Singapore, and Thailand. The Model Law is a model or standard only – imposing no obligations on states in international law.[93] The Model Law, if incorporated into domestic regimes, is designed to put in place procedures that encourage and facilitate cooperation between state institutions. Notably, the Model Law mandates that local courts cooperate 'to the maximum extent possible with foreign courts or foreign representatives' via the communication of information between courts, or between courts and insolvency administrators 'by any means considered appropriate'. The Model Law also aims at the coordination of the administration of the debtor's assets and affairs between courts, and the approval of the agreements concerning the coordination of proceedings between jurisdictions.[94]

At the same time, critics maintain that the Model Law, through its proposal that a court of a multinational debtor's 'home country' applies the law of the country to control the company's insolvency worldwide, imports the principle of universalism into domestic legal systems, for example, the US Chapter 15. The indeterminacy of the home country standard, they argue, will simply lead to forum shopping.[95]

At this point, it is too early to say whether jurisdictions across East Asia will embrace the Model Law. However, regardless of whether the territorial, universal or a modified approach is adopted by jurisdictions in the region, one thing is clear. There will only be a true harmonization of approaches to cross-border insolvency in the East Asian region if jurisdictions foster the judicial and professional culture necessary to implement the laws on cross-border insolvency. It has been noted that merely incorporating, wholesale, foreign insolvency laws has had little impact on a number of jurisdictions (for example, Indonesia, Vietnam, Thailand, Taiwan). The ADB's Regional Technical Assistance for Insolvency Law Reform, which is designed to allow officials, judges and insolvency practitioners a forum for exploring solutions to cross-border insolvency, is an example of where dialogue between jurisdictions in the region may encourage a more uniform, embedded approach to cross-border insolvency in East Asia.

Conclusion

National insolvency regimes in East Asia display the disparity of approach to resolving jurisdictional and enforcement issues in cross-border insolvencies evident in jurisdictions in other regions. The national insolvency regimes in East Asia are largely ill-prepared for the growing regional interdependence in trade and investment. Cross-border insolvency is a consequence of cross-border transactions. As trade increases in the region, national insolvency regimes that encourage cooperation in the resolution of these cases are needed to facilitate trade and investment. Whilst

---

93 Sekolec, J. (1999), 'The UNCITRAL Model Law on Cross-Border Insolvency', in Giovanoli, M. and Heinrich, G. (eds), *International Bank Insolvencies: A Central Bank Perspective*, The Hague: Kluwer Law International, 337–346, 339.

94 Leonard, B. (1998), 'Multijurisdictional Insolvencies and Reorganizations', 10 *Commercial Insolvency Reporter* 49, 54–55.

95 Lo Pucki, L. (2005), 'Global and out of control?', 79 *American Bankruptcy Law Journal* 79–103; Lo Pucki, L. (2005), 'Universalism unravels', 79 *American Bankruptcy Law Journal* 143–167.

differences of approaches based on territorism or universalism pose challenges to the effective resolution of cross-border insolvency cases, so do the ingrained differences between judicial officers and professionals. Greater dialogue is needed to cross this divide.

Index

For Product Safety Concerns and Information please contact our EU representative GPSR@taylorandfrancis.com
Taylor & Francis Verlag GmbH, Kaufingerstraße 24, 80331 München, Germany

www.ingramcontent.com/pod-product-compliance
Ingram Content Group UK Ltd.
Pitfield, Milton Keynes, MK11 3LW, UK
UKHW020025200926
475702UK00014B/2063
* 9 7 8 0 3 6 7 6 0 3 9 6 0 *